Robert Cox's writings have had a profound influence on recent developments in thinking in world politics and political economy in many countries. This book brings together for the first time his most important essays, grouped around the theme of world order. The volume is divided into sections dealing respectively with theory; with the application of Cox's approach to recent changes in world political economy; and with multilateralism and the problem of global governance. The book also includes a critical review of Cox's work by Timothy Sinclair, and an essay by Cox tracing his own intellectual journey. This volume will be an essential guide to Robert Cox's critical approach to world politics for students and teachers of international relations, international political economy, and international organization.

CAMBRIDGE STUDIES IN INTERNATIONAL RELATIONS: 40

Approaches to world order

CAMBRIDGE STUDIES IN INTERNATIONAL RELATIONS

Series list continues after index

Approaches to world order

Robert W. Cox
York University, Toronto

with Timothy J. Sinclair
University of Warwick

CAMBRIDGE
UNIVERSITY PRESS

Published by the Press Syndicate of the University of Cambridge
The Pitt Building, Trumpington Street, Cambridge CB2 1RP
40 West 20th Street, New York, NY 10011-4211, USA
10 Stamford Road, Oakleigh, Melbourne, 3166, Australia

First published 1996

Printed in Great Britain at the University Press, Cambridge

A catalogue record for this book is available from the British Library

Library of Congress cataloguing in publication data

Cox, Robert W., 1926–
    Approaches to world order / Robert W. Cox, with Timothy J. Sinclair.
        p.   cm. – (Cambridge Studies in international relations; 40)
    Includes bibliographical references and index.
    ISBN 0 521 46114 6 (hc)   ISBN 0 521 46651 2 (pb)
    1. International organization.   2. International cooperation.
    3. World politics.   I. Title.
    JX1954.C688   1995
    327.1'01 – dc20   94-37094 CIP

ISBN 0 521 4 6114 6 hardback
ISBN 0 521 4 6651 2 paperback

Contents

Contents

Preface

A subtitle for this book of essays might have been "Apart from the Mainstream." My work has developed apart from the dominant currents of thought in international studies. The approach I have called historical dialectic has for long been outside the mainstream of social science, especially in America. Latterly, I have sensed an interest, or at least a curiosity, among graduate students and younger colleagues, for exploring alternatives to what have been the prevailing theoretical frameworks, and for breaking down the barriers erected by consecrated academic divisions. Perhaps the essays collected here will help to encourage that continuing search.

The initiative for this book came from graduate students. Many of my previously published pieces were scattered in diverse journals and books, making them difficult to assemble for study or teaching. Also some students and colleagues, who found my *Production, Power, and World Order* (New York: Columbia University Press, 1987) a demanding read, thought my essays were a more attractive access to my thinking.

The idea for the book and the pressure for me to actually see it through came from several of my recent graduate students. The principal instigator has been Timothy J. Sinclair, now teaching international political economy at the University of Warwick, who was also prepared to do most of the work to bring the project to fruition. He has most carefully reviewed and reconstituted the essays we selected together and has annotated them in such a way as to maintain the integrity of the original text while making necessary abbreviations and adding explanatory footnotes where references might not be clear to a present-day reader.[a] He has also written an introductory essay

---

[a] The original notes, some of which have been edited, are reprinted as endnotes following the respective chapter.

commenting on my work and situating it in its larger context. Such an overview of a person's work is often written by a senior scholar, an act of scholarly legitimation. This somewhat heterodox author is most pleased to have it written by a promising member of the new generation of critical thinkers about world affairs.

Timothy Sinclair was joined by some fellow students in encouraging the project: Robert J. O'Brien, now teaching at the University of Sussex, Randall Germain, now of the University of Sheffield, Deborah Stienstra of the University of Winnipeg, and Hélène Pellerin, lately of the University of Amsterdam and now taking up a position at Glendon College of York University in Toronto. Robert O. Keohane, from whose critical comments on earlier work I have greatly benefited, suggested about the same time that I prepare something of this sort. Stephen Gill, my colleague at York University, brought the idea for the book to the attention of Cambridge University Press, who then suggested Sinclair and I proceed with the project.

The collection is organized into four parts. The first part, intended as background and context for the reader, includes Sinclair's essay commenting on major components of my thinking and situating it in relation to other work in the broad field of international studies. The other essay is a new one written by me for this book in which I reflect upon the development of my thinking over half a century in terms of the influences and commitments that have shaped it.

The essays reproduced here are then grouped by themes rather than chronologically. I hope that the influences and commitments essay will help the reader situate each of these essays in its historical context and to note the development of ideas between different essays. A few of these essays have become fairly well known and have been reproduced in other published collections. Other essays, which have been relatively ignored, nevertheless constitute moments in the dialectic of my own thinking under the pressures of political and personal events.

The second part, Theory, begins with a short piece so obscure (it was a book review written in 1953) that I had forgotten about it until the opportunity to comment on the manuscript of Craig Murphy's *International Organization and Industrial Change: Global Governance Since 1850* (New York: Oxford University Press, 1994) brought it back to mind. He suggested it might be a useful clue to the development of later thinking. It is followed by the postscript I wrote for the republication of "Social Forces, States, and World Orders" in the reader prepared by Robert O. Keohane, *Neorealism and Its Critics* (New York: Columbia University Press, 1986), under the new title of "Realism, Positivism, and Historicism." The juxtaposition of these two pieces suggests both a line of consistency and a measure of development between 1953 and 1985. The "Social Forces" essay which has been most widely disseminated appears here in abbreviated form, following a far less well known but for me equally important essay, "On Thinking about Future World Order" (1976). A new piece, not previously published, written in honor of Susan Strange, is also included.

Part III, Interpretations, brings together several essays that attempt to apply the framework of ideas developed in Part I to some of the salient concerns of world political economy in recent years: the social and economic polarization resulting from the hyperliberal tendency in national and global political economy; the rise and decline of "real socialism" and its possible consequences; the contest of rival capitalisms, especially in Europe; the potential role of Japan in the making of world order; the dialectic of production and security; and, in "Global Perestroika," the negation of the "end of history" thesis in an analysis of the troubles brewed by the juggernaut of economic globalization.

Part IV, Multilateralism, shifts from global structures of political economy and their regional variants to efforts towards global governance. These essays, written over a period of twenty-five years, reflect both personal involvement and detached observation – the term "objectivity" has little meaning for me in its positivistic implications of separation of subject and object of enquiry, of fact and value. Commitments are, I think, clearly evident in these pieces, as, I hope, is realism of analysis.

In Part IV, the theme that emerges is hegemony: how hegemony has been articulated in leadership and (in "Labor and Hegemony") through dominant coalitions of social forces, how it works through decision making, and the prospects and obstacles to counterhegemonic forces. I have been concerned with the ways in which international organization has contributed to particular structures of world order by reflecting and reinforcing dominant forms of state and preeminent social forces. Through this runs a practical interest in finding ways in which multilateralism may help construct alternative world orders more fully embodying the normative commitments I have articulated: social equity, mutual recognition of civilizations, nonviolence in dealing with conflict, and compatibility with the survival of the biosphere. The common aim in these essays is to conceptualize an adequate framework for this arena of global politics.

I acknowledge here my debt of intellectual companionship and friendship to Harold K. Jacobson. The essay on "Decision Making" included here was a joint effort reflecting after five years' interval on the book *The Anatomy of Influence: Decision Making in International Organization* (New Haven, Conn.: Yale University Press, 1972) which we produced together with Gerard and Victoria Curzon, Joseph S. Nye, Lawrence Scheinman, James P. Sewell, and Susan Strange. During the last few years, the United Nations University has given me the opportunity to serve as program coordinator for a program on multilateralism and the United Nations system (MUNS). The essay "Multilateralism and World Order" was written as a "concept paper" for that program and I have benefited greatly from the intellectual contacts it has made possible.

I wish to thank, at Cambridge University Press, Professor Steve Smith, managing editor of the Cambridge Studies in International Relations series, for his encouragement of the project, Michael Holdsworth for seeing it through the Press Syndicate, and John Haslam for his helpfulness during the production of the manuscript. Heather Chesnutt efficiently wordprocessed the manuscript, providing many thoughtful comments and useful suggestions along the way, bringing to bear her considerable experience in preparing manuscripts for publication. She was ably assisted by Rose Edgecombe.

I entered a full-time teaching career somewhat later than most people do, at the age of forty-five. I am now technically retired, though still teaching and working with graduate students. Teaching has been a great enrichment. The student–teacher relationship is a dialectic (a word that will appear recurrently below). Understanding grows for both through the relationship. I have learned much from students I have worked with over the years. Jeffrey Harrod's was the first doctoral dissertation I supervised. We subsequently worked together in a study on production relations that produced my *Production, Power, and World Order* (New York: Columbia University Press, 1987) and his *Power, Production and the Unprotected Worker* (New York: Columbia University Press, 1987). He is now at the Institute of Social Studies in The Hague and we keep in touch. Michael Schechter, who was my student later at Columbia University, has been working with me on the MUNS program. He teaches at James Madison College, Michigan State University. It was a graduate student at the University of

Toronto who first (in 1972) introduced me to the reading of Gramsci. As I said at the outset, this book project originated with students. It is, then, appropriate that I dedicate this book to those who have been my students. With thanks.

Acknowledgements

I am grateful to a number of publishers and academic journals for permission to reprint material that originally appeared elsewhere. *International Labour Review* gave permission for reprinting of "The Idea of International Labour Regulation" (chapter 3), vol. 67, no. 2 (February 1953), pp. 191–196. "Realism, Positivism, and Historicism" (chapter 4) is reprinted with the permission of Columbia University Press. It first appeared as a new postscript to the reprinting of "Social Forces, States, and World Orders: Beyond International Relations Theory; in *Neorealism and Its Critics*, edited by Robert O. Keohane (New York: Columbia University Press, 1986). The Johns Hopkins University Press gave permission for reprinting of "On Thinking about Future World Order" (chapter 5) which was first published by *World Politics*, vol. 28, no. 2 (January 1976), pp. 175–196. *Millennium: Journal of International Studies* first published "Social Forces, States, and World Orders: Beyond International Relations Theory" (chapter 6), vol. 10, no. 2 (Summer 1981), pp. 126–155, and "Gramsci, Hegemony, and International Relations: An Essay in Method" (chapter 7), vol. 12, no. 2 (Summer 1983), pp. 162–175. Cambridge University Press gave permission for reprinting of "Towards a Posthegemonic Conceptualization of World Order: Reflections on the Relevancy of Ibn Khaldun" (chapter 8), which first appeared in *Governance Without Government: Order and Change in World Politics*, edited by James N. Rosenau and Ernst-Otto Czempiel (Cambridge: Cambridge University Press, 1992), and "Structural Issues of Global Governance: Implications for Europe" (chapter 12), which was first published in *Gramsci, Historical Materialism, and International Relations*, edited by Stephen Gill (Cambridge: Cambridge University Press, 1993). "The Global Political Economy and Social Choice" (chapter 10) first appeared in *The New*

Era of Global Competition: State Policy and Market Power, edited by Daniel Drache and Meric S. Gertler (Montreal and Kingston: McGill-Queen's University Press, 1991), and is reprinted with the permission of McGill-Queen's University Press. " 'Real Socialism' in Historical Perspective" (chapter 11) was published for the first time in *Socialist Register 1991* (London: Merlin Press, 1991), as was "Global *Perestroika*" (chapter 15), which appeared in the 1992 volume. The Canadian Institute of International Affairs gave permission for reprinting of "Middlepowermanship, Japan, and Future World Order" (chapter 13), which was first published in its publication *International Journal*, vol. 44, no. 4 (Autumn 1989), pp. 823–862. "Production and Security" (chapter 14) was first published in *Building a New Global Order: Emerging Trends in International Security*, edited by David Dewitt, David Hagland, and John Kirton (Toronto: Oxford University Press, 1993), and is reprinted with permission of Oxford University Press. Four chapters first appeared as articles in *International Organization* and are reprinted with permission of the Massachusetts Institute of Technology Press. The first is "The Executive Head: An Essay on Leadership in International Organization" (chapter 16), vol. 23, no. 2 (Spring 1969), pp. 205–230. The second is "Ideologies and the New International Economic Order: Reflections on Some Recent Literature" (chapter 18), vol. 33, no. 2 (Spring 1979), pp. 257–302. The third article is "Labor and Hegemony" (chapter 19) which was published in vol. 31, no. 3 (Summer 1977), pp. 385–424. The last article reprinted is "Labor and Hegemony: A Reply" (chapter 20), vol. 34, no. 1 (Winter 1980), pp. 159–176. "Decision Making" (chapter 17), written with Harold K. Jacobson, is reprinted with permission of the United Nations Educational, Scientific, and Cultural Organization and first appeared in the *International Social Science Journal*, vol. 29, no. 1 (1977), pp. 115–135. *Review of International Studies* first published "Multilateralism and World Order" (chapter 21), vol. 18, no. 2 (April 1992), pp. 161–180. "Globalization, Multilateralism, and Democracy" was given as the John Holmes Memorial Lecture to the 1992 conference of the Academic Council on the United Nations System, Washington, D.C. on June 19, 1992, and appears with the permission of the Academic Council on the United Nations System.

The other material in the volume is published here for the first time: "Beyond International Relations Theory: Robert W. Cox and Approaches to World Order" (chapter 1), by Timothy J. Sinclair;

Acknowledgements

"Influences and Commitments" (chapter 2) and " 'Take Six Eggs':
Theory, Finance, and the Real Economy in the Work of Susan Strange"
(chapter 9).

Part I
Overviews

1 Beyond international relations theory: Robert W. Cox and approaches to world order

Timothy J. Sinclair

Robert W. Cox's work stands outside the usual parameters of international relations theory. Strongly historical in perspective, Cox's method of understanding global change represents a challenge to conventional ontological assumptions about international relations. These assumptions, the central of which is that states are the major actors whose interaction is to be explained, are qualified by Cox based on his observation that the major driving forces of world order change, albeit slowly, over time. Rather than discuss "the state," Cox's focus has been on forms of state and how these change under pressure from forces from above (world order) and from below (civil society). Cox considers states to be focal terrains of conflict and institutional means of action internationally and nationally. In Cox's worldview the future represents an opportunity to break with the structures of the past and thus the potential to escape the strictures that bind human potential.

This essay is intended to provide the reader with an introduction to Robert W. Cox's approach to the study of international relations. It has four sections in which this is pursued. In the first part, the importance of Cox's work is established by reference to the changing nature of world order and the critical stance of his work. Unlike other approaches, it is argued, Cox's intellectual stance makes change a central feature of the understanding of international relations. This gives it an advantage over status quo perspectives in a world order characterized by transformation. In the second section of the essay, Cox's rejection of positivism and endorsement of an historicist epistemology is evaluated. This is followed by a discussion of his method of historical structures, which embodies his assumptions about the basic components of an understanding of historical change. This is where Cox is most innovative, so most attention will be focused on this section of the essay. Finally, there is some brief consideration of the reception and criticism Cox's work has received. The reaction to his work raises sociology-of-knowledge questions about why his work is read, and why not, as the case may be.

Turning points and critical purposes

One senses that the course of history is at a turning point, a juncture where the opportunities for movement toward peaceful cooperation, expanded human rights, and higher standards of living are hardly less conspicuous than the prospects for intensified group conflicts, deteriorating social systems, and worsening environmental conditions.[1]

As Rosenau's comments suggest, the contemporary world order is characterized by change. In a trivial sense, of course, change never stops. There is, as Helleiner has paraphrased Braudel, a "world of events" in which to place the day-to-day changes that impact on us directly as individuals.[2] Second, there is the "conjunctural" time of trends that take place over ten, twenty or fifty years. This "history of gentle rhythms, of groups and groupings" has been the focus of social scientists and historians. Beyond this there is the very long run – the *longue durée* – that might cover a number of centuries and which focuses on the broadest patterns and structures.[3]

The most obvious recent instance of conjunctural change is the apparent end of the Cold War, which is perceived to have fundamentally transformed the preexisting pattern of relations between states. East–West tensions are no longer thought by most observers to dominate the inter-state system. Ethnic and related conflicts within states and former states are now widely understood to be significant. In fact, as Cox has observed, there is a change *in* the Cold War, not a change *from* the Cold War. Formally, the Cold War between the United States and USSR has passed into history, but there is a substantive meaning to the Cold War which has to do with the construction and maintenance of a set of structures – the national security state, the ideology of national security itself, intelligence and surveillance systems, and the co-optation of the political leadership of subordinate states, amongst other things. These structures remain in place, although they are now much less stable as events in Japan, Italy, Somalia, and the former Yugoslavia attest.[4] The inter-state certitude provided by the Cold War

4

has been mourned by some commentators.[5] Others seem to have sought solace in phenomena such as "Japan-bashing." This change in the form of world order tensions has been matched by the growth of competitive pressures within the global economy, connected to the advent of mobile financial capital. State policy making is now conditioned by the need to attract these financial flows, expressed in the commitment to an appropriate "business climate."[6]

These twin developments have altered the nature of authority in the global system and upset the intellectual means through which international relations is interpreted. The absence of formal superpower conflict and the emphasis on competitiveness within the global economy have decreased the leverage of states and seemingly increased that of corporations and other institutions of global civil society. Mainstream approaches to international relations have not lived up to their scientific aspirations and have failed to predict these developments. The change in the form of the Cold War came as more or less a complete shock to the policy intellectuals informed by neorealist and related frameworks. As Richard Falk has suggested, this "disciplinary 'oversight' was not a matter of a surprise development but represented the overnight collapse of the intellectual framework that had guided academicians and policymakers for decades and was expected to last indefinitely."[7] The demonstrated inadequacies of mainstream approaches to international relations place a premium on theoretical innovation in the study of international relations in the 1990s. The gap between predictive aspiration and predictive failure suggests new departures are required, that the assumptions that guided theory building in the postwar era were tied to the needs of that time. New times require new thinking. Robert W. Cox's work provides one cogent set of concepts with which to approach change in world order.

The crucial thing to understand about Cox's framework is that he begins with a different purpose in mind to that of neorealist international relations scholars. This is the key to the flexibility of his approach when considered beside that of neorealist orthodoxy, in the context of global change. Cox argues that there are two broad purposes for theory.[8] The first is problem solving. Problem solving assumes that the major components of the system, such as states, are not subject to fundamental change. They provide the limits of the system in which the action occurs. It is the action, not the limits of the system, that is the analytical focus of problem solving. Critical theory steps outside the confines of the existing set of relationships to identify the origins and developmental potential of these phenomena. While problem solving theory assumes the functional coherence of existing phenomena, critical theory seeks out the sources of contradiction and conflict in these entities and evaluates their potential to change into different patterns. There is an ethical dimension to the distinction as well, because problem-solving theory, in its concern with solving problems that arise in distinct parts of a complex whole aims to "smooth the functioning of the whole," whilst critical theory "allows for a normative choice in favour of a social and political order different from the prevailing order."[9]

Problem solving and critical theory are not necessarily mutually exclusive. They may be understood to address different concerns or levels within one overall story. However, as Cox argues, the salience of each approach to international relations will vary in relation to each other depending on historical conditions. In conditions of relative stability in the fundamental structures and relationships that constitute international relations, problem-solving work is likely to be more salient. There will be more of a fit between the explanations offered by the various theoretical approaches that make up the problem-solving mainstream and scholarly and public perceptions of international relations phenomena. As Cox observes, for problem solving, "The Cold War was one such period."[10] When this fit becomes too loose, as seems to be the case in the context of the global economy of the 1990s with its heightened competitiveness, the utility of problem-solving theory breaks down and scholars, the general public, and policy makers become more receptive as communities to new ideas that challenge conventional dogmas and received understandings about the limits of the system. Cox's ideas for such a critical theory are examined in the following section.

Coxian historicism[11]

Cox matches his interest in transformations in world order and his critical purpose to an historicist set of assumptions about acquiring knowledge. Historicism can be contrasted with positivism, which tends to provide the assumptions for those with problem-solving purposes. Positivism is that school within philosophy of science which holds that the only means by which claims to knowledge about the world can be sustained is through an appeal to experience, observation, and testing.[12] As Hollis and Smith and Cox comment, positivism, or behavioralism as it has been known in international relations, takes the methods of the natural sciences (specifically, Newtonian physics) as its guiding light. Adopting this approach, observes Cox,

> involves positing a separation of subject and object. The data of politics are externally perceived events brought about by the interaction of actors in a field. The field itself, being an arrangement of actors, has certain properties of its own which can be called "systemic." The concept of "cause" is applicable within such a framework of forces. Powerful actors are "causes" of change in the behavior of less powerful ones, and the structure of the system "causes" certain forms of behavior on the part of actors.[13]

The problem with this approach, according to Cox, is that it cannot account for significant, that is, structural, change which transcends Braudel's "world of events." As Cox writes, "insofar as this approach aspires to a general science of society, it cannot discriminate between times and places."[14] The problem with a "general (read: universally applicable) science of society" is that although it can allow for variance in technological capacities and the leverage of actors, it cannot allow for fundamental divergences in "either the basic nature of the actors (power-seeking) or in their mode of interaction (power-balancing)." In the positivist method, the

> universality of these basic attributes of the social system comes to be perceived as standing outside of and prior to history. History becomes but a mine of data illustrating the permutations and combinations that are possible within an essentially unchanging human story.[15]

Within international relations, this ahistorical worldview is evident in realism's transhistoricization of states as ever-present elements of world order. As Gill writes, by contrast, for Cox, "there are different forms of state and world orders, whose conditions of existence, constitutive principles and norms vary over time."[16] Accordingly, "no transhistorical essentialism or homeostasis is imputed to any given social system or world order."[17] Social science theories which postulate general or universally valid laws or human regularities are not sustainable, except where the temporal boundaries of these laws are acknowledged. Things change over time, including what might be thought of as basic driving forces. Positivism can be useful, but only within "defined historical limits." It is the research program or method of historicism, Cox notes, "to reveal the historical structures characteristic of particular eras within which such regularities prevail."[18] The next section considers this method.

Method of historical structures

The notion of a framework for action or historical structure is a picture of a particular configuration of forces. This configuration does not determine actions in any direct, mechanical way but imposes pressures and constraints. Individuals and groups may move with the pressures or resist and oppose them, but they cannot ignore them. To the extent that they do successfully resist a prevailing historical structure they buttress their actions with an alternative, emerging configuration of forces, a rival structure.[19]

Cox's method of historical structures is an innovative and significant contribution to the study of international relations. While others have written on Gramsci and the influence of social forces on global relations, Cox's unique method for understanding the structures of world order has not been matched elsewhere in the emerging critical tradition for its flexibility and adaptability to research problems. Unlike other methods, Cox's approach is designed to incorporate both the static and dynamic aspects of structures, and thus the use of historicist and positivist epistemologies is conceivable within the parameters of his method, in different instances.

There are two major moments in Cox's research program. The first moment is that of static or synchronic understanding. It has to do with contemplating the coherence of a social relationship within its own terms. Problem-solving theory can be put to a critical purpose here to evaluate how a relationship, an institution, a process operates in narrow or day-to-day terms. The second moment involves understanding the developmental potential in a whole. This diachronic moment seeks out the contradictions and conflicts inherent in a social structure and contemplates the characteristics of emerging social forces and the nature and extent of structural change that is feasible. Governing both these moments is a specification of the basic components, or ontology, which are understood to constitute and to interact within a structure.

How does Cox specify his ontology? In *Production, Power, and World Order* he begins by establishing the ontological significance, if not the primacy, of the production of material life.[20] Cox has been criticized by some for reductionism to production, where production is narrowly conceived. Cox certainly sees the production of the material basis of life as a fundamental activity for all human groups. Social practices evolve as collective human responses to the problem of group survival. In this sense, Cox is an historical materialist, although emphasizing Gramsci's distinction between historical materialism and historical economism. Production, for Cox, includes the production of ideas, of intersubjective meanings, of norms, of institutions and social practices, i.e., of the whole context of ideas and institutions within which the production of material goods takes place. Looking at production is simply a way of thinking about collective life, not a reference to the "economic" sectors of human activity (such as agriculture, commerce, industry, and so forth).[21]

Cox recognizes a level of ontological selection which transcends individual choice. This is the level of intersubjective or collective meanings. Considered in this way, ontologies are sets of shared meanings, which come to define reality. Because people – including scholars – tend to think in collective ways, our actions and words tend to reproduce this understood and shared reality, even if we do not approve of it. As Cox writes, "They [ontologies] are the parameters of our existence. Knowing them to be there means knowing that other people will act as though they are there."[22] The state is an historical example of an intersubjectively constituted entity created by collective human response to material conditions. This and other intersubjectively constituted entities constitute a prevailing ontology. "Ontologies are not arbitrary constructions; they are the specification of the common sense of an epoch."[23]

Cox's work reflects a willingness to sample from discordant intellectual traditions to create a method. For example, he sees no contradiction in using the Weberian notion of elite and the Marxist idea of class in the same analysis, based on the specification of an elite as the political and moral leadership of a class. Elites lead historic blocs understood in the Gramscian sense as coalitions of social forces bound by consent and coercion. Elites comprise the organic intellectuals (including political leaders) who lead hegemonic and counterhegemonic formations. One of Cox's major contributions to international relations is to demonstrate the utility of Weber's ideal type method in dissecting ontological constructs.[24] In doing so, Cox has provided the international relations scholar with a vehicle through which a much more thoroughgoing understanding of intersubjectively

9

constituted entities can be achieved. Ideal types are, in Cox's words, "a concrete and specific way of grasping the variety of actual forms" encountered in the contemporary world and in history. "Persistent patterns" amongst the selected intersubjectively constituted entities can be identified by stopping the movement of history, and "conceptually fixing a particular social practice." In simple terms, this means that the analyst must specify the core relationships and the parameters of the object in question in a systematic way before other considerations take place. The ideal type can now be compared and contrasted with other social practices to assess its significance. In the second moment, that of diachronic development, ideal types can be evaluated to assess the points of stress and conflict within respective practices.

Cox's "frameworks for action" are a development of his synchronic tool kit, incorporating a series of ideal types, as dictated by the particular circumstances under consideration. They are the gateway to diachronic understanding within his method. The task of the analyst is to specify the forces that interact in a structure, through the delineation of ideal types, and determine the "lines of force" between these different poles, which is "always an historical question to be answered by a study of the particular case."[25] There is no repetition of the reductionism inherent in the structural Marxist conception of a material or objective base determining an ideal or subjective superstructure (commonly referred to as the base–superstructure metaphor).[26] For Cox, historical structures

> are contrast models: like ideal types they provide, in a logically coherent form, a simplified representation of a complex reality and an expression of tendencies, limited in their applicability to time and space, rather than fully realised developments.[27]

Cox proposes that three broad categories of forces interact in a structure: material capabilities; ideas; and institutions. Material capabilities consist of dynamic productive capabilities (such as technology) and accumulated resources. There are at least two kinds of ideas: intersubjective meanings, which tend to cut across social divisions; and rival collective images of social order, which are specific to competing social forces based, amongst other things, on locality, ethnicity, and religion, and which relate to the material conditions of existence of the group. Institutions tend to stabilize and perpetuate a particular order. They may also acquire a degree of autonomy, take on their own life, and serve as agents of change.[28] They may become the "battleground" for opposing tendencies. Accordingly, institutions and the processes of struggle between contending social forces that occur within and around them have a close connection to Gramsci's discussion of hegemony.[29] Institutions provide the opportunity for dominant social forces to soften their social domination through the buying off of subordinate forces, thus strengthening their hold through a process of consensus building. Both hegemonic and nonhegemonic structures can be distinguished. In the latter case, social control may be maintained through explicit domination and terror.

An important consideration in Cox's method of historical structures is the limited nature of each structure. These "limited totalities" as Cox calls them, do not incorporate everything, but rather represent "a particular sphere of human activity in its historically located totality." The problem inherent in problem-solving theory, of holding everything static through the *ceteris paribus* invocation is avoided in Cox's method by "juxtaposing and connecting" historical structures in related spheres. Diachronic understanding is introduced by deriving structures from historical situations rather than abstract models of world order, and by anticipating the development of rival or counterhegemonic structures.

My research on the impact of wholesale credit rating in the global economy is an example of the exploration of just such a limited totality.[30] In this research I explore the ideas central to the rating process which derive from prevailing models of economic and financial analysis. The material capabilities of the process are evaluated, as they relate to the impact of downgrading on the cost of capital. Lastly, rating agencies and related institutions are examined as sources of authority in competition with other institutions involved in allocating capital, including governments. This work has suggested the existence of a nascent counterhegemonic structure in Europe opposed to some of the features of this existing limited totality, based on sources of material capability (the Euromarkets), and a different history of capital allocation practices from that prevailing in the United States.

The final element to Cox's research program or method is to place the hegemonic and counterhegemonic structures that have been identified by the analyst, comprising sets of material capabilities, ideas and institutions, into three broad "levels" or "spheres" of the social world.[31] These three spheres consist of the social forces related to production, forms of state, and world orders. These levels are not in any fixed relationship to each other, just as the three categories of forces identified by Cox exist only in relation to their historically endowed capacities. Perhaps the most familiar historical structure that we might contemplate through this method is the Cold War, a limited totality which contained a certain set of institutions (for example, NATO), ideas (McCarthyism and its derivatives), and material capabilities (the military-industrial complex, to use a familiar term). This hegemonic limited totality significantly impacted on the social forces of production (for example, constraining the development of social democratic or socialist consciousness in labor unions in the United States amongst other places), forms of state (elaborating forms of social control and surveillance) and world orders (liberal trading order and anti-communist alliances). The next step involves considering the relationships between these spheres under the pressures produced by the Cold War and other historical structures, and the changes in the historical structure as the Cold War evolved and as other totalities, such as the Third World demand for a New International Economic Order and subsequently the rise of a global economy, became significant.[32]

Reception and criticism

The reception of Cox's work has varied over time and place, as his thinking has developed, and as the world order in which he has developed his ideas has been transformed around him.[a] There seems to be something of a break in his work between the dominance of more problem-solving concerns to do with international organization which produced *The Anatomy of Influence* (written with Harold K. Jacobson), and subsequent work.[33] These were the times in which Cox was a member of the Board of Editors of *International Organization*. Positive citations to this earlier work abound in the American international relations literature of the 1970s and 1980s.

From the latter 1970s through the 1980s to the present, after Cox became professor of political science at York University in Toronto, he further developed his critical, historicist viewpoint, returning to his reading of history and political theory and elaborating on some of the themes he had begun exploring during his latter days at Columbia University, as suggested by an article in *World Politics* in 1976, amongst other work.[34] The latter Cox increasingly began to publish in British journals after previously publishing the bulk of his scholarly

[a] See Cox's discussion of his "Influences and Commitments," chapter 2 in this volume.

12

output in American periodicals. This new work included the two often-cited articles in *Millennium* which served to bring him to the attention of people interested in international relations theory in Britain.[35] His work is taught widely in the United Kingdom, including at the London School of Economics and at the University of Sussex, reflecting the relative openness to critical perspectives in research and teaching in that country.[36]

The reception of Cox's work has been more complex in the United States. Until recently Cox's critical work has been largely ignored by the problem-solving-dominated American academy. This is understandable. His concerns have largely differed from those of most US scholars concerned as they have been with the detail of hegemony maintenance, more narrowly conceived as "policy-relevant scholarship." A generation of international relations scholars has been trained in the United States in terms of a prevailing ethos of what Kuhn would call normal science, in which many of the analytical tools that have come to dominate public policy studies and the field of American politics more generally have been applied to "issue areas" within inter-state affairs, much as these were applied to relations between the US states. However, this state of affairs began to change with the republication of Cox's 1981 *Millennium* article, "Social Forces, States and World Orders" in the reader on neorealism edited by Robert O. Keohane.[37] The publication of this book reflected a growth in theoretical diversity in the American academy as the insularity and self-confidence of Cold War assumptions came under assault from the rise of a global economy, the increasing exhaustion of American hegemony, and the growth of transnational civil society which cast into increasing doubt the idea of states as the exclusive units of the global system. In other words, the shifting character of world order provided a broader context in which new patterns of thought became feasible, in which unexpected problems made the preexisting normal science less sustainable. In this context Cox's work has become more salient in the United States, and is now taught at some major American research universities, including the University of Michigan and the University of Minnesota, amongst others.[38]

Cox has been variously understood and portrayed. To Adams, his use of dialectical method means that Cox never breaks away from what Adams terms a "watery Marxism," incorporating notions of surplus, class forces, and hegemony which in Adams' words, "we have all seen before."[39] Others see the opposite approach in Cox, deploring the lack of "overdetermination" and the absence of "overall structure" amongst his variables such that the "true consequence" of Cox's position is to produce a "pluralist empiricism."[40] Other reviews have been favorable, celebrating his originality, including those in *Contemporary Sociology* and in *American Political Science Review*.[41] Feminists have responded positively to his work, praising his concern with emancipatory knowledge, despite thinking he has given insufficient weight to gender and related concerns.[42] Mark Hoffman has portrayed Cox as the field leader in the adaptation of the central themes of critical social and political thought – theory and its relationship to interests and emancipation – to international relations, using Cox's discussion of theory as a criterion by which to judge the efforts of others.[43] Cox's thinking about method seems to have had less impact on the American academy, where his work on the internationalization of production and of forms of authority has been more influential, as reflected in a recent article by Wendt.[44] This may be evidence of the greater effectiveness of his approach in the analysis of phenomena thrown up by a world order in which a multitude of actors and processes vie with each other, disturbing the intellectual consensus established by postwar problem-solving scholars.

Conclusion

Robert W. Cox's work is motivated by fundamentally different purposes from that of mainstream neorealist international relations scholarship. He seeks to understand transformation in historical structures in order to influence change along the lines of what Gill has called the "self defence of society."[45] To this critical purpose he marries an historicist epistemology, allocating positivism to the questions of detail and synchronic modeling. Indeed, perhaps uniquely amongst critical international relations theorists his work can in part be distinguished by the degree to which methods for synchronic analysis are developed. His approach is not a mere retreat to history or thick description. By constantly refining concepts through an exposure to changing circumstances he allows for deductive precision when appropriate. Yet what really marks his work as distinctive is his concern with diachronic development, with the dialectics or genealogy of change, that is, the tendencies to social transformation arising from the contradictions between ascendant and descendent social forces. His method of historical structures, tying together conceptual contri-

14

butions from Vico, Sorel, Weber, Gramsci, Polanyi, and Braudel, amongst others, brings this concern with the potential of world order change into graphic relief, because this method allows for the synchronic and the diachronic to be integrated. Understanding and using Cox's method to establish intellectual and political insight into the nature of world order is a demanding scholarly enterprise. But Coxian historicism offers more than description. Unlike mainstream or problem-solving international relations theory, Coxian historicism also contains an emancipatory project which means that it should be of the highest priority to anyone wishing to understand the world in order to change it.

Notes

This essay is original to this volume. I thank Robert W. Cox, Stephen Gill, Susan Strange, James H. Mittelman, John Maclean, and Robert J. O'Brien for comments. An earlier version of this essay was presented at the annual conference of the British International Studies Association, University of Warwick, Coventry, England, December 1993.

1 James N. Rosenau, "Governance, Order, and Change in World Politics," in James N. Rosenau and Ernst-Otto Czempiel (eds.), *Governance Without Government: Order and Change in World Politics* (Cambridge: Cambridge University Press, 1992), p. 1.

2 Eric Helleiner, "Fernand Braudel and International Political Economy," *International Studies Notes*, vol. 15, no. 3 (Fall 1990), p. 75.

3 Ibid.

4 This argument is derived from comments by Robert Cox in a private communication to the author, January 9, 1994.

5 John J. Mearsheimer, "Back to the Future: Instability in Europe after the Cold War," *International Security*, vol. 15, no. 1 (Summer 1990), pp. 5–56.

6 Stephen Gill and David Law, "Global Hegemony and the Structural Power of Capital," in Stephen Gill (ed.), *Gramsci, Historical Materialism, and International Relations* (Cambridge: Cambridge University Press, 1993).

7 Richard Falk, Review of Rosenau and Czempiel, *Governance Without Government*, in *American Political Science Review*, vol. 87, no. 2 (June 1993), p. 545.

8 See "Postscript 1985," in Robert W. Cox, "Social Forces, States, and World Orders: Beyond International Relations Theory," in Robert O. Keohane (ed.), *Neorealism and Its Critics* (New York: Columbia University Press, 1986), p. 244. The postscript is included in this volume as "Realism, Positivism, and Historicism" (chapter 4).

9 Robert W. Cox, "Social Forces, States, and World Orders: Beyond International Relations Theory," *Millennium: Journal of International Studies*, vol. 10, no. 2 (Summer 1981), pp. 129–130. This essay is included as chapter 6

in this volume. Subsequent page references are to the original *Millennium* version.

10 Cox, "Social Forces, States, and World Orders," p. 130.
11 This term was first used in Stephen Gill and James H. Mittelman, "Innovation in International Relations Theory: Coxian Historicism as an Alternative Paradigm," paper presented to the annual meeting of the International Studies Association, Acapulco, Mexico, March 1993.
12 Martin Hollis and Steve Smith, *Explaining and Understanding International Relations* (Oxford: Clarendon Press, 1990), p. 12.
13 Cox, "Postscript 1985," p. 242.
14 Ibid., p. 243.
15 Ibid.
16 Stephen Gill, "Epistemology, Ontology, and the 'Italian School,' " in Gill, *Gramsci, Historical Materialism, and International Relations*, p. 29.
17 Ibid.
18 Cox, "Postscript 1985," p. 244.
19 Robert W. Cox, "Critical Political Economy," lecture given to the United Nations University conference on Emerging Trends in Political Economy and International Relations Theory, Oslo, Norway, August 1993, p. 4.
20 Robert W. Cox, *Production, Power, and World Order: Social Forces in the Making of History* (New York: Columbia University Press, 1987), p. 1.
21 I am indebted to Robert Cox for clarifying his approach to this important issue in a private communication with the author, January 9, 1994.
22 Cox, "Critical Political Economy," p. 4.
23 Ibid., p. 5.
24 Cox, *Production, Power, and World Order*, p. 4.
25 Cox, "Social Forces, States, and World Orders," p. 136.
26 Cox distinguishes two divergent Marxist perspectives in an effort to distance himself from the subject–object distinction made in the base–superstructure metaphor and its attendant implication that consciousness and ideas are mere surface forms of material forces. This distinction is most forcefully stated in his essay, "Social Forces, States, and World Orders: Beyond International Relations Theory," included as chapter 6 in this volume. Cox explains:

> There is a Marxism which reasons historically and seeks to explain, as well as to promote, changes in social relations; there is also a Marxism, designed as a framework for the analysis of the capitalist state and society, which turns its back on historical knowledge in favour of a more static and abstract conceptualisation of the mode of production. The first we may call by the name under which it recognises itself: historical materialism. It is evident in the historical works of Marx, in those of present-day Marxist historians such as Eric Hobsbawm, and in the thought of Gramsci. It has also influenced some who would not be considered (or consider themselves) Marxist in any strict sense, such as many of the French historians

associated with the *Annales*. The second is represented by the so-called structural Marxism of Althusser and Poulantzas ("so-called" in order to distinguish their use of "structure" from the concept of historical structure in this essay) and most commonly take the form of an exegesis of *Capital* and other sacred texts. Structural Marxism shares some of the features of the Neorealist problem-solving approach such as its ahistorical, essentialist epistemology, though not its precision in handling data nor, since it has remained very largely a study in abstractions, its practical applicability to concrete problems. ("Social Forces, States, and World Orders," p. 133)

27 Ibid., p. 137.
28 For example, although nationalist and liberation movements spearheaded the struggle, the United Nations Committee of Twenty-Four played an important role in decolonization. I am indebted to James H. Mittelman for emphasizing this point in a private communication with the author, January 20, 1994.
29 Cox, "Social Forces, States, and World Orders," pp. 136–137.
30 Timothy J. Sinclair, "Passing Judgement: Credit Rating Processes as Regulatory Mechanisms of Governance in the Emerging World Order," *Review of International Political Economy*, vol. 1, no. 1 (Spring 1994), pp. 133–159.
31 Cox, "Social Forces, States, and World Orders," p. 138.
32 On the New International Economic Order see Robert W. Cox, "Ideologies and the New International Economic Order: Reflections on Some Recent Literature" included in this volume as chapter 18.
33 Robert W. Cox and Harold K. Jacobson, *The Anatomy of Influence: Decision Making in International Organization* (New Haven, Conn.: Yale University Press, 1972).
34 Robert W. Cox, "On Thinking About Future World Order," included in this volume as chapter 5.
35 These two articles, "Social Forces, States, and World Orders: Beyond International Relations Theory," and "Gramsci, Hegemony, and International Relations: An Essay in Method," are both reproduced in this volume as chapters 6 and 7.
36 Robert J. O'Brien, "International Relations and International Political Economy: Apprentice as Teacher?," in John McMillan and Andew Linklater (eds.), *New Directions in International Relations* (London: Pinter, 1995). O'Brien chronicles the relative penetration of *Production, Power, and World Order* and of works which incorporate Cox's thinking, for example, that of Stephen Gill and David Law, *The Global Political Economy: Perspectives, Problems and Policies* (Baltimore: Johns Hopkins University Press, 1988).
37 Keohane, *Neorealism and Its Critics*.
38 It should be mentioned in this regard that Cox's work was honored by an eminent scholar panel at the International Studies Association meeting in Acapulco, Mexico, March 1993. Those presenting papers on Cox's work were James N. Rosenau, James H. Mittelman and Stephen Gill, Craig

N. Murphy, V. Spike Peterson, and Mustapha Pasha. The panel was exceptionally well attended and at Cox's insistence was a challenging intellectual event, going far beyond the usual homilies to a genuine engagement with Cox's ideas. The panel also provided an opportunity for warm appreciation of the considerable contributions of Jessie Cox to be made. Thanks are due here to Stephen Gill for emphasizing the significance of this event to me.

39 John Adams, Review of Cox, *Production, Power, and World Order*, *Annals of the American Academy*, vol. 501 (January 1989), pp. 224–225.

40 Peter Burnham, "Neo-Gramscian Hegemony and the International Order," *Capital and Class*, no. 45 (Autumn 1991), pp. 77–78. Cited in Leo Panitch, "Rethinking the Role of the State in an Era of Globalization," paper presented to the workshop on Globalization: Opportunities and Challenges, The American University, Washington, D.C., March 1994, p. 22.

41 See Dietrich Rueschemeyer, "Macrosociology: Social Change, Social Movements, World Systems, Comparative and Historical Sociology," *Contemporary Sociology*, vol. 18, no. 5 (September 1989), pp. 693–696; Douglas E. Williams, Review of Cox, *Production, Power, and World Order*, *American Political Science Review*, vol. 83, no. 1 (March 1989), pp. 347–349. Both of these reviews comment on the innovativeness of Cox's approach, as does the review by Susan Strange in *International Affairs*, vol. 64, no. 2 (April 1988), pp. 269–270, which goes on to label Cox "an eccentric in the best English sense of the word, a loner, a fugitive from intellectual camps of victory, both Marxist and liberal." For a longer piece, which tries to show the originality of Cox's approach, compares it to that of Robert Gilpin, and traces the lineage of Cox's ideas, see Stephen Gill, "Two Concepts of International Political Economy," *Review of International Studies*, vol. 16, no. 4 (1990), pp. 369–381.

42 Susan Judith Ship, "And What About Gender? Feminism and International Relations Theory's Third Debate," in Claire Turenne Sjolander and Wayne S. Cox (eds.), *Beyond Positivism: Critical Reflections on International Relations* (Boulder, Colo.: Lynne Rienner, 1994). Also, comments by V. Spike Peterson, panelist, Eminent Scholar Panel Honoring Robert W. Cox, annual meeting of the International Studies Association, Acapulco, Mexico, March 1993.

43 Mark Hoffman, "Critical Theory and the Inter-Paradigm Debate," *Millennium: Journal of International Studies*, vol. 16, no. 2 (Summer 1987), pp. 231–249.

44 Alexander Wendt, "Collective Identity Formation and the International State," *American Political Science Review*, vol. 88, no. 2 (June 1994), p. 393.

45 Stephen Gill, "Gramsci and Global Politics: Towards a Post-Hegemonic Research Agenda," in Gill, *Gramsci, Historical Materialism, and International Relations*, p. 2.

2   Influences and commitments

In a review of *Production, Power, and World Order* Susan Strange wrote that I am "an eccentric in the best English sense of the word, a loner, a fugitive from intellectual camps of victory, both Marxist and liberal."[1] The unconventionality of my intellectual journey requires some explanation for those who would want to situate what I have written in the context of my life.

Two kinds of influence are at play. There is the influence of circumstances and events personally experienced; and the influence of authors and ideas encountered. The reader will have to judge whether or not there is consistency or rational development in the sequence of my commitments.

Conservatism and social democracy

Growing up in Montreal during the 1930s and 1940s shaped my outlook. From an early age, I was inclined to see the contradictions in the values of my milieu and to challenge its orthodoxies. My family were conservatives in politics, so I began to take a critical interest in conservatism. For Anglo-Canadians of that era, conservatism was the British connection, and for Anglo-Quebecers it was also a sense of complacent, self-satisfied superiority, with regard to French (and Catholic) Quebecers. These feelings were exaggerated during World War II because of lukewarm commitment or outright opposition to the war among much of the French-speaking population. Given my disposition to question the dominant attitudes of my milieu, I devoted my research interests to French-Canadian politics, and my theoretical interests to reading some classics of conservatism.

I read Edmund Burke from whom I derived the notion that conservatism meant an organic and solidaristic vision of society. Contrary to eighteenth-century rationalist notions of the social contract as an ever-renewable pact among a multitude of self-regarding individuals, for Burke the social contract had the more integral – one could say "romantic" in its eighteenth-century meaning – aura of "the great primaeval contract of eternal society," as he put it "a partnership in all science; a partnership in all art; a partnership in every virtue, and in all perfection."[2]

Here we have the notion of a hierarchical order but one with bonds of mutual obligation that transcend individual interests. Furthermore, the state and society are thought of as maintaining that spirit of solidarity while changing through history. As my political awareness developed, this conservatism, shedding its fixed hierarchical aspect, came to seem more consistent with socialism than with the possessive individualism of economic liberalism. The organic concept of society was the link between conservatism and socialism.

In addition, I discovered something consistent with Burke's vision in the experience of French Canada, a people whose political consciousness was focused on the solidarity and survival of a nation in an environment perceived to be hostile. I had little affinity with the doctrinaire ultramontanism of the clerical right in Quebec; but I discovered through my research and by looking around me a more humanist and pragmatic French-Canadian conservatism[3] that led towards a moderate nationalism with a social dimension. I read the nationalist newspaper *Le Devoir* and went to political meetings in the east end of Montreal. During the Quebec election of August 1944, I worked in support of my friend Gordon Rothney, candidate for the *Bloc populaire canadien* in Brome County. Rothney was a professor of history at what is now Concordia University in Montreal, and one of a handful of Quebec Anglophones committed to French-Canadian nationalist politics at that time. Through him I met briefly André Laurendeau, then provincial leader of the *Bloc* and, much later, the co-chair of the Royal Commission on Bilingualism and Biculturalism set up by the government of Lester Pearson.[4] Laurendeau was an intellectual in politics, a reasoner, not a demagogue. He had little success in electoral politics but made a great impact on the French-Canadian mind and on the future of federalism in Canada.

With Laurendeau, Quebec nationalism grew from a cultural-political anti-imperialist movement to embrace a social democratic view of an alternative to the Anglo-dominated capitalism of the 1940s. The *Bloc*, in the election of 1944, represented itself as Quebec's counterpart to the Cooperative Commonwealth Federation (CCF) which won the provincial election in Saskatchewan that year to become the first socialist government in North America. Unfortunately for Canada, the left in English-speaking Canada rarely and ineffectively made contact with or showed understanding of the left in Quebec.[5]

Universalism and relativism

My first job after graduating from university was with the International Labor Office. The ILO had passed the war years in Canada, a refugee from Nazi-dominated Europe, housed on the campus of McGill University where I was a student. One day the principal of the university, Cyril James, summoned me to his office to inform me the ILO wanted to begin to build up its postwar staff; and shortly thereafter I received an ILO appointment at the most junior professional level. A year later, I was married and settled in Geneva – temporarily, I thought, but the temporary lasted some twenty-five years.

I welcomed the move to Geneva with the ILO as a chance to live in Europe for a while and as a career experience; but there were two special reasons why I was ready to go. One was relief at the opportunity to distance myself from a milieu in which I had become quite alienated, my political commitments being so much at variance with anything acceptable within it. The other was that I thought my experience of trying to bridge two cultures, or at least trying to understand how the world looked through two quite distinct mental frameworks, should be good basic training for the work of an official in the newly established United Nations system.

I did not know then that this would be an unusual and sometimes resented attitude within international organizations. Wherever officials were able to rise above nationally conditioned reflexes, they tended to become exponents of a universalistic organizational ideology – a mode of thought that I would later call "hegemonic."

From my university studies in history, I had derived a certain relativism. One of my history professors, E. R. Adair, pointed out the contrast between the devout Catholic, Lord Acton, who judged and condemned Machiavelli and the Renaissance papacy in the light of the universal truths of Christian morality, and the Anglican historian,

21

Bishop Mandell Creighton, who judged the popes and Machiavelli in the context of their own times. Creighton looked for the consequences of words and actions, what Max Weber would later call an ethic of responsibility. Lord Acton held to absolute values.

One cannot lightly opt for one side only of this dilemma between principle and common practice. Integrity and understanding require a reconciliation between the absolute and the relative in morality. Much later, I found the dilemma nicely framed in a quotation by Isaiah Berlin from an unidentified author: "To realise the relative validity of one's convictions and yet stand for them unflinchingly is what distinguishes a civilized man from a barbarian."[6] The quotation gives no philosophical grounding for moral commitment; but it does avoid the ethical nihilism of some current postmodern writing. The risks in nothing but relativism are, on the one hand, an abdication of responsibility and, on the other, a disdain of all values as atavisms to be superseded by good managerial practice. My relativism called for mutual recognition of differences in value systems among cultures and civilizations.

This intellectual position often put me at odds with my new milieu in the ILO. The dominant ideology there was committed to the universality of some very obviously historically contingent European–American practices in labor–management relations. Any disposition to think of these practices as relative to time and place was frowned upon within the institution. They were taken to be the ultimate universal truth of production relations, and the western capitalism that had given birth to them was hidden in the blinding light of universal truth. I found myself in the moral position of the anthropologist – a participant observer of my new tribe. I was in it but could not be entirely of it insofar as I reflected upon the sources of the norms it espoused. This is a difficult position to maintain over a long period. For me the difficulty developed slowly, and culminated in rupture only after twenty-five years.

Labor and hegemony

During much of my career with the ILO, I was associated with Director-General David Morse, an American who presided over the evolution and expansion of the ILO's program during the postwar and Cold War years. I was his *chef de cabinet* (or principal staff officer) and then chief of the ILO's Program and Planning Division.

During the larger part of this career, I was directly involved in the politics of running an international agency by an American executive head during the Cold War. There were three inherently contradictory but essential bases for political survival in this context: (1) to maintain the support of the United States (essential especially to an American head who was recurrently being attacked as "soft on communism" by Cold War hard-liners in the US labor movement and as a cover for "creeping socialism" by the more reactionary elements of American business); (2) to maintain the principle of "universality" which meant trying to make Soviet bloc membership acceptable to the West in an organization where the majority of votes could always be mobilized behind the anti-communist exclusionary slogan of "tripartism"; and (3) to achieve and maintain a reasonable degree of program coherence in a bureaucracy that was segmented into feudal-type baronies politically sustained by distinct elements among the organization's constituents.

In 1964, I took a year's leave from the ILO to teach at the Graduate Institute of International Studies in Geneva and during that year wrote a paper, "The Executive Head," which was intended as an analytical exercise on the politics of leadership in the peculiar world of international organization. It instantly became a *cause celèbre* in the ILO milieu. I confess the title was a borrowing from Machiavelli's *Prince*; and critics of the paper bestowed upon me Machiavelli's popular reputation as an immoralist rather than crediting me with his merits as a political analyst. The paper touched the raw nerve of the organizational ideologists. They cried "sacrilege" and raised suspicion towards me, especially in the western trade union camp. From then on, I was a controversial figure in an organizational milieu that put a premium on conformity.

In the last phase of my ILO career, I took some distance from the day-to-day management of the organization. I was appointed by Morse as director of the International Institute for Labor Studies. I had taken a large part in designing and setting up this institute which was intended to become a research and educational center enjoying autonomy and intellectual freedom. However, whether or not such freedom could exist really depended upon who was director-general.

David Morse had accepted the notion that it would be healthy for a large bureaucracy with an established ideology to harbor some faculty for independent criticism of its norms and practices, especially since the critical faculty had only powers of expression, not of decision. For the orthodox, however, that was another instance of sacrilege; and the head of the orthodox faction became director-general in succession to Morse during 1970. It was evident to me that the role of the institute as I had conceived it, could not survive. Philosophical difference was compounded by personal incompatibility. This was not a person with whom I could maintain a civilized dialogue about our differences.

I had arranged, prior to the change of directors-general, to take a year's leave at the University of Toronto. During that year I completed, with Harold Jacobson of the University of Michigan, a collaborative work entitled *The Anatomy of Influence: Decision Making in International Organization.*[7]

The new director-general, a jurist who published copiously himself, held to the principle that the executive head had to approve – or, as he liked to put it, give his *nihil obstat* to – any publication of whatever kind by an ILO official.[8] I was alerted by a friend and colleague that the new boss, aware that I was engaged in a collective scholarly enterprise, was waiting to catch me in breach of this customary rule. I decided to take the initiative and to comply by half. I transmitted the manuscript for his information, but explicitly not for his approval. He replied with a refusal of the *nihil obstat* which I had not sought. This was for me the last in a series of interventions by him in the functioning of the institute that together constituted a denial of intellectual independence. I resigned, as I had anticipated I would when entering into this *dialogue de sourds.*[9]

A sense of liberation came with throwing off the constraints peculiar to this rather special international bureaucracy. I retained respect for many friends and former colleagues who continued to use their considerable talents for the best within an environment that had become impossible for me. I began full-time academic activity at Columbia University.

The problem for me with the ILO had become even broader than resistance to the attempt to discipline and censor what was done in the institute and my own work. I had gradually come to understand that my official role and the work of the ILO in general had become an accessory to what I soon came to call "hegemony."

This awareness began with the events of 1968. I was in Mexico when the news broke about the student revolt in France. I crossed the Atlantic from New York on an Italian liner, sitting at the same table with a young American woman who had been with Robert Kennedy's campaign in California when he was assassinated. I disembarked at Cannes; the French state and its services had ground to a halt but Swissair got me back to Geneva. In September, my wife and I went on official business to the Soviet Union as guests of the Soviet Academy of Sciences. In Moscow, apart from the formal toasts and receptions, we talked darkly and privately with a very few Soviet scholars who gave us their critical interpretation of the Soviet occupation of Czechoslovakia and the reasons behind the supression of the Prague spring. In the Academgorodok outside Novosibirsk, I had talks with the economist and later adviser to Gorbachev, Abel Aganbegyan, and with the sociologist and later author of an important document in the era of *perestroika*,[10] Tatyana Zaslavskaya. On returning to Geneva, we stopped in Prague and Bratislava. Soviet tanks surrounded the airports; our local contacts showed us the flowers strewn on the streets where Soviet bullets had felled citizens of Bratislava; and at a retreat in the Tatra Mountains, we heard staff from Slovak television, in retreat from the reimposition of Moscow rule, singing World War II German marching songs.

All of this gave pause for reflection. The movements of 1968 were all defeated, but they revealed that the convictions of Cold War ideology were transparent and fragile. The hiatus between ideology and reality was manifest.

In my immediate world, these contradictions became troubling. The labor movement was the political force behind social democracy – the organic and solidaristic form of society that corresponded to my earlier concept of conservatism. But the labor movement, in some of its international manifestations, bore little resemblance to this ideal vision. Indeed, the more one knew about the inner politics of international labor, the more what one saw negated the vision many rank-and-file union members had about the mission of the labor movement. The reality ranged from a kind of labor imperialism through which rich-country unions sought to dominate poor-country unions,[11] through collaboration with national employers and governments in a kind of Cold War corporatism, to active involvement in intelligence service activities designed to undermine and overthrow radical governments.[a]

I began to see that my work through the institute had implicitly promoted a perspective on labor and social policy that reflected the

---

[a] See "Labor and Hegemony" included in this volume (chapter 19).

dominant social forces in the rich countries and in the world. I now sensed the importance of a broader, more critical perspective. I had, indeed, begun, almost unconsciously, to work towards this in an enquiry initiated through the Institute for Labor Studies, on world trends in labor relations.[12] This ultimately became *Production, Power, and World Order: Social Forces in the Making of History*.[13] The book, published in 1987, spanned an evolution in my thinking over almost twenty years. It was an effort to integrate ideas and experience into a comprehensive way of thinking about social change. It took its final form only in the two years immediately preceding publication. That form represents but a moment in a continuing process. The book was lacking in respects that have since become important to me. It does not take account of the biosphere, nor does it consider the significance of the perspectives of different traditions of civilization. It may be inadequate in its treatment of gender. These would all be major gaps in any comprehensive view of world order today. But the book does show the interrelationship of social forces, forms of state, and structures of world order in processes of global transformation. It does look for the springs of future change through a type of class analysis that required liberation from the constraints of officialdom.

Retrospectively, I can see a gradual but fundamental shift in my thinking from the world events of 1968 and those more personally leading to my break with the ILO (which were interrelated), through my efforts thereafter to formulate a consistent basis in thought for a critical analysis of social change. I began, before this transition, with the tools of American political science, notably the functionalism of the comparative politics theorists that I had absorbed while teaching at the Graduate Institute in Geneva. This influence is evident in *The Anatomy of Influence*. I gradually shed this approach in favor of a return to the more historical mode of thinking I had adopted as a student and the Vichian and Marxian critical thought I came to appreciate in the course of the 1970s. These were better able to make sense of global and personal events that reshaped my outlook. This evolution covered at least a decade. The changed approach that grew out of it was articulated first and most fully in the two articles published in *Millennium* in 1981 and 1983.[b]

---

[b] See "Social Forces, States, and World Orders: Beyond International Relations Theory," and "Gramsci, Hegemony, and International Relations: An Essay in Method," included in this volume as chapters 6 and 7.

Realism and historicism

Production, Power, and World Order completed a phase of my thinking that arose out of concentration upon production relations – my ILO phase. I was now in a position to expand my thinking from this base into other areas. In this process, early influences merged with new readings and reflection upon events. Among the intellectual influences of my earlier university years, two stand out: Georges Sorel and Edward Hallett Carr. They seem contradictory figures in some ways. Sorel denounced the state, while Carr is now regarded as the father of state-centric international relations theory. In my view, they were both realists, but they told me different things about realism.

Many graduate students in international relations today come to Carr through the stylized pseudo-scientific neorealism that became fashionable during the Cold War.[14] I had the advantage of having read Carr closer to the time he was writing, and of only encountering "neorealism" when I was well prepared to react critically to it. Of course, I read the *Twenty Years' Crisis* which is what remains of Carr on graduate-course reading lists in international relations, but I also read Carr's books on Marx, Bakunin, and Dostoyevsky, on the nine-teenth-century Russian exiles, and on the Bolshevik Revolution – and his thoughts on the nature of history. There was no disposition in Carr to isolate "levels of analysis." He saw the interrelatedness of industrialization, change in forms of state, change in ideas, and change in world order.[15] Carr brought an historical mode of thought to what-ever he wrote about. He was equally alive to economic, social, cul-tural, and ideological matters. He studied individuals, especially those whose intellectual influence marked an era; but most of all, he brought all these elements to an understanding of structural change.

Sorel taught me that you could take some things from Marxism without swallowing the whole package. For a history student, Sorel had a much more perceptive understanding of historical process and of struggle as the moving force in history than was given in the crude economic determinism that often represented itself as Marxism in my youth.[16] For Sorel, historical materialism was to be understood as the relationship between mentalities and material conditions of existence. Later, E. P. Thompson put it as the relationship between social being and social consciousness.[17] Sorel was interested in the subjective movements in historical struggles. He knew that outcomes are always unpredictable, but that nothing will be achieved without passion, and

27

therefore to understand the sources of political passion is of the utmost importance.[18]

As for Marx, so for Sorel, the point in studying society was to change it. He also awakened in me a suspicion of positivism and pseudo-science applied to human affairs. I also liked the way he stood out as an exception, a "loner" to use Susan Strange's word, apart from the fashionable intellectuals of Paris.

While in university, I read R. G. Collingwood's *The Idea of History*.[19] In truth, I was more interested in history as a mode of understanding than in the study of any particular period and place in history. My work on Quebec politics was motivated by the form anti-imperialism took for me at that time and place and by the desire (which I would later encounter in Vico) to be able to enter into the mind of another culture. The theory of history was to be an enduring interest.

It seemed to me that a difficulty with many historians was their disposition to dismiss theory. An unavowed or unconscious theory can be an intellectual trap, an ideological prison. Collingwood argued that historiography consisted in rethinking the thought of the past. I did not understand this as a statement of idealism, that everything came out of the mind. With Sorel superimposed upon Collingwood, I understood it to mean a relationship between the experienced material world and the subjectivity through which people interpreted and acted upon that material world; and I took it as a guideline for my reflections upon social and political change.

People, in different times and places, have been collectively confronted by challenges arising from their material conditions of existence. Collectively, they have worked out different ways of interpreting and responding to these challenges through struggles pitting class against class, community against community. The social practices they collectively devised ranged from religion, through social and political organization, to technology. They embraced different rationalities and different normative orders. The formation of communities of struggle became the central issue of politics.

The mind is the privileged channel of access to understanding how social institutions are constructed to cope with material problems, how communities, in E. P. Thompson's phrase "make themselves." Better to say the relationship of idealism to materialism is dialectical. They are two necessary and complementary ways to approach reality.

Collingwood led me back in time to Vico. I began to read Vico on my return to university as a professor at Columbia after leaving the

ILO. Vico confirmed my view that there is an alternative historicist tradition to positivist social science, and that this historicist mode of understanding is the proper route towards the study of historical structures and structural change.

I have taken the term "historical structure" from Fernand Braudel.[20] It is not to be found in Vico. Vico used *cosa*, or thing, to have the same meaning, incidentally giving a material character to an institution or consecrated pattern of human relationships. *Cosa*, or historical structure, covered systems of language, of law, of religion, of morals, of economic organization, of family and social life. Vico negates universalism in one sense. He argues that social practices have changed through class struggles, and that human nature itself is not a fixed essence but the ensemble of social relations changing through the course of history.[21] But he also affirms a different kind of universalism: the potential for what he called a common mental dictionary. By this he meant concepts that grasped the common features that make history intelligible.

All peoples, according to Vico, have confronted similar problems in the course of their development. It should therefore be possible to derive concepts that help explain events occurring in the distinct histories of different peoples. The study of specific events is to be joined to ideas that make possible comparisons or generalizations about social change – the possibility of what we call social science. The unique and the general are combined; indeed, without the general it would be impossible to understand or explain the unique.[22]

This mode of understanding is so different from that of positivist social science that the term "science" creates some confusion. "Science" has been so far appropriated by positivism, by the separation of observing subject from observed object, that an interpretive, hermeneutic, historicist mode of knowledge lends itself to the epithet "unscientific."[23] Vico, however, argued that history is the most appropriate form of human knowledge, since history was made by men and therefore men are capable of understanding what they have made. In historical study (and by extension in a hermeneutical social science), the enquirer's mind enters into the historical process – observer and observed, agent and structure, become intertwined.

Reading Vico led me forward in time again to Sorel (whose reflections on Vico I now saw as a critical stage in Sorel's own thinking).[24] From this, I moved on to Gramsci. Gramsci stands in direct descent from Vico, with Sorel and Benedetto Croce as intermediaries, and

29

Marx as the thinker to be interpreted through this philosophical current.

Gramsci brought the idea of absolute historicism to challenge "scientistic" representations of Marx.[25] For Gramsci, philosophy and history are identical. Philosophy is the history of philosophy. The "truth" of philosophy lies in its fit with the configuration of social forces that shape history – a shared mental framework, or intersubjectivity,[26] constitutes the objectivity of an epoch. This must mean that "truth" changes with the movement of history. Marxism, or what Gramsci called the "philosophy of praxis," provides a method or avenue of understanding, but has to be thought of critically, i.e., in relation to its changing material supports. To represent Marxism as the embodiment of absolute truth would be to negate its very nature. Absolute historicism is juxtaposed to absolute truth.

Hyperliberalism and the double movement

Columbia University turned out to be a transitional resting place. My colleagues were a fine group and students were of a high caliber; but there were some irritants unconnected with the university. My tenure at Columbia was not reflected in my status with US immigration, and although living in the Greenwich, Connecticut, area was comfortable, the ideological homogeneity of the business executive class contrasted with the cultural mix of Geneva's international milieu. Sometime during 1976, I had a telephone call from John Holmes, who then played a key role in Canada's international studies network. He asked if I had thought of coming back to Canada. It was almost thirty years since I had left Canada and it struck me that if I did not take up his suggestion, it might not be repeated. By 1977, I was at York University in Toronto, in a lively and more youthful political science department. An additional incentive for the move was the *Parti québécois* victory in the 1976 provincial elections which rekindled my old interest in Quebec politics. I did indeed teach for a winter term at Laval University in Quebec City during the campaign on the sovereignty referendum in 1981. But York University became a congenial intellectual home.

The ideological milieu in the western nations, which had been shaken up in the late 1960s, hardened into a seemingly monolithic conformity during the 1980s and into the 1990s. In *Production, Power, and World Order*, I had contrasted two ideal types of society competing for future dominance: state capitalism and hyperliberalism. In state capitalism, the state functioned to guide capitalist development and to moderate capitalism's polarizing impact on society. Forms of state capitalism included corporatism and social democracy, and the "social market" capitalism of central and northern Europe. I called hyperliberalism what others have called neoliberalism (a term I reserved for the postwar versions of Keynesianism and what John Ruggie called "embedded liberalism"). Hyperliberalism, in the ideology if not always in the practice of Reaganism and Thatcherism, rejects state intervention to influence the results of market behavior and views the state only as the enforcer of market rules. This attempt of mine to depict the rivalry between projects of social order was written before the collapse of "real socialism." The dichotomy has since become more generally characteristic of the global political economy.

The hyperliberal ideology has become entrenched in international institutions, backed by American power, overshadowing the residues of the social democratic thinking that were more in evidence in the 1960s and 1970s. The key words in the currently dominant global ideology are competitiveness, deregulation, privatization, and restructuring. Restructuring refers to the reorganization of global production from Fordist economies of scale to post-Fordist economies of flexibility. It means fewer reasonably secure and high-income core workers and a larger proportion of precariously employed lower-income peripheral workers, the latter weakened by being divided by locations around the world, by ethnicity and religion, and by gender. It also means that a large part of the world's population exists in deepening poverty, outside the global economy. Privatization and deregulation refer to the removal of the state from a substantive role in the national or global economy, except as guarantor of free movement for capital and profits. Competitiveness is the justification for dismantling the welfare states built up in the post-World War II period – negating the effort in the more industrialized countries to legitimate capitalism by avoiding a recurrence of the immiseration that occurred during the Great Depression of the 1930s.

Present realities serve to revive interest in Karl Polanyi's analysis in *The Great Transformation*[27] of the social and political consequences of the industrial revolution in the nineteenth and early twentieth centuries. Polanyi described the self-regulating market of classical economic theory as the project of subordinating society to an abstract economic logic. This was a radical departure from the general historical rule in which economic processes were embedded in social relations, the economy being but one manifestation of the social order. The consequence of this disembedding of the economy was to disarticulate society, to make people vulnerable to forces over which they collectively had no control. This rending of the social fabric was the first phase of a double movement, the second phase of which was society's response, a movement to reconstitute coherence and solidarity through measures to reintegrate its fragmented components. These took the benign forms of labor legislation, industrial relations practices, and ultimately social democracy and the welfare state. Malignant developments also appeared in more extreme conditions of social breakdown: fascism and Stalinism.

Hyperliberalism today replicates the first phase of the double movement. Reflecting on Polanyi's dialectical framework, the problems now are (1) to identify the probable sources of response leading to a second phase of movement; and (2) to avoid the kinds of excessive breakdown that would generate malignant responses of the fascist type.

There are many indications of an approaching crisis of a political and ideological kind out of which the second phase of the double movement at the global level of political economy might be generated. The supremacy of hyperliberal ideology is accompanied by polarization of rich and poor which cuts across national borders. People who are linked into the core activities of the global economy do well. Those who are more peripheral within the global economy do poorly, suffering a decline in their living standards. Many are excluded altogether from the global economy.

Hyperliberalism, still monopolistic in the centers of ideological power, has lost some credibility among electorates in the main capitalist countries. This is evident in an erosion of respect for politicians of all stripes. In a few of these countries (for example, Italy and Japan), political establishments long sustained by Cold War politics have been rejected as corrupt and incompetent. What is to replace them in the medium or longer term is less certain. Other countries crack or fragment under pressures of local nationalisms. In the post-communist world, an initial infatuation with the most extreme market-oriented ideologies is giving place either to a nostalgia for the benign aspects of "real socialism" or for the allurements of authoritarian populism. In the poorest countries, people come to regard the local state and the formal agencies of international intervention as hostile forces responsible for their oppression and impoverishment. They opt out from state structures and the formal economy. The worst cases become "black holes"[28] – with Lebanon as prototype, followed by Somalia, Angola, Liberia, Mozambique, Rwanda, Burundi, Haiti, the former Yugoslavia, and much of the Caucasus.

The second Gulf War – the US and coalition campaign against Iraq – made transparent a change in the structure of global politics. The change was not the transition to a post-Cold War order proclaimed by US political leaders. Rather it was the shift from a hegemonic to a tributary system. This shift had been going on since the early 1970s. Retrospectively, it had begun with the US defeat in Vietnam, and the "Nixon shocks" that undid the Bretton Woods system. Since that time, the more or less spontaneous consensual hegemonic leadership the United States had commanded in the non-Soviet world turned into a sequence of bargained deals, mostly taking the form of financial quid pro quo for US military cover. In the Gulf War, the United States decided to go to war and retained control of the war, including its presentation as TV entertainment, while using pressure and side payments, for example, the rollover of Egypt's debt, to construct the coalition, controlling the Security Council to legitimate its decisions, and securing overall financing from Japan, Germany and the Gulf states. The hiatus between military strength and economic and financial inadequacy became transparent. The system has become unstable at the top. There is no assurance that a combination of pressures like that which made the Gulf War possible could be put together again. At the most, the war stands as a warning to Third World countries not to risk a confrontation with the protector of the global economy.

On January 16, 1991, my wife and I were in New York to attend a memorial service for David Morse. Since leaving the ILO, he had become a senior partner in a major law firm. I had maintained personal contact with him, though some of his new associations were very remote from my own world. In the Temple Emmanuel on Fifth Avenue that morning eulogies were delivered by notable associates including the secretary-general of the United Nations, Javier Perez de Cuellar.

When I reached home in Toronto that evening, I learned that the bombing of Baghdad had begun, precisely during East Coast prime time. The secretary-general had spent the whole morning commemorating a fellow executive head. That said something about his courtesy and loyalty, but also about how far the United Nations was associated with the management of the war.

The Cold War has not ended. The structures of Cold War power continue to exist in the West. Intelligence services remain in place as occult powers seeking new and as yet uncertain purposes. Abundant supplies of arms and local war lords subsidized by the Cold War contestants continue the bloodshed in Afghanistan, Somalia, Mozambique, Angola, Cambodia, and Rwanda. The overflow of small arms supply the insatiable demand in the US domestic market. Manichean mental frameworks preserve the Cold War form while searching for new content (the "Japan problem," "Islamic fundamentalism"). The economic warfare that broke the Soviet economy and overstrained the US economy is perpetuated on a global scale through the ideology of "competitiveness." The biosphere is under threat.

The continuing residue of the Cold War contributes to the progressive decay of the old world order. The outlines of a new world order are yet to be perceived. Two factors may, in the longer run, be formative of a new order. One is the rivalry among different forms of what Polanyi called "substantive economies," i.e., the different ways in which production and distribution are socially organized. The struggle between rival forms of capitalism (hyperliberal versus social market) in Europe[29] may be critical in determining the balance of social and economic power in the global economy. At stake are the prospects of subordinating the economy to social purpose, and the prospects of redesigning production and consumption so as to be compatible with a sustainable biosphere.

The other factor is the potential for recomposition of civil society in reaction to the disintegrating consequences of a residual Cold War and a polarizing economic globalism. Democratization is the condition for rebuilding structures of social equity and political authority. This would have to be something more than formal democracy. It would have to translate a revived spirit of community into a refounding of political authority. In Machiavellian terms, it will require *virtù*, the spirit of solidarity that makes it possible to found or sustain a state. Multilateralism is the way in which a plurality of socially grounded communities can become linked into a coherent global order.[30] This would have to be something more than the existing state-centered multilateralism. It would be the expression of the cultural diversity of reconstituted civil societies.

The feasibility of this project depends upon whether in this world a revival of *virtù* is possible. Machiavelli looked to the prince to implant a *virtù* that was no longer present in a decadent society.

34

Nearer to us, Gramsci placed that role upon the modern prince, the political party that could give momentum to all aspects of social, political, and cultural life. It is not easy at the end of the twentieth century to put full confidence in either of these solutions. I found a different and more pessimistic answer in the life of Ibn Khaldun, confronting the fourteenth-century decadence of a once-brilliant Islamic political culture: an affirmation of the ethical responsibility of an intellectual, a judge, to incarnate the values of civilization and to express them at the level of the local community, so that they might infuse a new *'asabiya*, a new social and political solidarity.[31] This is, perhaps, closer to those who today look to social movements as the means of revivifying civil society. Probably the answer lies in no one of these courses but in a combination of them – of leadership and organized political mobilization at one level, and of commitment to principles of civility through personal example and the stimulus of group involvement at another. If a new world order is to emerge out of the decadence of the old, it will have to be built from the bottom up. The alternative is acquiescence in impersonal, occult forms of power.

Notes

This essay is published for the first time in this volume.

1 Susan Strange, Review of Cox, *Production, Power, and World Order*, *International Affairs*, vol. 64, no. 2 (Spring 1988), pp. 269–270.

2 Edmund Burke, *Reflections on the French Revolution* (London: Dent, Everyman edition, 1950), pp. 93–94.

3 For example, in my MA thesis on the Quebec election of 1886. This pragmatic French-Canadian conservatism had severed affiliation with the Conservative Party by the end of the nineteenth century and was thenceforward expressed in a sequence of nationalist movements.

4 *Report of the Royal Commission on Bilingualism and Biculturalism* (Ottawa: Queen's Printer, 1967).

5 A friend from university years, Michael Oliver, who also became interested in French-Canadian nationalism and wrote a dissertation on Henri Bourassa, the foremost nationalist spokesman of the late nineteenth and early twentieth centuries, became director of research for the Royal Commission on Bilingualism and Biculturalism, where he came to know and respect André Laurendeau. Oliver was a theoretician of Canadian social democracy. He was the rare case where social democratic thinking of Quebec and English-speaking Canada met in one person.

6 The quotation in Berlin's *Two Concepts of Liberty* (Oxford: Clarendon Press, 1958) is, I think, from Schumpeter but I have not been able to trace it. Berlin added: "To demand more than this is perhaps a deep and incurable

metaphysical need; but to allow it to guide one's practice is a symptom of an equally deep, and far more dangerous, moral and political immaturity" (p. 57).

7 Robert W. Cox and Harold K. Jacobson, *The Anatomy of Influence: Decision Making in International Organization*, (New Haven, Conn.: Yale University Press, 1972). The other authors contributing to the book were Gerard and Victoria Curzon, Joseph S. Nye, Lawrence Scheinman, James P. Sewell, and Susan Strange.

8 He had observed this rule himself. While I was *chef de cabinet* for David Morse, I would signify on Morse's behalf that he was free to publish, a procedure I regarded as rather tiresome. Morse, in any case, had no disposition to read long, and in the event, innocuous manuscripts. The procedure served, in the new boss's mind, to reinforce the principle of the *nihil obstat*. My own view was that there should be a distinction between texts written in an official capacity, or which engaged the responsibility of the organization, and texts written in a personal or scholarly capacity. This distinction was not uncommon in other parts of the UN system.

9 My letter of resignation, dated June 12, 1972, after recounting the series of interventions that negated the expectation of autonomy and freedom of expression, contained the following concluding paragraph:

> The issues do, I think, go beyond the Institute and the ILO. International organisations are passing through a critical period in which it is evident they have lost some of the public and political support they enjoyed following the creation of the United Nations. The first requirement for a constructive transformation of existing international organisations such as would merit renewed support is a healthy spirit of self-criticism and responsiveness to the new demands of social change. An intellectually independent institute could have helped. But if instead of allowing the critical spirit to grow, the Institute is now to be caught up in the old game of bureaucratic politics and to begin to screen out opinions which do not show deference to the canons of official doctrine, it may, I fear, become of little use either to the ILO itself or to social policy thinking in the world at large.

10 The so-called Novosibirsk Report, 1984, circulated to the Central Committee on the need and prospects for transforming the social and attitudinal conditions of work. Published in translation in *Survey*, vol. 128, no. 1, pp. 88–108.

11 One such case is analyzed in Jeffrey Harrod, *Trade Union Foreign Policy: A Study of British and American Trade Union Activities in Jamaica* (London: Macmillan, 1972). This book originated as a doctoral dissertation I supervised at the Graduate Institute for International Studies, Geneva.

12 See Cox (with Jeffrey Harrod), "Approaches to a Futurology of Industrial Relations," *Bulletin*, no. 8, pp. 139–164 (Geneva: International Institute for Labor Studies, 1971).

13 Robert W. Cox *Production, Power, and World Order: Social Forces in the Making of History* (New York: Columbia University Press, 1987). A companion book by Jeffrey Harrod is *Power, Production, and the Unprotected Worker* (New York: Columbia University Press, 1987).

14 On neorealism, see Robert O. Keohane (ed.), *Neorealism and Its Critics* (New York: Columbia University Press, 1986).

15 Especially in E. H. Carr, *Nationalism and After* (London: Macmillan, 1945).

16 See especially Georges Sorel, *Système historique de Renan* (Paris, 1905; reprinted in Geneva: Slatkine Reprints, 1971).

17 E. P. Thompson, *The Poverty of Theory and Other Essays* (London: Merlin Press, 1978).

18 Especially in his best-known work: Georges Sorel, *Reflections on Violence*, trans. by T. E. Hulme (New York: Peter Smith, 1941).

19 R. G. Collingwood, *The Idea of History* (Oxford: Clarendon Press, 1946).

20 Fernand Braudel, *On History*, trans. by Sarah Matthews (Chicago: University of Chicago Press, 1980), pp. 25–54; and Braudel, *Civilisation matérielle, économie, et capitalisme, XVe–XVIIIe siècle*, 3 vols. (Paris: Armand Colin, 1979).

21 The phrase "ensemble of social relations" is, of course, that of Marx in the *Theses on Feuerbach*: "The human essence is no abstraction inherent in each single individual. In its reality it is the *ensemble* of social relations . . ."

22 *The New Science of Giambattista Vico*, trans. by Thomas Goddard Bergin and Max Harold Fisch (Ithaca, N.Y.: Cornell University Press, 1970). Vico's "new science" was to be based on joining philosophy (rational knowedge of the true) with philology (empirical knowledge of the certain).

23 My use of "historicism" here is obviously at odds with the use of the term by Karl Popper in *The Poverty of Historicism* (London: Routledge and Kegan Paul, 1957). The historicism criticized by Popper is a perversion of positivism, an attempt to discover "laws of history" comparable to the laws of physics that would make it possible to predict the future. It is history viewed externally as an object of enquiry rather than history known from within, from its making, as Vico taught.

24 Georges Sorel, "Etude sur Vico," *Le Devenir Social* (Paris), October, November, and December 1896 issues.

25 Antonio Gramsci, *Selections from the Prison Notebooks*, edited and trans. by Quintin Hoare and Geoffrey Nowell Smith (New York: International Publishers, 1971), p. 465.

26 The notion of intersubjective meanings is well expressed in Charles Taylor, "Hermeneutics and Politics," in Paul Connerton (ed.), *Critical Sociology* (Harmondsworth, Middlesex: Penguin, 1971).

27 Karl Polanyi, *The Great Transformation* (Boston: Beacon Press, 1944).

28 The term was, I think, first used by Richard Falk to describe a situation of total breakdown of political authority and fragmentation of society into warring parts.

29 See Michel Albert, *Capitalisme contre capitalisme* (Paris: Seuil, 1991).

30 I am grateful to the United Nations University for providing me with the opportunity to reflect upon the potential of future multilateralism when it invited me to coordinate a program on multilateralism and the United Nations system. The essay included in this volume as chapter 21 on "Multilateralism and World Order" is a contribution to this program.

31 See "Towards a Posthegemonic Conceptualization of World Order: Reflections on the Relevancy of Ibn Khaldun," included in this volume (chapter 8).

Part II
Theory

3 The idea of international labor regulation (1953)

The writing of history is primarily a matter of asking the right questions of your source material. It is this questioning mind of the historian which distinguishes history from mere chronology and from the "background information" found in the flimsy introductory chapters to the innumerable mass-produced economic surveys that purport to explain the complexities of the contemporary world. The history of ideas is especially challenging to the historian because it is sometimes difficult to treat ideas as source material and to subject them to the kind of questions that the historian is bound to ask. There is always a temptation to accord absolute value to some ideas, to cease being an historian and to become an apostle and an advocate. John W. Follows, in a book entitled *Antecedents of the International Labour Organisation*[1] which attempts to trace the origins and progress of the idea of international labor regulation, has not avoided the most important mistakes. He obviously wants to do honor to the ILO (a laudable motive, but not for an historian); and he considers international labor regulation to be a "good thing." This approach to his subject inhibits him from asking the rather unceremonious and impertinent questions which the historian must ask: Why did the idea of international labor regulation originate with certain industrial employers in the early nineteenth century? What significance did this idea have in relation to the early conflicts between industrial workers and their employers? What interest (personal, class, or other) did these particular employers have in advancing this idea? Why, in the last quarter of the nineteenth century, did certain governments such as that of Germany espouse the idea? What relationship did this have to the growth of popular nationalism and of the socialist movement? Why should the idea of international labor regulation grow to fruition in a period of increasing economic and social nationalism?

It is not unjust to say that these questions are never really raised in Follows' book. The first chapter of the book is entitled "Robert Owen" and on the first page we read: "This chapter has been written to disprove Owen's supposed authorship of the idea of international labor regulation . . ." The second chapter has been written largely to establish Charles Hindley's authorship. One of the preoccupations of subsequent chapters is to establish a connecting thread between Hindley and some of the early French exponents of this idea. The author takes pains to set forth the arguments used by the exponents of the idea, but there is no attempt to assess the meaning of this idea of international labor regulation in the particular social, economic, and political circumstances in which it was put forward.

The impression conveyed by the early chapters of the book is that the guiding motive of the first reformer advocates of international labor legislation was humanitarianism. Follows points out the parallel drawn by them between international action for abolition of the slave trade and their proposals for international labor laws. This is, however, only putting the question at one remove. Humanitarianism was one of the greatest social forces of the nineteenth century, and the historian, in attempting to understand the importance and meaning of this force, must follow his critical method and not treat the humanitarian idea as an absolute. This is not to suggest that the anti-slavery reformers and proponents of factory legislation had sordid motives of self-interest, hypocritically clothed in the language of morality; it is only to say that the historian must try to relate this moral force to the other forces of the age in which it developed. To take another example, a number of eminent scholars, such as Max Weber, Ernst Troeltsch, and R. H. Tawney, have produced penetrating studies of the relationship between Protestant morality and the development of modern capitalism. This is no reason to accuse Professor Tawney, for example, of questioning the sincerity of Protestant reformers. He was fulfilling one of the major tasks of the historian of ideas.

Even though it does not explore the relationship between the idea of international labor legislation and the social forces which accompanied early nineteenth-century industrialization, Follows' book provides evidence that such an investigation might prove fruitful. The religious background and moral intent of the early exponents of the idea of international labor regulation are abundantly evident. Charles Hindley himself studied for the ministry. He later transferred his attention from preaching to the management of a cotton-spinning

42

factory in Lancashire, but always took an active interest in the religious life of his workers and particularly in the religious education of their children. He was representative of the Nonconformist, Manchester-school, Liberal manufacturer – one of the mainsprings of the English early nineteenth-century reform movement.

"No church," wrote Elie Halévy, "can be successful except by coming to terms with the Devil. The evangelicalism of Wesley and Whitfield ... had learnt to adapt itself to the economic requirements of northwest England, and displayed the greatest indulgence towards all the business methods of the speculative financier or promoter."[2] Evangelicalism blunted the edge of industrialism, and in converting the working class, deflected into religious channels the emotional forces that might have flared into class war. This force became joined with the philosophical radicalism of Bentham and J. S. Mill; theoretically hostile, the two elements nevertheless became inextricably intertwined in the phenomenon of English humanitarianism. This combination of evangelicalism and radicalism was at once the force which disciplined the workers and which encouraged philanthropy in their masters – a philanthropy which was at least in part designed to prove the manufacturer respectable in the eyes of the landed classes who remained the social if not the economic arbiters. This was the mental and moral climate into which the idea of international labor regulation was born in England in the 1830s.

This English synthesis of evangelicalism and radicalism was unique. On the continent the French Revolution had created a deep cleavage between religion and radicalism. The liberal Catholic movement in France, for example, remained an anomaly in French politics throughout the nineteenth century; it failed to become an effective compromise. Industrialization was slower on the continent than in England, but as it progressed the sense of conflict between workers and employers was the more acute for lack of any emotional solidarity between the two groups such as evangelicalism produced in England, and because of dramatic clashes like those which occurred in 1848 and during the life of the Paris Commune in 1871.

In spite of the differences in setting there were certain personal similarities between Hindley and Daniel Legrand, who took up in France the idea of international labor legislation. Legrand was a Swiss from Basle who managed a ribbon-making factory in Alsace. He was a Protestant who, like Hindley, concerned himself with the religious life of his workers and administered religious instruction to them. In 1840 he expressed "the conviction that the success of all enterprises [and in this context he means industrial enterprises] is dependent before anything else upon divine blessing . . ." He urged limitation of hours of work on the grounds that the industrial system of his time had bad moral effects on the workers: "The destruction of the family is the festering wound of modern industry and measures calculated to restore family life would be one of the greatest benefits procurable for the working-classes." In his final "[A]ppeal" of 1855 to the governments of all industrial countries, he stated: "An international law concluded by the governments of all industrial countries is the only possible solution of the great social problem of restoring family life to the working-class." Legrand was no political radical; he was a supporter of the bourgeois monarchy of Louis Philippe, disapproved of the revolution of 1848, and only later gained a measure of confidence in the Second Empire.

When Legrand wrote these words the "great social problem of restoring family life to the working-class" was overshadowed by the tangible threat of open class war. The class struggle during the 1840s and 1850s was no theoretical invention of an extreme fringe of the socialist movement. It was not a concept advanced first by Marx but one which had already gained wide currency in the revolutionary movement and which Marx himself had borrowed from Weitling and others. Nor was it a concept known only to the revolutionaries; in 1845 Disraeli published his *Sybil*, subtitled *The Two Nations*, the central theme of which is the antagonism between the established classes and the working urban masses which burst out in the Chartist movement. The suppression of the workers' political uprisings in 1848, and the firm re-establishment of the bourgeois state, emphasized quite clearly the growing social antagonisms throughout western Europe.

It is clear where the nebulous notion of international labor legislation was situated in relation to the social conflicts and upheavals of the first half of the nineteenth century. In England it was associated with the Liberal factory owners, not with the Chartists or with the Tory proponents of factory legislation. It was humanitarian in expression; but is there not at least a suspicion that, by making national action conditional upon international agreement, the practical effect of the idea would be to delay improvement of conditions at home at a time when pressures were being brought to bear in that direction? On the continent this idea was to be found on the side of authority, as against the revolutionary and early socialist movements.

It was an expression of a longing for "social peace" which could be achieved by a "moral reform" of the working man; in its context this idea was clearly counterrevolutionary. A Congress of Benevolence held at Frankfurt in 1857 expressed this viewpoint:

> It is desirable that industrial leaders get together and reach agreement on the application of these measures [measures regarding maximum workday, medical certificates, regulated night labour, limitation on dangerous work, factory hygiene, workshop inspection, etc.] to all establishments operating under like conditions. This agreement will show their benevolent and paternal attitude toward their workers. In so using their liberty they will escape the intervention of laws requiring amelioration and guarantees. It is preferable from every point of view that they themselves take the initiative.

The concern to forestall class conflict and promote the moral solidarity of classes also lies behind the advocacy of international labor legislation by Catholic social reformers during the second half of the nineteenth century, such as Count Albert de Mun in France, the German Christian Social movement, and Bishop Mermillod of Fribourg. It is a pity that Follows, in a book which contains so much information incidental to these questions, should never think to raise them.

It is one of the paradoxes of the history of the idea of international labor regulation that it first began to gain official government support during the last decades of the nineteenth century, precisely at the time when European states were entering a phase of increasing nationalism in economic and social policy. The predominant characteristic of European countries during the years from about 1870 up to the outbreak of war in 1914 was the increasing power of the masses, and particularly of the urban industrial workers, within the state. Industry expanded; urban working populations grew in numbers and importance; workers' organizations gained strength and spread class consciousness; universal compulsory education and the extension of the franchise gave the urban masses the possibility of articulate political expression; the popular press came into being; and the first waves of mass emotion foreshadowed the great play of irrational forces in modern mass politics. These developments combined to revolutionize the nature and functions of the state in western European countries.

During the early part of the century the forces of production and the state in the great European countries were in middle-class control. The suppression of social revolution in 1848 confirmed the power of this class. This was the period when the Marxist analysis of society was made; and, whatever opinions one may hold of his economic theory and dialectical philosophy or of the validity of his predictions of the future course of the world, it must be conceded that, as an economic historian and social analyst of his own time, Marx was extraordinarily acute. Since the state was in the hands of the bourgeoisie, socialism looked to the international solidarity of the working classes. The worker had no fatherland; the worker's enemy was the state.

Marx predicted that the further development of capitalism would widen the conflict between the nationalism of big business and the internationalism of the workers; but the radical transformation of the state in the last quarter of the century falsified his prediction. During these years the nation ceased to be exclusively bourgeois, and the masses were incorporated into the nation. The strength of the state was based upon industrial power and the industrial worker came to occupy a strategic position. The state sought to increase its power by encouraging and protecting its industry through measures of intervention in economic life which it had shunned hitherto. The industrial workers sought protection by the state and the workers' movements directed their efforts to influencing government policy and gaining power through the control of state machinery. Only in revolutionary syndicalism did the earlier traditions of socialism as an anti-state movement survive. A new nationalism combined policies for industrial expansion, protection of the workers, and increased state power. It was economic and social as well as military: industry was protected by tariffs; free movement of workers from one country to another was severely limited so as to protect workers against the competition from cheaper foreign labor; and social insurance made its appearance with Bismarck's sickness insurance law of 1882, accident insurance law of 1884, and old-age and invalidity insurance law of 1889, and spread from Germany to other European countries before the end of the century. This new nationalism was based on the masses. Imperialism, far from being only a conspiracy of industrialists characteristic of the last and decadent stages of capitalism as Marx predicted, was a popular movement. As the masses became nationalistic, the internationalist character of socialism became diluted. The enigmatic figure of Ferdinand Lassalle presides over this transformation; the meetings between Lassalle and Bismarck were a symbol of the alliance between industrialism, nationalism, and socialism.

These radical transformations in the state and in the strength of social forces within the state during the last decades of the nineteenth century completely altered the meaning and significance of the idea of international labor regulation. Governments were now taking measures to protect workers, and these measures were part and parcel of a nationalistic movement which was bringing European states into conflict both within Europe and more especially in the areas of imperial expansion beyond Europe.

Follows does not reflect upon this complete change in the situation as compared with the early decades of the century, and so he is slightly surprised to see Bismarck and the kaiser considering international action on labor matters. He cites Bismarck's statement on the question of an internationally agreed limit to the working day, made before the Reichstag in 1885. A normal workday, said the German chancellor, could be established for Germany alone if that country were surrounded by a Chinese wall and were economically self-sufficient. Such was not the case. It would be necessary to establish a universal workday union analogous to the Universal Postal Union, and a universal wage union which would have to embrace the United States, Britain, and every industrial country. None of these countries, in the interests of competition, could permit its officials, inspectors, and workers to deviate from the internationally agreed standards in the least. Bismarck's conclusion was that such a proposal was impossible of achievement in the world in which he lived. "If we set out on this road alone, then we alone will have to suffer the consequences of our experiment: and I do not believe we will succeed in persuading our neighbours to follow our example."[3]

This conclusion was based on the question of practicability and did not challenge the argument that the best way to secure protection in these matters for German workers, without compromising the position of German industries, was by international agreement. International agreements on such matters, arrived at between the chief industrial states, would in no way conflict with the economic nationalism of state policy. Their purpose would be to strengthen the ties between state and workers by allowing the former to increase its guarantees to the latter, while in no way checking industrial expansion. There was therefore nothing incongruous in the espousal of the cause of international labor regulation both by the German socialists (it was adopted by Liebknecht's group in 1881 and included in the Erfurt program of the Social Democratic Party in 1891) and by the German kaiser when he convened the first international conference on labor questions at Berlin in 1890.

Notes

This text first appeared in the *International Labour Review*, vol. 68, no. 2 (February 1953), pp. 191–196. It is included here because it anticipates the method more fully developed in "Realism, Positivism, and Historicism," included in this volume (chapter 4).

1 John W. Follows, *Antecedents of the International Labour Organisation* (Oxford: Clarendon Press, 1951).
2 Elie Halévy, *A History of the English People in the Nineteenth Century*, Volume I, *England in 1815*, trans. by E. I. Watkin and D. A. Barker (London: Ernest Benn, 1949), p. 284.
3 Follows, *Antecedents*, p. 91.

4 Realism, positivism, and historicism (1985)

In the range of their different arguments, I find myself in agreement and in disagreement with aspects of each of the other authors' texts.[a] I am, however, left with the general impression that this is a specifically American debate even though it is couched in terms of international or world systems. Stanley Hoffmann put it that international relations is an *American* social science.[1] This is not (on my part any more than on Hoffmann's) to suggest that American thought is cast in a single mold. (I protest in advance my innocence of Robert Gilpin's strictures against lumping together authors whose views differ in important respects.)[2] What is common, it seems to me, is (1) the perspective of the United States as the preponderant of the two major powers in the system and consequently the sharing of a certain measure of responsibility for US policy, and (2) the organization of argument around certain obligatory themes of debates, notably those of power versus morality and of science versus tradition. The first of these is, to employ

[a] This text first appeared as a postscript to the article, "Social Forces, States, and World Orders: Beyond International Relations Theory" (included in this volume, chapter 6) as re-published in the reader edited by Robert O. Keohane, *Neorealism and Its Critics* (New York: Columbia University Press, 1986). Kenneth Waltz was the exemplar of neorealism in this collection; and Robert Gilpin, though perhaps more of a classical realist in the mold of E. H. Carr, figured in the defense of neorealism. Criticism by Keohane and John Gerrard Ruggie, both of whom accepted the centrality of states, stressed the static nature of the model presented by neorealism and its inability to explain change of systems (as distinct from change within systems). These two critics favored the liberal institutionalist position that international organizations and regimes matter, in contrast to the neorealists' exclusive concern with states. Richard Ashley's postmodernist critique challenged the form of knowledge on which neorealism was based and its linkage to the Cold War. Cox's article, first published in *Millennium: Journal of International Studies*, did not arise out of this debate but comes to it from outside. In it he points out the difference in its approach to those of the other contributors. The title is new, reflecting the content of the text rather than its position in the Keohane reader.

Waltz's language, a systemic conditioning of American thought. The second derives more from an explicitly American cultural process. One aspect of this process was the intellectual conversion of US policy makers to the use of the accumulated physical power of the United States for the performance of a world system-creating and system-maintaining role. Important influences in this conversion were European-formed thinkers like Reinhold Niebuhr and Hans Morgenthau who introduced a more pessimistic and power-oriented view of mankind into an American milieu conditioned by eighteenth-century optimism and nineteenth-century belief in progress. Another aspect was the need to legitimate this new-found realism in "scientific" terms. The second aspect can be read as the revenge of eighteenth-century natural-law thinking for the loss of innocence implicit in the first. Richard Ashley has well recounted the socializing process through which successive cohorts of American (and by assimilation Canadian) graduate students have been brought into this stream of thinking.[3]

At this point, following Gilpin's example, an autobiographical reference is in order: the reader should know that this author did not experience the above-mentioned process of intellectual formation. His introduction to international political processes came through practice as an "empathetic neutral" in his role of international official in one of the less salient spheres of policy.[b] His only formal academic training was in the study of history. Accordingly, he never shared a sense of responsibility for, nor aspired to influence, US policy or that of any other country, though he has been well aware that his destiny, like that of the rest of mankind, is profoundly shaped by what he cannot influence. These circumstances have inclined him toward an initial acceptance of the realist position. The political world is at the outset a *given* world. Men make history, as Marx wrote, but not in conditions of their own choosing. To have any influence over events, or at the very least to forestall the worst eventualities, it is necessary to begin with an understanding of the conditions not chosen by oneself in which action is possible.

The intellectual influences that contributed to the formation of this

[b] "Less salient" sphere of policy recalls conclusions in Robert W. Cox and Harold K. Jacobson, *The Anatomy of Influence: Decision Making in International Organization* (New Haven, Conn.: Yale University Press, 1972), pp. 420 and 428, which differentiated decision making models in international organizations according to the salience of the organizations' tasks to the interests of the most powerful governments. See "Influences and Commitments," chapter 2 in this volume, for further elaboration on intellectual and ethical sources of Cox's thought.

idiosyncratic view share with realism a common source in Machia-velli. They diverge in having followed a historicist current, through Giambattista Vico to Georges Sorel and, above all, Antonio Gramsci. These thinkers were not concerned primarily with international relations; they addressed the problem of knowledge about society and social transformations. Historians provided the more specific light on international structures – to some extent the twentieth-century British Marxist historians, and more particularly Fernand Braudel and the French *Annales* school. Intellectual points of contact with influences upon other contributors to this debate include E. H. Carr (especially with Gilpin), Friedrich Meinecke, Ludwig Dehio, and Karl Polanyi (especially with Ruggie). So much for autobiography: the point is that the itinerary to the *Millennium* article did not pass through neorealism; it contemplates neorealism from the destination reached.[c]

To change the world, we have to begin with an understanding of the world as it is, which means the structures of reality that surround us. "Understanding" is the key word here. The issues in the confron-tation of approaches are linked to different modes of knowledge: posi-tivism and historicism. Since these two terms have been used in con-tradictory ways in different texts included in *Neorealism and Its Critics*, I reiterate my own usage here.

By "positivism" I mean the effort to conceive social science on the model of physics (or more particularly, physics as it was known in the eighteenth and nineteenth centuries before it had assimilated the principles of relativity and uncertainty). This involves positing a sep-aration of subject and object. The data of politics are externally per-ceived events brought about by the interaction of actors in a field. The field itself, being an arrangement of actors, has certain properties of its own which can be called "systemic." The concept of "cause" is applicable within such a framework of forces. Powerful actors are "causes" of change in the behavior of less powerful ones, and the structure of the system "causes" certain forms of behavior on the part of the actors.

I use "historicism" to mean a quite different approach to knowledge about society which was well defined by Giambattista Vico[4] and has continued as a distinctive tradition to the present. In this approach, human institutions are made by people – not by the individual

---

[c] The *Millennium* article, "Social Forces, States, and World Orders: Beyond International Relations Theory," is collected in this volume (chapter 6).

gestures of "actors" but by collective responses to a collectively perceived problematic that produce certain practices. Institutions and
practices are therefore to be understood through the changing mental
processes of their makers. There is, in this perspective, an identity of
subject and object. The objective realities that this approach
encompasses – the state, social classes, the conflict groups that Robert
Gilpin (following Ralf Dahrendorf) refers to, and their practices – are
constituted by intersubjective ideas. As Gilpin says, none of these
realities exist in the same way that individuals exist, but individuals
act *as though* these other realities exist, and by so acting they reproduce
them. Social and political institutions are thus seen as collective
responses to the physical material context (natural nature) in which
human aggregates find themselves. They in turn form part of the
social material framework (artificial nature or the network of social
relations) in which historical action takes place. Historicism thus
understood is the same as historical materialism. The method of historical materialism – or, in Robert Keohane's term, its research
program – is to find the connections between the mental schema
through which people conceive action and the material world which
constrains both what people can do and how they can think about
doing it.

The two approaches – positivist and historicist – yield quite different versions of the task of science. There can be no dispute about
Kenneth Waltz's adherence to the positivist approach, and he lays out
clearly the tasks of a positivist science: to find laws (which are regularities in human activity stateable in the form of "if A, then B"); and
to develop theories which explain why observable laws hold within
specific spheres of activity. Laws and theories advance knowledge
beyond what would otherwise be "mere description," i.e., the cataloguing of externally observed events.[5]

Insofar as this approach aspires to a general science of society, it
cannot discriminate between times and places. All human activity is
its province (though this activity is arbitrarily divided among a priori
categories of activity of which international relations is one), all of it
treated as raw material for the finding of laws and the development
of theories. I believe this to be the root of the major deficit in Waltz's
approach pointed to by his critics (see especially Keohane and
Ruggie): the inability of his theory to account for or to explain structural transformation. A general (read: universally applicable) science
of society can allow for variations in technologies and in the relative

capabilities of actors, but not in either the basic nature of the actors (power-seeking) or in their mode of interaction (power-balancing). The universality of these basic attributes of the social system comes to be perceived as standing outside of and prior to history. History becomes but a mine of data illustrating the permutations and combinations that are possible within an essentially unchanging human story. Despite his wide historical learning, Waltz's work is fundamentally ahistorical. The elegance he achieves in the clarity of his theoretical statement comes at the price of an unconvincing mode of historical understanding.

The historicist approach to social science does not envisage any general or universally valid laws which can be explained by the development of appropriate generally applicable theories. For historicism, both human nature and the structures of human interaction change, if only very slowly. History is the process of their changing. One cannot therefore speak of "laws" in any generally valid sense transcending historical eras, nor of structures as outside of or prior to history.[6] Regularities in human activities may indeed be observed within particular eras, and thus the positivist approach can be fruitful within defined historical limits, though not with the universal pretensions to which it aspires. The research program of historicism is to reveal the historical structures characteristic of particular eras within which such regularities prevail. Even more important, this research program is to explain transformations from one structure to another. If elegance is what Robert Keohane writes of as "spare, logically tight" theory[7] then the historicist approach does not lead to elegance. It may, however, lead to better appraisal of historically specific conjunctures. One person's elegance is another's oversimplification.

In choosing between the two approaches, much depends upon one's idea of what theory is for. I have suggested two broad purposes corresponding to the two approaches: a problem-solving purpose, i.e., tacitly assuming the permanency of existing structures, which is served by the positivist approach; and a critical purpose envisaging the possibilities of structural transformation which is served by the historicist approach. The usefulness of all theory, whether problem-solving or critical, is in its applicability to particular situations. But whereas problem-solving theory assimilates particular situations to general rules, providing a kind of programed method for dealing with them, critical theory seeks out the developmental potential within the particular.

Developmental potential signifies a possible change of structure. It can be grasped by understanding the contradictions and sources of conflict within existing structures; and this task may be aided by an understanding of how structural transformations have come about in the past.[8] Thus the determination of breaking points between successive structures – those points at which transformations take place – becomes a major problem of method. John Ruggie raised this issue in pointing to the structural disjuncture between the medieval and modern world systems, and to the inability of Waltz's structural realism to even consider let alone explain this transformation. The case is extremely important, since it contrasts two worlds constituted by quite distinct intersubjectivities. The entities as well as the modes of relations among them are of different orders.[9]

This case of transformation can be contrasted to the frequent invocations of Thucydides in neorealist literature in support of the contention that a balance-of-power system is the universal condition. What these invocations do establish is that there have been other periods in history where structures analogous to the balance of power of the modern state system have appeared. They do not consider that there have likewise been otherwise-constituted historical structures of which the medieval order of European Christendom was one. The instinct of structural realism may be to reduce the medieval order to its power model; but if so that would be to reject an opportunity for scientific exploration.

Ruggie suspects – and I share his suspicions – that the transformation from the medieval to the modern order cannot be understood solely in terms of a general international-systems theory (indeed, one could point out that the very term "international," derived from modern practice, is inapposite to the medieval world) but probably has also to be explained in terms of changing state structures and changing modes of production. This joins the substantive point of my argument: I have tried to sketch out a research program that would examine the linkage between changes in production, in forms of state, and in world orders.

The relevancy of such a research program is strictly practical. It flows from the question whether the present age is one of those historical breaking points between world-order structures, whether the present world situation contains the development potential of a different world order. If this were to be the case, what then would be the range of future structural possibilities? What social and political forces would have to be mobilized in order to bring about one or another of feasible outcomes? The practical use of political theory should be to help answer such questions. That they are present in the minds of the contributors to *Neorealism and Its Critics* is clear – for instance in Keohane's primary concern to discover the means of bringing about peaceful change, and Gilpin's with the problems of change under conditions of declining hegemony. Neither of these authors sees clearly how structural realism can be a guide to the answers. My suggestion is that the approach of historical structures would be more apposite.

For Fernand Braudel, a historical structure is the *longue durée*, the enduring practices evolved by people for dealing with the recurrent necessities of social and political life and which come by them to be regarded as fixed attributes of human nature and social intercourse.[10] But, particularly with regard to the world system, how long is the *longue durée*? Ruggie pointed to the breaking point between medieval and modern world orders, but have there been other breaking points since then? What is the proper periodization of world orders? I am inclined to answer that yes, there have been further breaking points, and to suggest a succession of mercantilist, liberal (*pax britannica*), neo-imperialist, and neoliberal (*pax americana*) orders. At the same time, I would not want to give the impression that this was in some manner the uncovering of an ontological substratum of world history, that these successive world orders were real entities fixed in order of time within some immutable world-historic plan. This periodizing is an intellectual construct pertinent to the present and useful for the purpose of understanding how changes in economic and political practices and in the relations of social groups contribute to the genesis of new world orders. The approach is not reductionist in the sense of making one single factor or set of factors the explanation of all changes. It is grounded in the notion of reciprocal relationships among basic forces shaping social and political practice.[11]

Ruggie made another point in suggesting that Waltz's exclusive stress on power capabilities precludes consideration of other significant factors differentiating international systems, in particular the presence or absence of hegemony. Indeed, in neorealist discourse the term "hegemony" is reduced to the single dimension of dominance, i.e., a physical-capabilities relationship among states. The Gramscian meaning of hegemony which I have used[12] and which is important in distinguishing the *pax britannica* and *pax americana* from the other world orders of the sequence suggested above, joins an ideological and intersubjective element to the brute power relationship. In a hegemonic order, the dominant power makes certain concessions or compromises to secure the acquiescence of lesser powers to an order that can be expressed in terms of a general interest. It is important, in appraising a hegemonic order, to know both (a) that it functions mainly by consent in accordance with universalist principles, and (b) that it rests upon a certain structure of power and serves to maintain that structure. The consensual element distinguishes hegemonic from nonhegemonic world orders. It also tends to mystify the power relations upon which the order ultimately rests.

The hegemonic concept has analytical applicability at the national as well as the international level (indeed, Gramsci developed it for application at the national level). I would differ from Gilpin when he (and Stephen Krasner,[13] in line with him) suggest that it is possible to distinguish a national interest from the welter of particular interests, if they mean that such a general will exists as some form of objective reality. I can accept their proposition if national interest is understood in a hegemonic sense, i.e., as the way in which the dominant groups in the state have been able – through concessions to the claims of sub-ordinate groups – to evolve a broadly accepted mode of thinking about general or national interests. Unfortunately, Gilpin (and Krasner) end their enquiry with the identification of national interests. When the concept of hegemony is introduced, it becomes necessary to ask what is the form of power that underlies the state and produces this particular understanding of national interest, this particular *raison d'état* – or in Gramscian terms, what is the configuration of the historic bloc?

Finally, there is the troublesome question of the ideological nature of thought – troublesome insofar as the imputation of ideology may appear to be insulting to the positivist who draws a line between his science and another's ideology. I should make it clear that I do not draw such a line; I accept that my own thought is grounded in a particular perspective; and I mean no offense in pointing to what appears to be a similar grounding in other people's thought. Science, for me, is a matter of rigor in the development of concepts and in the appraisal of evidence. There is an inevitable ideological element in science which lies in the choice of subject and the purposes to which analysis is put. The troublesome part comes when some scientific enterprise claims to transcend history and to propound some univer-sally valid form of knowledge. Positivism, by its pretensions to escape from history, runs the greater risk of falling into the trap of unconscious ideology.

There are two opposed concepts of history, each of which is intellectually grounded in the separation of subject and object. One is a methodological separation wherein events are conceived as an infinite series of objectified data. This approach seeks universal laws of behavior. Structural realism, as noted, is one of its manifestations. The other sees the subjectivity of historical action as determined by an objectified historical process. It seeks to discover the "laws of motion" of history. Both of these concepts of history lend themselves readily to ideology: the one becoming an ideology reifying the status quo; the other an ideology underpinning revolution by revealing the certainty inherent in the historicist expectation of dialectical development arising out of the contradictions of existing forces – a conception in which, as argued above, subject and object are united.

Neorealism, both in its Waltzian structuralist form and in its game-theoretic interactionist form, appear ideologically to be a science at the service of big-power management of the international system. There is an unmistakably Panglossian quality to a theory published in the late 1970s which concludes that a bipolar system is the best of all possible worlds. The historical moment has left its indelible mark upon this purportedly universalist science.

To the American social science of international relations, Marxism is the great "other," the ideology supportive of the rival superpower. It is also that most readily associated with the alternative mode of separation of subject and object. In the works of this American social science, Marxism is politely recognized but usually reduced to a few simple propositions which do not impinge upon its own discourse. If there is any dialogue between the American science of international relations and Marxism, it is a *dialogue de sourds*. Gilpin was justified in protesting the richness and diversity of realist thought, but it is at least as justifiable to point to the diversity of Marxist thought. It cuts across all the epistemological distinctions discussed above. There is a structuralist Marxism which, as Richard Ashley has indicated,[14] has analogies to structural realism, not in the use to which theory is put but in its conception of the nature of knowledge. There is a determinist tradition (perhaps less evident at present) which purports to reveal the laws of motion of history. And there is a historicist Marxism that rejects the notion of objective laws of history and focuses upon class struggle as the heuristic model for the understanding of structural change. It is obviously in the last of these Marxist currents that this writer feels most comfortable. Were it not for the contradictory diversity of Marxist thought, he would be glad to acknowledge himself (in a parody of Reaganite rhetoric) as your friendly neighborhood Marxist-Leninist subversive. But as things stand in the complex world of Marxism, he prefers to be identified simply as a historical materialist.

Notes

1 Stanley Hoffman, "An American Social Science: International Relations," *Daedalus*, vol. 106, no. 3 (Summer 1977), pp. 41–60.

2 Robert Gilpin, "The Richness of the Tradition of Political Realism," in Robert O. Keohane (ed.), *Neorealism and Its Critics* (New York: Columbia University Press, 1986), pp. 301–321.

3 Richard Ashley, "The Poverty of Neorealism," in Keohane, *Neorealism and Its Critics*, pp. 255–300.

4 *The New Science of Giambattista Vico*, trans. by Thomas Goddard Bergin and Max Harold Fisch (Ithaca, N.Y.: Cornell University Press, 1970).

5 The term "description" as used in positivist discourse (often preceded by "mere") is meaningless in historicist discourse. Description, for the historicist, is inseparable from interpretation or understanding – i.e., the appraisal of a unique fact through the medium of an explanatory hypothesis. The task of theory is to develop hypotheses and the concepts of limited historical applicability in which they are expressed – i.e., concepts like mercantilism, capitalism, fascism, etc. The difference between "description" (positivist) and "understanding" (historicist) is reflected in the words used to denote the object of study: datum (positivist) versus fact (historicist). The distinction is less self-evident in English than in Latin languages, where the corresponding words are past participles of the verbs "to give" and "to make." Positivism deals with externally perceived givens; historicism with events or institutions that are "made" – i.e., that have to be understood through the subjectivity of the makers as well as in terms of the objective consequences that flow from their existence.

6 Nor can one speak of "cause" in historicist discourse, except in a most trivial sense. The "cause" of a murder is the contraction of the murderer's finger on a trigger which detonates a charge in a cartridge, sending a bullet into the vital parts of the victim. Explanation is the purpose of historicist enquiry. It is much more complex, requiring an assembling of individual motivations and social structures to be connected by explanatory hypotheses.

7 Robert O. Keohane, "Theory of World Politics: Structural Realism and Beyond," in Keohane, *Neorealism and Its Critics*, p. 197.

8 This does not imply the presumption that the future will be like the past. But there can be (in the historicist approach) no complete separation between past and future. The practical utility of knowledge about the past

is in the development of explanatory hypotheses about change. In *Longue Durée* Fernand Braudel employed the metaphor of a ship for such hypotheses. The hypothesis sails well in certain waters under a range of conditions; it remains becalmed or it founders in others. The task of theory is to explore the limits of validity of particular hypotheses and to devise new hypotheses to explain cases in which they fail: Fernand Braudel, "History and the Social Sciences: The *Longue Durée*," in *On History*, trans. by Sarah Matthews (Chicago: University of Chicago Press, 1980), pp. 25–54.

9 John Gerard Ruggie, "Continuity and Transformation in the World Polity: Toward a Neorealist Synthesis," in Keohane, *Neorealism and Its Critics*, pp. 131–157.

10 Braudel, "History and the Social Sciences."

11 Waltz writes of reductionism and reification in a curious way in saying that systems are reified by political scientists when they reduce them to their interacting parts. In my reading of his work, Waltz comes close to the opposite of this position, reifying the international system by treating it not as an intellectual construct but as a "cause," and deriving the behavior of its parts, i.e., states, from the system itself; thus international relations is reduced to the workings of a reified system: Kenneth N. Waltz, "Reductionist and Systemic Theories," in Keohane, *Neorealism and Its Critics*, p. 61.

12 See "Gramsci, Hegemony, and International Relations: An Essay in Method," collected in this volume (chapter 7).

13 Stephen Krasner, *Defending the National Interest: Raw Materials Investment and US Foreign Policy* (Princeton, N.J.: Princeton University Press, 1978).

14 See Ashley's "Poverty of Neorealism."

5 On thinking about future world order (1976)

Daniel Halévy used the term "acceleration of history" in the title of an essay which he conceived at the onset of World War II and revised for republication in its aftermath.[1] Oswald Spengler's diagnosis of a cyclical rise and fall of cultures and civilizations was then well known to Halévy and his contemporaries among the European intelligentsia.[2] Arnold Toynbee had also already published a substantial part of his enquiry into the loss of creativity in civilizations, and the conditions for rebirth.[3] All three were concerned with the problem of world order. They were deeply affected by a pessimistic view of the prospects for western societies. Perhaps their pessimism arose from apprehension that an agreeable and civilized way of life had been irremediably disturbed. Whatever particular sentiments may have sparked their efforts, in order to understand the nature of the crisis they each turned naturally to a reflection upon history. The fact that so many professional historians proclaimed agnosticism concerning the meaning of history was provocation and incentive to take up what these skeptics had eschewed.[4] Indeed, the agnosticism of the professionals appeared as a thin veil covering a declaration of bankruptcy in the linear progressive view of history that had optimistically envisaged the universal triumph of liberal parliamentary polities – a bankruptcy consequent upon the political and economic defaults of liberalism in the Europe of the 1930s.

Following World War II, professional historians have been readier to take up the challenge of broad reinterpretation. Geoffrey Barraclough, for instance, has left aside the comparative civilizations approach of Spengler and Toynbee in favor of a view of contemporary history that is comprehensive both in the way he conceives the world as a structural totality and in his manner of linking together the

60

different aspects of social life.[5] Like his predecessors, however, Barraclough seems to find a perception of the structures and processes of history a useful point of departure for thinking about the shaping of the future.

A newer current of literature, also concerned about future world order but renouncing the historical approach, fits into the general rubric of "futurology." (Bertrand de Jouvenel, seeking to avoid the deterministic implications of "futurology," offers the term – derived from the French – *futuribles*: possible futures, or perhaps better, alternative futures.) The literature of futurology may be seen as reflecting an impatience with the failure of the behavioral sciences (despite massive injections of foundation money), to come up with a scientific basis for predicting the social future. As a practical matter, businesspeople and policy makers have to make some assumptions about the future as a basis for their own planning. Futurology tries to compensate for the inadequacy or diffidence of overly cautious behavioral scientists by offering some explicit assumptions to meet the demand. In general, futurology relies heavily upon forecasting new developments in technology,[6] and tends to consider social organization as a dependent variable that must adapt to new technology. It takes account of those aspects of social life which can be most easily measured, such as demography and production. And it is concerned with the problems of individual psychology that occur when individuals are under pressure to make rapid adjustments to continually novel environments. But futurology, as a literary genre, has shown no interest in enquiries into the structure and process of history. It seems firmly committed to the notion that the past can be no guide to the future.

There is, of course, nothing very new about a concern for the human future, although this concern may be perceived as more acute at some times than at others. Such a perception, occurring at a time when intellectual pursuits are specialized and compartmentalized, has, in futurology, spun off a new "discipline." But the modes of thought that can be applied to the problem of reasoning about the future have long roots in the past. The sense of urgency which currently surrounds this exercise inclines its practitioners to stress their conclusions rather than the logical basis from which these conclusions are derived. This essay, which has nothing new to say about the mental processes for speculating about the future, attempts to sort out distinctively different approaches and to discuss some of the implications of each.

Approaches to thinking about the future

We shall discuss three types of approaches to thinking about the future of world order: the natural-rational, the positivist-evolutionary, and the historicist-dialectical. Each conceives the future in terms of some combination of constraints and purposive action. Each has a distinctive theory of knowledge and method, leading to different techniques of enquiry. And each has, implicitly or explicitly, a distinctive model of historical process through which the future may be conceived.

The natural-rational approach

This approach is founded in the concept of a duality distinguishing the inward nature from the outward appearance of human institutions and events. The inward nature is knowable by reason, which is our avenue toward understanding the real essence of man and the polity. The standard given by reason derives from a conviction of the universality of essential human nature, and by this standard the observable differences in human institutions and behavior, which constitute the historical record of various attempts to realize the human potential, may be appraised.

Corresponding to this inwardness and outwardness are two conflicting principles of politics: the subjective principle, which is the creative ability of individuals and peoples, the intelligence, energy, and degree of concord they manifest in building and preserving the polity; and the objective principle, which is the concatenation of conditions and events or circumstances against which the subjective principle has to work.[7]

The problem of how this duality is resolved on the historical plane has been given different emphases. When the objective principle appears predominant, and the potentiality of political action appears limited or futile, a doctrine of Providence offers the explanation that the objective circumstances may be intelligible by a suprahuman extension of reason (St. Augustine, Tolstoy). When, on the other hand, there is a strong will to master the objective principle, attention focuses upon the means of arousing and enhancing creative ability in politics, so that through it objective circumstances may be understood and manipulated (cf. Machiavelli's concept of *necessità*).

Two lines of enquiry which derive from the natural-rational approach are, first, the normative task of designing polities consistent with the rational nature of man (utopianism), and second, the analysis of politics so as better to understand the conditions that must be taken into account in the effort to construct the ideal polity. Political science, in this conception, is not opposed to normative theory, but is a complement to it. Normative theory gives the goals of politics, and political science the conditions under which these goals can be attained.

A cyclical model of the historical process corresponds to this approach. Politics strives toward the ideal when invested with creative energy or *virtù*; such hopeful periods are followed by phases of progressive corruption of political structures as this vital energy is superseded by a subordination of civic spirit to the pursuit of particular interests. The positive content of the ideal is often constructed with elements from the remote past. Dante's *De Monarchia* and Machiavelli's *Discorsi*, for example, refer to a golden age some thirteen or fifteen hundred years earlier.

The positivist-evolutionary approach

Positivism denies the relevancy, for an understanding of the social world, of the inward and outward duality of human institutions and events. Scientific method for the study of society is conceived as analogous to that evolved for the study of the world of nature. Human agents and actions are to be reduced to their outward phenomenal aspects, and science is thought of as a rationality to be discovered in the form of regularities in the relationships among externally observed phenomena. The progress of social science is equated to the cumulative discovery of laws in the form of consequences that are predictable under prescribed conditions.

In order to pursue this approach, historical events have to be converted into objects. Even mental states can be reduced to object form as measurable, comparable units – e.g., by the use of opinion surveys (which extract a statement of opinion from the total context of an individual mind and then consider this as an object similar to many others). Positivism requires *data* – i.e., externally observed "givens" – whereas other approaches to understanding the social world deal with *facts* – i.e., events or institutions which are intelligible to people because they have been made by people.[8]

From the subjective standpoint, actions are explainable in terms of a total context of conscious and unconscious influences. The positivist approach, seeking objective data, fragments this subjective totality into a number of distinct observations that can be classified as variables. In the simplest case, changes in one variable are observed to be associated with changes in another; causal inferences can be drawn from this observation if it is assumed that other factors are either irrelevant or constant. Generally, however, social life is too complex to be reducible to two variables. It is therefore necessary to devise a linkage among a number of supposedly relevant variables, all thought of as interacting with each other: hence the device of a system. In considering the problems of thinking about the future, it is important to make clear how the assumptions that are built into the notion of a system can shape our ideas of social change.

Two variants of systems models may be compared. The first is a structural-functionalist variant, in which social roles are conceived as being linked together through the performance of functions that complement each other in the achievement of equilibrium at the level of the system. The system, from being simply a nominalist framework for organizing data, implicitly becomes a real entity with a finality of its own – i.e., the maintenance of its own equilibrium. Homeostatic mechanisms reassert equilibrium against the destabilizing consequences of dysfunctional activity. The normative consensual content of the system is an important regulating mechanism that socializes the actors to their roles and controls deviant behavior.

The latent status quo bias which the equilibrium concept gives to the functionalist model is modified by its particular manner of conceiving development of the system, namely in terms of the system's progressive "integration." This notion of social change derives from nineteenth-century sociology, particularly Tönnies and Durkheim, in which social evolution was conceived as a movement away from a traditional, rural, organic community toward a more complex urban and industrial division of labor. Integration, in that framework, is seen as the emergence of structures capable of ensuring a harmonious complementarity among functionally specific roles in a society characterized by a high degree of interdependence of its parts.[9]

Integration is a technological concept that specifies the final state toward which the system is drawn. By deductive reasoning, various problems to be overcome en route toward this final state can be defined, and their solutions planned with a view to facilitating its attainment. Functionalism lends itself to problem solving – diagnosing technical obstacles and engineering appropriate adjustments – where the end goal is taken as given by the system itself.

But how did the end goal get into the system in the first place? We can only answer in historical terms: from the system's own ideological origin. In functionalist models, the future is meant to achieve the maximum of productive efficiency with a minimum of social conflict in industrial societies of the western type.[10]

The second variant of systems models abandons the equilibrium bias of functionalism by giving pride of place to the notion of a "feedback loop." The interactions of the system are thereby seen as producing certain outputs or consequences which "feed back" by modifying the inputs for the next round of outputs. This use of the feedback loop justifies the appellation "system dynamics," and lends itself to quantitative applications with apparent potential for simulating the future. The Club of Rome group has used such a model in preparing the study on *The Limits to Growth*.[11] The method extrapolates a series of outputs – population growth, production, resource depletion, pollution – taking account of the feedback effects of these outputs on each other. What the method in a way conceals, or at least does not make explicit, is that these outputs and the rates of change in them depend upon specific forms of social organization and social relations. Extrapolation of recent rates of growth in these outputs assumes implicitly that existing social relations (and the distribution of social power that they express) will remain unchanged.

The model of historical process common to both variants of the positivist-evolutionary approach is based upon a projection of the observed tendencies of contemporary society. The existing distributions of power, existing forms of social relations, and currently dominant norms are considered as given, and the future is thought of as the fulfilment of their inherent tendencies. The bias of the approach is in favor of the status quo, by contrast with the critical potential of the natural-rational approach which holds up the ideal as a challenge to the status quo.

The historicist-dialectical approach

Historicism reverts to the dualism of subjectivity. The social world is intelligible as the creation of the human mind. Historicism deals with facts, not data. Whereas the natural-rational method contrasts a subjectively conceived universal ideal with the objective conditions of social existence, historicism looks for the idea within the actual: its aim is not critical appraisal of the actual, but understanding and explanation.[12] Historicism is a method for understanding historical process in terms of the workings of the human mind in its inward aspect, while the positivist-evolutionary approach looks for trends or predictable regularities in objective data.[13]

The historicist is a "holist" who considers individual events as intelligible only within the larger totality of contemporaneous thought and action. Each individual mind has a partial, more or less comprehensive view of the totality of which any event is a part. The historicist approach attempts to achieve a certain level of generality with reference to particular historical periods and places through the use of concepts like feudalism, capitalism, liberalism, fascism, and so forth.[14] These suggest a coherent structural arrangement of ideas, behavior patterns, and institutions. Such concepts do not represent the thought of any historical actors in particular (although they may best be derived from an examination of the thought of the most perceptive minds of a period), but may be taken as ideal types expressive of the dominant orientations to actions of a whole period. The dialectical element in this approach arises when historical change is seen as the result of conflict between two such contrasting conceptions. The model of historical process is, then, a conflict model. Ralf Dahrendorf has expressed this simply: "[T]he idea of a society which produces in its structure the antagonisms that lead to its modification appears as an appropriate model for the analysis of change in general."[15]

This is not to say that conflict always originates in ideas. There is always tension between a widely held conception of the world and the realities of existence for particular groups of historical people. Gaps develop between changing material conditions and old intellectual schemata. Such gaps suggest latent conflict, the actualizing of which depends upon a change of consciousness on the part of the potential challengers and their adoption of a contrast image of society. The historical-dialectical analyst's role is thus as much to arouse consciousness and the will to act as to diagnose the condition of the world.[16]

Some ideas about future world order

What follows is a discussion of some applications of the three intellectual orientations just outlined. The ideas considered in this connection are images of the future which can be found in the words of politicians and analysts (mainly contemporary social scientists), rather than the more explicit anticipations of utopian literature.

A normative perspective: liberal pluralism as a condition for world peace

The idea that a normative view of the good polity can be a condition of world order seems to have become distinctly unfashionable.[17] It does, however, have a distinguished genealogy in the history of ideas and was readily accepted as recently as the early postwar years. Even if the idea is now in intellectual eclipse, residues of it remain, and revival may be anticipated.

The major premise of this normative view is that the whole – the world political order – cannot be inconsistent with its parts, i.e., with the nature of the polities of which it is composed. Justice at the global level would depend upon justice in the polities. Injustice or disorder in the parts would threaten the maintenance of order and justice at the global level; therefore it is held that the global order – insofar as power and influence can be mobilized on its behalf – may legitimately act to ensure justice and order in deviant polities. The minor premise is that liberal pluralism is the political arrangement most conducive to the good life. Liberal pluralism in the component polities thus becomes the normative condition for world order.[a]

First, we must note the antiquity and prestige of the major premise in normative political theory. Dante wrote: "Whatever relation a part bears to its whole, the structure of that part must bear to the total structure." And he continued, "if the form of this structure is found among the partial associations of men, much more should it be found in the society of men as a totality...."[18] Some two centuries later, Machiavelli confronted the same general problem with the different political perspective of his time. His practical vision of order was limited geographically to the unification of Italy, whereas Dante's extended in principle to the larger concept of Christendom. But on the major premise of the necessity for conformity between the nature of order in the parts with order in the whole, Machiavelli and Dante were in agreement. Machiavelli thought the republic to be the highest form of polity, but considered his contemporaries too corrupt to sustain a republic. His appeal to the prince was the creation of a social

---

[a] One extension of this line of thinking has been to conclude that the "end of history" has arrived now that the postwar conflict between East and West has ended with the political dissolution of the Soviet Union: Francis Fukuyama, "The End of History?," *National Interest*, no. 16 (Summer 1989), pp. 3–18, and his *The End of History and the Last Man* (New York: Free Press, 1992).

myth, through which he hoped for a regeneration of the civic spirit.[19] The same assumption – that there are internal conditions of polities required to sustain the larger world order – is found in Kant's reflections, *Eternal Peace*. Kant considered this essential condition to be the existence of a republican form of government in each state, by which he meant constitutional government, representative and respectful of law and right.[20]

The basic idea was common enough in the rhetoric of political leaders after World War II, and was reinforced among western spokesmen with the onset of the Cold War. As applied particularly to the emerging nations, it could be reduced to a series of linked propositions: technical and economic aid is conducive to economic development; development creates conditions conducive to democracy; democratic polities provide the condition for world peace. Each of these linked propositions has been demolished by critics,[21] and sometime during the 1960s the argument dropped out of western justifications for development assistance.[22]

This change even at the local level of rhetoric calls for some explanation. International relations theorists never did give much credence to the idea that the internal characteristics of a polity might influence its international behavior. In their international relations, states pursued national interests which had little to do with their forms of government. When international relations analysts began to look within states for an explanation of conduct, it was bureaucratic processes that claimed their attention rather than the broader internal structure and processes of power.

Among politicians, a necessary respect for the postwar structure of world power inclined toward a historicist relativism. President Wilson had sought to make the world safe for democracy; President Lyndon Johnson offered the goal of making the world safe for diversity.[23] Meanwhile, among those nations of the Third World toward which development assistance from the liberal pluralist polities of the West was directed, authoritarian regimes became increasingly common.[24] And the United States, which had been most ready to export its national ideology and which represented its world power in terms of leadership of democratic forces, found itself by the late 1960s the chief external support for many of these authoritarian regimes. All of this required a revision of the thesis that world peace could be built on the foundations of economic development and democratic pluralism.

The theorists of comparative politics and political modernization undertook that revision by an attack on the minor premise – at least to the extent of discouraging belief in the feasibility of liberal pluralism in poor countries. The vehicle for this ideological revision was the application of one of the methods derived from the positivist-evolutionary approach: functionalism. The overload of demands upon underdeveloped political structures inclined them toward authoritarian solutions. Authoritarianism was accordingly to be expected, save for some exceptional situations, as a characteristic of early stages of modernization. David E. Apter, whose analysis is one of the most sophisticated in comparative politics theory, considers authoritarian types optimal for long-term modernization, adding that this "may well result in a rebirth of fascism, stripped of its more atavistic qualities."[25] (Possibly, in a future revision of his text, more recent events will suggest to him the deletion of the qualifying clause.)[b]

Functionalist theories seemed to sweep aside the normative inconsistency in which the western countries, and especially the United States, found themselves by asserting a doctrine of long-term convergence toward what Apter called "reconciliation systems," and what Clark Kerr and others named "pluralistic industrialism."[26] Normatively congenial outcomes were thus assured, without any purposive action in support of these norms being required. Historical inevitability or the functional logic of systemic development would do the work of morality. The liberal conscience need not be troubled by active support of fascism abroad.

Other, less theoretically sophisticated interests continued to support the implantation abroad of those elements of the pluralist polity most dear to them: business in its concern for freedom from politically imposed constraints on economic activity, and trade unions in support of autonomy for labor organizations.[27] Even in the absence of well-developed competing political parties, the pluralist polity might be founded upon an independent organization of interests. The practical consequences of such externally induced pluralism in poor countries are now fairly well known: the creation of enclaves of relative power and privilege subject to external control, a lopsided minority pluralism that has been no obstacle to repressive authoritarianism.[28]

[b] The sentence in parentheses was inspired by the trend noted above towards authoritarianism during the 1960s. (Apter's book was published in 1965 and probably was not able to assess the full strength of the trend.) Of course, this trend seemed to have been moderately reversed during the 1980s as more elected governments appeared in LDCs. One can question the durability of this reversal insofar as the social-political

69

Advocates of liberal pluralism as a condition for world order are now in serious trouble; their claims are rejected in fashionable theory, and their program perverted in practical applications. Tentatively, it is suggested that formalism has been the root of the weakness of the normative position. The institutions of pluralism presuppose a diffusion of power, but where power is very unevenly distributed – because of a social structure based upon concentrated land ownership, for example, or because foreigners hold powerful economic levers which they manipulate with the connivance of strategically placed domestic groups – institutions with a formal appearance of pluralism will be but a facade for tyranny. This inference does not invalidate the major premise of the natural-rational approach – that justice in the parts is a condition for justice in the whole – but it does imply that there has been an inadequacy in understanding how justice may be promoted in the parts. The Machiavellian analysis of *necessità*, of the material constraints that must be taken into account in shaping action toward the normative goal, has been deficient. At least part of the responsibility for that deficiency lies with the dominant positivist tendency in political science, which in renouncing the subjective aspect of politics has unwittingly become a justifier of the status quo.

Toward global integration: visions derived from positivist social science

Functionalist theories elaborated during the past two decades have held forth visions of a more centralized international system, which will be brought about through a continuing process of integration, part regional, part global. The origin of this development of functionalism is traceable to an essentially normative theory evolved through the League of Nations period and propounded, toward the end of World War II, by David Mitrany in his pamphlet, *A Working Peace System*.[29] Mitrany regarded the nation-state, with its representatives who thought in terms of "national interest," as the major obstacle to world order. The nation-state was too firmly anchored in public mores to succumb to a frontal attack through the route of world federalism. But it might possibly be outflanked by removing certain practical problems from its effective control and organizing the solution of these problems on an international basis. As the internationally linked

basis of elected regions is undermined by the consequences of "structural adjustment," etc., in the 1980s and 1990s.

areas expanded, the role of the nation-state would diminish, and the prospects of world government become more real. What could not be achieved by the direct approach might come about indirectly, by stealth. Mitrany, in his overriding concern with the problem of world peace, undoubtedly underestimated the extent to which the nation-state had become the guarantor of welfare. The state was unlikely to abandon its welfare role willingly in favor of international authorities;[30] and the expectations of the public would not allow the state to devolve its responsibility for welfare to any international body. Mitrany's normatively inspired prescriptions achieved a more scientific appearance during the 1950s in a revised form which political scientists termed "neofunctionalism."[31] Neofunctionalism was concerned primarily with analysis of the political process which would transform a less integrated into a more integrated international system. Whereas Mitrany had envisaged a mere addition of problem-solving tasks, neofunctionalism introduced as a key concept the notion of "spillover." In practice, the tasks of administration are linked, so that if the performance of some particular function becomes organized internationally, this will create the opportunity to raise the question of similarly organizing the performance of related tasks. Perceptive leaders in the internationally integrated sectors could use these linkages among related functions so as to precipitate or take advantage of crises to bring about a step-by-step expansion of internationally performed tasks. As this happened, the various client groups within countries would increasingly focus their interests upon the international agencies carrying out these tasks, thereby expanding the authority of the international institutions at the expense of national institutions.

The model from which this image was derived was the *relance européenne* of the late 1950s. The common market for coal and steel spilled over into a general common market. After the Suez crisis, a policy for coal, one source of energy, spilled over into a joint policy for atomic energy through Euratom. Around 1958, neofunctionalist theory seemed to have pointed to an historical trend. What was manifestly happening in western Europe might, more remotely, be anticipated on a global scale.

As the continuing progress of European integration faltered during the 1960s, theory was revised. The concept of "spillback" had to be introduced when member countries of the EEC resorted to national measures to deal with recession in the coal industry.[32] And when

General de Gaulle intervened to obstruct the interbureaucratic processes envisaged in the neofunctionalist model, a new category, the
"dramatic-political actor," was brought into the picture – a *deus ex
machina* who burst into the system to alter its rules. By this time, neofunctionalism had lost the clear (but now clearly wrong) ability to
predict which it appeared to have in its original formulation. It had
become largely a checklist of concepts drawn up in relation to the
question as to whether the international system was becoming more
centralized.

Currently, two derivatives of functionalism present alternative
visions of the future. They correspond broadly to the ways in which,
according to the earlier functionalists, the nation-state could be outflanked: one was by the transnational action of nongovernmental
organizations, the other by a splitting away of specialized agencies
of government from central political control. The first is called the
transnational approach to integration, the second the *transgovernmental*
(or multibureaucratic) approach.

The current hero of the transnational approach is the multinational
corporation. The MNC has been hailed as the emergent structure of
efficient management operating on a global scale and capable both
of organizing global economic development and of submerging the
ideological conflict of the Cold War by demonstrating a transideologi-
cal harmony of interests. These structures, potentially (if not altogether
actually) "geocentric" in the attitudes and loyalties of their management, correspond to the functional requirements of the increasingly
interdependent global system. The more peaceful and abundant
future they herald is being held back (in the minds of their supporters)
only by the nationalistic reflexes of an obsolescent structure of nation-
states. The practical issue is therefore how to ease the inevitable transition toward a world organized by several hundred large corporations, whose rivalries can be thought of as creating welfare and as
involving competition within a homogeneous set of values.[33] The
global economic integration to be brought about by MNCs will require
steps toward political integration which would supersede the nation-
state system.

This vision is an extrapolation from some economic trends of the
late 1960s, particularly the expansion of international production with
the substantial increases of foreign and especially American investment in Europe and some of the less-developed areas. It takes little
account of the response to that same tendency: an increased determi-

72

nation by states in both host and home countries to reassert more effectively their control over national economies, which seemed to be slipping from states as MNCs enhanced their ability to maximize their advantages among different national jurisdictions. Now, by the mid-1970s, as governments pressed by powerful domestic interest groups engage in what Helmut Schmidt has called the "struggle for the world product,"[34] the political emancipation of the MNC seems a less likely prospect than it did a decade ago. This appears to be an apposite illustration of the dialectical quality of historical change and consequential error of extrapolating observed trends. Widespread consciousness of a trend may indeed be a signal that the trend is about to be reversed.

The transgovernmental approach is an extension of the bureaucratic-politics analysis of national foreign policy. It takes account of the increase in transnational economic activity by MNCs and of the growing propensity of states to control this activity. It envisages not a demise of the nation-state as such, but a growing disaggregation of governmental activity and merging of policy making among states – in which process international organizations will play important roles. Stated simply, the argument runs: control of transnational activity increases the range of action of a large number of agencies of government; the increasing sensitivity of national economies to each other means that foreign governments are concerned about the effects of national policies and these become matters for intergovernmental negotiations; the national agencies of government concerned with specific kinds of policy enter into direct contact with each other in preference to communicating through foreign offices; transgovernmental policy making leads to the formation of transgovernmental coalitions, through which specialized agencies of national governments advance their preferred policies with the support of their opposite numbers abroad; intergovernmental organizations are convenient forums for the formation of transgovernmental coalitions, and provide agencies of national governments with potential external support for their policy goals. The older neofunctionalism envisaged that international organizations would become autonomous actors in the international system, with increasing authority as interests and loyalties of subnational groups became more and more focused upon them, until they outclassed nation-states. The transgovernmental revision of neofunctionalism withdraws the claims for the autonomy of intergovernmental organizations – they are seen more as forums for mobilizing national policy makers than as distinct entities – but puts more stress upon a fragmentation of national government or weakening of the effective control by the central authorities over the proliferating roles of the government.[35] The integration that will be achieved is less clearly identifiable with concrete institutions; it will be the product of more anonymous multinational networks of bureaucrats.

The limitation of the transgovernmental approach as a vision of the future is similar to that of the preceding transnational approach: it perceives the future in terms of the magnification of one currently observable tendency. The approach usefully focuses upon one sector of political activity which has been neglected in the past and which, for some of the reasons mentioned, has come to have particular importance at the present time. By concentrating upon the interactions of bureaucrats, however, the approach takes as given the parameters of bureaucratic action. It can have little or nothing to say about changes in these parameters, which may come from outside the multibureaucratic system. Notable among such exogenous changes affecting the parameters of bureaucracy are changes in the nature of the state, which are traceable to social movements or disturbances, that is, to changes in the balance of social forces within the state. The New Deal can be seen in retrospect as a comprehensive change in the personnel and structure of government administration which came from such a social disturbance. Movements toward secession or regional autonomy in various countries today could also change the structure of governments and the conditions in which bureaucracies operate.

The larger questions concern the basis of power in societies. Do we envisage a concentration of organized economic interests, business, and labor, in the management of modern economies through a new corporatism? Or a populist or revolutionary reversal of these tendencies? Will Third World countries be increasingly or decreasingly controlled by authoritarian coalitions of the military and externally oriented economic interests? Answers to such questions would determine the conditions in which the multibureaucratic politics envisaged by the transgovernmental-relations approach will take place.

Furthermore, the approach must consider a contradiction implicit in its own premise. The progress of transgovernmental relations comes from a losing struggle by the central political authorities to ensure a coherence in its control of national policies, and a shift of power toward segmented bureaucratic networks. Is not a growing consciousness of this tendency likely to strengthen public support behind political leaders in their determination to regain control, and to lead to public pressures for more effective accountability of bureaucratic policy makers?

Geoffrey Barraclough, in delineating the salient features of contemporary history, directs attention first to what he calls structural changes – among which he includes changes in the nature of industrialism and imperialism, shifts in the demographic balance of the world's regions, changes in the nature of the state, and movements of ideologies and attitudes – since these "fix the skeleton or framework within which political action takes place."[36] Thinking about the future should give precedence to speculation about such structural changes over a focus on a subset of political actors and their interactions.

The systems-dynamics variant of the positivist-evolutionary approach gives us a different kind of view of future world order, cast in the more openly pessimistic terms of "limits to growth" or "endangered planet." The world is an ecological system whose material components and processes determine its finite limits. For all of history up to the very recent past, the system has contained a good deal of slack for human activity. The consequences of man-made disasters as well as of natural disasters have been remedied over time through the natural cycle of the system. That is no longer the case, as the consequences of human activity begin to press against the limits of the system. The human population is approaching the limit of life-sustaining resources. Production is depleting mineral resources faster than they are being replenished. Pollutants being produced exceed the absorptive and recycling capacity of the system. If present rates of growth in population, production, resource depletion, and pollution continue, the system will break down at some foreseeable and not too distant date. The form of breakdown will be a sudden drop in population and production.

Political and social variables form no part of the model from which these predictions are derived. But the implication of the model is clearly political: population and production must be brought under collective control and reduced to a zero rate of growth if the anticipated disaster is to be averted. Only the attainment of a stable state will allow survival. On this analysis, a new justification for international organization can be constructed, and a more urgent one than

75

those of the past. Global monitoring and management will be required in order to achieve and maintain the optimum state of the global system.[37]

The proposed remedies raise as many grave problems at the political level as they purport to solve at the ecological level. Poor people and poor countries can point to the lopsided distribution of the key variable, with the rich having consumed most of the nonreplaceable resources and contributed most of the nonabsorbable pollution, and the poor having contributed most of the population increase. The policy prescriptions seem to affect the poor most of all: they are to have fewer children and they are not to get richer through industrializing in the way some of them had hoped. If zero growth is necessary for the future, the poor may well argue, justice requires a critical look at the distribution of costs and benefits. The clear political implication of zero growth is conflict over redistribution, both among and within nations. Growth attenuated such conflict in the past by making possible a sharing of increments, thus avoiding the more intractable issues of the basic redistribution of wealth and power.

The rich, by contrast, are naturally inclined to take their own privileged position as an unstated point of departure. From that perspective, the performance of the poor is to be judged by how far they adjust to the changes required by the total system. Jay W. Forrester's thesis of the "counterintuitive nature of social systems" comes in here.[38] He maintains that in complex systems with a number of feedback loops, purposive action directed to the solution of specific ills may have the unintended effect of making those ills worse. (For instance, housing renewal in the urban centres, he argues, will extend the urban blight by encouraging further crowding into these areas.) So, it may be inferred, economic assistance by rich countries to the poorest countries may merely encourage a continuance of the "dysfunctional" behavior that leads to population increase and inefficient agriculture. It would be more in accordance with the interests of the global system to aid only those among the poor who demonstrate that they are reforming their behavior in accordance with the requirements of the system. The argument already commends itself in the affluent suburbs.[39]

The systems-dynamics variant shares a common defect with the other approaches to thinking about future world order that are derived from positivism: the power relations of the status quo are taken as given, and the process models on which reasoning about future prospects can be based do not include anything relevant to a consideration of how these power relations may change, or even how they may be maintained. Power is simply left out of account. Yet order refers, in the first instance, to the distribution and mechanism of power.

Conflict and historical change

The question of power relations suggests a remedy for the defects of the normative approach as well as an alternative to the models derived from positivism. The historicist-dialectical mode of thought places power at the centre of its attention. It sees historical change as the result of conflicts, in which the emergence of a new form of consciousness leads to a shift in power relations which makes this new form of consciousness supreme over the erstwhile dominant form of consciousness. Power represents a conjunction of the outward and inward, of material capabilities and consciousness leading to purposive action.

This mode of thought looks backward in order to explain the present by the structural changes (in Barraclough's usage of the term) which, from the standpoint of the present, can be seen as arising from the past. Since each major period, and thus each successive pattern of "world" order,[40] is to be explained by a specific set of structural changes, there is no general model that can account for past, present, and future. The structural changes that explain one order are not the same as those that explain another; even though some common dimensions recur – technology, production relations, ideologies, and so forth – their precise form differs from case to case.

The future, therefore, necessarily – and perhaps reassuringly – appears indeterminate. We cannot be sure, following the historicist-dialectical mode of thought, which of the structural changes we perceive as going on at present will, in the perspective of the future order, appear as the significant explanatory ones. Some relief from total indeterminism is offered by the idea of conflict as the origin of change. We can follow a method of identifying the crises in which conflict is actual or potential. The kinds of crises we should focus upon are not crises in international relations *per se* – i.e., conflicts arising among the actors of a particular system – but conflicts affecting the parameters of the system – i.e., those that might lead to a change of the system rather than merely changes within the system.

Posing the matter in this way connects with the normative approach and gives it greater realism. These crises in the parameters arise within societies and extend their effects into the international system. Changes in the principles by which societies are organized into polities can thereby be related to changes in the international system. But these changes within societies are now seen in terms of power relations rather than merely formally in terms of institutions, hitherto suggested as the weakness of the normative approach.

Identifying crises is a first step. The next is to consider possible outcomes – alternative directions of historical change which would be conditioned by differences in power relations among the social forces involved.[41] The form of thought within which these steps are taken has both synchronic and diachronic dimensions. In the synchronic dimension, the structural elements that link national societies into a particular historical world order are identified. These are the elements that, as Barraclough says, constitute the framework within which political action takes place. The diachronic dimension shows those points of critical change in the social and political landscape where power is moving from one configuration to another – points from which a nascent order may extend over the broader landscape of a future time.[42] To identify such points and then to consider what paths of change are imaginable in the light of the power relations bearing upon these crises would be a valid method of thinking toward the future.

Notes

This text was first published in *World Politics*, vol. 28, no. 2 (January 1976), pp. 175–196.

1 Daniel Halévy, *Essai sur l'accélération de l'histoire* (2nd ed.; Paris: Plon, 1949).
2 Oswald Spengler, *The Decline of the West*, trans. by C. F. Atkinson (New York: Knopf, I, 1926; II, 1928). The original two-volume edition, *Der Untergang des Abendlandes*, was published by Baumuller in Munich in 1918 and 1922.
3 Arnold Toynbee, *A Study of History* (London: Oxford University Press, 1933–61). This work was published in twelve volumes between 1933 (first three volumes) and 1961 (XII, *Reconsiderations*).
4 Recall particularly the preface, dated January 1936, to H. A. L. Fisher, *A History of Europe* (London: Eyre and Spottiswoode, 1936), in which history is seen as "only one emergency following upon another." Fisher is unwilling to abandon the notion of progress, but warns that progress is not a

law of nature and the "ground gained by one generation may be lost by the next."

5 Geoffrey Barraclough, *An Introduction to Contemporary History* (Harmondsworth, Middlesex: Penguin, 1967); first published London: C. A. Watts, 1964.

6 Using sometimes a form of expert opinion survey genially named the Delphi method.

7 C. N. Cochrane, *Christianity and Classical Culture* (Toronto: Oxford University Press, 1944), deals with the duality of "virtue" and "fortune," and the subjective and objective in classical political thought. See especially 99ff. and 122ff.

8 Giambattista Vico, in his criticism of Descartes, distinguished understanding from perception. R. G. Collingwood summarizes his argument thus: "[T]he condition of being able to know anything truly, to understand it as opposed to merely perceiving it, is that the knower himself should have made it . . . It follows from the *verum factum* principle that history, which is emphatically something made by the human mind, is especially adapted to be an object of human knowledge" (Collingwood, *The Idea of History* (Oxford: Clarendon Press, 1946), pp. 64–65).

9 For a criticism of the logical foundations of functionalism, see W. G. Runciman, *Social Science and Political Theory* (London: Cambridge University Press, 1963), ch. 6.

10 Two illustrations of the manner in which the dominant ideology of a contemporary society has been imported into a functionalist model of historical process are provided by Talcott Parsons and by Clark Kerr and his co-authors. Parsons, in his article, "Evolutionary Universals in Society," *American Sociological Review*, vol. 29, no. 3 (June 1964), pp. 339–357, includes among the "evolutionary universals" which provide societies with adaptive advantages over those that do not possess them, both "money and markets" (which could be roughly equated with free enterprise) and democratic association with elective leadership and fully enfranchised membership. He adds: "I realize that to take this position I must maintain that communist totalitarian organization will probably not fully match 'democracy' in political and integrative capacity in the long run" (p. 356). Kerr and his co-authors project an ultimate convergence of all societies, which begin from different points of departure under different industrializing elites, toward a single ultimate type called "pluralistic industrialism" – that which is best able to solve the functional problems of industrialism. Not surprisingly, the type looks familiar ("The elites all wear grey flannel suits"): Clark Kerr, John T. Dunlop, Frederick H. Harbison, and Charles A. Myers, *Industrialism and Industrial Man* (Cambridge, Mass.: Harvard University Press, 1960).

11 D. H. Meadows *et al.*, *The Limits to Growth* (New York: Universe Books, 1972). The systems-dynamic model was devised by Jay W. Forrester and

described in *World Dynamics* (Cambridge, Mass.: Wright-Allen Press, 1971).

12   The most a historian can do is to take the particular processes of the historical world which he is supposed to elucidate, and let these events be seen in the light of higher and more general forces which are present behind and develop these events; his task is to show the concrete *sub specie aeterni*. But he is not in a position to determine the relationship it bears to concrete reality. Thus he can only say that in historical life he beholds a world which, though unified, is bipolar: a world which needs both poles to be as it appears to us. Physical nature and intellect, causality according to law and creative spontaneity, are these two poles, which stand in such sharp and apparently irreconcilable opposition. But historical life, as it unfolds between them, is always influenced simultaneously by both, even if not always by both to the same degree.

Friedrich Meinecke, *Machiavellism: The Doctrine of* Raison d'État *and Its Place in Modern History*, trans. by Douglas Scott (London: Routledge and Kegan Paul, 1957), p. 8. The original German edition, *Die Idee der Staatrason*, was published in Munich in 1924. For Meinecke, the implications of moral relativism were a torturing problem (pp. 9, 424ff.). Collingwood states the matter in somewhat simpler terms:

The historian, investigating any event in the past, makes a distinction between what may be called the outside and the inside of an event. By the outside of the event I mean everything belonging to it which can be described in terms of bodies and their movements: the passage of Caesar, accompanied by certain men, across a river called the Rubicon at one date, or the spilling of his blood on the floor of the senate-house at another. By the inside of the event, I mean that in which it can only be described in terms of thought: Caesar's defiance of Republican law, or the clash of constitutional policy between himself and his assassins. The historian is never concerned with either of these to the exclusion of the other. He is investigating not mere events (where by a mere event I mean one which has only an outside and no inside) but actions, and an action is the unity of the outside and the inside of an event . . . his main task is to think himself into this action, to discern the thought of its agent.

This reenactment of past thought, Collingwood continues, "is not a passive surrender to the spell of another's mind: it is a labour of active and therefore critical thinking . . . This criticism of the thought whose history he traces is not something secondary to tracing the history of it. It is an indispensable condition of the historical knowledge itself": Collingwood, *Idea of History*, pp. 213–215 (fn. 8).

13 Karl Popper, in his well-known critique, *The Poverty of Historicism* (London: Routledge and Kegan Paul, 1957), includes under the rubric of "historicism" attempts at a positivist sociology of history as well as the

approach characteristic of Meinecke and Collingwood discussed here. Popper's criticism would have fallen on the efforts of Parsons and Kerr mentioned in fn. 10. On this point, see John H. Goldthorpe, "Theories of Industrial Society: Reflections on the Recrudescence of Historicism and the Future of Futurology," *Archives européenes de sociologie*, vol. 12, no. 2 (November 1971), pp. 263–288.

14 Reinhard Bendix calls them "limited applicability concepts" and "contrast concepts." See his essay, "The Comparative Analysis of Historical Change," in Michael Argyle *et al.*, *Social Theory and Economic Change* (London: Tavistock Publications, 1967).

15 Ralf Dahrendorf, *Class and Class Conflict in Industrial Society* (Stanford, Calif.: Stanford University Press, 1959), p. 125. The original German edition was published in 1957.

16 That is, of course, especially true of Marxists in the Hegelian and historicist tradition, most notably Georg Lukács, *History and Class Consciousness*, trans. by Rodney Livingston (Cambridge, Mass.: MIT Press, 1971). Meinecke's conservative enquiry into the history of the doctrine of *raison d'état* concludes also with a consideration of the problems of consciousness and action: in this case the moral dilemma between a sterile idealism which is totally ineffective as a limitation on state action, and a relativism which sees some merit or justification in every action. Positivist writers do not bother themselves with such problems.

17 For instance, at a conference on conditions of world order held in 1965 at the Villa Serbelloni – a site which certifies the intellectual respectability of the event – Raymond Aron introduced the discussions by considering various meanings of the term "world order." Two were purely descriptive: order as any arrangement of reality and order as the relations between the parts. Two were part descriptive, part normative: order as the minimum conditions for existence and order as the minimum conditions for coexistence. A further meaning was purely normative: order as the conditions for the good life. This last meaning was ruled "out of order" at the start as likely to lead discussion in too many divergent directions. The conference agreed to concentrate on the issue of coexistence, thereby implicitly accepting that existing polities were "givens," and ruling out the idea that the internal aspects of a polity might have to be adjusted to a desirable world order. See Stanley Hoffman (ed.), *Conditions of World Order* (Boston: Houghton Mifflin, 1968).

18 Dante, *De Monarchia*, trans. by Herbert W. Schneider (New York: Bobbs-Merrill, 1957), pp. 9–10.

19 In this interpretation of Machiavelli, I lean upon the writings of Federico Chabod and Antonio Gramsci. See Chabod, *Machiavelli and the Renaissance*, trans. by David Moore, with an introduction by A. P. d'Entreves (London: Bowes and Bowes, 1958); Gramsci, *Quaderni del carcere* (Turin: Einaudi, 1975).

20 C. J. Friedrich, *Inevitable Peace* (Cambridge, Mass.: Harvard University

Press, 1948), includes a new translation of Kant's essay. See also F. H. Hinsley, *Power and the Pursuit of Peace* (London: Cambridge University Press, 1963), ch. 4.

21 For example, Inis L. Claude, Jr., "Economic Development Aid and International Political Stability," in Robert Cox (ed.), *The Politics of International Organization* (New York: Praeger, 1970); also, Edward C. Banfield, in Robert A. Goldwin (ed.), *Why Foreign Aid?* (Chicago: Rand McNally, 1963).

22 The point that political development doctrines were always more rhetoric than substance in the administration of US aid programs was made by Robert A. Packenham, "Approaches to the Study of Political Development," *World Politics*, vol. 17, no. 1 (October 1964), pp. 108–120.

23 President Johnson in his first State of the Union message to Congress, January 1964 (*Public Papers of the Presidents of the United States, Lyndon B. Johnson, 1963–64*, I (Washington: US Government Printing Office, 1965), p. 116).

24 Harold Jacobson and I went through the exercise of classifying 154 countries in the world political system as to their economic level and type of polity – using three types: competitive, mobilizing, and authoritarian – at five-year intervals between 1950 and 1970. The trend toward authoritarianism in the Third World countries was marked in the 1960s. It came from two sources: (1) most newly independent countries came into the system with authoritarian regimes and (2) of those independent countries that experienced changes of regime, the largest number moved in the direction of authoritarian polities, usually as a consequence of military coups. Both sources of change were concentrated in countries at the lower economic levels.

25 David E. Apter, *The Politics of Modernization* (Chicago: University of Chicago Press, 1965), p. 416.

26 Kerr, Dunlop, Harbison, and Myers, *Industrialism and Industrial Man*.

27 International action in support of autonomous labor unions has been carried out through international trade union organizations and by the International Labor Organization. Issues within the ILO concerning the goal of promoting pluralism were analyzed in N. M., "International Labor in Crisis," *Foreign Affairs*, vol. 49, no. 3 (April 1971), pp. 519–532. The article signed N. M. was written anonymously by Cox while still director of the International Institute for Labor Studies (part of the ILO). It became one of the sources of tension between him and the then director-general of the ILO (see "Influences and Commitments," chapter 2 in this volume). The far-flung activities of the United States Central Intelligence Agency using "autonomous" labor organizations as cover for political penetration in other countries, long a well-known story to people active in international trade union affairs, are described in some detail in Philip Agee, *Inside the Company: CIA Diary* (London: Penguin, 1975).

28 A detailed study of the consequences of trade union penetration from a developed to a less-developed country is in Jeffrey Harrod, *Trade Union Foreign Policy: A Study of British and American Unions in Jamaica* (London:

Macmillan, 1972). A pessimistic evaluation of the consequences in Latin America of promoting cooperative organizations on the autonomous models evolved in European countries was made by Orlando Fals Borda in *International Institute for Labour Studies Bulletin*, no. 7 (Geneva, 1970).

29 David Mitrany, *A Working Peace System: An Argument for the Functional Development of International Organisation* (London: Royal Institute of International Affairs/Oxford University Press, 1943).

30 This argument was cogently presented in Gunnar Myrdal, *Beyond the Welfare State* (New Haven, Conn.: Yale University Press, 1960).

31 The most systematic statement is in Ernst B. Haas, *Beyond the Nation-State: Functionalism and International Organization* (Stanford, Calif.: Stanford University Press, 1964).

32 A significant revision within the neofunctionalist school was in Leon N. Lindberg and Stuart A. Scheingold, *Europe's Would-be Polity: Patterns of Change in the European Community* (Englewood Cliffs, N. J.: Prentice-Hall, 1970).

33 Among the abundant literature hailing the MNC as the wave of the world's future, the following are particularly interesting in defining aspects of an ideology which this paragraph tries to summarize: George W. Ball, "Multinational Corporations and Nation-states," *Atlantic Community Quarterly*, vol. 5, no. 2 (Summer 1967), pp. 247–253, and "Cosmocorp: The Importance of Being Stateless," *Atlantic Community Quarterly*, vol. 6, no. 2 (Summer 1968), pp. 163–170; Frank Tannenbaum, "The Survival of the Fittest," *Columbia Journal of World Business*, vol. 3, no. 2 (March–April 1968), pp. 13–20; Howard Perlmutter, "The Tortuous Evolution of the Multinational Corporation," *Columbia Journal of World Business*, vol. 4, no. 1 (January–February 1969), pp. 9–18.

34 Helmut Schmidt, "The Struggle for the World Product," *Foreign Affairs*, vol. 52 (April 1974).

35 The transgovernmental approach was foreshadowed by Robert O. Keohane and Joseph S. Nye in the introductory section of their edited book, *Transnational Relations and World Politics* (Cambridge, Mass.: Harvard University Press, 1972), and presented more explicitly by them in a paper prepared for the 1974 annual meeting of the American Political Science Association, subsequently published as "Transgovernmental Relations and International Organizations," *World Politics*, vol. 27, no. 1 (October 1974), pp. 39–62. I do not wish to imply that these authors have presented the transgovernmental approach as a contribution to futurology. They offer it primarily as a framework for analysis of current affairs. Nor do they assume that transgovernmental relations are all-determining. They take account of the possibility that the lower-level bureaucrats who are the object of their attention may at times be brought under control by top political leadership. The criticisms of the transgovernmental relations approach in the following paragraphs are not directed at the careful formulation of the concept by Keohane and Nye (which has the merit of

delineating a relatively neglected area of political activity), but are directed rather at the consequences this formulation may have for research priorities from the standpoint of the usefulness of research as an aid to thinking about the future.

36 Barraclough, *Introduction to Contemporary History*, p. 16.

37 This new concept of the role of international organization is presented in Philippe de Seynes, "Prospects for a Future Whole World," *International Organization*, vol. 26, no. 1 (Winter 1972), pp. 1–17. Maurice F. Strong, "One Year after Stockholm: An Ecological Approach to Management," *Foreign Affairs*, vol. 51, no. 4 (July 1973), pp. 690–707, wrote of "the need to develop at the national and international levels the kinds of structures and institutions required for societal management" (p. 702). He added that "the environment cannot be sectoralized. It is a system of interacting relationships that extend through all sectors of activity, and to manage these relationships requires an integrative approach for which present institutional structures were not designed" (p. 703). Not surprisingly, he foresaw the central role of this concept of global management for the United Nations and the Environmental Program that he heads.

38 Jay N. Forrester, "Counterintuitive Nature of Social Systems," *Technology Review*, vol. 73 (1971), p. 53.

39 See Wade Green, "Triage: Who Shall Be Fed? Who Shall Starve?," *New York Times Magazine* (January 5, 1975). A countermodel to that used by the MIT–Club of Rome group is reported on by Alexander King, "The Club of Rome – Setting the Record Straight," *Center Magazine*, vol. 7 (September–October 1974), pp. 15–24. Constructed by Latin American social scientists, it has different distributionist assumptions, and its predictions do not bear out the contention that population growth is catastrophic.

40 The quotation marks are required on "world" because it can well be argued that only the present system, emerging sometime after World War II, is truly global. Previous historical systems referred to more limited areas, more or less sealed off from external influences, which were the relevant "worlds" for the people in them, e.g., Roman, Chinese, Indian, and European systems.

41 An impressive effort to discover the conditions for change in the societal parameters of polity is Barrington Moore, Jr., *The Social Origins of Dictatorship and Democracy* (London: Penguin, 1967). Although his work is confined to the national level, it is illustrative of the approach I attempt to outline here.

42 A masterly historical work incorporating the synchronic and diachronic dimensions is Fernand Braudel, *Civilization matérielle, économie, capitalisme, XVe–XVIIIe siècle*, 3 vols. (Paris: Armand Colin, 1979). Although it is much more narrowly "political," R. R. Palmer, *The Age of the Democratic Revolution* (Princeton, N.J.: Princeton University Press, vol. I, 1959; vol. II, 1964), also adopts the synchronic/diachronic approach.

6 Social forces, states, and world orders: beyond international relations theory (1981)

Academic conventions divide the seamless web of the real social world into separate spheres, each with its own theorizing; this is a necessary and practical way of gaining understanding. Contemplation of undivided totality may lead to profound abstractions or mystical revelations, but practical knowledge (that which can be put to work through action) is always partial or fragmentary in origin. Whether the parts remain as limited, separated objects of knowledge, or become the basis for constructing a structured and dynamic view of larger wholes, is a major question of method and purpose. Either way, the starting point is some initial subdivision of reality, usually dictated by convention.

It is wise to bear in mind that such a conventional cutting up of reality is at best just a convenience of the mind. These segments, however, derive indirectly from reality insofar as they are the result of practices, that is to say, the responses of consciousness to the pressures of reality. Subdivisions of social knowledge thus may roughly correspond to the ways in which human affairs are organized in particular times and places. They may, accordingly, appear to be increasingly arbitrary when practices change.

International relations is a case in point. It is an area of study concerned with the interrelationships among states in an epoch in which states, and most commonly nation-states, are the principal aggregations of political power. It is concerned with the outcomes of war and peace and thus has obvious practical importance. Changing practice has, however, generated confusion as to the nature of the actors involved (different kinds of state, and non-state entities), extended the range of stakes (low as well as high politics), introduced a greater diversity of goals pursued, and produced a greater complexity in the modes of interaction and the institutions within which action takes place.

One old intellectual convention which contributed to the definition of international relations is the distinction between state and civil society. This distinction made practical sense in the eighteenth and early nineteenth centuries when it corresponded to two more or less distinct spheres of human activity or practice: to an emergent society of individuals based on contract and market relations which replaced a status-based society, on the one hand, and a state with functions limited to maintaining internal peace, external defense, and the requisite conditions for markets, on the other. Traditional international relations theory maintains the distinctness of the two spheres, with foreign policy appearing as the pure expression of state interests. Today, however, state and civil society are so interpenetrated that the concepts have become almost purely analytical (referring to difficult-to-define aspects of a complex reality) and are only very vaguely and imprecisely indicative of distinct spheres of activity ... There has been little attempt within the bounds of international relations theory to consider the state/society complex as the basic entity of international relations. As a consequence, the prospect that there exists a plurality of forms of state, expressing different configurations of state/society complexes, remains very largely unexplored, at least in connection with the study of international relations ...

Some historians, quite independently of theorizing about either international relations or the state, have contributed in a practical way toward filling the gap. E. H. Carr and Eric Hobsbawm have both been sensitive to the continuities between social forces, the changing nature of the state, and global relationships. In France, Fernand Braudel has portrayed these interrelationships in the sixteenth and seventeenth centuries on a vast canvas of the whole world. Inspired by Braudel's work a group led by Immanuel Wallerstein has proposed a theory of world systems defined essentially in terms of social relations: the exploitative exchange relations between a developed core and an underdeveloped periphery, to which correspond different forms of labor control, for example, free labor in the core areas, coerced labor in the peripheries, with intermediate forms in what are called semi-peripheries. Though it offers the most radical alternative to conventional international relations theory, the world-systems approach has been criticized on two main grounds: first, for the tendency to under-value the state by considering it as merely derivative from its position in the world system (strong states in the core, weak states in the periphery); second, for the alleged, though unintended, system-maintenance bias. Like structural-functional sociology, the approach is better at accounting for forces that maintain or restore a system's equilibrium than identifying contradictions which can lead to a system's transformation.[1]

The above comments are not, however, the central focus of this essay but warnings prior to the following attempt to sketch a method for understanding global power relations: look at the problem of world order in the whole, but beware of reifying a world system.[2] Beware of underrating state power, but in addition give proper attention to social forces and processes and see how they relate to the development of states and world orders. Above all, do not base theory on theory but rather on changing practice and empirical-historical study, which are a proving ground for concepts and hypotheses.

On perspective and purposes

Theory is always *for* someone and *for* some purpose. All theories have a perspective. Perspectives derive from a position in time and space, specifically social and political time and space. The world is seen from a standpoint definable in terms of nation or social class, of dominance or subordination, of rising or declining power, of a sense of immobility or of present crisis, of past experience, and of hopes and expectations for the future. Of course, sophisticated theory is never just the expression of a perspective. The more sophisticated a theory is, the more it reflects upon and transcends its own perspective; but the initial perspective is always contained within a theory and is relevant to its explication. There is, accordingly, no such thing as theory in itself, divorced from a standpoint in time and space. When any theory so represents itself, it is the more important to examine it as ideology, and to lay bare its concealed perspective.

To each such perspective the enveloping world raises a number of issues; the pressures of social reality present themselves to consciousness as problems. A primary task of theory is to become clearly aware of these problems, to enable the mind to come to grips with the reality it confronts. Thus, as reality changes, old concepts have to be adjusted or rejected and new concepts forged in an initial dialogue between the theorist and the particular world he or she tries to comprehend. This initial dialogue concerns the *problematic* proper to a particular

87

perspective. Social and political theory is history-bound at its origin, since it is always traceable to a historically conditioned awareness of certain problems and issues, a – problematic – while at the same time it attempts to transcend the particularity of its historical origins in order to place them within the framework of some general propositions or laws.

Beginning with its problematic, theory can serve two distinct purposes. One is a simple, direct response: to be a guide to help solve the problems posed within the terms of the particular perspective which was the point of departure. The other is more reflective upon the process of theorizing itself: to become clearly aware of the perspective which gives rise to theorizing, and its relation to other perspectives (to achieve a perspective on perspectives); and to open up the possibility of choosing a different valid perspective from which the problematic becomes one of creating an alternative world. Each of these purposes gives rise to a different kind of theory.

The first purpose gives rise to *problem-solving theory*. It takes the world as it finds it, with the prevailing social and power relationships and the institutions into which they are organized, as the given framework for action. The general aim of problem solving is to make these relationships and institutions work smoothly by dealing effectively with particular sources of trouble. Since the general pattern of institutions and relationships is not called into question, particular problems can be considered in relation to the specialized areas of activity in which they arise. Problem-solving theories are thus fragmented among a multiplicity of spheres or aspects of action, each of which assumes a certain stability in the other spheres (which enables them in practice to be ignored) when confronting a problem arising within its own. The strength of the problem-solving approach lies in its ability to fix limits or parameters to a problem area and to reduce the statement of a particular problem to a limited number of variables which are amenable to relatively close and precise examination. The *ceteris paribus* assumption, upon which such theorizing is based, makes it possible to arrive at statements of laws or regularities which appear to have general validity but which imply, of course, the institutional and relational parameters assumed in the problem-solving approach.

The second purpose leads to *critical theory*. It is critical in the sense that it stands apart from the prevailing order of the world and asks how that order came about. Critical theory, unlike problem-solving theory, does not take institutions and social power relations for granted but calls them into question by concerning itself with their origins and how and whether they might be in the process of changing. It is directed toward an appraisal of the very framework for action, or problematic, which problem-solving theory accepts as its parameters. Critical theory is directed to the social and political complex as a whole rather than to the separate parts. As a matter of practice, critical theory, like problem-solving theory, takes as its starting point some aspect or particular sphere of human activity. But whereas the problem-solving approach leads to further analytical subdivision and limitation of the issue to be dealt with, the critical approach leads toward the construction of a larger picture of the whole of which the initially contemplated part is just one component, and seeks to understand the processes of change in which both parts and whole are involved.

Critical theory is theory of history in the sense of being concerned not just with the past but with a continuing process of historical change. Problem-solving theory is nonhistorical or ahistorical, since it, in effect, posits a continuing present (the permanence of the institutions and power relations which constitute its parameters). The strength of the one is the weakness of the other. Because it deals with a changing reality, critical theory must continually adjust its concepts to the changing object it seeks to understand and explain.[3] These concepts and the accompanying methods of enquiry seem to lack the precision that can be achieved by problem-solving theory, which posits a fixed order as its point of reference. This relative strength of problem-solving theory, however, rests upon a false premise, since the social and political order is not fixed but (at least in a long-range perspective) is changing. Moreover, the assumption of fixity is not merely a convenience of method, but also an ideological bias. Problem-solving theories can be represented, in the broader perspective of critical theory, as serving particular national, sectional, or class interests, which are comfortable within the given order. Indeed, the purpose served by problem-solving theory is conservative, since it aims to solve the problems arising in various parts of a complex whole in order to smooth the functioning of the whole. This aim rather belies the frequent claim of problem-solving theory to be value-free. It is methodologically value-free insofar as it treats the variables it considers as objects (as the chemist treats molecules or the physicist forces and motion); but it is value-bound by virtue of the fact that it implicitly accepts the prevailing order as its own framework. Critical theory contains problem-solving theories within itself, but contains them in the form of identifiable ideologies, thereby pointing to their conservative consequences, not to their usefulness as guides to action. Problem-solving theory stakes its claim on its greater precision and, to the extent that it recognizes critical theory at all, challenges the possibility of achieving any scientific knowledge of historical processes.

Critical theory is, of course, not unconcerned with the problems of the real world. Its aims are just as practical as those of problem-solving theory, but it approaches practice from a perspective which transcends that of the existing order, which problem-solving theory takes as its starting point. Critical theory allows for a normative choice in favor of a social and political order different from the prevailing order, but it limits the range of choice to alternative orders which are feasible transformations of the existing world. A principal objective of critical theory, therefore, is to clarify this range of possible alternatives. Critical theory thus contains an element of utopianism in the sense that it can represent a coherent picture of an alternative order, but its utopianism is constrained by its comprehension of historical processes. It must reject improbable alternatives just as it rejects the permanency of the existing order. In this way critical theory can be a guide to strategic action for bringing about an alternative order, whereas problem-solving theory is a guide to tactical actions which, intended or unintended, sustain the existing order.

The perspectives of different historical periods favor one or the other kind of theory. Periods of apparent stability or fixity in power relations favor the problem-solving approach. The Cold War was one such period. In international relations, it fostered a concentration upon the problems of how to manage an apparently enduring relationship between two superpowers. However, a condition of uncertainty in power relations beckons to critical theory as people seek to understand the opportunities and risks of change. Thus the events of the 1970s generated a sense of greater fluidity in power relationships, of a many-faceted crisis, crossing the threshold of uncertainty and opening the opportunity for a new development of critical theory directed to the problems of world order. To reason about possible future world orders now, however, requires a broadening of our enquiry beyond conventional international relations, so as to encompass basic processes at work in the development of social forces and forms of state, and in the structure of global political economy. Such, at least, is the central argument of this essay.

Realism, Marxism, and an approach to a critical theory of world order

Currents of theory which include works of sophistication usually share some of the features of both problem-solving and critical theory but tend to emphasize one approach over the other. Two currents which have had something important to say about inter-state relations and world orders – realism and Marxism – are considered here as a preliminary to an attempted development of the critical approach.

The realist theory of international relations had its origin in a historical mode of thought. Friedrich Meinecke in his study on *raison d'état*, traced it to the political theory of Machiavelli and the diplomacy of Renaissance Italian city-states quite distinct from the general norms propagated by the ideologically dominant institution of medieval society, the Christian church.[4] In perceiving the doctrines and principles underlying the conduct of states as a reaction to specific historical circumstances, Meinecke's interpretation of *raison d'état* is a contribution to critical theory. Other scholars associated with the realist tradition, such as E. H. Carr and Ludwig Dehio, have continued this historical mode of thought. They delineated the particular configurations of forces which fixed the framework of international behavior in different periods; and they tried to understand institutions, theories, and events within their historical contexts.

Since World War II, some American scholars, notably Hans Morgenthau and Kenneth Waltz, have transformed realism into a form of problem-solving theory. Though individuals of considerable historical learning, they have tended to adopt the fixed ahistorical view of the framework for action characteristic of problem-solving theory, rather than standing back from this framework, in the manner of E. H. Carr, and treating it as historically conditioned and thus susceptible to change. It is no accident that this tendency in theory coincided with the Cold War, which imposed the category of bipolarity upon international relations, and an overriding concern for the defense of American power as a bulwark of the maintenance of order.

The generalized form of the framework for action postulated by this new American realism (which we shall henceforth call neorealism, which is the ideological form abstracted from the real historical framework imposed by the Cold War) is characterized by three levels, each of which can be understood in terms of what classical philosophers would call substances or essences, that is, fundamental and unchanging substrata of changing and accidental manifestations or phenomena. These basic realities were conceived as: (1) the nature of man, understood in terms of Augustinian original sin or the Hobbesian "perpetual and restless desire for power after power that ceaseth only in death";[5] (2) the nature of states, which differ in their domestic constitutions and in their capabilities for mobilizing strength, but are similar in their fixation with a particular concept of national interest (a Leibnizian *monad*) as a guide to their actions; and (3) the nature of the state system, which places rational constraints upon the unbridled pursuit of rival national interests through the mechanism of the balance of power.

Having arrived at this view of underlying substances, history becomes for neorealists a quarry providing materials with which to illustrate variations on always-recurrent themes. The mode of thought ceases to be historical even though the materials used are derived from history. Moreover, this mode of reasoning dictates that, with respect to essentials, the future will always be like the past.[6]

In addition, this core of neorealist theory has extended itself into such areas as game theory, in which the notion of substance at the level of human nature is presented as a rationality assumed to be common to the competing actors who appraise the stakes at issue, the alternative strategies, and the respective payoffs in a similar manner. This idea of a common rationality reinforces the nonhistorical mode of thinking. Other modes of thought are to be castigated as inapt; and there is no attempt to understand them in their own terms (which makes it difficult to account for the irruption into international affairs of a phenomenon like Islamic integralism for instance).

The "common rationality" of neorealism arises from its polemic with liberal internationalism. For neorealism, this rationality is the one appropriate response to a postulated anarchic state system. Morality is effective only to the extent that it is enforced by physical power. This has given neorealism the appearance of being a non-normative theory. It is "value-free" in its exclusion of moral goals (wherein it sees the weakness of liberal internationalism) and in its reduction of problems to their physical power relations. This non-normative quality is, however, only superficial. There is a latent normative element which derives from the assumptions of neorealist theory: security within the postulated inter-state system depends upon each of the major actors understanding this system in the same way, that is to say, upon each of them adopting neorealist rationality as a guide to action. Neorealist theory derives from its foundations the prediction that the actors, from their experiences within the system, will tend to think in this way; but the theory also performs a proselytizing function as the advocate of this form of rationality. To the neorealist theorist, this proselytizing function (wherein lies the normative role of neorealism) is particularly urgent in states which have attained power in excess of that required to balance rivals, since such states may be tempted to discard the rationality of neorealism and try to impose their own moral sense of order, particularly if, as in the case of the United States, cultural tradition has encouraged more optimistic and moralistic views of the nature of man, the state, and world order.[7]

The debate between neorealists and liberal internationalists reproduced, with up-to-date materials, the seventeenth-century challenge presented by the civil philosophy of Hobbes to the natural-law theory of Grotius. Each of the arguments is grounded in different views of the essences of man, the state, and the inter-state system. An alternative which offered the possibility of getting beyond this opposition of mutually exclusive concepts was pointed out by the eighteenth-century Neapolitan Giambattista Vico, for whom the nature of man and of human institutions (among which must be included the state and the inter-state system) should not be thought of in terms of unchanging substance but rather as a continuing creation of new forms. In the duality of continuity and change, where neorealism stresses continuity, the Vichian perspective stresses change; as Vico wrote, "this world of nations has certainly been made by men, and its guise must therefore be found within the modifications of our own human mind."[8]

This should not be taken as a statement of radical idealism, (that is, that the world is a creation of mind). For Vico, ever-changing forms of mind were shaped by the complex of social relations in the genesis of which class struggle played the principal role, as it later did for Marx. Mind is, however, the thread connecting the present with the past, a means of access to a knowledge of these changing modes of social reality. Human nature (the modifications of mind) and human institutions are identical with human history; they are to be understood in genetic and not in essentialist terms (as in neorealism) or in teleological terms (as in functionalism). One cannot, in this Vichian perspective, properly abstract man and the state from history so as to define their substances or essences as *prior to* history, history being but the record of interactions of manifestations of these substances. A proper study of human affairs should be able to reveal both the coherence of minds and institutions characteristic of different ages, and the process whereby one such coherent pattern – which we can call a historical structure – succeeds another. Vico's project, which we would now call social science, was to arrive at a "mental dictionary," or set of common concepts, with which one is able to comprehend the process of "ideal eternal history," or what is most general and common in the sequence of changes undergone by human nature and institutions.[9] The error which Vico criticized as the "conceit of scholars," who will have it that "what they know is as old as the world," consists in taking a form of thought derived from a particular phase of history (and thus from a particular structure of social relations) and assuming it to be universally valid.[10] This is an error of neorealism and more generally, the flawed foundation of all problem-solving theory. It does not, of course, negate the practical utility of neorealism and problem-solving theories within their ideological limits. The Vichian approach, by contrast, is that of critical theory.

How does Marxism relate to this method or approach to a theory of world order? In the first place, it is impossible, without grave risk of confusion, to consider Marxism as a single current of thought. For our purposes, it is necessary to distinguish two divergent Marxist currents, analogous to the bifurcation between the old realism and the new. There is a Marxism which reasons historically and seeks to explain, as well as to promote, changes in social relations; there is also a Marxism, designed as a framework for the analysis of the capitalist state and society, which turns its back on historical knowledge in favor of a more static and abstract conceptualization of the mode of production. The first we may call by the name under which it recognizes itself: historical materialism. It is evident in the historical works of Marx, in those of present-day Marxist historians such as Eric Hobsbawm, and in the thought of Gramsci. It has also influenced some who would not be considered (or consider themselves) Marxist in any strict sense, such as many of the French historians associated with the *Annales*. The second is represented by the so-called structural Marxism of Althusser and Poulantzas ("so-called" in order to distinguish their use of "structure" from the concept of historical structure in this essay) and most commonly takes the form of an exegesis of *Capital* and other sacred texts. Structural Marxism shares some of the features of the neorealist problem-solving approach such as its ahistorical, essentialist epistemology, though not its precision in handling data nor, since it has remained very largely a study in abstractions, its practical applicability to concrete problems. To this extent it does not concern us here. Historical materialism is, however, a foremost source of critical theory and it corrects neorealism in four important respects.

The first concerns dialectic, a term which, like Marxism, has been appropriated to express a variety of not always compatible meanings, so its usage requires some definition. It is used here at two levels: the level of logic and the level of real history. At the level of logic, it means a dialogue seeking truth through the exploration of contradictions.[11] One aspect of this is the continual confrontation of concepts with the reality they are supposed to represent and their adjustment to this reality as it continually changes. Another aspect, which is part of the method of adjusting concepts, is the knowledge that each assertion concerning reality contains implicitly its opposite and that both assertion and opposite are not mutually exclusive but share some measure of the truth sought, a truth, moreover, that is always in motion, never to be encapsulated in some definitive form. At the level of real history, dialectic is the potential for alternative forms of development arising from the confrontation of opposed social forces in any concrete historical situation.

Both realism and historical materialism direct attention to conflict. Neorealism sees conflict as inherent in the human condition, a constant factor flowing directly from the power-seeking essence of human nature and taking the political form of a continual reshuffling of power among the players in a zero-sum game, which is always played according to its own innate rules. Historical materialism sees in conflict the process of a continual remaking of human nature and the creation of new patterns of social relations which change the rules of the game and out of which – if historical materialism remains true to its own logic and method – new forms of conflict may be expected ultimately to arise. In other words, neorealism sees conflict as a recurrent consequence of a continuing structure, whereas historical materialism sees conflict as a possible cause of structural change.

Second, by its focus on imperialism, historical materialism adds a vertical dimension of power to the horizontal dimension of rivalry among the most powerful states, which draws the almost exclusive attention of neorealism. This dimension is the dominance and subordination of metropole over hinterland, center over periphery, in a world political economy.

Third, historical materialism enlarges the realist perspective through its concern with the relationship between the state and civil society. Marxists, like non-Marxists, are divided between those who see the state as the mere expression of the particular interests in civil society and those who see the state as an autonomous force expressing some kind of general interest. This, for Marxists, would be the general interest of capitalism as distinct from the particular interests of capitalists. Gramsci contrasted historical materialism, which recognizes the efficacy of ethical and cultural sources of political action (though always relating them to the economic sphere), with what he called historical economism or the reduction of everything to technological and material interests.[12] Neorealist theory in the United States has returned to the state/civil society relationship, though it has treated civil society as a constraint upon the state and a limitation imposed by particular interests upon *raison d'état*, which is conceived of, and defined as, independent of civil society.[13] The sense of a reciprocal relationship between structure (economic relations) and superstructure (the ethico-political sphere) in Gramsci's thinking contains the potential for considering state/society complexes as the constituent entities of a world order and for exploring the particular historical forms taken by these complexes.[14]

Fourth, historical materialism focuses upon the production process as a critical element in the explanation of the particular historical form taken by a state/society complex. The production of goods and services, which creates both the wealth of a society and the basis for a state's ability to mobilize power behind its foreign policy, takes place through a power relationship between those who control and those who execute the tasks of production. Political conflict and the action of the state either maintain, or bring about changes in, these power relations of production. Historical materialism examines the connections between power in production, power in the state, and power in international relations. Neorealism has, by contrast, virtually ignored the production process. This is the point on which the problem-solving bias of neorealism is most clearly to be distinguished from the critical approach of historical materialism. Neorealism implicitly takes the production process and the power relations inherent in it as a given element of the national interest, and therefore as part of its parameters. Historical materialism is sensitive to the dialectical possibilities of change in the sphere of production which could affect the other spheres, such as those of the state and world order.

This discussion has distinguished two kinds of theorizing as a preliminary to proposing a critical approach to a theory of world order. Some of the basic premises for such a critical theory can now be restated:

(1) An awareness that action is never absolutely free but takes place within a framework for action which constitutes its problematic. Critical theory would start with this framework, which means starting with historical enquiry or an appreciation of the human experience that gives rise to the need for theory.[15]

(2) A realization that not only action but also theory is shaped by the problematic. Critical theory is conscious of its own relativity but through this consciousness can achieve a broader time-perspective and become less relative than problem-solving theory. It knows that the task of theorizing can never be finished in an enclosed system but must continually be begun anew.

(3) The framework for action changes over time and a principal goal of critical theory is to understand these changes.

(4) This framework has the form of a historical structure, a particular combination of thought patterns, material conditions, and human institutions which has a certain coherence among its elements. These structures do not determine people's actions in any mechanical sense but constitute the context of habits, pressures, expectations, and constraints within which action takes place.

(5) The framework or structure within which action takes place is to be viewed, not from the top in terms of the requisites for its equilibrium or reproduction (which would quickly lead back to problem solving), but rather from the bottom or from outside in terms of the conflicts which arise within it and open the possibility of its transformation.[16]

Frameworks for action: historical structures

At its most abstract, the notion of a framework for action or historical structure is a picture of a particular configuration of forces. This configuration does not determine actions in any direct mechanical way

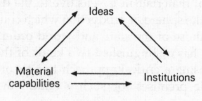

Fig. 6.1

but imposes pressures and constraints. Individuals and groups may move with the pressures or resist and oppose them, but they cannot ignore them. To the extent that they do successfully resist a prevailing historical structure, they buttress their actions with an alternative, emerging configuration of forces, a rival structure.

Three categories of forces (expressed as potentials) interact in a structure: material capabilities, ideas, and institutions (see figure 6.1). No one-way determinism need be assumed among these three; the relationships can be assumed to be reciprocal. The question of which way the lines of force run is always a historical question to be answered by a study of the particular case.

Material capabilities are productive and destructive potentials. In their dynamic form these exist as technological and organizational capabilities, and in their accumulated forms as natural resources which technology can transform, stocks of equipment (for example, industries and armaments), and the wealth which can command these.

Ideas are broadly of two kinds. One kind consists of intersubjective meanings, or those shared notions of the nature of social relations which tend to perpetuate habits and expectations of behavior.[17] Examples of intersubjective meaning in contemporary world politics are the notions that people are organized and commanded by states which have authority over defined territories; that states relate to one another through diplomatic agents; that certain rules apply for the protection of diplomatic agents as being in the common interest of all states; and that certain kinds of behavior are to be expected when conflict arises between states, such as negotiation, confrontation, or war. These notions, though durable over long periods of time, are historically conditioned. The realities of world politics have not always been represented in precisely this way and may not be in the future. It is possible to trace the origins of such ideas and also to detect signs of a weakening of some of them.[18]

The other kind of ideas relevant to a historical structure are collective images of social order held by different groups of people. These are differing views as to both the nature and the legitimacy of prevailing power relations, the meanings of justice and public good, and so forth. Whereas intersubjective meanings are broadly common throughout a particular historical structure and constitute the common ground of social discourse (including conflict), collective images may be several and opposed.[19] The clash of rival collective images provides evidence of the potential for alternative paths of development and raises questions as to the possible material and institutional basis for the emergence of an alternative structure.

Institutionalization is a means of stabilizing and perpetuating a particular order. Institutions reflect the power relations prevailing at their point of origin and tend, at least initially, to encourage collective images consistent with these power relations. Eventually, institutions take on their own life; they can become a battleground of opposing tendencies, or rival institutions may reflect different tendencies. Institutions are particular amalgams of ideas and material power which in turn influence the development of ideas and material capabilities.

There is a close connection between institutionalization and what Gramsci called hegemony. Institutions provide ways of dealing with conflicts so as to minimize the use of force. There is an enforcement potential in the material power relations underlying any structure, in that the strong can destroy the weak if they think it necessary. But force will not have to be used in order to ensure the dominance of the strong to the extent that the weak accept the prevailing power relations as legitimate. This the weak may do if the strong see their mission as hegemonic and not merely dominant or dictatorial, that is, if they are willing to make concessions that will secure the weak's acquiescence in their leadership and if they can express this leadership in terms of universal or general interests, rather than just as serving their own particular interests.[20] Institutions may become the anchor for such a hegemonic strategy since they lend themselves both to the representations of diverse interests and to the universalization of policy.

It is convenient to be able to distinguish between hegemonic and nonhegemonic structures, that is to say, between those in which the power basis of the structure tends to recede into the background of consciousness, and those in which the management of power relations is always in the forefront. Hegemony cannot, however, be reduced to an institutional dimension. One must beware of allowing a focus upon institutions to obscure either changes in the relationship of material forces, or the emergence of ideological challenge to an erstwhile prevailing order. Institutions may be out of phase with these other aspects of reality and their efficacy as a means of regulating conflict (and thus their hegemonic function) thereby undermined. They may be an expression of hegemony but cannot be taken as identical to hegemony.

The method of historical structures is one of representing what can be called limited totalities. The historical structure does not represent the whole world but rather a particular sphere of human activity in its historically located totality. The *ceteris paribus* problem, which falsifies problem-solving theory by leading to an assumption of total stasis, is avoided by juxtaposing and connecting historical structures in related spheres of action. Dialectic is introduced, first, by deriving the definition of a particular structure, not from some abstract model of a social system or mode of production, but from a study of the historical situation to which it relates; and second, by looking for the emergence of rival structures expressing alternative possibilities of development. The three sets of forces indicated in figure 6.1 are a heuristic device, not categories with a predetermined hierarchy of relationships. Historical structures are contrast models; like ideal types they provide, in a logically coherent form, a simplified representation of a complex reality and an expression of tendencies, limited in their applicability in time and space, rather than fully realized developments.

For the purpose of the present discussion, the method of historical structures is applied to the three levels, or spheres of activity: (1) organization of production, more particularly with regard to the *social forces* engendered by the production process; (2) *forms of state* as derived from a study of state/society complexes; and (3) *world orders*, that is, the particular configurations of forces which successively define the problematic of war or peace for the ensemble of states. Each of these levels can be studied as a succession of dominant and emergent rival structures.

The three levels are interrelated. Changes in the organization of production generate new social forces which, in turn, bring about changes in the structure of states; and the generalization of changes in the structure of states alters the problematic of world order. For instance, as E. H. Carr argued, the incorporation of the industrial workers (a new social force) as participants within western states from the late

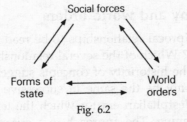

Fig. 6.2

nineteenth century accentuated the movement of these states toward economic nationalism and imperialism (a new form of state), which brought about a fragmentation of the world economy and a more conflictual phase of international relations (the new structure of world order).[21]

The relationship among the three levels is not, however, simply unilinear. Transnational social forces have influenced states through the world structure, as evidenced by the effect of expansive nineteenth-century capitalism, *les bourgeois conquérants*, upon the development of state structures in both core and periphery.[22] Particular structures of world order exert influence over the forms which states take: Stalinism was, at least in part, a response to a sense of threat to the existence of the Soviet state from a hostile world order; the military-industrial complex in core countries justified its influence by pointing to the conflictual condition of world order; and the prevalence of repressive militarism in periphery countries can be explained by the external support of imperialism as well as by a particular conjunction of internal forces. Forms of state also affect the development of social forces through the kinds of domination they exert, for example, by advancing one class interest and thwarting others.[23]

Considered separately, social forces, forms of state, and world orders can be represented in a preliminary approximation as particular configurations of material capabilities, ideas, and institutions (as indicated in figure 6.1). Considered in relation to each other, and thus moving toward a fuller representation of historical process, each will be seen as containing, as well as bearing the impact of, the others (as in figure 6.2).[a]

[a] At the time of writing this essay, I was engaged (with Jeffrey Harrod) in a study of production relations on a world scale which subsequently took the form of two books: *Production, Power, and World Order: Social Forces in the Making of History* (New York: Columbia University Press, 1987) by me; and *Power, Production, and the Unprotected Worker* (New York: Columbia University Press, 1987) by Harrod. This study began with an examination of distinctive patterns of power relations in the production

Hegemony and world orders

How are these reciprocal relationships to be read in the present historical conjuncture? Which of the several relationships will tell us the most? A sense of the historicity of concepts suggests that the critical relationships may not be the same in successive historical periods, even within the Westphalian era for which the term "state system" had particular meaning. The approach to a critical theory of world order, adumbrated here, takes the form of an interconnected series of historical hypotheses.

Neorealism puts the accent on states reduced to their dimension of material force and similarly reduces the structure of world order to the balance of power as a configuration of material forces. Neorealism, which generally dismisses social forces as irrelevant, is not much concerned with differentiating forms of state (except insofar as "strong societies" in liberal democratic polities may hamper the use of force by the state or advance particular interests over the national interest), and tends to place a low value on the normative and institutional aspects of world order.

One effort to broaden the realist perspective to include variations in the authority of international norms and institutions is the theory of "hegemonic stability," which, as stated by Robert Keohane, "holds that hegemonic structures of power, dominated by a single country, are most conducive to the development of strong international regimes, whose rules are relatively precise and well-obeyed."[24] The classical illustrations of the theory discussed by Keohane are the *pax britannica* of the middle of the nineteenth century and the *pax americana* of the years following World War II. The theory appears to be confirmed by the decline in observance of the norms of the nineteenth-century order which accompanied Britain's relative decline in state power from the late nineteenth century. Exponents of the theory see a similar decline, since the early 1970s, in the observance of norms of the postwar order, relating it to a relative decline in US power. Robert Keohane has tested the theory

process as separate historical structures and which then leads to a consideration of different forms of state and global political economy. Bringing in these last two levels is necessary to an understanding of the existence of the different patterns of production relations and the hierarchy of relationships among them. One could equally well adopt forms of state or world orders at the point of departure and ultimately be required to bring in the other levels to explain the historical process.

in particular issue areas (energy, money, and trade) on the grounds that power is not a fungible asset, but has to be differentiated according to the contexts in which a state tried to be influential. He finds that, particularly in the areas of trade and money, changes in US power are insufficient to explain the changes that have occurred and need to be supplemented by the introduction of domestic political, economic, and cultural factors.

An alternative approach might start by redefining what is to be explained, namely, the relative stability of successive world orders. This can be done by equating stability with a concept of hegemony that is based on a coherent conjunction or fit between a configuration of material power, the prevalent collective image of world order (including certain norms) and a set of institutions which administer the order with a certain semblance of universality (that is, not just as the overt instruments of a particular state's dominance). In this formulation, state power ceases to be the sole explanatory factor and becomes part of what is to be explained. This rephrasing of the question addresses a major difficulty in the neorealist version signaled by Keohane and others, namely, how to explain the failure of the United States to establish a stable world order in the interwar period despite its preponderance of power. If the dominance of a single state coincides with a stable order on some occasions but not on others, then there may be some merit in looking more closely at what is meant by stability and more broadly at what may be a necessary but not a sufficient condition of hegemony.

The two periods of the *pax britannica* and the *pax americana* also satisfy the reformulated definition of hegemony. In the middle of the nineteenth century, Britain's world supremacy was founded on its sea power, which remained free from challenge by any continental state as a result of Britain's ability to play the role of balancer in a relatively fluid balance of power in Europe. The norms of liberal economics (free trade, the gold standard, free movement of capital and persons) gained widespread acceptance with the spread of British prestige, providing a universalistic ideology which represented these norms as the basis of a harmony of interests. While there were no formal international institutions, the ideological separation of economics from politics meant that the City could appear as administrator and regulator according to these universal rules, with British sea power remaining in the background as potential enforcer.

The historical structure was transformed in its three dimensions during the period running from the last quarter of the nineteenth century through World War II. During this period British power declined relatively, losing its undisputed supremacy at sea, first with the German challenge and then with the rise of US power; economic liberalism foundered with the rise of protectionism, the new imperialisms, and ultimately the end of the gold standard; and the belated and abortive attempt at international institutionalization through the League of Nations, unsustained either by a dominant power or a widely accepted ideology, collapsed in a world increasingly organized into rival power blocs.

The power configuration of the *pax americana* was more rigid than that of the earlier hegemony, taking the form of alliances (all hinging on US power) created in order to contain the Soviet Union. The stabilization of this power configuration created the conditions for the unfolding of a global economy in which the United States played a role similar to that of Britain in the middle of the nineteenth century. The United States rarely needed to intervene directly in support of specific national economic interests; by maintaining the rules of an international economic order according to the revised liberalism of Bretton Woods, the strength of US corporations engaged in the pursuit of profits was sufficient to ensure continuing national power. The *pax americana* produced a greater number of formal international institutions than the earlier hegemony. The nineteenth-century separation of politics and economics had been blurred by the experience of the Great Depression and the rise of Keynesian doctrines. Since states now had a legitimate and necessary overt role in national economic management, it became necessary both to multilateralize the administrative management of the international economy and to give it an intergovernmental quality.

The notion of hegemony as a fit between power, ideas, and institutions makes it possible to deal with some of the problems in the theory of state dominance as the necessary condition for a stable international order; it allows for lags and leads in hegemony. For example, so appealing was the nostalgia for the nineteenth-century hegemony that the ideological dimension of the *pax britannica* flourished long after the power configuration that supported it had vanished. Sustained, and ultimately futile, efforts were made to revive a liberal world economy along with the gold standard in the interwar period.

Social forces, hegemony, and imperialism

Represented as a fit between material power and institutions, hegemony may seem to lend itself to a cyclical theory of history; the three dimensions fitting together in certain times and places and coming apart in others. This is reminiscent of earlier notions of *virtù*, or of the *Weltgeist* migrating from people to people. The analogy merely points to something which remains unexplained. What is missing is some theory as to how and why the fit comes about and comes apart. It is my contention that the explanation may be sought in the realm of social forces shaped by production relations.

Social forces are not to be thought of as existing exclusively within states. Particular social forces may overflow state boundaries, and world structures can be described in terms of social forces just as they can be described as configurations of state power. The world can be represented as a pattern of interacting social forces in which states play an intermediate though autonomous role between the global structure of social forces and local configurations of social forces within particular countries. This may be called a political-economy perspective of the world: power is seen as *emerging* from social processes rather than taken as given in the form of accumulated material capabilities, that is as the result of these processes. (Paraphrasing Marx, one could describe the latter, neorealist view as the "fetishism of power.")[25] In reaching for a political-economy perspective, we move from identifying the structural characteristics of world orders as configurations of material capabilities, ideas, and institutions (figure 6.1) to explaining their origins, growth, and demise in terms of the interrelationships of the three levels of structures (figure 6.2). It is, of course, no great discovery to find that, viewed in the political economy perspective, the *pax britannica* was based both on the ascendancy of manufacturing capitalism in the international exchange economy, of which Britain was the centre, and on the social and ideological power, in Britain and other parts of northwest Europe, of the class which drew its wealth from manufacturing. The new bourgeoisie did not need to control states directly; its social power became the premise of state politics.[26]

The demise of this hegemonic order can also be explained by the development of social forces. Capitalism mobilized an industrial labor force in the most advanced countries, and from the last quarter of the nineteenth century industrial workers had an impact on the structure of the state in these countries. The incorporation of the industrial workers, the new social force called into existence by manufacturing capitalism, into the nation involved an extension in the range of state action in the form of economic intervention and social policy. This in turn brought the factor of domestic welfare (i.e., the social minimum required to maintain the allegiance of the workers) into the realm of foreign policy. The claims of welfare competed with the exigencies of liberal internationalism within the management of states; as the former gained ground, protectionism, the new imperialism, and ultimately the end of the gold standard marked the long decline of liberal internationalism.[27] The liberal form of state was slowly replaced by the welfare-nationalist form of state.

The spread of industrialization, and the mobilization of social classes it brought about, not only changed the nature of states but also altered the international configuration of state power as new rivals overtook Britain's lead. Protectionism, as the means of building economic power comparable to Britain's, was for these new industrial countries more convincing than the liberal theory of comparative advantage. The new imperialisms of the major industrial powers were a projection abroad of the welfare-nationalist consensus among social forces sought or achieved within the nations. As both the material predominance of the British economy and the appeal of the hegemonic ideology weakened, the hegemonic world order of the middle of the nineteenth century gave place to a nonhegemonic configuration of rival power blocs . . .

James Petras, in his use of the concept of an imperial state system, has posed a number of questions concerning the structural characteristics of states in the present world order.[28] The dominant imperial state and subordinate collaborator states differ in structure and have complementary functions in the imperial system; they are not just more and less powerful units of the same kind, as might be represented in a simple neorealist model. A striking feature in Petras' framework is that the imperial state he analyzes is not the whole US government; it is "those executive bodies within the 'government' which are charged with promoting and protecting the expansion of capital across state boundaries." The imperial system is at once more than and less than the state. It is more than the state in that it is a transnational structure with a dominant core and dependent periphery. This part of the US government is at the system's core, together (and here we may presume to enlarge upon Petras' indications) with

inter-state institutions such as the IMF and the World Bank symbiotically related to expansive capital, and with collaborator governments (or at any rate parts of them linked to the system) in the system's periphery. It is less than the state in the sense that nonimperial,
or even anti-imperial, forces may be present in other parts of both core
and periphery states. The unity of the state, posited by neorealism, is
fragmented in this image, and the struggle for and against the
imperial system may go on within the state structures at both core
and periphery as well as among social forces ranged in support and
opposition to the system. The state is thus a necessary but insufficient
category to account for the imperial system. The imperial system itself
becomes the starting point of enquiry ...

At this point, it is preferable to revert to the earlier terminology
which referred to hegemonic and nonhegemonic world order structures. To introduce the term "imperial" with reference to the *pax americana* risks both obscuring the important difference between hegemonic and nonhegemonic world orders and confusing structurally
different kinds of imperialism (e.g., liberal imperialism, the new or
colonial imperialism, and the imperial system just outlined). The contention here is that the *pax americana* was hegemonic: it commanded
a wide measure of consent among states outside the Soviet sphere and
was able to provide sufficient benefits to the associated and subordinate elements in order to maintain their acquiescence. Of course, consent wore thin as one approached the periphery where the element of
force was always apparent, and it was in the periphery that the challenge to the imperial system first became manifest.

It was suggested above how the particular fit between power, ideology, and institutions constituting the *pax americana* came into being.
Since the practical issue at the present is whether or not the *pax americana* has irretrievably come apart and if so what may replace it, two
specific questions deserving attention are: (1) what are the mechanisms for maintaining hegemony in this particular historical structure?
and (2) what social forces and/or forms of state have been generated
within it which could oppose and ultimately bring about a transformation of the structure?

The internationalization of the state

A partial answer to the first question concerns the internationalization
of the state. The basic principles of the *pax americana* were similar to

those of the *pax britannica*: relatively free movement of goods, capital, and technology and a reasonable degree of predictability in exchange rates. Cordell Hull's conviction that an open trading world was a necessary condition of peace could be taken as its ideological text, supplemented by confidence in economic growth and ever-rising productivity as the basis for moderating and controlling conflict. The postwar hegemony was, however, more fully institutionalized than the *pax britannica* and the main function of its institutions was to reconcile domestic social pressures with the requirements of a world economy. The International Monetary Fund was set up to provide loans to countries with balance-of-payments deficits in order to provide time in which they could make adjustments, and to avoid the sharp deflationary consequences of an automatic gold standard. The World Bank was to be a vehicle for longer-term financial assistance. Economically weak countries were to be given assistance by the system itself, either directly through the system's institutions or by other states after the system's institutions had certified their conformity to the system's norms. These institutions incorporated mechanisms to supervise the application of the system's norms and to make financial assistance effectively conditional upon reasonable evidence of intent to live up to the norms.

This machinery of surveillance was, in the case of the western allies and subsequently of all industrialized capital countries, supplemented by elaborate machinery for the harmonization of national policies. Such procedures began with the mutual criticism of reconstruction plans in western European countries (the US condition for Marshall aid funds), continued with the development of annual review procedures in NATO (which dealt with defense and defense support programs), and became an acquired habit of mutual consultation and mutual review of national policies (through the OECD and other agencies).

The notion of international obligation moved beyond a few basic commitments, such as observance of the most-favored-nation principle or maintenance of an agreed exchange rate, to a general recognition that measures of national economic policy affect other countries and that such consequences should be taken into account before national policies are adopted. Conversely, other countries should be sufficiently understanding of one country's difficulties to acquiesce in short-term exceptions. Adjustments are thus perceived as responding to the needs of the system as a whole and not to the will of dominant countries. External pressures upon national policies were accordingly internationalized . . .

The practice of policy harmonization became such a powerful habit that when the basic norms of international economic behavior no longer seemed valid, as became the case during the 1970s, procedures for mutual adjustment of national economic policies were, if anything, reinforced. In the absence of clear norms, the need for mutual adjustment appeared the greater.[29]

State structures appropriate to this process of policy harmonization can be contrasted with those of the welfare nationalist state of the preceding period. Welfare nationalism took the form of economic planning at the national level and the attempt to control external economic impacts upon the national economy. To make national planning effective, corporative structures grew up in most industrially advanced countries for the purpose of bringing industry, and also organized labor, into consultation with the government in the formulation and implementation of policy . . .

The internationalization of the state gives precedence to certain state agencies – notably ministries of finance and prime ministers' offices – which are key points in the adjustment of domestic to international economic policy. Ministries of industry, labor ministries, and planning offices, which had been built up in the context of national corporatism, tended to be subordinated to the central organs of internationalized public policy. As national economies became more integrated in the world economy, it was the larger and more technologically advanced enterprises that adapted best to the new opportunities. A new axis of influence linked international policy networks with the key central agencies of government and with big business. This new informal corporative structure overshadowed the older, more formalized national corporatism and reflected the dominance of the sector oriented to the world economy over the more nationally oriented sector of a country's economy . . .[30]

The internationalization of production

The internationalization of the state is associated with the expansion of international production. This signifies the integration of production processes on a transnational scale, with different phases of a single process being carried out in different countries. International production currently plays the formative role in relation to the structure of states and world order that national manufacturing and commercial capital played in the middle of the nineteenth century.

International production expands through direct investment, whereas the *rentier* imperialism, of which Hobson and Lenin wrote, primarily took the form of portfolio investment. With portfolio investment, control over the productive resources financed by the transaction passed with ownership to the borrower. With direct investment, control is inherent in the production process itself and remains with the originator of the investment. The essential feature of direct investment is possession, not of money, but of knowledge – in the form of technology and especially in the capacity to continue to develop new technology. The financial arrangements for direct investment may vary greatly, but all are subordinated to this crucial factor of technological control. The arrangements may take the form of wholly owned subsidiaries, joint ventures with local capital sometimes put up by the state in host countries, management contracts with state-owned enterprises, or compensation agreements with socialist enterprises whereby, in return for the provision of technology, these enterprises become suppliers of elements to a globally organized production process planned and controlled by the source of the technology. Formal ownership is less important than the manner in which various elements are integrated into the production system.

Direct investment seems to suggest the dominance of industrial capital over finance capital. The big multinational corporations which expand by direct investment are, to some degree, self-financing, and to the extent that they are not, they seem capable of mobilizing money capital in a number of ways, such as through local capital markets (where their credit is better than that of national entrepreneurs), through the Eurocurrency markets, through infusions of capital from other multinationals linked to technology and production agreements, through state subsidies, and so forth. And yet, particularly since the 1970s, finance capital seems to be returning to prominence through the operations of the multinational banks, not only in the old form of *rentier* imperialism administering loans to peripheral states, but also as a network of control and private planning for the world economy of international production. This network assesses and collectivizes investment risks and allocates investment opportunities among the participants in the expansion of international production; that is, it performs the function of Lenin's collective capitalist in the conditions of late twentieth-century production relations.

International production and class structure

International production is mobilizing social forces, and it is through these forces that its major political consequences vis-à-vis the nature of states and future world orders may be anticipated. Hitherto, social classes have been found to exist within nationally defined social formations, despite rhetorical appeals to the international solidarity of workers. Now, as a consequence of international production, it becomes increasingly pertinent to think in terms of a global class structure alongside or superimposed upon national class structures.

At the apex of an emerging global class structure is the transnational managerial class. Having its own ideology, strategy, and institutions of collective action, it is a class both in itself and for itself. Its focal points of organization, the Trilateral Commission, World Bank, IMF, and OECD, develop both a framework of thought and guidelines for policies. From these points, class action penetrates countries through the process of internationalization of the state. The members of this transnational class are not limited to those who carry out functions at the global level, such as executives of multinational corporations or as senior officials of international agencies, but include those who manage the internationally oriented sectors within countries, the finance ministry officials, local managers of enterprises linked into international production systems, and so on.[31]

National capitalists are to be distinguished from the transnational class. The natural reflex of national capital faced with the challenge of international production is protectionism. It is torn between the desire to use the state as a bulwark of an independent national economy and the opportunity of filling niches left by international production in a subordinate symbiotic relationship with the latter.

Industrial workers have been doubly fragmented. One line of cleavage is between established and nonestablished labor. Established workers are those who have attained a status of relative security and stability in their jobs and have some prospects of career advancement. Generally they are relatively skilled, work for larger enterprises, and have effective trade unions. Nonestablished workers, by contrast, have insecure employment, have no prospect of career advancement, are relatively less skilled, and confront great obstacles in developing effective trade unions. Frequently, the nonestablished are disproportionately drawn from lower-status ethnic minorities, immigrants, and women. The institutions of working class action have privileged established workers . . .

The second line of cleavage among industrial workers is brought about by the division between national and international capital (i.e., that engaged in international production). The established workers in the sector of international production are potential allies of international capital. This is not to say that those workers have no conflict with international capital, only that international capital has the resources to resolve these conflicts and to isolate them from conflicts involving other labor groups by creating an enterprise corporatism in which both parties perceive their interest as lying in the continuing expansion of international production.

Established workers in the sector of national capital are more susceptible to the appeal of protectionism and national (rather than enterprise) corporatism in which the defense of national capital, of jobs, and of the workers' acquired status in industrial relations institutions, are perceived to be interconnected.[32]

Nonestablished labor has become of particular importance in the expansion of international production. Production systems are being designed so as to make use of an increasing proportion of semi-skilled (and therefore frequently nonestablished) in relation to skilled (and established) labor.[33] This tendency in production organization makes it possible for the center to decentralize the actual physical production of goods to peripheral locations in which an abundant supply of relatively cheap nonestablished labor is to be found, and to retain control of the process and of the research and development upon which its future depends.

As a nonestablished workforce is mobilized in Third World countries by international production, governments in these countries have very frequently sought to preempt the possibility of this new social force developing its own class-conscious organizations by imposing upon it structures of state corporatism in the form of unions set up and controlled by the government or the dominant political party. This also gives local governments, through their control over local labor, additional leverage with international capital regarding the terms of direct investment. If industrial workers in Third World countries have thus sometimes been reduced to political and social quiescence, state corporatism may prove to be a stage delaying, but in the long run not eliminating, a more articulate self-consciousness.

Even if industry were to move rapidly into the Third World and local governments were, by and large, able to keep control over their industrial workforces, most of the populations of these countries may see no improvement, but probably a deterioration, in their conditions. New industrial jobs lag far behind increases in the labor force, while changes in agriculture dispossess many in the rural population. No matter how fast international production spreads, a very large part of the world's population in the poorest areas remains marginal to the world economy, having no employment or income, or the purchasing power derived from it. A major problem for international capital in its aspiration for hegemony is how to neutralize the effect of this marginalization of perhaps one-third of the world's population so as to prevent its poverty from fueling revolt.[b]

Social forces, state structures, and future world order prospects

It would, of course, be logically inadmissible, as well as imprudent, to base predictions of future world order upon the foregoing considerations. Their utility is rather in drawing attention to factors which could incline an emerging world order in one direction or another. The social forces generated by changing production processes are the starting point for thinking about possible futures. These forces may combine in different configurations, and as an exercise one could consider the hypothetical configurations most likely to lead to three different outcomes as to the future of the state system. The focus on these three outcomes is not, of course, to imply that no other outcomes or configurations of social forces are possible.

First is the prospect for a new hegemony being based upon the global structure of social power generated by the internationalizing of production. This would require a consolidation of two presently powerful and related tendencies: the continuing dominance of international over national capital within the major countries, and the continuing internationalization of the state. Implicit in such an outcome

[b] The armed insurrection in southern Mexico that began in January 1994 is a case in point.

is a continuance of monetarism as the orthodoxy of economic policy, emphasizing the stabilization of the world economy (anti-inflationary policies and stable exchange rates) over the fulfilment of domestic sociopolitical demands (the reduction of unemployment and the maintenance of real-wage levels).

The inter-state power configuration which could maintain such a world order, provided its member states conformed to this model, is a coalition centering upon the United States, the Federal Republic of Germany, and Japan, with the support of other OECD states, the co-optation of a few of the more industrialized Third World countries, such as Brazil, and of leading conservative OPEC countries, and the possibility of revived detente allowing for a greater linkage of the Soviet sphere into the world economy of international production. The new international division of labor, brought about through the progressive decentralization of manufacturing into the Third World by international capital, would satisfy demands for industrialization from those countries. Social conflict in the core countries would be combated through enterprise corporatism, though many would be left unprotected by this method, particularly the nonestablished workers. In the peripheral countries, social conflict would be contained through a combination of state corporatism and repression.

The social forces opposed to this configuration have been noted above. National capital, those sections of established labor linked to national capital, newly mobilized nonestablished workers in the Third World, and social marginals in the poor countries are all in some way or another potentially opposed to international capital, and to the state and world-order structures most congenial to international capital. These forces do not, however, have any natural cohesion, and might be dealt with separately, or neutralized, by an effective hegemony. If they did come together under particular circumstance in a particular country, precipitating a change of regime, then that country might be dealt with in isolation through the world structure. In other words, where hegemony failed within a particular country, it could reassert itself through the world structure.

A second possible outcome is a nonhegemonic world structure of conflicting power centers. Perhaps the most likely way for this to evolve would be through the ascendancy in several core countries of neomercantilist coalitions which linked national capital and established labor, and were determined to opt out of arrangements designed to promote international capital and to organize their own power and welfare on a national or sphere-of-influence basis. The continuing pursuit of monetarist policies may be the single most likely cause of neomercantilist reaction. Legitimated as anti-inflationary, monetarist policies have been perceived as hindering national capital (because of high interest rates), generating unemployment (through planned recession), and adversely affecting relatively deprived social groups and regions dependent upon government services and transfer payments (because of budget-balancing cuts in state expenditures). An opposing coalition would attack monetarism for subordinating national welfare to external forces, and for showing an illusory faith in the markets (which are perceived to be manipulated by corporate-administered pricing). The likely structural form of neomercantilism within core states would be industry-level and national-level corporatism, bringing national capital and organized labor into a relationship with the government for the purpose of making and implementing state policy. Peripheral states would have much the same structure as in the first outcome, but would be more closely linked to one or another of the core-country economies.

A third and more remotely possible outcome would be the development of a counterhegemony based on a Third World coalition against core country dominance and aiming toward the autonomous development of peripheral countries and the termination of the core–periphery relationship. A counterhegemony would consist of a coherent view of an alternative world order, backed by a concentration of power sufficient to maintain a challenge to core countries. While this outcome is foreshadowed by the demand for a New International Economic Order, the prevailing consensus behind this demand lacks a sufficiently clear view of an alternative world political economy to constitute counterhegemony.[c] The prospects of counterhegemony lie very largely in the future development of state structures in the Third World.

The controlling social force in these countries is, typically, what has been called a "state class,"[34] a combination of party, bureaucratic, and military personnel and union leaders, mostly petty bourgeois in origin, which controls the state apparatus and through it attempts to gain greater control over the productive apparatus in the country. The state class can be understood as a local response to the forces gener-

---

[c] See Robert W. Cox, "Ideologies and the New International Economic Order: Reflections on Some Recent Literature," included in this volume (chapter 18).

ated by the internationalizing of production, and an attempt to gain some local control over these forces. The orientation of the state class is indeterminate. It can be either conservative or radical. It may either bargain for a better deal within the world economy of international production, or it may seek to overcome the unequal internal development generated by international capital.

State classes of the first orientation are susceptible to incorporation into a new hegemonic world economy, and to the maintenance of state corporatist structures as the domestic counterpart to international capital. The second orientation could provide the backing for counter-hegemony. However, a state class is only likely to maintain the second and more radical orientation if it is supported from below in the form of a genuine populism (and not just a populism manipulated by political leaders). One may speculate that this could come about through the unfolding social consequences of international production, such as the mobilization of a nonestablished labour force coupled with the marginalization of an increasing part of the urban populations. The radical alternative could be the form of response to international capital in Third World countries, just as neomercantilism could be the response in richer countries. Each projects a particular state structure and vision of world order.

Notes

This text was first published in *Millennium: Journal of International Studies*, vol. 10, no. 2 (Summer 1981), pp. 126–155. It was republished with a postscript in Robert O. Keohane (ed.), *Neorealism and Its Critics* (New York: Columbia University Press, 1986). The abridged version presented here is based on the 1986 text.

1 Among critics of the world systems approach, note especially Theda Skocpol, "Wallerstein's World Capitalist System: A Theoretical and Historical Critique," *American Journal of Sociology*, vol. 82, no. 5 (March 1977), pp. 1075–1090; and more generally, her major study, *States and Social Revolutions* (Cambridge: Cambridge University Press, 1979). Also see Robert Brenner, "The Origins of Capitalist Development: A Critique of Neo-Smithian Marxism," *New Left Review*, no. 104 (July–August 1977), pp. 25–92.

2 I use the term "world order" in preference to "inter-state system," as it is relevant to all historical periods (and not only those in which states have been the component entities) and in preference to "world system" as it is more indicative of a structure having only a certain duration in time and avoiding the equilibrium connotations of "system." "World" designates the relevant totality, geographically limited by the range of probable inter-

actions (some past "worlds" being limited to the Mediterranean, to Europe, to China, etc.). "Order" is used in the sense of the way things usually happen (*not* the absence of turbulence); thus disorder is included in the concept of order. An inter-state system is one historical form of world order. The term is used in the plural to indicate that particular patterns of power relationships which have endured in time can be contrasted in terms of their principal characteristics as distinctive world orders.

3 E. P. Thompson argues that historical concepts must often "display extreme elasticity and allow for greater irregularity." His treatment of historical logic develops this point in his essay, "The Poverty of Theory," in *The Poverty of Theory and Other Essays* (London: Merlin Press, 1978), especially pp. 231–242.

4 Friedrich Meinecke, *Machiavellism: The Doctrine of* Raison d'Etat *and Its Place in Modern History*, trans. by Douglas Scott (London: Routledge and Kegan Paul, 1957).

5 Hobbes, *Leviathan*, part I, ch. xi.

6 Kenneth Waltz, in a paper presented to a panel discussion at the American Political Science Association in August 1980 for which a first version of the present essay was written, asked the question, "will the future be like the past?," which he answered affirmatively – not only was the same pattern of relationships likely to prevail, but it would be for the good of all that this should be so. It should be noted that the future contemplated by Waltz was the next decade or so.

7 A recent example of this argument is Stephen Krasner, *Defending the National Interest: Raw Materials Investments and US Foreign Policy* (Princeton, N.J.: Princeton University Press, 1978). The normative intent of the new realism is not apparent as a polemic response to liberal moralism. This was also the case for E. H. Carr's *The Twenty Years' Crisis, 1919–1939* (London: Macmillan, 1946) which offered a "scientific" mode of thinking about international relations in opposition to the "utopianism" of the supporters of the League of Nations in Britain. Dean Acheson and George Kennan, in laying the foundations for US Cold War policy, acknowledged their debt to Reinhold Niebuhr whose revival of a pessimistic Augustinian view of human nature challenged the optimistic Lockean view native to American culture. Krasner's chosen target is "Lockean liberalism" which he sees as having undermined the rational defense of US national interests.

8 *The New Science of Giambattista Vico*, trans. Thomas Goddard Bergin and Max Harold Fisch (Ithaca, N.Y.: Cornell University Press, 1970), p. 62, para. 349.

9 Ibid., p. 6, para. 35; p. 22, para. 145; p. 25, para. 161; p. 62, para. 349.

10 Ibid., p. 19, para. 127.

11 See, for instance, R. G. Collingwood's distinction between dialectical and eristical reasoning, *The New Leviathan* (Oxford: Oxford University Press, 1942). Collingwood takes dialectic back to its Greek origins and spares us the assertions of theological Marxism concerning "Diamat."

12 Antonio Gramsci, *Selections from the Prison Notebooks*, edited and trans. by Quintin Hoare and Geoffrey Nowell Smith (New York: International Publishers, 1971), especially pp. 158–168. The full critical Italian edition *Quaderni del carcere* (Turin: Einaudi, 1975) contains additional passages on this point, e.g., pp. 471, 1321, 1492.

13 As in Krasner, *Defending the National Interest*, and Peter Katzenstein (ed.), *Between Power and Plenty: Foreign Economic Policies of Advanced Industrial States* (Madison, Wis.: University of Wisconsin Press, 1978). The United States is represented by these authors as a state weak in relation to the strength of civil society (or more particularly of interests in civil society), whereas other states, e.g., Japan or France, are stronger in relation to their societies. Civil society is thus seen in the US case as limiting the effectiveness of the state.

14 Gramsci saw ideas, politics, and economics as reciprocally related, convertible into each other and bound together in a *blocco storico* (historic bloc). "Historical materialism," he wrote, "is in a certain sense a reform and development of Hegelianism. It is philosophy freed from unilateral ideological elements, the full consciousness of the contradictions of philosophy": *Quaderni*, p. 471, my translation.

15 The notion of a framework for action recalls what Machiavelli called *necessità*, a sense that the conditions of existence require action to create or sustain a form of social order. *Necessità* engenders both the possibility of a new order and all the risks inherent in changing the existing order. "[F]ew men ever welcome new laws setting up a new order in the state unless necessity makes it clear to them that there is a need for such laws; and since such a necessity cannot arise without danger, the state may easily be ruined before the new order has been brought to completion": Niccolo Machiavelli, *The Discourses*, edited by Bernard Crick (Harmondsworth, Middlesex: Penguin Books, 1970), pp. 105–106.

16 In this regard, Stanley Hoffman has written:

> Born and raised in America, the discipline of international relations is, so to speak, too close to the fire. It needs triple distance: it should move away from the contemporary world toward the past; from the perspective of a superpower (and a highly conservative one), toward that of the weak and the revolutionary – away from the impossible quest for stability; from the glide into policy science, back to the steep ascent toward the peaks which the questions raised by traditional political philosophy represent.

In "An American Social Science: International Relations," *Daedalus*, vol. 106, no. 3 (Summer 1977), p. 89.

17 On intersubjective meaning, see Charles Taylor, "Hermeneutics and Politics," in Paul Connerton (ed.), *Critical Sociology* (Harmondsworth, Middlesex: Penguin Books, 1965), ch. 6. Also relevant is Peter L. Berger and Thomas Luckman, *The Social Construction of Reality* (Harmondsworth, Middlesex: Penguin, 1971).

18 C. Taylor, "Hermeneutics and Politics," points out that expectations with regard to negotiating behavior are culturally differentiated in the present world. Garrett Mattingly, *Renaissance Diplomacy* (London: Cape, 1955), studies the origins of the idea outlined in this paragraph which are implicit in the modern state system.

19 Collective images are not aggregations of fragmented opinions of individuals such as are compiled through surveys; they are coherent mental types expressive of the world views of specific groups such as may be reconstructed through the work of historians and sociologists – e.g., Max Weber's reconstructions of forms of religious consciousness.

20 Gramsci's principal application of the concept of hegemony was to the relations among social classes – e.g., in explaining the inability of the Italian industrial bourgeoisie to establish its hegemony after the unification of Italy and in examining the prospects of the Italian industrial workers establishing their class hegemony over peasantry and petty bourgeoisie so as to create a new *blocco storico*, a term which in Gramsci's work corresponds roughly to the notion of historic structure in this essay. The term "hegemony" in Gramsci's work is linked to debates in the international communist movement concerning revolutionary strategy and in this connection its application is specifically to classes. The form of the concept, however, draws upon his reading of Machiavelli and is not restricted to class relations; it has a broader potential applicability. Gramsci's adjustment of Machiavellian ideas to the realities of the world he knew was an exercise in dialectic in the sense defined above. It is an appropriate continuation of his method to perceive the applicability of the concept to world order structures as suggested here. For Gramsci, as for Machiavelli, the general question involved in hegemony is the nature of power, and power is a centaur, part man, part beast, a combination of force and consent. See Machiavelli, *The Prince*, Norton Critical Edition, edited by Robert M. Adams (New York: W. W. Norton, 1977), pp. 49–50; Gramsci, *Selections*, pp. 169–170.

21 E. H. Carr, *Nationalism and After* (London: Macmillan, 1945).

22 Charles Morazé, *Les bourgeois conquérants* (Paris: Armond Colin, 1957).

23 A recent discussion of the reciprocal character of these relations is in Peter A. Gourevitch, "The Second Image Reversed: The International Sources of Domestic Politics," *International Organization*, vol. 32, no. 4 (Autumn 1978), pp. 881–911.

24 Robert O. Keohane, "The Theory of Hegemonic Stability and Changes in International Economics Regimes, 1967–77," in Ole Holsti, Randolph Siverson, and Alexander George (eds.), *Change in the International System* (Boulder, Colo.: Westview Press, 1981). Keohane cites as others who have contributed to this Charles Kindleberger, Robert Gilpin, and Stephen Krasner. "Hegemony" is used by Keohane here in the limited sense of dominance by a state. This meaning is to be distinguished from its meaning in this article, which is derived from Gramsci – i.e., hegemony as a

119

structure of dominance, leaving open the question of whether the dominant power is a state or a group of states or some combination of state and private power, which is sustained by broadly based consent through acceptance of an ideology and of institutions consistent with this structure. Thus a hegemonic structure of world order is one in which power takes a primarily consensual form, as distinguished from a nonhegemonic order in which there are manifestly rival powers and no power has been able to establish the legitimacy of its dominance. There can be dominance without hegemony; hegemony is one possible form dominance may take. Institutional hegemony, as used in this essay, corresponds to what Keohane calls a "strong international regime." His theory can be restated in our terms as: dominance by a powerful state is most conducive to the development of hegemony. In this present text, the term "hegemony" is reserved for a consensual order and "dominance" refers only to a preponderance of material power. Keohane's discussion of hegemony is developed in his later work but without affecting the distinction made here.

25 The basic point I am making here is suggested by a passage in Gramsci's *Selections* which reads:

> Do international relations precede or follow (logically) fundamental social relations? There can be no doubt that they follow. Any organic innovation in the social structure, through its technical-military expressions, modifies organically absolute and relative relations in the international field too.

Gramsci used the term "organic" to refer to relatively long-term and permanent changes, as opposed to "conjunctural": *Selections*, pp. 176–177. In *Quaderni*, the original is to be found in vol. III, p. 1562.

26 E. J. Hobsbawm writes: "The men who officially presided over the affairs of the victorious bourgeois order in its moment of triumph were a deeply reactionary country nobleman from Prussia, an imitation emperor in France, and a succession of aristocratic landowners in Britain" (*The Age of Capital, 1843–1875*, London: Sphere, 1977, p. 15).

27 Among analysts who concur in this are Karl Polanyi, *The Great Transformation: The Political and Economic Origins of Our Time* (Boston: Beacon Press, 1957); Gunnar Myrdal, *Beyond the Welfare State* (New Haven, Conn.: Yale University Press, 1960); Carr, *Nationalism and After*; and Geoffrey Barraclough, *An Introduction to Contemporary History* (Harmondsworth, Middlesex: Penguin, 1967).

28 James Petras, "The Imperial State System," paper presented to the American Political Science Association, Washington, D.C., August 1980.

29 Max Beloff was perhaps the first to point to the mechanisms whereby participation in international organizations altered the internal policy-making practices of states in his *New Dimensions in Foreign Policy: A Study in British Administration Experience, 1947–59* (London: George Allen and Unwin, 1961). Robert W. Cox and Harold K. Jacobson, *et al.*, *The Anatomy of Influence: Decision Making in International Organization* (New Haven, Conn.: Yale

University Press, 1972), represented the political systems of international organization as including segments of states. Robert O. Keohane and Joseph S. Nye, "Transgovernmental Relations and International Organizations," *World Politics*, vol. 27, no. 1 (October 1974), pp. 39–62, pointed to the processes whereby coalitions are formed among segments of the apparatuses of different states and the ways in which international institutions facilitate such coalitions. These various works, while they point to the existence of mechanisms for policy coordination among states and for penetration of external influences within states, do not discuss the implications of these mechanisms for the structure of power within states. It is this structural aspect I wish to designate by the term "internationalization of the state." Christian Palloix refers to "L'internationalisation de l'appareil de l'Etat national, de certains lieux de cet appareil d'Etat ... ," *L'internationalisation du capital* (Paris: Maspero, 1975), p. 82, by which he designates those segments of national states which serve as policy supports for the internationalization of production. He thus raises the question of structural changes in the state, though he does not enlarge upon the point. Keohane and Nye, subsequent to "Transgovernmental Relations," linked the transgovernmental mechanism to the concept of "interdependence": *Power and Interdependence* (Boston: Little, Brown, 1977). I find this concept tends to obscure the power relationships involved in structural changes in both state and world order and prefer not to use it for that reason. Peter Gourevitch, "Second Image Reversed," does retain the concept of interdependence while insisting that it be linked with power struggles among social forces within states.

30 There is, of course, a whole literature implicit in the argument of this paragraph. Some sketchy references may be useful. Andrew Shonfield, *Modern Capitalism* (London: Oxford University Press, 1965), illustrated the development of corporative-type structures of the kind I associate with the welfare-nationalist state. The shift from industry-level corporatism to an enterprise-based corporatism led by the big public and private corporations has been noted in some industrial relations works, particularly those concerned with the emergence of a "new working class," e.g., Serge Mallet, *La nouvelle classes ouvrière* (Paris: Seuil, 1963), but the industrial relations literature has generally not linked what I have elsewhere called enterprise corporatism to the broader framework suggested here (see R. W. Cox, "Pour une étude prospective des relations de production," *Sociologie du Travail*, no. 2, March 1977). Erhard Friedberg, "L'internationalisation de l'économie et modalités d'intervention de l'état: la 'politique industrielle,' " in *Planification et Société* (Grenoble: Presses universitaires de Grenoble, 1974), pp. 94–108, discusses the subordination of the old corporatism to the new. The shift in terminology from planning to industrial policy is related to the internationalizing of state and economy. Industrial policy has become a matter of interest to global economic policy makers: see William Diebold, Jr., *Industrial Policy as an International Issue* (New

York: McGraw-Hill for the Council on Foreign Relations, 1980), and John Pinder, Takashi Hosomi, and William Diebold, *Industrial Policy and the International Economy* (New York: Trilateral Commission, 1979). If planning evokes the spectre of economic nationalism, industrial policy, as the Trilateral Commission study points out, can be looked upon with favor from a world economy perspective as a necessary aspect of policy harmonization:
> We have argued that industrial policies are needed to deal with structural problems in the modern economies. Thus, international action should not aim to dismantle these policies. The pressure should, rather, be toward positive and adaptive industrial policies, whether on the part of single countries or groups of countries combined. Far from being protectionist, industrial policy can help them to remove a cause of protectionism, by making the process of adjustment less painful. (p. 50)

It may be objected that the argument and references presented here are more valid for Europe than for the United States, and that, indeed, the very concept of corporatism is alien to US ideology. To this it can be replied that since the principal levers of the world economy are in the United States, the US economy adjusts less than those of European countries and peripheral countries, and the institutionalization of adjustment mechanisms is accordingly less developed. Structural analyses of the US economy have, however, pointed to a distinction between a corporate internationally oriented sector and a medium- and small-business nationally oriented sector, and to the different segments of the state and different policy orientations associated with each. See John Kenneth Galbraith, *Economics and the Public Purpose* (London: Andre Deutsch, 1974), and James O'Connor, *The Fiscal Crisis of the State* (New York: St. Martin's Press, 1973). Historians point to the elements of corporatism in the New Deal, e.g., Arthur M. Schlesinger, Jr., *The Age of Roosevelt*, Volume II, *The Coming of the New Deal* (London: Heinemann, 1960).

31 The evidence of the existence of a transnational managerial class lies in actual forms of organization, the elaboration of ideology, financial supports, and the behavior of individuals. Other structures stand as rival tendencies – e.g., national capital and its interests sustained by a whole other structure of loyalties, agencies, etc. Individuals or firms and state agencies may in some phases of their activity be caught up now in one, now in another, tendency. Thus the membership of the class may be continually shifting, though the structure remains. It is sometimes argued that this is merely a case of US capitalists giving themselves a hegemonic aura, an argument that by implication makes of imperialism a purely national phenomenon. There is no doubting the US origin of the values carried and propagated by this class, but neither is there any doubt that many non-US citizens and agencies also participate in it nor that its world view is global and distinguishable from the purely national capitalisms which exist alongside it. Through the transnational managerial class, American cul-

ture, or a certain American business culture, has become globally hegemonic. Of course, should neomercantilist tendencies come to prevail in international economic relations, this transnational class structure would
wither.

32 Some industries appear as ambiguously astride the two tendencies – e.g.,
the automobile industry. During a period of economic expansion, the international aspect of this industry dominated in the United States, and the
United Auto Workers union took the lead in creating world councils for
the major international auto firms with a view to inaugurating multinational bargaining. As the industry was hit by recession, protectionism
came to the fore.

33 R. W. Cox, "Labour and Employment in the Late Twentieth Century," in
R. St. J. Macdonald, *et al.* (eds.), *The International Law and Policy of Human
Welfare* (The Hague: Sijthoff and Noordhoff, 1978). This tendency can be
seen as the continuation of long-term direction of production organization
of which Taylorism was an early stage, in which control over the work
process is progressively wrested from workers and separated out from the
actual performance of tasks so as to be concentrated with management.
See Harry Braverman, *Labor and Monopoly Capital* (New York: Monthly
Review, 1974).

34 I have borrowed the term from Hartmut Elsenhans, "The State Class in
the Third World: For a New Conceptualization of Periphery Modes of Production" (unpublished).

7 Gramsci, hegemony, and international relations: an essay in method (1983)

Some time ago I began reading Gramsci's *Prison Notebooks*. In these fragments, written in a fascist prison between 1929 and 1935, the former leader of the Italian Communist Party was concerned with the problem of understanding capitalist societies in the 1920s and 1930s, and particularly with the meaning of fascism and the possibilities of building an alternative form of state and society based on the working class. What he had to say centered upon the state, upon the relationship of civil society to the state, and upon the relationship of politics, ethics, and ideology to production. Not surprisingly, Gramsci did not have very much to say directly about international relations. Nevertheless, I found that Gramsci's thinking was helpful in understanding the meaning of international organization with which I was then principally concerned. Particularly useful was his concept of hegemony, but valuable also were several concepts which he had worked out for himself or developed from others. This essay sets forth my understanding of what Gramsci meant by hegemony and these related concepts, and suggests how I think they may be adapted, retaining his essential meaning, to the understanding of problems of world order. It does not purport to be a critical study of Gramsci's political theory but merely a derivation from it of some ideas useful for a revision of current international relations theory.[1]

Gramsci and hegemony

Gramsci's concepts were all derived from history – both from his own reflections upon those periods of history which he thought helped to throw an explanatory light upon the present, and from his personal

124

experience of political and social struggle. These included the workers' councils movement of the early 1920s, his participation in the Third International, and his opposition to fascism. Gramsci's ideas have always to be related to his own historical context. Moreover, he was constantly adjusting his concepts to specific historical circumstances. The concepts cannot usefully be considered in abstraction from their applications, for when they are so abstracted different usages of the same concept appear to contain contradictions or ambiguities.[2] A concept, in Gramsci's thought, is loose and elastic and attains precision only when brought into contact with a particular situation which it helps to explain, a contact which also develops the meaning of the concept. This is the strength of Gramsci's historicism and therein lies its explanatory power. The term "historicism" is however, frequently misunderstood and criticized by those who seek a more abstract, systematic, universalistic, and non-historical form of knowledge.[3]

Gramsci geared his thought consistently to the practical purpose of political action. In his prison writings, he always referred to Marxism as "the philosophy of praxis."[4] Partly at least, one may surmise, it must have been to underline the practical revolutionary purpose of philosophy. Partly too, it would have been to indicate his intention to contribute to a lively developing current of thought, given impetus by Marx but not forever circumscribed by Marx's work. Nothing could be further from his mind than a Marxism which consists in an exegesis of the sacred texts for the purpose of refining a timeless set of categories and concepts.

Origins of the concepts of hegemony

There are two main strands leading to the Gramscian idea of hegemony. The first ran from the debates within the Third International concerning the strategy of the Bolshevik Revolution and the creation of a Soviet socialist state, the second from the writings of Machiavelli. In tracing the first strand, some commentators have sought to contrast Gramsci's thought with Lenin's by aligning Gramsci with the idea of a hegemony of the proletariat and Lenin with a dictatorship of the proletariat. Other commentators have underlined their basic agreement.[5] What is important is that Lenin referred to the Russian proletariat as both a dominant and a directing class, dominance implying dictatorship and direction implying leadership with the consent of allied classes (notably the peasantry). Gramsci, in effect, took over an idea that was current in the circles of the Third International: the workers exercised hegemony over the allied classes and dictatorship over enemy classes. Yet this idea was applied by the Third International only to the working class and expressed the role of the working class in leading an alliance of workers, peasants, and perhaps some other groups potentially supportive of revolutionary change.[6]

Gramsci's originality lies in his giving a twist to this first strand: he began to apply it to the bourgeoisie, to the apparatus or mechanisms of hegemony of the dominant class.[7] This made it possible for him to distinguish cases in which the bourgeoisie had attained a hegemonic position of leadership over other classes from those in which it had not. In northern Europe, in the countries where capitalism had first become established, bourgeois hegemony was most complete. It necessarily involved concessions to subordinate classes in return for acquiescence in bourgeois leadership, concessions which could lead ultimately to forms of social democracy which preserve capitalism while making it more acceptable to workers and the petty bourgeoisie. Because their hegemony was firmly entrenched in civil society, the bourgeoisie often did not need to run the state themselves. Landed aristocrats in England, Junkers in Prussia, or a renegade pretender to the mantle of Napoleon I in France, could do it for them so long as these rulers recognized the hegemonic structures of civil society as the basic limits of their political action.

This perception of hegemony led Gramsci to enlarge his definition of the state. When the administrative, executive, and coercive apparatus of government was in effect constrained by the hegemony of the leading class of a whole social formation, it became meaningless to limit the definition of the state to those elements of government. To be meaningful, the notion of the state would also have to include the underpinnings of the political structure in civil society. Gramsci thought of these in concrete historical terms: the church, the educational system, the press, all the institutions which helped to create in people certain modes of behavior and expectations consistent with the hegemonic social order. For example, Gramsci argued that the Masonic lodges in Italy were a bond amongst the government officials who entered into the state machinery after the unification of Italy, and therefore must be considered as part of the state for the purpose of assessing its broader political structure. The hegemony of a dominant class thus bridged the conventional categories of state and civil society, categories which retained a certain analytical usefulness but ceased to correspond to separable entities in reality.

As noted above, the second strand leading to the Gramscian idea of hegemony came all the way from Machiavelli and helps to broaden even further the potential scope of application of the concept. Gramsci had pondered what Machiavelli had written, especially in *The Prince*, concerning the problem of founding a new state. Machiavelli, in the fifteenth century, was concerned with finding the leadership and the supporting social basis for a united Italy; Gramsci, in the twentieth century, with the leadership and supportive basis for an alternative to fascism. Where Machiavelli looked to the individual prince, Gramsci looked to the modern prince: the revolutionary party engaged in a continuing and developing dialogue with its own base of support. Gramsci took over from Machiavelli the image of power as a centaur: half man, half beast, a necessary combination of consent and coercion.[8] To the extent that the consensual aspect of power is in the forefront, hegemony prevails. Coercion is always latent but is only applied in marginal, deviant cases. Hegemony is enough to ensure conformity of behavior in most people most of the time. The Machiavellian connection frees the concept of power (and of hegemony as one form of power) from a tie to historically specific social classes and gives it a wider applicability to relations of dominance and subordination, including, as will be suggested below, relations of world order. It does not, however, sever power relations from their social basis (i.e., in the case of world-order relations by making them into relations among states narrowly conceived), but directs attention towards deepening an awareness of this social basis.

War of movement and war of position

In thinking through the first strand of his concept of hegemony, Gramsci reflected upon the experiences of the Bolshevik Revolution and sought to determine what lessons might be drawn from it for the task of revolution in western Europe.[9] He came to the conclusion that the circumstances in western Europe differed greatly from those in Russia. To illustrate the differences in circumstances, and the consequent differences in strategies required, he had recourse to the military analogy of wars of movement and wars of position. The basic difference between Russia and western Europe was in the relative strengths of state and civil society. In Russia, the administrative and coercive apparatus of the state was formidable but proved to be vulnerable, while civil society was undeveloped. A relatively small working class led by a disciplined vanguard was able to overwhelm the state in a war of movement and met no effective resistance from the rest of civil society. The vanguard party could set about founding a new state through a combination of applying coercion against recalcitrant elements and building consent among others. (This analysis was particularly apposite to the period of the New Economic Policy before coercion began to be applied on a larger scale against the rural population.)

In western Europe, by contrast, civil society, under bourgeois hegemony, was much more fully developed and took manifold forms. A war of movement might conceivably, in conditions of exceptional upheaval, enable a revolutionary vanguard to seize control of the state apparatus; but because of the resiliency of civil society such an exploit would in the long run be doomed to failure. Gramsci described the state in western Europe (by which we should read state in the limited sense of administrative, governmental, and coercive apparatus and not the enlarged concept of the state mentioned above) as "an outer ditch, behind which there stands a powerful system of fortresses and earthworks."

> In Russia, the State was everything, civil society was primordial and gelatinous; in the West, there was a proper relation between State and civil society, and when the State trembled a sturdy structure of civil society was at once revealed.[10]

Accordingly, Gramsci argued that the war of movement could not be effective against the hegemonic state-societies of western Europe. The alternative strategy is the war of position which slowly builds up the strength of the social foundations of a new state. In western Europe, the struggle had to be won in civil society before an assault on the state could achieve success. Premature attack on the state by a war of movement would only reveal the weakness of the opposition and lead to a reimposition of bourgeois dominance as the institutions of civil society reasserted control.

The strategic implications of this analysis are clear but fraught with difficulties. To build up the basis of an alternative state and society upon the leadership of the working class means creating alternative institutions and alternative intellectual resources within existing society and building bridges between workers and other subordinate classes. It means actively building a counterhegemony within an established hegemony while resisting the pressures and temptations to relapse into pursuit of incremental gains for subaltern groups within the framework of bourgeois hegemony. This is the line between war of position as a long-range revolutionary strategy and social democracy as a policy of making gains within the established order.

Passive revolution

Not all western European societies were bourgeois hegemonies. Gramsci distinguished between two kinds of societies. One kind had undergone a thorough social revolution and worked out fully its consequences in new modes of production and social relations. England and France were cases that had gone further than most others in this respect. The other kind were societies which had so to speak imported or had thrust upon them aspects of a new order created abroad, without the old order having been displaced. These last were caught up in a dialectic of revolution-restoration which tended to become blocked as neither the new forces nor the old could triumph. In these societies, the new industrial bourgeoisie failed to achieve hegemony. The resulting stalemate with the traditionally dominant social classes created the conditions that Gramsci called "passive revolution," the introduction of changes which did not involve any arousal of popular forces.[11]

One typical accompaniment to passive revolution in Gramsci's analysis is caesarism: a strong man intervenes to resolve the stalemate between equal and opposed social forces. Gramsci allowed that there were both progressive and reactionary forms of caesarism: progressive when strong rule presides over a more orderly development of a new state, reactionary when it stabilizes existing power. Napoleon I was a case of progressive caesarism, but Napoleon III, the exemplar of reactionary caesarism, was more representative of the kind likely to arise in the course of passive revolution. Gramsci's analysis here is virtually identical with that of Marx in *The Eighteenth Brumaire of Louis Bonaparte*: the French bourgeoisie, unable to rule directly through their own political parties, were content to develop capitalism under a political regime which had its social basis in the peasantry, an inarticulate and unorganized class whose virtual representative Bonaparte could claim to be.

In late nineteenth-century Italy, the northern industrial bourgeoisie, the class with the most to gain from the unification of Italy, was unable to dominate the peninsula. The basis for the new state became an alliance between the industrial bourgeoisie of the north and the landowners of the south – an alliance which also provided benefits for petty-bourgeois clients (especially from the south) who staffed the new state bureaucracy and political parties and became the intermediaries between the various population groups and the state. The lack of any sustained and widespread popular participation in the unification movement explained the "passive revolution" character of its outcome. In the aftermath of World War I, worker and peasant occupations of factories and land demonstrated a strength which was considerable enough to threaten yet insufficient to dislodge the existing state.[12] There took place then what Gramsci called a "displacement of the basis of the state" towards the petty bourgeoisie, the only class of nationwide extent, which became the anchor of fascist power. Fascism continued the passive revolution, sustaining the position of the old owner classes yet unable to attract the support of worker or peasant subaltern groups.

Apart from caesarism, the second major feature of passive revolution in Italy Gramsci called *trasformismo*. It was exemplified in Italian politics by Giovanni Giolitti, who sought to bring about the widest possible coalition of interests and who dominated the political scene in the years preceding fascism. For example, he aimed to bring northern industrial workers into a common front with industrialists through a protectionist policy. *Trasformismo* worked to co-opt potential leaders of subaltern social groups. By extension *trasformismo* can serve as a strategy of assimilating and domesticating potentially dangerous ideas by adjusting them to the policies of the dominant coalition and can thereby obstruct the formation of class-based organized opposition to established social and political power. Fascism continued *trasformismo*. Gramsci interprets the fascist state corporatism as an unsuccessful attempt to introduce some of the more advanced industrial practices of American capitalism under the aegis of the old Italian management.

The concept of passive revolution is a counterpart to the concept of hegemony in that it describes the condition of a nonhegemonic society, one in which no dominant class has been able to establish a hegemony in Gramsci's sense of the term. Today this notion of passive revolution, together with its components, caesarism and *trasformismo*, is particularly apposite to industrializing Third World countries.

Historic bloc (*blocco storico*)

Gramsci attributed the source of his notion of the historic bloc (*blocco storico*) to Georges Sorel, though Sorel never used the term or any other in precisely the sense Gramsci gave to it.[13] Sorel did, however, interpret revolutionary action in terms of social myths through which people engaged in action perceived a confrontation of totalities – in which they saw a new order challenging an established order. In the course of a cataclysmic event, the old order would be overthrown as a whole and the new be freed to unfold.[14] While Gramsci did not share the subjectivism of this vision, he did share the view that state and society together constituted a solid structure and that revolution implied the development within it of another structure strong enough to replace the first. Echoing Marx, he thought this could come about only when the first had exhausted its full potential. Whether dominant or emergent, such a structure is what Gramsci called an historic bloc.

For Sorel, social myth, a powerful form of collective subjectivity, would obstruct reformist tendencies. These might otherwise attract workers away from revolutionary syndicalism into incrementalist trade unionism or reformist party politics. The myth was a weapon in struggle as well as a tool for analysis. For Gramsci, the historic bloc similarly had a revolutionary orientation through its stress on the unity and coherence of sociopolitical orders. It was an intellectual defense against co-optation by *trasformismo*.

The historic bloc is a dialectical concept in the sense that its interacting elements create a larger unity. Gramsci expressed these interacting elements sometimes as the subjective and the objective, sometimes as superstructure and structure.

> Structures and superstructures form an "historic bloc." That is to say the complex contradictory and discordant *ensemble* of the superstructures is the reflection of the *ensemble* of the social relations of production.[15]

The juxtaposition and reciprocal relationships of the political, ethical, and ideological spheres of activity with the economic sphere avoid reductionism. It avoids reducing everything either to economics (economism) or to ideas (idealism). In Gramsci's historical materialism (which he was careful to distinguish from what he called "historical economism" or a narrowly economic interpretation of history), ideas and material conditions are always bound together, mutually influencing one another, and not reducible one to the other. Ideas have to be understood in relation to material circumstances. Material circumstances include both the social relations and the physical means of production. Superstructures of ideology and political organization shape the development of both aspects of production and are shaped by them.

An historic bloc cannot exist without a hegemonic social class. Where the hegemonic class is the dominant class in a country or social formation, the state (in Gramsci's enlarged concept) maintains cohesion and identity within the bloc through the propagation of a common culture. A new bloc is formed when a subordinate class (e.g., the workers) establishes its hegemony over other subordinate groups (e.g., small farmers, marginals). This process requires intensive dialogue between leaders and followers within the would-be hegemonic class. Gramsci may have concurred in the Leninist idea of an vanguard party which takes upon itself the responsibility for leading an immature working class, but only as an aspect of a war of movement. Because a war-of-position strategy was required in the western countries, as he saw it, the role of the party should be to lead, intensify, and develop dialogue within the working class and between the working class and other subordinate classes which could be brought into alliance with it. The "mass line" as a mobilization technique developed by the Chinese Communist Party is consistent with Gramsci's thinking in this respect.

Intellectuals play a key role in the building of an historic bloc. Intellectuals are not a distinct and relatively classless social stratum. Gramsci saw them as organically connected with a social class. They perform the function of developing and sustaining the mental images, technologies, and organizations which bind together the members of a class and of an historic bloc into a common identity. Bourgeois intellectuals did this for a whole society in which the bourgeoisie was hegemonic. The organic intellectuals of the working class would perform a similar role in the creation of a new historic bloc under working-class hegemony within that society. To do this they would have to evolve a clearly distinctive culture, organization, and technique, and do so in constant interaction with the members of the emergent block. Everyone, for Gramsci, is in some part an intellectual, although only some perform full-time the social function of an intellectual. In this task, the party was, in his conception, a "collective intellectual."

In the movement towards hegemony and the creation of an historic bloc, Gramsci distinguished three levels of consciousness: the economico-corporative, which is aware of the specific interests of a particular group; the solidarity or class consciousness, which extends to a whole social class but remains at a purely economic level; and the hegemonic, which brings the interests of the leading class into harmony with those of subordinate classes and incorporates these other interests into an ideology expressed in universal terms.[16] The movement towards hegemony, Gramsci says, is a "passage from the structure to the sphere of the complex superstructures," by which he means passing from the specific interests of a group or class to the building of institutions and elaboration of ideologies. If they reflect a hegemony, these institutions and ideologies will be universal in form, i.e., they will not appear as those of a particular class, and will give some satisfaction to the subordinate groups while not undermining the leadership or vital interests of the hegemonic class.

Hegemony and international relations

We can now make the transition from what Gramsci said about hegemony and related concepts to the implications of these concepts for international relations. First, however, it is useful to look at what little Gramsci himself had to say about international relations. Let us begin with this passage:

> Do international relations precede or follow (logically) fundamental social relations? There can be no doubt that they follow. Any organic innovation in the social structure, through its technical-military expressions, modifies organically absolute and relative relations in the international field too.[17]

By "organic" Gramsci meant that which is structural, long-term, or relatively permanent, as opposed to the short-term or "conjunctural." He was saying that basic changes in international power relations or world order, which are observed as changes in the military-strategic and geopolitical balance, can be traced to fundamental changes in social relations.

Gramsci did not in any way bypass the state or diminish its

importance. The state remained for him the basic entity in international relations and the place where social conflicts take place – the
place also, therefore, where hegemonies of social classes can be built.
In these hegemonies of social classes, the particular characteristics of
nations combine in unique and original ways. The working class,
which might be considered to be international in an abstract sense,
nationalizes itself in the process of building its hegemony. The emergence of new worker-led blocs at the national level would, in this line of
reasoning, precede any basic restructuring of international relations.
However, the state, which remains the primary focus of social struggle
and the basic entity of international relations, is the enlarged state
which includes its own social basis. This view sets aside a narrow
or superficial view of the state which reduces it, for instance, to the
foreign-policy bureaucracy or the state's military capabilities.

From his Italian perspective, Gramsci had a keen sense of what we
would now call dependency. What happened in Italy he knew was
markedly influenced by external powers. At the purely foreign-policy
level, great powers have relative freedom to determine their foreign
policies in response to domestic interests; smaller powers have less
autonomy.[18] The economic life of subordinate nations is penetrated by
and intertwined with that of powerful nations. This is further complicated by the existence within countries of structurally diverse regions
which have distinctive patterns of relationship to external forces.[19]

At an even deeper level, those states which are powerful are precisely those which have undergone a profound social and economic
revolution and have most fully worked out the consequences of this
revolution in the form of state and of social relations. The French Revolution was the case Gramsci reflected upon, but we can think of the
development of US and Soviet power in the same way. These were
all nation-based developments which spilled over national boundaries
to become internationally expansive phenomena. Other countries have
received the impact of these developments in a passive way, an
instance of what Gramsci described at the national level as a passive
revolution. This effect comes when the impetus to change does not
arise out of a "vast local economic development . . . but is instead the
reflection of international developments which transmit their ideological currents to the periphery."[20]

The group which is the bearer of the new ideas, in such circumstances, is not an indigenous social group which is actively engaged
in building a new economic base with a new structure of social

134

relations. It is an intellectual stratum which picks up ideas originating from a prior foreign economic and social revolution. Consequently, the thought of this group takes an idealistic shape ungrounded in a domestic economic development; and its conception of the state takes the form of "a rational absolute."[21] Gramsci criticized the thought of Benedetto Croce, the dominant figure of the Italian intellectual establishment of his own time, for expressing this kind of distortion.

Hegemony and world order

Is the Gramscian concept of hegemony applicable at the international or world level? Before attempting to suggest how this might be done, it is well to rule out some usages of the term which are common in international relations studies. Very often "hegemony" is used to mean the dominance of one country over others, thereby tying the usage to a relationship strictly among states. Sometimes "hegemony" is used as a euphemism for imperialism. When Chinese political leaders accuse the Soviet Union of "hegemonism," they seem to have in mind some combination of these two. These meanings differ so much from the Gramscian sense of the term that it is better, for purposes of clarity in this chapter, to use the term "dominance" to replace them.

In applying the concept of hegemony to world order, it becomes important to determine when a period of hegemony begins and when it ends. A period in which a world hegemony has been established can be called hegemonic and one in which dominance of a nonhegemonic kind prevails, nonhegemonic. To illustrate, let us consider the past century and a half as falling into four distinguishable periods, roughly,[22] 1845–1875, 1875–1945, 1945–1965, and 1965 to the present.[a]

The first period (1845–75) was hegemonic: there was a world economy with Britain as its center. Economic doctrines consistent with British supremacy but universal in form – comparative advantage, free trade, and the gold standard – spread gradually outward from Britain. Coercive strength underwrote this order. Britain held the balance of power in Europe, thereby preventing any challenge to hegemony from

---

[a] In *Production, Power, and World Order*, three successive structures of world order are substituted for the periodization given above, based on the dialectical relation of production, forms of state, and different configurations of world order. These three structures are: (1) the liberal international economy (1789–1873); (2) the era of rival imperialisms (1873–1945); and (3) the neoliberal world order (post-World War II). See Robert W. Cox, *Production, Power, and World Order: Social Forces in the Making of History* (New York: Columbia University Press, 1987), pp. 107–109.

a land-based power. Britain ruled supreme at sea and had the capacity to enforce obedience by peripheral countries to the rules of the market.

In the second period (1875–1945), all these features were reversed. Other countries challenged British supremacy. The balance of power in Europe became destabilized, leading to two world wars. Free trade was superseded by protectionism; the gold standard was ultimately abandoned; and the world economy fragmented into economic blocs. This was a nonhegemonic period.

In the third period, following World War II (1945–65), the United States founded a new hegemonic world order similar in basic structure to that dominated by Britain in middle of the nineteenth century but with institutions and doctrines adjusted to a more complex world economy and to national societies more sensitive to the political repercussions of economic crises. Sometime from the later 1960s through the early 1970s it became evident that this US-based world order was no longer working well. During the uncertain times which followed, three possibilities of structural transformation of world order opened up: a reconstruction of hegemony with a broadening of political management on the lines envisaged by the Trilateral Commission; increased fragmentation of the world economy around big-power-centered economic spheres; and the possible assertion of a Third World-based counterhegemony with the concerted demand for the New International Economic Order as a forerunner.

On the basis of this tentative notation, it would appear that, historically, to become hegemonic, a state would have to found and protect a world order which was universal in conception, i.e., not an order in which one state directly exploits others but an order which most other states (or at least those within reach of the hegemony) could find compatible with their interests. Such an order would hardly be conceived in inter-state terms alone, for this would likely bring to the fore oppositions of state interests. It would most likely give prominence to opportunities for the forces of civil society to operate on the world scale (or on the scale of the sphere within which hegemony prevails). The hegemonic concept of world order is founded not only upon the regulation of inter-state conflict but also upon a globally conceived civil society, i.e., a mode of production of global extent which brings about links among social classes of the countries encompassed by it.

Historically, hegemonies of this kind are founded by powerful states which have undergone a thorough social and economic revolution. The revolution not only modifies the internal economic and political structures of the state in question but also unleashes energies which expand beyond the state's boundaries. A world hegemony is thus in its beginnings an outward expansion of the internal (national) hegemony established by a dominant social class. The economic and social institutions, the culture, the technology associated with this national hegemony become patterns for emulation abroad. Such an expansive hegemony impinges on the more peripheral countries as a passive revolution. These countries have not undergone the same thorough social revolution, nor have their economies developed in the same way, but they try to incorporate elements from the hegemonic model without disturbing old power structures. While peripheral countries may adopt some economic and cultural aspects of the hegemonic core, they are less able to adopt its political models. Just as fascism became the form of passive revolution in the Italy of the interwar period, so various forms of military-bureaucratic regime supervise passive revolution in today's peripheries. In the world-hegemonic model, hegemony is more intense and consistent at the core and more laden with contradictions at the periphery.

Hegemony at the international level is thus not merely an order among states. It is an order within a world economy with a dominant mode of production which penetrates into all countries and links into other subordinate modes of production. It is also a complex of international social relationships which connect the social classes of the different countries. World hegemony can be described as a social structure, an economic structure, and a political structure; and it cannot be simply one of these things but must be all three. World hegemony, furthermore, is expressed in universal norms, institutions, and mechanisms which lay down general rules of behavior for states and for those forces of civil society that act across national boundaries, rules which support the dominant mode of production.

The mechanisms of hegemony: international organizations

One mechanism through which the universal norms of a world hegemony are expressed is the international organization. Indeed, international organization functions as the process through which the institutions of hegemony and its ideology are developed. Among the features of international organization which express its hegemonic role are the following: (1) the institutions embody the rules which facilitate the expansion of hegemonic world orders; (2) they are themselves the product of the hegemonic world order; (3) they ideologically legitimate the norms of the world order; (4) they co-opt the elites from peripheral countries; and (5) they absorb counterhegemonic ideas.

International institutions embody rules which facilitate the expansion of the dominant economic and social forces but which at the same time permit adjustments to be made by subordinated interests with a minimum of pain. The rules governing world monetary and trade relations are particularly significant. They are framed primarily to promote economic expansion. At the same time they allow for exceptions and derogations to take care of problem situations. They can be revised in the light of changed circumstances. The Bretton Woods institutions provided more safeguards for domestic social concerns like unemployment than did the gold standard, on condition that national policies were consistent with the goal of a liberal world economy. The current system of floating exchange rates also gives scope for national actions while maintaining the principle of a prior commitment to harmonize national policies in the interests of a liberal world economy.

International institutions and rules are generally initiated by the state which establishes the hegemony. At the very least they must have that state's support. The dominant state takes care to secure the acquiescence of other states according to a hierarchy of powers within the inter-state structure of hegemony. Some second-rank countries are consulted first and their support is secured. The consent of at least some of the more peripheral countries is solicited. Formal participation may be weighed in favor of the dominant powers as in the International Monetary Fund and World Bank, or it may be on a one-state–one-vote basis as in most other major international institutions. There is an informal structure of influence reflecting the different levels of real political and economic power which underlies the formal procedures for decisions.

International institutions perform an ideological role as well. They help define policy guidelines for states and legitimate certain institutions and practices at the national level. They reflect orientations favorable to the dominant social and economic forces. The Organization for Economic Cooperation and Development, in recommending monetarism, endorsed a dominant consensus of policy thinking in the core countries and strengthened those who were determined to combat inflation this way against others who were more concerned about unemployment. The International Labor Organization, by advocating tripartism, legitimates the social relations evolved in the core countries as the desirable model for emulation.

Elite talent from peripheral countries is co-opted into international institutions in the manner of *trasformismo*. Individuals from peripheral countries, though they may come to international institutions with the idea of working from within to change the system, are condemned to work within the structures of passive revolution. At best they will help transfer elements of "modernization" to the peripheries but only as these are consistent with the interests of established local powers. Hegemony is like a pillow: it absorbs blows and sooner or later the would-be assailant will find it comfortable to rest upon. Only where representation in international institutions is firmly based upon an articulate social and political challenge to hegemony – upon a nascent historic bloc and counterhegemony – could participation pose a real threat. The co-optation of outstanding individuals from the peripheries renders this less likely.

Trasformismo also absorbs potentially counterhegemonic ideas and makes these ideas consistent with hegemonic doctrine. The notion of self-reliance, for example, began as a challenge to the world economy by advocating endogenously determined autonomous development. The term has now been transformed to mean support by the agencies of the world economy for do-it-yourself welfare programs in the peripheral countries. These programs aim to enable the rural populations to achieve self-sufficiency, to stem the rural exodus to the cities, and to achieve thereby a greater degree of social and political stability amongst populations which the world economy is incapable of integrating. Self-reliance in its transformed meaning becomes complementary to and supportive of hegemonic goals for the world economy.

Thus, one tactic for bringing about change in the structure of world order can be ruled out as a total illusion. There is very little likelihood of a war of movement at the international level through which radicals would seize control of the superstructure of international institutions. Daniel Patrick Moynihan notwithstanding, Third World radicals do not control international institutions.[b] Even if they did, they could

---

[b] Moynihan was US ambassador to the UN during the Carter administration. He made speeches deploring that the United States was "in opposition" in the UN, which he represented as being run by a majority of Third World countries. See *New York Times*, January 28, 1976.

achieve nothing by it. These superstructures are inadequately connected with any popular political base. They are connected with the national hegemonic classes in the core countries and, through the intermediacy of these classes, have a broader base in these countries. In the peripheries, they connect only with the passive revolution.

The prospects for counterhegemony

World orders – to return to Gramsci's statement cited earlier in this essay – are grounded in social relations. A significant structural change in world order is, accordingly, likely to be traceable to some fundamental change in social relations and in the national political orders which correspond to national structures of social relations. In Gramsci's thinking, this would come about with the emergence of a new historic bloc.

We must shift the problem of changing world order back from international institutions to national societies. Gramsci's analysis of Italy is even more valid when applied to the world order; only a war of position can, in the long run, bring about the structural changes, and a war of position involves building up the sociopolitical base for change through the creation of new historic blocs. The national context remains the only place where an historic bloc can be founded, although world-economy and world-political conditions materially influence the prospects for such an enterprise.

The prolonged crisis in the world economy (the beginning of which can be traced to the late 1960s and early 1970s) is propitious for some developments which could lead to a counterhegemonic challenge. In the core countries, those policies which cut into transfer payments to deprive social groups and generate high unemployment open the prospects of a broad alliance of the disadvantaged against the sectors of capital and labor which find common ground in international production and the monopoly-liberal world order. The policy basis for this alliance would most likely be post-Keynesian and neomercantilist. In peripheral countries, some states are vulnerable to revolutionary action, as events from Iran to Central America suggest. Political preparation of the population in sufficient depth may not, however, be able to keep pace with revolutionary opportunity and this diminishes the prospect for a new historic bloc. An effective political organization (Gramsci's modern prince) would be required in order to rally the new working classes generated by international production and build a bridge to peasants and urban marginals. Without this, we can only envisage a process where local political elites, even some which are the product of abortive revolutionary upheavals, would entrench their power within a monopoly-liberal world order. A reconstructed monopoly-liberal hegemony would be quite capable of practicing *trasformismo* by adjusting to many varieties of national institutions and practices, including nationalization of industries. The rhetoric of nationalism and of socialism could then be brought into line with the restoration of passive revolution under new guise in the periphery.

In short, the task of changing world order begins with the long, laborious effort to build new historic blocs within national boundaries.

Notes

This text was first published in *Millennium: Journal of International Studies*, vol. 12, no. 2 (Summer 1983), pp. 162–175. An earlier version was presented to the Panel on Hegemony and International Relations, convened by the caucus for a New Political Science at the 1981 annual meeting of the American Political Science Association, New York, September 1981.

1 For citation here, I refer where possible to Antonio Gramsci, *Selections from the Prison Notebooks*, edited and trans. by Quintin Hoare and Geoffrey Nowell Smith (New York: International Publishers, 1971), hereafter cited as *Selections*. The full critical edition, *Quaderni del carcere* (Turin: Einaudi, 1975), is cited as *Quaderni*.

2 This seems to be the problem underlying Perry Anderson's "The Antinomies of Antonio Gramsci," *New Left Review*, no. 100 (November 1976–January 1977), which purports to find inconsistencies in Gramsci's use of concepts.

3 On this point see E. P. Thompson, "The Poverty of Theory," in his *The Poverty of Theory and Other Essays* (London: Merlin Press, 1978), which represents an historicist position analogous to that of Gramsci's in opposition to the abstract philosophical Marxism of Louis Althusser. For Althusser's position see "Marxism is not Historicism," in Louis Althusser and Etienne Balibar, *Reading Capital*, trans. by Ben Brewster (London: New Left Books, 1979).

4 It is said that this was to avoid confiscation of his notes by the prison censor, who, if this is true, must have been particularly slow-witted.

5 Christine Buci-Gluckmann, *Gramsci et l'état. Une théorie matérialiste de la philosophie* (Paris: Fayard, 1975), places Gramsci squarely in the Leninist tradition. Hughes Portelli, *Gramsci et le bloc historique* (Paris: Fayard, 1972), and Maria Antonietta Macciocchi, *Pour Gramsci* (Paris: Fayard, 1973), both contrast Gramsci with Lenin. Buci-Gluckmann's work seems to me to be more fully thought through. See also Chantal Mouffe and Anne Showstack Sassoon, "Gramsci in France and Italy – A Review of the Literature," *Economy and Society*, vol. 6, no. 1 (February 1977), pp. 31–68.

6 This notion fitted well with Gramsci's assessment of the situation in Italy in the early 1920s; the working class was by itself too weak to carry the full burden of revolution and could only bring about the founding of a new state by an alliance with the peasantry and some petty bourgeois elements. In fact, Gramsci considered the workers' council movement as a school for leadership of such a coalition and his efforts prior to his imprisonment were directed towards building this coalition.

7 See Buci-Gluckmann, *Gramsci et l'état*, p. 63.

8 Machiavelli, *The Prince*, Norton Critical Edition, edited by Robert M. Adams (New York: W. W. Norton, 1977), pp. 49–50; and Gramsci, *Selections*, pp. 169–170.

9 The term "western Europe" refers here to the Britain, France, Germany and Italy of the 1920s and 1930s.

10 Gramsci, *Selections*, p. 238.

11 Gramsci borrowed the term "passive revolution" from the Neopolitan historian Vincenzo Cuocco (1777–1823), who was active in the early stages of the Risorgimento. In Cuocco's interpretation, Napoleon's armies had brought a passive revolution to Italy.

12 Buci-Gluckmann, *Gramsci et l'état*, p. 121.

13 Gramsci, *Quaderni*, vol. IV, p. 2632.

14 See Sorel's discussion of myth and the "Napoleonic battle" in the letter to Daniel Halévy which introduces his *Reflections on Violence*, trans. by T. E. Hulme (New York: Peter Smith, 1941).

15 Gramsci, *Selections*, p. 366

16 Ibid., pp. 180–195.

17 Ibid., p. 176.

18 Ibid., p. 264.

19 Ibid., p. 182.

20 Ibid., p. 116.

21 Ibid., p. 117.

22 The dating is tentative and would have to be refined by enquiry into the structural features proper to each period as well as into factors deemed to constitute the breaking points between one period and another. These are offered here as mere notations for a revision of historical scholarship to raise some questions about hegemony and its attendant structures and mechanisms.

Imperialism, which has taken different forms in these periods, is a closely related question. In the first, *pax britannica*, although some territories were directly administered, control of colonies seems to have been incidental to rather than necessary for economic expansion. Argentina, a formally independent country, had essentially the same relationship to the British economy as Canada, a former colony. This, as George Lichtheim noted, may be called the phase of "liberal imperialism." In the second period, the so-called "new imperialism" brought more emphasis on direct political controls. It also saw the growth of capital exports and of the finance capital identified by Lenin as the very essence of imperialism. In the third period, which might be called that of the neoliberal or monopoly-liberal imperialism, the internationalizing of production emerged as the preeminent form, supported also by new forms of finance capital (multinational banks and consortia). There seems little point in trying to define some unchanging essence of imperialism, but it would be useful to describe the structural characteristics of the imperialisms which correspond to successive hegemonic and nonhegemonic world orders.

8 Towards a posthegemonic conceptualization of world order: reflections on the relevancy of Ibn Khaldun (1992)

In the beginning was the Word.

John 1.1

When there is a general change of conditions, it is as if the entire creation had changed and the whole world been altered, as if it were a new and repeated creation, a world brought into existence anew.

Ibn Khaldun, *The Muqaddimah*

Ontology lies at the beginning of any enquiry. We cannot define a problem in global politics without presupposing a certain basic structure consisting of the significant kinds of entities involved and the form of significant relationships among them. We think, for example, about a system whose basic entities are states and of an hypothesized mechanism called the balance of power through which their relationships may be understood to constitute a certain kind of world order. From such ontological beginnings, complex theories have been built and specific cases – particular inter-state relationships – can be examined. There is always an ontological starting point.

Any such ontological standpoint is open to question. All of the terms just used have ontological meanings: global politics, structure, system, states, balance of power, world order. I choose "global politics" deliberately to avoid certain ontological presuppositions inherent in other terms such as "international relations," which seems to equate nation with state and to define the field as limited to the interactions among states; or "world system," which has been given a specific meaning by certain writers, notably by Immanuel Wallerstein. "Global politics" is looser and broader as a starting point than these other terms, although the reader will soon see that even "politics"

144

constitutes an ontological limitation for me. My thinking would prefer something like "political economy."

Theory follows reality. It also precedes and shapes reality. That is to say, there is a real historical world in which things happen; and theory is made through reflection upon what has happened. The separation of theory from historical happenings is, however, only a way of thinking, because theory feeds back into the making of history by virtue of the way those who make history (and I am thinking about human collectivities, not just about prominent individuals) think about what they are doing. Their understanding of what the historical context allows them to do, prohibits them from doing, or requires them to do, and the way they formulate their purposes in acting, is the product of theory. There is a grand theory written by scholars in books; and there is a common-sense theory which average people use to explain to themselves and to others why they are doing what they do.

The ontologies that people work with derive from their historical experience and in turn become embedded in the world they construct. What is subjective in understanding becomes objective through action. This is the only way, for instance, in which we can understand the state as an objective reality. The state has no physical existence, like a building or a lamp-post; but it is nevertheless a real entity. It is a real entity because everyone acts as though it were; because we know that real people with guns and batons will enforce decisions attributed to this nonphysical reality.

These embedded structures of thought and practice – the nonphysical realities of political and social life – may persist over long periods of time, only to become problematic, to be called into question, when people confront new sets of problems that the old ontologies do not seem able to account for or cope with. In such periods, certainties about ontology give place to skepticism. As the European old regime passed its peak and entered into decline, Pyrrhonism, a revival of skepticism from the ancient world, became an intellectual fashion.[1] Now postmodernism, more attuned to a generation that disdains to seek models from the past, performs the function of disestablishing (or, in its terms, deconstructing) the heretofore accepted ontologies.

In a recent work,[2] Richard Ashley argued that there is no indubitable Archimedean point, no single firm foundation, on which to build a science of global politics.[3] Every purported firm ground is to be doubted in the eyes of eternity. We are not, however, working with the eyes of eternity but with a myopia particular to the late twentieth century. Indeed, our perspectives may be strongly influenced by a sense of the invalidity of former certainties – those of the Cold War, of a bipolar structure of world power, of US hegemony. Our challenge is not to contribute to the construction of a universal and absolute knowledge, but to devise a fresh perspective useful for framing and working on the problems of the present.

There is a lingering absolutism in the very denial of the possibility of absolute knowledge – a regret, a striving to approximate something like it, to endow our practical wisdom with universality. As intellectuals and theorists, we are disposed to think of our task as that of *homo sapiens*, though we might be more effective were we to see our task as that of an adjunct to *homo faber*, the maker of history. To deconstruct the ontological constructs of the passing present is a first step towards a more pertinent but still relative knowledge. The task of clearing the ground should not become an obstacle to constructing a new perspective that can be useful even though it in turn will ultimately be open to critical reevaluation.

Homo faber is also *homo sapiens*. There is a cumulative as well as a disjunctive quality to history. Distinct historical phases, with their historically specific ontologies, are not sealed off from one another as mutually incomprehensible or mutually irrelevant constructs.[4] Historical phases in our own current of civilization are produced, one following the other, in a process of contradiction. The contradictions and conflicts that arise within any established structure create the opportunity for its transformation into a new structure. This is the simplest model of historical change. The successive phases of other currents of civilization can be understood by the human mind's capacity for analogy. The encounters and merging of civilizations can be understood by a combination of process and analogy. These capacities of thought make the historical process intelligible. Knowledge of history, not just of events but of the regularities or general principles that help explain historical change, can, in turn, become a guide for action. History thus generates theory. This theory is not absolute knowledge, not a final revelation or a completeness of rational knowledge about the laws of history. It is a set of viable working hypotheses. It is a form of knowledge that transcends the specific historical epoch, that makes the epoch intelligible in a larger perspective – not the perspective of eternity which stands outside history, but the perspective of a long sweep of history.[5]

There are special epistemological as well as ontological issues to be resolved in working within an era of structural change. Positivism offers an epistemological approach congenial to periods of relative structural stability. The state of the social whole can be taken as given in order to focus upon those particular variables that frame the specific and limited object of enquiry. Positivism allows for detailed empirical investigation of discrete problems. The observing subject can be thought of as separated from, as not directly involved with, what is investigated. The purpose of enquiry is to bring the aberrant activity that focused attention as an object of study back into a compatible relationship with the relatively stable whole. Although this is not always clearly recognized, in positivism there is an implicit identity between the observer-analyst and the stable social whole. This identity at the level of the whole allows for the fiction of a separation between subject and object at the level of the specific issue.

Positivism is less well adapted to enquiry into complex and comprehensive change. For this we need an epistemology that does not disguise but rather explicitly affirms the dialectical relationship of subject and object in historical process. Intentions and purposes are understood to be embodied within the objectified or institutionalized structures of thought and practice characteristic of an epoch. Where positivism separates the observing subject from the observed object of enquiry, this other historically oriented, interpretative, or hermeneutic epistemology sees subject and object in the historical world as a reciprocally interrelated whole. Such an epistemology is more adequate as a guide to action towards structural change, even though it may not attain the degree of precision expected of positivism. This essay is an attempt to develop such an approach.

A shift of ontologies is inherent in the very process of historical structural change. The entities that are significant are the emerging structures and the processes through which they emerge. Reflection upon change discredits old ontologies and yields an intimation of a possible new ontology. Use of the new ontology becomes the heuristic for strategies of action in the emerging world order.

One reason to reexamine the thought of Ibn Khaldun is that he confronted this kind of situation. He was aware of living and acting in a period of historical change, a period of decline and disintegration of the social and political structures that had been the underpinnings of past glory and stability; and he wanted to understand the reasons that lay beneath the brute facts of historical events, reasons that, when understood, could become guidelines for action. Following the reasonings of such a mind while appreciating the differences between his fourteenth-century Islamic world and our own time and place in history is one good reason for rethinking his thought.[6] Other reasons will appear in due course.

Knowledge about global politics

As a preliminary to discussing the writings of a sophisticated fourteenth-century Islamic scholar whose sense of the basic entities and relationships of his world was different from ours, it is necessary to find some categories that can be assumed to be applicable to both our worlds. I have already used some terms – world order, institutions, structures – which, though not common to both Ibn Khaldun and ourselves, may be understood to be of such generality and comprehensiveness that they can be held to apply transhistorically for purposes of comparison.

Hedley Bull defined "order" to mean "that [the constituents of order] are related to one another according to some pattern, that their relationship is not purely haphazard but contains some discernible principle."[7] This suggests a dimension ranging from something just short of the "purely haphazard" to a condition of stasis. Even the notion of the haphazard can be contested, as scientists now perceive order within chaos.[8] Some kind of order may be perceived in anarchy. Order is thus not to be perceived as a limited range of social situations, e.g., those which are free from turbulence or conflict. Order is whatever pattern or regularity of interaction is to be found in any social situation.

Bull proceeded to introduce a normative element or the promotion of certain goals or values into the concept of order. That is to say, different orders promote different goals or values. This is consistent with the hermeneutic approach. Purpose or intention is inherent in individual and collective human activity and so it is natural to enquire what goals or values inspire or are promoted by any particular order. He then goes one step further to maintain that three specific values transcend all differences among orders: security against violence, *pacta sunt servanda*, and relative stability of possessions (or property). In this last step, I think he introduces too much normative specificity. This is not a given but a problem: how to introduce into order the norms of behavior that will come to inform individual and collective conduct.

He also distinguishes usefully between "world order" and "international order." World order is genuinely transhistorical. It refers to the order prevailing in all mankind, without prejudging the manner in which mankind is institutionalized. International order refers to a particular historically limited condition of institutionalization: that of a system of nation-states.[9]

Institutions and institutionalization are the next concepts applicable to a comparative study of world orders. Institutions are the broadly understood and accepted ways of organizing particular spheres of social action – in our own era, for instance, from marriage and the nuclear family, through the state, diplomacy and the rules of international law, to formal organizations like the United Nations and the International Monetary Fund. In other eras and in different cultures, the set of institutions has been otherwise. Even where institutions within different orders bear the same names, e.g., family or state, the meanings behind the names have been different.

Institutions are the ways in which social practices developed in response to particular problems confronting a society become routinized into specific sets of rules. They may be more or less formally organized, and the sanctions that sustain rules may range from the pressure of opinion to enforceable law. At the global level this includes practices with a conventional backing in the law of nations like diplomacy, those enduring arrangements regulating actions in particular spheres that are now commonly referred to as "regimes," and formal international organizations with explicit rules and enforcement procedures.

Institutions are sustained within something broader called structures. Structures are the product of recurrent patterns of actions and expectations, the *gestes répétées* of Braudel's *longue durée*.[10] Structures exist in language, in the ways we think, in the practices of social and economic and political life. Any particular way of life in time and place, when analyzed, will reveal a certain structure. Any particular sphere of life will have its structure. Structures are then the larger context within which institutions are to be located.

Structures are socially constructed, i.e., they become a part of the objective world by virtue of their existence in the intersubjectivity of relevant groups of people. The objective world of institutions is real because we make it so by sharing a picture of it in our minds quite independently of how we value it, whether we approve or disapprove of it. Intersubjectively shaped reality, the institutions that structure how material life is organized and produced, is as much a part of the material world and as independent of individual volition as the brute physical material upon which those institutions work. Marx expressed this in terms of the interaction of relations of production (inter-subjectively constituted reality) and productive forces.

How this objective world is made and remade through changes in intersubjectivity is the principal question to be answered in any attempt to understand the process of historical change. Such a study will focus upon the relationship between (a) the stock of ideas people have about the nature of the world and (b) the practical problems that challenge them, on the aptitude or inaptitude of ideas to provide an effective and acceptable means of acting on problems that cannot be ignored because they do not go away. Where there appears to be a disjuncture between problems and hitherto-accepted mental con-structs, we may detect the opening of a crisis of structural transform-ation. Thus some of us think the erstwhile-dominant mental construct of neorealism is inadequate to confront the challenges of global poli-tics today, while others, of course, think it still works.

It is impossible to predict the future; but it may be possible to con-struct a partial knowledge that can be helpful in making a future, i.e., in channeling the direction of events towards a desired option from among those that appear feasible. Such practical knowledge as a guide to political action is to be derived from an attempt to understand his-torical change.

To be useful, this knowledge must be specifically relevant to salient practical problems, the handling of which will condition the kind of future to be made. Thus, a first emphasis should be upon identifying the salient problems of the present. Problems are not just *given* as in a positivist epistemology. Problems are *perceived*, that is to say, they arise in the encounter of social being with social consciousness.[11] Thus awareness of new problems makes us sensitive to the inadequacies of conventional mental structures that tend to make us focus on prob-lems other than those of emerging salience.

Revision of conventional ontologies

Because we cannot know the future, we cannot give a satisfactory name to future structures. We can only depict them in terms of a negation or potential negation of the dominant tendencies we have known. I use "negation" here in the sense of dialectical overcoming –

Aufhebung in Hegel's usage,[12] i.e., in which the past stage is both annulled and preserved in the succeeding stage. This sense of transition away from known structures towards an as yet unnameable future accounts for the large number of approaches in different fields of study that begin with "post" – postindustrial, postmodern, poststructural, postcapitalist, post-Marxist, etc.

There are three still dominant tendencies of thought that are candidates for negation in the emergence of future world order: hegemony, the Westphalian state system, and the globalization trend in world political economy. I shall therefore suggest some implications of an order that would become posthegemonic, post-Westphalian, and postglobalizing.

Posthegemonic

I do not use "hegemonic" in the conventional international relations meaning of a dominant state's relationship with other less powerful states. "Dominance" will do for that. Nor, consequently, do I use the term "hegemon" which refers to the dominant state in a relationship of dominance. I use "hegemony" to mean a structure of values and understandings about the nature of order that permeates a whole system of states and non-state entities. In a hegemonic order these values and understandings are relatively stable and unquestioned. They appear to most actors as the natural order. Such a structure of meanings is underpinned by a structure of power, in which most probably one state is dominant but that state's dominance in itself is not sufficient to create hegemony. Hegemony derives from the ways of doing and thinking of the dominant social strata of the dominant state or states insofar as these ways of doing and thinking have acquired the acquiescence of the dominant social strata of other states. These social practices and the ideologies that explain and legitimize them constitute the foundation of hegemonic order (Ashley's Archimedean point that is a candidate for deconstruction).[13]

Hegemony expands and is maintained by the success of the dominant social strata's practices and the appeal they exert to other social strata, through the process that Gramsci described as passive revolution. Hegemony frames thought and thereby circumscribes action.

The prospect of a posthegemonic order implies doubt as to the likelihood that a new hegemony can be constructed to replace a declining hegemony.[14] It suggests doubt as to the existence of an Archimedean point around which a new order could be constructed. Previous hegemonic orders have derived their universals from the dominant society, itself the product of a dominant civilization. A posthegemonic order would have to derive its normative content in a search for common ground among constituent traditions of civilization.

Is there a basis for common ground? The question takes us back to Hedley Bull's concern with the normative content of a world order. We raise it now, not as a matter of prior definition, but as a matter of historical contingency. What common ground is conceivable?[15]

A first condition would be mutual recognition of distinct traditions of civilization, perhaps the most difficult step especially for those who have shared a hegemonic perspective, and who are unprepared to forsake the security of belief in a natural order that is historically based on universalizing from one position of power in one form of civilization. The difficulty is underlined by the way political change outside the West is perceived and reported in the West, the tendency to view everything through western concepts which can lead to the conclusion that the "end of history" is upon us as the apotheosis of a late western capitalist civilization. Mutual recognition implies a readiness to try to understand others in their own terms.

Incidentally, speculation concerning Japan as a future hegemonic leader[16] raises implicitly this question of universalizing from a particular form of civilization. Whereas US history and Soviet history have both exhibited a strong tendency to self-universalization, Japan's civilization has been tenaciously particularistic. Japan has the economic power to pursue a hegemonic project, but seems to lack the intent to assimilate the rest of the world to its sociocultural practices. This self-restraint at the threshold of universalization could give Japan an advantage in showing the way towards a posthegemonic form of order provided it does not degenerate into a new nationalistic striving for dominance.[17]

A second condition for a posthegemonic order would be to move beyond the point of mutual recognition towards a kind of supra-intersubjectivity that would provide a bridge among the distinct and separate subjectivities of the different coexisting traditions of civilization. One can speculate that the grounds for this might be: (1) recognition of the requisites for survival and sustained equilibrium in global ecology – though the specific inferences to be drawn from this may remain objects of discord; (2) mutual acceptance of restraint in the use of violence to decide conflicts – not that this would eliminate organized political violence, though it might raise the costs of

152

resorting to violence; and (3) common agreement to explore the sources of conflict and to develop procedures for coping with conflict that would take account of distinct coexisting normative perspectives.

For those who have shared a common hegemonic perspective, the search for the common ground for a posthegemonic order can best begin with an effort to understand those perspectives that have appeared most to challenge the existing hegemonic ways of understanding and acting in world politics. This is another reason for revisiting the thought of Ibn Khaldun. The Islamic tradition is the "other" in relation to the western tradition which is both the closest and the most difficult for the western-conditioned mind to understand. A rationalist and historicist Islamic philosopher and historian can be the point of access to empathy with that other.

Post-Westphalian

To foresee a post-Westphalian world order seems initially to contradict the revival of interest in the state that has been common to both liberals and Marxists in recent decades.[18] It is, however, all the more important to give attention to the nature of the state if it is to be assumed that the role of the state and its relationship to non-state forces may be in process of significant change, that the essence of global politics may no longer be conceivable solely in terms of the inter-state system (and of the principal powers within it at that).

One indication of a changed position of states is the dramatic increase in the number of state entities. That number seemed to be declining up to the early decades of the twentieth century[19] but has greatly expanded in the second half of the twentieth century. The neo-realist responds that middle and small states do not matter;[20] they can be ignored in calculating the configuration of effective power relations.

Lesser powers do, however, alter the milieu of inter-state relations. They have a collective interest in erecting limits on great-power activity; and they encourage norms of international behavior that are anti-colonial and anti-interventionist, and which favor redistribution of global resources. Even as victim, the small state highlights a shift from hegemony to dominance, undermining moral certainties, underlining arbitrariness and departure from rule – consider the undermining of hegemonic beliefs in the cases involving Vietnam, Afghanistan, Grenada, Nicaragua, El Salvador, and Panama.

Territoriality was the defining feature of the Westphalian state. The contemporary state retains this feature, but its importance has diminished in relation to nonterritorial power.[21] Even those neorealists who predict a new mercantilist world order do not conceive it on the model of the autarkic territorially defined blocs of the 1930s. The new mercantilism would be a struggle among some territorially located centers of nonterritorial political-economic power. It would be a struggle for markets and investment opportunities over the whole globe, including the domestic territories of the rival centers of power. Each of these power centers has a stake within the others. Nonterritoriality gives a greater scope for action to economic and social organizations of civil society whose activities cross territorial boundaries.

In the last half of the twentieth century, the relationship of states to the world political economy has altered. Formerly, the state's role was conceived as bulwark or buffer protecting the domestic economy from harmful exogenous influences. Latterly, the state's role has been understood more as helping to adjust the domestic economy to the perceived exigencies of the world economy. "Competitiveness" is the key word indicative of this shift in perspective. The state is tributary to something greater than the state. The state has become "internationalized" as a consequence, a transmission belt from world economy to domestic economy. Evidently, the process of adaptation is uneven. Some states use their powers to resist adaptation by attempting to force other states to adjust to their interests. Some states seize the new economic environment as an opportunity to control their own adjustment and advance their own economies. Many have adjustment thrust unwillingly upon them. All, however, reason about state policy from the premise of the world economy.

In these changes in the role and capacities of states, it is increasingly meaningless to speak of "the" state as do neorealists, or even (as among Marxists) of "the capitalist" state. It becomes more useful to think in terms of *forms* of state – different forms which condition the ways in which different societies link into the global political economy.[22]

Moreover, the changes taking place in state roles give new opportunity for self-expression by nationalities that have no state of their own, in movements for separation or autonomy; and the same tendencies encourage ethnicities and religiously defined groups that straddle state boundaries to express their identities in global politics. Multinational corporations and transnational banks develop their autonomy, partly exploiting the opportunities of a deregulated international environment, partly falling back upon state support in difficulties. Social movements like environmentalism, feminism, and the peace movement transcend territorial boundaries. Transnational cooperation among indigenous peoples enhances their force within particular states. These various developments lend credibility to Bull's vision of a "new medievalism."[23]

Postglobalization

Karl Polanyi discerned a double movement in the economic and social history of Europe during the nineteenth century.[24] The thrust behind the utopian vision of a self-regulating market was the first phase of movement. The market was conceived as bursting free from the bonds of society, a newly unleashed natural force that would subject society to its laws. Then came, unplanned and unawaited, a second phase of movement: society's response of self-preservation, curbing the disintegrating and alienating consequences of market-oriented behavior. Society set about to tame and civilize the market.

In the late twentieth century, we can discern a similar recurrence of the double movement. A powerful globalizing economic trend thrusts toward the achievement of the market utopia on the global scale. At the present moment, the protective response of society appears to be less sure, less coherent. Yet the elements of opposition to the socially disruptive consequences of globalization are visible. The question remains open as to what form these may take, as to whether and how they may become more coherent and more powerful, so that historical thesis and antithesis may lead to a new synthesis. Globalization is not the end of history but the initiation of a new era of conflicts and reconciliations.[25]

The characteristics of the globalization trend include the internationalizing of production, the new international division of labor, new migratory movements from South to North, the new competitive environment that accelerates these processes, and the internationalizing of the state (referred to above) making states into agencies of the globalizing trend.

Looking to the future of global politics, it is of the first importance to consider the sources of conflict that may be exacerbated by the globalization trend. Conflicts arising from ecological issues (pollution, waste disposal, preempting of depletable resources, etc.); from migration; from social polarization produced by new structures of production; from vulnerabilities to competition; and from ethnic, gender, and other group differentiations that become identified with and manipulated in the interest of economic and social cleavages. Conflicts from such sources can break out directly within societies and can become extended into the inter-state system through the differential responses of particular states and the transnational linkages of social groups.

It is equally important to identify probable sources of opposition to globalization – the relatively disadvantaged who will affirm the right of social forces to make economy and polity serve their own self-determined goals. The confrontation precipitated by globalization presages a new synthesis in which economic efficiency may better serve social goals and buttress the identities of self-defined social groups. The relevant sources of opposition include the new social movements, those labor movements that have been capable of transcending what Gramsci[26] called the economic-corporative level of consciousness, democratization movements that strive to enhance popular control over those aspects of social organization that directly affect people's lives. Forms of struggle also change, and emerging cleavages become aligned with ideologies in new ways.

Ibn Khaldun: roots of an Islamic perspective on historical change

The foregoing outlines the perspective from which I enquire into the thought of Ibn Khaldun and something of the reasons for choosing this object of enquiry as part of a collective project of rethinking the contemporary meaning of international relations. Let us now turn more directly to the relevancy of Ibn Khaldun.

Ibn Khaldun was born in May 1332 in Tunis of a distinguished family which had emigrated from Seville to the Maghreb some years previously, before the fall of Seville to the *reconquista*. Both his parents died in the Black Death while he was still a young man. He was educated by some of the best minds of his time, and made a career in the court politics of a turbulent era in the history of North Africa and Andalusia.

As a participant observer of politics, he had excellent opportunity to develop his judgement, with access to many of the prominent personalities of the time, both within the Arabic-Islamic world and beyond it. From another point of view, his political career was tumultuous and on the whole unsuccessful. His political projects failed; and at a certain point he withdrew from active politics in order to pursue an effort at deeper understanding of politics through history. It was during this phase that he composed *Muqaddimah* or prolegomena to his world history,[27] entitled *Kitab al-'Ibar*, which was completed in 1377 while he was living in refuge in a fortress village in the province of Oran.

Soon thereafter he obtained permission to make the pilgrimage to Mecca and traveled as far as Cairo, then the most brilliant remaining center of a contracting Islamic world. He accepted appointment to a prestigious judgeship. Family tragedy struck again when his wife and children died in shipwreck on their way to join him. He continued the pilgrimage to Mecca and on his return to Cairo was appointed first to a most eminent academic charge and then again to a judgeship.

The latter part of his career was thus in the judicial sphere, where the first had been in court politics and diplomacy, the two spheres of activity being separated by the phase of reflections on history. He died in Cairo in March 1406.[28]

Why should Ibn Khaldun's thought be of interest to us today? One reason already suggested is that he provides a point of access to the understanding of Islamic civilization; and Islamic civilization is asserting its presence in the shaping of any future world order. There are also some reasons that derive from analogies between Ibn Khaldun's times and our own. He enables us to examine how a differently constituted mind confronted similar problems to those we now face and what factors shaped his understanding of and response to these problems.

He confronted the problem of decline. The *reconquista* had reduced the Islamic hold on Spain to Granada. The North African states were hard pressed by nomadic tribes on one side and by the Christian states to the north controlling the Mediterranean seaways on the other. Christians and Jews were the middlemen in international trade. To the east, Mongol invasion shattered the existing structures, even though the invaders ultimately became absorbed into Islamic culture. Major cities were ruined; irrigation systems were disrupted or destroyed; oppressive taxation and the practice of tax farming fragmented power and undermined administrative organization. Although the cultural preeminence of Islam remained, the material foundations of Islamic hegemony were much weakened.

During his own career, Ibn Khaldun had personal encounters with

Pedro the Cruel of Castile in Seville, and with the Mongol conqueror Tamerlane outside of Damascus. Both sought his advice and collaboration and both were discreetly refused. The challenge to understand the composite nature of decline was a principal incentive for Ibn Khaldun to undertake his studies on the meaning of history.[29]

The state was a focus of his interest; but the state could not be taken by Ibn Khaldun as a given, as the unquestioned basis of world order.[30] The construction and maintenance of states was problematized in his work. He perceived a process of emergence, maturity, and decline of states. States had to be seen and understood in the context of broader-ranging political processes. The *polis* was not, as for the Greeks, the beginning and end of politics. Politics emerged from the tribal community; and it extended to the empire. The state was a critical phase of political process, but only one phase, and that phase one of mutation, not of finality. There is little in common between Ibn Khaldun and our contemporary neorealism. There is much in common with the effort to conceive of a post-Westphalian world.

There is a profoundly material basis to Ibn Khaldun's political thought. He is keenly aware of the relationship of political forms to ecology. The prospects of civilized life are seen by him to be conditioned by matters of climate. The alternation of forms of state depend upon the balance between steppe and sown, nomadic and sedentary life, each generating its specific political culture.

This perspective is more congenial to our present than it would have been to the two centuries that preceded our time. Uniquely in world history, those two hundred years knew continuous growth. The doctrine of progress, child of material growth, is now challenged by a new awareness of ecological limits and a fear that perhaps that awareness may have come too late. Globalization is the expression of latter-day confidence in material growth. Ibn Khaldun may have something to say to those endeavoring to think in terms of postglobalization.

The political ontology of medieval Islam

A first problem in approaching Ibn Khaldun's thought is to grasp the intersubjective meanings that would be shared as points of reference among his contemporaries. This is, in other words, to attempt to define the ontological content of his world.

This world would have been understood by contemporaries in

terms of a primary cleavage between Islam and the non-Islamic world. In its origins, Islam connoted a sense of community, of religious fellowship, that transcended narrower communities centered on kinship.[31] Common faith overcame the limitations of blood bonds.

It also drew a line between believers and non-believers outside the pale of Islam. Community within contrasted to war without. Indeed, the identity of religion and politics characteristic of Islam is conditioned by this cleavage. The Prophet had to found a new political community in Medina, following the *hijra*, as a base for the propagation of God's message. The Caliphate, succeeding the rule of the Prophet, upheld the injunction to pursue *jihad*, holy war, through the fusion of the Law with military-political power. This fusion distinguished the Islamic whole from the European-Christian, with the latter's distinction of religious and secular authorities, symbolized by the dualism of papacy and empire.

In historical experience, the cleavage between Islam and infidels may not have been quite so extreme. Certainly, Islamic political identity was reinforced by military pressure from Christian Europe and from Asian Mongol invaders. However, diplomatic, trade, and cultural exchanges between Islamic and non-Islamic worlds constituted factors of coexistence. Ibn Khaldun himself participated in such exchanges. Nevertheless, Islam constituted the broadest entity with which a Middle Easterner or North African individual would identify. In much the same manner, a European would identify with the *respublica Christiana*, a religious-cultural entity to which no specific political institution corresponded, but which was nonetheless intersubjectively real.

In another dimension (the vertical by contrast to the horizontal), Islam expressed the linkage between the conditions of material existence, the forms of human organization, and the realm of the angels and of God. Prophecy consummated this linkage. The Prophet was the messenger of God. God was unity, suffering no separation into distinct persons such as occurred in Christian trinitarianism. The Prophet conveyed the Law through which human society was to be shaped; and taught how mankind was to cope with the problems of material existence under the Law. In the time of the Prophet, there was an identity between religion, law, politics, and social organization; and this identity remained the Islamic ideal.

From the time of the Prophet, however, this identity became fragmented in practice. The fragmentation did not destroy the ideal of unity. Rather it took a dialectical form in which different aspects assumed what today might be called a "relative autonomy," emphasizing some aspects of the whole at the expense of others, but not separating out from the whole. The relationship between these aspects took the form of what Croce called a dialectic of distincts, as contrasted with a dialectic of opposites.[32] These different aspects were constituted by the distinct traditions that were encompassed by Islam as an historical phenomenon.

The basic elements that united in Islam with the religious-political tradition of prophesy, yet remained distinct to constitute its historical dialectic were (1) the sociopolitical organization of the pre-Islamic bedouin Arab clan, (2) the administrative and political structure of the pre-Islamic (notably Sasanian Persian) empires, (3) the Sultanate or emergent states that represented both the transcendence of the clan group and the disintegration of the imperial administration, (4) the social and economic organization of urban society, (5) the intellectual rationalist tradition of classical Greek philosophy, and (6) a mode of production continuous from pre-Islamic times which remained substantially unchanged though permitting an oscillation between the satisfaction of bare necessities and a cyclical appearance of instances of relative luxury. Each of these distinct elements in the Islamic tradition in turn lent itself to contradictory perspectives.

In the Sunni tradition, unity of political and religious authority embodied in the Caliphate remained as an ideal, but the rule of kingship that emerged in independent states succeeding the Caliphate had a relative legitimacy. It was still the higher duty of rulers to uphold the Law, but kingly rule also had rational justification as the means of maintaining order. The state and the Islamic tradition became historicized.

The Shi'ite tradition embodied by contrast an essentially ahistorical eschatological view of politics. The believer awaited the coming of the Mahdi, the Islamic messiah, the hidden Twelfth Imam, who would inaugurate the reign of heaven on earth. In this conception, all states were fundamentally illegitimate with no more than a spurious claim upon the transitory allegiance of the believer.

Politicized and non-politicized perceptions of Islam coexisted in distinct social milieus quite apart from the Sunni/Shi'a distinction. The milieu of the kingly courts fostered a politicized form, tending even at times, despite the hostility of the Islamic tradition to any form of organized church, towards a state religion.[33] Popular piety, on the other hand, was more consistently represented by the *ulama*, local elites of religious teachers and judges, respected for their learning and probity. For most people, membership in a universal Islamic fellowship became concretized less in the state than in the local urban community. This localization of identity was further reinforced by the appeal of Sufi mysticism among rural as well as urban populations.

The educated elites had to wrestle also with the rival claims of prophecy, religious revelation, and mysticism, on the one hand, and rationalism, on the other. Islam preserved the classical Greek texts of Plato and Aristotle, and developed the ideas contained in them through the works of Avicenna, Averroes, and others. It was through contact with the higher culture of Islam that the Christian West recovered knowledge of Greek philosophy. Ibn Khaldun's education was in this rationalist tradition. He, along with others of the educated elite, did not regard the rival claims of revelation and rationalism as mutually exclusive. Both had their place in Islamic thought. To some extent it was a question of to whom you were speaking.[34] The discourse of rationalism was appropriate for the educated elite, and the discourse of revealed authority for the masses. Ultimately both discourses ought to be consistent one with the other. The Law, revealed by the Prophet as the guidelines for human life, was the basis for the state. Politics, the construction and maintenance of the state, was a matter for rational scientific enquiry. A prophet, indeed, to be effective, would need to function rationally in being able to communicate and to build the human foundation for the revealed message.[35]

Finally, there is a contradiction inherent in two forms of society, each grounded in a different ecology and economy: the nomadic bedouin culture and the urban culture. This contradiction became the central theme of the *Muqaddimah*. The bedouin culture is one of blood relations and relative economic equality. All members of such populations are satisfied with a minimum of material necessities. All male members share in the tasks of defense and expansion in relation to other communities. Morals are simple and pure. There is a kind of military equality under patriarchal leadership. The urban culture begins with the division of labor in the development of specialized arts and crafts. It culminates in luxury, dissolution, and effeminate decline. Since the mode of production did not admit of cumulative growth, the two cultures were condemned to a continuing oscillation. The limits to growth were quickly reached in urban expansion, precipitating a reversion to the regime of primitive necessity. Urban decadence opened the way to nomadic incursions and a restarting of the cycle.

The epistemology of Ibn Khaldun

Ibn Khaldun entitled his major work *Kitab al-'Ibar* which is usually rendered as "world history." Muhsin Mahdi comments on the meaning of the key word *'Ibar*: it signifies to pass from the outside to the inside of a thing.[36] The concept suggests that Ibn Khaldun's aim is to pass from the immediate world of sensible things, the world of events, to penetrate into the world of rationally intelligible explanation that lies behind events. Ibn Khaldun called what he was doing a "new science." What he envisaged was a critical, scientific knowledge of history. Knowledge of events was a basis for reasoning about underlying causes. The rationally knowable principles conditioning such causes, once demonstrated, could serve as critical standards of the validity of evidence about events.[37]

The enquiry was directed, not to individual historical actions, but to collective human action in history. The object of enquiry was *'umran* or culture. *'Umran* represented the ways in which human communities confronted their specific problems of material existence. These problems varied according to climate and ecology. Culture could only develop in propitious circumstances, where the climate was neither too hard nor too easy. In these temperate zones, different peoples, influenced by their environment, have adopted different modes of association and economic activity, some nomadic and practicing animal husbandry, some sedentary and agricultural.

Prophecy played a critical role of stimulus in bringing about the diverse existing patterns of human organization. The prophet is the legislator and teacher who adjusts human organization to material conditions, showing a people how they should live, instructing them in new attitudes and founding new institutions.

Prophecy is not, however, a sufficient cause. It is inoperative in the absence of *'asabiya*. The concept of *'asabiya* in Ibn Khaldun is the subject of as much discussion and shades of meaning as the concept of *virtù* in Machiavelli. It has been roughly but probably inadequately translated as "group feeling" in Franz Rosenthal's standard English translation of *Muqaddimah*. In Yves Lacoste's[38] reading of Ibn Khaldun's text, *'asabiya* arises with the emergence of a de facto aristocracy within a tribal community. It is a form of military solidarity congruent

162

with the passage from a classless to a class structure. In the terms I have employed above, *'asabiya* is the form of intersubjectivity that pertains to the founding of a state. It is the creative component in this critical phase of human development; and in this respect *'asabiya* has (for a Westerner) some relationship to Machiavelli's *virtù*.

This vital component is, however, subject to decay, and therein lies the dialectical character of the concept. The expansion of the power of the founders of a state leads to their corruption; they become accustomed to urban luxury, abandon their military habits to depend upon mercenaries, resort to tax farming and bribery, and lose touch with their followers. Lacoste writes: "*'Asabiya* is the motor of development of the state, *and* it is destroyed by the emergence of the state."[39]

In Islam, an insistent monotheism, exclusive of any intermediary or distinct theological personalities such as figure in Catholic Christianity, is the mirror of the unity of the faithful. Monotheism transcends tribal or ethnic blood bonds; it becomes the ideological basis for unity in a multiethnic world order. The political basis was, however, rooted in tribal society, the *'asabiya* of the nomadic bedouin conquerors. The social structure resulting from the fusion of these political and ideological elements was what the Moroccan sociologist Mohammed Al-Jabri,[40] building on Ibn Khaldun's work, called the "invasion economy." The nomadic tribesman extracted surplus from the sedentary agricultural and urban societies to maintain their rule. This relationship became, in turn, the cause of their own decline.

To summarize Ibn Khaldun's epistemology: (1) reason can discern explanatory principles of history that make events intelligible to the retrospective enquirer; (2) human natures, and thus human capacities for understanding, take different forms as human collectivities confront the problems of material existence in different ways; (3) *'asabiya* is the necessary intersubjective condition for the creation of a higher form of collective existence, i.e., the state; (4) prophecy superimposed on *'asabiya* creates the fullest potentiality for the founding of a world order; (5) the state is the form in relation to which culture is the matter, the state having the capacity to shape a higher culture; and (6) the development of a state contains the seeds of its own destruction, from which it may be inferred that the intersubjectivity that was the basis of state power will cease to exist.

Although Ibn Khaldun does not state this explicitly, one must infer that the knowledge comprised in the "new science" could only come about as a consequence of this historical development of human

163

understanding. Knowledge, in other words, must be historically conditioned. In the sequel to decline, the historian-philosopher who knows about the no-longer-existent *'asabiya*, is left in a lonely position.[41] He can be neither prophet nor state-builder and is possessed of a knowledge that may not be well received by his contemporaries.

Perceptions of world order and the philosopher-historian's role

Ibn Khaldun's life story says something about the relationship of the philosopher to world history in an era of decline. His career, as indicated above, encompassed three phases: (1) a period of intense political-diplomatic activity, of involvement in the life of the courts; (2) a phase of withdrawal and reflection during which he composed his major study of history; and (3) a final phase devoted to the piecemeal amelioration of existing society through the application of the Law.

This suggests that he had tested the possibility of achieving a desirable political order through the political process, through the state, and found that wanting. From his own reasoning, the failing could not lie with individuals or miscalculated events. It would have to lie with the inadequacies of the prevailing culture. *'Asabiya* had eroded as an underpinning of political structures. Thus one could not look to the existing forms of state for the creative force necessary to raising culture to a higher level. In this situation, two possibilities remained. One was the potential of the enlightened individual in an era of decline. This could be exercised through the *ulama*, the role of an educated and devout elite, that persistent element within Islamic society which had acted as a counterpoint to the state. The *ulama* could be the voice of the Law, appealing to the source of religious belief for authority. The philosopher would conceal his faculty of reason without abandoning it. Reason would remain as esoteric among initiates. The philosopher would express himself to the public through Plato's noble lie.

The other possibility was a future revival of *'asabiya* under the aegis of a new world force. The new force would not come from among those peripheral semi-barbarous Arab and Berber tribes whose incursions into the diminishing sphere of the North African states had reduced them to an unstable residue of their one-time glory. These tribes were too primitive and undisciplined to found a state.

There was, however, the possibility of a new emerging world power reinstituting order. Muhsin Mahdi writes:

> A Messiah might very well appear at some future time. But if he is to put into effect the expected reforms, he must come at the head of a powerful people with great solidarity. He might even need to bring a new religion to unite and inspire his people. Ibn Khaldun thus intimates that such a Messiah could not appear among the Arabs where he is expected and might not even be a Muslim . . . He will have to possess the qualifications necessary for a leader and must be born in circumstances conducive to the creation of a powerful state, which in turn must follow the natural course of rise and decline.[42]

Ibn Khaldun analyzed the political role of religion. Under this aspect, the rational science of culture could yield knowledge concerning the circumstances in which prophecy combined with *'asabiya* could be politically effective, and the circumstances in which this efficacy ceased. Circumstances of political efficacy, however, could say nothing about the truth of religious revelation. Ibn Khaldun could remain a devout Muslim while being pessimistic about the prospects of the Islamic world. In historical experience, the decay of the institutions of his world system enhanced the importance of moral action at the local level.

Ibn Khaldun's reflections on world history contemplated the "world" that would have been intelligible to him, just as ours contemplate the "world" intelligible to us. Any such reflections are historically conditioned. A first requirement, accordingly, is to become conscious of the nature of that conditioning. One way of achieving this awareness is to rethink the thought of someone who has attempted to do this in the past, and especially in the circumstances of a different tradition of civilization from our own. That is the initial purpose of turning to Ibn Khaldun.

Recent decades have seen a number of works about Ibn Khaldun, and references to his work by contemporary scholars. These various readings of Ibn Khaldun find interesting things in his work; but none of them is concerned directly with the question raised here about how to understand change in world order.[43]

In this latter perspective, enquiry focuses upon what the constituent elements of world order are (or were at any given time) and how and why the relationships among these elements have changed during critical phases of structural transformation. In the world of Ibn

Khaldun, order begins with a unity of message and power, the rule of the Prophet and its succession in the Caliphate. That order is then transformed in a dispersion of power among states, and a separation of political power from the propagation of the message. The message instead becomes embedded in society, while court circles are motivated by the gaining and preservation of power more than by the application of the message.

The status of the state in this process of transformation is worth underlining. The state might have become the focal point of power and the principal object of Ibn Khaldun's enquiry;[44] but the state in Muslim history never attained the absolute claims accorded it in European history. The claims of world order and the image of the Caliphate never completely vanished from the intersubjectivity of Islam despite the prolonged absence of institutional embodiment. This is particularly significant at the present time, when states, though repositories of organized power, are perceived as intermediate between the *telos* of Islamic peoples and the achievement of a reunified Islam.

Much of the fluidity among institutional forms and ideal conceptions in the Islamic political ontology Ibn Khaldun finds to be explainable in terms of how human groups relate to economic conditions of survival (pastoral, agricultural, and urban artisan and commercial forms of social life), and to the formation of rival dominant classes – both political-military-administrative classes linked to the state, and an urban-commercial class outside the state. This decentralization of power has left the message as a thin bond of fellowship with no corresponding institutionalized support, a residue of intersubjectivity awaiting some future possible but not necessarily probable revival through the coming of the Mahdi.

The above changes can be understood rationally in terms of human thought reflecting upon human behavior. They are not to be interpreted as determined by some extra-human transcendent or immanent force, neither by a Divine Providence nor by a Hegelian Reason. There is thus a science of politics which is in practice the science of history, i.e., the rational understanding of collective human practices. Under distinct circumstances, ideas and material conditions come together to form consistent patterns of action or structures which in their turn are worn out by experience and changing circumstances and replaced by other structures.

What is, then, the relationship of this rational understanding of history to the Law, i.e., to the revealed message about good and evil in human action? By putting together Ibn Khaldun's text with his life, we may reply that the two are distinct but not irreconcilable. A person can have both an understanding of why things are the way they are and a conviction that some things are morally reprehensible and stand to be corrected. One of our contemporaries, Isaiah Berlin, has stated this dilemma succinctly in terms applicable to the late twentieth century:

> In the end, men choose between ultimate values; they choose as they do, because their life and thought are determined by fundamental moral categories and concepts that are as much a part of their being and conscious thought and sense of their identity, as their basic physical structure.
>
> Principles are not less sacred because their duration cannot be guaranteed. Indeed, the very desire for guarantees that our values are eternal and secure in some objective heaven is perhaps only a craving for the certainties of childhood or the absolute values of our primitive past. "To realise the relative validity of one's convictions," said an admirable writer of our time, "and yet stand for them unflinchingly, is what distinguishes a civilized man from a barbarian." To demand more than this is perhaps a deep and incurable metaphysical need; but to allow it to guide one's practice is a symptom of an equally deep, and far more dangerous, moral and political immaturity.[45]

There are certain rules of prudence suggested by Ibn Khaldun in the situation of conflict or inconsistency between moral principles held with conviction and the practical possibilities of politics. His rule is to pursue moral principle within the realm of the feasible. This is not a counsel of despair. It need not imply passivity or defeatism. Analysis of feasibility may reveal opportunities for a new departure. The moment of prophecy seizes the historical opportunity when the message can become political reality. This is the moment when the rational and the revealed again attain unity. Such moments mark a new beginning in historical process, the founding of a new order; but the new order will, in the rational understanding of the laws of historical change, itself be subject to fruition and decay. It has no eternal guarantee, even though its proponents act as though it should have.

What Ibn Khaldun does not explicitly contemplate is the possibility of alternative intersubjective worlds coexisting without losing, each of them, their internal conviction and dynamism; and without one coming to dominate and absorb the others through its superior *asa-biya*. This is the essence of our problem of conceiving a posthegemonic world on the threshold of the twenty-first century.

Can there be distinct, thriving macro-societies, each with its own solidarity, each pursuing a distinct *telos*, which could coexist through a supra-intersubjectivity? This supra-intersubjectivity would have to embody principles of coexistence without necessarily reconciling differences in goals. It would have to allow for a degree of harmonization of the trajectories of the different macro-societies.

Or is the only model of the future one in which differences become absorbed into a new unity, a new global hegemony, perhaps the creation of a new global Mahdi? (The global Mahdi could take the form of a collectivity rather than an individual.)[46] Ibn Khaldun does not answer, but perhaps his skepticism concerning the coming of a Mahdi and his apparent preference for action at the level of local societies can give us a clue.

Notes

This text was first published in James N. Rosenau and Ernst-Otto Czempiel (eds.), *Governance Without Government: Order and Change in World Politics* (Cambridge: Cambridge University Press, 1992). I would like to thank James Rosenau, Janice Thomson, Oran Young, and Ahmed Samatar, for critical comment on an earlier draft of this essay, with the usual disclaimer that they bear no responsibility for the final product.

1 Paul Hazard, *La crise de la conscience européene, 1680–1715* (Paris: Fayard, 1961); trans. as *The European Mind, 1680–1715* (Cleveland, Ohio: World Publishing Co., 1963).

2 Richard Ashley, "Imposing International Purpose: Notes on a Problematic of Governance," in Ernst-Otto Czempiel and James N. Rosenau (eds.), *Global Changes and Theoretical Challenges: Approaches to World Politics for the 1990s* (Lexington, Mass.: Lexington Books, 1989) pp. 251–290.

3 Czempiel and Rosenau, *Global Changes and Theoretical Challenges*, pp. 257, 286. For a critique of postmodernism in world politics studies see Pauline Rosenau, "Once Again into the Fray: International Relations Confronts the Humanities," *Millennium: Journal of International Studies*, vol. 19, no. 1 (Spring 1990), pp. 83–110.

4 This point is well made by Joseph Femia, drawing upon the "absolute historicism" of Antonio Gramsci, in his article "An Historicist Critique of 'Revisionist' Methods for Studying the History of Ideas," *History and Theory*, vol. 20, no. 2 (1981), pp. 113–134.

5 This perspective on history as the unifying field of social sciences was pioneered in western thought by Giambattista Vico, *The New Science of Giambattista Vico*, trans. by Thomas Goddard Bergin and Max Harold Fisch

(Ithaca, N.Y.: Cornell University Press, 1970), and has perhaps best been explained in a contemporary context by Fernand Braudel, "History and the Social Sciences: The *Longue Durée*," in *On History*, trans. by Sarah Matthews (Chicago: University of Chicago Press, 1980), pp. 25–54.

6 R. G. Collingwood, *The Idea of History* (Oxford: Clarendon Press, 1946), influences my approach to rethinking the thought of the past.

7 Hedley Bull, *The Anarchical Society: A Study of Order in World Politics* (New York: Columbia University Press, 1977), ch. 1.

8 James Gleick, *Chaos: Making a New Science* (New York: Penguin, 1987).

9 Writing in January 1991, I cannot ignore that the term "world order" has been used by the US administration of President George Bush in one of several justifications of its war against Iraq. Bush's "new world order" would be an order enforced by US power. It is pertinent to recall words written by E. H. Carr almost half a century ago: "To internationalise government in any real sense means to internationalise power; and international government is, in effect, government by that state which supplies the power necessary for the purpose of governing" (*The Twenty Years' Crisis, 1919–1939* (London: Macmillan, 1946), p. 107). One might add, at this later date: . . . and which has the power to compel other governments to finance the cost of the use of power. The general category "world order" should not become reduced to one specific and politically manipulative use of the term.

10 Fernand Braudel, *Civilisation matérielle, économie, et capitalisme, XVe–XVIIIe siècle*, 3 vols. (Paris: Armand Colin, 1979).

11 Marx and Engels, in *The German Ideology*, said that social being determines social consciousness. E. P. Thompson formulated the relationship in a more balanced and interactive way which I follow here. See especially "The Poverty of Theory," in E. P. Thompson, *The Poverty of Theory and Other Essays* (London: Merlin Press, 1978). He writes: "Changes take place within social being, which give rise to changed *experience*: and this experience is *determining*, in the sense that it exerts pressures upon existent social consciousness, proposes new questions, and affords much of the material which the more elaborated intellectual exercises are about" (p. 200).

12 As explicated, e.g., in Charles Taylor, *Hegel and Modern Society* (Cambridge: Cambridge University Press, 1979), p. 49.

13 This point is developed in Robert W. Cox, "Gramsci, Hegemony, and International Relations: An Essay in Method," collected in this volume (chapter 7).

14 Whether or not the *pax americana* is declining is, of course, a matter of open debate. I am taking here the proposition that it is declining. Susan Strange contests this proposition (see her article "Towards a Theory of Transnational Empire," in Czempiel and Rosenau (eds.), *Global Changes and Theoretical Challenges*, pp. 161–176) but her use of "hegemony" is different from mine, more akin to that of the theorists of hegemonic stability, more like my "dominance." We differ in the use of words, not, I think, in

substance. When she points to a tendency towards unilateralism in US behavior as an irresponsible use of US power, that, in my usage, would indicate an abdication of hegemonic leadership. Of course, the tendency is not irreversible. There is a question whether, if reversed, the new direction would be towards an attempt to reestablish *pax americana*, or towards US adaptation to a posthegemonic world.

15 Ibn Khaldun wrote: "We must distinguish the conditions that attach themselves to the essence of civilization as required by its very nature; the things that are accidental and cannot be counted on; and the things that cannot possibly attach themselves to it" (Ibn Khaldun, *The Muqaddimah: An Introduction to History*, trans. by Franz Rosenthal (Princeton, N.J.: Princeton University Press, 1967), p. 38). This may sound very like Bull's basic normative principles. I prefer to think, not of principles which can be deduced from the nature of civilization, but rather of principles which, in the actuality of the historic encounter of civilizations, can be accepted as common.

16 For instance, Ezra Vogel, "Pax Nipponica?," *Foreign Affairs*, vol. 64, no. 4 (Spring 1986), pp. 752–767.

17 Robert W. Cox, "Middlepowermanship, Japan, and Future World Order," collected in this volume (chapter 13).

18 I refer, e.g., to Marxian theorizing on the state by Nicos Poulantzas, *Pouvoir politique et classes sociales* (Paris: Maspero, 1968), and Ralph Miliband, *The State in Capitalist Society* (London: Weidenfeld and Nicolson, 1969); and to Stephen Krasner, *Defending the National Interest: Raw Materials Investments and US Foreign Policy* (Princeton, N.J.: Princeton University Press, 1978), and Theda Skocpol, *States and Social Revolutions* (Cambridge: Cambridge University Press, 1979). See in particular, Mark W. Zacher, "The Decaying of the Westphalian Temple: Implications for International Order and Governance," in Rosenau and Czempiel, *Governance Without Government*, pp. 58–101.

19 Indeed, E. H. Carr, *Conditions of Peace* (London: Macmillan, 1944), assumed that one of the causes of World War II was the breakup of pre-World War I empires into a number of weak states, and that a future peace would depend upon a reconcentration of power into a more limited number of economically and militarily viable states.

20 I recall Kenneth Waltz saying "Denmark doesn't matter."

21 See Susan Strange, "Towards a Theory of Transnational Empire"; also Richard Rosecrance, *The Rise of the Trading State: Commerce and Conquest in the Modern World* (New York: Basic Books, 1986). I have discussed the dualism of territorial and interdependence principles in "Production and Security," which is collected in this volume (chapter 14).

22 Robert W. Cox, *Production, Power, and World Order: Social Forces in the Making of History* (New York: Columbia University Press, 1987), pp. 105–109.

23 Bull, *Anarchical Society*, pp. 254–255.

24 Karl Polanyi, *The Great Transformation: The Political and Economic Origins of Our Time* (Boston: Beacon Press, 1957).

25 I have discussed this in "The Global Political Economy and Social Choice," which is collected in this volume (chapter 10).

26 Antonio Gramsci, *Selections from the Prison Notebooks*, edited and trans. by Quintin Hoare and Geoffrey Nowell Smith (New York: International Publishers, 1971), pp. 131–132, 173–175, 181–182.

27 The standard English translation is *The Muqaddimah: An Introduction to History*, trans. by Franz Rosenthal (Princeton, N.J.: Princeton University Press, 1967).

28 Currently available works on Ibn Khaldun include Aziz Al-Azmeh, *Ibn Khaldun in Modern Scholarship: A Study in Orientalism* (London: Third World Centre for Research and Publishing, 1981), which includes an extensive bibliography; Aziz Al-Azmeh, *Ibn Khaldun: An Essay in Reinterpretation* (London: Frank Cass, 1982); Majallat Et-Tarikh, *Actes du colloque international sur Ibn Khaldun*, Algiers, June 1978 (Algiers: Société nationale d'édition et de diffusion, 1982); Charles Issawi, *An Arab Philosophy of History* (London: J. Murray, 1950); Yves Lacoste, *Ibn Khaldun: The Birth of History and the Past of the Third World* (London: Verso, 1984); Muhsin Mahdi, *Ibn Khaldun's Philosophy of History: A Study in Philosophical Foundations of the Science of Culture* (London: George Allen and Unwin, 1957); Nathaniel Schmidt, *Ibn Khaldun: Historian, Sociologist, and Philosopher* (New York: AMS Press, 1967); and Heinrich Simon, *Ibn Khaldun's Science of Human Culture*, trans. by Fuad Baali (Lahore: Sh. Muhammad Askraf, 1978).

29 Mahdi, *Ibn Khaldun's Philosophy of History*, pp. 18–26.

30 For Ibn Khaldun, the state was not conceived as an abstraction; it was always a concrete historical phenomenon equated with a dynasty. The dynasty created the state and the state ceased to exist with the collapse of the dynasty. The Arabic word for "state" and for "dynasty" was the same (*dawlah*): introduction by Franz Rosenthal to the *Muqaddimah*, p. xi.

31 Ira M. Lapidus, *A History of Islamic Societies* (Cambridge: Cambridge University Press, 1988), p. 251, suggests that in the twentieth century the continuing strength of Islam is demonstrated in its ability to give a new social identity to peoples severed from their traditional social structures. Other works I have found useful towards an understanding of the political ontology of Islam are Ernest Gellner, *Muslim Society* (Cambridge: Cambridge University Press, 1981); and R. M. Savory (ed.), *Introduction to Islamic Civilization* (Cambridge: Cambridge University Press, 1976).

32 Benedetto Croce, *Ce qui est vivant et ce qui est mort de la philosophie de Hegel*, trans. by Henri Buriot (Paris: V. Giard and E. Brière, 1910).

33 In different historical phases, Shi'ism in Persia was taken over and domesticated by the state as a form of state religion. Throughout such phases, it did, however, remain a latent subversive force in relation to the state.

34 Mahdi, *Ibn Khaldun's Philosophy of History*, pp. 103–125.

35 Ibid., pp. 89–91.

36 Ibid., pp. 64–71.

37 The resemblance between Ibn Khaldun's work and that of Giambattista Vico, who composed his *New Science* in Naples in the early years of the eighteenth century, has been contested by some scholars of Ibn Khaldun. The grounds on which they discard the comparison are the ontological positions of the two theorists concerning a cyclical interpretation of history. There are undoubtedly differences between Ibn Khaldun's and Vico's cycles. There is also a similarity in the interpretation of decadence, the problem that most concerned both. More striking to me is their resemblance on epistemological grounds, notably in Vico's joining of certainty (concerning events) with a rational understanding of principles of "ideal eternal history" underlying events and providing a hermeneutical guide for the understanding of events. There is, of course, no evidence that Vico knew Ibn Khaldun's work directly. The intriguing question remains whether he might have, whether at first or second hand. Vico's prudence in avoiding censure by the Inquisition, still active in Naples during his lifetime, would have precluded his acknowledging an Islamic author. But Naples, as a crossroads of Mediterranean cultures, would also have been a privileged position in Europe for contact with Islamic literature.

38 Lacoste, *Ibn Khaldun*, pp. 110–117.

39 Ibid., p. 116. Ibn Khaldun discerned a circulation of *'asabiya* among dominant and subordinate groups linked together through political power. A decadent dynasty could be confronted by the gathering strength of a hitherto subordinate group which could overcome and displace it, founding a new dynasty: *Muqaddimah*, p. 108.

40 Mahmoud Dhaouadi, "Ibn Khaldun: The Founding Father of Eastern Sociology," *International Sociology*, vol. 5, no. 3 (September 1990), pp. 316–335. Gellner, *Muslim Society*, writes: "The traditional Muslim state is simultaneously and without contradiction both a Robber State, run for the benefit of the dominant group, and a moralistic state, bound to promote good and proscribe evil. It is carried by and identified with a dominant group, yet it also has an inbuilt vocation towards the implementation of a sharply identified divine order on earth" (p. 47). The necessary relationship between these two aspects was clear to Ibn Khaldun when he wrote: "The truth one must know is that no religious or political propaganda can be successful, unless power and group feeling ['asabiya] exist to support the religious and political aspirations and to defend them against those who reject them" (*Muqaddimah*, p. 258).

41 Mahdi, *Ibn Khaldun's Philosophy of History*, pp. 125–132.

42 Ibid., p. 256.

43 Arnold Toynbee praised Ibn Khaldun as a great, perhaps the greatest, philosopher of history. Toynbee certainly borrowed from him some of his leading ideas, including the principle that physical environments must not be either too hard or too lush in order that they stimulate the development of civilization (Arnold Toynbee, *A Study of History*, abridgement of volumes I–IV by D. C. Somervell (Oxford: Geoffrey Cumberledge, 1946), vol.

I, ch. 7 and 8; and vol. XII, *Reconsiderations* (London: Oxford University Press, 1961), p. 205). Gellner considers Ibn Khaldun to be the best interpreter of Islamic society and a sociologist whose theoretical insights are comparable to those of Durkheim and Weber. A recent Foucauldian interpretation, on the other hand, finds little in Ibn Khaldun's work that would not have been common knowledge in his time – no paradigmatic unity, no epistemological break, no coherent discourse, but only a cluster of conventional discourses (Aziz Al-Azmeh, *Reinterpretation*, pp. 146–162).

Some commentators have pictured Ibn Khaldun as the father of sociology, and have emphasized the rationalist, empirical element in his work, perceiving him as continuous with the Aristotelian–Averroist current of Islamic thought and a forerunner of a modernist secular Islam (Simon, *Ibn Khaldun's Science of Human Culture*). Others, by contrast, stress his religious commitment (H. A. R. Gibb, "The Islamic Background of Ibn Khaldun's Political Theory," *Bulletin of the School of Oriental and African Studies*, vol. 7 (1933–35), pp. 23–31).

The revival of Ibn Khaldun has also nourished the revival of Arab and Islamic nationalism. He has been read as showing the means of Arab renaissance through an *'asabiya* capable of creating unity in a modern pan-Arab state. This interpretation has been seen as strengthening both the Ba'ath concept of a secular Islam, and the Qadafist and Muslim Brothers' notion of Islam providing the cohesive force for national restoration on the scale of the whole Islamic world (Olivier Carre, in Majallat Et-Tarikh, *Actes*, pp. 264–65).

One recent study views Ibn Khaldun's analysis of the fourteenth-century Maghreb as probing the underlying causes of underdevelopment and as giving a clue why economic development in Third World conditions has taken a different course from western capitalism (Lacoste, *Ibn Khaldun*).

44 Aziz Al-Azmeh, *Reinterpretation*, pp. 11–33.
45 Isaiah Berlin, *Two Concepts of Liberty* (Oxford: Clarendon Press, 1958), p. 57. The "admirable writer of our time" was, I think, Joseph Schumpeter, but I have not been able to trace the source of the quotation.
46 Much as Gramsci envisaged the modern prince not as an individual but as the party.

9 "Take six eggs": theory, finance, and the real economy in the work of Susan Strange (1992)

In the April 1970 issue of the Chatham House journal *International Affairs* there appeared an article by Susan Strange entitled "International Economics and International Relations: A Case of Mutual Neglect."[1] In retrospect, it has the appearance of a manifesto. It challenged the dividing and enclosing practice that is characteristic of academic disciplines. It pointed to a gap in understanding of the economic power relationships that underpin world politics. It directed the way towards the definition of an area of study that soon became identified as international political economy.

Academia, in turn, moved to assimilate and consecrate IPE as yet another compartment of knowledge with its own certified practitioners. New orthodoxies watched over by new hierarchies of initiates took charge of it. Susan Strange never gave them her official blessing. They never succeeded in taming her iconoclasm. She continued swift as a corsair to harass the plodding convoys of the new conventional thinking.

Her initiative of 1970 was followed up by other authors in a variety of ways. It found a response among some political scientists who began to explore international economic relations as a special sphere of politics – the methods of political analysis brought to a new domain. An early major textbook by Joan Spero, published first in 1977, is called *The Politics of International Economic Relations*.[2] Much American scholarship continued to be grounded in political science perspectives, in the framework of actors and interactions, the political processes of international economic relations, who does what to whom.

Meanwhile, in another intellectual world, reflection upon imperialism from the sources of Rosa Luxemburg and Lenin was generating a different perspective, this one focusing upon structures rather than actors and interactions. Immanuel Wallerstein's *The Modern World-System*,[3] a key work in this current of scholarship, was published in 1974. The Marxian tradition was more comfortable with the term "political economy." The origin of the term lay in the classical theorists of the late eighteenth and early nineteenth century whom Marx subjected to his "critique of political economy." The term brought power back into a formal economics that had been abstracted out of a real world – the power relations of capital, land, and labor, of core and periphery.

Yet the two currents of scholarship had no common point of contact. The adoption of the term "political economy" by the American current did not mean a departure from the positivism of the actors/interactions perspective, from methodological individualism. Robert Gilpin's *The Political Economy of International Relations*[4] attempted, if not a reconciliation, at least a confrontation of perspectives; but it remained squarely in the American tradition.

Nor did the Marxian current go much beyond discussion of accumulation at the world level.[5] Susan Strange meanwhile had taken some distance from the concept of accumulation. The critical factor, for her, was credit, not accumulation. Power in the world economy lay as she saw it in the ability to create credit and to have access to credit.

Perhaps the most promising advance from the Marxian side was an article by Bernadette Madeuf and Charles-Albert Michalet called "A New Approach to International Economics,"[6] which suggested the emergence of a global economy, superimposed upon and interrelated with the international economy of conventional economics. The global economy is characterized by global production systems and global financial networks that transcend territorial boundaries, while the international economy is conceived in terms of flows of trade, investments, and money among territorial entities. The problem of understanding now focused upon the interrelationships of the two.

In *States and Markets*,[7] Susan Strange came back to the problem of defining an approach to IPE. Mutual neglect, which posits two distinct fields, gave place to an attempt to ground work in the field in a unifying perspective – not unifying in the sense of some overarching definitive theory, but unifying in the sense of the search for common concepts and alternative approaches to understanding and explaining what goes on in an arena of human activity that is unified by structures, institutions, activities, and outcomes. *States and Markets* carries the search for understanding one step further and cheers us on to the next step. That was its purpose and its achievement.

Six eggs and the role of theory[8]

How does a new field of academic enquiry come into existence? Not surely through some form of intellectual parthenogenesis whereby existing realms of academic enquiry subdivide and multiply on their own. The new field is born from the fertilization of experienced reality. Something important is going on that the academy cannot explain to our satisfaction. Sensitivity to the real world is the primary ingredient, a sensitivity that is the salient qualification of the good journalist.

The journalist is also concerned with how things actually work, and interviews the people who are doing things to find out what they think they are doing. The next stage goes beyond the general practice of journalism. It is to draw back from the action in order to try to perceive the structures within which action takes place. The best journalism rises to this level which is that of the historian, or, as Vico would have it, the adding of philosophy (the search for sustainable generalizations) to the achievements of philology (the discovery of what actually happens).[9]

This approach to theory, which I take to be that of Susan Strange, is very different from some of the grander notions of theory. There is a kind of Theory (with a capital "T") that we can call theological, whose adepts conceive it as the revelation of the inner essence of the universe, the deep and abstract explanation of everything. The theological vision is common to some Marxists and some liberals. Theological Marxists go on about the "law of value" and the "laws of motion of capital" not as hypotheses but as absolute knowledge. Louis Althusser wrote: "It has been possible to apply Marx's theory with success because it is 'true'; it is not true because it has been applied with success."[10] Theological liberals have a vision of a universal human nature and a heaven of perfect markets with perfect information from which economic behavior can be deduced and which is the ultimate guarantee of human freedom.

This is all very different from the approach which sees theory as the construction of explanatory hypotheses that can be used heuristically in trying to understand better what is going on, or what went on at some earlier time. Braudel used the metaphor of a ship to characterize such hypotheses.[11] The trick was to find out in which set of circumstances the ship would sail well. You do not scuttle a ship because it will not sail in every circumstance. You take care not to use it where it will not work, but you do use it where it will. Susan Strange's sense of theory is similar to that of Braudel.

First, we have to know what it is we are setting out to do. Then we need to know what probably are the relevant factors that enter into the doing of it (the required six eggs). Then we need to imagine (hypothesize) some of the possible relationships among the factors that determine outcomes.

The first question is of practical importance: what are we setting out to do? Susan Strange's answer is that theory should be a help in dealing with some practical question that does not have a self-evident answer, e.g., "why do states fail to act to regulate and stabilize an international financial system which is known to be vitally necessary to the 'real economy' but which all the experts in and out of government now agree is in dangerous need of more regulation for its own safety?"[12] Indeed, this particular practical question may be read as the consistent theme of Susan Strange's work.

I would add another question to her series leading up to theory. This question concerns purpose. Is the purpose to fix something that is putting the existing order at risk, i.e., to conserve the existing order by reforming it? Or is the purpose to make a critical analysis of the existing order so as to be able to change it?[13] *States and Markets* does not entirely evade the issue, but leaves it as a matter of taste. *De gustibus non disputandum.*

The sociology of theorizing: loners and groupies

As Susan Strange frequently pointed out, often innovative thinking has come from people outside the more recognized schools of academic thought. Some were public officials, whether of national governments or international organizations, who were able to stand apart from their practical experiences to reflect upon the dynamics and relationships at work. Business-school economists were often more alive to the power factor and the importance of organization and process than were the academically more "pure" economists. Some stimulus came from other disciplines. The historian Fernand Braudel's vast study of structural changes through the centuries illuminated the

177

contemporary world, raising different kinds of questions than those prompted by the rational-choice calculations of political scientists or economists. The field for investigation was not a subdivision of political science or of economics, nor was it some amalgam of the two. It had to be defined in its own distinctiveness; and it should remain an open field.

A number of the authors Susan Strange considers favorably she describes as loners. Since the idea occurs so regularly, it is perhaps of interest to consider its implications for theorizing. The loner does not fit into any predefined category, does not fit into conventional classifications like left and right, is not easily assimilated to any school or sect.

The contrast type I shall call the groupie. Groupies are the more common type, so they should be considered first. Graduate education is more or less designed to produce groupies. They speak within a consecrated discourse, i.e., the concepts and issues recognized as legitimate by a prominent school of academics. Students are socialized to the discourse by professional training and career ladders that inspire a desire for affiliation and acceptance, and which unconsciously are conducive to conformity.

There is something of a choice the neophyte can make among groups, schools, and sects, although the student will become aware of the hierarchy of respect (and attendant fundraising potential) accorded these different intellectual networks. Thus there may be a natural desire for emulation on the part of the student, or a more cynical tradeoff of convictions and professional opportunities. All this is not very new. Max Weber raised these issues, though he did not resolve them, in discussing the academic career in his essay on science as a vocation.[14]

To become a groupie, you have to be admitted by the gatekeeper. This is where the key questions are asked. Do you use the right concepts? Have you addressed the correct issues? Have you taken account of the previous debate among members of the group? (It doesn't much matter what people outside the group may have written.) Once properly endorsed with the unwritten certification of the invisible network, then you may be considered for publication in the recognized journals and find peer reviewers from among members of the group for your longer manuscripts.

Loners live on the margins. They may have an unconventional background. They may not have been trained in the particular department of the "discipline." Sometimes, they are people who have had experience outside academia. They may come from another "discipline." In the IPE field, Susan Strange has noted the contributions of people who have backgrounds in history, management studies, development economics, and sociology. Loners tend to define their own issues and their own conceptual frameworks. For this reason, they are sometimes "difficult" to read, i.e., one encounters the unexpected and the unfamiliar. They do not recount the debates of the groups or write primarily for the attention of the groups.

Individual loners may influence other loners, may even occasionally be noticed (with appropriate qualifications) by some groups. Groupies may become organic intellectuals (in Gramsci's sense) of particular social forces, or at least they may aspire to play that role. Loners may think as organic intellectuals but often it is their fate to remain politically unconnected. One risk for a loner is inadvertently to become a guru, attracting a new set of groupies and thereby forfeiting status as a loner. In the emergence of a new way of looking at the world, or a new paradigm, loners may have something to say. One might even speculate that a proliferation of loners is an indicator of crisis in received opinion, perhaps even a crisis of hegemony.

Real and symbolic economies

Susan Strange's work since her early publications[15] has focused primarily on finance. Money is a symbol. Goods and services are the products of the "real economy." The relationship between real and symbolic economies – the economy understood in terms of production and the economy understood in terms of finance – is always a fundamental question. There is, of course, no uniform answer to the question. We cannot say that finance, or alternatively production, is always the determining force. It is crucial to know which, at any particular historical juncture, is of paramount importance.

I have been asked to comment on "[t]he differences that you and she have over the primacy of credit versus production." These are certainly differences in the object of enquiry. Whether they are differences in the evaluation of the relative weight of the real and the symbolic in the present world conjuncture I am less certain.

I start from the position that the existence and the health of the real economy is fundamental. The observation is not trite. We can see that a real existing economy can be reduced to a shambles and thereby cause enormous misery to a large mass of people. *Perestroika* achieved this. It is quite possible that financial mismanagement and ideological fixation could achieve comparable devastation in the capitalist West. (It seems less likely to happen, as a practical matter, in the capitalist East.) The real economy requires a guidance and regulatory mechanism. Politics and finance can provide this – or destroy it.

I have been inclined to think that the resources that make for financial and political power depend ultimately upon the real economy. "Ultimately" in the sense that without a healthy real economy, financial and political power will become dissolved. But the real economy can just as surely be damaged by political and financial mismanagement. The key question is not which is the more important, but what is the relationship between them.

There is a third factor: the social. It intervenes between the real economy on one side, and financial and political power on the other. The social is often equated with the spirit of generosity – with idealism in a world of realism. That is a nice, if condescending, way of thinking of it but not what I have in mind here. The social factor concerns the coherence, the inner strength and resilience of a society and its capacity to sustain a political superstructure.

Nineteenth-century realist conservative politicians like Bismarck and Disraeli understood this well. They practiced their art during a period of deep transformation in modes of living, in class structures, and in movements of peoples. The Bismarcks and Disraelis knew they had to secure the support of the working population, to lay the foundations for personal and family security of those upon whose work the real economy depended, and upon whose loyalty the state rested. The same quality of perception is not so evident among politicians today, especially among the "neoconservatives" who intone the words "globalization," "competitiveness," and "structural adjustment" while their populations face, with reduced public help, transformations of an intensity comparable to those of the nineteenth century.

The social factor is intrinsically linked to the real economy, the economy of production. If the guiding mechanisms of finance and politics fail to sustain the real economy, then the social factor becomes the conduit of feedback to politics; and politics, in crisis, is the only power able to take hold of finance. In *Casino Capitalism*,[16] Susan Strange made this point forcefully. The problem she diagnosed is that the symbolic economy has (since the mid-1970s) become decoupled from the real economy.[17] It has become the playground for junk-bond dealers, leveraged-buyout specialists, and risk arbitragers.

The issue between accumulation and credit fits in here. We need not think of accumulation as the amassing of profits that firms invest in new productive capacity. Susan Strange is surely right to argue that the ability to tap credit, more than the profits earned in the last cycle of production, determine a firm's ability to expand.

Accumulation can rather be thought of in non-monetary, even nonquantifiable terms as the hierarchy of social structures of production.[a] At the bottom of the hierarchy is the household that reproduces labor, both in the sense of a new generation of producers and in the sense of a reviving of the ability to produce from day to day. Then there are the poorly rewarded, the precariously employed, who, in turn, provide the services and the inputs for the more skilled and securely employed; and those skilled and securely employed provide the scope for the innovators, designers, and organizers of the real economy. Each step up the scale commands greater resources. Those at the bottom have no plastic (i.e., credit cards). Those in the middle have green plastic. Those at the top have gold. Accumulation, in this sense, is a social hierarchy that defines the power structure of the real economy. It has a certain relationship to credit; but when credit at the top behaves in unpredictable and unstable ways, feeding on itself rather than nourishing the real economy, the social structure and the financial structure become dangerously severed.

Financial manipulators operate within an entirely different timeframe than that of the organizers of production. The distinction is between the synchronic and the diachronic. Financial calculations take place in an instantaneous global electronic network in which fortunes are made and lost at the speed of electricity. Production takes time to plan, research, develop, install, train, and put into operation. Its efficacy is influenced by local cultures and the social climate.[18]

The decoupling of finance from production made production vulnerable to the unpredictable effects of financial speculation. Much of the effect of unregulated global finance is destructive of production.

---

[a] On Cox's use of "accumulation" also see *Production, Power, and World Order: Social Forces in the Making of History* (New York: Columbia University Press, 1987), pp. 5–9. In that text Cox observes, "To explain the mechanisms of accumulation in each mode and the crises to which each is subject delineates the physiology of power in ... society" (p. 6).

Leveraged buyouts followed by the selloff of assets increase paper profits and speculative fevers while reducing the productive capacity of the real economy.[b] (The military factor is also a drain on the real economy. Military production is the accumulation of waste. Even the development of military technology, which once had a spillover effect into civilian production, now seems to depend more on civilian research.)[c]

Finance has been allowed to become decoupled not only from production but also from politics – a condition consecrated by the neoconservative dogma that there should be no political intervention in the working of the abstract but intractable laws of economics (Milton Friedman *dixit*). Politicians today are trying to entrench constitutional impediments to states intervening in economic and monetary affairs, so strong is faith in the virtue of the impersonal workings of the market.

The creation of credit depends upon confidence. Confidence rests on power. The United States is the center of world power in its various aspects – military, financial, and productive – but US productive power is lagging rather seriously behind its military power, and US financial power may be in a vulnerable condition. Danger lies in an unstable, disconnected relationship between productive, financial, and military power at the top of the world system.

It seems doubtful that you can pick one element, credit, and make it the key factor. I do not think Susan Strange does this, though others may read this meaning into her emphasis on global finance. Certainly credit is a big part of the problem; but the credit problem hangs upon political changes in which the role of the United States is crucial.

The real question, and the one concerning which Susan Strange has appeared as Cassandra, is whether the US domestic political system is capable of the decisions that would make a global solution possible. The US economy has become used to a level of consumption both military and civilian that is not sustained by US production.

---

[b] Here Cox is in disagreement with the literature supporting the thesis that predatory financial manipulators have made capitalism "better" or more efficient. An example of this view, which focuses on the pressure LBOs place on management to perform, is Glen Yago, *Junk Bonds: How High Yield Securities Restructured Corporate America* (New York: Oxford University Press, 1991). In Cox's view, predatory financial activities are an aspect of the broader issue of whether the financial "mentality" can be creative in real economy terms. On this issue, see Cox's reference to Sorel in endnote 18 of this essay.

[c] On this theme, see "Production and Security," chapter 14 in this volume.

Foreigners, and recently especially Japanese, have paid the difference. No US politician will tell the electorate they must face a reduction in living levels, although many voters sense that is happening anyway. At the same time as they are more dependent upon the flow of Japanese capital, Americans are becoming more fearful of Japanese penetration into their real economy, more hostile to their creditor. The contradictions of US economy and society are becoming more and more evident – wealth and poverty, external power and internal impotence. When this happens in the world's preeminent military power everyone has cause for concern.

The ontology of world order

Susan Strange proclaims herself a realist; but she certainly cannot be classified with those theorists who posit an exclusively state-centered view of world political economy or with the oversimplifications of neorealism. Her realism is a search for the effective entities of world politics, whatever they may turn out to be. Instead of defining the world exclusively in terms of states, she sees power as the basic concern of realism and asks: Where does power lie? With states certainly, to some degree, but also with markets. With firms, too, and possibly with some other entities. The answer is not given with the question, and the answer is subject to change.

Indeed, she, like some others, has observed that the contemporary world is beginning to look more like the European Middle Ages than the Westphalian system that has served as a paradigm for international relations scholars these many years. Cities are again meaningful centers of global interactions. Provinces achieve autonomy as states lose efficacy; and macro-regions take on some of the roles hitherto performed by states. The loyalties of individuals are multiple, not unique – loyalties to nation, to firm, to ideology, to ethnicity or gender. The "business civilization"[19] with its universal norms of economic and political conduct, and its homogeneity of tastes and hierarchy of values molded in global consumerism, is the tawdry latter-day counterpart to theological universalism and disputes over the primacy of papacy or empire.

Furthermore, she is not content with the narrowly political science actors–interactions approach to political process. Relational power (the ability of one actor to influence others) is encompassed within structural power (the ability to shape the frameworks of interaction).

Perhaps her structural power sometimes seems to retain too much of relational power, when she speaks of the United States as determining the frameworks. Perhaps she appears to underestimate the autonomy of frameworks, their basis in intersubjective meanings, in acquired and deeply rooted habits of thought, sustained, to be sure by a hierarchy of real power, but not necessarily shaped consciously by powerful states. This, however, is a quibble that in no way detracts from the importance of drawing attention to structures and the power inherent in structures, which may not always be the power consciously to make structures. This is surely an area of investigation that will be fruitful in discerning what kind of world order may be emerging.

She has, indeed, been raising some questions for this investigation. There are, in her ontology, four forms of power: security (military), production, finance, and knowledge. She calls these "structures," a term I would prefer to reserve for the ways these forms of power are combined in particular historical configurations; but her meaning is clear.

Two of these forms, I would argue, constitute the immediate or short-term forms of power: military-political and financial. These forms of power are most determining of outcomes of events. They correspond most to the synchronic dimension of history. The other two forms of power, production and knowledge, are of longer-term importance. They are constitutive of what Fernand Braudel called the *longue durée*. The knowledge form has to be broadened beyond science and technology to embrace the ways in which people understand the world, the construction and maintenance of the intersubjective meanings that make communication possible.

This is a vast program for a study that goes beyond the meaning of that Westphalian-era term "international relations." It envisages a redefinition of the object of enquiry in terms meaningful for the late twentieth century.

The world according to Susan Strange

The central theme of her work in recent years has been the shift of power from states to markets – and particularly from that most powerful of states, the United States, to that most influential of markets, the global financial market. There are other forms of power as well – military power, productive capacity, and technology – but the focal point of her interest lies in the relationship of states to global finance.

The shift was not something buried deep in the impersonal dynamics of history or in the laws of motion of capital. It was something brought about by the action of the United States government and the collateral action of other governments, notably the British.[20] It was initiated by a deliberate decision to allow the growth of an unregulated Eurodollar market, and furthered by subsequent measures of financial deregulation. States are now limited in their options by this financial power they have allowed to take over.

There are, however, no inexorable laws of history, and no necessary irreversibility of trends. It is not inconceivable that this new global financial market can become reregulated, and domesticated to serve the human community.

Susan Strange's injunction to the scholar is to ask the question: *Cui bono?* Who wins in the globalizing of finance and the globalizing of production? Who loses? Although she does not lean heavily upon the point, it is clear that she sees this process as generating social and economic polarization; and it is a small further step to recognize that such polarization of winners and losers can engender political conflict. Military power is, of course, a deterrent, but there are ways of fighting dominant military power without building up a comparable power, ways of making it difficult to govern a reluctant population. Both Palestine and eastern Europe offer recent examples.

Following upon *cui bono?*, the next question is "What is to be done?" Susan Strange has some tentative answers. The first is negative: put not your trust in international organizations, especially those concerned with finance. They are little more than facades for real power. Ultimately, the only power capable of reregulating the world financial order, in her analysis, is the United States government.

If this were to occur, it would surely revive the postwar battle between the Treasury in Washington and Wall Street. But it seems unlikely to occur. The US political system, as I have suggested, stands in the way. Ordinary Americans have benefited too long from their country's abuse of the dollar's world role and the ability it has given them to extract savings from other people to compensate their own unknowing profligacy. US politicians will not confront them with the hard choices. In the perspective of foreigners, elections bring out the most intractable features in the American psyche; and American elections are frequent and of long duration. Furthermore, other people, deferential to US military-political power, continue to acquiesce (but for how long?) in the extraction of tribute.

Susan Strange has exhorted Americans, in government especially and in business, to cease using their power in a unilateral and manipulative way as they have during the past couple of decades and to resume a leadership of the postwar kind that would be for the benefit of the world system as a whole and not least for the long-term interests of the United States. Her analysis may not be very flattering for Americans, but there can be no denying that she is pro-American. She would like nothing better than to see the United States become the effective center of a transnational invisible empire.[21]

There seems little prospect of this happening, that is to say, of the United States accepting the tough discipline that would be the condition, as she sees it, for taking this leadership.

There is, however, a fall-back position: currency blocs.[22] Trade blocs of the 1930s kind are highly unlikely in a globalized economy in which, as she says, struggle for market shares is "the name of the game"; but faced with a persistence of an unregulated global financial system, the yen and the ecu are most likely to want to build defenses against vulnerability to erratic and manipulated movements of the dollar. These other currency blocs could put external pressure on the United States to mend its fiscal ways. One could even imagine a movement towards Japanese–European cooperation to initiate a different leadership in global finance, to challenge what Susan Strange sees as the persistent but abused structural power of the United States over global finance. But this latter development, in the current climate of edginess Europeans seem to feel towards Japanese economic expansionism, may be as unlikely as renewed US consensual leadership.

One gnawing question remains. To what end would reform of the global financial system be undertaken? In whose interest? Is it primarily in the interest of a stable and predictable environment for transnational corporations to go about their business?

One can come away with the impression that Susan Strange sees this as the optimum future; that global business will make the best of all possible worlds for most people. Is trickle-down the best hope? Or is it possible that global finance could be reregulated so as to make it possible for states to regain the control over domestic social and economic futures that is being lost in the struggle for world market shares? Susan Strange has not yet addressed this question; and those of us who are unprepared to confide our grandchildren's fates to the all-too-visible hands of transnational business must hope that she and others will take up the issue. Pessimism of the intellect has given us a good picture of the limits of the possible. We await the optimism of the will that can show with some realism the way ahead.

Notes

This essay is published here for the first time. It was first presented at a panel to celebrate Susan Strange as eminent scholar at the International Studies Association conference, Atlanta, March–April 1992.

1 Susan Strange, "International Economics and International Relations: A Case of Mutual Neglect," *International Affairs*, vol. 46, no. 2 (April 1970), pp. 304–315.

2 Joan Spero, *The Politics of International Economic Relations* (New York: St. Martin's Press, 1977).

3 Immanuel Wallerstein, *The Modern World-System: Capitalist Agriculture and the Origins of the European World-Economy in the Sixteenth Century* (New York: Academic Press, 1974).

4 Robert Gilpin, *The Political Economy of International Relations* (Princeton, N.J.: Princeton University Press, 1987).

5 Samir Amin, *Accumulation on a World Scale* (New York: Monthly Review Press, 1974).

6 Bernadette Madeuf and C.-A. Michalet, "A New Approach to International Economics," *International Social Science Journal*, vol. 30, no. 2 (1978), pp. 253–283.

7 Susan Strange, *States and Markets: An Introduction to International Political Economy* (London: Pinter, 1988).

8 In case anyone has not read *States and Markets*, "Take six eggs" is the heading (p. 230) that introduces the summation of Strange's theoretical framework.

9 *The New Science of Giambattista Vico*, trans. by Thomas Goddard Bergin and Max Harold Fisch (Ithaca, N.Y.: Cornell University Press, 1970). This work of the eighteenth-century Neapolitan philosopher-philologist still has a lot to tell us about method in social science.

10 Louis Althusser and Etienne Balibar, *Reading Capital*, trans. by Ben Brewster (London: New Left Books, 1979), p. 59. Jean Guitton, the French Catholic theologian who was Althusser's teacher when, in his youth, Althusser was a member of *Action catholique*, and with whom Althusser kept contact throughout his career, believed that Althusser retained the same theological cast of mind throughout his adult life.

11 Fernand Braudel, "History and the Social Sciences: The *Longue Durée*," in *On History*, trans. by Sarah Matthews (Chicago: University of Chicago Press, 1980), pp. 25–59.

12 Strange, *States and Markets*, p. 11.

13 I have made the distinction between problem-solving and critical theory in

"Social Forces, States, and World Orders: Beyond International Relations Theory," chapter 6 in this collection.

14 H. H. Gerth and C. Wright Mills (eds.), *From Max Weber* (London: Routledge and Kegan Paul, 1948), pp. 129–156.

15 Especially, Strange, *Sterling and British Policy: A Political Study of an International Currency in Decline* (London: Oxford University Press for the Royal Institute of International Affairs, 1971); also, Strange, "The Meaning of Multilateral Surveillance," in Robert W. Cox (ed.), *International Organization: World Politics. Studies in Economic and Social Agencies* (London: Macmillan, 1969).

16 Susan Strange, *Casino Capitalism* (Oxford: Basil Blackwell, 1986).

17 Peter Drucker, "The Changed World Economy," *Foreign Affairs*, vol. 64, no. 4 (Spring 1986), pp. 768–791, made the same point. David Gordon, "The Global Economy: New Edifice or Crumbling Foundations," *New Left Review*, vol. 168 (March–April 1988), p. 55, placed the shift from real productive investment to paper investment as happening during the late 1960s and early 1970s. A fall in corporate profit rates accompanied by more uncertainty about exchange rates and interest rates encouraged this switch.

18 The synchronic and the diachronic are more than two dimensions of time. The synchronic framework fits with the market mentality (which Karl Polanyi rather prematurely called "outmoded"). The diachronic, the time of duration, encompasses complex social processes. Georges Sorel touched upon this distinction when he wrote that in every significant body of knowledge a clear and an obscure region can be distinguished. In ethics, maxims about equitable relations between people can, he wrote, be clearly stated; while the obscure part concerns sexual relations. Similarly, he argued, in economics, the easy part concerns exchange, whereas the difficult and obscure part concerns production. The former can be expressed in theorems more or less valid everywhere; the latter requires an intimate knowledge of historical process and particular cases: *Reflections on Violence*, trans. by T. E. Hulme (New York: Peter Smith, 1941), pp. 159–161. It is important not to try to reduce the understanding of the difficult part to the deductive formulas that have been applied to the easy part.

19 Susan Strange, "The Name of the Game," in Nicholas X. Rizopoulos (ed.), *Sea Changes: American Foreign Policy in a World Transformed* (New York: Council on Foreign Relations, 1990).

20 Susan Strange, "An Eclectic Approach," in Craig Murphy and Roger Tooze (eds.), *The New International Political Economy* (Boulder, Colo.: Lynne Rienner, 1991).

21 Susan Strange, "Towards a Theory of Transnational Empire," in Ernst-Otto Czempiel and James N. Rosenau (eds.), *Global Changes and Theoretical Challenges: Approaches to World Politics for the 1990s* (Lexington, Mass.: Lexington Books, 1989), pp. 161–176.

22 Susan Strange, "The Transnational Financial System of the 1990s," unpublished paper presented to the International Studies Association Conference, Vancouver, March 1991.

Part III
Interpretations

10 The global political economy and social choice (1991)

In the late twentieth century, a powerful globalizing economic trend thrusts toward the achievement of a market utopia on the world scale. At the present moment, no counter-tendency effectively challenges the globalization thrust. The market appears to be bursting free from the bonds of national societies, subjecting a global society to its laws. Yet, as Karl Polanyi discerned of nineteenth-century Britain, the freeing of the market can in the longer run provoke an equally powerful reaction as society seeks to curb its disintegrating and alienating consequences. Already, elements of opposition to the socially disruptive consequences of globalization are visible. The question remains open as to what form these may take, as to when and how they may become more coherent and more powerful.

The answer hinges on changes in the power relationships among social groups on the world scale.[1] In particular, it implies a weakening of the arrangements for management of international economic relations as put in place during the *pax americana* of the postwar world. But, the taming and civilizing of the market presupposes a development of social and political forces that are global in their reach. Such social forces are emerging among women, environmentalists, peace activists, indigenous peoples, trade unions, and churches, to name but a few examples of popular sector movements that increasingly are opposed to the harmful consequences of globalization. These movements present a dramatically different range of social choices and have the potential, if they can merge their consciousness and concerns, for a new political discourse.

Unfortunately, the left has either remained mired in its Keynesian positions of the 1960s, even more than usually fragmented by polemical sectarianism, or else (as in the case of some social democrats) has seemingly accepted the neoconservative rationale of globalization without being very clear about how this is to be reconciled with socialism's commitment to social equity. There is an intellectual vacuum to be filled – a challenge to critical thinking on the left.

At the heart of the challenge is the question of the motive force for change. One effect of the globalization of production is that one can no longer speak very meaningfully of the "working class" as a unified social force on the national, let alone world, level. The working class now has a fragmented objective existence and a very problematic common consciousness. In the new emerging social structure, categories defined solely in relation to production are complicated by the categories of gender, ethnicity, religion, and region, since these are often the basis for segmentation. These categories do not displace production as a primordial factor in the structuring of society. They become intermediate factors, the basis for self-awareness of group identities, between production relations and social forces.

Thus, the political basis for social action to confront the emerging global trends has to be rethought and recomposed in relation to the strategies of the past. By analyzing the dynamics of the restructuring of social relations on a world scale, it is possible to see how changes in production become the basis for social movements for change, and for new forms of state and of world order.

The globalization thrust

The analysis of globalization must begin with the internationalization of production. The internationalizing process results when capital considers the productive resources of the world as a whole and locates elements of complex globalized production systems at points of greatest cost advantage. The critical factor is information on how to combine most profitably components in the production process.

Multinational corporations have encouraged this kind of thinking and planning, but the component elements now include joint enterprises, industrial cooperation agreements between multinationals and socialist-country enterprises, and world-class cottage industries as well as huge corporations. Producing units take advantage of abundant, cheap, and malleable labor where it is to be found, and of robotization where it is not. Transnational production requires an environment in which capital, technology, and inputs to the production process (whether raw materials or component parts), as well as finished goods, can cross borders relatively freely.

A second major development is the internationalizing of the state. Throughout most of this century, the role of states has been conceived as a buffer protecting the national economy from disruptive external forces so as to be able to encourage internal levels of economic activity sufficient to sustain adequate domestic employment and welfare. The state's priority was domestic welfare. In the past couple of decades, the priority has shifted to one of adapting domestic economies to the perceived exigencies of the world economy.

This has had an impact within the structures of national governments. Central agencies that act as conduits for the world economy (and in the cases of North America and of Europe, the continental economy) have become preeminent within governments over those agencies that deal with primarily internal affairs. Ministries of industry and ministries of labor used to combine with their respective domestic constituencies to guide and implement national economic policies. These domestic-oriented agencies have in practice been subordinated to ministries of finance and offices of presidents and prime ministers that provide the direct links between world-economy negotiations (through bodies like the OECD, the IMF, and the economic summits) and the development of national policies that implement the international consensus reached in these negotiations. Domestic economic and social interests have as a result been diminished as policy influences. The domestic-oriented agencies of the state are now more and more to be seen as transmission belts from world-economy trends and decision making into the domestic economy, as agencies to promote the carrying out of tasks they had no part in deciding.

Thirdly, the new international division of labor is creating a new pattern of uneven development. The concept of a "Third World" no longer has a clear meaning, since many of the countries once considered as belonging to it have either found some niche as producers of manufactures or natural resources (especially energy), or else have been relegated to a "Fourth World" sunken irretrievably in poverty. This "Fourth World" has become a concern of the world system not as a potential partner in future growth but as an object of poor relief and riot control.

The World Bank shifted its emphasis in the 1970s towards "absolute poverty" in the Fourth World, which it perceived as threatening social and political turmoil that could spill over into zones more integrated with the world economy in the form of regional conflicts and internal warfare. Economic aid for these countries became geared towards keeping people employed in low-productivity jobs (the celebrated "informal economy"), towards enabling them to provide for their own basic needs through do-it-yourself welfare, and towards limiting population growth so as to reduce the future size of the problem. A central concern of world-economy institutions became to prevent poverty somewhere becoming disruptive of growth elsewhere. This was the "poor relief" component of multilateral world-system policy. The "riot control" aspect was taken care of by bilateral military aid to repressive regimes for counterinsurgency and support of "low intensity" conflict.

Fourthly, the world economic crisis of the mid-1970s which ended a long phase of economic expansion stimulated by Keynesian demand management and Fordist industrialism brought about a new economic conjuncture. The rise in oil prices in the 1970s, combined with recession in the advanced capitalist countries, vastly increased liquidities held by the transnational banks which became avid lenders. Corporations were big borrowers, financing the restructuring of production through debt. Governments of newly industrializing economies (NICs) also borrowed heavily, because borrowing from private banks involved less onerous public policy conditions than borrowing from the IMF, and because they hoped to be able to service their debt by exporting the products of debt-financed industries.

The United States became the world's largest debtor nation, effectively internationalizing its public debt. The United States, however, escaped the fiscal pressures that bore more heavily on other countries because it was the source of the world's most widely used transaction and reserve currency. Americans could enjoy through debt a higher level of consumption than their production would otherwise have paid for because foreigners were ready to accept a flow of depreciating dollars. The longer-run consequence for Americans was growing foreign ownership of their economy, as depreciating dollars held by foreigners could best be used in buying US industries and real estate. The American economy lost its one-time lead in productivity, but its hour of reckoning was postponed by the dollar's hegemonic role in world finance.

As the debt problem for debtor countries other than the United States became critical during the 1980s, it accelerated all of the foregoing tendencies. Conditions for access to borrowing and for roll-over of existing debt became more closely tied to integration with the global economy and to the adoption of economic policies conducive to world-economy interests. Governments' accountability to foreign creditors came to outweigh accountability to their own citizens. They became the reluctant agents of international finance, which required of them freedom for transnational movements of capital, facility for the development of international production, devaluation of national currencies, raising of domestic prices, and allowing increased unemployment. The onus of adjustment has thus been placed upon labor and the more vulnerable social groups through cuts in government services, price rises in basic consumption items, and unemployment or pressures to accept substandard employment as the means of existence.

Fifthly, a global migration from South to North has been under way for some decades and may now be accelerating. By and large, our mindset has not adjusted to seeing this as a long-term trend; we prefer to think of it in terms of an apparently episodic "refugee problem." During the late nineteenth century (1870–1900), Europe's population grew by one hundred million. This increase was accommodated by Europe's shift from a predominantly rural to an increasingly urban civilization, and by the emigration of forty million persons in an era of imperialist expansionism. In the late twentieth century, a reverse movement of perhaps even larger proportions is in progress.

It would be more realistic to see migratory pressures as bound up with the other structural changes noted above. The internationalizing of production, as it penetrates into the peripheries of the world economy, benefits some social groups and disadvantages others. Peasants become marginalized as the more well-to-do farmers or cattle ranchers who produce cash crops for exports are able to take over land. Production of basic foods for local markets takes a low priority with governments strapped by debt and concerned above all with increasing export income. Export-oriented manufacturing provides low-income jobs for some of those displaced from rural life, especially women. The gap between loss of rural work opportunity and new industrial jobs is considerable, creating a migratory pressure directed, first, toward the nearby urban areas, and then outward towards other countries wherever access, legal or (more usually) illegal, is possible.

The typical form taken by the internationalizing of states in the Third World was until recently the military-bureaucratic regime that sought to encourage export-oriented development together with the enforcement as necessary of domestic austerity upon the politically excluded elements of society. Physical repression, ranging from widespread violations of human rights to open civil wars, generates the "refugee problem." In part, it may be explained by a political psychology of authoritarianism, but in its broadest terms, the refugee problem has to be understood as a systemic consequence of the globalization trend. Even where bureaucratic authoritarianism has been succeeded by fragile elected regimes, the impersonal pressures of the market and fears of insecurity continually replenish the migratory flow.

The new migratory movements from Third World to First World countries, combined with the downgrading of job opportunities in advanced capitalist countries (the McDonaldization of the workforce) constitute what has been called the "peripheralization of the core."[2] The new masses of low-paid, insecurely employed, unprotected workers are segmented into groups defined by gender, ethnicity, religion, and national origin.[3] They often perceive each other as enemies, rather than the system which subordinates them all. Segmentation perpetuates their political and economic weakness.

Finally, the cumulative result of all the above structural tendencies in the global political economy have rendered invalid the intellectual framework with which the state managers of the advanced capitalist countries confronted, relatively successfully, the problems of the postwar world. The neoclassical synthesis in economics ran aground on the stagflation of the 1960s and 1970s. Monetarism and supply-side economics claim succession to its hegemonic aura.

The left has yet to retool intellectually and develop a new critical perspective on the relationship between global change and social power. Take, for example, the concept of a core/periphery structuring of the world economy. The terms "core" and "periphery" were originally given a geographical meaning, distinguishing the economic-political metropoles from their dependent countries and territories.[4] These terms increasingly have to be given a social meaning as territorial boundaries and the efficacy of state regulation recede before the advance of the global economy and the big continental economies.

In the newer meaning, a relatively small core of personnel, closely integrated with capital in forms of enterprise corporatism, is to be distinguished from a segmented periphery of relatively disposable short-term, temporary, part-time, subcontracting, putting-out, and underground-economy producers, and also from the temporarily and permanently unemployed. Production organizations have shifted from the economies of scale of Fordist mass production, to the economies of flexibility of post-Fordism. These new technologies maximize the use of segmented workforces. The new semi-skilled workforces of the NICs' export platforms are predominantly female; ethnic differentiation in employment opportunities among various segments of peripheral labor is a universal phenomenon; and regional disparities provide the rationale for the differential location of labor-intensive and technology-intensive kinds of economic activity.

Alternatives in forms of state: hyperliberalism or state capitalism

The same tendencies as are bringing about the core/periphery restructuring of the production process also manifest themselves in mutations in the forms of states.[5]

It has become a commonplace on both left and right of the political spectrum that the capitalist state has both to support capital in its drive to accumulate and to legitimate this accumulation in the minds of the public by moderating the negative effects of accumulation on welfare and employment. As growth stagnates, the contradiction between the two functions of accumulation and legitimation sharpens. The contradiction manifests itself internally in the advanced capitalist country as a fiscal crisis, whereas for the late-industrializing Third World country it manifests itself as an exchange crisis. In the Soviet Union, socialist legitimacy underwritten by job security and equal access to basic needs is threatened by economic reform measures deemed necessary by the leadership to relaunch economic growth.[a]

As growth stagnated in advanced capitalist countries, governments in effect denounced the social contract worked out with capital and labor during the postwar economic boom. Governments had to balance the fear of political unrest from rising unemployment and exhaustion of welfare reserves against the fear that business would refrain from leading a recovery that would both revive employment and enlarge the tax base. In this circumstance they bent before the interests of capital.

---

[a] This has not abated under the Russian Republic and other Soviet successor states since the abolition of the Soviet Union on January 1, 1992.

During the postwar years, a neoliberal form of the state took shape in countries of advanced capitalism based on a negotiated consensus among the major industrial interests, organized labor, and government. It was "neo" in the sense that classical liberalism was modified by Keynesian practice to make market behavior consistent with social defense of the more disadvantaged groups. In the neoliberal consensus it had become accepted wisdom that society would not tolerate high unemployment or any dismantling of the welfare state. If these things were to occur, it would, it was said, cost the state the loss of its legitimacy. The truth of this statement has not been demonstrated uniformly. Indeed, it would more generally seem to be the case that the legitimacy of state welfare and of labor movements has been undermined in public opinion, not the legitimacy of the state. Large-scale unemployment has produced fear and concern for personal survival rather than collective protest. The unions are in strategic retreat, losing members, and unable, in general, to appeal to public opinion for support.

The disintegration of the neoliberal historic bloc was prepared by a collective effort of ideological revision undertaken through various unofficial agencies – the Trilateral Commission, the Bilderberg conferences, the Club of Rome, and other less prestigious forums – and then endorsed through more official consensus-making agencies such as the OECD. These agencies of latter-day neoliberalism prepared its demise. A new doctrine defined the tasks of states in relaunching capitalist development out of the depression of the 1970s. There was, in the words of a blue-ribbon OECD committee, a "narrow path to growth," bounded on one side by the need to encourage private investment by increasing profit margins, and bounded on the other by the need to avoid rekindling inflation.[6]

The government–business alliance formed to advance along this narrow path ruled out corporative-type solutions like negotiated wage and price policies and also the extension of public investment. It placed primary emphasis on restoring the confidence of business in government and in practice acknowledged that welfare and employment commitments made in the framework of the postwar social contract would have to take second place.

The restructuring of production has accentuated segmentation and divisions within the working class, but this tendency has not been uniform. In many western European countries, a long history of ideological education has maintained a sense of solidarity. The force of this tradition is much weaker in North America although it remains stronger in Canada than in the United States. In both Italy and France there have been instances where unions have maintained solidarity of action between migrant workers and local established workers, whereas in other instances these groups have been juxtaposed in opposition one to another. Segmentation has, however, been the underlying trend that explains the weakness of labor in preventing the disintegration of the neoliberal social consensus and in opposing the program put in its place by the government–business alliance.[7]

If the strains tending toward a disintegration of the neoliberal historic bloc have been visible since the mid-1970s, it would be premature to define the outlines of a new historic bloc likely to achieve any durability as the foundation of a new form of state. Two principal directions of movement in political structures are visible in the erstwhile neoliberal states: the confrontational tactics of Thatcherism in Britain and Reaganism in the United States toward removing internal obstacles to economic liberalism; and the more consensus-based adjustment process as in Japan, West Germany, and some of the smaller European countries.

Hyperliberalism

The Thatcher–Reagan model can be treated ideologically as the anticipation of a hyperliberal form of state, in the sense that it seems to envisage a return to nineteenth-century economic liberalism and a rejection of the neoliberal attempt to adapt economic liberalism to the sociopolitical reactions that classical liberalism produced. It takes the "neo" out of neoliberalism. The whole paraphernalia of Keynesian demand-support and redistributionist tools of policy are regarded with the deepest suspicion in the hyperliberal approach. Government-imposed regulations to protect the public with respect to industrial activities (antipollution, safety, and health controls, and so on) are also to be weakened or dismantled. The market is to determine how much protection the public really wants.

The hyperliberal tendency actively facilitates a restructuring, not only of the labor force, but also of the social relations of production. It renounces tripartite corporatism. It also weakens bipartism by its attack on unions in the state sector and its support and encouragement to employers to resist union demands in the oligopolistic sector. Indirectly, the state encourages the consolidation of enterprise corporatist relations for the scientific-technical-managerial workers in the oligopolistic sector, a practice for which the state itself provides a model in its treatment of its own permanent cadres. Finally, state policies are geared to an expansion of employment in short-term, low-skill, high-turnover jobs that contribute to further labor-market segmentation.

The political implications are a complete reversal of the coalition that sustained the neoliberal state. That state rested on its relationship with trade unions in the oligopolistic sector (the social contract), an expanding and increasingly unionized state sector, readiness to support major businesses in difficulty (from agricultural price supports to bailouts of industrial giants), and transfer payments and services for a range of disadvantaged groups. The neoliberal state played a hegemonic role by making capital accumulation on a world scale appear to be compatible with a wide range of interests of subordinate groups. It founded its legitimacy on consensual politics. The would-be hyperliberal state confronts all those groups and interests with which the neoliberal state came to terms. It does not shrink from open opposition to state-sector employees, welfare recipients, and trade unions.

The government–business alliance that presides over the transformation of the neoliberal into a would-be hyperliberal form of state generates an imposing list of disadvantaged and excluded groups. State-sector employees made great gains in collective bargaining and wages during the years of expansion and they have now become front-line targets for budgetary restraint. Welfare recipients and nonestablished workers, socially contiguous categories, are hit by reduced state expenditure and unemployment. Farmers and small businessmen are angry with banks and with governments as affordable finance becomes unavailable to them. Established workers in industries confronting severe problems in a changing international division of labor – textiles, automobiles, steel, shipbuilding, for example – face unemployment or reduced real wages.

As long as the excluded groups lack strong organization and political cohesion, ideological mystification and an instinctive focus on personal survival rather than collective action suffice to maintain the momentum of the new policy orthodoxy. If a small majority, or even an articulate minority of the population remains relatively satisfied, it can be politically mobilized as necessary to maintain these policies in place against the dissatisfaction of a large minority or a slim majority that is divided and incoherent.

State capitalism

While the hyperliberal model reasserts the separation of state and economy, the alternative state form that some see as capable of renewed capitalist development promotes a fusion of state and economy. This state-capitalist path may take several forms all according to different national positions within the world economy and different institutional structures and ideologies. The common thread lies in a recognition of the indispensible guiding role of the state in the development of the nation's productive forces. The advancement of these forces in the world economy can only be achieved through a conscious industrial policy, arrived at by a negotiated understanding among the principal social forces and through the mediation of the state in a corporative process. Such an understanding would have to produce agreement on the strategic goals of the economy and also on the sharing of burdens and benefits in the effort to reach those goals.

The state-capitalist approach is grounded in an acceptance of the world market as the ultimate determinant of development. No single national economy, not even the largest, can control the world market or determine its orientation. Furthermore, unlike the neoliberal approach, the state-capitalist approach does not posit any consensual regulation of the world market as regards multilateral trade and financial practices. States are assumed to intervene not only to enhance the competitiveness of their nations' industries but also to negotiate or dictate advantages for their nations' exporters. The world market is the state of nature from which state-capitalist theory deduces specific policy.

The broad lines of this policy consist of, in the first place, development of the leading sectors of national production so as to give them a competitive edge in world markets, and in the second place, protection of the principal social groups so that their welfare can be perceived as linked to the success of the national productive effort.

The first aspect of this policy – industrial competitiveness – is to be achieved by a combination of opening these industrial sectors to the stimulus of world competition, together with state subsidization and orientation of innovation. Critical to the capacity for innovation is the condition of the knowledge industry; the state will have a major responsibility for funding technological research and development.

The second policy aspect – balancing the welfare of social groups – has to be linked to the pursuit of competitiveness. Protection of disadvantaged groups and sectors (industries or regions) would be envisaged as transitional assistance for their transfer to more profitable economic activities. Thus training, skill upgrading, and relocation assistance would have a preeminent place in social policy. The state would not indefinitely protect declining or inefficient industries but would provide incentives for the people concerned to become more efficient according to market criteria. The state would, however, intervene between the market pressures and the groups concerned so that the latter did not bear the full burden of adjustment. By contrast, the hyperliberal model would exclude the state from this cushioning and incentive-creating function, letting the market impose the full costs of adjustment upon the disadvantaged.

Where internally generated savings were deemed to be essential to enhanced competitiveness, both investors and workers would have to be persuaded to accept an equitable sharing of sacrifice, in anticipation of a future equitable sharing of benefits. Thus incomes policy would become an indispensible counterpart to industrial policy. Similarly, the managerial initiative required to facilitate innovation and quick response to market changes might be balanced by forms of worker participation in the process of introducing technological changes. The effectiveness of such a state-capitalist approach would, accordingly, depend on the existence of corporative institutions and processes, not only at the level of enterprises and industries, but also of a more centralized kind capable of organizing interindustry, intersectoral, and interregional shifts of resources for production and welfare.

The state-capitalist form involves a dualism between a competitively efficient world-market-oriented sector, and a protected welfare sector. The success of the former must provide the resources for the latter; the sense of solidarity implicit in the latter would provide the drive and legitimacy for the former. State capitalism thus proposes a means of reconciling the accumulation and legitimation functions brought into conflict by the economic and fiscal crises of the 1970s and by hyperliberal politics.

In its most radical form, state capitalism beckons toward the prospect of an internal socialism sustained by capitalist success in world-market competition. This would be a socialism dependent on capitalist development – that is, on success in the production of exchange values. But, so its proponents argue, it would be less vulnerable to external destabilization than were socialist strategies in economically weak countries (Allende's Chile or Portugal after the "carnation revolution"). The more radical form of state-capitalist strategy presents itself as an alternative to defensive, quasi-autarkic prescriptions for the construction of socialism which would aim to reduce dependency on the world economy and to emphasize the production of use values for internal consumption.[8]

Different countries are more or less well equipped by their historical experience to adopt the state-capitalist developmental path with or without the socialist coloration.[9] Those best equipped are the late-industrializing countries (from France and Japan in the late nineteenth century to Brazil and South Korea in the late twentieth), in which the state (or a centralized but autonomous financial system as in the German case) has played a major role in mobilizing capital for industrial development. Institutions and ideology in these countries have facilitated a close coordination of state and private capital in the pursuit of common goals. Those least well equipped are the erstwhile industrial leaders, Britain and the United States, countries in which hegemonic institutions and ideology kept the state by and large out of specific economic initiatives, confining its role to guaranteeing and enforcing market rules and to macroeconomic management of market conditions. The lagging effects of past hegemonic leadership may thus be a deterrent to the adoption of state-capitalist strategies.

The corporatist process underpinning state-capitalist development, which would include business and labor in the world-market-oriented sector and workers in the tertiary welfare-services sector, would at the same time exclude certain marginal groups. These groups frequently have a passive relationship to the welfare services and lack influence in the making of policy. They are disproportionately to be found among the young, women, immigrant or minority groups, and the unemployed. The restructuring of production tends to increase their numbers. Since these groups are fragmented and relatively powerless, their exclusion has generally passed unchallenged. It does, however, contain a latent threat to corporatist processes. Part of this threat is the risk of anomic explosions of violence, particularly on the part of the young male unemployed element. Such explosions often strengthen the established authority by reinforcing the demand for law and order.

The other part of the threat is the risk of political mobilization of the marginals, which would pit democratic legitimacy against corporatist economic efficiency. These dangers are foreshadowed in the writings of neoliberal ideologues about the "ungovernability" problem of modern democracies.[10] The implication is that the corporatist processes required to make state-capitalist development succeed may have to be insulated from democratic pressures. To the extent this becomes true, the prospects of internal socialism sustained by world-market state capitalism would be an illusion.

In short, the state-capitalist alternative has some potential for reconstructing national hegemonies and overcoming the impasse that hyperliberalism tends to rigidify. The narrowing basis of corporatism (particularly as regards its labor component) on which state capitalism must rest does, however, contain a latent contradiction to democratic legitimacy. Its historic bloc would be thin. The excluded groups available for mobilization into a counterhegemony would be considerable, though the fragmentation and powerlessness of these groups would make the task formidable. In the medium term, state-capitalist structures of some kind seem a feasible alternative to the hyperliberal impasse. The long-term viability of these forms is a more open question.

Social forces counteracting globalization

Hyperliberalism is the ideology of the globalization thrust in its most extreme form. State capitalism is an adaptation to globalization that responds at least in part to society's reaction. We must ask ourselves whether there are longer-term prospects that might come to fruition following a medium-term experiment with state capitalism.

This is best approached dialectically: by enquiring how the conditions created by the globalizing thrust could generate a response from a *crise de conscience* among those elements of societies that are made more vulnerable or are more exploited by it. Beginning with the constraints placed by globalization on national policies, we can proceed to popular responses.

The main external constraint on national policy is the international financial network. The very hint of a threat by a government to control capital movements or foreign exchange can lead to an investment strike and capital flight, precipitating thereby an exchange crisis that will require foreign borrowing and possibly devaluation of the national currency. Reluctance to follow a policy of openness to global economic movements makes foreign or domestic borrowing by the state difficult, as does a perception in the financial markets that the state is not managing its expenditures in relation to its revenues. The British Labour government was forced in 1976 to reduce state expenditures as a proportion of GNP by a combination of IMF pressures and the high cost of borrowing in the domestic finance market. The alternative to borrowing would have been to print more money and provoke a run on the pound.[11] The French Socialist government under President François Mitterrand introduced (1981/82) a number of new social measures and carried out nationalizations of banks and industrial groups. In its second year, however, the government had to face deficits in the social services and unemployment insurance, in public enterprises, and in the balance of payments of the country, which resulted in an alignment of state policies to those of the other advanced capitalist countries: priority to anti-inflation measures, imposition of a wage freeze and abandonment of wage indexation, and cutbacks in government spending in general and in social expenditures in particular.

A combination of internal pressures from the more powerful domestic social forces and external constraints operating through financial markets and institutions of the world economy sets practical limits to the options of governments. If a government were determined not to heed the external forces, it would have to be prepared to rely exclusively on internal means of stimulating and coordinating the productive forces in its society. In the extreme case, this would mean mass mobilization, collective and egalitarian austerity, and the organization of production geared to use (or the basic needs of society) rather than exchange (or the possibility of profits on world markets). This would imply a shift toward what Polanyi called a redistributive society.

There is no indication that public opinion in advanced capitalist countries is psychologically prepared for such an alternative. The ethic of personal choice that nourishes the hope of a personal salvation on earth, as well as in heaven, is too widespread to succumb to a collectivist solution except perhaps under conditions of social and economic catastrophe.

Nor is there much prospect that governments in less-developed or newly industrializing countries would be prepared for such a choice. A return to right-wing authoritarianism which reimposed an austerity intended to revive confidence among foreign creditors risks popular explosions. The food riots of 1989 in Venezuela, Brazil, and Argentina were a warning.[b] A left-wing nationalism that would turn its back on foreign credits and try to compensate for them by inward-turning autarkic mobilization of human resources lacks credibility. Elected governments in Third World countries have neither the will nor the authority to pursue either course.

The situation in the countries formerly self-designated as socialist is equally contradictory. Pressures are coming from the top for economic restructuring of a kind that would reduce the complexity of central planning by giving more scope to domestic markets and to incorporation into the global market economy. The hope of the economic reformers is that this will raise productivity and allocate resources more efficiently. At the same time, democratic movements from below challenge all forms of central direction and are likely to rise against the adverse consequences of economic reforms. They welcome markets as a means of overthrowing the autocracy and the shortage economy of planning; but they will surely protest the counterpart to liberalizing the economy in the introduction of the typical hazards of capitalism, inflation, and unemployment.

Three outcomes seem possible. One is a return to political repression, either as a means of continuing economic liberalization or of reviving Stalinist-type central planning. Another outcome could be a birth of corporatist politics in which particular groups try to take advantage of their strategic positions in industries or in regions to get as much as they can from the state. The notion of the state's commitment to the general interest of society as a whole thus risks becoming eroded in a *sauve qui peut* among rival claimants for whatever returns may be gained from economic reform. This outcome may be consistent with current trends in Poland and Hungary and conceivably even in the Soviet Union. A third possibility could be found within the democratization movement. It would lead towards a more democratically participant kind of economic management and planning inspired by the egalitarian idea innate in socialism.

In all of these cases, the prospect of turning around the segmenting, socially disintegrating, and polarizing effects of the globalization

---

[b] The revolt in southern Mexico which began in January 1994 is a further instance of this phenomenon.

thrust rests upon the possibility of the emergence of an alternative political culture that would give greater scope to collective action and place a greater value on collective goods. For this to come about, whole segments of societies would have to become attached, through active participation and developed loyalties, to social institutions engaged in collective activities. They would have to be prepared to defend these institutions in times of adversity.

The condition for a restructuring of society and polity in this sense would be to build a new historic bloc capable of sustaining a long war of position until it is strong enough to become an alternative basis of polity. This effort would have to be grounded in the popular strata. The activities that comprise it will not likely be directed to the state because of the degree of depoliticization and alienation from the state among these strata. They will more likely be directed to local authorities and to collective self-help. They will in many cases be local responses to global problems – to problems of the environment, of organizing production, of providing welfare, of migration. If they are ultimately to result in new kinds of state, these forms of state will arise from the practice of non-state popular collective action rather than from extensions of existing types of administrative control.

To the extent that such popular responses to the existing thrust of globalization come to fruition, they will change the meaning and the form of the polity. Such a long-term result could hardly be achieved in one national society alone; it would have to move forward simultaneously in several countries, and draw sufficient support in the world system to protect its various national bases. The existing globalization thrust grounded in the economic logic of markets would be countered by a new globalization embedded in society.

Notes

This text was first published in Daniel Drache and Meric S. Gertler (eds.), *The New Era of Global Competition: State Policy and Market Power* (Montreal and Kingston: McGill-Queen's University Press, 1991).

1 I have discussed this in *Production, Power, and World Order: Social Forces in the Making of History* (New York: Columbia University Press, 1987).

2 See, for example, Robert Ross and Kent Trachte, "Global Cities and Global Classes: The Peripheralization of Labor in New York City," *Review*, vol. 6, no. 3 (1983), pp. 393–431.

3 Jeffrey Harrod, *Power, Production, and the Unprotected Worker* (New York: Columbia University Press, 1987).

4 See, for example, Immanuel Wallerstein, *The Modern World-System: Capitalist Agriculture and the Origins of the European World-Economy in the Sixteenth Century* (New York: Academic Press, 1974).
5 This section is based on parts of ch. 8 of *Production, Power, and World Order*.
6 The McCraken Report, *Toward Full Employment and Price Stability* (Paris: OECD, 1977).
7 On the segmentation trend see, *inter alia*: Frank Wilkinson (ed.), *The Dynamics of Labour Market Segmentation* (London: Academic Press, 1981).
8 Some French writers have probed these questions, for example, Christian Stoffäes, *La grande menace industrielle* (Paris: Calmann-Levy, 1978), and Serge-Christolphe Kolm, *La transition socialiste: la politique économique de gauche* (Paris: Éditions du cerf, 1977).
9 Some recent US studies that have compared the institutional characteristics of leading capitalist countries include Peter Katzenstein (ed.), *Between Power and Plenty: Foreign Economic Policies of Advanced Industrial States* (Madison, Wis.: University of Wisconsin Press, 1978), and John Zysman, *Governments, Markets, and Growth* (Ithaca, N.Y.: Cornell University Press, 1983).
10 Michel J. Crozier, Samuel P. Huntington, and Joji Watanuki, *The Crisis of Democracy: Report on the Governability of Democracies to the Trilateral Commission* (New York: New York University Press, 1975).
11 Laurence Harris, "The State and the Economy: Some Theoretical Problems," *The Socialist Register* (London: Merlin Press, 1980).

11 "Real socialism" in historical perspective (1991)

> It is not the business of the historian to award prizes for virtue, to propose the erection of statues, or to establish any catechism whatever; his business is to *understand what is least individual* in the course of events . . .
>
> Georges Sorel, *Reflections on Violence* (1906)

The death of socialism is affirmed everywhere today as a matter of common knowledge, from yesterday's newspaper to the neo-Hegelian "end of history" proclaimed by Francis Fukuyama,[1] and the neo-Burkian reflections on revolution in eastern Europe by Ralf Dahrendorf.[2] The events of eastern Europe are read as the definitive seal of closure upon something much broader than the regimes of "real socialism."[3] They signal the end of an historical project that had its origins in the response of nineteenth-century industrial society to the disintegrating impact of capitalism.[4] Or so it would seem.

Those who retain socialist convictions must treat the proclamation seriously, even in offering Mark Twain's rejoinder that it is greatly exaggerated. Two lines of argument are weak responses. One is that Soviet (or by extension, Chinese, or Cuban or . . .) socialism was never true socialism. It was from the beginning, or from some later stage, a deformation, a perversion, of the true thing. Like Christianity, socialism has never been tried. The other weak rejoinder is that the failure of socialism was the fault of evil men – Stalin in the first place and secondarily of a corrupted *nomenklatura*. A corollary of these arguments is the fragmentation of socialism into a multitude of quarreling groups, each convinced of its possession of the "truth" of socialism.

Whatever validity there may be in these judgements on the failures of "real socialism," they are inconsistent with a socialist view of history and a socialist mode of reasoning. Socialism is both a project of society and a method of social and historical analysis – and there has to be some consistency between its two aspects. The project of society is not a Platonic intellectual construct given in advance which is to be put into effect by enlightened leadership of a mass movement being led towards the light. The project of society is itself a product of historical struggles which have to be understood as a conflict of social forces the precise outcome of which is never altogether predictable. Individuals and leadership groups are important, but must also be seen as the product of impersonal forces. All revolutions create opportunities for individuals whose aggressive and deviant proclivities would be controlled and repressed in a more stable social situation. We have the right to moral outrage at what these individuals may do, but we should not let this obscure the impersonal forces that unleash their vicious tendencies. Both lines of apology for the failings of "real socialism" forsake historical materialism to fall into the trap of idealism. They thereby endorse the death certificate of socialism.

The most serious present task of socialism is to analyze what went wrong and not to try to avoid the issue idealistically by defining it out of socialism. "Real socialism" was shaped and conditioned by the world into which it came and in which it developed. What were these shaping forces? What historical social structures may survive the débâcle of "real socialism" to be available for the making of the future? Which configurations of forces delineate feasible future options, including, perhaps, socialist options? These are pertinent questions for socialism today.

The impersonal shaping forces have operated at three levels: production, the state, and world order.[5] These three levels are conceptually distinct but interrelated in practice. Production creates the material basis for all forms of social existence, and the ways in which human productive efforts are combined in productive processes affect all other aspects of social life, including the polity. Production generates the capacity to exercise power, but power in the form of state determines the manner in which production takes place. The structure of world order, in turn, conditions the possibilities of formation and development of different forms of state and of production. Socialism as an historical experience arose from a particular crisis of world order. It aspired to be at the same time a system of political rule and of production. The organization of production lies at the heart of socialist politics.

Two intertwined historical processes affected the course of socialist development: (1) external constraints from the world order influenced the origins of socialist experiments, the course they took, and their possibilities of survival; and (2) internal dynamics of socialist development generated new social forces with actual or latent conflicting interests and they raised new problems to be confronted. The socialist state faces both inward, attempting to reach a modus vivendi or historic compromise with the emerging social forces, and outward, attempting to secure the political space and the material resources required to confront internal demands. As Machiavelli long ago warned, the necessity of reforms can never be acted upon without danger, the danger being that the state may be destroyed before having perfected its constitution.[6]

Machiavelli also underlined the importance of events in demonstrating the necessity of reforms in the state. It is well, in our present context, to reflect upon the relationship of events to historical structures. Braudel expressed this relationship as a dialectic of duration, an interaction of the immediacy of events with the slower-moving structures of the *longue durée*.[7] A gathering of 800,000 people massed in and about Wenceslas Square in Prague manifesting opposition to the government is a salient event. When they walk home or to work, structures reemerge, though the continuity of these structures may have been called into question. At one moment there is "the people." "The people" is not a structure but an unstructured energized mass, a moment when structures are suspended, only to reappear again. Structures are the means whereby we get from one day to the next, but events may shake and cumulatively may transform structures.

The historical dialectic of "real socialism" comprises four moments: (1) the military-political conditions requisite to survival of a socialist experiment initiated in relatively underdeveloped territories; (2) an organization of state and production shaped and reshaped in the context of this military-political struggle for survival; (3) the emergence of contradictions within this organization of state and production which block its ability both to produce adequately and to guarantee order; and (4) a struggle among internally generated social forces over the restructuring of state and economy in which external forces also play an influential role.

The analysis which begins with the state of world order in which a socialist experiment becomes possible, proceeds to the internal

211

dynamic of socialist development, to return again to the implications of the *dénouement* of the crisis of existing socialism for the world order and for the prospects of socialism in the larger world.

The primacy of the military-political

Survival was the categorical imperative of socialist construction since the Bolsheviks seized power in a collapsing Russian state during the autumn of 1917.[8] The subsequent collapse of the Central powers and the limited willingness or ability of the victorious western powers to sustain a long civil and interventionist war on Russian territory provided the conditions of inter-state relations in which the Soviet state could establish itself. The first socialist revolution gained a precarious existence because the world military-political balance was not propitious for its suppression. Western statesmen, fearing an advance of the revolutionary movement through Europe, settled for a defensive strategy.

The military-political factor thus was dominant in the initial stages of the socialist experiment. This factor remained dominant in subsequent socialist revolutions. They all occurred in economically backward societies in conditions of internal military débâcle and armed struggle and of external hostility to the socialist project. The political, economic, and at times military forces of the developed capitalist world have been mobilized to harass, destabilize, and defeat efforts to consolidate socialist revolutions. Where the socialist experiment was supported or imposed from without, as in eastern Europe following World War II, the military-political configuration was again dominant.

External pressures have the effect of privileging those internal forces that appear to respond effectively to them. External opposition to established socialist regimes, whether or not intended, whether or not justified, provoked responses from the socialist leaderships in the realms of foreign policy, production, and the form of state that have nothing intrinsically to do with the socialist idea *per se*.[9] Real historical socialism, in other words, has not been the gradual putting into effect of a socialist idea. Real socialism has grown through an historical dialectic with the forces of world capitalism within the framework of the inter-state system. Socialism has internalized the marks of this dialectic.

Two models of state and production emerged from the Bolshevik experience both of which have lived on to influence the shapes of historical socialism. One is War Communism (1917–21); the other, the New Economic Policy (NEP; 1921–28).

War Communism was the creation of military necessity, though some Bolshevik leaders saw a virtue in it independent of necessity. Its characteristics were economic autarky; requisitioning and rationing rather than market allocation in a money economy; nationalization of industry as a preemptive strike against private capital and foreign control; the reconstituting of trade unions as agencies of labor discipline and labor control; the militarization of labor as an obligation to perform national service with administrative allocation to jobs rather than allocation through a labor market. Under War Communism administrative coercion replaced market coercion.

The NEP was also a creation of necessity; and other Bolshevik leaders saw virtue in it independently of its necessity. The limits of War Communism were demonstrated by the Kronstadt rising in the navy in March 1921 and by peasant resistance to the exactions from the rural economy. The NEP was, in the phrase of Lenin's collaborator, Ryazanov, "a peasant Brest-Litovsk," a necessary surrender and concession to the country's most numerous class and the one on which the revolution had to depend for physical survival.[10] The characteristics of the NEP were reliance upon market forces and material inducements to peasants to increase agricultural supply; encouragement of foreign trade and foreign investment; and emphasis on increasing industrial productivity.

Two foreign policies corresponded to the two models of economy. The policy of world revolution threatened from within the capitalist states which menaced the beleaguered autarky of War Communism. It aimed at transforming the inter-state system away from its identification with a capitalist world order. But when the Soviet Union sought to establish economic intercourse with the outside world in the interest of repairing wartime damage, the strategy of world revolution became dangerously provocative. The NEP required a normalizing of the Soviet Union's relations in the inter-state system. Soviet security would be best assured if the Soviet Union were to appear as a state like other states, not one bent upon transforming the structure of world power. A strategy of taking advantage from divisions among the capitalist powers and of encouraging economic relations with those which were willing would serve to gain a pause for internal recovery better than one that united capitalist powers in hostility to Soviet survival. The Soviets negotiated trade agreements with Britain and several other European countries and made a secret treaty with Germany for mutual assistance in developing the military strength of both powers.

The military factor was also influential in the organization of production. The workers' militia concept and the Red Guards expressed the initial form of revolutionary military organization, just as workers' soviets constituted the initial form of production organization. Both were changed into a disciplined hierarchical mode of organization in the testing ground of armed conflict. The Red Guards might be effective in gaining control of major cities; they were ineffective in waging a war against organized military forces over vast distances. The Red Army was constituted along classical military lines, incorporating many regular Russian officers who were placed under the surveillance of political commissars. Similarly, the workers' soviets were displaced by a hierarchical system of management in which many former owners and "bourgeois experts" paralleled the roles of tsarist officers in the army. The pressures of war initially foreclosed any experimentation with alternative modes of production organization, either as the spontaneous outgrowth of working-class action or as a planned introduction of socialist ideas. This initial impetus became institutionalized in *edinonachalie* or the system of one-man-management which survived through the NEP in large-scale industry to become integrated into the central planning of the 1930s and after. Capitalism had achieved the highest development of productive forces through hierarchical management structures of industry. The Bolsheviks took over and developed the model of the capitalist labor process for its organization of industry.

The Stalinist "revolution from above" was a return to the War Communism model, more fully institutionalized as a systematic organization of state and production. The state was centralized and, along with the Party, subjected to police power. A new "people's intelligentsia" was recruited to manage state and economy, learning on the job through trial and error to construct and operate a central planning system. The new cadres, who displaced the purged "Old Bolsheviks" and the residual pre-revolutionary "bourgeois experts," depended exclusively on service to the autocrat in the manner of the prebendary Muscovite tsardom of the sixteenth century.

It is possible to understand the features of this system of power without attributing it altogether to Stalin's personality. The coercive-repressive character of the system flowed from the political power struggle within the Party that preceded it; from the spillover of coercive practices from grain seizures and forced collectivization; from the use of coercive discipline in the formation of a new industrial working class of ex-peasants (which in comparative historical terms concentrated the coercion of the British enclosure movement into a single decade); and from a world environment perceived as hostile to Soviet survival and thus as requiring a forced pace of industrialization to prepare the military basis for resisting the inevitable attack.

Revisionist history has challenged and rejected the Stalinist arguments for the policies imposed from 1929 through the 1930s. It questions the economic efficacy of the collectivization of agriculture, and the reality of the external threat, and charges that Stalin's military purges weakened rather than strengthened Soviet defenses.[11] These matters are not in dispute here. My point is that, wisely or unwisely, necessarily or unnecessarily, the Soviet system in its form of state and production as well as in its armed force was shaped in the consciousness of military threat. Soviet socialism was the product of the world system – a capitalist-dominated system – as much as of internal political forces. The whole responsibility cannot be attributed to the personality of Stalin. Revolutionary situations give opportunities for power to personalities who would be excluded in more stable times – to both utopian visionaries and perverse jailors. We should not ignore the circumstances by explaining everything in terms of the individuals. Nor is it useful to speculate about what might have been. (Suppose, for example, that Bukharin had won out over Stalin.) Counterfactual histories can never be refuted because they cannot be tested. They are the stuff of idealism rather than of historical materialism.

Coercion consolidated the new system of power. It survived the Nazi onslaught during World War II and maintained its momentum during the postwar decades. But coercion left its impact on a very large part of the population whose surviving friends and family members had bitter cause for grievance against Stalinist rule. This suppressed anger would find expression when the pressure of authority slackened and it would be supported by others dismayed by the historical record and hopeful for a more open society.

The Chinese revolution followed a different pattern in its organization of production, although also shaped by its (rather different) military experience. China's revolutionary military power was built up after the Long March in the remote rural zone of Yenan. It was a new kind of army, adapted to the conditions in which it came to exist. The army lived in symbiosis with peasant communities and engaged in a guerrilla type of warfare. These conditions, very different from those of the civil war following the Bolshevik revolution, shaped the revolutionary theory and practice of the People's Liberation Army (PLA) long before it moved to occupy the coastal cities in the final stages of revolutionary war.

The PLA was organized for production, side by side with the peasantry of the zones it controlled. The leadership type it cultivated was the versatile head of a guerrilla unit who was required to assimilate fully the goals of the struggle and then to improvise autonomously in carrying them out. These characteristics defined the Chinese model of the cadre. It carried over into the organization of civilian production as a tendency to rely on ideologically assimilated leadership at all levels – an assimilation recurrently revised through "rectification" campaigns – together with relative autonomy of work groups and coordination through committees rather than line hierarchy.

In effect, two models of production organization were rivals in China following the establishment of the People's Republic (in 1949). One was the model just mentioned, a product of the experience of revolutionary war. The other was the Soviet model of one-man-management under central planning. Just as the Bolsheviks took over the only available model of industrial management – the capitalist model – so the Chinese leadership had as the most obviously available model, the Soviet one. Furthermore, in the first phase of the People's Republic, China's leadership depended heavily upon Soviet aid to develop industry, particularly in the Manchurian region. The implantation into that region of the Soviet model led to a struggle that was both political and industrial, in which the Soviet model and its supporters were defeated.

This victory was more than an assertion of an indigenous Chinese way. It was also the proclamation of a heresy in relation to Soviet Marxism: the doctrine that production relations, not productive forces, could spearhead revolutionary change. It was, furthermore, an affirmation that the Chinese way would be more relevant than the Soviet way for economically backward Third World countries which, like China, did not have the numbers of technically trained staff required to manage central planning and industry in the Soviet manner.

As a corollary to the primacy of the military factor in shaping the forms of state and production in "real socialism," the military have had a prior claim upon the resources of socialist societies. Since socialism has come about in relatively poor and less-developed societies whose leaders have felt compelled to prepare to resist a military threat from much wealthier capitalist societies, it follows that they have consistently allocated a higher proportion of their total product to the military.

One consequence is that in order to undertake any large-scale measures of structural economic or political reform, the socialist state requires both a relaxation of the external threat and a shift of resources from military to civilian production. From the 1960s onward, the socialist countries confronted the issue of reform, as the structures of production brought into being during the earlier phase of defense of their revolutions produced declining increments of growth. The challenge from the capitalist world, military in form, was economic in its consequences, whether it confronted the Soviet Union itself or a small peripheral aspirant to socialism. The arms race provoked by the Reaganite phase of the Cold War was too much for an unreformed Soviet economy to sustain; and efforts to keep up with the arms race blocked economic reform. The "low intensity" conflict maintained by the United States against the Sandinista government in Nicaragua was directed primarily against economic targets and local economic leadership, while requiring the Nicaraguan government to abandon economic and social investment by putting its resources into the military. The Sandinistas made a strategic withdrawal by abandoning power in elections carried out in conditions of war weariness and economic collapse. The Soviet Union, reminiscent of the NEP period, made an about shift in foreign policy to acquiesce in US and western European concerns, to seek technological and financial assistance from the capitalist world, and to devote more attention to internal structural change.

The social structure of accumulation

It is commonly asserted today that socialist central planning has been an unmitigated disaster. In the context of this general condemnation, some appraisal of the balance of achievements and failures of central planning seems a necessary prelude to any consideration of future options.

Socialist revolutions confronted two basic problems. One was to give work to all who were able. The socialist state took responsibility for the sustenance and welfare of its citizens, and determined to

217

mobilize the whole of society into the production process. Even those who could not produce their keep would add something to the social product upon which everyone depended.

The other basic problem was to break the agricultural barrier to expanded development. Since socialist revolutions occurred in peasant societies, it was necessary to raise agricultural productivity in order to be able to shift employment to industry and to finance industrial development.

By and large, socialist economic organization went a long way towards resolving these two problems. In doing so, "real socialism" created the human resource for economic development in backward societies: an educated public whose health was adequately cared for and amongst whom the basic necessities of life were more equitably distributed. The human costs of these achievements were great, especially in the collectivization of agriculture, in police repression, and in the casualties of war. As these costs were in part determined by internal political decisions, responsibility for pain and suffering can be directly attributed to political leaders. But was the cost more terrible than the suffering caused by the impersonal market forces of capitalist industrialization? There is little basis to conclude that it was, though the socialist experience was compressed into a shorter space of time.

The success of socialist growth did, however, manifest diminishing returns in virtually all the countries of "real socialism" from the mid-1960s. There is, of course, much scope for quarreling over the quantitative figures for growth rates. The pattern, however, seems clear enough. Return on investment of about 20 percent of national income during the first Five-Year Plans of the 1930s was high, as high as or higher than growth rates during the peak periods of growth of the major capitalist countries. These high growth rates continued during the reconstruction of the post-World War II period, not only in the Soviet Union but in the other countries practicing central planning. These growth rates began to decline from the 1960s through the 1980s. Higher investment ratios produced lower and lower increments of growth.[12]

During the same period, those areas in which socialism had produced its greatest achievements also began to manifest problems. The quality of health services deteriorated. There were recurrent shortages of basic consumer goods. There was a growing mismatch between skills produced by the education system and job opportunities. All of these factors built growing frustration into society.

These developments coincided with changes in deep social structure. In the first phase of revolution, the Party confronted a crumbling and disarticulated pre-revolutionary society. This is the phase Gramsci called the war of movement. The old structures of political authority were quickly swept aside because they had weak support in the old-regime society. The Party was able to take the initiative to create new social structures. By the early 1930s, new directing cadres, the "people's intelligentsia," assumed the functions of a ruling group. They were not a class in the sense that they were not a self-perpetuating entity possessing power as a group. Rather they were an agglomeration of individuals whose positions of authority depended on their loyalty and effectiveness. They worked in conditions of extreme personal insecurity.

In a subsequent phase, however, civil society gradually reemerged. This new form of civil society was in large measure the result of the ways in which the revolution had become institutionalized in the state and in production. In the Brezhnev period, the tension and personal insecurity of the ruling cadres was relaxed. Not only the small leadership group but also the much larger stratum of officials and managers in Party, state, and economy felt more secure. Their access to forms of relative privilege was guaranteed. The chances of their children to accede to the status of their parents was enhanced. The *nomenklatura*, in other words, was becoming a stabilized ruling class.

The lower echelons of Soviet society were also settling into a more permanent stratification. The era of rapid transformation of ex-peasants into a new industrial working class had passed. Two strata of workers emerged. An upper stratum was closely integrated into the economic system, with more permanent stability and privilege; and a lower stratum was less firmly attached to the organizations of production. A new large service sector was staffed substantially by women workers. The better-off agricultural workers were becoming assimilated to the status of industrial workers, while the less-well-off rural population remained more disadvantaged than urban residents.

Similar trends affected the populations of the eastern European countries. The cycle of initial suppression of civil society, followed by its emergence in a reshaped form has been common to all the countries of "real socialism." In China, Mao twice launched an offensive against what he perceived as the challenge to the continuity of revolution from a renascent civil society – first in the Great Leap Forward (1956–58), then in the Cultural Revolution (1965–76). But by the 1970s, the war of movement in China was spent and the Party came to terms with the existence of civil society.

The revival of civil society modified the role of the Party. It could no longer play the role of active shaper of a passive social mass. The Party's new role became that of mediator between social forces and state power. The Party's ultimate goal in this phase was to achieve an "historic compromise" whereby the most articulate elements of civil society would acquiesce in its continuing rule in return for a substantial degree of toleration of their own autonomy.[13] The contradictions in the emergent civil society were either internalized within the Party, leading to intra-Party conflict, or they erupted outside the Party where opposition was more vulnerable to repression.

The historic compromise consecrated a social structure of accumulation. Socialist societies (like the Soviet Union and China) accumulate like capitalist societies for the purpose of investment and growth. Both capitalist and socialist societies grow by extracting a surplus from the producers. In market-driven capitalist societies, this surplus is invested in whatever individual capitalists think is likely to produce a further profit. In socialist societies, investment decisions are politically determined according to whatever criteria are salient at the time for the decision makers, e.g., welfare or state power. The social structure of accumulation is the particular configuration of social power through which the accumulation process takes place. This configuration delineates a relationship among social groups in the production process through which surplus is extracted. This power relationship underpins the institutional arrangements through which the process works.[14]

To grasp the nature of the social structure of accumulation at the moment of the crisis of existing socialism in the late 1980s, one must go back to the transformation in the working class that began some three decades earlier. The new working class composed largely of ex-peasants that carried through the industrialization drive of the 1930s and the war effort of the 1940s worked under an iron discipline of strict regulation and tough task masters recruited from the shop floor. During the 1950s a new mentality reshaped industrial practices. Regulations were relaxed and their modes of application gave more scope for the protection of individual workers' interests. Managerial cadres began to be recruited mainly from professional schools and were more disposed to the methods of manipulation and persuasion than to coercion. The factory regime passed from the despotic to the hegemonic type.[15]

The historic compromise worked out by the Party leadership included a social contract in which workers were implicitly guaranteed job security, stable consumer prices, and control over the pace of work, in return for their passive acquiescence in the rule of the political leadership. Workers had considerable structural power, i.e., their interests had to be anticipated and taken into account by the leadership, though they had little instrumental power through direct representation. This arrangement of passive acquiescence in time generated the cynicism expressed as: "You pretend to pay us. We pretend to work."

The working class comprised an established and a nonestablished segment. One group of workers, the established-worker segment, were more permanent in their jobs, had skills more directly applied in their work, were more involved in the enterprise as a social institution and in other political and civic activities. The other group, the nonestablished-worker segment, changed jobs more frequently, experienced no career development in their employment, and were nonparticipant in enterprise or other social and political activities. The modalities of this segmentation varied among the different socialist countries. In China, it was more explicitly institutionalized.[16] In the Soviet Union, it was more a question of job relations, attitudes, and behavior.

Hungarian sociologists discerned a more complex categorization of nonestablished workers: "workhorses" willing to exploit themselves for private accumulation (newly marrieds, for instance); "hedonists" or single workers interested only in the wage as the means of having a good time; and "internal guest workers," mainly women, or part-time peasant workers, or members of ethnic minorities allocated to the dirty work.[17] In practice, labor segmentation under "real socialism" bore a striking similarity to labor segmentation under capitalism.[18]

This differentiation within the working class had a particular importance in the framework of central planning. Central planning can be thought of in abstract terms as a system comprising: (a) redistributors in central agencies of the state who plan according to some decision-making rationality, that is maximizing certain defined goals and allocating resources accordingly; and (b) direct producers who

221

carry out the plans with the resources provided them. In practice, central planning has developed an internal dynamic that defies the rationality of planners. It has become a complex bargaining process from enterprise to central levels in which different groups have different levels of power. One of the more significant theoretical efforts of recent years has been to analyze the real nature of central planning so as to discern its inherent laws or regularities.[19]

Capital is understood as a form of alienation: people through their labor create something that becomes a power over themselves and their work. Central planning also became a form of alienation. Instead of being a system of rational human control over economic processes, it too became a system that no one controlled but which came to control planners and producers alike.

A salient characteristic of central planning as it had evolved in the decades just prior to the changes that began to be introduced during the late 1980s was a tendency to overinvest. Enterprises sought to get new projects included in the plan and thus to increase their sources of supply through allocations within it. Increased supplies made it easier to fulfil existing obligations but at the same time raised future obligations. The centrally planned economy was an economy of shortages; it was supply-constrained, in contrast to the capitalist economy which was demand-constrained. The economy of shortages generated uncertainties of supply, and these uncertainties were transmitted from enterprise to enterprise along the chain of inputs and outputs.

Enterprise managers became highly dependent upon core workers to cope with uncertainties. The core workers, familiar with the installed equipment, were the only ones able to improvise when bottlenecks occurred. They could, if necessary, improvise to cope with absence of replacement parts, to repair obsolescent equipment, or to make use of substitute materials. Managers also had an incentive to hoard workers, to maintain an internal enterprise labor reserve that could be mobilized for "storming" at the end of a plan period. Managers also came to rely on their relations with local Party officials to secure needed inputs when shortages impeded the enterprise's ability to meet its plan target.

These factors combined to make the key structure at the heart of the system one of management dependence on local Party cadres together with a close interrelationship between management and core workers in a form of enterprise corporatism. From this point, there were downward linkages with subordinate groups of nonestablished workers, with rural cooperatives, and with household production. There were upward linkages with the ministries of industries and the state plan. And there was a parallel relationship with the "second economy" which, together with political connections, helped to bypass some of the bottlenecks inherent in the formal economy.

Several things can be inferred from this social structure of accumulation. One is that those constituting its core – management, established workers, and local Party officials – were well entrenched in the production system. They knew how to make it work and they were likely to be apprehensive about changes that would introduce further uncertainties beyond those that they had learned to cope with. Motivation for change was most likely to come from those at the top who were aware that production was less efficient than it might have been, and who wanted to eliminate excess labor and to introduce more productive technology. (Those at the core of the system had a vested interest in existing obsolescent technology because their particular skills made it work.) Motivation for change might also arise among the general population in the form of dissatisfaction with declining standards of public services and consumer goods; and among a portion of the growing "middle class" of white-collar service workers. The more peripheral of the nonestablished workers – those most alienated within the system – were unlikely to be highly motivated for change. There was, in fact, no coherent social basis for change but rather a diffuse dissatisfaction with the way the system was performing. There was, however, likely to be a coherent social basis at the heart of the system that could be mobilized to resist change.

Economic reform and democratization

Socialist systems, beginning with the Soviet Union, have been preoccupied with reform of the economic mechanism since the 1960s. The problem was posed in terms of a transition from the extensive pattern of growth that was producing diminishing returns to a pattern of growth that would be more intensive in the use of capital and technology. Perception of the problem came from the top of the political-economic hierarchy and was expressed through a sequence of on-again/off-again experiments. Piecemeal reform proved difficult because of the very coherence of the system of power that constituted central planning. Movement in one direction, for example, granting more decision-making powers to managers, ran up against obstacles in other parts of the system, for example, in the powers of central ministries and in the acquired job rights of workers.

Frustrations with piecemeal reforms encouraged espousal of more radical reform; and radical reform was associated with giving much broader scope to the market mechanism. The market was an attractive concept insofar as it promised a more effective and less cumbersome means of allocating material inputs to enterprises and of distributing consumer goods. It was consistent with decentralization of management to enterprises and with a stimulus to consumer-goods production. The market, however, was also suspect insofar as it would create prices (and thus inflation in an economy of shortages), bring about greater disparities in incomes, and undermine the power of the center to direct the overall development of the economy. Some combination of markets with central direction of the economy seemed to be the optimum solution, if it could be done.

Following in the tracks of the reform movement came pressures for democratization. These came from a variety of sources: a series of movements sequentially repressed but cumulatively infectious in East Germany, Poland, Hungary, and Czechoslovakia; the rejection of Stalinism and the ultimate weakening of the repressive apparatus installed by Stalinism; and the consequences of the rebirth of civil society and of the historic compromise allowing more autonomy to the intelligentsia. The two movements – *perestroika* and *glasnost* in their Soviet form – encountered and interacted in the late 1980s. Would they reinforce each other or work against each other?

Some economic reformers saw democratization as a means of loosening up society which could strengthen decentralization. Some of these same people also saw worker self-management as supporting enterprise autonomy and the liberalizing of markets. Humanist intellectuals tended to see economic reform as limiting the state's coercive apparatus and as encouraging a more pluralist society. For these groups, economic reform and democratization went together.

Other economic reformers recognized that reform measures would place new burdens on people before the reforms showed any benefits. There would be inflation, shortages, and unemployment. The social contract of mature "real socialism" would be discarded in the process of introducing flexibility into the labor market and the management of enterprises. The skills of existing managers would be rendered obsolete, together with those of many state and Party officials engaged in the central planning process. Anticipating the backlash from all these groups, the "realist" reformers recognized that an authoritarian power would be needed to implement reform successfully. Without it, they reasoned, reform would just be compromised and rendered ineffective, disrupting the present system without being able to replace it.[20] The economic Thatcherites of real socialism would become its political Pinochets.

The initial effects of both economic reform and democratization have produced some troublesome consequences. Relaxing economic controls towards encouraging a shift to market mechanisms has resulted in a breakdown of the distribution system with a channeling of goods into free markets and black markets, rampant gangsterism, and a dramatic polarization of new rich and poor. This is hardly surprising, since many of those who had any previous market experience had been involved in the often shady activities of the underground economy. The relaxing of political controls gave vent to conflicts long suppressed, mobilizing people around ethnic nationalisms, various forms of populism, and, at the extreme, right-wing fascist movements. Furthermore, the outburst of public debate, while it has severely shaken the legitimacy of the Soviet state and its sustaining myths, has also demonstrated its inability to come to grips with the practical reorganization of economy and society. The reform process has itself made things worse, not better. (One Soviet journalist in the United States summed this up by observing that while the radical-leaning municipal council in Leningrad debated for months whether or not to change the city's name back to St. Petersburg, the shops became more and more empty.)

The legitimacy of "real socialism" was destroyed by Stalinism and the anti-Stalinist backlash. Civil society is reemergent but its component groups have not achieved any articulate organized expression. This is a condition Gramsci called an organic crisis; and the solution to an organic crisis is the reconstitution of a hegemony around a social group which is capable of leading and acquiring the support or acquiescence of other groups. What does our analysis of the structure of Soviet society tell us about the prospects of this happening?

There are three distinct meanings that can be given to "democracy" in the context of the collapse of "real socialism." One is the conventional "bourgeois" meaning of liberal pluralism. It has a strong demonstration effect, particularly in eastern Europe. Liberal pluralism has a history and many examples. Two other meanings arise out of socialist aspirations.

One is producer self-management. It has been expressed in spontaneous action by workers in many different revolutionary situations – in the original Russian soviets, in the *Ordine Nuovo* movement of northern Italy in 1919, in workers' control of factories during the Algerian revolution, in the works councils set up in Poland following the events of 1956, and in factory movements in Hungary during the 1956 revolution and Czechoslovakia in 1968. These experiences were all short-lived. The only long experience with worker self-management is the Yugoslav one and, despite continuing debate, it cannot be considered persuasive. There is a strong point about producers being able to determine their own conditions; but there is also evidence of a tendency for such experiences, assuming they survive repression by a higher political authority, to turn in the direction of self-serving corporatism.

The other socialist meaning is popular participation in central planning. No historical experience can be cited; it would have to be invented. And yet it is perhaps the most attractive prospect in the spirit of socialism. Alec Nove suggested a form of compromise between democratic planning and producer self-government: consumers would decide what to produce; producers would decide how.[21]

Georg Lukács wrote a text that was posthumously published in Hungary as *Demokratisierung Heute und Morgen*.[22] Rejecting both the Stalinist past and the liberal concept of democracy, he speculated about the conditions in which a democratization of socialism might be possible.

A first condition was an increase in productivity such that the production of the necessities of life would not absorb the totality of human effort. In Marxian terms, this would mean a shift in the balance of human activity from the realm of necessity to the realm of freedom. This condition is recognized also by others who have thought about the problem. Kornai posited that sufficient slack in production would be necessary to undertake reform in an economy of shortage.[23] Bahro argued that a state of "surplus consciousness," i.e., the existence of a margin of time and effort over and above the satisfaction of basic wants, was requisite for the pursuit of "emancipatory interests" as an alternative to the "compensatory interests" of consumerism.[24]

The next condition would be a coalition of social forces upon which the structure of democratic socialism might be based. At this point, Lukács' prescription becomes obscure. Like Bahro and like Gorz in the West, he did not, in this last phase of his thought, look to the workers as the leading social class around which democratic socialism could take form. He spoke rather of liberating the "underground tendencies" hitherto repressed. The Party could, he hoped, reconstitute itself to achieve this.

This was a hope inspired by the reform movement led by the intelligentsia in Czechoslovakia in 1968. It had a brief revival again in East Germany during the time *Neues Forum* and similar groups were building the popular movement that overturned the Honecker regime. The project lives on for now in the Soviet Union, though its plausibility is diminished. The Party is an object of cynicism and the idea of socialism no longer has a secure basis of legitimacy.

Two other routes towards democratization in recent eastern European experience have been, first, a movement from outside a moribund Party led by an independent workers' movement to which an intelligentsia attached itself (Poland); and second, an enlargement of scope for independent decision making in the economy through a strategic withdrawal by the Party from direct control over certain aspects of civil society (Hungary). Both of these routes now in retrospect seem to be leading towards a restoration of capitalism. The former East Germany shows a third route to capitalism: total collapse of the political structures of "real socialism" and full incorporation of its economy into West German capitalism.

For the remaining countries of "real socialism," options for the future can be grouped broadly into three scenarios. Each of these should be examined in terms of the relationship of the projected form of state and economy with the existing social structure of accumulation.

The first scenario is a combination of political authoritarianism with economic liberalization leading towards market capitalism and the integration of the national economy into the global capitalist economy. In its most extreme form, this is a project favored by some segments of the intelligentsia who recognize that a "shock therapy" in the Polish mode will be necessary to carry through privatization and the freeing of market forces; and that dictatorial powers will be needed to prevent elements of existing civil society, notably workers and segments of the bureaucracies, from political protest and obstruction in response

227

to the bankruptcies of enterprises, unemployment, inflation, and polarization of rich and poor that would occur as the inevitable accompaniment to this kind of restructuring. This is the option encouraged by the western consultants pullulating through the world of "real socialism" as the whiz-kid offspring of private consulting firms and agencies of the world economy. It is encouraged by the revival of von Hayek's ideas in eastern Europe and by the mythology of capitalism and of a pre-environmentalist fascination with western consumerism.

More moderate and mature political leadership might hesitate before enforcing the full measure of market-driven adjustments upon the more resistant elements of civil society. The compromise envisaged by this leadership would likely be a form of corporatism that would aim at co-opting core workers into the transition to capitalism, separating the more articulate and more strategically placed segments of the working class from the less articulate and less powerful majority. The enterprise-corporatist core of "real socialism's" social structure of accumulation would thus lend itself to facilitating the transition to capitalism.

Some intellectuals have entertained the possibility of a transition to capitalism combined with a liberal pluralist political system. This vision most probably underestimates the level of conflict that would arise in formerly socialist societies undergoing the economic stresses of a transition to capitalism in the absence of a corporatist compromise. The choice then would become which to sacrifice, democracy or the free market. The historical record, as Karl Polanyi presented it in *The Great Transformation*, suggests that democracy is first sacrificed but the market is not ultimately saved. This setting was, for Polanyi, the opening of the path towards fascism; and some observers from eastern Europe raise again this spectre as a not unlikely outcome of the social convulsions following the breakdown of "real socialism."[25]

The second scenario is political authoritarianism together with a command-administrative economic center incorporating some subordinate market features and some bureaucratic reform. This would leave basically intact the enterprise-corporatist heart of the existing planning system, which would also constitute its main political roots in civil society and its continuing source of legitimation in the "working class." China seems to be following this route; and the "conservatives" of the Soviet Union (with the backing of influentials in the military and the KGB) could also be counted among its supporters.

The long-term problem for this course would be in the continuing exclusion of the more peripheral segments of the labor force from any participation in the system, though these elements might be calmed in the short run if the revival of authority in central planning were to lift the economy out of the chaos resulting from the removal of authority in both economic planning and political structures.

The third scenario is the possibility of democratization plus socialist reform. As suggested above, this could take the form either of producer self-management, or of a democratization of the central planning process, or conceivably of some combination of the two. Of the three scenarios, this one, with its two variants, is the least clearly spelled out. One reason for this may be, as David Mandell has suggested, that the power of the media in the Soviet Union has been monopolized by the adherents of the first two and especially by the radical market reformers.[26]

Self-management has been claimed by both economic liberals and socialists. It has lost ground among the liberals without noticeably gaining conviction among socialists. Some of those economic reformers who once thought of self-management as a support to economic liberalization now appear to have drawn back from this option.[27] Nevertheless, from a socialist perspective, the possibility must remain that self-management in the absence of some larger socialist economic framework is likely to evolve towards a form of enterprise corporatism within a capitalist market, i.e., the moderate variant of the first scenario.

The position of workers in relation to these three scenarios remains ambiguous and fragmented. In this there is a striking resemblance to the position of workers under capitalism since the economic crisis of the 1970s. The same question is to be raised: does the unqualified term "working class" still correspond to a coherent identifiable social force? The potential for an autonomous workers' movement was demonstrated in Poland by Solidarity; but in the hour of its triumph that movement fragmented. The Soviet miners' strike of July 1989 revived the credibility of a workers' movement; but it has not definitively answered the question.

Projects for managing and reorienting the working class that emanate from members of the intelligentsia are more readily to be found than clear evidence of autonomous working-class choice. David Mandell reports that the Soviet government tried to channel the miners' strike towards demands for enterprise autonomy, only subsequently

229

to abandon self-management as part of market reform.[28] Academician Zaslavskaya, in the internal Party Novosibirsk Report that was attributed to her authorship, prescribed a planned reorientation of worker attitudes:

> [i]t is in the interests of socialist society, while regulating the key aspects of the socio-economic activity of the workers, to leave them a sufficiently wide margin of freedom of individual behaviour. Hence the necessity for directing behaviour itself, i.e. the subjective relationship of the workers to their socio-economic activity. Administrative methods of management are powerless here. The management of behaviour can only be accomplished in an oblique fashion, with the help of incentives which would take into account the economic and social demands of the workers and would channel their interests in a direction which would be of benefit to our society.[29]

Some economic liberal reformers, no longer interested in self-management, entertain the notion of collective bargaining by independent trade unions as a counterpart to a capitalist economy.

Workers, it seems, may not have very much of an active, initiating voice in the reform process. They may continue as previously to be an important passive structural force that reforming intelligentsia will have to take into account. Their attitudes might be remolded over time as Zaslavskaya and others would envisage. For the present they are, as a structural force, likely to remain committed to some of the basic ideas of socialism: egalitarianism in opportunities and incomes, the responsibility of the state to produce basic services of health and education, price stability, and availability of basic wage goods. (In this respect, they would have to be classified, in the new vocabulary with which *perestroika* is discussed, as "conservatives.") Workers, like other groups, are critical of bureaucracy and irritating instances of privilege. These are the basic sentiments that future options for socialism could most feasibly be built upon.

World order and the future of socialism

The condition of the world system now seems singularly unpropitious to a socialist future anywhere. The United States remains the strongest military power, though it is moving into the same kind of difficulties that beset the Soviet economy – declining rates of productivity, high military costs, and an intractable budgetary deficit. US military power serves as enforcer for deregulation and unrestricted movement of capital in the global economy. The financial mechanism of the global economy disciplines all countries except the United States, whose deficits continue for the moment to be financed by other countries, notably Japan. Third World countries as well as countries of "real socialism" insofar as their external economic linkages grow are subject to the policies promulgated through the main agencies of the global economy – the IMF, World Bank, OECD, G7, and so on.

This phase of apparent unification of military and economic power behind a capitalist structure of world order is, in the sweep of history, necessarily transitory, though none can say with certainty how long the transition may last or towards what future structure of world order it may tend.

An underlying dynamic is at work in the global economy that gives some indication about possible futures. Its present manifest effect is globalization in production and in finance sustained by US military power. The further consequences of this globalizing movement are also predictable: more acute polarization of rich and poor within the global economy; and lines of social cleavage that will cut across boundaries thanks to the restructuring of production and to world migratory movements, transforming the geographical core/periphery structure of the past into a social core/periphery structure.

This polarization is likely to proceed apace before it provokes a concerted response because it generates a segmentation of peripheral social groups rather than a clear global class cleavage. The segmentation of the more disadvantaged groups will likely form around various distinct identities – ethnic, religious, nationalist, and gender identities, in particular. These distinct identities may find new grounds of unification. Islam, for instance, can become a metaphor for Third World revolt against western capitalist domination. In this respect, the situation of countries of "real socialism" is not different from that of other countries. The same global tendencies are at work.

The long-term challenge to socialism will be to bridge these various identities so as to arrive at a common understanding of the global economic forces that place all of them in a subordinate position. Bridging identities means preserving them, while allowing them to develop their distinctive personalities by removing the causes of their subordination. This socialism would have room for diversity – for mutual support in the pursuit of distinct projects of society.

Two tendencies apparent at present may open opportunities for the rebirth of socialism. One is the decline of hegemony in the global

231

system. This undermines conviction in the legitimacy of the principles upon which the globalization thrust is grounded. The cloak of common values becomes a transparent veil revealing the dominance of power, not the impersonal functioning of the order of nature. Such events as the collapse of the GATT negotiations[a] and the mobilization by the United States of military intervention in the Persian Gulf contribute in different ways to the erosion of global hegemony.[30]

The other tendency, not unrelated to the first, is toward a world of economic blocs. Insofar as this would imply a decentralization of power, it could give room for diversity in projects of economy and society. The balance of social forces is different in Europe, East Asia, and North America. Opportunities in social struggle will be different in different parts of the world. The survival and transformation in some form of "real socialism" is conceivable in this context. The struggles going on in the Soviet Union and China towards the definition of a new project of society could have a longer range importance not just for those countries.

Effective containment or limitation of the central military enforcer of the present global economy will be a necessary condition for any devolution of power or economic decentralization in the world system. This can happen only through internal resistance within US society combined with external resistance, perhaps in parts of the Third World that reject the IMF medicine and the US-dominated "new world order." For the future, the Gramscian war of position becomes the appropriate strategy for socialist construction, most particularly in targeting the heartlands of capitalism, but carried on in coordination with movements in the Third World and in the countries of "real socialism." The struggle will be at once internal and global.

Notes

This text was first published in Ralph Miliband and Leo Panitch (eds.), *The Socialist Register 1991* (London: Merlin, 1991).

1 Francis Fukuyama, "The End of History?," *National Interest*, no. 16 (Summer 1989), pp. 3–18.

2 Ralf Dahrendorf, *Reflections on the Revolution in Europe* (New York: Random House, 1990).

3 The cumbersome and redundant term "actually existing socialism" became current in English-language discourse after the publication of the

---

[a] The Uruguay Round of the General Agreement on Tariffs and Trade was eventually successfully concluded on December 15, 1993, as a result of concerted US–European bilateral negotiations over agriculture and communications.

English translation of Rudolph Bahro's *The Alternative in Eastern Europe* (trans. by David Fernbach; London: NLB, 1978). It applied to those social formations shaped since the Bolshevik Revolution by Leninist and Stalinist types of political parties and by economic central planning. This term now seems outdated as well as cumbersome since the continuing "actuality" and "existence" of this type of formation were placed in question by the events of 1989 in eastern Europe. Gordon Skilling suggested to me that a more accurate term is "real socialism" (from *realsocialismus*). "Real socialism" both designates a concrete historical phenomenon (whether past or present) and avoids confusion with measures introduced by social democratic and socialist party governments in capitalist social formations. The quotation marks signify a borrowed term designating an historical phenomenon open to critique, which the author does not consecrate with the meaning of a real essence.

4 Karl Polanyi, *The Great Transformation: The Political and Economic Origins of Our Time* (Boston: Beacon Press, 1957).

5 I use here the framework for analysis applied more specifically to capitalism in Robert W. Cox, *Production, Power, and World Order: Social Forces in the Making of History* (New York: Columbia University Press, 1987).

6 Machiavelli, *The Discourses*, Book 1, ch. 2.

7 Fernand Braudel, "History and the Social Sciences: The *Longue Durée*," in Braudel, *On History*, trans. by Sarah Matthews (Chicago: University of Chicago Press, 1980), pp. 25–54.

8 I have not included footnoting for factual or historical information in this article. Such footnoting, if carried through consistently, would result in a series of appended essays on each point of historical interpretation or evaluation – a distracting encumbrance in what is intended as an essay in theory rather than in historical research. Critics need no encouragement to strike where the shield is down.

9 R. W. Davies in a recent article points out that the three major principles of the nineteenth-century vision of socialism – common ownership, democratic management, and equality – were all either rejected or drastically modified in the construction of the Soviet model of "real socialism": "Gorbachev's Socialism in Historical Perspective", *New Left Review*, vol. 179, January–February 1990.

10 E. H. Carr, *The Bolshevik Revolution*, Volume II, *1917–1923* (London: Macmillan, 1952), p. 278. Lenin's longer phrasing was: "Only an agreement with the peasantry can save the socialist revolution in Russia until the revolution has occurred in other countries."

11 There is evidence that collectivization, far from enabling agriculture to contribute a surplus to the state during the First Five-Year Plan, actually drained resources from the nonagricultural sector through the need to supply agricultural machinery. The chief aim of collectivization was probably to break the power of the peasantry, the power of a social force independent of the state to determine what grain to produce and what to sell.

Stalin was prepared to incur loss of production to gain state power over agriculture. As in the sphere of control over the military, Stalin's policies opened a period of extreme Soviet vulnerability to outside attack. He must have gambled that the depression in the capitalist world would deter aggression while Soviet power was being consolidated. This opening of vulnerability has to be read in the context of a speech in 1931 in which Stalin declared (*Works*, vol. 13, pp. 40–41): "We are fifty or a hundred years behind the advanced countries. We must make good this distance in ten years. Either we do it, or we shall go under." Ten years later, Germany invaded the Soviet Union.

12 CMEA figures showed an average annual rate of growth in aggregate output for the USSR from the early 1930s to the beginning of World War II of 16 percent. This was about twice that of capitalist countries during their boom periods of development, e.g., the United States during the second half of the 1880s, Russia in the 1890s, or Japan between 1907 and 1913. During the years following World War II, the USSR and the eastern European countries maintained annual growth rates of industrial production in the range of 10 to 16 percent with investment ratios somewhat in excess of 20 percent of national income. The most backward (Bulgaria and Romania) grew the fastest during the 1950s and 1960s. From the 1960s on, high and even increasing investment ratios began to yield lower rates of growth in industrial production. Soviet industrial growth averaged 13.2 percent annually in the 1950s, 10.4 percent in the 1960s, and 8.5 percent in the 1970s, while the investment ratio had risen from 23.9 percent in the 1950s to 29.5 percent in the 1970s. The combined rate of growth in national income (measured in Net Material Product) for the USSR and eastern European CMEA members declined steadily from the mid-1960s. From a rate of 10 percent annually in the 1950s, it dropped to 7 percent in the 1960s, and 5 percent in the 1970s (6 percent in the first half of the decade and 4.2 percent in the second), down to about 2 to 3 percent in the early 1980s. These figures do not appear disastrous compared to the economic performance of some major capitalist countries during the years of economic crisis, but they contrast markedly with earlier socialist performance and indicate a trend towards stagnation. The editors of *Monthly Review* (vol. 41, no. 10 (March 1990), p. 12) cite Soviet Academician and Gorbachev economic adviser Abel Aganbegyan to the effect that the official figures for 1981–85 are flawed because of a failure to take account of hidden inflation, with the inference that in that economic period there was practically no economic growth. (Sources for the above figures include Silviu Brucan, "The Strategy of Development in Eastern Europe," IFDA Dossier 13 (November 1979), for historical comparisons; Alec Nove *et al.*, *The Eastern European Economics in the 1970s* (London: Butterworth, 1982), p. 215; A. Bergson, "Soviet Economic Slowdown and the 1981–85 Plan," *Problems of Communism*, vol. 30 (May–June 1981); and T. Colton, *The Dilemma of Reform in the Soviet Union* (New York: Council on Foreign Relations, 1984), p. 15.)

13 The concept of "historic compromise," borrowed from the lexicon of the Italian Communist Party (*compromesso storico*), was applied to this phase of "real socialism" by George Konrád and Ivan Szelényi, *The Intellectuals on the Road to Class Power* (Brighton: Harvester, 1979), especially pp. 186–187.

14 I have taken the concept of social structure of accumulation from David Gordon, "Stages of Accumulation and Long Economic Cycles," in Terence K. Hopkins and Immanuel Wallerstein (eds.), *Processes of the World System* (Beverly Hills, Calif.: Sage, 1980), pp. 9–45. My use of it focuses more specifically on the relationship of social forces, whereas Gordon uses it more broadly to encompass, for example, the institutions of the world economy. I have applied the concept to the capitalist world economy in *Production, Power, and World Order*, ch. 9.

15 The terms are taken from Michael Burawoy's use of Gramsci's concept of hegemony. See Burawoy, *The Politics of Production* (London: Verso, 1985).

16 William Hinton, *Fanshen* (New York: Vintage Press, 1966), p. 287, called the formal categorization of people as workers or peasants (with correspondingly different rights and responsibilities) a form of "hereditary social status." Industry in China was also organized on a core/periphery basis in which core enterprises employing established workers had satellite enterprises employing peasant-workers, and core enterprises could also employ teams of temporary peasant-workers in their main plants alongside established workers but with lower pay and benefits. The "iron rice bowl" of permanent job tenure and *buyuan* system whereby a worker is entitled to pass on his job to a qualified family member are Chinese counterparts to the social contract of Soviet post-Stalinist practice.

17 See Hungarian Academy of Sciences, Institute of Economics, 1984, *Studies*, nos. 23 and 24, *Wage Bargaining in Hungarian Firms*.

18 One study covering capitalist countries that comes from an International Working Party on Labor Market Segmentation is Frank Wilkinson (ed.), *The Dynamics of Labour Market Segmentation* (London: Academic Press, 1981).

19 Prominent among those who have opened up this line of theoretical enquiry are Wlodzimierz Brus, *The Economics and Politics of Socialism* (London: Routledge and Kegan Paul, 1973); János Kornai, *Economics of Shortage* (Amsterdam: North-Holland, 1980) and *Growth, Shortage, and Efficiency: A Macrodynamic Model of the Socialist Economy* (Oxford: Basil Blackwell, 1982).

20 The positions of various groups in Soviet society with regard to reforms are reviewed in Davies, "Gorbachev's Socialism."

21 Alec Nove, *The Economics of Feasible Socialism* (London: George Allen and Unwin, 1983), p. 199.

22 Georg Lukács, *Demokratisierung Heute und Morgen* (Budapest: Akadémiai Kiadó, 1985). I am indebted to Dr. A. Bródy, Director, Institute of Economics, Hungarian Academy of Sciences, for drawing this text to my attention. It proved to be difficult to trace a copy of it.

23 János Kornai, *Anti-Equilibrium: On Economic Systems Theory and the Tasks of Research* (Amsterdam: North-Holland, 1971).

24 Bahro, *Alternative in Eastern Europe.*

25 For example, Milan Vojinovic, "Will There Be a Palingenesis of Extreme Rightist Movements?," paper prepared for the conference, "After the Crisis," University of Amsterdam, April 1990. Ralf Dahrendorf, while arguing the possibility of capitalism with liberal pluralism, is also concerned by the possibility of a fascist revival (*Reflections on the Revolution in Europe*, pp. 111–116).

26 David Mandell, " 'A Market Without Thorns': The Ideological Struggle for the Soviet Working Class," *Studies in Political Economy*, vol. 33 (Autumn 1990), pp. 7–38.

27 Davies, "Gorbachev's Socialism," p. 23, reports this of, for example, Aganbegyan.

28 Mandell, " 'Market Without Thorns,' " p. 18.

29 Novosibirsk Report, 1984; trans. published in *Survey*, vol. 128, no. 1, pp. 88–108. Quotation from pp. 95–96.

30 There is a substantial literature about the decline of hegemony, mostly American. Much of the debate is about whether or not there has been a relative decline of US economic, financial, and military power. More basic to the question of hegemony, in a Gramscian sense, is the extent to which the principles of world order on which the *pax americana* has been based are broadly shared, especially among the more powerful capitalist countries. Susan Strange (for example, in *States and Markets: An Introduction to International Political Economy* (London: Pinter, 1988), pp. 235–240) argues that US power is still relatively great, but that the United States has misused its power in narrow national interests by following unilateralist policies. I would agree in large part with her assessment, but consider this trend in policy to be an indication of declining hegemony. There is a formally hegemonic aspect to the United Nations Security Council decisions in the Persian Gulf crisis; but since in brute fact they express a temporary coalition put together by diplomatic arm-twisting and side payments rather than a basic consensus on global order, this too must be considered an indication of US dominance rather than of hegemony.

12 Structural issues of global governance: implications for Europe (1991)

Europe and the world

... The future of Europe has been considered here in terms of the options for forms of state and society as they are conditioned by existing social forces within Europe – forces which are the European manifestation of global tendencies discussed in the first part of this essay.[a] Europe's relationship to the rest of the world will depend upon how Europeans define their own social and political identity by making their choices among these options; but at the same time external influences from the world system are affecting the internal European balance of social forces in the making of these choices.

The emerging European macro-region will have a formal political structure different from the more informal authority structure of the other two macro-regions, the US and Japanese spheres. Whereas the United States and Japan are economically and politically dominant in their spheres, the European core area in economic terms is a corridor running from Turin and Milan in the south through Stuttgart in the east and Lyons in the west up to the low countries and the southeast of England, spanning seven states. In political terms authority rests in a consultative confederalism in which participant states have often differing policy preferences and micro-regions are asserting their autonomy. This makes it less likely that Europe can speak in a unified way, especially on foreign policy matters – witness the divergences over the Gulf War and over a common response to Yugoslavia's

[a] This is a substantially abbreviated version of the original text. The arguments that have been deleted are considered in "The Global Political Economy and Social Choice" and " 'Real Socialism' in Historical Perspective," included in this volume as chapters 10 and 11.

237

disintegration – although pressure from the other macro-regions could become a recurrently unifying force.

The central issue in defining the future European identity will be the extent to which it is based on a separation of the economy from politics. Strong forces urge that this separation become the basic ontology of the new European order; and that a European-level political system be constructed that would limit popular pressures for political and social control of economic processes. These processes would then be left to a combination of the market and a Brussels-based technocracy which would, in turn, reflect the dominance of big capital and the "core" states, especially Germany. These forces have the initiative within Europe, and they have the external backing of the United States as the enforcer of global economic liberalism.[1] Europe has, however, a deeply rooted tradition of political and social control over economic processes, both in western social democracy and in eastern "real socialism." This is why the transformation of eastern European societies can be so important, despite their current weakness, in the overall balance of social forces shaping the future. East and West are no longer isolated compartments. Political processes will flow from one to the other; and although now the dominant flow is from West to East, a counterflow may be anticipated in migration and in political movements. Despair generating right-wing extremism in the East could both challenge and encourage right-wing extremism in the West. The emergence of a firmly based and clearly articulated democratic socialism from the transformation of real socialism in the East could likewise strengthen western social democracy.

Europe's relation with the United States will in the long run be redefined as Europeans recreate their own identity. The Gulf War and President Bush's "new world order" placed Europe in an ambiguous position. Britain and France followed the US lead, intent on regaining a position near the center of global politics as these were envisaged in the 1940s. Neither country appears to have gained status or other rewards as a consequence. Germany held back, conscious of a divided domestic opinion and of the overwhelming need to give priority to absorbing the impact of the collapse of real socialism in the East. Italy, in a certain manner, followed both courses.

Will Europe continue to accept the role of the United States as enforcer of global-economy liberalism? Will Japan continue to subscribe to the US deficit? The United States, despite its unquestioned economic and political power, is moving into the same kind of difficulties as beset the Soviet economy: declining rates of productivity, high military costs, and an intractable budgetary deficit. The role of enforcer is not sustainable by the United States alone; and there is a real question whether Europeans and Japanese would want to perpetuate and to subsidize this role for long.

Reconsidering Europe's relationship to the United States links directly to Europe's relationship to the Third World. The Gulf War was, in one of its manifold aspects, an object lesson to the Third World that the global political economy was capable of mustering sufficient military force to discipline and punish a Third World country that sought to become an autonomous military power and to deviate from acceptable economic behavior. The subsequent decision by NATO to establish a European rapid deployment force under British command can be read as a reaffirmation of this lesson.

This is consistent with a view that sees the Third World from the perspective of the dominant forces in the global economy: some segments of the Third World become integrated into the globalization process; other segments which remain outside must be handled by a combination of global poor relief and riot control. Poor relief is designed to avoid conditions of desperation arising from impoverishment which could threaten to politically destabilize the integrated segments. Riot control takes the form of military-political support for regimes that will abide by and enforce global economy practices, and, in the last instance, of the rapid deployment force to discipline those that will not.

Europe, in historical and in geopolitical terms, has a particular relationship to the Third World: the relationship of Islamic to Christian civilizations. Europe's vocation for unity can be traced to the medieval *respublica Christiana*, a concept of unity that had no corresponding political authority. Islam's vocation for unity looks to an equally distant past and to the ephemeral political authority of the Caliphate. Its unity also transcends states. Islam is for Christendom the great "other." In contemporary terms, Islam also appears as a metaphor for the rejection of western capitalism as a developmental mode.

The canceling of the schism between East and West in Christendom, symbolized by the collapse of "real socialism" but reappearing in the war between Serbs and Croats, leaves unresolved the European confrontation with Islam. The global economy perspective sees the Third World as a residual, marginal factor, a non-identity. The historical experience and perspective of Europe confronts Islam as a real identity,a different civilization. Islam returned to Europe its lost origins in Greek philosophy, taught Europe science and medicine, and showed Europe a cultivated style of living, yet remained fundamentally alien and never, unlike Europe, germinated its own capitalism.

The confrontation with Islam is not only external, across borders and the Mediterranean sea. It is also becoming internalized within European societies, in migration and in the responses to migration by such political phenomena as the Front National in France. The new Europe is challenged to free itself from the residual, marginalized view of the Third World and to confront directly the cultural as well as economic and political issues in a recognized coexistence of two different civilizations.[2]

Europe, in sum, can be a proving ground for a new form of world order: posthegemonic in its recognition of coexisting universalistic civilizations; post-Westphalian in its restructuring of political authority into a multi-level system; and postglobalization in its acceptance of the legitimacy of different paths towards the satisfaction of human needs.

Notes

This text was first published in Stephen Gill (ed.), *Gramsci, Historical Materialism, and International Relations* (Cambridge: Cambridge University Press, 1993). It is a revised version of a paper originally prepared for a conference on "A New Europe in the Changing Global System," convened in September 1991 in Velence, Hungary, under the auspices of the United Nations University and the Hungarian Academy of Sciences. I am indebted to Stephen Gill and Susan Strange for their close critical reading of the original text and their suggestions. I doubt that either will be satisfied with my revisions.

1 Stephen Gill, "The Emerging World Order and European Change: The Political Economy of European Union," paper presented to the XVth World Congress of the International Political Science Association, Buenos Aires, July 1991.
2 A thoughtful introduction to such a perspective can be found in Yves Lacoste, *Ibn Khaldun: The Birth of History and the Past of the Third World* (London: Verso, 1984). First published in French by Maspero, Paris, 1966.

13   Middlepowermanship, Japan, and future world order (1989)

"Middle power" and "functionalism" were key terms in John Holmes' work. His was perhaps the most articulate expression of the thought behind Canadian diplomacy in the reconstruction of international organization after World War II. Although the great powers, and in the first place the United States, were, in Dean Acheson's words, "present at the creation," Canada and other middle and smaller powers were, as Holmes underscored, "also present."

Canada's contribution, in Holmes' thinking, should not be just to claim a place for the assertion of particularistic national interests. Beyond such particulars, Canada had an overriding interest in the development of institutions and practices conducive to peace, tranquility, and orderly adjustment in world politics. Middle powers, the general category of which Canada was an exemplar, could be an important influence to this end because, unlike great powers, they were not suspected of harboring intentions of domination, and because they had resources sufficient to enable them to be functionally effective.

This in substance was the Canadian doctrine of functionalism,[1] although "doctrine" is a word that rests uneasily in relation to the flexible subtlety of John Holmes' mind. In coining the term "middlepowermanship," reminiscent of "brinksmanship" and "one-upmanship," he introduced a note of irony and autocriticism in the affirmation of the middle-power role. He was impatient with a certain smugness tending to hypocrisy that he sometimes perceived in the professional advocacy of Canada's external relations. Yet he never lost confidence in the basic rightness of his view of world order as an historical process (*not* an ideal final condition) in which some states could serve the community of nations by their readiness to assist in the adjustment of conflicts – recurrent conflict being inherent in the very processes of life. Such service was not to be seen as an unlikely altruism, but as an awareness that the primary national interest of the middle power lay in an orderly and predictable world environment that embodied some limits to the ambition and the reach of dominant powers.

Holmes' exposition of middle-power functionalism has spawned a debate about Canadian foreign policy, in which the middle-power role has been juxtaposed to the thesis of Canada as a dependent satellite of the United States; and in which a third position holds that both images have been superseded by Canada as a "principal power" participating in the management of the inter-state system and world economy through the economic summits of the Group of Seven (G7) and bilateral relations with other "principal powers."[2] The debate, perhaps inadvertently, tended to box Holmes unduly into the first of these categories, a victim of what he himself deplored as "hardening of the categories." Mindful that ideal types express historical tendencies rather than final and separate distinctive entities, Holmes' sense of paradox allowed for Canada's role being a bit of all three.

I propose in this essay to dissociate middlepowermanship (let us take the ironic, somewhat skeptical form of the term) from Canadian foreign policy in order to examine its validity more broadly in relation to world order. This is, I think, consistent with Holmes' own vision. He cited with sympathetic understanding Voltaire's "J'aime mieux la paix que le Canada."[3] He underscored that the middle-power role is not a fixed universal but something that has to be rethought continually in the context of the changing state of the international system. So let us try to put the middle-power thesis to the test of the present problem of emerging world order by taking what I think to be a pertinent but hard case – that of Japan. To do this, we have to take up three questions: (1) What is the essence of the middle power's functional relationship to world order? (2) What are the key elements in the current problem of world order and how would middlepowermanship relate to this problem? and (3) What are Japan's options and the prospects of it performing the middle-power function?

The middle-power concept

In successive world orders, some powers have striven for or imposed their dominance. Other powers have attached primacy to institutionalizing regularity and predictability, within which their own interests and those of their populations could be pursued in a semblance of order and tranquility. Where a major power has successfully established such an order, we can give it the name of hegemony. The rules and practices and ideologies of a hegemonic order conform to the interests of the dominant power while having the appearance of a universal natural order of things which gives at least a certain measure of satisfaction and security to lesser powers. Such a hegemonic order rests ultimately upon superior force, but this force can most often remain hidden in the background. The order does not usually need to be enforced by direct violence or threat of violence on the part of the founding power. Middle powers may play a supporting role in such a hegemonic order. Holmes cited an External Affairs colleague saying: *"pax americana* is better than no *pax* at all."

There have also been situations in which no dominant state power has universalized itself in hegemony, yet some powers of lesser rank in military capability have worked more or less effectively to promote an orderly environment. In the midst of the dynastic and emergent national struggles of seventeenth-century Europe, the Netherlands, with its far-flung maritime commercial interests, nourished the law of nations.[4] Earlier, in the fourteenth century, the Catalan bourgeoisie, through the codification of the Consulate of the Sea, furthered the spread of maritime law from Barcelona through the Mediterranean and up to the Baltic.[5] Both were centers of moderate power on the scale of their times; neither had ambition for political-military dominance but rather for independence from more powerful neighbors; in both cases civil society was highly developed in relation to the apparatus of political rule; and both had a strong interest in a stable and tranquil environment as a condition for the pursuit of goals inherent in their civil societies.

In modern times, the middle-power role, conceived on this model, has become linked to the development of international organization. International organization is a process, not a finality; and international law is one of its important products. The middle power's interest is to support this process, whether in the context of a hegemonic order or (even more vitally) in the absence of hegemony.

Commitment to the process of building a more orderly world system is quite different from seeking to impose an ideologically preconceived vision of the ideal world order. Holmes described the process as "lapidary" in the sense of building from the bottom up, stone upon stone, a structure that grows out of the landscape, not imposing from above some architectonic grand design.[6]

The middle power is likely to be in the middle rank of material capabilities, but it also stands in the middle in situations of conflict. It seeks to expand the area of common ground which will make it possible to curtail risk in the management of conflict. Possessing middle-range capability (military and economic) is a necessary condition of ability to play this role; but it is not an adequate predictor of a disposition to play it. An ability to take a certain distance from direct involvement in major conflicts, a sufficient degree of autonomy in relation to major powers, a commitment to orderliness and security in inter-state relations and to facilitating of orderly change in the world system are the critical elements for fulfilment of the middle-power role. With apologies to Pirandello, we can say that the middle power is a role in search of an actor.[a]

The transformation of the state system

As the reference above to fourteenth-century Catalonia may suggest, the middle-power role can be considered to have existed prior to the coming into existence of the modern or Westphalian inter-state system. In its post-World War II form, the middle-power thesis was an amendment to the realist or Rankean view of world politics as bounded by the state system and in practice confined to the great powers.[b] Now it may be useful to begin thinking about the potentiality of the middle-power concept in the transition to a post-Westphalian world order.

When Holmes elaborated middle-power functionalism as a foundation for Canadian foreign policy, it was in the context of state power. States were conceived in a hierarchy of superpowers, other great powers (whose qualifications owed more to their historical status than to actual capabilities), middle powers, and small powers. Middle powers combined with small powers to avert the creation of a world council which would have conferred managerial responsi-

---

[a] Luigi Pirandello was an Italian author and dramatist from Sicily. One of his better-known plays is "Six Characters in Search of an Author."

[b] Leopold von Ranke was an early nineteenth-century German historian, known for affirming that history should be written *wie es eigentlich gewesen* ("as what actually happened"). His work *Die grossen Machte* was a precursor of twentieth-century realism.

bility for world affairs upon the big powers alone. At the same time, middle-power functionalism claimed special consideration for states like Canada, Sweden, and Brazil in relation to small powers joining the postwar United Nations.

This hierarchical conception left the middle powers in a tenuous position, lacking any collective impact on decisions, unlikely to have their claims for special status recognized either by big powers or by small powers. During the Cold War years, the United Nations saw its security function displaced by balancing alliances outside the United Nations, and its other functions came to be dealt with in the main through the interaction of regional groupings. Middle powers had a secondary role in the alliances and had no special place in regional blocs. Through most of the period between World War II and the present, the middle-power thesis has been more of an idea, a potentiality, than a realized and effective strategy of world politics.

Now we may plausibly ask if there are not some prospects of a transformation of the Westphalian system into something different, something whose shape is at present neither clear nor predictable. Present uncertainties may open an opportunity for middle-power initiative operating through a revivified process of international organization to resume the lapidary task of order building in a more complex and extended environment. The Westphalian system which reduces everything to states would give place to a multi-level system in which states are but one kind of entity in a global system of interaction that encompasses a variety of different identities and forces defined by region, ethnicity, culture, religion, gender, and relationship to production.

A current theme of international relations writing is hegemonic decline. Most commonly, this is discussed in terms of the evidence for or against a relative diminution of dominance of the United States.[7] But hegemony is more than dominance. A hegemonic order is inscribed in the mind. It is an intersubjective sharing of behavioral expectations. A leading nation's conception of the world becomes universalized to the point where its own leaders stand by the universalized principles where they conflict with particularistic domestic interests. The evidence for a decline of hegemony is to be sought less in loss of power than in a tendency towards unilateralism in furtherance of specific interests. Susan Strange, who rejects the argument that US power has declined, cites the late Hedley Bull: "The problem

America presents for us is not, as so many Americans appear to think, the relative decline of its power, but the decline of its capacity for sound judgement and leadership."[8]

If there is indeed a crisis of hegemony, its origins may be traced to the mid-1970s. They became apparent at the level of the world economy in the conjunction of oil shocks, disarray in the international monetary system, the international transmission of inflation, and the downturn in growth in the advanced capitalist countries that also had consequential negative effects for Third World trading partners. Even more fundamental than these symptoms of crisis at the global level were indications of breakdown of hegemony *within* the dominant states, together with concurrent crises emerging within Third World and socialist countries.

I would argue that hegemony at the world level is a creation of, an expression of, hegemonic societies in the dominant countries of the world system. A hegemonic society, following Antonio Gramsci's thinking, is one in which a dominant class has made its conception of social order acceptable to subordinate classes. Social conflict is not eliminated (it never could be), but it is institutionalized and regulated. This institutionalization of conflict within the dominant power or powers becomes the basis for an institutionalization of conflict at the global level.

A dominant society must be capable of universalizing its own constitutive principles, it must be supremely self-confident in its own internal strength and expansive potential, before it can become the founder and guarantor of a world order grounded on these same principles. The American society that emerged out of the New Deal and World War II had this measure of self-confidence. It saw the future of war-ravaged Europe in terms of American practices. The Marshall Plan and US encouragement for European integration were based on the premises of a market of US size and on American standards of productivity.[9] Subsequently, the incorporation of the Third World into the hegemonic order was understood in terms of its assimilation to US business and industrial practices. This has been the aim of bilateral and multilateral development assistance, in which the United Nations and the specialized agencies have played a salient role.

When hegemony within dominant societies is strained, the discomfiture is transmitted to the global hegemony. Confidence wanes. The regulatory mechanisms of the global system begin to break down.

246

Pursuit of solutions in a notion of general interest appears to be more illusory, and states, corporations, and others more openly have confidence only in their own wits and their own strength. There is evidence that such tendencies emerged within the dominant western societies during the late 1960s and the 1970s and have come to affect the global system. In the United States, the tendency found expression in the opposition to the Vietnam War and in the civil rights movement, both of which undermined the assumption of American moral rectitude and universalism. The Reaganite reaction to this disillusionment took the form of nationalist assertiveness and unilateralism inconsistent with a revival of hegemonic leadership. In western Europe, the events of May 1968 exposed a ferment of social protest within societies that had hitherto appeared as stable, progressive, and successful. Subsequent economic growth clouded the visibility of social cleavage without healing the breach.

The twin bases of the postwar social hegemony were, firstly, a social contract, and secondly, economic growth. The social contract guaranteed employment, adequate incomes, and welfare supports for the bulk of the working population in return for its support for or acquiescence in an economic system of regulated capitalism. The institutional basis of the social contract was a close association of business and trade unions with government in economic management. The state regulated the economy through Keynesian demand management and social transfer payments. These ensured a healthy environment for capital expansion as well as social protection. Growth, albeit punctuated by moderate recessions, made it possible through these state policies to provide rewards to the various social groups out of increments to growth, without having to face the divisive issues of basic distribution of wealth and income.

In advanced capitalism, the crisis of the 1970s initiated a renunciation by governments of the social contract with labor and business that had been the bedrock of the post-World War II welfare state. This tendency reached its most extreme form in Thatcherism–Reaganism but manifested itself in some manner in virtually all advanced capitalist countries. Governments backed capital's demand for priority to investment incentives and weakening of unions.

New investment went into the restructuring of production that would further weaken labor's power. Increasingly, production became organized on a core/periphery basis, with a relatively small core of producers linked by interest and loyalty to capital through forms of enterprise corporatism, and a broadening periphery of more precariously employed workers fragmented into downgraded blue-collar workers, temporary and part-time workers, subcontracting and outsourcing enterprises, putting-out workers, and the labor reserves of the underground economy and of the export platforms of the Third World. This core/periphery restructuring was characteristic of international production systems but also of production within advanced capitalist countries. Postal franchising, fast-food outlets, and temporary office help are typical of the expanding areas of employment. Ethnic and gender divisions accentuate occupational segmentation. The "working class" has come to have a fragmented objective existence and a problematic common consciousness.

Labor segmentation and high unemployment during the crisis of the 1970s affected particularly youth, women, minorities, and economically declining regions. Societies that had been based on a fairly broad consensus slipped into a condition of polarization. The dominant, politically more participant part of the population was satisfied and supportive of state policies. The segmented periphery was alienated and nonparticipant. Depoliticization in this part of the population masked the extent to which hegemonic consent had become undermined.

In the Third World, a tide of populism that followed World War II was all but spent by the mid-1960s. Regime after regime succumbed to internal conflict and external destabilization – in South America, in Indonesia, the Congo, Egypt, Ghana. Populism was generally succeeded by military-bureaucratic regimes that excluded popular participation and sought an export-led development with the support of foreign capital. During the 1970s, elected governments reemerged in some of these countries, aided by the greater availability of liquidity from private transnational banks that relaxed the constraints hitherto conditioning international credit. This financial facility ended with the debt crisis of the 1980s.

These countries now confront a cruel dilemma. One prospect is resurgent repression to enforce the austerity that is the domestic counterpart to meeting conditions for renewal of credit. Another is to renounce further credit in an inward-turning popular mobilization to produce basic domestic needs rather than export earnings. Elected regimes may prove to have neither the authority nor the will either for repressive austerity or for nationalist mobilization. They confront an unresolved stalemate between hostile social forces: disintegrating

agrarian structures, newly mobilized industrial workers, and burgeoning urban marginal populations.

The socialist countries are engaged in their own process of restructuring production – a major effort to make the transition from extensive growth to more capital- and technology-intensive growth. Their
economies have stalled and their world position is threatened unless
they can make this transition. It will almost certainly involve a
revision of the social contract that has linked state and workers in the
post-Stalin era. In this social contract, workers granted acquiescence
and loyalty; they received in return job security, basic necessities at
subsidized prices, and tolerance of a relatively slack pace of work.
These acquired rights are all threatened by projects of economic
reform, which could make workers allies of bureaucrats resisting
change, while intellectuals more readily identify with reform. Meanwhile, the opening of a reform process has aroused demands among
the hitherto largely politically inarticulate, most strongly mobilized
around ethnic and religious identities.

Thus, in the 1980s, severe internal crises have arisen in all the main
categories of countries. The advanced capitalist countries confront
options of continuing social polarization or of rising to the challenge
to work out a new social contract, a new social hegemony. The Third
World countries confront options of conformity with debt-service
requirements at the probable cost of renewed repression, or the devising of some form of greater autonomy and locally controlled linkage
with the world economy that would be based upon popular support.
The options of the socialist countries are drastic reorganization for
accelerated growth that risks provoking potentially destructive
internal conflicts, or being satisfied with a low growth rate, an economy of shortages, and a lesser economic basis for their power position
in the world.

We may infer that the future shape of world order will depend very
largely upon how these internal crises work out. Further, we may infer
that the crises in these three kinds of countries are interdependent
in their courses and their outcomes. Continuing polarization within
advanced capitalist countries could be transmuted into aggressive
external behavior that would lock these societies into their present
impasse, block attempted reform in socialist societies, and force Third
World regimes into either renewed repression or chaotic opting out
of the world economy. A slackening of international tensions could
have the reverse effect, encouraging an alternative within advanced

capitalism and reforms within socialist planning, and allowing Third World societies more time to work out their internal conflicts without external interference.

This interdependence in the process of change opens a new opportunity for middle-power initiative in the development of international organization. The future shape of world order is conditioned in the first place by the existing world and the options it allows, and in the second place by the normative aims behind the preponderant formative initiatives. I have tried to sketch the options. As normative goals for a posthegemonic world, I suggest (1) greater social equity and (2) a greater diffusion of power. This would mean greater scope for self-determination by social groups as well as by small nations.

These normative goals are inherent in the notion of middle-power initiative towards a new world order. The middle-power role is to affirm the principle of adherence to acceptable rules of conduct by all powers, great and small. Now we rethink this notion in a context where the very form of state is at issue in the movement of social forces. The state is no longer the only center, the exclusive point of impetus. It is also the product of non-state forces at work, and these non-state forces assert their own identities and claim recognition and tolerance within the world system. The principle of adherence to acceptable rules of conduct would, for instance, allow Central American conflicts to be settled by Central Americans and east European or Korean conflicts to settled by east Europeans and Koreans respectively. It would respect the emergence of internally generated new political structures. This is not utopianism; since the time of Grotius it has been the *Realpolitik* of those states that cannot and do not aspire to dominance. It is a condition for the diffusion of power among and within societies.

International institutions are the vehicles through which middle-power initiative could help form such a world order. These institutions labor, however, under a very serious impediment. They have one foot mired in the past while the other tries to test out the ground of the future. They are creations of the inter-state system and formally accountable to existing states. Yet facilitating the emergence of a new world order would require them to become *interlocuteurs valables* for the social forces transforming existing states. A certain schizophrenia in international institutions is the condition for the coexistence of these two functions.

It corresponds to the two kinds of time in which international institutions operate. As Fernand Braudel pointed out, history comprises a relatively fast-moving events-time (*histoire événementielle*), and a much slower-moving time of structural change (*longue durée*). In the events-time of current politics, international institutions function in the context of the Westphalian inter-state system. For such matters, control is necessarily centralized in the office of the secretary-general of the United Nations or the executive heads of other organizations. The point of accountability is clear. Our concern here is rather with the potential of international institutions for facilitating the emergence of post-Westphalian world structures and for guiding this process in line with the normative goals just mentioned. The *interlocuteurs valables* for the social forces at work cannot be the centers of accountability to states. This argues for a decentered, fragmented structure of international institutions in which some relatively autonomous segments of international organization can become agencies of reflection and dialogue that can respond to emerging social forces and help work out strategies and goals for change in polity, economy, and society.[10]

Japan's options

There is no iron determinism or historical inevitability at work in the process of structural transformation of the world system. There is rather a balance of constraints inherent in the existing order, with opportunity inherent in the process of change itself. The Westphalian system could reassert itself, perhaps in the modified form of strong regional blocs. Hegemony could conceivably be reconstructed, led by a collective of great powers rather than by the United States alone, as in the project of trilateralism or the vision of "complex neorealism" associated with the principal powers thesis. Or a multi-level post-Westphalian order could emerge from a greater diffusion of power in which the nation-state becomes decentered with effective subnational and otherwise-defined identities achieving effective participation. The pre-Westphalian medieval order suggests such an alternative paradigm in which the Holy Roman Emperor and the pope represented concepts of order more than effective territorial power, and towns, corporations, universities, and monastic orders coexisted as authorities with kings and princes. Middlepowermanship, as redefined above, could work as an agent of change towards the multi-level order, though nothing ensures it would be successful.

To think of Japan as a middle power is quite incongruous, if one's notion of "middle" relates to capabilities. Japan is often called an economic superpower; and even though in military terms there is a widespread impression that Japan has only modest self-defense forces, its expenditure of just over one percent of gross national product on defense makes Japan number three in world defense spending by some counts.[11] By no standard of capabilities can Japan be considered to be in the middle range.

Nevertheless, by the behavioral test of "middlepowermanship" outlined above, a *prima facie* case can be made out that Japan could become an exemplar of this category.[12] Japan has manifested a growing interest in international institutions as a focus for its diplomacy. Though spending appreciably on armaments, Japan still appears as a reluctant military power. The armed forces are not highly esteemed and are seldom in public view. The US military presence has been a domestic political issue and its bases are not popular with their neighbors. Japan has increasingly been emphasizing its growing contribution to international development assistance, in which quantitatively it is becoming a world leader.[13] Japan has an aroused public opinion concerned with environmental issues and has made strides towards cleaning up the home environment. Japan has taken initiatives towards a multilateral resolution of the Third World debt problem which challenge other advanced capitalist countries to be more generous. Japan has also taken some quiet initiatives and shown a disposition to commit resources towards the moderating of regional conflicts, notably in Cambodia and Korea. Most of all, perhaps, Japan has an evident interest in a relatively open world-trading system and the avoidance of rival trading blocs that would exclude Japan.[14]

There is another side to this picture. Critics see Japanese development aid as a means of underwriting and strengthening Japanese economic penetration of less-developed countries, especially in Asia.[15] More recently, the expansion of Japanese aid, especially outside Asia, is seen as a response to US pressures, with a view to moderating the tendencies of the US Congress to institute restrictions on Japanese imports. Japan has followed the United States agenda for "strategic aid" to targeted countries (Egypt, Pakistan, El Salvador, and so on). As regards the environment, critics point to Japan's export of polluting industries and its voracious appetite for resources which leads to deforestation and soil erosion in some Asian countries and depletion of world fisheries. In this perspective, Japan's international posture appears a benign front for the consolidation of a political-economic structure of dominance with a Japan–United States relationship at the core and a cascading sequence of dependent economies at its periphery.

Let us consider some possible world order futures and Japan's relationship to them. Then we may speculate about internal developments or tendencies in Japanese society that would predispose Japan's choice in one direction or the other. Schematically, we may look at four conceivable world order futures: (1) a revived US dominance supported by Japan; (2) world-economy management by the G7 major capitalist powers including Japan but expanded to include some form of participation by a more market-oriented Soviet Union and China; (3) a neomercantilist world of rival and partially self-contained economic-military blocs; and (4) a multi-level order with a wide diffusion of power among nations and social groups.

The first future – revived US dominance – would be possible only in a form incorporating an integrated US–Japan economy. This seems, indeed, to be the outcome most consistent with current practices.[16] The American economy continues to grow and US military-political strength to be reasserted on the basis of Japanese financing of US trade, payments, and budget deficits. Japan's surpluses are lent to and invested in the United States. This maintains Japanese access to the US market. The Japanese people accept a lower level of consumption than they might otherwise afford, while Americans are able to consume more than their production would otherwise enable them to pay for.[17] The political counterpart is Japanese inclusion in a subordinate capacity in the US military-strategic system of the Pacific.

Although the plausibility of this future is enhanced by the momentum of its actual existence, it has increasingly apparent disadvantages for both parties. It is bad for the United States because it enables political leaders to postpone and try to evade facing some difficult problems – the painful adjustment to lower levels of private consumption consistent with actual productivity, and the social adjustments that would be necessary to enable a substantial part of the population to participate effectively in economy and polity that is the principal requirement for raising future productivity.[18] It is bad for Japan insofar as it may delay Japan's adjustment to a new economic role by perpetuating its dependency on the US market and on the continuation of export-led growth, and more generally adjustment towards a restructured economy led by services and social investments.

The second future – an enlarged G7 vision of global management – could be presented as an evolution from the first. Its conditions would be a Japanese affirmation of greater economic autonomy vis-à-vis the United States together with the achievement of a cohesive sense of mutual responsibility among all the major powers involved. It is this last condition that seems so unlikely. The G7 have at the maximum been able to make symbolic affirmations of good intentions and temporary understandings about exchange-rate and macroeconomic management. While occasionally becoming something more than a photo opportunity, economic summits have fallen far short of initiating a reform of international economic institutions and procedures or becoming an effective means of global economic management. There is little prospect of change in this respect among the existing G7, and *a fortiori* in any expanded consultative arrangement that might include the Soviet Union and China.

Some analysts have focused with avowed pessimism on the third future – a world of rival blocs.[19] While the mental image in which this scenario has been conceived derives from the fragmentation of the world economy in the 1930s, it seems more likely that concentrations of economic power in regional centers in the late twentieth century would not take the form of encapsulated blocs with minimal extra-bloc transactions. It is more probable that they would take the form of centers of political-economic power competing aggressively for shares of a world market and access to investment on a world scale. Powerful centers of coordinated business–government power would use all available instruments of political-military-financial-economic influence to gain advantage for their own interests on a world scale.[20]

This vision contrasts with the liberal view of a world economy operating according to rules of economic comparative advantage and political non-intervention. Critics of the liberal vision from Friedrich List to Karl Polanyi have pointed out that the separation of economics from politics and society is an illusion that contains grave risks, especially for the weaker party. It deprives society of the intellectual possibility of self-defense because it decrees the primordial character of economic relations to which social structures must inevitably adjust.

Canadian opponents of the free-trade agreement with the United States have made the point that the US demand for a "level playing field" means that Canadian social policies and state intervention for social protection will henceforth be judged by and adjusted to US

254

practice. Canada is relatively vulnerable to the hegemonic impact of US social and economic practices. Japan's case is quite otherwise. Japan is the first case of a non-western, nonliberal society that has developed its economy sufficiently to compete successfully with western capitalism. US demands for changes in Japanese economic practices are perceived more clearly by the Japanese people as demands for change in the very basis of their social organization. They may thus be more actively resisted, although United States advocacy of liberalizing imports could undermine support among Japanese consumers for existing practices. The close business–government relationship that has developed Japan's economy and led its expansion in trade and investment throughout the world means that Japan is well-equipped by experience and ideology to cope successfully in a world of rival political-economic blocs. This prospect raises, however, the question of whether more aggressive economic competition in a relatively unregulated world economy would not generate pressures within Japan for the acquisition of a stronger military force; and this could trigger serious internal conflict within Japanese society.

Some readers may wonder why I have not included Japanese global hegemony, a *pax nipponica*, among the possible world order futures. There is, indeed, a school of Japanese nationalists close to the former prime minister, Yasuhiro Nakasone, which envisages Japan replacing a defunct United States hegemony based on Japan's superior economic power. They believe the military component of hegemony to be declining in importance. Their argument (somewhat similar to that of Paul Kennedy in his *Rise and Fall of the Great Powers*) is that hegemony goes to the country that develops the dominant productive system. Japan, they argue, is taking the central place in global production organization in the post-Fordist era of microelectronics and is becoming a pattern for other countries just as the United States was after World War II.[21]

The notion of *pax nipponica* derives from the classic realist usage of hegemony as equivalent to the dominance of a single world power. It does not fit with the concept of hegemony presented above as the establishment of universal norms of order. A Japanese novelist observed to me that Japan could not become hegemonic in this sense because its traditional culture had not generated universal norms.[c]

---

[c] The novelist was Kenzaburo Oe, who was awarded the Nobel prize for literature in 1994. Cox met him during the autumn of 1988 when he had discussions with a study group composed of Japanese scholars of various disciplines and backgrounds of which

Japanese dominance would likely take the form of one people's mastery over others, not of the establishment of a universally acceptable concept of order. The culture of the United States did give root to universal norms, the extreme demonstration being that Vietnamese rebels could appeal to the principle of self-determination (a strand in America's traditional universalism) in their struggle against the United States. Because I am using hegemony in the sense of an order based on universals, this reasoning leads me to exclude a Japanese hegemony from potential futures. The assertion of Japanese economic power finds its place in the neomercantilist option.[22]

The fourth future – a counterhegemonic vision of greater diffusion of power and acceptance of diversity – could be regarded as the apotheosis of middlepowermanship. In the former hegemonies of *pax britannica* and *pax americana*, a dominant nation/culture was in each case able to express the essence of its own values in universal terms. The counterhegemonic vision begins with a recognition of necessary equality of civilizations and cultures while seeking some common ground among them, a basis for coexistence.

The principal problem in envisaging this option is to find a cohesive political base for it. There are a number of counterhegemonic tendencies at work in the world, though at present they lack coherence. These include the new social movements in advanced capitalist countries (environmentalism, feminism, and the peace movement); the affirmation of separate cultural identities within established multinational or multicultural states; the revival of Islam as a world movement; the demand for a New International Economic Order on the part of Third World countries and their desire to approach this through multilateral negotiations rather than by a series of individual poor countries confronting their combined creditors and aid-givers; the struggle of some poor countries – Mozambique and Nicaragua, for example – for the right to pursue an autonomous pattern of development free from external destabilization; the movements for restructuring and democratization in socialist countries; and a new disposition on the part of states to make the United Nations system a more important center of international relations.

The question asked here is whether Japan is a potential leader in giving coherence and a better chance for the multi-level counter-

Oe was a member. Professor Yoshikazu Sakamoto introduced the author to this group. Oe's position, as he has made clear in his speech accepting the Nobel award, favors a nonmilitary role for Japan in world affairs.

hegemonic world order, or whether Japan is more likely to choose one of the other options. Japan's choice could be decisive for others, but by the same token, others' influence through relations with Japanese society could incline that choice.

External relations consistent with such a leadership role for Japan would include a more independent foreign policy with a more equal orientation to all parts of the world (towards Europe and socialist countries as well as the United States, and especially towards the Third World); a strong commitment to multilateralism through the United Nations system; capital exports designed to moderate the unevenness of world development; and a readiness to act as a lender and consumer of last resort for Third World countries. Whether or not such external policies are adopted is likely to depend upon the condition of Japan's domestic society and its readiness to support them. This implies that politics would be placed on a broad popular base. What are the prospects?

Japan has been widely regarded as enjoying a highly stable social structure, which is credited with being the basis for its economic success. The two key factors in this social stability have been the Japanese job structure and the relationship between government and business in the management of the economy. Production has been organized through a dualism in the structure of employment in which a substantial part of the labor force enjoys job security through an employers' commitment in the big firms to provide lifetime employment, while another substantial part of the labor force is employed more precariously in small-scale, subcontracting, or temporary work which gives flexibility for expansion and contraction in the more established sector. In the relationship between business and government, the long dominance of the Liberal-Democratic Party (LDP) over state office has ensured access by business to government, and the economic state bureaucracy, principally in the Ministry of International Trade and Industry (MITI) and the Ministry of Finance, has, through its close relationship to big business, been an effective planner and guide of economic growth and overseas expansion of an export-led economy.

There have long been predictions, chiefly from US and other western economists, that the dual employment structure and the lifetime employment system would not survive the postwar expansion of the Japanese economy. These predictions were ill founded insofar as they were based on reasoning from a liberal economic model of labor-market behavior according to which acquisitive economic man would seek the highest return on his labor in a process of upward job mobility and employers would compete with one another to obtain scarce labor by offering higher wages. Japanese workers and employers, guided by the state bureaucrats, did not behave according to this economic model. They conformed much more closely to a Polanyian model in which their economic activity was embedded in a social structure that maximized security and cohesiveness.

More recently, however, some Japanese have become concerned that the pattern of social stability – what we may call the implicit Japanese social contract – is subject to serious strains from other causes than those predicted from the liberal model. These are the same causes as have been bringing about a restructuring of production on a world scale, in western advanced capitalist countries, in Third World countries, and in socialist countries as well as in Japan. In this post-Fordist restructuring, large-scale mass production is being displaced by complex production systems able to produce a variety of outputs quickly in response to changes in demand in a global market. This requires well-coordinated production systems with a central brain activating a wide variety of flexibly connected productive components, some highly technology- and capital-intensive and some relatively standardized and labor-intensive.[23] In a certain sense, Japan pioneered this kind of production organization with its dual structure of the labor force, part established and secure, part nonestablished and precarious. The global restructuring process has taken over Japanese practice (but without its commitment to social and employment stability) and has extended it by reducing the privileged core and expanding the segmented peripheries of employment. The result has been a global shift in power relations to the advantage of capital and the disadvantage of labor.

Japanese participation in this global trend has resulted in a number of consequences that cumulatively weaken the social system underlying production in Japan. The proportion of core workers enjoying the security of lifetime employment has declined and the number of those in more "flexible" employment has proportionally increased. The unionized workforce has declined, especially in the labor strongholds like steel and shipbuilding. These industries have tended to shift towards the newly industrializing countries (NICs) like South Korea that follow in Japan's wake, developing the more labor-intensive and more environmentally polluting industries that Japan is gradually shedding.

Overall there has been a relative decline in manufacturing and a rise in services; and while organized labor remains stable in big manufacturing industry, it is very weak in small industry and services where the volatility of employment is correspondingly great. Organized labor has responded defensively to these trends. Formerly rival union confederations in the private sector have combined in a single confederation (Rengo), but organized labor has been more ready to grant concessions to employers in order to protect jobs from the heightened competition of the NICs. Increasing use of "network production," that is, the outsourcing of components located (mostly abroad) on a cost-advantage basis, constitutes a continuing threat to jobs in Japan and thus further reduces union power.[24]

The conventional view of Japan as a racially homogeneous society is being threatened by the transnationalizing of the Japanese economy.[25] The homogeneous view survived despite the existence of groups subject to various forms of exclusion and discrimination: the Ainu, the former outcastes (or *burakumin*), and Koreans descendent from forced laborers brought into the Japanese homeland during the period of Japanese imperial expansionism. In the more recent period of economic expansion in manufacturing, Japanese corporations preferred to move abroad to make use of sources of cheap labor for the labor-intensive phases of production rather than to import labor as did western European and the US manufacturers. In the most recent phase, however, with the need for labor in services, exceptions to this practice have become current. The demand for construction workers, bar girls, and prostitutes, and for people to do other service work unattractive to Japanese nationals, is growing in the home islands. Immigration, a relatively new problem, has introduced new complexity, hierarchy, and discrimination – a new level of challenge to adaptation of entrenched social attitudes and practices. Initially, it seems to have broadened the scope of the organized criminal element in society (the *yakuza*) which thrives on the control and exploitation of those suffering social discrimination.

At the present time, immigration is more of a challenge to Japanese consciousness than a statistically significant problem of public policy. It has provoked some responses towards an opening of Japanese society and understanding of the needs of immigrants; and probably more significantly, other responses towards learning to live without immigrants. These include drawing more upon the pool of women remaining outside the Japanese labor force. They also include moves toward robotizing aspects of construction work and the promotion of sex tourism,[26] both of which are ways of reducing the demand for foreign service workers in the Japanese homeland.

These dislocating tendencies in Japan's postwar social structure of production are being counteracted by a response of state, business, and labor that has been called neocorporatism. Government has urged unions to exercise restraint in wage negotiations in return for improvements in the social security system and commitments to employment security. Neocorporatism would imply strong autonomous union power; but the foundation for this reaffirmation of collaborative industrial relations remains the Japanese pattern of enterprise corporatism characterized by a muted sense of class distinctions within the corporation and a strong sense of worker involvement in the competitive success of the enterprise.[27] Enterprise corporatism is being reaffirmed and strengthened in the core of the Japanese production system, while the size of that core is diminishing in relation to the expanding periphery of more precarious employment. The segmented nature of peripheral employment, together with the strong economy and high level of employment, however, preserves quiescence among the periphery even though these workers are not included in the bonds of social solidarity that guarantee security among the core.

The other main aspect of the Japanese postwar social contract, close government–business coordination of economic strategy, has also been weakened as a consequence of the transnationalizing of the Japanese economy. As with the social relations of production, the strength of the economy has concealed the implications of these changes. The guiding role of the state bureaucracy, especially MITI, diminishes as Japanese multinationals increasingly generate their investment capital abroad.[28] MITI, once the influential source of state-capitalist developmental strategies, has become a less authoritative exponent of free-trade thinking. A large part of the small business sector, hitherto dependent upon links with big corporations, is threatened by the movement of labor-intensive production overseas.

The weakening of state influence in relation to big business has to be seen within the larger picture of the nature of the Japanese state. The neorealist imagery of the fundamental likeness of states is particularly misleading in the case of Japan. The Dutch journalist Karel van Wolferen, has argued that Japan has a structure of power with no top, no ultimately responsible head or center.[29] Like many Japanese, he presents a case for the uniqueness of Japan, but perhaps because of a somewhat abrasive style, his argument has been much resented in official Japan.[30] Yet his central point has been made by Japanese scholars themselves.

In part, the explanation can be sought in the consequences of the postwar occupation during which the structures and functions of the present Japanese state were shaped. In part, it can be sought in the survival of a longer political tradition, the emperor system.

The occupation regime went through two phases. In the first phase, radical reformist forces, released from the repression of the militarist regime, gained influence, including Marxist-inspired political and trade union movements. This brief period came to an end as Japan was mobilized by its American tutors into the anti-communist front in the Cold War.[31] The Japan Communist Party became marginalized and the Japan Socialist Party was consigned to a seemingly endless opposition status. Enterprise unionism restrained the radical tendencies of central trade union leadership. Erstwhile war criminals were rehabilitated as potentially useful anti-communist supports. The long uninterrupted tenure of government control by the conservative coalition of political fiefdoms known as the Liberal-Democratic Party became securely anchored, and Japanese politics moved incrementally to the right, sustained by high levels of economic growth.

The trend was at times contradicted by grass-roots popular movements. Unions, student groups, and intellectuals led a popular movement against the "Red purge" in mid-1951 when the occupation regime switched from encouragement of democratic forces in Japan to a more single-minded anti-communism. Another large-scale movement in 1951 opposed the separate peace with the West alone, and favoured a comprehensive peace and neutralism. In 1960 a broad popular movement opposed the revision of the security treaty with the United States under which US military bases have existed in Japan. Throughout the 1960s, opposition to US bases, particularly in Okinawa, and anti-nuclear sentiment – both enhanced by opposition to the war in Vietnam – continued to activate popular protests. Movements against environmental degradation made considerable impact on municipal and prefectural politics in the 1970s. Popular movements demonstrated they could exercise a kind of veto by placing limits on what elected politicians could get away with, and the LDP's political managers responded by adopting redistributive measures to give some satisfaction to popular protest. These popular movements, however, had little staying power and were subject to factionalism and fragmentation.

Under the occupation, the Japanese state seemed to have been assigned the task of economic recovery. This task it performed to perfection and the state agencies directly involved, the Ministry of Finance and MITI, became the most influential bureaucracies with the most powerful clients. The Japanese state was not assigned in the same way the usual state functions of defense and foreign policy. In substance, the United States looked after these functions. The occupation regime paved the way for the incorporation of Japan into the US military-strategic system for the Pacific. The Japanese Self-Defense Forces are effectively integrated within US military planning, and they seem to function without effective accountability to Japanese civilian power. The Foreign Ministry is lower on the scale of domestic prestige and influence than the principal economic ministries. This cannot be surprising in view of the origins of the contemporary Japanese state, but it bears underscoring as an antidote to conventional international relations theorizing about the state as a unitary actor.

Japan is better understood by foreigners as a status society in Weberian terms than as a class society. Or perhaps better, a substructure of classes objectively differentiated by evolving relations of production is overlaid by the persistence of *stände* (status groups) characterized by specific styles of life and conceptions of honor – not associations pursuing group interests but traditions of behavior and characteristic attitudes.[32]

The traditional structure of status placed warriors at the top, farmers in the middle, and merchants at the bottom. This bore little similarity to the structure of incomes, since merchants might well become very wealthy without thereby gaining prestige. The traditional warrior status became transmuted over time into an ethic of commitment to service transcending ends/means calculations, an ethic of dedicated loyalty. The state evoked such loyalty among its officials; and the big corporations inspire the same commitment among their staffs.

The merchant, by contrast, was expected to devote himself to ends/means calculations in the pursuit of personal wealth. He might be very successful, although success did not in this case merit admiration. Today politics is held in low repute by most Japanese people, but they do not expect it to be different from what it is. The old ethical status of the merchant finds a present-day counterpart in the interface between business and politics, the realm of political money which has been the life-blood of Liberal-Democratic control of office.

Within the state, two contradictory ethics have coexisted. State economic and financial policy has been constructed and carried out by a bureaucracy dedicated to service working with corporate bureaucracies similarly motivated. At the same time, the fruits of political office are distributed through a brokerage system based on pork-barrel politics operating through other agencies of the state (for example, the Ministries of Construction and Post and Telecommunications) and also on illicit funding and political relationships that descend even into gangsterdom. In the depths of the Recruit–Cosmos scandal that brought down the Takeshita government in 1989, a public opinion survey revealed that only 3.9 percent of the population thought the government worthy of support. Yet no one really thought a change of regime to be imminent. This was a measure of the depoliticization of the Japanese, of the low expectations people held of the electoral system, of the apparent lack of any credible alternative. It does not necessarily betoken a loss of confidence in the integrity of the bureaucracies.

The Japanese intellectual historian and analyst of political culture, Maseo Maruyama, diagnosed the particularity of Japanese fascism as a "system of irresponsibilities."[33] His perceptive discussion of the subject, in his post-World War II writings, is recalled to mind by the mood which gripped Japan during the long public illness preceding the death of Emperor Hirohito.[34] Much of what he wrote seems as relevant to the present political system managed through the LDP as it was to fascism.

Maruyama's principal point is that the Japanese political tradition has impeded the development of a sense of subjective responsibility. It has not evolved universal values which, whether adhered to or flouted, can constitute criteria of individual responsibility. Values have rather been represented as radiating from the emperor as from the center of a circle, and individuals' standings in relation to these values depend upon their proximity or distance from this center. Value in this conception is equated with power, so that power cannot be judged by the criterion of value. "Morality is not summoned up from the depths of the individual; on the contrary, it has its roots outside the individual and does not hesitate to assert itself in the form of energetic outward movement."[35] The feeling of being close to the

263

center of value conveys a strong sense of efficacy and a justification of aggressive action. Although the lowest in the Japanese social hierarchy are positioned at the circumference of the circle, receiving all the pressures from those nearer the center, Japan is conceived as the center of a series of concentric circles encompassing the rest of the world in an almost infinite sequence of subordinations. Outward expansion – imperialism – constituted the psychological compensation for internal conformity and submissiveness. An important feature of this representation of the emperor system is that not even the center is responsible. The center is not a single point but an axis of ordinates (the time dimension) perpendicular to the plane of the circle. The emperor transmits the tradition inherited from the remote past. No one is responsible; there is no identifiable head. Japanese fascism was not a dictatorship, because the very notion of dictatorship implies a head. Decisions were shaped irresponsibly by an interplay of factional influences gyrating about the center of power.

These forces were, Maruyama elaborated, of three types: the Portable Shrine representing authority, the Official exercising power, and the Outlaw (*ronin*) perpetrating violence. Broadening his analysis beyond fascism, Maruyama observed that Japanese politics was never integrated through an explicit, open, institutionalized rational process. (Here he may, perhaps, have idealized the European political tradition, but no matter.) He writes: "A more irrational arrangement prevailed in which decisions depended on fortuitous human relations, psychological coercion by the Elder Statesmen and other 'officials close to the Throne,' shifts in the relative strength of cliques, deals among wire-pullers and bosses, assignation-house politics, and so forth."[36] The structure of politics in fascist Japan, minus its militaristic imperialism, can be seen to survive in the political culture of LDP-managed Japan. This helps to interpret the relationship of bureaucratic to political types suggested above. Neither type is the result of subjective commitment. Both are the expression of a role. It is in this sense that their respective ethics are to be understood. Individuals are not precluded from changing roles. Circumstances will dictate.

Public behavior during the illness of Emperor Hirohito during late 1988 has been seen as a reaffirmation of past tradition. Japanese society, which had virtually ignored the existence of the emperor for at least a generation,[37] suddenly appeared to stop in its tracks. With few exceptions, the public pattern of behavior was one of reverential unquestioning conformity. Media encouragement of this mood was reinforced by aggressive acts of the extreme right factions (Maruyama's Outlaws) against the minority of dissenters. However, further probing in surveys revealed a gap between outward show and actual feelings on the part of the public.[38] Outward conformity could be interpreted as one more manifestation of depoliticization.

This depoliticization, sustained as it is by economic expansion, is the force of inertia obstructing a transformation of political culture. It is also the obstacle to Japanese self-definition of their role in the world, their option for a future world order. The two issues of political culture and world role go together. For Japan to embrace middlepowermanship would require a transformation in its political culture, a repoliticization of Japanese society. Past experience seems to negate this possibility. Yet it is not inconceivable as a dialectical response to the basic social changes being brought about by the transnationalizing of Japanese production; and to the challenge Japan confronts in the world from the hiatus between its strong economy and its lopsided and uncertain state structure.

Japanese political culture should not be considered to be immutably determined in the form analyzed by Maruyama. The first phase of the occupation released forces that had been repressed under fascism, and these continued, even after the occupation policy had turned against "leftists" in its anti-communist phase, through popular movements for peace and environmentalism in successive waves of politicization. The occupation made some important and enduring institutional changes: land reform, reform of the family system that opened the way for an affirmation of a woman's identity, inauguration of relatively free (though rather conformist) mass media. Yet the legacy of the occupation was a return to the structure of politics of the 1930s and 1940s, shorn of its militarism, and with the nation's energies channeled into economic expansion.

The occupation, in the mode of democratization it bequeathed, was a "passive revolution" in Gramsci's meaning of the term. The institutional changes brought about through the occupation were imported, and the more authentically Japanese impulse to democratization was in large part stifled by a combination of external pressures and internal forces of conservatism. A transformation of political culture today would imply an authentic revolution, a product of the Japanese psyche more than an imported model.

In fact, Japan today no longer has a model to follow. Japan's predicament is to make for itself a new model for future development.

Since World War II, Japan's model for the purpose of overtaking the US economic lead has been what Chalmers Johnson has called the capitalist developmental state,[39] a model bequeathed by Japan to newer late developers like Taiwan and South Korea. Japan has now outgrown that model and must redefine its goals as a society. This absence of a clear goal (which contrasts with the energetic embrace of economic growth as the goal of the postwar decades) marks the political vacuum of which depoliticization is the outward symptom.

Some are apprehensive lest, in casting about for a purpose, Japan be tempted to revert to a conviction of its "uniqueness" for which the emperor system's veneration of the state provided a model. There have indeed been indications of a revival of nationalism, in Prime Minister Nakasone's official visit in 1984 to the Shintoist Yasukuni Shrine, a symbol evocative of the war period; in the Ministry of Education programs and textbooks which have evoked protests from other Asian countries that had been victims of Japanese militarism; and in the support by some politicians for greater military expenditures. But a return to the 1930s seems an unlikely prospect, given the public's widespread abhorrence of militarism and rejection of nuclear weapons. Moreover, external pressures, both from the United States and from Japan's Asian neighbors, would work against this outcome.[40] The combination of internal and external opposition would seem to preclude this possibility.[41]

A case can be made, to the contrary, that Japan's primary interest as a world trading nation lies in promoting a reduction of military tensions in the western Pacific. This could include negotiated arms reductions, revision of existing strategic doctrines like the forward maritime strategy of the United States Navy, establishment of a nuclear-weapons-free zone, relaxation of military-political alliance systems, and resolution of the Korean conflict (for example, through steps towards a neutralization of the peninsula).[42] Japan's claim to recovery of the Soviet-held islands off Hokkaido is hostage to such developments.

More likely than a revival of a nationalist-militarist state is that the conformity and commitment generated by the Japanese political tradition now finds its focus not in the state but in the big corporations. The inertia of existing attitudes and practices would continue to sustain aggressive economic expansion on a global scale. Lacking any change in political culture, this kind of conformity can be manipulated by business and government elites. This would strengthen the prospect of a neomercantilist future world.

Is there an alternative prospect? Is it possible to conceive realistically of Japanese leadership towards a counterhegemonic multi-level world order, of a real Japanese commitment to middlepowermanship? We may reason, on the basis of history, that the political culture that might sustain this alternative would have to be built from the bottom up, from a revitalizing of citizens' movements concerned both with global problems – global ecology, the injustice and dangers to peace arising from unequal social development and economic exploitation, and the problem of common security – and with local Japanese manifestations of the same broad issues. "Think globally. Act locally.": this slogan finds nourishment in Japan's alternative culture.

If the last weeks of Emperor Hirohito's illness seemed to bring forward a resurgence of the traditional political culture, at least in outward manifestations, the elections to the senate in July 1989 showed the presence of a countermovement in which old norms broke down and international opinion became internalized in domestic politics. The situation behind the so-called sex scandal involving Prime Minister Sosuko Uno was no novelty among the Japanese political elite. The novelty was that it became a political issue. It did so when Japanese mass media reported what United States and British newspapers had published about the affair. The politicization of the issue was triggered by Japanese concern over the possible disgrace of Japanese leaders in the eyes of foreigners. The election showed the political efficacy of Japanese women, not as an organized movement but as an aroused consciousness. Women reacted to the scandal and, as household managers, even more perhaps to the new 3-percent sales tax. Apart from the women's revolt, farmers broke from their clientelistic loyalty to the LDP because of the government's apparent willingness to liberalize agricultural import controls. Organized labor seemed to revive its fortunes. Rengo, the new private-sector union confederation, ran candidates and elected a group of deputies. This was the first time a trade union had participated directly in a election; hitherto unions had merely supported political parties with which they were aligned. Rengo, as an autonomous political force, may have a role to play in future coalition building. These various constituencies – women, farmers, established labour – have little in common as interest groups. What they may share is not only a sense of disgust with LDP corruption but also a suspicion of the LDP's readiness to adapt to world-market influences, to be the transmission belt of globalizing capitalism. This suspicion could as easily turn towards neomercantilist nationalism as towards more socially inspired internationalism.

The election result signals less a turning point than the opening of an opportunity. It is more symptomatic of potential for change in Japanese political culture than indicative of the future course of electoral politics. The result was more of a rebuke to the LDP than an endorsement of the Socialist Party as a viable alternative. Clearly the old LDP faction leaders – the Elder Statesmen of Maruyama's typology – hope that a phase of remorseful penitence and political reconstruction will enable them to return openly to control the political system which they must now manipulate from the shadows. Almost as clearly, the aroused but fragmented opposition forces reveal the potential for an alternative political culture – a potential that could, however, only be brought to fruition by what Gramsci called a prolonged war of position.

One condition for the development of this alternative political culture is for the Japanese people to come to terms with their own past. They will have to confront the political system analyzed by Maruyama in full self-awareness in order to develop a conscious alternative that understands Japanese uniqueness as one among many forms of civilization contributing to a multiform world order rather than as a center presiding over rings of national and ethnic subordination. They will have to recognize explicitly the hurt done by Japanese militarism in order to merit the confidence of the other peoples of Asia and to secure their participation in globally oriented initiatives. Japanese resources and energies that make such initiatives possible are still negated by suspicions of Japanese motives rooted in past experience. The "special relationship" between the United States and Japan has been absorbed into the concentric-circles image of the world in traditional Japanese culture. Instead of Japan alone and the emperor at the center, it has become Japan with the United States in their symbiotic complementarity at the center. To maintain this image would negate the possibility of Japanese initiative towards the multi-level world order.

A further condition of an alternative political culture is the capacity to construct the knowledge upon which the reform of domestic politics, the framing of a new social contract, and the definition of an autonomous world-oriented foreign policy can be based. Japanese pol-

itical science lies at the heart of this condition. The generation of Maruyama and his students made a start on developing a critical understanding of the obstacles deriving from past political culture, a
necessary first step towards overcoming these obstacles. The "passive
revolution" in Japanese politics that followed did not build on this
foundation. The trend in political science shifted towards the import
of US models and methodologies and their uncritical application to
Japan. Where Maruyama had drawn comparatively upon a European
tradition midway between the hermeneutical and the positivist, a tradition represented by Max Weber and Karl Mannheim, the emphasis
now became more exclusively positivist, losing thereby the sense of
the particularity of Japanese experience and of the special problems
it presented.

More recently, a new generation of Japanese political scientists,
many of them having done their graduate work abroad, have been
using the comparative approach once again to reinterpret the Japanese
experience with a view to reform of domestic and international practices. The recent expansion in university faculties of international
relations is not just the reflex of a self-congratulatory world power. It
is also the expression of the concern among a new generation of teachers and students that Japan should play a constructive and innovative
world role. The new internationalism faces resurgent nationalism and
the outcome of their confrontation is at this moment by no means
clear.

The lineaments of an alternative political culture exist in present-
day Japan. They have not yet taken form in such a way as to change
the dominant pattern of politics; and it is unlikely they will develop
through the existing institutions of electoral politics. This means they
will work at best slowly to transform a deeply rooted traditionalist
political culture in such a way as to produce an effect in Japan's international role. The question we are left with is: Will the global economic forces reshaping world order outpace this potential for change
within Japan so as to preclude these internal forces developing? Will
global economic forces instead stimulate nationalist or neomercantilist
responses? Or is there the prospect that global social forces may interact with internal Japanese social and intellectual changes to reinforce
the development of both? Those who are committed to work towards
the vision of a counterhegemonic, multi-level world will realize that
the outcome depends not only upon the efforts of the Japanese to
create a new political culture but also upon foreigners coming to

understand the potentialities within Japanese society the better to work with these internal forces.

Notes

This text was first published in *International Journal*, vol. 44, no. 4 (Autumn 1989), pp. 823–862.

1 It is to be distinguished from the "functionalism" advocated by David Mitrany in his pamphlet, *A Working Peace System: An Argument for the Functional Development of International Organisation* (London: Royal Institute of International Affairs/Oxford University Press, 1943), which envisaged the erosion of national sovereignties through the proliferation of functional international agencies carrying out specific and large technical tasks.

2 David B. Dewitt and John J. Kirton, *Canada as a Principal Power: A Study in Foreign Policy and International Relations* (Toronto: John Wiley, 1983).

3 John W. Holmes, *The Better Part of Valour: Essays on Canadian Diplomacy* (Toronto: McClelland and Stewart, 1970), p. 1. Holmes was prepared to place general good (peace) above specific national interest; and this is the meaning of middlepowermanship.

4 Hugo Grotius, by birth a Dutchman, lived as an exile in France and was employed as a diplomatist by the Swedish Crown. He was, as G. N. Clark wrote, "an international man": Clark, *The Seventeenth Century* (London: Oxford University Press, 1947), p. 127. One may see his work as a product of Dutch society, though not as dependent upon the Dutch state.

5 Edward P. Cheyney, *The Dawn of a New Era, 1250–1453* (New York: Harper and Row, 1936), pp. 31–34.

6 John W. Holmes, *The Shaping of Peace: Canada and the Search for World Order, 1943–1957*, vol. I (Toronto: University of Toronto Press, 1979), p. 307.

7 This is succinctly put in the title of a book review article by Paul Kennedy, "Can the US Remain Number One?" (*New York Review of Books*, March 16, 1989). Kennedy is, of course, one of the main contributors to the debate in his *Rise and Fall of the Great Powers* (New York: Random House, 1987).

8 In Susan Strange, "Protectionism and World Politics," *International Organization*, vol. 39, no. 2 (Spring 1985), p. 256.

9 Charles S. Maier, "The Politics of Productivity: Foundations of American International Economic Policy after World War II," *International Organization*, vol. 31, no. 4 (Fall 1975).

10 By "social forces" I do not mean to imply existing nongovernmental organizations that have formal consultative status with international organizations. Many NGOs are institutions of the established order integrated with the existing states and inter-state system. The need stressed here is for dialogue with those as yet imperfectly organized groups that are becoming socially and politically self-aware through developing conflicts within societies. This process is now most clearly visible in the current reemergence of civil society within socialist countries, but is also pre-

sent within advanced capitalism and in societies of dependent capitalist development. We need to see civil society as evolving, as continually creating its own future, and to avoid the mistake of confining it to structures congruent with the past.

11 Methods of accounting differ, for example as to whether or not pensions of military personnel are counted. Japan probably has higher costs of military procurement than some other big powers. Moreover, the range of weaponry acquired by Japan is limited to the non-nuclear although Japan has the technological capacity to "go nuclear" in a matter of months. Japan is unquestionably in the same category as Britain and France as regards overall military expenditures. The arms industry has been straining at the bit to become competitive in the world arms market (arms exports are banned at present): Nikos Tzermis, "Japan's Arms Industry Gears Up," *Swiss Review of World Affairs*, vol. 38, no. 6 (September 1988), p. 38.

12 Japan is, for instance, treated as a "middle power" (as are also Germany and Italy) by Donald J. Puchala and Roger A. Coate in reports they have prepared for the Academic Council on the United Nations System (ACUNS), although these authors question whether Japan is yet ready to play a leadership role in international organization. See *The State of the United Nations, 1988* (Hanover, N. H.: ACUNS, 1988), especially pp. 32–33, 41–44; and "The Challenge of Relevance: The United Nations in a Changing World Environment" (Hanover, N. H.: ACUNS, photocopied draft report, 1989), pp. 47–50.

13 *Le Monde*, December 13, 1988.

14 This point is stressed in Richard Rosecrance, *The Rise of the Trading State: Commerce and Conquest in the Modern World* (New York: Basic Books, 1986).

15 Critics link Japanese aid with the overseas expansion of the Japanese economy. Jun Nishikawa, professor of economics at Waseda University, had proposed that the exploitive expansionism of business and government be counteracted by promoting people-to-people contact: "Japan's Expansionism and the Role of People's Movements," *Waseda Journal of Asian Studies*, vol. 6 (1984), pp. 1–14. Yoko Kitazawa of the Pacific Asia Resource Center, Tokyo, argued (in an unpublished paper presented to the Conference on Common Security and the Role of the State, Yokohama, December 1987) that aid relationships with less-developed countries have the effect of undermining social welfare and employment security in Japan while exploiting cheap unprotected labor abroad, and giving Japan control over other countries' resources.

16 Robert Gilpin has christened this the Nichibei economy (from the Japanese characters for Japan, *Nihon*, and United States, *Beikoku*, or rice country) in *The Political Economy of International Relations* (Princeton, N.J.: Princeton University Press, 1987), pp. 336–339.

17 The French Nobel laureate for economics, Maurice Allais, estimates that external financing by Japan and others has financed a US average standard of living 3 percent higher than would otherwise be possible: *Le Monde*, June 29, 1989.

18 This is the problem of 25 million functional illiterates and the attendant problems of crime and drugs. Proportionally, the problem of illiteracy is not very different in Canada. It compares with the total educational mobilization of Japan. At the top levels, there is, of course, no question but that US elite educational institutions are in the forefront of the world. It is in the density of the educational base of society that the weakness of productivity lies. For some critical comments on the US productivity problem, see Peter G. Peterson, "The Morning After," *Atlantic Monthly*, vol. 260, no. 4 (October, 1987).

19 Gilpin (*Political Economy of International Relations*, pp. 404–405) distinguishes benign from malevolent mercantilisms, the former designed to protect the autonomy of the values and social organization of a country, the latter being aggressive use of economic levers for power and domination.

20 Contrary to the assumptions of liberal economic theory, Susan Strange argues that a world economy organized in a "web of contracts" put together by combined political pressures and economic incentives would not necessarily result in any marked reduction in the value of world trade. See her "Protectionism and World Politics."

21 This argument links with Kondratieff long-wave theories of global political-economic history. See, for example, Carlota Pérez, "Microelectronics, Long Waves, and World Structural Change: New Perspectives for Developing Countries," *World Development*, vol. 13, no. 3 (March 1985), pp. 441–463.

22 On the thesis of *pax nipponica*, see the chapter by Kenneth Pyle, "Japan, the World, and the Twenty-First Century," in T. Inoguchi and D. Okimuto (eds.), *The Political Economy of Japan*, vol. II: *The Changing International Context* (Stanford, Calif.: Stanford University Press, 1988), pp. 446–486. Also Ezra Vogel, "Pax Nipponica?," *Foreign Affairs*, vol. 64, no. 4 (Spring 1986), pp. 762–767, and David E. Sanger, in the *New York Times* of August 4, 1989, citing Shintaro Ishihara's book, *The Japan That Can Say No*, trans. by Frank Baldwin (New York: Simon and Schuster, 1991).

23 I have discussed this process more fully in Cox, *Production, Power, and World Order: Social Forces in the Making of History* (New York: Columbia University Press, 1987), especially ch. 9. Between the secure corporate lifetime-commitment sector and the vulnerable dependent small-scale sector, post-Fordism has made a place for a new technologically sophisticated sector of small-scale enterprises – world-class cottage industries that earn good incomes and have benefited from the internationalizing of the economy.

24 See, for example, Mikio Sumiya, president, Japan Institute of Labor, in *Japan Labor Bulletin*, vol. 27, no. 5 (May 1988), pp. 5–8; also Yasuo Kuwahara, in the March 1988 issue and Machiko Osawa's report on the 1988 conference on Japanese industrial relations in the June 1988 issue.

25 Yasuo Kuwahara, Professor of Economics at Dokkyo University and

Senior Researcher at the Japan Institute of Labor, has written a brief survey of the foreign-workers situation in *Japan Labor Bulletin*, vol. 27, no. 11 (November, 1988), pp. 4–8.

26 The foundation of the booming sex tourism industry in Southeast Asia can be traced to the United States military program of R&R (rest and recreation) during the Vietnam War. The industry continues and develops not only by attracting individual clients but also with a certain corporate sponsorship as one means of encouraging the commitment of male staff.

27 Professor Kuwahara points out that Japanese corporate structure is different from that prevailing in western capitalist countries where managers are accountable to shareholders and board members are often drawn from outside the corporation. In Japan managers are usually promoted from within and are more insulated from outside pressures. In the Japanese firm, there is correspondingly a greater perception of social proximity between managers and other employees, blue-collar and white-collar. The enterprise union embraces them all and accepts the interest of the corporation as its primary concern. Japanese practice suggests a model of employee-managed firms. This, of course, extends only to the core of permanent employees. See *Japan Labor Bulletin*, vol. 27, no. 6 (June 1988), pp. 4–8, and vol. 27, no. 12 (December 1988), pp. 4–8.

28 Peter F. Drucker, "Japan's Choices," *Foreign Affairs*, Summer 1987.

29 Karel van Wolferen, "The Japan Problem," *Foreign Affairs*, vol. 65, no. 2 (Winter 1986–87), pp. 288–303; and *The Enigma of Japanese Power: People and Politics in a Stateless Nation* (New York: Knopf, 1989).

30 See comments in a review article by James Fallows in *New York Review of Books*, July 20, 1989. Japanese critics of van Wolferen also suggest that the "no top" thesis results from an occidental misreading of Japan's decision-making practice which operates behind the scenes in a complex and informal way through multiple consultations but does (or can) nevertheless lead to effective decisions. They cite former prime minister Nakasone as a deviant case whose ineffectiveness in the eyes of foreigners resulted from a personalized decision-making system that did not observe conventional practice. The Japanese decision-making system explained by van Wolferen's critics is consistent with the model discussed in this essay, which is derived from Masao Maruyama.

31 Yoshikazu Sakamoto, "The International Context of the Occupation of Japan," in Robert E. Ward and Yoshikazu Sakamoto (eds.), *Democratizing Japan: The Allied Occupation* (Honolulu: University of Hawaii Press, 1987).

32 Chie Nakane, in her book, *Japanese Society* (Harmondsworth, Middlesex: Penguin, 1973), stresses the predominance of vertical (hierarchical-ranking) over horizontal (class and status-group) concepts of social differentiation in Japan. I am suggesting here that class, as determined by relative power in the production process, is a factor in shaping the long-term trends in Japanese social structure just as it is in other societies. But this is class in the objective (*in* itself) sense much more than class as a group

consciousness (*for* itself). Status, conceived as adherence to norms of behavior – an ethic – expected of persons, holding certain social positions (high officials, professors, salarymen, etc.), is the conscious form of social differentiation. These horizontal distinctions are, in turn, overlaid by vertically structured identities that Nakane classifies as "frame" distinctions (corresponding to the Japanese *ba*), that is, the corporation, ministry, or other work unit to which a person belongs. At the broadest level, the frame can coincide with the nation. Frame identities evoke loyalties, and these loyalties are superimposed on status ethics without negating those ethics. Takeshi Ishida discusses how the class consciousness which emerged in Japan in the early 1930s and in the immediate postwar years became submerged in national consciousness in each period, although for different reasons in the two cases ("Socialism and National Consciousness: The Case of Japan in the Periods before and after World War II," conference paper, 1987). In his book, *Japanese Culture: Change and Continuity* (New Brunswick, N.J.: Transaction Books, 1983), Ishida derives the Japanese sense of conformity (consistent with Nakane's notion of frame) from the group orientation of the premodern rice-growing community which the Meiji state builders mobilized into the doctrine of the family-state.

33 Maseo Maruyama, *Thought and Behaviour in Modern Japanese Politics*, edited by Ivan Morris (London: Oxford University Press, 1969).

34 Yoshikazu Sakamoto (ed.), *The Emperor System as a Japan Problem: The Case of Meiji Gakuin University*, Occasional Papers No. 5 (Meigaku: PRIME, the International Peace Research Institute, 1989), especially the articles by Sakamoto and Takeshi Ishida.

35 Maruyama, *Thought and Behaviour*, p. 9.

36 Ibid., p. 232.

37 I had an opportunity to discover this personally while in Japan during this period. I was given the chance to ask members of a graduate seminar what the emperor meant to them. Their responses indicated that the question had only been brought into their consciousness by the press coverage of the illness, and that they had rarely heard discussion about the emperor's role, in the war or otherwise, either at school or in their families.

38 An NHK (Japan Broadcasting Corporation) survey conducted in June 1988, that is, before the emperor's illness, revealed that 47 percent of respondents were indifferent to the emperor, 28 percent expressed respect for the emperor, and 22 percent said they had a favorable impression of the emperor. On February 8, 1989, *Aashi Shimbun* published the results of a poll taken two weeks after the emperor's death in which 57 percent said the media had created too much of a stir, 28 percent said a natural manifestation of popular feelings had occurred, and 5 percent felt uneasy lest Japan be taking the road back to the prewar period (Sakamoto, *Emperor System*, pp. 17 and 47).

39 Chalmers Johnson, *MITI and the Japanese Miracle: The Growth of Industrial Policy, 1925–1975* (Stanford, Calif.: Stanford University Press, 1982).

40 US policy toward Japan on defense matters has been ambivalent. On the one hand, US pressures have supported increases in Japanese defense spending, although only within the framework of the 1960 security treaty, while on the other hand, some voices (including that of former United States secretary of state Henry Kissinger) propose that Japan put more resources into development aid rather than defense: Nikos Tzermias, "Japan's Defense Buildup," *Swiss Review of World Affairs*, vol. 38, no. 3 (June 1988), pp. 12–15.

41 Yoshikazu Sakamoto, "Conditions for Peace in the Asia-Pacific Region," paper presented to the Conference on Common Security and the Role of the State, Yokohama, December 1987. Strategic matters affecting the area are examined in Robert W. Reford, "Canada's National Security Interests in the North Pacific," mimeo, 1989.

42 The recent resurgence of a nationalist perspective on Japan's future has caused radical critics of its foreign policy dependency on the United States to be wary of advocating an independent foreign policy lest it move in a nationalist-militarist direction. Former prime minister Nakasone has been cast by some in the role of a Japanese de Gaulle, that is, a leader who will define a independent Japanese role in the world. This purports to depict Nakasone as a future prime minster. Nakasone as a past prime minister demonstrated a very non-Gaullist readiness to accede to pressures from the United States and to give tactical advantage precedence over long-term strategic planning.

14   Production and security (1993)

Production and security, the linked themes of this essay, are not to be thought of as independent and dependent variables. Their relationship is reciprocal or dialectical. Furthermore, the relationship of these two terms should be understood as taking place within a third term: the changing structures of world order. This paper sketches a framework for thinking about these relationships in structural terms by placing the contemporary world in its historical dimension. It offers not an empirical study but some linked hypotheses that may be suggestive for more empirical investigation.

Fordism and post-Fordism

What is the relationship of "production" to military power and world order? Two critical thresholds in the contemporary history of production are separated by about one hundred years.[1] During the last decades of the nineteenth century, a new system of production was initiated, which (with a certain anachronism in naming) is now called Fordism. Following a similar break in the dominant pattern of production, the era of post-Fordism is being initiated now, in the last decades of the twentieth century.

Fordism is a complex phenomenon.[2] In purely technological terms it is based on mass production, the assembly line, and the replacement of the skilled worker under factory discipline by a large proportion of semi-skilled quickly trainable workers in Taylorized production systems. This new structure of production was linked to new structures of economic organization, consumption and income distribution,

276

welfare, and the consolidation of the territorial basis of state power. Fordism meant the concentration of economic power in large corporations, and the adoption of employment, wage, and welfare policies that would enable mass consumption of standardized goods to sustain mass production.

From its early stages, Fordism encouraged measures of economic nationalism to protect national labor and product markets. In its later stages, Keynesian demand-management policies helped to sustain an alliance of corporate management and organized labor with the state based on full employment and welfare. Fordism was part and parcel of the world order of rival imperialisms that displaced the putative liberal order of the middle of the nineteenth century; and it was consistent with the state system of the middle of the twentieth century. Fordism was the basis for international economic relations, the inter-state arrangements to regulate transactions among national economies. Fordism was also an integral part of the military security system of the middle of the twentieth century: it produced the material basis of military power, provided a model for military organization, and was essential to the national interests of the states constituting the inter-state system.

Fordist production began to give way to a new kind of production organization, particularly in the most technologically advanced sectors, following the economic crisis of 1973–74. Business became concerned about restructuring capital, so as to become more competitive in world markets and pressed its concern upon governments. The international economic relations of the Fordist era were gradually displaced by the emergence of a world economy of transnationalized production and finance that could either escape inter-state regulation or become self-regulating with the support or connivance of states.[3]

Post-Fordism meant a shift away from large plants mass-producing standardized goods, towards shorter-run production for a greater variety of more specialized markets. No longer were large numbers of semi-skilled workers to be brought together in big plants. The need now was to combine the outputs of a large number of smaller production units according to shifting demands. The high overhead cost of plant, employed labor, and inventory was to be minimized in favor of greater flexibility in staffing and subcontracting. Post-Fordism is built upon a segmentation of labor markets. It has been accompanied by a weakening of organized labor (whose strength lay very largely in the mass-production industries) and an attack on the welfare state (regarded by business as a cost, obstructing international competitiveness).

Post-Fordist production lends itself to international production: i.e., to linking groups of producers and plants in different territorial jurisdictions in order to supply markets in many countries. It is promoted and sustained by an international financial system that is global in scope with focal points in major cities – New York, Tokyo, London, Frankfurt. Post-Fordism is the production mode congruent with interdependence within a global economy, just as Fordism was congruent with the system of rival state sovereignties. Whereas Fordism encouraged the organization of national economies under state management, post-Fordism encourages the internationalizing of the state; making the state an instrument for adjusting national economies to the exigencies of world-economy expansion. This has, of course, implications for world order and for the concept of military security.

Two concepts of world order stand in conflict: the territorial concept and the globalization concept.[4] Of course, this opposition puts the question more starkly than reality will admit. These are two tendencies rather than two completed structures. And they are not just opposed but also interrelated. The globalizing economy requires the backing of territorially based state power to enforce its rules.

Globalization results in a realignment of powers. The United States has assumed the preeminent role in promotion and enforcement of its conception of a global economy which is largely self-regulated by the interactions of private economic agents. Most other states, especially those that are economically more dependent, are constrained to apply internally the adjustment mechanisms that will integrate their economies more fully into this kind of world economy. The United States, however, cannot alone determine the rules and practices of the global economy, and must try to negotiate these with other major economic powers – Europe and Japan notably, and perhaps also China. These other major economic powers hedge their bets as between the globalizing and the territorial principles of world order. Their economic practice is conditioned by a higher degree of state involvement. Enforcement of the rules of economic globalization is thus problematical because there is no firm agreement concerning these rules and probable conflicts of interest among the major powers over particular instances of enforcement.

If observers take a longer historical perspective than the one hundred years of the contemporary era, stretching it backward to two hundred years, then Fordism and its related social and political structures can be seen as a reaction to the socially polarizing effects of what Karl Polanyi called the self-regulating market.[5] In *The Great Transformation*, Polanyi analyzed how the British state used its legal force to create free markets in goods, money, land, and labor. For Polanyi as an economic historian and anthropologist, the self-regulating market was never a natural phenomenon but the artificial creation of coercive power in the pursuit of a utopian idea. In response traditionalists, moralists, and the newly deprived subaltern classes supported political efforts to counteract the market, and to build through the state and state-supported institutions, like collective bargaining, the means of social protection. What we now call "Fordism" was the ultimate shape of this response.

What happened on the scale of the national economy during the nineteenth century could be repeated on the scale of the global economy in the twenty-first century. By polarizing the satisfied and the deprived within and among national societies, and indeed across territorial boundaries in an increasingly global society, post-Fordism could well arouse a reaction by the disadvantaged and the dispossessed with support from a segment of the competing dominant groups. This could revive the aim of regulating the global economy with the interests of these groups more clearly in mind – a revival of the aim of the New International Economic Order that was on the global agenda in the mid-1970s – and of organizing local economies with a view to social equity.

If and when this reaction occurs, it is likely to have one or more territorial bases that will take steps to insulate themselves from world-economy pressures. Such secessionist territorial powers would use their authority to control finance, trade, investment, production, and access to their country's resources in the interests of explicit national goals.[6] Various names may be applied to such state forms: state capitalism, socialism, and corporatism are some of the well-worn terms that may be replaced by new ones. The common factor is rejection of the notion of the state as servicing world-economy exigencies, as being the agency that ensures that global market pressures operate without constraint. This reaffirmation of the territorial principle of economic and social organization will be perceived as challenging the structures of global economy, and will thus encounter the hostility of the territorial power that stands as the military bulwark for globalization.

Fordism and military power

There is no inevitability in the course of history. If analysts can discern patterns in the past that can serve as indicators for future possibilities it is because, while outcomes are unpredictable, there are powerful pressures that shape the circumstances in which the future is decided. Knowing these pressures can help distinguish the feasible from the impractical, and thus may enable observers to try to channel events in whichever of the feasible directions appear to be desirable.

In this vein, there was no inevitability in the transformation of manufacture into mass production. In the more industrially advanced European countries, a craft tradition of high-quality manufacture was well entrenched in the small-scale manufacturing of Birmingham, the steel of Sheffield, and the silk of Lyons, all of which produced varieties of goods for segmented markets. The major factors encouraging mass production were, in the first instance, the American market, which was ready for mass consumption of standard goods; and, in the second place, military demand for standardized weapons and munitions.[7] The Singer sewing machine, the Colt, and the Winchester were the harbingers of a new industrial era. In retrospect, the American Civil War provided the necessary threshold and stimulus for future economic organization.

Economies of scale gave mass production of consumer articles a cost advantage over shorter-run specialized manufacture, which guaranteed the spread of mass production. The military demand was particularly important, since, once it was established, any country without a mass-production industry would be vulnerable. Both factors can be assimilated to competition: competition for shares of consumer markets and competition between states. Competition led not to greater differentiation and choice, but to greater uniformity, to homogenization. This effect of competition among capitalist powers was extended in unlikely manner through the adoption of Fordist production organization by Lenin and the Bolsheviks in Russia.

The social correlates of mass production were also perceived as essential to national security. A modern industrial state could only sustain its world-power position to the extent that it could counter the Communist Manifesto's appeal for the workers of the world to unite by binding them through loyalty and interest to the state. Bismarck was among the first national leaders to understand that the new industrial working class had to be incorporated within the nation in order to enhance state power. He made overtures to the nascent German socialist movement, introduced a whole series of social insurance measures, and formulated a concept of corporatism, linking workers and employers with the state, as a basis for his drive for German unification and primacy in Europe. Bismarck's approach was closely followed by conservative statesmen in Britain, France, and Italy.[8] The success of this line of policy was demonstrated on the outbreak of World War I when the national labor movements of the western and Central powers came to the defense of their respective states.[9] The same broad tendency, through national corporatism or tripartism, culminated in the welfare states of the post-World War II period. The Fordist contribution to national security was the integration of industrial labor into the pursuit of national goals.

If military demand was a driving force behind Fordism, productive capacity even more than population became the basis for measuring military capability. Paul Kennedy has recently argued the point in his *Rise and Fall of the Great Powers*.[10] Kennedy advances a cyclical theory: economic and productive capacity is the basis for developing military power, but beyond a certain point overinvestment in military means becomes a drag upon the nation's economy. A great power whose military might is disproportionately great in relation to its economic performance is on the verge of decline.

The Kennedy thesis can be read into the latter-day Reagan Cold War strategy. The Reagan administration's determination to build up US military force and pursue the Strategic Defense Initiative (SDI) increased the competitive pressure on the Soviet Union to what in retrospect must have been an intolerable level. With smaller productive capacity, the Soviet Union had to devote a much larger proportion of its capacity than the United States to military consumption, and it had fewer external resources on which to call for its effort. In the final analysis, the outcome of the political-ideological contest was conditioned by economic-productive capacity to sustain high levels of military expenditure.

In the relationship between productive and military capabilities, military demand was for a long time the stimulant of new ways of organizing production. The case of munitions requirements as shaper of mass production in the early stages of Fordism has been paralleled in more recent times in the development of nuclear power and space technology. The great powers (to employ the term Kennedy borrowed from Ranke) have subsidized research and development in these fields, and these subsidies had spinoffs in civilian industrial production. It would be difficult to estimate the full extent to which the direction of technological development since the middle of the twentieth century has been determined by military demand, but it is not unreasonable to accord it the status of a primary determinant.

In more recent years, however, the direction of technological flow has become more ambiguous. Military innovations have become more and more dependent upon the progress of civilian technologies. The flow has to a considerable extent been reversed. Military demand is still important, but military R&D now has to draw heavily upon civilian technological development. Nowhere is this more clear than in the aerospace field, and in the relationship between the United States and Japan in this field.

One major industry which did not develop in Japan after World War II was the aircraft industry. The base for aircraft production in those few countries that supply the world market for civilian aircraft has been the demand from their states for military aircraft. Article 9 of Japan's postwar constitution limited Japan's military force to self-defense and precluded export of arms so there was no basis for an aircraft industry.

The initiative towards the introduction of an aircraft industry came only in the 1980s; and it was prompted by changes in the civilian economy rather than from security considerations. Those large corporate enterprises which were to become the centers of Japan's aerospace industry had until then been the leaders in steel and heavy machinery, industries that were coming under growing competition from the newly industrializing countries (NICs). The need to adjust to a changed world-market environment suggested aerospace as potential new territory. This coincided with US pressure on Japan to circumvent Article 9 (which had originated under US dictation), so as to allow Japan to assume a larger share of defense costs. The Japanese initiative in aerospace took advantage of these changed political circumstances, but was precipitated by an oncoming global crisis of Fordism: the spread of labor-intensive heavy industries into the lower-cost labor zones of the NICs. Aerospace offered Japan a chance to break into a world market from which it had hitherto been excluded; and to enter this market, the military point of access was indispensable.

The complexity of the United States–Japan security arrangement enters the picture here. Japan depended upon US military protection. US military aircraft development was, however, becoming less and less able to advance on the basis of its own technological resources alone; it was more and more dependent upon being able to mobilize foreign contributions to its technological growth. The aircraft industry's problem was part of a broader problem, illustrated by US efforts to secure foreign participation in the SDI project. The US government and American industry accordingly sought Japanese technology, but at the same time wished to bind any Japanese technological contribution within the framework of security secrecy. The United States also wished (for balance-of-payments reasons) to remain the chief military supplier for the aircraft needs of the Japanese self-defense force. A nascent Japanese military-industrial complex, for its part, envisaged independent Japanese aircraft development, drawing upon existing US technology, as the foundation for a civilian aircraft industry. Japan would do in aircraft what it had already done in automobiles (and what Europe was doing with the Airbus).

The result of these conflicting goals was a compromise. For Japan to go it alone would have provoked a furor in the US Congress and run the risk of a protectionist attack on Japanese access to the US market. Instead, Japan is producing a Japanese development of a US design of a fighter aircraft with a US component of production, and with US access to the new Japanese technology built into the new design.[11] One can see this compromise as either leading to a continuation of a highly integrated US–Japanese aerospace industry or as a step towards a more autonomous Japanese aerospace industry, one whereby Japan can expand its production capacity and technology in this sphere. Both Japan and the United States have military and commercial interests in mind, but for the Japanese, the commercial motive may be the dominant consideration for the future.

This sketch has suggested several propositions concerning the relationship between production and security in the Fordist era:

(1) Military demand, along with the opening of broad-based civilian markets, was a major determinant of the shift from manufacture to mass production.
(2) Fordist social and economic organization created the political basis for sustaining national security interests.
(3) Military subsidizing of R&D acted as a major stimulus to the development of civilian production.

(4)   Overinvestment in military consumption became a drain on the economic capabilities of the great powers.

(5)   In the most dynamic economies, i.e., in countries whose strength lay in the economic, rather than in the military, field, civilian technologies took the lead in innovation so that further development of military technologies became dependent upon the development of civilian production.

Security implications of post-Fordism

A general crisis in Fordism began with the economic downturn in the world economy of the mid-1970s, which stimulated a restructuring of production organization. Broadly speaking, the large integrated plant mass-producing standardized articles ceased to be the model for the most advanced industries. Markets became more fragmented and specialized and production technologies shifted to supplying shorter runs and greater diversity. This required a more flexible type of production organization based on a relatively small core of permanent workers with polyvalent skills, able to adapt themselves to shifting product design and demand, and a larger proportion of ancillary workforce that could be linked into the production system according to need.

This ancillary workforce – peripheral in relation to the integrated core workforce – is fragmented (or segmented in the terminology of labor economists).[12] Some have less secure jobs in core plants; some are in subcontracted maintenance jobs or temporary employment; some are employed by subcontracting suppliers, or as putting-out workers, or in the underground economy. Frequently, to the fragmentation of production tasks corresponds a fragmentation of group identities: for example, on an ethnic or gender basis.

Post-Fordist production organization thus generates social relations that contrast with those of Fordism. Fordism concentrated workers from different origins in a common mass, providing a basis for strong industrial trade unions. Post-Fordist production organization takes a core of skilled, stably employed workers and integrates them with capital in a relatively privileged status; and it fragments the larger proportion of peripheral workers into a mix of often competing identities. Post-Fordism thereby undermines the strong industrial trade unions that were a force in the making of state policy. The class struggle of post-Fordism is latent, but it is there.

284

This new pattern of social organization of production has become characteristic of the most technologically advanced sectors. It has also begun to change public-service employment, with the contracting-out of some government services (for example, franchising of postal work) increasing recourse to private consultants, and so on. It is accompanied by some geographical shifts in production within countries, mainly the shift of labor-intensive work to areas where union organization is weak. It is also accompanied by the growth of international production systems based on labor-intensive, energy-intensive, and polluting operations in low-wage countries.

Post-Fordism is congruent with the globalization trend towards greater interdependence not only among countries, but in the operations of individual production organizations. (Globalized production organizations include not only multinational corporations, but also production systems constructed ad hoc to link many individual producing units in different countries providing components and assembly of a particular product.) It thus implicitly contradicts the territorial principle that was congruent with Fordism.

Along with this transnational mixing of producing units comes a greater mixing of peoples. A large-scale migration from South to North is in progress, from the Third World to the old core areas of the world economy. This migration obviously generates new social tensions that reinforce the fragmenting tendency of production relations, while obstructing the possibility of a coherent articulated viewpoint on the part of peripheral workers. There is frustration, but no effective outlet for it in social demands. The politics of distant regions surface within the countries of immigration. Local politics come to have a global reach.

The environment becomes an issue. The old Fordist industries were polluters. Post-Fordism cleans up pollution in the core areas, but it generates more pollution in the peripheries. The energy-intensive as well as labor-intensive (usually the same) operations are located in areas less able or willing to defend their interests. Resource extraction proceeds apace in zones that are politically unprotected. Petroleum and other mineral reserves, the trees of the forests, and the fish of the seas are appropriated by the relatively rich without much concern for ecological consequences. The environmental power relationship of exploiters and exploited is charged with a conflict that is only beginning to be articulated, most notably by indigenous peoples, from the Amazon to northern Canada.

The post-Fordist complex is dismantling the welfare state that Fordism built. Together, the erosion of organized labor's strength and capital's insistence that welfare costs are a burden upon international competitiveness overturn the tripartite alliance of government, big labor, and big industry upon which the welfare state and Keynesian demand-management of the economy were grounded. Government now acts to provide internationally oriented business with the best possible conditions, and conspires to obstruct labor's demands. The symbolic signal was given by President Reagan in his action against the air-traffic controllers; but any number of actions by any number of governments could be cited as following that lead.

In the leading capitalist powers, post-Fordist employment structures and politics have left a large part of the population relatively satisfied, while another large part has been economically and socially marginalized, fragmented, and, in effect, depoliticized.[13] Here again, conflict is largely submerged. The alternative to post-Fordist politics has not been formulated and articulated. Fordism thrived in cohesive national societies intent upon embracing all effective social forces within the nation. Post-Fordism deprives the national entity of its social unity; ideologically, it can substitute only a jingoism empty of social content.

The security implications of post-Fordism thus become clear:

(1) Greater international interdependence in sophisticated production processes makes these processes more vulnerable to disruption, whether to supplies of energy or of technological components.

(2) Greater international mingling of populations creates potential for dissent by minorities from state goals and, at the extreme, for political use of hostages.

(3) New sources of conflict are generated by the core–periphery structuring of production, some identified as centering on ethnic, some on gender, some on environmental issues, all of which undermine the concept of national identity.

(4) Jingoism may produce a momentary psychological impact in an economically fragmented population, but cannot have much staying power in public opinion where it has no material foundation (the late nineteenth-century British worker and the US hard-hat during the Vietnam era were both benefici-

aries, in a way, of their countries' imperial strategies, but the peripheral worker of post-Fordism is not).

(5) There is a contradiction inherent in post-Fordism: the globalizing interdependence principle is strengthened as the territorial national principle is weakened; but ultimately the security of globalization depends upon military force with a territorial basis.

The United States and global security

US Secretary of State James Baker is reported as saying that the Persian Gulf crisis that began in the summer of 1990 was the first crisis of the post-Cold War world. It was a perceptive comment, even if the crisis was not favorable for the future world order projected by the US administration. United States intervention in the Gulf did, however, reveal in action the structure of world power underpinning globalization in the post-Fordist era.

The conflict began at the regional level between forces based on the territorial principle challenging forces deeply embedded in globalizing interdependence. Iraq's goals were to use territorial power to secure economic resources for its own economic recovery from the Iran–Iraq war, and for consolidation of a strong Middle East territorial power that could control resources (oil) required by the world economy, and thereby extract from the world economy a rent that could be used to further its own developmental and security goals. Palestinian claims for statehood are an extension of that goal. (Post-revolutionary Iran's goals, while distinct and potentially conflicting, are also territorially oriented: i.e., to use its economic resources and to control its economic links to the outside world in the interests of nationally determined priorities.)

Kuwait, Saudi Arabia, and the other Gulf states are fully integrated into the interdependent world economy. Indeed, these states are more analogous to large holding companies than to territorial states. The revenues they derive from oil are invested by their rulers through transnational banks into debt and equities around the world. Within the territories of these countries, the workforce is multinational. The region thus contains the elements of conflict between territorial and globalizing principles, both struggling to align themselves with the other major sources of conflict. In this struggle, the territorial principle has the advantage of being more readily able to mobilize the demands of the poor versus the rich, and the claims of cultural specificity versus the homogenizing tendencies of globalism.

The trigger to the conflict was Iraq's effort to constrain Kuwait, through OPEC and other negotiations, to restrict its deliveries of oil to the world market so as to raise the world price of oil. This would have benefited Iraq's goal of reconstruction and development. The issue pitted territorial development against world-economy stability. When Kuwait resisted, Iraq asserted historical claims to Kuwait as an excuse for occupation and annexation. The United States responded as the principal guarantor and enforcer of the globalizing world economic order and, in that role, rallied support from other states deeply concerned about the stability of the world economy.[14]

The role of principal enforcer has, however, evolved as one beset by some basic contradictions. US projection of military power on the world scale has become more salient, while the relative strength of US productive capacity has declined.[15] As a consequence, US military power in defense of world-economy interests has become a quid pro quo for foreign support of the US economy.

Two main means of coercion are available to enforce compliance with the exigencies of a globalizing world economy: financial and military. These two have become intertwined, particularly since the mid-1960s. The Vietnam War was a turning point in their relationship as concerns the United States. President Lyndon Johnson proved able to choose *both* guns and butter – both a substantial military commitment abroad and the Great Society program at home. He was able to do this because foreigners paid for the war. Foreign central banks bought US Treasury bills to roughly the same extent that the US government spent on the war. The US national debt became increasingly a debt held by foreigners, a trend that has continued ever since.[16]

At that time, President de Gaulle of France objected that an unrestrained accumulation of payments deficits by the United States constituted an abuse of the special privilege inherent in the dollar's status as the principal international currency. He signaled his unwillingness either to finance a US war in Indochina that France did not support or to assist in a US takeover of European businesses by accepting an unlimited supply of dollars. France had some leverage at the time in its ability, under the rules of the Bretton Woods system, to exchange dollars for gold, at a time when dollars held by foreigners had come to exceed the value of US gold reserves. The rules then prevailing placed some restraint upon US policy, at least potentially.

Although it shared the French concern over undisciplined US monetary behavior, West Germany was in effect a US military protectorate. In the mid-1960s, the United States was able to make German acceptance of US public debt the quid pro quo for the US military presence in the heart of Europe as a counter to a perceived Soviet threat.[17]

By the 1980s, the rules of the Bretton Woods system, which had some potential for restraint on US policy, ceased to be operative. The link of the dollar to gold was severed in the summer of 1971, and from 1973 the exchange rates of the major world currencies were afloat. Management of the dollar became a matter of negotiation among the treasuries and central banks of the chief industrial powers, and in these negotiations the military power and world role of the US could not but be a factor. Under the Reagan presidency, the build-up of US military strength contributed to growing budget deficits. A US trade deficit had also appeared during the 1970s, and it continued to grow apace during this period. The US economy was consuming far beyond its ability to pay.

The accumulating gap continued to be bridged by borrowing from foreigners. At the end of 1981, the United States was in a net world creditor position of $141 billion. By the end of 1987, the United States had become the world's biggest debtor nation to the tune of some $400 billion,[18] and the debt has remained high ever since. In the interplay of political pressures among the industrial states, US military power and commitments to allies became counterweights to the compliance of allies with US financial needs. Whereas in the postwar world, US hegemonic leadership had been the means of reviving the economies of the other non-communist industrial countries, now military power could be seen as the justification for exacting tribute. A hegemonic system was becoming transformed into a tributary system.

There is a striking contrast between the US situation as the largest debtor nation and the situation of other debtor nations. While the United States has been able to attract, cajole, or coerce other nations' political leaders, central bankers, and corporate investors to accept its IOUs, other countries become subject to the rigorous discipline imposed by market forces and by the agencies of the world economy, notably the IMF. Under the euphemistic name of "adjustment programs," they are required to impose domestic austerity with the effect of raising unemployment and domestic prices, which fall most heavily on the economically weaker segments of the population. Through the financial mechanism, these debtor states are constrained to play the role of instruments of the world economy, opening their national economies more fully to external pressures. By acquiescing, they contribute to undermining the territorial principle: i.e., the possibility of organizing collective national self-defense against external economic forces. Any show of resistance in favor of an alternative developmental strategy can be met by a series of measures beginning with a cutoff of foreign credit, and progressing through political destabilization, to culminate in covert and ultimately overt military attack.

The uniqueness of the US position in relation to debt cannot be attributed solely, or perhaps even primarily, to willful policy. It results from a structural inability of the US policy to change certain parameters of the military-debt relationship. Americans have been able to enjoy, through debt, a higher level of consumption than their production would otherwise permit, because foreigners were ready to accept a flow of depreciating dollars. Part of the debt-causing US deficit is attributable to military expenditure (or military-related, i.e., payments to client states that provide military staging grounds, like Egypt or the Philippines); and part is attributable to domestic transfer payments (so-called entitlement programs) which by and large benefit the American middle class.

The peace dividend anticipated as a result of the end of the Cold War seems a much less likely prospect since the Gulf crisis has underscored the US role as enforcer in the world economy. Domestic political resistance to cuts in the entitlement programs is on a par with resistance to tax increases. Public funds on an unprecedented scale can be taken to cover a government–business scandal in the savings and loan sector, but the rising price of oil resulting from the Gulf conflict effectively precluded any increase in fuel tax that might have been a gesture towards alleviating the deficit. American politicians cannot confront their electors with the prospect of a necessary reduction in their living standards when the Middle East confrontation has been presented as the defense of the American way of life. With no relief in the deficit, there can be no prospect of Washington's undertaking the massive investment in human resources that would be necessary in the long run to raise US productivity by enabling the marginalized quarter or third of the population to participate effectively in the economy so that the United States might gradually move out of its dependence on foreign debt sustained by military power. All elements of the military-debt syndrome conspire to prevent an American initiative to transform it.[a]

The structural obstacles to change extend outside the United States, but not quite so obstinately. Those foreigners who hold US debt are increasingly locked in as the exchange rate of the dollar declines. They would suffer losses by shifting to other major currencies; and their best immediate prospect may be to exchange debt for equity by purchase of US assets. In the longer run, however, foreigners may weigh more seriously the option of declining to finance US debt; and if this were to happen it would force the United States into a painful domestic readjustment. Indeed, it is probably the only thing that could precipitate such an adjustment. But there are serious risks for the rest of the world in forcing the world's preeminent military power into such a painful course. They are the risks inherent in assessing self-restraint in the use of military power.

Japan is in a particularly delicate position as the major financer of the US deficit. There is a commercial incentive for Japan to hold US debt. By continuing to subscribe to US Treasury bills, Japan maintains access to the US market and appeases the protectionist proclivities of the US Congress. On the other hand, resistance to the conversion of debt into equity has arisen within the United States. There is evidence of intolerance in US domestic opinion for increased Japanese ownership of US assets. (Such intolerance does not arise in the same way, for example, regarding British or Dutch ownership of US assets, which is also considerable.)

Japan, like the former West Germany, has also been subject to the US quid pro quo of financial support for military protection. This incentive is reduced as dependence on US military cover seems less significant for Japan now that the Cold War has abated and the sense of Soviet, now Russian, threat has weakened. By contrast, Japan's security would be more seriously threatened by a prolonged disruption in the flow of oil from the Persian Gulf. It is not surprising that influential voices are raised in Japan to criticize the lack of discipline in US domestic and economic policy, to urge Japan to diversify economic relations away from dependence upon the US market, and to

[a] The Clinton administration's gestures toward infrastructure investment continue the pattern of subsidization of the established, privileged sector at the expense of the peripheral components of the population.

advocate an independent political-military position.[19] The risks are, however, still considerable for Japan. The asymmetry in the relationship of the two powers (Japan's relative economic dynamism and the US preponderance of military power) brings to the back of the mind the spectre of Japan as America's Kuwait.

Conclusion

This sketch of the structural model of a crisis in world power relations grounded in the relationship of production to military power is uncomplicated by debate about the motives of actors and moral judgement on their behavior. There are no good guys or bad guys in this model. Indeed, the model is not so much concerned with actors as with the objective forces that condition actions.

The distinction around which these forces cluster is that between the territorial and the globalizing principles of world order. This essay argues that although the globalizing principle is now dominant, the contradictions within it are likely to lead, not next year or even during the present decade but in the course of several decades, to a different kind of world order produced by the interaction of the two principles.

The United States stands at the heart of the contradiction between these two principles: it is the champion of globalization, yet its role as military enforcer is territorially based. Within the US state, the globalizing policies and ideology of the executive branch and the big corporations and banks are contested by territorial protectionism in the Congress, the states, and a sector of domestic business and labor.

The Japanese and European economies have become globalized in practice without entirely sacrificing the territorial principle, retaining it as a safeguard and insurance against risk. Neither (with the exception of Britain in Europe) has assimilated the ideology of globalization to the degree common in the United States. The tradition of a corporatist relationship of state to productive forces remains strong in Europe and Japan. In their economies, aggressive economic expansionism in world markets coexists with social protectionism at home.[20] Russia and China aspire to globalization (or at any rate to further integration into the world economy), but, in the light of their past, find it difficult to dismantle the controls over external economic forces affecting them.

Those countries with the least defenses against the socially and economically polarizing consequences of globalization are the Third World countries. For them, assertion of the territorial principle is the

292

only means of undertaking an alternative development strategy; and only a few – those with valuable natural resources – can have a chance to survive if they were to pursue such a strategy. When Iraq tried to seize this chance, its action threatened the globalizing world economy's reliance on cheap oil, and its fragile financial structure. It also threatened the balance of domestic forces determining US policy. The Iraqi action accordingly provoked military confrontation.

The Middle East crisis showed the kind of conflict situation that could become characteristic of the transition from globalization to a postglobalization world order. The conflict had the external features of a territorial confrontation; but its implications lie in the transformation of societies through the spread of new production relations, the disturbance and mixing of peoples that has unleashed an affirmation of suppressed identities (ethnic, religious, gender), and the challenge this poses to existing forms of state. This challenge, most visible now in parts of the Third World and in the disintegration of the Soviet empire, will in due time appear within the most powerful centers of the world economy. When it does, the ability of military force to obstruct change will itself be challenged. Power in the world system will become fragmented, and the possibility of culturally diverse alternatives to global homogenization will become more real.

Notes

This text was first published in David Dewitt, David Hagland, and John Kirton (eds.), *Building a New Global Order: Emerging Trends in International Security* (Toronto: Oxford University Press, 1993).

1 The usage "contemporary history" is borrowed from Geoffrey Barraclough, *An Introduction to Contemporary History* (Harmondsworth, Middlesex: Penguin, 1967). He meant by "contemporary" a structural shape of the world which is recognizable in its main features today, and that he dated from the last decades of the nineteenth century.

2 Antonio Gramsci, in *Selections from the Prison Notebooks*, edited and trans. Quintin Hoare and Geoffrey Nowell Smith (New York: International Publishers, 1971), used the term "Fordism" to designate a particular technological-economic-social-moral-political organization of production. It has been adopted by economists of the French regulation school, for example, Alain Lipietz, *Mirages and Miracles* (London: Verso, 1987), and by some American political economists, for example, Charles Sabel, *Work and Politics: The Division of Labor in Industry* (Cambridge: Cambridge University Press, 1982).

3 On the distinction between international economy and world economy, see Bernadette Madeuf and Charles-Albert Michalet, "A New Approach

to International Economics," *International Social Science Journal*, vol. 30, no. 2 (1978), pp. 253–283.

4 The point has been argued by Richard Rosecrance, *The Rise of the Trading State: Commerce and Conquest in the Modern World* (New York: Basic Books, 1986).

5 Karl Polanyi, *The Great Transformation: The Political and Economic Origins of Our Time* (Boston: Beacon Press, 1957).

6 Stephen Hymer, "The Multinational Corporation and the Law of Uneven Development," in Jagdish N. Bhagwati (ed.), *Economics and World Order: From the 1970s to the 1990s* (London: Macmillan, 1972). Hymer discussed the grounds of conflict between two forms of economic organization; the multinational corporation and national planning, or, in our terms, the globalizing and territorial principles of organization.

7 See Sabel, *Work and Politics*, p. 44, and David S. Landes, *The Unbound Prometheus: Technological Change and Industrial Development in Western Europe from 1750 to the Present* (Cambridge: Cambridge University Press, 1969), p. 308.

8 E. H. Carr, *Nationalism and After* (London: Macmillan, 1945); Franz Borkenau, *Socialism, National or International* (London: George Routledge and Sons, 1942); Robert Cox, *Production, Power, and World Order: Social Forces in the Making of History* (New York: Columbia University Press, 1987), ch. 6. Bismarck, it may be noted, was consistent with Clausewitz, who understood that the French Revolution had created a threshold beyond which military power had to be based upon the solidarity of a nation's people, and could no longer, as in eighteenth-century Europe, be the activity of a military caste employing mercenaries, i.e., distinct from the nation. See Peter Paret, *Clausewitz and the State* (Oxford: Clarendon Press, 1976).

9 The exception was Italy, where the socialist movement split, and only that fraction led by Mussolini rallied to the defense of the state.

10 Paul Kennedy, *The Rise and Fall of the Great Powers* (New York: Random House, 1987).

11 George R. Packard, "The Coming US–Japan Crisis," *Foreign Affairs*, vol. 66, no. 2 (Spring 1987), pp. 348–367; Richard J. Samuels and Benjamin C. Whipple, "Defense Production and Industrial Development: The Case of Japanese Aircraft," from *MIT–Japan Science Technology Program*, 1988; Toshiyuka Toyoda, *A Study on Military R&D: Concerns About Japan's Participation in the Strategic Defense Initiative* (Yokohama: PRIME, 1988).

12 David M. Gordon, Richard Edwards, and Michael Reich, *Segmented Work, Divided Workers: The Historical Transformation of Labor in the United States* (Cambridge: Cambridge University Press, 1982); Frank Wilkinson (ed.), *The Dynamics of Labour Market Segmentation* (London: Academic Press, 1981); Cox, *Production, Power, and World Order*, ch. 9.

13 There is an ideological current within the rich countries that argues for a degree of depolitization as being essential to the "governability" of western-style democracies. Too active participation, in this argument, would

place demands upon governments that would preclude the possibility of their carrying out the economic policies required to adjust their countries to the world economy (Michel J. Crozier, Samuel P. Huntington, and Joji Watanuki, *The Crisis of Democracy: Report on the Governability of Democracies to the Trilateral Commission* (New York: New York University Press, 1975)). This can be read as a premonition of the coming "Polanyi effect" discussed above.

14 It has been objected that Iraq could hardly embody the territorial principle, because it violated the territorial integrity of another state, Kuwait; also that Iraq's economy could not be taken as an example of Fordism, since Iraq's economy relies on oil exports, not manufacturing. These points are quite apart from this essay's argument. My point is that Iraq's strategy has been to consolidate territorial power within which control of oil could be used as a basis for development of economic and military strength; and that these territorial aims threatened a sensitive sector of global economic organization. There is nothing in the territorial principle of economic organization that implies respect for boundaries. Indeed, respect for the sanctity of boundaries, by removing territorial matters from conflict, favors the globalizing principle of economic organization.

15 There is a burgeoning literature debating the question of US decline. Suffice to mention two contributions giving opposing views: Kennedy, *Rise and Fall of the Great Powers*, and Joseph S. Nye, Jr., *Bound to Lead: The Changing Nature of American Power* (New York: Basic Books, 1990). There is very little disagreement on the basic facts: the decline of US productivity relative to European and Japanese productivity; and the extent of functional illiteracy and nonparticipation in economically productive work among the US population. The debate is mainly between optimists and pessimists as to whether these conditions can be reversed: Paul Kennedy, "Fin-de-siècle America," *New York Review of Books*, June 28, 1990.

16 Michael Hudson, *Global Fracture: The New International Economic Order* (New York: Harper and Row, 1977).

17 David P. Calleo, *The Imperious Economy* (Cambridge, Mass.: Harvard University Press, 1982), pp. 51–56; Hudson, *Global Fracture*, pp. 53–54.

18 Peter G. Peterson, "The Morning After," *Atlantic*, vol. 260, no. 4 (October 1987), pp. 43–69.

19 Akio Morita and Shintaro Ishihara, *The Japan that Can Say "No"* (Tokyo: Kobunsha, 1989); also see Robert W. Cox, "Middlepowermanship, Japan, and Future World Order," included in this volume (chapter 13).

20 This was aptly argued by Christian Stoffäes, *La grande menace industrielle* (Paris: Calmann-Levy, 1978).

15 Global *perestroika* (1992)

Mikhail Gorbachev's *perestroika* was a revolution from above, a decision by political leadership to undertake a reform of the economic organization of "real socialism" which, once initiated, got out of control and spun into entropy. Underlying that decision was a vague idea that some kind of socialism could be rebuilt in the context of market forces. No one had a clear strategy based upon real social forces as to how this result could be achieved. The consequence has been a devastating destruction of the real economy, i.e., the productive capacity and the economic organization of real (albeit ailing) socialism, and a disarticulation of social forces. Soviet *perestroika* aggravated the decay of public services, created large-scale unemployment, polarized new wealth and new poverty, generated inflation, and made a former superpower dependent upon foreign relief. Those who gained from the "market" were preeminently well-placed members of the former *nomenklatura*, speculators, and gangsters. The market is the mafia.

Perestroika in the now-defunct Soviet empire is perhaps the worst case of what has become a global phenomenon – worst not in an absolute sense but in the most dramatic descent from production to entropy. Global *perestroika*, more euphemistically called "globalization," is not the consequence of a conscious decision of political leadership. It is a result of structural changes in capitalism, in the actions of many people, corporate bodies, and states, that cumulatively produce new relationships and patterns of behavior. The project of global *perestroika* is less the conscious will of an identifiable group than the latent consequence of these structural changes. These consequences form a coherent interrelated pattern; but this pattern contains within itself contradictions that threaten the persistence of this structural whole in formation. Those of us who abhor the social and political implications of the globalization project must study its contradictions in order to work for its eventual replacement.

Sources of globalization

It has been fashionable, especially in the Anglo-Saxon tradition, to distinguish states and markets in the analysis of economic forces and economic change. Where this distinction leads to the privileging of one to the exclusion of the other, it always departs from historical reality. States and political authorities have had a variety of relationships to economic activity, even when proclaiming non-intervention; and the market is a power relationship. (As François Perroux wrote: "Il n'y a pas de sosie en économie" – Economic agents are not look alikes.) Where the distinction serves to assess the relative weight of the visible hand of political authority and of the latent outcome of an infinity of private actions, it has some analytical merit.[1]

In the capitalist core of the world economy, the balance has shifted over time from the mercantilism that went hand in hand with the formation of the modern state, to the liberalism of *les bourgeois conquérants*[2], and back again to a more state-regulated economic order, first in the age of imperialism and then, after a postwar interlude of aborted liberalism, during the Great Depression of the 1930s. During the 1930s the state had to assume the role of agent of economic revival and defender of domestic welfare and employment against disturbances coming from the outside world. Corporatism, the union of the state with productive forces at the national level, became, under various names, the model of economic regulation.

Following World War II, the Bretton Woods system attempted to strike a balance between a liberal world market and the domestic responsibilities of states. States became accountable to agencies of an international economic order – the IMF, World Bank, and GATT – as regards trade liberalization, and exchange-rate stability and convertibility; and were granted facilities and time to make adjustments in their national economic practices so as not to have to sacrifice the welfare of domestic groups. Keynesian demand management along with varieties of corporatism sustained this international economic order through the ups and downs of the capitalist business cycle. Moderate inflation attributable to the fine-tuning of national economies stimulated a long period of economic growth. War and arms production played a key role: World War II pulled the national economies out of the Depression; the Korean War and the Cold War underpinned economic growth in the 1950s and 1960s.

The crisis of this postwar order can be traced to the years 1968–75. During this period, the balanced compromise of Bretton Woods shifted towards subordination of domestic economies to the perceived exigencies of a global economy. States willy-nilly became more effectively accountable to a *nébuleuse* personified as the global economy; and they were constrained to mystify this external accountability in the eyes and ears of their own publics through the new vocabulary of globalization, interdependence, and competitiveness.

How and why did this happen? It is unlikely that any fully adequate explanation can be given now. The matter will be long debated. It is, however, possible to recognize this period as a real turning point in the structural sense of a weakening of old and the emergence of new structures. Some key elements of the transformation can be identified.

The structural power of capital Inflation, which hitherto had been a stimulus to growth, beneficent alike to business and organized labor, now, at higher rates and with declining profit margins, came to be perceived by business as inhibiting investment. Discussions among economists as to whether the fault lay in demand pull or in cost push were inconclusive. Business blamed unions for raising wages and governments for the cycle of excessive spending, borrowing, and taxing. Governments were made to understand that a revival of economic growth would depend upon business confidence to invest, and that this confidence would depend upon "discipline" directed at trade unions and government fiscal management. The investment strike and capital flight are powerful weapons that no government can ignore with impunity. A typical demonstration of their effectiveness was the policy shift from the first to the second phase of the Mitterand presidency in France.

The restructuring of production Insofar as government policies did help restore business confidence, new investment was by and large of a different type. The crisis of the postwar order accelerated the shift from Fordism to post-Fordism – from economies of scale to economies of flexibility. The large integrated plant employing large numbers of semi-skilled workers on mass-production of standardized goods became an obsolete model of organization. The new model was based on a core–periphery structure of production, with a comparatively small core of relatively permanent employees handling finance, research and development, technological organization, and inno-vation, and a periphery consisting of dependent components of the production process.

While the core is integrated with capital, the fragmented compo-nents of the periphery are much more loosely linked to the overall production process. They can be located partly within the core plant, for example, as maintenance services, and partly spread among differ-ent geographical sites in many countries. Periphery components can be called into existence when they are needed by the core and dis-posed of when they are not. Restructuring into the core–periphery model has facilitated the use of a more precariously employed labor force segmented by ethnicity, gender, nationality, or religion. It has weakened the power of trade unions and strengthened that of capital within the production process. It has also made business less control-lable by any single state authority. Restructuring has thereby acceler-ated the globalizing of production.

The role of debt Both corporations and governments have relied increasingly on debt financing rather than on equity investment (in the case of corporations) or taxation (in the case of governments). Fur-thermore, debt has to an increasing extent become *foreign* debt. There was a time when it could be said that the extent of public debt did not matter "because we owed it to ourselves." However plausible the attitude may have been, it no longer applies. Governments now have to care about their international credit ratings. They usually have to borrow in currencies other than their own and face the risk that depreciation of their own currency will raise the costs of debt service.

As the proportion of state revenue going into debt service rises, governments have become more effectively accountable to external bond markets than to their own publics. Their options in exchange rate policy, fiscal policy, and trade policy have become constrained by financial interests linked to the global economy. In Canada, among the very first acts of the heads of the *Parti québecois* government elected in Quebec in 1976 and of the New Democratic Party government elected in Ontario in 1990, both of them appearing as radical challenges to the preexisting political order, was to go to New York to reassure the makers of the bond market. In Mexico, the government had to abandon an agricultural reform designed to expand medium-sized farming for local consumption goods, and revert to large-scale production of luxury export crops in order to earn dollars to service the country's debt.

Corporations are no more autonomous than governments. The timing of an announcement by General Motors just prior to Christmas 1991 that it was going to close 21 plants and cut 74,000 jobs was hardly prompted by a particularly Scrooge-like malevolence.[3] By informed accounts, it was intended, by appearing as a token of the corporation's intention to increase competitiveness, to deter a downgrading of its bond rating which would have increased the corporation's cost of borrowing. A large corporation, flagship of the US economy, is shown to be tributary to the financial manipulators of Wall Street. Finance has become decoupled from production to become an independent power, an autocrat over the real economy.[4]

And what drives the decision making of the financial manipulators? The short-range thinking of immediate financial gain, not the long-range thinking of industrial development. The market mentality functions synchronically; development requires a diachronic mode of thought. Financial markets during the 1980s were beset by a fever of borrowing, leveraged takeovers, junk bonds, and savings-and-loan scandals – a roller coaster of speculative gains and losses that Susan Strange called "casino capitalism."[5] The result of financial power's dominance over the real economy was as often as not the destruction of jobs and productive capital. This is western capitalism's counterpart to *perestroika*'s destruction of the residual productive powers of real socialism.

The structures of globalization

The crisis of the postwar order has expanded the breadth and depth of a global economy that exists alongside and incrementally supersedes the classical international economy.[6] The global economy is the system generated by globalizing production and global finance. Global production is able to make use of the territorial divisions of the international economy, playing off one territorial jurisdiction against another so as to maximize reductions in costs, savings in taxes, avoidance of anti-pollution regulation, control over labor, and guarantees of political stability and favor. Global finance has achieved a virtually unregulated and electronically connected 24-hour-a-day network. The collective decision making of global finance is centered in world cities rather than states – New York, Tokyo, London, Paris, Frankfurt – and extends by computer terminals to the rest of the world.

The two components of the global economy are in potential contradiction. Global production requires a certain stability in politics and finance in order to expand. Global finance has the upper hand because its power over credit creation determines the future of production; but global finance is in a parlously fragile condition. A calamitous concatenation of accidents could bring it down – a number of failures on the Robert Maxwell scale combined with government debt defaults or a cessation of Japanese foreign lending.[a] For now governments, even the combined governments of the G7, have not been able to devise any effectively secure scheme of regulation for global finance that could counter such a collapse.

There is, in effect, no explicit political or authority structure for the global economy. There is, nevertheless, something there that remains to be deciphered, something that could be described by the French word *nébuleuse* or by the notion of "governance without government."[7]

There is a transnational process of consensus formation among the official caretakers of the global economy. This process generates consensual guidelines, underpinned by an ideology of globalization, that are transmitted into the policy-making channels of national governments and big corporations. Part of this consensus-formation process takes place through unofficial forums like the Trilateral Commission, the Bilderberg conferences, or the more esoteric Mont Pèlerin Society. Part of it goes on through official bodies like the OECD, the Bank for International Settlements, the International Monetary Fund, and the G7. These shape the discourse within which policies are defined, the terms and concepts that circumscribe what can be thought and done.

[a] Maxwell is thought to have siphoned around $1.2 billion from Maxwell company pension plans to support the price of Maxwell Communications stock prior to his death in 1991. Bankruptcy proceedings and litigation will continue for several years (Anita Raghavan, "Goldman's Partners Contend with Maxwell Legacy," *Wall Street Journal*, April 12, 1995, p. C1). The collapse of confidence in Mexico's peso in late 1994 led to its 40 percent depreciation by early 1995 and great difficulty in financing Mexican debt, placing all Latin American economies on the brink of "horrific collapse." G7 and IMF assistance was notable for its tardiness and small size (Craig Torres, "Mexico's Debt-Restructuring Plan Stalls; Problems in Repackaging $2 Billion of 'Tesobonos' Add to Nation's Woes," *Wall Street Journal*, February 15, 1995, p. A14).

They also tighten the transnational networks that link policy making from country to country.[8]

The structural impact on national governments of this global centralization of influence over policy can be called the internationalizing of the state. Its common feature is to convert the state into an agency for adjusting national economic practices and policies to the perceived exigencies of the global economy. The state becomes a transmission belt from the global to the national economy, where heretofore it had acted as the bulwark defending domestic welfare from external disturbances. Power within the state becomes concentrated in those agencies in closest touch with the global economy – the offices of presidents and prime ministers, treasuries, and central banks. The agencies that are more closely identified with domestic clients – ministries of industries, labor ministries, and so on – become subordinated. This phenomenon, which has become so salient since the crisis of the postwar order, needs much more study.

Different forms of state facilitate this tightening of the global–local relationship for countries occupying different positions in the global system. At one time, the military-bureaucratic form of state seemed to be optimum in countries of peripheral capitalism for the enforcement of monetary discipline. Now IMF-inspired "structural adjustment" is pursued by elected presidential regimes (Argentina, Brazil, Mexico, Peru) that manage to retain a degree of insulation from popular pressures. India, formerly following a more autocentric or self-reliant path, has moved closer and closer towards integration into the global economy. Neoconservative ideology has sustained the transformation of the state in Britain, the United States, Canada, and Australasia in the direction of globalization. Socialist party governments in France and in Spain have adjusted their policies to the new orthodoxy. The states of the former Soviet empire, insofar as their present governments have any real authority, seem to have been swept up into the globalizing trend.

In the European Community, the ongoing debate over "social Europe" indicates a present stalemate in the conflict over the future nature of the state and of the regional authority. There is a struggle between two kinds of capitalism:[9] the hyperliberal globalizing capitalism of Thatcherism and a capitalism more rooted in social policy and territorially balanced development. The latter stems from the social democratic tradition and also from an older conservatism that thinks of society as an organic whole rather than in the contractual individualism of so-called neoconservatism.[b]

In Japan, the guiding and planning role of the state retains initiative in managing the country's relationship with the world outside its immediate sphere, and will likely be of increasing significance in lessening that economy's dependence upon the US market and the US military. The EC and Japan are now the only possible counterweights to total globalization at the level of states.

Globalization and democracy

The issues of globalization have an important implication for the meaning of democracy. The ideologues of globalization are quick to identify democracy with the free market. There is, of course, very little historical justification for this identification. It derives almost exclusively from the coincidence of liberal parliamentary constitutionalism in Britain with the industrial revolution and the growth of a market economy. This obscured in a way the necessity of state force to establish and maintain the conditions for a workable market – a new kind of police force internally and sea power in the world market. It also ignored the fact that the other European states following the British lead in the nineteenth century, for example, the French Second Empire, were not notably liberal in the political sense. In our own time, the case of Pinochet's Chile preconfigured the role of military-bureaucratic regimes in installing the bases for liberal economic policies. Ideological mystification has obscured the fact that a stronger case can probably be made for the pairing of political authoritarianism with market economics. It is perhaps worth reflecting upon this point when undertaking the task of constructing the socialist alternative for the future.

Since the crisis of the postwar order, democracy has been quietly redefined in the centers of world capitalism. The new definition is grounded in a revival of the nineteenth-century separation of economy and politics. Key aspects of economic management are therefore to be shielded from politics, that is to say, from popular pressures. This is achieved by confirmed practices, by treaty, by legislation, and

---

[b] For elaboration of these points see "The Global Political Economy and Social Choice," chapter 10 in this volume.

by formal constitutional provisions.[10] By analogy to the constitutional limitations on royal authority called limited monarchy, the late twentieth-century redefinition of pluralist politics can be called "limited democracy."

One of the first indications of this development can now in retrospect be traced to the fiscal crisis of New York city in 1975. The 1960s saw the emergence of three strong popular movements in New York city: a middle-class reform movement, a black civil-rights movement, and a movement to unionize city employees. Reformers captured the mayoralty with the support of blacks and subsequently had to come to terms with the unions in order to be able to govern effectively. The city could not pay through its own revenues for the new public services demanded by the coalition and for the wage and benefits settlements reached with the unions. It had to borrow from the banks. Without a subsidy that the state of New York was unwilling to provide, the city was unable to service and renew these loans. To avoid a bankruptcy that would have been detrimental to all parties, from the bankers to the unions, the city was placed in a kind of trusteeship with members of the banking community in control of the city budget and administration. Retrenchment was directed at programs with black clienteles and at labor costs. Blacks, who then lacked effective political organization, were abandoned by the middle-class reformers who had mobilized them into city politics. Municipal unions were better organized, but vulnerable to their corporatist involvement with the city, and not likely to risk a bankruptcy that would threaten city employees' future incomes and pensions.[11]

This episode showed that: (1) corporatism can provide a way out of a fiscal crisis provoked by the demands of new political groups; (2) this decision requires a restriction of decision power to elements acceptable to the financial market; (3) this, in turn, requires the political demobilization or exclusion of elements likely to challenge that restriction; and (4) this solution is vulnerable to a remobilization of the excluded elements.

During the same year 1975, three ideologues of the Trilateral Commission produced a report to the Commission that addressed the issue of the "ungovernability" of democracies.[12] The thesis of the report was that a "democratic surge" in the 1960s had increased demands on government for services, challenged and weakened governmental authority, and generated inflation. The Trilateral governments, and especially the United States, were suffering from an "excess of democracy," the report argued; and this overloading of demands upon the state could only be abated by a degree of political demobilization of those "marginal" groups that were pressing new demands.[13]

The underlying ideology here propounded became expressed in a variety of measures intended to insulate economic policy making from popular pressures. Cynicism, depoliticization, a sense of the inefficacy of political action, and a disdain for the political class are current in the old democracies.

Although the tendency towards limited democracy remains dominant, it has not gone unchallenged. Prime Minister Brian Mulroney of Canada sold the Free Trade Agreement with the United States in the oil-producing region of Alberta with the argument that it would forevermore prevent the introduction of a new national energy policy; but opposition to free trade, though defeated in the elections of 1988, did mobilize many social groups in Canada more effectively than ever before. In Europe, the "democratic deficit" in the EC is at the center of debate. Business interests are, on the whole, pleased with the existing bureaucratic framework of decision making, remote from democratic pressures – apart, of course, from the more paranoid hyperliberals who see it as risking socialism through the back door. But advocates of the social charter and of more powers for the European parliament are sensitive to the long-term need for legitimation of a European form of capitalism.

One can question the long-term viability of the new limited or exclusionary democracies of peripheral capitalism. They must continue to administer an austerity that polarizes rich and poor in the interests of external debt relationships. Very likely, they will be inclined to resort to renewed repression, or else face an explosion of popular pressures. Nowhere is this dramatic alternative more apparent than in the former Soviet empire. Whereas *glasnost* has been a resounding success, *perestroika* has been a disastrous failure. The race is between the constitution of pluralist regimes grounded in the emergence of a broadly inclusionary civil society, and new fascist-type populist authoritarianism.

The changing structure of world politics

Out of the crisis of the postwar order, a new global political structure is emerging. The old Westphalian concept of a system of sovereign states is no longer an adequate way of conceptualizing world

politics.[14] Sovereignty is an ever looser concept. The old legal defi-
nitions conjuring visions of ultimate and fully autonomous power are
no longer meaningful. Sovereignty has gained meaning as an affirmation of cultural identity and lost meaning as power over the economy. It means different things to different people.

The affirmation of a growing multitude of "sovereignties" is
accompanied by the phenomena of macro-regionalism and micro-
regionalism. Three macro-regions are defining themselves respectively
in a Europe centered on the EC, an East Asian sphere centered on
Japan, and a North American sphere centered on the United States
and looking to embrace Latin America. It is unlikely that these macro-
regions will become autarkic economic blocs reminiscent of the world
of the Great Depression. Firms based in each of the regions have too
much involvement in the economies of the other regions for such
exclusiveness to become the rule. Rather the macro-regions are political-economic frameworks for capital accumulation and for organizing
interregional competition for investment and shares of the world
market. They also allow for the development through internal
struggles of different forms of capitalism. Macro-regionalism is one
facet of globalization, one aspect of how a globalizing world is being
restructured.

These macro-regions are definable primarily in economic terms but
they also have important political and cultural implications. The EC,
for instance, poses a quandary for Switzerland whose business elites
see their future economic welfare as linked to integration in the EC,
but many of whose people, including many in the business elites,
regret the loss of local control upon which Swiss democracy has been
based. On the other hand, people in Catalonia, Lombardy, and Scot-
land look to the EC as an assurance of greater future autonomy or
independence in relation to the sovereign states of which they now
form part. And there have been no more fervent advocates of North
American free trade than the Quebec *indépendentistes*. Globalization
encourages macro-regionalism, which, in turn, encourages micro-
regionalism.

For the relatively rich micro-regions, autonomy or independence
means keeping more of their wealth for themselves. The *lega* in Lombardy would jealously guard northern wealth against redistribution
to the south of Italy. Such motivations in other relatively wealthy
regions are less overtly proclaimed. An institutionalized process of
consultation (an incipient inter-micro-regional organization) among

the "four motors" of Europe – Catalonia, Lombardy, Rhône-Alpes, and Baden-Württemberg – has been joined by Ontario.

Micro-regionalism among the rich will have its counterpart surely among poorer micro-regions. Indeed, some of the richer micro-regions have, as a gesture of solidarity, "adopted" poor micro-regions. Micro-regionalism in poor areas will be a means not only of affirming cultural identities but of claiming payoffs at the macro-regional level for maintaining political stability and economic good behavior. The issues of redistribution are thereby raised from the sovereign-state level to the macro-regional level, while the manner in which redistributed wealth is used becomes decentralized to the micro-regional level.

At the base of the emerging structure of world order are social forces. The old social movements – trade unions and peasant movements – have suffered setbacks under the impact of globalization; but the labour movement, in particular, has a background of experience in organization and ideology that can still be a strength in shaping the future. If it were to confine itself to its traditional clientele of manual industrial workers, while production is being restructured on a world scale so as to diminish this traditional base of power, the labor movement would condemn itself to a steadily weakening influence. Its prospect for revival lies in committing its organizational and ideologically mobilizing capability to the task of building a broader coalition of social forces.

New social movements, converging around specific sets of issues – environmentalism, feminism, and peace – have grown to a different extent in different parts of the world. More amorphous and vaguer movements – "people power" and democratization – are present wherever political structures are seen to be both repressive and fragile. These movements evoke particular identities – ethnic, nationalist, religious, gender. They exist within states but are transnational in essence. The indigenous peoples' movement affirms rights prior to the existing state system.

The newly affirmed identities have in a measure displaced class as the focus of social struggle; but like class, they derive their force from resentment against exploitation. There is a material basis for their protest, a material basis that is broader than the particular identities affirmed. Insofar as this common material basis remains obscured, the particular identities now reaffirmed can be manipulated into conflict with one another. The danger of authoritarian populism, of reborn fascism, is particularly great where political structures are crumbling and the material basis of resentment appears to be intractable. Demo-cratization and "people power" can move to the right as well as to the left.

Openings for a countertrend: the clash of territorial and interdependence principles

The emerging world order thus appears as a multi-level structure. At the base are social forces. Whether they are self-conscious and articulated into what Gramsci called an historic bloc, or are depoli-ticized and manipulable, is the key issue in the making of the future. The old state system is resolving itself into a complex of political-economic entities: micro-regions, traditional states, and macro-regions with institutions of greater or lesser functional scope and formal auth-ority. World cities are the keyboards of the global economy. Rival transnational processes of ideological formation aim respectively at hegemony and counterhegemony. Institutions of concertation and coordination bridge the major states and macro-regions. Multilateral processes exist for conflict management, peace keeping, and regu-lation and service providing in a variety of functional areas (trade, communications, health, and so on). The whole picture resembles the multi-level order of medieval Europe more than the Westphalian model of a system of sovereign independent states that has heretofore been the paradigm of international relations.[15]

The multi-level image suggests the variety of levels at which inter-vention becomes possible, indeed necessary, for any strategy aiming at transformation into an alternative to global *perestroika*. It needs to be completed with a depiction of the inherent instability of this emerging structure. This instability arises from the dialectical relationship of two principles in the constitution of order: the principle of interdepen-dence and the territorial principle.

The interdependence principle is nonterritorial in essence, geared to competition in the world market, to global finance unconstrained by territorial boundaries, and to global production. It operates in accordance with the thought processes of what Susan Strange has called the "business civilization."[16] The territorial principle is state-based, grounded ultimately in military-political power.

Some authors have envisaged the rise of the interdependence prin-ciple as implying a corresponding decline of the territorial principle;[17]

but the notion of a reciprocal interactive relationship of the two principles is closer to reality. The myth of the free market is that it is self-regulating. As Karl Polanyi demonstrated, it required the existence of military or police power for enforcement of market rules.[18] The fact that this force may rarely have to be applied helps to sustain the myth but does not dispense with the necessity of the force in reserve. Globalization in the late twentieth century also depends upon the military-territorial power of an enforcer . . .[c]

The new world order of global *perestroika* is weak at the top. The next few years will likely make this weakness more manifest. There is a kind of utopian optimism abroad that sees the United Nations as coming to play its "originally intended" role in the world. But the United Nations can only be the superstructure or the architectural facade of an underlying global structure of power. It could never sustain a breakdown of that structure, nor should it be asked to do so. The United Nations, for all its recent achievements in the realm of regional conflicts and in resolution of the hostage crisis in Lebanon (1990–92), is probably today at greater risk than it was during the years of Cold War and North–South impasse when it was substantially sidelined. If the United Nations is to become strengthened as an institution of world order, it will have to be by constructing that order on surer foundations than those presently visible.

Terrains of struggle for an alternative world order

Global *perestroika* penetrates the totality of structures constituting world order. It can only be effectively countered by a challenge at several levels, by a Gramscian war of position probably of long duration.

The basic level is the level of social forces. The globalizing economy is polarizing advantaged and disadvantaged, while it fragments the disadvantaged into distinct and often rival identities. The challenge here is to build a coherent coalition of opposition. Such a coalition must, most likely, be built at local and national levels among groups that are aware of their day-to-day coexistence, and are prepared to

---

[c] A discussion of the United States and global security that appeared in the original text of this essay has been cut. The substance of this part can be found in "Production and Security," chapter 14 in this volume.

work to overcome what keeps them apart. Labor movements have an experience in organizing capability and ideological work that can be used in this task, provided they are able to transcend narrow corporative thinking to comprehend the requirements of a broader-based social movement.

A new discourse of global socialism – that could become a persuasive alternative to the now dominant discourse of globalizing capitalism remains to be created. It is the task of organic intellectuals not just to deconstruct the reigning concepts of competitiveness, structural adjustment, and so on, but to offer alternative concepts that serve to construct a coherent alternative order. This goes beyond the strictly economic to include the political foundations of world order. An alternative future world order implies a new intersubjective understanding of the nature of world order and its basic entities and relationships.

Part of this intersubjectivity to be created will be an alternative model of consumption. Consumerism has been the driving force of capitalist *perestroika*, not only in the advanced capitalist societies but in the ex-Soviet East and in the Third World. Perhaps the greatest failure of "real socialism" was its failure, in its fixation upon "overtaking" capitalism, to generate alternative aspirations to those of capitalist consumerism. This paralleled real socialism's failure to envisage alternative ways of organizing production to those of the hierarchical capitalist factory system. An alternative model of consumption would be one in balance with global ecology, which minimised energy and resources consumption and pollution, and maximized emancipatory and participatory opportunities for people.

The local basis for political and ideological action, while indispensable, will by itself be ineffective. Since the globalising tendency extends everywhere, the countertendency could be rather easily snuffed out if it were isolated in one or a few places. Many locally based social forces will have to build transnational arrangements for mutual support. The alternative to capitalist globalization will need to build upon the productive forces created by capitalism by converting them to the service of society. The counterforce to capitalist globalization will also be global, but it cannot be global all at once.

The macro-regional level offers a prospectively favorable terrain, most of all in Europe.[19] It is at the macro-regional level that the confrontation of rival forms of capitalism is taking place. Those who are

looking beyond that phase of struggle have to be aware of the ideological space that is opened by this confrontation of hyperliberal and
state-capitalist or corporatist forms of capitalism. A similar kind of
confrontation is developing between Japanese and American forms of
capitalism. The long-term strategic view has to take account of opportunities in the medium-term encounter of forces.

Another major source of conflict lies in the rising power of Islamism
(or what western journalists like to call Islamic fundamentalism).
Islam, in this context, can be seen as a metaphor for the rejection of
western capitalist penetration in many peripheral societies. Some of
its aspects – the penal code, the place of women in society, the concept
of *jihad* – are incomprehensible or abhorrent to western progressives.
Yet Islam has superseded socialism as the force rallying the disadvantaged of much of the populations in North Africa, the Middle East,
and parts of Asia. One of the more difficult challenges in building a
global counterforce is for western "progressives" to be able to come
to terms on a basis of mutual comprehension with the progressive
potential in contemporary Islam.[20]

The fragility of the existing global structure is felt particularly at
two points: military and financial. These are the instruments of power
that shape the behavior of states today both structurally and instru-
mentally. They need to be more fully understood in their relationship
to the goal of a future world social order.

On the military side, the struggle is bound to be asymmetrical
against a concentrated monopoly of high-technology military power.
Strategies that rely upon a different kind of power will be required.
Experience has been gained with relatively nonviolent methods of
opposition, for example, the *intifada*.

Finally, rather more thought needs to be devoted to financial strategies that could be brought into play in the event of a global financial
crisis. A financial crisis is the most likely way in which the existing
world order could begin to collapse. A new financial mechanism
would be needed to seize the initiative for transcending the liberal
separation of economy from polity and for reembedding the economy
in a society imbued with the principles of equity and solidarity.

Notes

This text was first published in Ralph Miliband and Leo Panitch (eds.), *New World Order? The Socialist Register 1992* (London: Merlin, 1992).

1 See, for example, Susan Strange, *States and Markets: An Introduction to International Political Economy* (London: Pinter, 1988); and Charles E. Lindblom, *Politics and Markets* (New York: Basic Books, 1977).

2 Charles Morazé, *Les bourgeois conquérants* (Paris: Armand Colin, 1957).

3 *Globe and Mail* (Toronto), December 19, 1991.

4 Peter Drucker, "The Changed World Economy", *Foreign Affairs*, vol. 64, no. 4 (Spring 1986), p. 783, wrote; "[I]n the world economy today, the 'real' economy of goods and services and the 'symbol' economy of money, credit, and capital are no longer bound tightly to each other; they are, indeed, moving further and further apart."

5 Susan Strange, *Casino Capitalism* (Oxford: Basil Blackwell, 1986).

6 Bernadette Madeuf and Charles-Albert Michalet, "A New Approach to International Economics," *International Social Science Journal*, vol. 30, no. 2 (1978), pp. 253–283.

7 James Rosenau and Ernst Otto Czempiel (eds.), *Governance Without Government: Order and Change in World Politics* (Cambridge: Cambridge University Press, 1992). This collection deals with many aspects of the problem of world order, although not explicitly with global finance. Susan Strange, *Casino Capitalism*, pp. 165–169, argues that effective regulation over finance is unlikely to be achieved through international organization, and that only the US government, by intervening in the New York financial market, might be capable of global effectiveness. But, she adds, US governments have behaved unilaterally and irresponsibly in this matter and show no signs of modifying their behavior.

8 There is a growing interest in the nature and processes of this *nébuleuse*. See, e.g., the work of the University of Amsterdam political economy group, especially Kees van der Pijl, *The Making of an Atlantic Ruling Class* (London: Verso, 1984); Stephen Gill, *American Hegemony and the Trilateral Commission* (Cambridge: Cambridge University Press, 1990); and an unpublished Ph.D dissertation at York University, Toronto, by André Drainville, "Monetarism in Canada and in the World Economy" (1991).

9 See, for example, Michel Albert, *Capitalisme contre capitalisme* (Paris: Seuil, 1991).

10 Stephen Gill has referred to the "new constitutionalism." See his "The Emerging World Order and European Change: The Political Economy of European Union," paper presented at the XVth World Congress of the International Political Science Association, Buenos Aires, July 1991.

11 Martin Shefter, "New York City's Fiscal Crisis: The Politics of Inflation and Retrenchment," *Public Interest*, no. 48 (Summer 1977), pp. 98–127.

12 Michel J. Crozier, Samuel P. Huntington, and Joji Watanuki, *The Crisis of Democracy: Report on the Governability of Democracies to the Trilateral Commission* (New York: New York University Press, 1975).

13 Ralf Dahrendorf, to his credit, criticized these findings in a plea "to avoid the belief that a little more unemployment, a little less education, a little more deliberate discipline, and a little less freedom of expression would

make the world a better place, in which it is possible to govern effectively" (Crozier, Huntington, and Watanuki, *Crisis of Democracy*, p. 194).

14 International relations analysts use the term Westphalian to refer to an inter-state system supposed to have come into existence in Europe after the Peace of Westphalia in 1648.

15 In *The Anarchical Society: A Study of Order in World Politics* (New York: Columbia University Press, 1977), Hedley Bull projected a "new medievalism" as a likely form of future world order.

16 Susan Strange, "The Name of the Game," in Nicholas X. Rizopoulos (ed.), *Sea Changes: American Foreign Policy in a World Transformed* (New York: Council on Foreign Relations, 1990).

17 For example, Richard Rosecrance, *The Rise of the Trading State: Commerce and Conquest in the Modern World* (New York: Basic Books, 1986).

18 Karl Polanyi, *The Great Transformation: The Political and Economic Origins of Our Time* (Boston: Beacon, 1957).

19 Björn Hettne, "Europe in a World of Regions," paper for the United Nations University/Hungarian Academy of Sciences conference on "A New Europe in the Changing Global System," Velence, Hungary, September 1991.

20 An interesting work raising philosophical-ideological aspects of this problem is Yves Lacoste, *Ibn Khaldun: The Birth of History and the Past of the Third World* (London: Verso, 1984).

Part IV
Multilateralism

16 The executive head: an essay on leadership in international organization (1969)

The quality of executive leadership may prove to be the most critical single determinant of the growth in scope and authority of international organization. Now sufficiently long and varied to allow a comparative approach, the history of international organization may provide elements for a theory of leadership. This essay is but a preliminary effort in that direction. It is concerned not only with how the executive head protects and develops his position as top man but also with how, by doing so, he may be the creator of a new (if yet slender) world power base.

The origin of the comparative study of executive heads of international organizations was the observation that Albert Thomas was a very different kind of man from Sir Eric Drummond and had very different ideas about how to carry out his job.[a] From this observation stemmed a number of speculations. The failure of the League of Nations in the late thirties was contrasted with the apparent success of the International Labor Organization (ILO). Would the story have been different had a Thomas been secretary-general of the League? Or would – as seems to have been Sir Eric Drummond's view – the nature of the job have led a Thomas to fail in the League? Whatever disagreement surrounds this speculation there is a greater measure of agreement that with the Drummond approach the ILO would have become nothing more than a technical information bureau.[1]

The interest of the comparison is not confined to curiosity about the consequences of different styles of leadership. It lies also in the possibility that the executive head may be the explanatory key to the

---

[a] Albert Thomas was director of the International Labor Office, 1919–32. Sir Eric Drummond was first secretary-general of the League of Nations, 1919–32.

emergence of a new kind of autonomous actor in the international system. If we want to answer the question, "Are international organizations merely the instruments of national foreign policies or do they influence world politics in their own right?," then we must take a closer look at the executive head.

This question has both ontological and systemic implications. The ontological implication may be illustrated by a second question: "What is the United Nations going to do about it?" (for example, as applied to Hungary, Suez, apartheid, Cuba, Czechoslovakia); or alternatively, "What can the United Nations do about it?" The form of the question itself behooves us to define the meaning of "United Nations" in it. Political analysts will usually take the nominalist position that "United Nations" is just a name, not a real essence. Instead of saying "United Nations," the questioner should specify what persons, what procedural processes, what committees or assemblies he has in mind. Yet by the very fact that he puts the question the questioner protests against such nominalism. The questioner is a realist,[b] a believer in real essences. For him the United Nations either actually or potentially is more than just a name covering a multitude of exogenously determined activities. He knows why the Security Council does nothing: because the states represented on it have conflicting interests, because of a big-power veto. But he still thinks, as a realist, that there must be some fundamental essence in the United Nations that ought to receive expression. Most probably he expects the executive head – the secretary-general – to express this latent reality. A few years ago it would have been bad form to put a problem in political analysis this way. But Professor Herbert Marcuse has taught us we are wrong to continue to discount the realists.

The "systemic" implication of the original question concerns how an international system based upon nation-states may become transformed in the direction of greater integration. Since it is common in literature about systems to find diagrams, figure 16.1 is offered as an outline of the hypothetical process of integration.

The hypothesis within the hypothesis is that among possible conversion variables at X and Y the executive head is especially important. It may be through his leadership that an international organization is transformed from being a forum of multilateral diplomacy

[b] "Realist" is used here in the scholastic tradition of Thomas Aquinas as meaning belief in real essences or universals. The opposite to this realism is not idealism (with which it has an affinity) but nominalism.

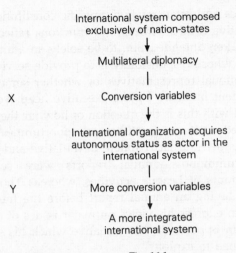

International system composed
exclusively of nation-states

↓

Multilateral diplomacy

|

X   Conversion variables

↓

International organization acquires
autonomous status as actor in the
international system

|

Y   More conversion variables

↓

A more integrated
international system

Fig. 16.1

into something which is more than the sum of its inputs and that this new potency continues to take on more common tasks and make more decisions on behalf of the whole community of nation-states, thereby gradually bringing formerly anarchic inter-state relations under a common regulatory power.

The ontological and systemic implications become joined if we regard the emergence of a new and more integrated world order as the culmination of a dialectical process in which conflicts between nations are resolved through the discovery of higher common interests and the creation of international agencies to promote and regulate them. The real essence of international organization then becomes not a commitment to the performance of specific tasks but a commitment to bring about the new, more integrated world order. The executive head, in this vision, is cast in a role comparable to that of the proletariat in a better-known dialectical proposition – a heavy load of historical expectations for a rather lonely figure to bear.

These are not points of view to be defended in what follows. They are some of the reasons why the study of executive heads may be found interesting. Now, how to go about it?

Until recently the literature about executive heads could have been divided according to three characteristic emphases: legal-institutional, idiosyncratic (personality or leadership style), and ethical-normative.

The legal-institutional studies stress the formal constitutional powers of the executive head and how these have been contained or

319

enlarged by practice and interpretation. Specific constitutional references to the executive head's powers and functions reflect whether
the constitution makers intended him to be solely an administrative
officer, the limit of whose responsibility is to provide services for the
deliberations of national representatives, or whether some opportunities for independent initiative by the executive head were clearly
anticipated. Linked with this is the question of how far the executive
head has in fact used whatever constitutional opportunities he had in
order to expand his own de facto sphere of initiative and influence.
For example, Drummond's annual reports were self-effacing
administrative accounts of League activities, whereas Thomas used
his opportunity of laying an annual report before the International
Labor Conference to express his views on major issues of social and
economic policy – an opportunity for initiative which his successors
in ILO have continued to exploit.[2]

The opportunity for political initiative by the secretary-general of
the United Nations is seen as founded upon Article 99 of the Charter,
which empowers the secretary-general to "bring to the attention of
the Security Council any matter which in his opinion may threaten
the maintenance of international peace and security." Studies of the
legal-institutional kind have been particularly interested in the apparent expansion of the secretary-general's executive functions, particularly in regard to peace-keeping activities but also in the administration of economic and technical aid to developing countries. Michel
Virally has buttressed a legal argument concerning an enlarged
interpretation of Article 99 with an analysis of the different types of
political activity undertaken by the secretary-general and of the doctrine concerning his role elaborated by Dag Hammarskjöld.[3]

The weakness in the legal approach is its tendency to be unilinear
and cumulative, arguing from precedent to precedent toward the
steady expansion of the secretary-general's role and his emergence (in
Virally's terms) as a *gouvernant* rather more than a *fonctionnaire*. The
idea of cumulative institutional development is, however, of doubtful
application to the history of the UN. More evident has been the impact
of the major shifts in the configuration of world power and in the
pattern of cleavages on salient world issues which have changed the
balance within the United Nations Organization among its major
organs – the Security Council, the General Assembly, and the
secretary-general. Every such shift has changed their respective roles
and practical powers. The difference between Trygve Lie's role in the

Korean conflict and Hammarskjöld's in the Congo conflict is to be explained more by reference to the Organization's changed relationship to the two big-power blocs and the emergence of a better-articulated neutralist group than by differences in the interpretation held by the respective incumbents of the institutional responsibilities of the secretary-general. Throughout the history of the Organization the world pattern of conflict and alignment appears as the independent variable and the institutional development of the United Nations as the dependent variable.[c] The weakness of the legal approach has been its implicit assumption (a natural consequence of a lawyer's preoccupation with institutional machinery) that the relationship is reversed.

A second emphasis in the literature has been upon the personalities of the executive heads themselves. The implicit assumption here is that it is the man who makes the institution. One might call it the "great-man theory of international organization."[4] Much discussion in this connection has revolved about the point of an executive head's origins. Was he, before his appointment, a national political figure of some stature or was he primarily a diplomat, an administrator, or a technician? Another point of discussion concerns his style of leadership. In the case of both the League and the United Nations early thoughts turned in the direction of a forceful role for a prominent statesman, and in both cases the governments in the end settled for something a little less ambitious (in the case of the League rather more explicitly than in the case of the United Nations).[5] In the Organization for European Economic Cooperation (OEEC) and in the North Atlantic Treaty Organization (NATO) cases United States representatives advocated a more demonstrative role for the executive head and the appointment of a prominent political personality while the United Kingdom's policy was to confine the international secretariat's role to something like that of the cabinet secretariat at home.[6]

Yet despite the controversy this ground of comparison does not always seem to have been very significant. Dag Hammarskjöld entered the UN with the public image of an administrator who would keep the United Nations' house in order and avoid rash political

---

[c] These references to dependent and independent variables are evidence of the somewhat positivist epistemology which was characteristic of Cox's work during the 1960s and early 1970s, as discussed in Sinclair, "Beyond International Relations Theory: Robert W. Cox and Approaches to World Order," included as chapter 1 in this volume.

initiatives – on both grounds probably contrasting with his predecessor in the minds of those who appointed him. Yet it was Hammarskjöld, responding to the opportunities thrown up by world
events following his appointment, who gave effective political content
to the office of the secretary-general.

The ILO has had directors-general of both the "political" and the
"administrative" background. Edward Phelan might be considered
the archetype of the civil servant. Yet while he never attempted to cut
a public figure in the more flamboyant style of Thomas, it was in no
small measure his diplomatic skill and political understanding which
enabled the ILO to traverse the war period and to survive as part of
the new system of international organizations linked with the United
Nations, despite considerable political disadvantages, for example, the
ILO's prewar Geneva associations, the hostility of the Union of Soviet
Socialist Republics, and competition for influence within the new UN
system from the newly organized World Federation of Trade Unions
(WFTU).

The executive leadership of an international organization is preeminently a political task – but of a special kind, requiring particular apti-
tudes and knowledge on the part of its exponents. A background in
national politics may be an advantage, but the contrast between the
civil servant and "political" types is not in itself a valid indicator of
leadership potential in the international sphere. The individual's inter-
personal and "cross-cultural" sophistication and his access to the
highest levels in diplomacy and government are better criteria.

An executive head who behaves in the manner of a local politician
may lack capacity for leadership in an arena of larger and more vari-
egated dimensions. On the other hand, executive heads who have conceived their roles primarily as technicians have not been notably successful. Their projects, for all the intrinsic merit they may possess, may
fail either because of bad judgement on timing or because they have
not taken sufficient account of effective opinion among the Organization's membership: Sir John Boyd-Orr's[d] scheme for a world food
board was a case in point.

---

[d] Sir John Boyd-Orr, an Australian, was the first director-general of the Food and Agriculture Organization (FAO). He staked his leadership upon a bold and imaginative
proposal for a world food-price stabilization scheme which would have funded purchase of basic foodstuffs in times of surplus and sold them in times of shortage. The
concept was to promote "the marriage of health and agriculture," linking nutrition
and farming on a global basis. The plan failed because the major agricultural
exporting countries would not consider it at a time of postwar rising agricultural
prices.

On styles of leadership the classic contrast is between charismatic and bureaucratic types. The ILO during the interwar period became identified with Thomas' personality and the doctrine he preached even though much of what he proposed was never consecrated formally by the votes of the ILO Conference. He infused his staff with a sense of devotion to a cause of which he appeared to them as a world leader. He traveled widely, not only to talk with the official political and diplomatic representatives of member countries but even more to contact workers' leaders and to speak to the people. Yet for all that it warms the heart, the charismatic style seems out of fashion in international organizations of the postwar period. This is mainly because of the heterogeneous world in which executive heads have to operate. The responsibility they have for preserving and continually reconstructing a slender basis of consensus among the members of their organizations has encouraged "quiet diplomacy" and discouraged a policy of continuous self-assertion.

There are, however, moments when the executive head can effectively give verbal leadership: when, for example, major powers are known to be prepared to accept a course of action though unable or disinclined themselves to advocate it. The creation of the United Nations Emergency Force (UNEF) in the Suez crisis is an example. (Whether the idea originated with the executive head is not so important as that he became identified with it and his office with its implementation.) The leadership of the executive head may, in such rather exceptional circumstances, lead to the creation of a new consensus among the powers. The rational use of personal initiative may be distinguished from cultivating charisma as a political style.

Personality is in this as in all spheres of politics a significant variable. But it would be a distortion to regard it as the independent variable, just as it would be wrong so to regard legal-institutional forms and practices. The problem we are left with is to formulate better the relationship of the personality and style of the executive head with other possibly weightier variables.

A third current of literature concentrates upon the concept of the international character of the role and responsibilities of the international secretariat and its executive head. Much of it welled out over the *troika* controversy of 1960 when the Soviet Union attacked Hammarskjöld over his handling of the Congo situation and proposed his replacement by a three-man executive composed of representatives of the three main divisions of world politics (at least as they appeared to Soviet viewers): socialist, western, and nonaligned. The controversy

323

revolved about two doctrinal positions: the first, conveyed by the statement Nikita Khrushchev, chairman of the Council of Ministers of the Soviet Union, is supposed to have made to Walter Lippmann that "there are neutral nations but there are no neutral men" – a statement which greatly incensed Hammarskjöld who saw it as a personal attack upon his integrity; and the second, defended by Hammarskjöld and most western participants, of an exclusively international secretariat whose actions are guided by the principles of the Charter, a secretariat which can be developed as a neutral executive instrument of the Organization and whose international character, in the words of Hammarskjöld, "is not tied to its composition, but to the spirit in which it works and to its insulation from outside influences . . . "[7] The Hammarskjöld argument immerses the executive head within the larger concept of the international secretariat which it views in monolithic and moral terms.

In historical perspective the two opposing arguments lose their absolute character and will be seen as ideologies buttressing particular sides in a global conflict; but both are very inadequate descriptions of actual behavior and are of very little use to the analyst.

A different perspective on this particular conflict results from considering the UN as one case of a broader trend in modern political institutions. This is the tendency in international organization as in national government for bureaucracies to expand their functions, which is accompanied by a growing difficulty for the parliamentary or representative organs holding formal power to supervise and control in detail many of these functions. In national affairs this is particularly true in connection with the broadening intervention of the state in economic life, for example, in the recent attempts of government in many industrialized countries to control or influence prices and incomes. In response to this problem new types of bodies are being created which are neither bureaucracies in the old sense of "civil service" nor are they representative in the old sense of elected. They are appointed by governments but composed in such a way as to be considered representative of significant segments of national opinion. The efficacy of these new agencies (such as prices and incomes boards) depends upon the confidence they inspire in their representative character.

The analogy applies to international secretariats. Specifically, the UN had, through the agency of the secretary-general, taken on peace-keeping functions and broad executive functions for economic and social development. The representative organs of the UN – in particular the Security Council with respect to peace-keeping – were unable to control or direct these tasks. The abortive *troika* proposal was an expression of the lack of confidence of one major segment of world-power opinion in the way the job was being done and a warning that a condition for reestablishing consensus was to make the new locus of decision making more representative.

These three approaches, which reflect traditional scholastic analyses of political leadership, do not exhaust the subject. Richard Neustadt in his *Presidential Power*[8] has studied the actual extent and limitations of the influence of a political executive in decision making. From the direction of organization theory, stimulated in particular by Chester Barnard in *The Functions of the Executive*,[9] another current of analysis throws light on executive leadership. These approaches, in contrast with those just discussed, put emphasis on the informal rather more than the formal, on process rather more than norm, and on role rather more than idiosyncrasy.

Among studies of international organization a great step beyond the three traditional approaches to executive leadership was made by Ernst Haas in *Beyond the Nation-State*.[10] Haas views an international organization as a structure within a world environment. The inputs to the structure come from the demands and expectations of the states and other organized forces in the environment. It is the configuration of these input pressures – the elements of overt and potential conflict and consensus among them – which defines opportunities for action through the organization. The executive head is in the key position to maximize these opportunities, in other words to interpret the input pressures in such a way as to bring about an expansion of the tasks and of the authority of the organization. Haas is thus concerned with executive leadership as a politically adapted function, not about its legal bases, personal styles, or ethical principles.

How does the executive head fulfil this role? According to Haas he makes use of conflict in the environment to propose actions which were not part of the contestants' original intentions but in which they can be persuaded to acquiesce as at any rate less harmful than a continuation of conflict. These actions, undertaken by the international organization, expand its task and enhance its authority. The classic illustrations are the creation of UNEF in the Suez conflict and the mounting of the Congo operation by Hammarskjöld. In both cases the secretary-general interpreted the conflict in the environment in such a way as to expand the task of the UN and more specifically to expand his own executive functions. At the same time Hammarskjöld elaborated a doctrine to explain and justify this expansion: the doctrine of the UN as an actively neutral intervening force or interposing force in situations of potential big-power conflict, a doctrine in which the concept of an actively neutral international secretariat was an essential element. Another example can be taken from the ILO: the two major program expansion areas of the ILO in the postwar era, human rights and manpower, grew out of the ILO leadership's interpretation of Cold War pressures and the opportunities they offered.

Haas distinguishes three critical variables in the executive head's strategy for maximizing opportunities for task expansion. First, the executive head must define an ideology which gives clear goals to the organization and prescribes methods for attaining these goals. This ideology must respond to a wide range of demands and expectations from the constituents. He must not be satisfied with a program that is a mere accumulation of odds and ends of projects, some appealing to one, some to another, group of constituents. Pursuit of such subgoals may be useful in retaining support in specific quarters; but the organizational ideology, in order to perform its function of expanding the task and enhancing the authority of the organization, must point to a few clear and overriding objectives with which the executive head is identified. Second, he must build a bureaucracy committed to this ideology and having a sense of its own independent international role. Third, he must make coalitions and alliances – which of their nature will be more implicit than formalized – to ensure support from a sufficient proportion of the constituents. Building a supporting coalition is a difficult business. International organizations work by separating issues. Quite different majorities may be formed on different issues. But to be assured of the kind of support he needs for attainment of his major goals the executive head must be able to retain over a period of time – perhaps throughout his tenure of office – the support of the same basic coalition. The requirements of ideology and of coalition building coincide here: the executive head can and probably should refrain from involvement in lesser issues in order to concentrate on those which link with the major goals he has defined. Hammarskjöld again serves as prototype: he concentrated his attention on a limited range of issues to do with peace keeping and related functions – a reserved area which he dealt with helped by a small personal staff – leaving the many other functions of the UN under the care of undersecretaries.[11]

For any concrete application, theory has to be placed in a historical context. The utility of a theory lies in the extent to which it draws attention to the significant explanatory factors in a particular historical situation. The Haas model of executive leadership is in this respect a big advance over earlier thinking. Its weakness may lie in encouraging on the part of the researcher who uses it a presumption that the executive head has more effective initiative than in fact he often does have. By presenting almost a formula for integrative leadership it may lead to an underestimation of the constraints which are inherent in the set of relationships of which the executive head is a part. It is the purpose of this article to complement the Haas model by trying to specify and to begin to analyze the key relationships in executive leadership.

The three relationships analyzed here are those of the executive head with:

(1) the international bureaucracy;
(2) the member states (and especially the most powerful among them); and
(3) the international system.

Leadership and control of the international staff

The first problem of the executive head is to establish his leadership of the staff of the organization. In doing this he has to deal with two related sets of problems. The first concerns the relationship of the staff to outside pressures from the constituents of the organization. The second concerns the executive head's relationship to the top officials of his own staff. It is convenient to deal with these separately.

The staff and the constituents

Out of the interwar experience of international organization grew a set of opinions broadly accepted among international officials concerning the ideal of an international civil service. Alexander Loveday's *Reflections on International Administration*,[12] for example, embodies this orthodoxy. The staff of an international organization, in this conception, should be an autonomous entity having no links with national administrations, and its members should cultivate a distinct "international" viewpoint. In order to achieve this the international civil service must be a career service; and a career service can be built securely only on the basis of individual merit and uniformly fair treatment under regulations which allow for no arbitrary intervention. This orthodoxy exalted the notion of a eunuch-like detachment from "politics." A major concern was to protect the staff from political intervention; and in this connection Loveday views the head of an international administration with some suspicion. "There is no *a priori* reason," he warns,

> for assuming that the head of an international organization will prove competent and judicious. In all probability he will have been appointed as a result of a political compromise and will not be the strongest candidate available.

And further:

> When the organization is a reflection of a divided world . . . he may endeavor to ingratiate himself with one camp or another, and the staff may suffer . . . *The more politically minded the Secretary-General, the greater the danger.*[13]

The attitude betrayed by these lines is worth stressing because it has been characteristic of many international civil servants.

The career-service thesis has not, however, had a monopoly. The NATO international staff was composed largely of officials on short-term secondment from national administrations.[14] This practice may increase the intensity of intergovernmental cooperation by familiarizing a growing number of national officials with the workings of NATO. It is clearly more appropriate to an organization in which there is a relatively great commonness of purpose among its members than to one more heterogeneous. It also produces the least permanent organizational effect since it creates no institutional interest concerned exclusively with the perpetuation and development of the organization itself.

In a more broadly based international organization with greater diversity among its members this secondment system would tend to produce an unmanageable cacophony. It is in this more universal context that the development of a career service cultivating a distinct loyalty to the organization seems most necessary. Short-term secondments are not conducive to this concept of international loyalty since each temporary official would naturally be influenced by his own long-term career prospects in national service. Thus, the universal organizations have introduced the practice of permanent contracts of employment for international staff and of career development in international service as a means of strengthening the staff's capacity to resist outside pressures.

A long period of gradual growth under dynamic leadership can enable an organization to assimilate officials of widely diverse origins into a common pattern of behavior and outlook. ILO officials in the immediate postwar period sometimes exhibited a distinct feeling of their own organization's superiority in this respect to the newly established United Nations whose larger staff had perforce been quickly assembled. Indeed, strong organizational tradition seems to be a more potent influence toward staff discipline and conformity than is a marked degree of ideological homogeneity among the membership. The relatively strong sense of unity within the early postwar staff of the ILO (which was working in a world of sharp ideological divisions, especially prominent among the labor movements with which it had to deal) contrasts with the internal divisions present now within the secretariats of the European Communities, divisions which follow national, political party, and pressure group lines.[15] The narrower range of ideological divergency within the Europe of the Six seems to have encouraged a franker policy of representation of interests within the secretariat with a consequently greater measure of diversity than exists where an established tradition exercises its formative power in the education of newcomers in conformity.

The concept of loyalty to the international organization calls for some further comment. It is a general principle enshrined in the regulations governing international staffs that no international official should seek or accept instructions from any authority external to the organization. That is the law, and every official is bound to it by oath of office. But there is a political reality which modifies the law. Appointments are made so as to effect a certain balance within the staff between different nationalities, geographical areas, and sectional interest groups. This applies both at the very top level of officials and at lower levels as well. All member countries (and in some cases major interest groups as well) consider themselves entitled to "representation" on the staff. An executive head will normally try to give satisfaction to these pressures (and sometimes a government may impose its choice of officials upon him). In part he is motivated by a desire not to alienate by a negative attitude any important segment of opinion within the organization. But in a more positive sense part of the value to the executive head of a diversified staff is as a sounding board for national, regional, or sectional reactions to his policy ideas.

The "representative" function of the staff normally does not take the form of a crude violation of the pledge not to seek or accept outside instructions though sometimes it must come very close to that. Certain officials will enjoy the confidence of the official national representatives of their country or of pressure groups such as international trade union organizations. They may have access to information of a confidential or semi-confidential nature from two sources: the internal network of the international organization and the external national or pressure group network. The way in which they adjust their conduct in the light of what they know, and the extent to which they reveal information from one network to the other, measures the balance of their loyalties. Even officials from the most monolithic of states acquire some degree of commitment to the organization; and even the most disciplined of loyal international officials has to give some small change to retain the confidence of his outside contacts.

Thus "conflict of loyalties" is rarely nowadays a drama of personal conscience. At one time perhaps it was: in the case, for example, of League officials of German or Italian nationality confronted with Nazi or Fascist reaction to the League. Yet in more recent years one can sense a tendency of the universal organizations of the United Nations system to abandon gradually their normative content. Staff members are more easily able to espouse a variety of personal ideologies, knowing that each has the degree of respectability conferred upon it by some national or regional interest represented in the organization while none has an imperative universal sanction.

The Loveday conception cited earlier represents the secretariat as an automatically functioning and self-regulating machine in which attempts by an executive head to assert leadership are to be discouraged. Once the problem of adaptation of the secretariat is posed, however, it is the executive head who must give the leadership and direction. And his efforts toward redefining the ideology of the organization and toward adjusting its political base will encounter the resistance of bureaucratic *immobilisme*. The executive head faces a problem which is typical in any bureaucratic situation: his orders will not be carried out in the way he intends them; they will be twisted in the course of execution to conform with the prior intentions of subordinate officials. The executive head may take special precautions in particular instances, but his personal influence cannot be everywhere all the time.

The very factors which are supposed to strengthen the international character of the staff – long-term tenure of appointment, judicially interpreted administrative regulations, etc. – reinforce this *immobilisme*. The executive head has very little latitude to dismiss officials who are patently undisciplined; he will often be reluctant to take any sanctions against them for fear of displeasing particular member states or pressure groups. His only recourse is to place recalcitrant officials as far as possible in positions where they can do little harm to his plans and to maneuver them out of the effective circuit of communications within the bureaucracy; but even in doing this he must often be careful to avoid arousing the protests of outside interests.

A direct consequence is the great difficulty of dislodging special limited goals and programs (what Haas calls "subgoals") once they have been incorporated into an organization's regular activities. Such limited goals are served within the bureaucracy by technical specialists and are supported outside by particular pressure groups. This combination of paired internal resistance to changes and external pressures for the maintenance of existing goals and activities makes it very difficult for the executive head to effect real adjustments in the work of an international organization in line with his redefinition of major goals and priorities. The changes he makes in the ideology tend to remain verbal only; and the "back-scratching" tendency of international conferences makes delegates reluctant to oppose individual projects which are dear to the hearts of others for fear of a hostile attitude towards their own. Thus it is rarely advisable or profitable for an executive head to risk a confrontation with the membership and with a segment of his own staff in order to eliminate redundant activities. These activities tend to continue but to atrophy slowly to the extent the executive head is able to deny them the impetus of fresh and renovating thought. This is one reason why international agencies carry so much deadwood.

Thus, if stability and conformity in outlook among the staff are elements in strengthening its international loyalty to the organization, these same qualities are in latent antithesis with the desire of the executive head to lead in new directions, redefining the major objectives of the organization and readjusting its political base. This is an instance of a more general conflict between innovators and established bureaucracies. In national settings radically new policies usually have been put into effect by an influx of new administrators. This was, for example, the case of the New Deal in the United States in the 1930s. It is also the case today of countries initiating the new policies of economic planning[e] where conflict develops between the established bureaucracies and those seeking to put into effect the new policies. The same type of conflict is to be anticipated in international bureaucracies led by innovating executive heads.

The only practical way an executive head can combat these tendencies toward stabilization of programs and inertia of policy is to surround himself with new staff committed to his objectives and to give this new staff as far as possible the initiative for program innovation within the bureaucracy and throw the weight of his influence, to the extent the political constraints upon him permit, behind the innovating group.

Relations with top officials

The second set of problems referred to concerns the executives head's relations with the top officials within the organization. Two difficulties arise from a tendency toward "feudalism" characteristic of international secretariats: there are conflicting poles of authority at the top level of staff and a corresponding division of loyalties into clusters of informal groups within, converging on top staff members. While these may be factors in any large organization, they are given special weight in international bureaucracies when senior officials base their position upon support from outside constituencies.

Internal opposition or passive resistance to new policies by the executive head may thus originate within the bureaucracy. Such internal opposition will be fortified by the ability of the top officials concerned to activate a group of the organization's constituents to put pressure on the executive head. Conflict within the bureaucracy can thus spread to the constituency. Within the staff it is based not only upon the fact that the "opposition" is hierarchically in command of a sector of the staff; even more it is based upon informal networks of

---

[e] The reference is to the 1960s when economic planning was being introduced in many Third World countries. It reads strangely in the 1990s when the neoliberal policies of the IMF and World Bank, agents of the consensus among the G7 countries, urge dismantling of government intervention. The parallel today would be in the attempt to install "economic reformers" in key decision-making roles in the former Soviet empire.

communications and personal loyalties which top officials can build up around themselves. (Apart from the nobler sentiments of identification with specific policies or goals, subordinate officials look to the top officials to advance their own careers.)

Now it is in the nature of the political position of these top officials to be closely identified with subgoals. There are occupational and political reasons for this. Occupationally, each top official is responsible for a limited sector of the organization's activity; his interests will be inclined into this sector and his contacts will be with those most concerned with the subgoals characteristic of that sector. He may come subjectively to consider these sectoral subgoals as the main purposes of the organization. Politically, he will look for support to a limited group of the organization's constituents and must therefore give special prominence to satisfying the expectations of these constituents.

There are legal-institutional differences among organizations in the relationship of the executive head to his top-level subordinates. Formally, in the United Nations and the specialized agencies each organization has one executive head – the secretary-general or the director-general – and other officials usually have status only as his appointees. In fact, procedures have normally become established and accepted whereby the executive head consults formally or informally with a politically representative body before making top appointments, and understandings exist as to the regions or pressure groups to be given satisfaction in such appointments.[16] The executive head's freedom in such appointments is always limited. Sectors of the bureaucracy's work will have to be allocated to these top officials.

At the other extreme, in the legal sense, are the executives of the European Communities which are collegial bodies on which provision is made for the representation of separate national and political interests. In fact, these executives cannot work on all questions as a collegial body and so they operate on the principle of a division of labor, each member of the executive body being responsible for a sector of work.[17]

Thus, underlying differences in legal form, there appears to be a common resemblance in the internal political processes of international bureaucracies.

There are three ways in which the executive head may seek to control the top staff so as to maintain his political initiative. These are:

(1) *Complete domination and centralization of power in his own hands.*

This would mean effectively overcoming the "feudal" tendencies by reducing the top officials to a position in which they would be dependent on the executive head, holding their appointments at pleasure and carrying out subordinate technical functions. Albert Thomas seems to have aimed at something like this when he first refused to accept Harold Butler as deputy director, offering him instead an appointment as a chief of one of the divisions he intended to create. But Thomas was soon convinced that the confidence and support of important member governments – and in particular of the British government – depended upon his appointing Butler as deputy director.[18] It is doubtful whether any executive head has or could achieve a position in which his top subordinates hold their posts at pleasure; but one means of preventing them from developing a power base within the bureaucracy is to make frequent changes of responsibilities and to prevent the emergence of well-defined continuous sectors within the bureaucracy. While this may achieve the political objective of preventing the identification of top officials with major bureaucratic sectors, the costs in administrative inefficiency may be high.

(2) *Presiding over a cabinet of top officials.* Usually an executive head will want to meet with his senior staff periodically to discuss matters of general concern to the organization. This will be a means of pulling individual top officials out from under their preoccupation with subgoals by keeping them informed about important matters outside their own particular sphere. It will also oblige conflicting elements among the top staff to have at least a minimum of contact with each other. And it may help the executive head – if he is skilled at this – to smoke out differences among his staff about which he is not adequately informed. Collective discussion can be used as an instrument favoring a certain conformity of policy. But it would be an unwise executive head who did not take his major decisions on policy *after* consultation rather than *in* consultation with his top officials. The cabinet technique is, at best, an instrument of communication and of limited control over the top-level officials. It has not proven to be an effective instrument of decision making.[19]

(3) *The "reserved area" of policy.* By this is meant that the executive

head reserves certain types of decisions to himself and equips himself with a personal staff so as to be able to act within this area of policy. Following from the prescriptions implicit in the Haas model the questions which an executive head would reserve in this way include:

(a) those relating to the definition of the major goals and policy orientation (including program priorities) and the development of organizational ideology; and

(b) matters of direct concern to the executive head's base of political support and his coalition policy for the construction of alliances to support his program.

Everything else he would delegate to his top officials and interfere as little as possible with them; but to the extent that he allows top officials to encroach upon the reserved areas he would undermine his own capacity for leadership. This is the most usual method for executive heads to follow, using it in some combination with the cabinet system, as described, for communications and general supervision.

The "reserved area" implies that the executive head acquires his own staff distinct from the staff controlled, in fact, by his senior officials (while the latter staff is formally under the executive's supreme control, in fact he is inhibited from exercising his authority over it). This personal staff can provide an executive head with several essential, effective components to his job:

(a) A few people in whom he has virtually complete confidence, with whom he can talk frankly about all the issues arising within the organization. With his top officials, because of their political position, he is usually in a posture of negotiating.

(b) Channels of intelligence providing accurate assessment of the expectations and demands from the membership of the organization. His top officials provide a sounding board for sectional reactions, but in addition the executive head needs his own research and intelligence network to assess the possibilities and limits presented by the world situation in terms of the policy objectives which he determines to pursue.

(c) Competent advisers to help him redefine as necessary the major aims which the organization is to pursue and to explain these in such a way as to gain the necessary political support. In other words, the staff would effectively command program and policy development and avoid determination of the program by specialists committed to subgoals and subject to the special influence of particular outside pressure groups.

Relations with member states

The executive head's relationship with the bureaucracy determines his capability for action and initiative. His relationship with the national constituents determines the political support he will have for his action and thus the limits to which it can go. Some of the analytical features of this relationship emerge from a comparison of cases involving the executive heads of the ILO during a period of almost fifty years.

Albert Thomas came to the directorship of the ILO with the acquiescence, though not with the wholehearted political support, of the French government. The French government wanted a Frenchman as director; it could hardly have desired Thomas who was politically in opposition to it. Thomas' appointment was secured on the initiative of the western European trade unions, supported by employer representatives, at a time when the governments had no concerted policy on the directorship. Thomas identified the ILO with his ideology of reformist socialism, stressing educational action among workers, the development of trade unions, and reforms such as worker participation in management, social insurance, and nationalization. He made the trade unions of the International Federation of Trade Unions (IFTU) in Amsterdam his political base.

Thomas soon became embroiled in a controversy with the French government before the Permanent Court of International Justice (PCIJ) in the course of which he appeared in person to contest the French government's position. This conflict between the director and the government of his country has to be seen within the context of French domestic politics. Thomas never gave up the intention of returning to active political life in France. He maintained his political affiliation with the Socialist Party, the Section Française de l'Internationale Ouvrière (SFIO), and, more particularly, retained the support of Léon Jouhaux and the Confédération Générale du Travail (CGT). It was this domestic political support which gave Thomas his freedom to criticize his political opponents who were occupying the seats of power in the government.

Harold Butler, Thomas' successor, contributed to the development of the organizational ideology of the ILO in the 1930s. He redirected ILO thinking along lines similar to those of the American New Deal, advocating a broader role for the ILO in the field of international economic policy particularly as regards measures to fight the Depression. This major contribution to ILO ideology prepared and solidified his principal political success, the acquisition of United States membership.

Nevertheless, Butler's position had political weaknesses. To some extent these may have been a question of personality. Temperamentally he was an intellectual and a civil servant, closer to the men of government – particularly to upper-middle-class reformers such as the New Deal brought to the fore – rather than to the trade unions, closer, indeed, in many ways to some of the employers than to the trade unions.

Butler's last ILO battle, concerning an apparently trivial matter of an appointment to the ILO staff, brought out these weaknesses. Four consecutive French governments during the period from the autumn of 1937 through the spring of 1938 – the Camille Chautemps Popular Front government, the Chautemps Radical government, the short-lived Léon Blum government of March 1938, and the Edouard Daladier government of National Union – pressed Butler to appoint as his representative in the Paris office of the ILO a person in whom Butler had no confidence. Butler, in this situation, had no political leverage within France, such as Thomas had enjoyed through the favour of the CGT. The French employers, who appeared to share Butler's views, either could not intervene to change the official position or did not consider it worth their while to do so when they had more vital interests at stake. Butler's only weapons were the threat to resign and the possibility of mobilizing outside pressure. He tried both and both failed to change the French position.[20] Butler first threatened to resign over this issue in March 1938 at a time when on the broader international scene Hitler was menacing Austria. Though Butler himself might not have come so well out of it, the French government might equally have been implicated in a blow at the remains of the Geneva edifice of international cooperation. Butler was persuaded to withdraw his resignation at this time on the understanding he would be supported by the officers of the Governing Body and by the British government in resolving the issue which had brought him into conflict with the French government. This attempt to "internationalize" a conflict between the director and a major member state was resented in

French circles. Butler again pressed his resignation, advancing personal grounds, as the only way out for him. His purely diplomatic position, lacking a solid base of political support, left him powerless in a crisis with a member state.

John Winant, Butler's successor, was a leading American political personality, having been governor of New Hampshire and holding the respect and confidence of President Franklin Roosevelt. Winant was only for a brief period director of the ILO, but he had to handle the major crisis into which the outbreak of war plunged the organization. Winant was determined, contrary to the decision taken by the League, to remove the ILO from the threat that its resources might be seized or its capacity for action destroyed by the Axis powers; consequently, he decided to transfer the organization to North America. Indeed, destiny seemed to have given him this role to play. In June 1940, as the Nazis advanced into France, Winant appealed to Secretary of State Cordell Hull, and through him to Roosevelt, to permit the removal of the ILO to the United States. He met with their refusal; the ILO was low on their list of preoccupations and they were unprepared to face isolationist, anti-League hostility in Congress. As things worked out, the result was politically satisfactory for the ILO, which went to Canada with the support of Prime Minister Mackenzie King and thus became located in a belligerent country from the very earliest phase of the war, a major factor in the ILO's survival into the postwar world. But the refusal of the Roosevelt administration was a blow for Winant, who resigned shortly thereafter. It underlines the point that personal relationships of confidence between a director and the head of the government of a major state are not a sufficient guarantee of support when domestic political currents, to which national leaders will be more sensitive, are working against the policy of the director.

David Morse, the present director-general, has had to deal with a series of crises, in all of which the ILO's relationship to the United States was crucial.[f] Shortly after he assumed office an anti-ILO campaign became active among right-wing business circles in the United States allied with the forces advocating the Bricker Amendment to the Constitution of the United States.[g]

[f] Morse was ILO director-general 1948 to 1970.
[g] A major political controversy of the 1950s, the Bricker Amendment was intended to protect the sovereignty and independence of the United States from treaties and international agreements, many of them emanating from United Nations institutions.

This attack reached its critical phase in 1956–57. The ILO had the sympathy of the Eisenhower administration; yet the White House, while taking a position against the Bricker Amendment, did not risk antagonizing a large body of Congressional opinion by actively supporting the ILO, for example, on the question of the ceiling fixed by Congress on the United States' contribution to the ILO budget.

Morse had, however, the support of certain domestic forces which could independently influence Congress. These included liberal businessmen (David Zellerbach, Paul Hoffmann, and others), certain Catholic groups (for example, the National Catholic Welfare Conference), and, above all, the American Federation of Labor-Congress of Industrial Organizations (AFL-CIO).

The domestic attack on the ILO within the United States became accentuated in reaction to the Soviet Union's reentry into the ILO after 1954. The fact that Morse was able to arouse sufficient domestic support for the ILO within the United States enabled him not only to counter the threat of reduced participation or even withdrawal of the United States from the organization but also to maintain personally the confidence of both the United States and the Soviet governments. The key factor in the situation was the support Morse had, not from the United States administration (which while favorable would not actively support the ILO in the face of any major challenge from public opinion or influential pressure groups) but from the domestic groups, principally the trade unions.

This position has certain inherent difficulties, particularly that of a possible conflict between the primary aims in the international sphere of AFL-CIO and those of the ILO as articulated by its executive head. During the United States domestic crisis on ILO matters in 1956–57 the policies advanced by Morse conformed with those of the AFL-CIO: notably, the abolition of forced labor and the promotion of freedom of association for trade unions, both of which were seen at that time primarily in terms of a challenge to the Communist world. However, the gravity and extent of the problems confronting an international organization and the perspective from which an executive head has to deal with them makes it increasingly difficult for him to maintain a firm doctrinal alliance with particular domestic interests in a major

On the amendment, see Duane Tanabaum, *The Bricker Amendment Controversy: A Test of Eisenhower's Political Leadership* (Ithaca, N.Y., Cornell University Press, 1988).

member state. Yet lacking such domestic support, the executive head may find himself defenseless in a major crisis since governments will be far less responsive to the appeal of an executive head than they will to powerful domestic pressure groups.[h]

From this outline of the relationships between executive heads and member states the following propositions may be drawn:

(1) The issues which are most important to the executive head are seldom of the same order of importance to national governments.

(2) Strong local pressure groups or local political factors are more likely to influence a government's attitude toward an international organization than any sense of commitment to the personality at the head of the organization.

(3) The interests of international organizations have to be advanced within the domestic context of its major member states by making use of such favorable currents of domestic opinion as present themselves, i.e., the executive head must exercise the sailor's skill in using available winds and currents to advance in the direction of his choice.

(4) Thus, the executive head needs to fortify his position by alliance with domestic pressure groups. He must not limit himself to "foreign" politics but know how to make domestic politics work in favor of his policies.

In order to be able to work in this way the executive head must have great political skill. He needs also a personal confidential intelligence network reaching into domestic politics of key countries. Of necessity these networks of contacts will be limited for any single individual to a very few countries; and taking this into account, the ideal executive head is one who is able to engage in political confrontation in those countries which at the particular time are crucial in the evolution of the organization.

Finally, the executive head, because this is inherent in political confrontation, must be able when necessary to compromise on nonessentials in his program and his definition of the aims of the organization.

---

[h] Support for Morse from the AFL-CIO during the Bricker Amendment debate quickly evaporated when Morse came under pressure to appoint a Soviet citizen to a post of assistant director-general, considered by the Soviet Union to be their "right" as a great-power member of the ILO. It was in this context that Morse resigned as director-general. See "Labor and Hegemony", chapter 19 in this volume.

This is a difficult matter of judgement since he must be able to reconcile any compromise with the need for ideological clarity in his leadership of the bureaucracy and the organization's constituents. When compromising he must appear to be acting on principle, consistent with his professed organizational aims. He must not appear to be too much of a bargainer.

The international system

The basic personal qualification for effective leadership is clear perception of what action and initiative the state of the international system at any time permits. The definition of organizational ideology and the establishment of the political base for an organization's action have to be determined in the light of the executive head's reading of the constraints imposed and the opportunities opened by the world political situation. His perception will determine the balance between an executive head's role as a negotiator in "quiet diplomacy" and as a taker of personal political initiatives.

The oldest and most regularly recurrent political function of an executive head is to be a mediator in negotiating agreement among different constituents' interests. In order to do this effectively the executive head must:

(1) acquire and maintain the confidence of all major segments of opinion;

(2) be identified with a definite, though to some extent flexible, ideology representing a consensus within the organization, i.e., his suggestions must be seen as conforming with the aims and purposes of the organization and not as seeking merely agreement for its own sake and at any price; and

(3) have an adequate intelligence at his disposal so that he can make constructive suggestions and avoid pitfalls.

These conditions are not easy to combine. There is a potential conflict between maintaining the confidence of major powers or interests and standing forth as spokesman of a clear organizational ideology. Furthermore, adequate intelligence cannot easily be acquired solely through the services of an international organization. Thus, the executive head will have to rely on supplementary intelligence from the diplomatic services of major powers or other sources outside the organization. The extent to which he has to rely on particular outside

341

sources may adversely affect confidence in his impartiality on the part of those powers to which he is less close.

Much greater difficulty arises when the executive head is in the position of taking political initiative for which he and the organization will bear the full responsibility. Such was the initiative of 1956 to create UNEF in the Suez crisis. At this point the secretary-general emerged dramatically from the role of chief administrator and "quiet diplomat" to take on that of an independent actor in world affairs. The Suez initiative was carried through successfully, with considerable enhancement to the prestige of his office. It was the kind of initiative which met with a broad degree of support or acquiescence. In the Congo, by contrast, attempting a second time to bear the same kind of political responsibility, the secretary-general was not able to maintain the same degree of consensus behind his actions. He became a political casualty before his tragic death in the air crash of September 1961.

Hammarskjöld had a keen sense of the risks of his position. Five years before his death he had written in a personal letter to Max Ascoli:[21]

> It is one thing that, in the vacuum which suddenly developed in the Suez crisis, I had, for what it was worth, to throw in everything I had to try to tide us over; it was one of those irrational and extremely dangerous situations in which only something as irrational on a different level could break the spell. But it is an entirely different thing, every time the big powers run into a deadlock, to place the problem in the Secretary-General's hands with the somewhat naive expectation that he can continue to turn up with something. It is a matter of course that a continued use of the office of the Secretary-General in that way sooner or later leads to a point where he must break his neck, politically. If, as in the Suez situation, the very facts, as established by the policy of the various big powers, force the Secretary-General into a key role, I am perfectly willing to risk being a political casualty if there is an outside chance of achieving positive results. But if the Secretary-General is forced into a similar role through sheer escapism from those who should carry the responsibility, there is a place for solid warning. Politically, the Secretary-General should be, and is, most expendable, but he should not be expended just because somebody does not want to produce his own money.

An initiative-taking secretary-general cannot become a substitute for a Security Council that does not work because no consensus exists. When the major powers are deadlocked, the secretary-general may try to play a role. In fortuitous circumstances, such as the Suez crisis, he may succeed, but it is a risky formula. The secretary-general can be the most significant contributing factor toward building up a working consensus within the United Nations, but his success in this depends upon maintaining the confidence of all the major powers and groups of countries. Once a risky action has led to this confidence being withdrawn by any major party, then – even though the others may feel honor-bound to support him – the secretary-general's ability to be the architect of consensus is expended.[22]

The executive head needs to be able to count upon a working majority of the organization's constituents in support of his policies. In order to build majorities he may, as suggested earlier, have to engage quietly in domestic politics in key countries. But he cannot afford either to appear as the spokesman of a coalition of countries or as the supporter of domestic factions. He has to limit his coalition policy at the point where he risks alienating a major power or interest within the organization, and he has to limit his personal political initiative at the same point. Once he becomes the prisoner of any particular coalition which divides the organization, he can no longer perform his primary function of consensus formation. The potential conflict between his function as catalyst of consent and his personal political initiative constitutes the executive head's most troublesome dilemma and that most likely to lead to his downfall.

In his introduction to the secretary-general's report to the 1961 session of the General Assembly Hammarskjöld set forth ideas which appeared to suggest the political base for UN action would be the emerging nations of Asia and Africa.[23] He attempted to reconcile subtly the notion of a universal rule of law in international relations with a notion of the will of the international community reminiscent of Rousseau. This ideology – though one should not impute to Hammarskjöld personally what is not explicitly stated by him – could lead to the use of Assembly majorities as a means of putting pressure upon the industrialized countries. The United Nations would become the gadfly of the great powers, an international pressure group of the poor used to secure concessions from the rich.[i]

An alternative political strategy would be to rest the political base of the system upon the industrial powers, using it as an instrument

---

[i] This was, of course, what the United States objected to during the period of Third World pressure for the NIEO.

of building consensus between western countries and the Soviet Union. The corresponding ideology would stress functional areas of common interest between East and West and move from broadening functional cooperation toward a concerted policy of industrialized powers to facilitate economic development of the poorer nations. It is a less demagogic policy, more skeptical of majorities unless they are majorities which represent negotiated agreement.

Within international organizations there is now some evidence of disenchantment with majoritarianism although it is difficult to discern a consistent alternative strategy. In the UN Conference on Trade and Development (UNCTAD) the "77," realizing that majority votes could not compel real concessions from the rich countries, accepted a conciliation procedure in case of division between blocs on substantive issues. Retreat from majoritarianism would imply a reversal of the doctrine espoused by United States administrations from the late 1940s which could bring the United States closer to Soviet and French views on the UN system. But the distinction to be brought out in the context of this essay is that while the policy of alignment with the emerging nations calls for continued use of initiative on the part of the secretary-general at the risk of a growing impatience of the industrialized countries of both East and West and a growing disillusionment of the emerging nations at the hiatus between aims and results, the policy of East–West reconciliation would give the primacy in the secretary-general's role to quiet diplomacy and consensus formation.[j]

In the foregoing, the executive head has been used as a focus for the study of some problems of international organization and as a means to sketch out a framework of analysis for the purpose. It is now useful to turn back to the notions enunciated at the start. The first of these is that the executive head plays a key role in converting an international organization conceived as a framework for multilateral diplomacy into one which is an autonomous actor in the international system. The Haas strategy (organizational ideology *plus* committed bureaucracy *plus* supporting coalition) offers valid guidelines, but in seeking

---

[j] An appearance of consensual direction by the western countries led by the United States through the UN Security Council and the economic agencies (the IMF and the World Bank) came about following the collapse of the Soviet Union. It is more accurate to see this as consecrating a global division between rich and poor countries accompanied by a weakening of the influence of the poor countries. Consensus is more in appearance than reality.

to follow them the executive head must be conscious of and work within constraints. The first of these constraints is bureaucratic *immobilisme* which is to some extent amenable to effective leadership. The second, less amenable, is the limitation on the executive head's control which comes from institutionalizing client interests within the bureaucracy. As the executive tasks of international organization expand, client control will come to depend more and more upon an intrabureaucratic balance of influences, and thus issues of representation within the bureaucracy are likely to become more salient and the primacy of the executive head more hemmed in. The third constraint – and the most determining in the short run – is the world pattern of conflicts and alignments. In a tight bipolar situation, such as prevailed during the early 1950s, the executive head may try to play a role of intermediary between rival blocs but is most likely to become aligned with one of them. This may give the illusion of strength to the organization (as to the UN in the Korean conflict) but in the perspective of the system as a whole the international organization appears as the instrument of the bloc which succeeds in dominating it. In a looser system the executive head may be able to mobilize uncommitted supporters in order to follow a line independent of the rival blocs, the limits of which will be fixed by big-power tolerance or willingness to acquiesce. In a system characterized by several, for example, five or six, concentrations of more equally balanced effective power it is conceivable that an executive head might play an important brokerage role. The personal idiosyncratic dimension enters both in the form of the executive head's ability to maintain himself as top man in bureaucratic politics and in the clarity of his perception of the significance for international organization of the prevailing pattern of conflicts and alignments.

The second notion advanced earlier was that the executive head may be a key factor in bringing about a transformation of the system in the direction of greater integration. The test of whether he can do this lies in his ability to bring about changes in national policies so that they conform more with the decisions and interests of the international organizations. A diplomatic go-between or brokerage role, useful as it may be for helping to preserve peace within the system, does not meet this test because it does not bring about change in the system. In performing it the executive head acts as the instrument of the powers for reaching their own accommodation.[24] In this essay only a limited number of crisis situations in the relations between an executive head and member states have been examined, admittedly not a representative or typical sample. Yet the tentative conclusion seems indicated that an executive head's ability to bring effective influence to bear on government policy depends upon his ability to exert influence through actors *within* the domestic political system. The requisites for this are: (1) access to domestic groups having influence; (2) adequate intelligence concerning their goals and perceptions; and (3) ability to manipulate international action so that these groups can perceive an identity of interests with it. The cases cited all involve pluralistic polities, in respect of which the requisites might conceivably be met. But what about noncompetitive and especially ideological polities which succeed in subjecting internal groups to a common political direction and in insulating the polity from external influences? The prospects of system change through the agency of international organizations and their executive heads would seem to be linked with the progress of pluralism in polities. The long-term possibilities of penetrating ideological regimes may, if we follow David Apter's reasoning, lie through the scientific elites, a group likely to lose patience with political orthodoxies which cramp the search for new knowledge, to demand free access to information necessary for scientific work, and to see advantages in contacts with scientists abroad.[25] The potentiality of scientific elites as a channel of penetration depends not only on their receptivity to external influences but also on whether they have real influence upon the political leadership at home, and in this last respect recent events suggest that the long term may be quite long indeed.

Notes

This text was first published in *International Organization*, vol. 23, no. 2 (Spring 1969), pp. 205–230.

1 The fact that the ILO, particularly under the leadership of its first director-general, Albert Thomas, has been held up as a model of dynamic leadership in international organization may excuse the prominence of the ILO case in this article. Of Thomas' leadership the best study is still E. J. Phelan, *Yes and Albert Thomas* (London: Cresset Press Limited, 1949). More recent is B. W. Schaper, *Albert Thomas: trente ans de réformisme social* (Assen, Netherlands: Van Gorcum and Co., 1959).

2 Phelan, *Yes and Albert Thomas*, pp. 124–127.

3 Michel Virally, "Le rôle politique du secrétaire-général des Nations-Unies," *Annuaire français de droit international*, vol. IV (Paris: Centre National de la Recherche Scientifique, 1958), pp. 360–399.

4 This is a natural bias in most biographical studies, for example, those on

Albert Thomas, and would seem to be the central idea in Stephen M. Schwebel, *The Secretary-General of the United Nations: His Political Powers and Practice* (Cambridge, Mass.: Harvard University Press, 1952).

5 Jean Siotis, *Essai sur le secrétariat international*, Publications de l'Institut Universitaire de Hautes Etudes Internationales, No. 41 (Geneva: Librairie Droz, 1963), pp. 60–64, 135ff.; and Leon Gordenker, *The UN Secretary-General and the Maintenance of Peace* (New York: Columbia University Press, 1967), pp. 5–6, 18ff.

6 Max Beloff, *New Dimensions in Foreign Policy: A Study in British Administrative Experience, 1947–59* (London: George Allen and Unwin, 1961), pp. 39, 58–59.

7 Dag Hammarskjöld, *Introduction to the Annual Report of the Secretary-General on the Work of the Organisation, 16 June 1960–15 June 1961* (General Assembly *Official Records* [16th session], Supplement No. 1A), p. 6; also Dag Hammarskjöld, *The International Civil Servant in Law and in Fact* (Oxford: Clarendon Press, 1961), *passim*; a study written in the same context is Sydney D. Bailey, *The Secretariat of the United Nations*, United Nations Study No. 11 (New York: Carnegie Endowment for International Peace, 1962).

8 Richard E. Neustadt, *Presidential Power: The Politics of Leadership* (New York: John Wiley and Sons, 1960). The author describes his book as a contribution to analysis of "the classic problem of the man on top in any political system: how to be on top in fact as well as in name" (p. vii). Arthur M. Schlesinger, Jr., *The Age of Roosevelt*, Volume II, *The Coming of the New Deal* (Boston: Houghton Mifflin, 1959), especially Part 8, "Evolution of the Presidency," adopts a similar approach. Gordenker follows Neustadt's approach in his stress on process and influence.

9 Chester Barnard, *The Functions of the Executive* (Cambridge, Mass.: Harvard University Press, 1946).

10 Ernst B. Haas, *Beyond the Nation-State: Functionalism and International Organization* (Stanford, Calif.: Stanford University Press, 1964), especially pp. 119ff.

11 Bailey, *Secretariat of the United Nations*, pp. 57–58; Gordenker, *UN Secretary-General and the Maintenance of Peace*, p. 103.

12 Alexander Loveday, *Reflections on International Administration* (Oxford: Clarendon Press, 1956).

13 Loveday, pp. 118–119. My italics.

14 Cf. Lord Hastings Ismay, *NATO: The First Five Years, 1949–1954* (Paris: NATO, 1954), p. 64.

15 Jean Siotis, "Some Problems of European Secretariats," *Journal of Common Market Studies*, vol. 2, no. 3 (March 1964), especially pp. 245ff.

16 Concerning the arrangements for top appointments in the UN see Gordenker, *UN Secretary-General and the Maintenance of Peace*, pp. 91ff.

17 There is a "written procedure" in force in the European Commission whereby files with decisions by each member are circulated to all the

others. Anyone with experience of official bodies would assume that the principle of non-intervention would become the rule. Rarely would any member of the executive college interfere in the work of another member for fear of others crossing his own jurisdictional boundaries.

18 Phelan, *Yes and Albert Thomas*, pp. 28–33.

19 The parallel with President Franklin D. Roosevelt's use of the cabinet is evident from Schlesinger:

> The meetings evidently retained some obscure usefulness for the President. The reaction he got from this miscellany of administrators perhaps gave him some idea of the range of public opinion. It also helped him to measure the capacity of his subordinates ... But, like all strong Presidents, Roosevelt regarded his cabinet as a body of department heads, to be dealt with individually – or, sometimes, as a group of representative intelligent men, useful for a quick canvass of opinion – not as a council of constitutional advisers.
>
> (*Coming of the New Deal*, p. 504)

The similarity of UN practice under Lie, Hammarskjöld, and Thant is pointed out by Gordenker.

20 It is, of course, difficult to disentangle at this distance in time the personal motives of Butler as regards his resignation. But these motives do not materially enter into the political analysis of the use of resignation as a weapon.

21 Letter from Hammarskjöld, quoted in Max Ascoli, "The Future of the UN – An Editorial," *Reporter* (New York), October 26, 1961, p. 12.

22 Leland M. Goodrich, "The Political Role of the Secretary-General," *International Organization*, vol. 16, no. 4 (Autumn 1962), pp. 720–735, stresses the secretary-general's role as consensus builder and concludes that dangers to the UN might be avoided

> if governments assume their responsibilities in the General Assembly and Security Council and do not place upon the Secretary-General or make it necessary for him to assume responsibilities beyond his powers and of such a nature as to expose him to serious political attack.
>
> (pp. 734–735)

23 Hammarskjöld, *Introduction to the Annual Report, 16 June 1960–15 June 1961*.

24 Perceptive executive heads have realized this, as for example in former ILO Director-General Edward Phelan's comment to Schwebel:

> The Secretary-General's activity behind the scenes is useful. But multiple consultations decide nothing. They keep the Secretary-General informed and they exercise a gentle influence. This is not the same as influencing an international, collective decision.
>
> (Schwebel, *Secretary-General of the United Nations*, p. 211)

Nor is it the same as influencing a government to change its policy.

25 David E. Apter, *The Politics of Modernization* (Chicago: University of Chicago Press, 1965), pp. 432–463.

17 Decision making (with Harold K. Jacobson) (1977)

The analysis of decision making is one way of studying power relations. Decisions, of course, do not reveal power directly.[a] What they may show directly is influence, or the way in which power is translated into action. The relative power of contending forces is an inference that can be drawn from a careful observation of the workings of influence.

In drawing this inference, one must include "non-decisions" within the concept of decisions. When an individual or group or government refrains from taking some initiative or action, this is usually because they have made a calculation showing it likely to be fruitless or possibly damaging to the attainment of their goals because it would encounter opposition too powerful to overcome.[1] Thus, likely opposing power has been taken into account and one possible action eliminated before it ever became part of a record of visible actions. All decision makers, individual or collective, carry in their consciousness a picture of prevailing power relations, and these images of the way power is structured are initial determinants of the decision process.

---

[a] This essay was written by Robert W. Cox and Harold K. Jacobson for a volume edited by Georges Abi-Saab and published as a special issue of the *International Social Science Journal*, vol. 29, no. 1 (1977), pp. 115–135. It represents a development of their thinking beyond the analysis of decision making in their book, *The Anatomy of Influence: Decision Making in International Organization* (New Haven, Conn.: Yale University Press, 1972). This essay puts more emphasis on the process of global structural change whereas the book, reflecting the rigidities of the Cold War phase of world-power relations, analyzed influence within relatively fixed parameters. In Cox's work, it marks the introduction of concern for hegemony and a preliminary statement of his view of a world system structured by production – a perspective developed further in his *Production, Power, and World Order: Social Forces in the Making of History* (New York: Columbia University Press, 1987) and in the essay, "Social Forces, States, and World Orders: Beyond International Relations Theory," chapter 6 in this volume.

The "pre-influence" stage of decision making is a mental picture of power relations.

The decision process can thus be seen as both a test of the power relations assumed at the start of the action (the mental picture), and as a means toward changing these power relations.[2] Decisions can change power relations either by changing the resources available to the actors or by changing the procedures through which they interact so as to give some actors a more advantageous position than others. The study of decision making is, accordingly, a study of the dynamics of power relations. It begins with an analysis of the structure of existing power relations; and it seeks to understand how the decision process may tend to sustain or to change that structure.

The choice of contexts: narrow or broad?

Quite obviously, power relations and decision making take place within a variety of contexts, more or less broad in scope, more or less consequential. Towards the simple and less consequential end of the scale would be a local friendly society; towards the complex and more consequential, economic policy in a major modern state. The more confined the context studied, the more precision can be given to the concept of a decision. Making an *ex gratia* payment to someone would clearly be a specific decision in the friendly society. National economic policy by contrast involves a multitude of actions all of which might be called decisions, taken by distinct but frequently overlapping sets of people, with different degrees of importance and effectiveness. In such a complex and extensive context, the concept of decision tends to lose the specificity associated with the more simple context. General categories are required to differentiate the kinds of actions which cumulatively constitute a policy – symbolic declarations, strategic programming, tactical allocations, and so forth. The larger the context, the more the specificity of decisions tends to become swallowed up into the decision process as a whole.

This consideration applies to enquiry into power relations at the global level as well as at local or national level. The choice of a context that is relatively limited in scope and precisely defined implies, on the part of the investigator, an assumption of stability in those other factors in world politics into which the specific decision context fits. It is, of course, possible to allow for changes in the environment of such a limited decision context, but these environmental changes have to be treated as given, as beyond the scope of enquiry. In times of relative stability, a narrower focus with the greater precision of detail it allows, seems like the best way to gain understanding about the inner workings of specific institutions. But in times of more profound and pervasive change, a broader angle of vision is desirable, one that sacrifices detail the better to grasp the shifting outline of the whole into which the separate institutions fit and in relation to which they make sense. This whole is the world system of power relations.

The authors of this essay completed in 1972 a study of decision making in international organization which they began in the late 1960s and carried out with the collaboration of several others.[3] It was a comparative study of how decisions were made in eight specialized international institutions of universal or quasi-universal scope: the International Telecommunication Union (ITU), the International Labor Organization (ILO), the United Nations Educational, Scientific, and Cultural Organization (UNESCO), the World Health Organization (WHO), the International Atomic Energy Agency (IAEA), the International Monetary Fund (IMF), the General Agreement on Tariffs and Trade (GATT), and the United Nations Conference on Trade and Development (UNCTAD). By contrast with the world system of power relations, these specialized organizations provided a set of relatively limited and specific decision contexts. The study covered a period of history, 1945–70, that was one of relative stability in the basic framework of world power relations, although some important changes did modify this framework. The United States and the USSR remained the dominant powers in the world system during the period, and while the USSR moved toward parity with the United States in some respects, both declined in their power relative to other states. The main modifications were the increased power and potential for autonomy of western Europe, and the increased articulation of Third World concerns. The eight organizations studied reflected the structure of world power and adapted to the two major modifications in the framework of world-power relations.

As a consequence of this relative stability in the environment our analysis could and did devote primary attention to the interaction among individuals who participated directly in the political processes of the eight international organizations. Building on the tradition of studies of decision making within local communities and national states,[4] our study sought to explain how influence was acquired and exercised in international organization by analyzing how decisions were made. We sought to determine if there were persistent patterns and structures of influence.

We developed a common analytical framework so that our analyses of decision making in the eight agencies would be comparable. To determine whether or not patterns and structures of influence differed depending on the issue that was being decided we utilized a tax-onomy of decisions involving seven categories: representational, sym-bolic, boundary, programmatic, rule-creating, rule-supervisory, and operational. Decision making within each of the categories showed certain distinctive patterns common to most of the agencies studied. Differences among the agencies seemed to arise from differences in the importance to each of the various categories of decision – differences, that is, in the emphasis on certain categories of decisions and also in the practical consequences in terms of real resources affec-ted that flow from decisions. For instance, symbolic decisions were quite important in the ILO and UNCTAD (a category of decisions that by definition does not have significant practical consequences), but relatively unimportant to GATT and the IMF. On the one hand, though all of these agencies engaged in rule creating, the practical consequences of their rules were greater in the cases of the IMF and GATT than in those of the ILO or UNCTAD, and this affected the way in which decisions were made.

The individuals who were directly involved in decision making within international organizations (the actors in decision making) were classified into the following categories: (a) representatives of national governments; (b) representatives of national and inter-national private associations; (c) the executive heads of the organiza-tions; (d) high officials and other members of the bureaucracy of each organization; (e) individuals who serve in their own capacity formally or informally as advisers; (f) representatives of other international organizations; and (g) employees of the mass media.

Individuals in the first four categories were active in decision making in all of the organizations throughout the period studied. Those in the fifth and sixth categories were active in some of the organizations some of the time, but those in the final category played virtually no role, reflecting the minimal attention that public opinion gave to these eight agencies prior to the 1970s.

Different categories of actors tended to be influential in different types of decision. For example, representatives of national govern-ments were influential in symbolic, representational, and rule-creating decisions. Executive heads were particularly influential in boundary and programmatic decisions. Members of international bureaucracies were more influential in operational decisions than in programmatic ones.

Various measures were used to gauge the influence of different individuals and categories of individuals. One technique that was utilized was simply examining the formal structure of authority: those who held positions of authority in an agency were assumed to be influential. Another technique of analysis was to ask knowledgeable individuals to list the individuals with the greatest general influence in a particular organization. Attempts were also made to construct behavioral indices of influence for individuals in some organizations on the basis of scores achieved for success in initiating and obstructing proposals. Finally, case studies of the interactions involved in particular decisions were used to assess influence in several instances. Each of the techniques had limitations, but relying on several measures, we were able to obtain a broad and, we felt, reasonably reliable understanding of the relative influence of individuals who directly participated in decision making in the eight organizations.

We were, of course, more interested in learning what general characteristics make for influence than in identifying which particular individuals appeared to be most influential. Accordingly, we sought to determine how certain general attributes relating respectively to position and personality contributed to the influence of different individuals. Our concept of position included role in the formal structure of authority and in the case of representatives the power of the unit that they represented. In this connection we assessed the changing stratification of the power of the states in the global system. Personal attributes included such factors as charisma, experiences, expert knowledge, doggedness, and negotiating skill.

Our interest went beyond the static measurement, the comparison, and the analysis of influence of individual actors. We also sought to determine how influence was aggregated behind particular policy orientations. Organizational ideologies were investigated as means of legitimating particular goals and strategies for their attainment. Persistent groupings of actors (whether formal as in the case of caucusing groups, or informal as in recurrent voting patterns) were examined.

Finally, we sought explanations outside the internal interaction processes within agencies by considering the environment that set the constraints or framework for the politics of each agency. This environment was conceived as having two aspects. One was the general environment of world politics affecting all intergovernmental organizations. The other was an environment specific to each agency in terms of the conditions most directly relevant to its specific tasks. Each of these environments could be conceived in terms of a stratification of capabilities of states, distinctive patterns of organization or ideology, and configurations of alignments and cleavages of interests among states. This mode of analysis was admittedly "state-centric" in the sense that it assumed states to be the basic entities coordinating the expression of interests through international agencies, but it did, of course, take into account non-state factors in the environment and non-state actors participating in decision making.

In summary, we sought explanations for how influence was gained and utilized within international organization on two levels: (a) that of the individual actors, those who participated directly in the making of decisions, and (b) that of the environment. The emphasis was on internal processes within agencies. The environment was taken as the given point of departure that set the framework for action and might be expected to explain a large part of the outcome. What could not be explained by the environment was to be understood as the result of the internal decision-making processes.

The principal general findings were first that these eight universal international organizations fell into two broad categories: those in which what we termed "representative subsystems" dominated decision making and those in which the "participant subsystems" dominated decision making. The "representative subsystems" are composed of the individuals in the different countries whose interactions (taking place mainly in the countries) determine the policy pursued by that country's representatives through the agency in question. The "participant subsystem" comprises the interactions taking place (mainly at the headquarters of the agency) among these representatives, the high officials of the agency, and any others directly involved in the internal processes of the agency. The first category (representative-subsystem dominated) included GATT, IMF, ITU, and IAEA, and the second, ILO, UNCTAD, WHO, and UNESCO. The policies that were pursued by the organizations in the first category were determined and closely controlled by their most powerful member states. The representatives of the most powerful states constituted an oligarchical elite within these organizations. However these individuals generally enjoyed little autonomy; rather they were required to adhere to detailed instructions formulated by their representative sub-systems. Representatives of the most powerful member states were also influential in the organizations within the second category, but beyond setting broad limits the governments of the most powerful member states allowed these organizations considerable autonomy. Within these limits policies were determined by those who participated directly in making decisions within the organizations. These organizations consequently offered considerable scope for executive heads, for members of international bureaucracies, and for representatives of less powerful member states. An essential difference between the two categories of organizations was that the activities of GATT, IMF, ITU, and IAEA had important consequences for the governments of their most powerful member states while the activities of ILO, UNCTAD, WHO, and UNESCO were less consequential to them.

Other principal general findings were that these universal international organizations broadly, though in varying degrees, became increasingly involved in activities directed towards the Third World, while individuals reflecting the values associated with rich, industrial, non-socialist societies retained dominant influence. In this sense the organizations became agencies of a type of collective colonialism. At the same time, the governments of these western societies whose nationals dominated the patterns and structures of influence in the eight organizations were increasingly coming to use separate, limited-membership organizations to deal with the matters of greatest mutual concern to themselves – the Group of 10[b] paralleling the IMF, for example, and the Development Assistance Committee of OECD paralleling UNCTAD. The study of decision making in this set of relatively limited contexts thus led to a question that went beyond the study's own framework: how do the decisions of different international organizations relate to each other and to decisions taken in other settings of the broader context of world-power relations?

Since the above-mentioned study was concluded, further develop-

[b] The Group of 10 industrial countries (Belgium, France, Germany, Italy, the Netherlands, Sweden, Canada, Japan, the United Kingdom, and the United States) was first set up at a meeting in Paris in December 1961 for the purpose of controlling the use of additional liquidities created outside the IMF's jurisdiction through the General Arrangements to Borrow. It soon became a forum for these financially powerful countries to reach consensus outside the IMF concerning actions to be taken through the IMF. In this, it overlapped with Working Party Three of the OECD.

ments have occurred that seem to indicate a period of more profound and accelerating change in world power relations, including the breakdown of the Bretton Woods system of fixed exchange rates, the dramatic increase in the price of petroleum and the consequential changes in the monetary position of states, the US withdrawal from Indochina, the crumbling of the outer ring surrounding the white minority bastion in southern Africa, continuing momentum of the non-aligned countries in advocating a new international economic order (NIEO), and the more active participation of the People's Republic of China in world affairs.[c] These developments cut across the conventional distinctions between the political and the economic, between state and society. Political and economic, public and private, have to be linked together within the structuring notion of the world system. Whereas the focus of interest in the earlier study was on the interactions of individuals in the internal processes of existing intergovernmental agencies, now the decision process is to be conceived in broader terms as the generating of new and modified forms of international organization. What goes on within particular agencies can only be a small part of the total process that is to be seized by the analyst. Such an enlargement of the scope of enquiry calls for some redefinition of the concepts appropriate to it.

The thesis presented here is that for the late 1970s. A somewhat different approach to the study of decision making in international organization is required than the approach we adopted in the late 1960s. This statement is not to be read as a disavowal of previous work, but as awareness that changes in the world require a further advance from the position reached then.

An approach commensurate with the preoccupations of the present must begin with the world system of power relations. International institutions have to be seen as functioning within that larger system. The starting-point would be a structural picture of power relations which is always the starting-point of the decision process. The approach would then focus on the points of conflict within the system that seem to suggest a potential for structural transformation. Then attention would concentrate on the role of international organization, particularly as to (a) whether international organization tended to stabilize or to transform the existing power relations and (b) what factors

---

[c] Robert W. Cox, "Ideologies and the New International Economic Order: Reflections on Some Recent Literature," included this volume (chapter 18).

determine the development of international organization. What follows is a sketch of a possible approach along these lines.

Power

The first problem in designing an appropriate model is to define the nature of power. To say in purely abstract terms that power is the capacity to influence the action of others and to achieve autonomy of one's own actions does not advance us very far. It is necessary to enter the historical plane so as to consider the sphere in which the kind of power relevant to this enquiry is exercised. Traditionally, this has been thought to be the sphere of the state and of inter-state relations. Those who regard state power as providing the only hard facts in the study of world politics have as their model the states of the European balance-of-power system that emerged in the seventeenth century and extended by the nineteenth to include North America, Russia, and Japan.[5] They can hardly in the same breath include the "soft states," of which Gunnar Myrdal wrote, that came into existence in the second half of the twentieth century.[6] The "state-centric" approach implicitly, though rarely explicitly, refers to a privileged minority among the number of entities now juridically regarded as states.

Criticism of the "state-centric" approach has led to definition of a "transnational" approach that would take fuller account of non-state factors in relations among peoples, notably economic relations and movements of people and ideas.[7] Such non-state factors assume increasing importance among other reasons because of the nuclear stand-off among those states possessing weapons of mass destruction and the generally decreasing utility of military force in inter-state relations (as distinct from its impact on domestic politics). If "state-centric" relations can be thought of as a first level of power relations, corresponding to the political-security sphere, then it will be useful to distinguish two further levels both in the "transnational" category. One corresponds to the distinction between high and low politics, or roughly between political-security and economic-welfare politics.

In the economic-welfare sphere – the second level of power relations – we remain within the sphere of the state, in that area where the state plays a role of shaping and channeling the development of society or of responding to the pressures of society. At this second level, financial policy in modern capitalist states has come to play the determining role, and acts as the link between domestic economic-welfare policies of individual states and their international economic relationships.[8]

The third level of power relations arises conceptually outside the sphere of the state, in the realm of society. This is the level of social power or of the dominant and subordinate relationships of classes and social groups. Social power can be expressed in terms both of production and of consumption.

In production relations some groups control others, and increasingly with the internationalizing of production, these control relationships operate between social groups in different countries. There is, accordingly, an international structure of production relations. A control structure of the world economy is implicit in the notion of interdependence now so widely accepted. It is more explicitly present in theories of dependency.[9] The dependency concept is concerned with social power in transnational relations.

It is a moot question whether this control structure is properly thought of as state or non-state in nature. The answer is that it is difficult and decreasingly relevant to try to disentangle how much is state and how much non-state. What, for instance, is the significance of this distinction in considering an industrial cooperation agreement between a European- or American-based multinational and a socialist state enterprise? States can muster resources to encourage, strengthen, or modify the behavior of non-state actors. Social groups or non-state interests can influence state policy in these matters. We have to think of social power and the control structure of the world economy as composed of both.

If production is the determining aspect of social power, consumption is its counterpart. We frequently speak loosely of rich countries and poor countries when what we mean is that some countries contain more of the powerful social groups, those able to command the largest share of the world product, while other countries contain more of the powerless, those least able to command a share of the world product. We know that there are rich people in poor countries and poor people in rich countries, but the fact that accounts are made up on a country basis lends a territorial bias to the way we have come to measure social power, for instance by comparing GNP per capita.

To summarize, a working definition of world power relations has to bridge the conventional distinction between state and society. An appropriate conceptualization of the world system would take

358

account of (a) the structure of international production relations, from the standpoint of control over production; (b) the consequences of political-security policies of states on their economic-welfare policies; and (c) the consequences of economic-welfare policies on international production relations. Thus production relations can be a common yardstick, to which the other levels of power can be reduced. This approach views the world system primarily in terms of social power.

A model of the world system

World power relations have generally been thought of in terms of the dichotomies of East/West and North/South, corresponding first, to the Cold War beginning in the late 1940s, and second, to the debate over international economic relations arising during the 1960s. By taking production relations as the starting-point, it is possible to define a single world system, encompassing but going beyond these two simple dichotomies. The internationalizing of production is the underlying historical process that has linked these segments of the world together and determined their relationships within the whole system.

Very briefly, the internationalizing of production is bringing about a global division of labor in which technological development is concentrated in a core area, while physical production of goods is moving increasingly into peripheral areas, the two being linked by control mechanisms located in the core area. The multinational corporations are now perceived as technology and control mechanisms of this kind. Between core and periphery are semi-peripheral areas struggling not to lose the ability to attain core status.[10]

This world system is to be defined in terms of functional positions in production relations. These functional positions can also be seen as fitting over a territorial map, so that specific functional positions correspond to certain countries. This does not, of course, mean that the activities characteristic of specific functional positions necessarily occupy most of the people in these countries. It does mean that they are the dominant activities, to which other local activities are subordinate, and that they determine the relationship of the country within the world system. In this sense, we can move from speaking of functional positions to speaking about countries. The concepts "core" and "periphery" are at the same time functional and geographic. These categories are in the nature of ideal types, which can be thought of as expressing a latent potential rather than a definitive classification of countries.

The structure and the direction of movement of the present world system, from the standpoint of international production relations, can be seen in terms of five categories.

First are the richest countries, moving towards an essentially postindustrial pattern of society. Here are concentrated the research and development capabilities of innovation in production and the control centers of multinational corporations. The United States is the core of the core, and some countries of western Europe and Japan might also be assimilated to this status. At most 10–15 percent of world population live in countries on the threshold of postindustrialism.

Second is a category of advanced industrial countries. The Council for Mutual Economic Assistance (COMECON) group of countries would now be the largest component of this category, but industrialized capitalist countries would now be candidates for it in so far as they fail to make the postindustrial category.[11] The status of this second category of countries in the world system is semi-peripheral. Their typical state policies are mercantilist. Their governments seek to reconcile a need for greater links with international production (as a means of acquiring more advanced technology) with a jealous regard to preserve their own autonomy of development so they do not become dependent upon the first generation of postindustrial societies, and are eventually able to make their own transition independently to this status. This category would account for perhaps 15-20 percent of world population.

Third are the countries of dependent capitalism, those that accept industrialization under the management control of postindustrial centers.[12] These include less-developed countries with a fairly large elite domestic market for consumer durables and now more particularly the export platforms manufacturing for the rich country markets of the world – countries like Brazil, Iran, South Korea, Mexico, Singapore, Spain, and others. Potentially, they could include another 20 percent of world population.

These first three categories, which together account for about half of world population, include the most closely integrated or interdependent elements in international production relations. The remaining half of world population live in countries less fully integrated into international production. This population can be divided into two further categories.

Fourth, about 25 percent of world population live in poor countries that have at present only very limited development prospects within the perspective of existing international production relations, i.e., under the present world structure of social power. The world system makes only very limited use of their labor power or their markets. They do not seem essential to the system. Yet they are there, and any disturbances arising from their condition of frustrated development might be disruptive to the system. Once the niceties of diplomatic dialogue are stripped away, the problems of these countries tend to be regarded by those more integrated into international production as problems of global poor relief and potentially of global riot control.

Fifth, one-quarter of the world population lives in the People's Republic of China, a country that cannot be fitted into the preceding categories. China by conventional statistical measures is poor, but the extent to which its population has been mobilized differentiates it from the undeveloped poor of the fourth category. China is seeking its own autonomous development, rejecting dependent capitalism. In the longer term, it is conceivable that China could connect with the world system in semi-peripheral status, comparable to the way in which the USSR expanded its links with the world economy from the late 1960s. It is equally conceivable that China will serve as a contrast model rallying those disaffected by the way the system of international production works and promoting its dialectical contradiction.

The potential sources of conflict within the present world system are grave indeed. Postindustrial societies face the problem of securing a meaningful participation in production, in incomes, in decision making for that large part of their populations not engaged in the core economic activities. Alienation menaces the heart of the system. The mercantilism characteristic of semi-peripheral countries' defensive postures in the system could spark international conflict. Dependent capitalism is generating increasing income disparities within countries of this category. The capital–labor mix characteristic of transferred technology tends to reduce employment in agriculture, while increasing it only modestly in industry, thus leading to a dramatic rise in the destitute marginal population. Growing income disparities and growing marginality encourage repression. When the alienated at the core begin to understand and sympathize with the reactions of the destitute in the peripheries, the crisis of the system can be said to have arrived.

Ideologies of international organization

Power can never be defined exclusively in physical or material terms. The material aspect of power has its counterpart in ideas. Those who at any time seek to change power relations have to struggle not only against entrenched material interests but also against the legitimacy that accrues to the status quo. Existing power relations define in large measure what problems are worthy of attention, in terms of eliminating what is deemed to be dysfunctional to the existing order. The problematic for science and technology is framed within the parameters of existing power relations. These orientations to behavior and to applied science we call ideology. Ideology sustains the existing structure or power by mobilizing opinion in favor of it and by directing practical efforts towards solving the problems that arise in the workings of existing power relations.[13]

Ideologies have played an important role in the history of international organization. If we consider only its recent history since World War II, functionalism was an esoteric doctrine of marked influence in shaping the structure and policies of international institutions emerging in the 1940s.[14] Functionalism in essence sought to base international organization upon interests inherent in society rather than making them dependent upon the goodwill of states. In retrospect, functionalism can be seen as the projection upon the world as a whole of the pluralist concept of society which is a prominent aspect of the western European and North American political tradition.

Functionalism's appeal was mainly to a small number of senior international officials and active promoters of international institutions. Its influence could be seen to wane during the 1960s, to be outclassed by a new dominant ideology of international organization, developmentalism. Developmentalism can be defined as the promotion of economic growth in poor countries by methods consistent with the expansion of a liberal world economy.[15] In practice, this meant creating conditions propitious to the flow of private direct investment, or, in other words, encouraging dependent capitalism.

In the 1970s, developmentalism was succeeded by two newer ideologies, transnationalism and globalism. Transnationalism did not depart radically from developmentalism, but shifted the emphasis from developing growth-oriented public services and public policy to the supposed engines of growth themselves, the multinational corporations.[16] Globalism added something new: the ecological perspective. Globalism introduced the notion that there were limits to the total population the world could sustain, to the amount of man-made pollution the ecosystem could cope with. The policy inferences from globalism were restraint in the growth of population and industrial production, and a need for global monitoring and ultimately for global management of the ecosystem.[17]

The fundamental question to ask about ideologies is: do they sustain the status quo of power relations, or do they tend to undermine and revise them? All of the foregoing were status quo-supporting ideologies. They all took existing social power relations and the existing structures of the world economy as the given framework. Functionalism would have exalted economic interests and diminished the ability of states to intervene and control these interests. Developmentalism and transnationalism offered programs for growth within existing structures.

Globalism alone stood on the threshold of a contradiction. It seemed to be saying that the thoughtless growth policies of the past had brought the world into great danger, which could only be averted if the poor of the world were to have fewer children and abandon hopes for rapid industrialization. But latent within the notion of limiting growth is the issue of sharing. Growth-oriented ideologies rely on dividing increments as a means of solving problems and reducing tensions. With no growth, the more intractable problem of redistribution is posed. Globalism, which began as a concern among the affluent minority, becomes readily transformed into an attack on privileges they acquired through the appropriation of a disproportionate share of the world's resources. The demand for a new international economic order (NIEO) formulates this challenge from the Third World as a new revisionist ideology of international organization.

Hegemony and international organization: the environment

The material and ideological aspects of power are united in the concept of hegemony. The hegemony of a particular social group reflects that group's dominance over the material components of power, but it is a dominance expressed through a consensus (i.e., in ideological form) in which the dominant group takes account of the interests of

363

subordinate groups so as to yield them some satisfactions without at the same time endangering their own position of dominance.[18] The interests of subordinate groups are merged in some measure into a program that can be plausibly represented as of universal interest. This will usually be a program of expansion under existing power relations in which, though benefits will be unequally distributed, there will be something for all participating groups.

International organization here is regarded as a process that takes place in world power relations – a process in which hegemony becomes institutionalized. When a particular formal intergovernmental institution is established, it crystallizes the hegemonic consensus of a particular time in relation to a particular global task or set of global tasks. Hence hegemony comprises the environmental variables relevant to decision making in international organization. Hegemony thus replaces the three variables which we used to characterize the general environment in our previous study: the stratification of states in terms of their power, the distribution of states and nonindependent territories according to their political and economic characteristics, and the pattern of conflicts and alignments. Hegemony is a historical moving force; it is readjusted as the material and ideological components of world power relations change over time. The specific institutions spawned by hegemony at one point in time face a problem of adjustment to the altered hegemony at a later point in time. Institutions are visible. Hegemony is invisible, a latent force that can only be seized intellectually. Yet hegemony is the secret of the vitality of institutions. Some institutions successfully adapt to a changing hegemony, others fail to. The effectiveness of international institutions is to be gauged by their fit to prevailing hegemony.

The issue of change in institutions is thus secondary to the question of change in hegemony. A change in hegemony can come about through the emergence of a counterhegemonic force. Bearing in mind the dual nature of power – the conjunction of material and ideological elements – the counterhegemonic force will result from a combination of (a) an increase in the material resources available to a subordinate group and (b) a coherent and persistent articulation of the subordinate group's demands that challenges the legitimacy of the prevailing consensus.

The first response of the hegemonic group once it becomes aware that the counterhegemonic force has to be contended with is to try to co-opt it, giving its leading elements a fuller place in the system without really changing the system. Co-optation reestablishes the old hegemonic legitimacy. This is the most likely result in a "moderate" international system.[19] It results in some gradual change within the world system but no radical change of the system as a whole. The alternative of a violent revolutionary change of the international system is hardly conceivable other than through a nuclear war, the consequences of which are predictable only as making survival for humanity, and thus of any international system, problematic. Intermediate between co-optation and violent revolution, a negotiated restructuring of power relations may be conceived; one could designate this possibility by the term that evokes the 1976 demand by the opposition for a restructuring of the Italian political system to reflect a perceived change in the balance of social forces – the demand for a *compromesso storico*. Effective counterhegemonic challenges may thus lead either to co-optation or to a historic compromise.

At the present juncture, the demand for a NIEO expresses a counterhegemonic force in the form of a consensus among a large number of Third World countries. To maintain this consensus is the first condition for an effective challenge. This is difficult because in the existing world economy the interests of Third World countries are to some degree competitive. Moreover, it is a consensus among governments with very different policies – from those seeking growth through attracting foreign investment to those favoring greater self-reliance, from those seeking to mobilize domestic populations and widen popular participation to those using coercion to obstruct any such developments. Nevertheless, the consensus has been maintained and encouraged by such manifestations of a shift in world power as the rise in petroleum prices, the withdrawal of the United States from Indochina, and the setbacks to white minority government in southern Africa.

The more radical elements behind the Third World consensus seek a historic compromise, one that would give the Third World countries a greater share of control over real resources. The powerful within the existing hegemony respond by attempting to co-opt some elements of the Third World consensus, to offer them some satisfaction within the existing order without prejudicing their own control, a tactic that might prove attractive to those Third World country regimes fearful of arousing popular pressures.[20]

The question of the reform or reconstruction of international institutions has to be approached in the perspective of interinstitutional

365

relations. Study of any particular institution, for instance the IMF or the ILO to mention but two within which issues of institutional reform have been raised, quickly leads outside the initial object of study to the broader problematic of hegemony.

Currently, a division of labor is apparent among the variety of institutions participating in the process of institutionalizing a new hegemony. OPEC and the International Atomic Energy Agency group countries have specific interests.[d] They are directly concerned with the use of real resources. Negotiations between representatives of these two groups and others take place through the institutionalized North–South dialogue meeting in Paris, the Conference on International Economic Cooperation. The nonaligned countries meet to maintain the Third World consensus and define its content (for example, the conference held in Lima in August 1975), and try to maintain a common platform for those countries that have leverage through their resources (especially petroleum) and those poor countries that lack such leverage. The secretariats of UNCTAD and the United Nations Industrial Development Organization provide intellectual support for the countries of the South in the form of data and ideas. The General Assembly of the United Nations, which has no control over real resources, confers legitimacy upon the aims of a NIEO and thereby acts as a spur to the North–South dialogue which does deal with real resources. When the General Assembly does produce widely agreed conclusions, it is registering through formal proceedings the results of an intricate informal process of negotiations amongst groups of countries, groups defined by mutual and persisting interests.

When one comes to consider some specific institutional issue like the reform of voting rights in the IMF, it now has to be seen as conditioned by all these other activities. The decision process through which a new hegemony becomes institutionalized encompasses existing international institutions and what could be called quasi-institutions (various ad hoc forums for negotiation). The process extends, of course, well beyond the central meeting places to include the networks of public officials and private interest groups that shape international policy from within countries. In short, the decision process of international organization is interinstitutional and it also tran-

---

[d] See also Robert O. Keohane, *After Hegemony: Cooperation and Discord in the World Political Economy* (Princeton, N.J.: Princeton University Press, 1984), pp. 219–240.

scends existing institutions, since it must include the explanation for the creation of new or reformed institutions.

Proximate factors in decision making: individuals and groups

Certain individuals and groups merit special attention since they may play a crucial role in how the institutionalization of world power relations is being shaped, and thus how hegemony is being adjusted. For convenience, these can be called the proximate factors in the decision process. They replace the actors in our previous study.

A first category is that of foreign-policy directors of powerful states. These are the individuals whose role requires an accurate assessment of existing hegemony as a basis for action at all times. The preeminence of functionalist thinking has perhaps given a bias against paying much attention to personalities like de Gaulle and Kissinger in earlier studies of international organization. Most of these studies have included the middle-level officials of foreign offices and functional ministries who take part in decision making within international institutions.[21] In times of relative stability, this may suffice. What it implies is that the frameworks for action by these middle-level bureaucrats are fixed. In times of change in the structure of world power relations, it is important to consider how the heads of government and foreign secretaries envisage the role and potential for international institutions. Their intervention can change the limits of action of the middle-level officials. The first category of proximate factors includes only the highest level of national foreign-policy makers, those with authority to fix the framework of policy for lower-level officials.

A second category includes special-interest groups whose activities transcend national boundaries. These include both private or nongovernmental interest groups and segments of governmental bureaucracies that serve particular specialized interests. Private- and public-interest group activities that cross national boundaries have been distinguished as transnational and transgovernmental relations respectively.[22] Keohane and Nye have pointed out that intergovernmental institutions are privileged forums for transgovernmental relations. Transnational relations of the nongovernmental kind take place through a variety of international interest groups (for example, the International Chamber of Commerce) or religious, charitable, or scientific associations, "invisible colleges," and clubs (for example, the Club of Rome).

The level of consciousness characteristic of this second category is likely to differ from that of the first. The first category thinks in terms of hegemony, of the overall structure of world power. The consciousness of the second category is of the economic-corporative type, concerned with the solidarity of interests of particular groups. The various economic-corporative interests are assigned their place within any particular hegemony. But the construction of hegemony is analytically separate from the pursuit of economic-corporative interests. In general, the action of special-interest groups tends to maintain the status quo in hegemony to the extent that satisfaction for particular interests is built into hegemony.

A third category can be called the "empathetic neutral." The first identified components of this category were executive heads of international institutions. Executive heads have been represented as able to play a critical role in the development of their institutions.[23]

The ground for looking to executive heads for leadership in international organization is similar to the ground on which Karl Mannheim placed the role of the intellectual in a world of conflicting socioeconomic interests and ideologies – both can be relatively free from the constraints of particular interests and better than others able to comprehend the conflicting viewpoints of competing interests.[24] The executive head can perform this role not by virtue of his office alone, but to the extent that he has been able to approximate the ideal type of relative detachment.

Thinking of the ideal type rather than one of the offices that may be most conducive to its attainment, this category might be extended to include certain notable individuals who are not executive heads of international institutions but may be placed by events in situations of ad hoc players of similar roles. Indeed, one need not even be restricted to individuals, since the foreign policies of some small countries may play such a role.

Since we are concerned with organization as a process rather than as a set of formal institutions, it is best to define this category in the broadest possible manner as the empathetic neutral. The particular question of interest here is whether a period of profound change in world power relations is more or less propitious for effective initiative by empathetic neutrals than are times of relative stability.

Empathetic neutrals can be thought of as links between economic-corporative and the hegemonic levels of actions. Their role in times of change in world power relations would be to help adjust hegemony – to achieve either co-optation or a historic compromise with counterhegemonic forces by reformulating the hegemonic consensus and program so as to embrace successfully all the relevant elements. It is a mediating role between the complex of economic-corporative interests and foreign-policy makers of the most powerful states.

The fourth and final category is what can loosely be called "public opinion." International institutions are bureaucracies built upon national bureaucracies. The normal political process of international institutions are intrabureaucratic processes. The nongovernmental interests which impinge upon these institutions are expressed through interest-group bureaucracies. Rarely is there any occasion for accountability to any more broadly based opinion. Even those international institutions that ostensibly serve the interests of broad segments of populations, for example, the ILO in relation to industrial labor, or the FAO in relation to farmers, have in practice had little or no direct audience with mass constituencies.

In contemplating present and future change, however, it seems useful to enquire to what extent the mobilization of mass-based concern with certain world issues is capable of affecting the reformulation of hegemony and providing a political base for certain forms of international action. It is not inconceivable that the development of forces at work in the world economy could provide conditions propitious for mass-based concern in controlling international production. Popular participation in the process of international organization has clearly not arrived, but it may be wise to retain an open mind as to its future possibility.[25]

In so far as public opinion may be in the picture, the question must be asked: whose public opinion? This may well be a means of mobilizing new political resources behind rich country positions, since it is in the richer countries that public opinion can most easily become a political force. The poor of the world, as a whole, remain very largely inarticulate. Insofar as public opinion becomes a factor in the decision process of international organization, it could under present conditions be to their disadvantage.

This prospect would be altered to the extent that social mobilization extends into the Third World and is expressed through a greater

identification of people and governments and a fuller public consciousness in these countries of how international issues impinge
upon their own welfare. In the short run, the proponents of a New
International Economic Order have to patch together through diplomatic activity a rather heterogeneous coalition of radical mobilizing
and repressive authoritarian regimes. In the long run, they may have
to build a more durable popular base of support for their program
among the people of the Third World as a whole, as well as among
the populations of the richer countries. At some point along this road,
active stimulus to social mobilization will come into conflict with the
diplomatic task of maintaining support for the program from those
regimes in the coalition that view mobilization as a threat to established elites. In so far as the balance tips towards a more articulate
popular support for Third World goals, the prospects of a historic
compromise – a renegotiated hegemony with all the institutional
consequences that flow from it – are enhanced. In so far as the balance
tips in favor of the non-mobilizing authoritarian regimes, the likelihood that these will be co-opted into the existing hegemony is high.

In summary, the decision-making approach to international organization analyses how these key proximate factors interact with the
prevailing hegemony – the environment – and it seeks to understand
the extent to which these interactions support the status quo or promote change in the structure of existing power relations.

Notes

1 The concept of "non-decision" has been used by Peter Bachrach and
Morton S. Baratz in *Power and Poverty, Theory and Practice* (New York:
Oxford University Press, 1970).

2 "Power relations" is used here to include both (a) the structure of power,
i.e., the relative capability of individuals, social groups, states, etc., and (b)
the process of power or patterns of interaction in which power is used.
Decisions can thus change power relations either by changing relative
access to resources, or by altering the procedures of interaction to the
advantage of one party or another.

3 Robert W. Cox and Harold K. Jacobson, *The Anatomy of Influence: Decision
Making in International Organization* (New Haven, Conn.: Yale University
Press, 1972). Others contributing to the volume are Gerard and Victoria
Curzon, Joseph S. Nye, Lawrence Scheinman, James P. Sewell, and Susan
Strange. Earlier studies of decision making include: Chadwick F. Alger,
"Interaction in a Committee of the United Nations General Assembly," in
J. David Singer (ed.), *Quantitative International Politics* (New York: Free
Press, 1968), pp. 51–81; Hayward R. Alker, Jr., and Bruce M. Russett, *World*

Politics in the General Assembly (New Haven, Conn.: Yale University Press, 1965); John Hadwen and Johan Kaufmann, *How United Nations Decisions Are Made*, 2nd ed. (Leiden, Netherlands: A. W. Sitjoff, 1962); Arend Lijphart, "The Analysis of Bloc Voting in the General Assembly: A Critique and a Proposal," *American Political Science Review*, vol. 55, no. 4 (December 1963), pp. 902–917; Johan Kaufmann, *Conference Diplomacy: An Introductory Analysis* (Leiden, Netherlands: A. W. Sitjoff, 1968); Robert O. Keohane, "Political Influence in the General Assembly," *International Conciliation*, vol. 557 (March 1966), pp. 5–64.

4 See especially Robert A. Dahl, *Who Governs? Democracy and Power in an American City* (New Haven, Conn.: Yale University Press, 1963), and Richard C. Snyder, H. W. Bruck, and Burton Sapin (eds.), *Foreign Policy Decision Making: An Approach to the Study of International Politics* (New York: Free Press, 1962).

5 A point of view which in the United States is commonly associated with Hans Morgenthau, *Politics Among Nations* (New York: Alfred Knopf, 1948). This is also the perspective of many European scholars of international relations, for example, Ludwig Dehio, *The Precarious Balance: The Politics of Power in Europe, 1494–1945* (New York: Knopf, 1962). Originally published in German, 1948, as *Gleichgewicht oder Hegemonie*.

6 Gunnar Myrdal, *The Challenge of World Poverty* (Harmondsworth, Middlesex: Penguin, 1970). Myrdal writes:

> The term "soft state" is understood to comprise all the various types of social indiscipline which manifest themselves by: deficiencies in legislation and in particular law observance and enforcement, a wide-spread disobedience by public officials on various levels to rules and directives handed down to them, and often their collusion with powerful persons and groups of persons whose conduct they should regulate. Within the concept of the soft state belongs also corruption . . . (p. 211)

7 Robert O. Keohane and Joseph S. Nye (eds.), *Transnational Relations and World Politics* (Cambridge: Harvard University Press, 1972).

8 The new primacy of finance ministries in the modern capitalist state arises from the way domestic economic welfare policies are conditioned by external economic conditions. Finance ministries are the link between external and internal economies. This has been noted in French scholarship, for example, Erhard Friedberg, "L'internationalisation de l'economie et modalités d'intervention de l'état: la Politique industrielle," *Planification et Société* (Grenoble: Presses universitaires de Grenoble, 1974), pp. 94–108, and Christian Palloix, *L'internationalisation du capital* (Paris: Maspero, 1975), especially pp. 81–83.

9 This is not the place to give a full bibliography on dependency theory. Suffice it to say that insofar as the study of international organization is to be placed within the larger framework of the world system of power relations, and power is to be understood primarily in terms of what we

have called social power, dependency theorists have been particularly pro-
lific in suggesting structural models of the world system. Some of those
works which have influenced the authors' thinking in drawing up the present outline are referred to in notes below.

10 The core/periphery model outlined here may be found also in Immanuel
Wallerstein, *The Modern World-System: Capitalist Agriculture and the Origins
of the European World-Economy in the Sixteenth Century* (New York: Academic Press, 1974), and his article "The Rise and Future Demise of the
World Capitalist System: Concepts for Comparative Analysis," *Comparative Studies in Society and History*, vol. 16, no. 4 (September 1974), pp. 387–
415. Wallerstein's thesis that capitalism became a world system in the sixteenth century would be contested by historians, for example, the Marxist
Perry Anderson, *Lineages of the Absolutist State* (London: NLB–Atlantic
Highlands Humanities Press, 1974), who saw this period as the consolidation of centralized feudal states on which mercantile capitalism had only
limited impact, and Geoffrey Barraclough, *An Introduction to Contemporary
History* (Harmondsworth, Middlesex: Penguin, 1967), who sees the emergence of something that might be called a "world system" as an aspect of
contemporary history, which begins only on the threshold of the twentieth
century. The argument over when the model becomes applicable does not
diminish the usefulness of the model for analysis of contemporary world
power relations. The application of the core/periphery conceptualization
to international production relations fits well with the work of Christian
Palloix and of Stephen Hymer, "The Multinational Corporation and the
Law of Uneven Development," in Jagdish N. Bhagwati (ed.), *Economics
and World Order: From the 1970s to the 1990s* (London: Macmillan, 1972);
and Keith Griffin, "The International Transmission of Inequality," *World
Development*, vol. 2, no. 3 (March 1974), pp. 3–15, among others.

11 The semi-peripheral status of the Soviet Union is suggested in Wallerstein,
"The Rise and Future Demise of the World Capitalist System." A somewhat fuller rationale might be given by reference to the innovations in
Soviet economic policy observable from the late 1960s when technology
was perceived by Soviet economic management as a bottleneck to further
growth. Continuing extensive use of capital and labor seemed to be reaching limits that could only be passed through a more technologically intensive use of capital. To acquire such technology, industrial cooperation
agreements with European- and United States-based multinationals were
encouraged. In order to acquire the foreign exchange to purchase technology, Soviet exports were encouraged; and some industrial cooperation
agreements included provision that the western partner firm should be
paid in goods produced by the new technology which it would then
undertake to market. Soviet trade and industrial links with the world economy have thus increased markedly during the mid-1970s. Of course, the
managers of the Soviet economy do not want such increased intercourse
or "interdependency" to reduce their ultimate control over the Soviet

economy. These developments in policy and economic relations conform to the semi-peripheral type in the model outlined.

12 Fernando Henrique Cardoso has put aside the notion of "development of underdevelopment" of André Gunder Frank, and substitutes for it the notion of "dependent capitalist development" that occurs in the sectors of the Third World integrated into the expanding economy of international production. See Cardoso, "Imperialism and Dependency in Latin America," in Frank Bonilla and Robert Girling (eds.), *Structures of Dependency* (Nairobi, Calif.: Nairobi Bookstore, 1973).

13 Karl Mannheim, *Ideology and Utopia* (New York: Harcourt Brace, 1936). Original German edition, 1929.

14 On functionalism as an approach to international organization, the classic text is David Mitrany, *A Working Peace System: An Argument for the Functional Development of International Organization* (London: Royal Institute of International Affairs/Oxford University Press, 1943). Important commentaries and developments in functionalist thinking are in Inis L. Claude, Jr., *Swords into Plowshares* (New York: Random House, 1964), ch. 17, and Ernst B. Haas, *Beyond the Nation-State: Functionalism and International Organization* (Stanford, Calif.: Stanford University Press, 1964). Cox and Jacobson, *The Anatomy of Influence*, pp. 403–406, contains a critical discussion of functionalism and developmentalism as ideologies of international organization.

15 The report entitled *Partners in Development* prepared for the World Bank by a commission under the chairmanship of Lester B. Pearson is an exemplary statement of developmentalist ideology. See also Robert W. Cox, "The Pearson and Jackson Reports in the Context of Development Ideologies," *The Year Book of World Affairs, 1972*, vol. 26 (London: Stevens, 1972), pp. 187–202.

16 There is now an abundant literature which could be bracketed under the heading of transnationalism, which sees the multinational as the engine of global development breaking through the restrictions of an obsolescent nation-state. Most of this literature, to be sure, is American. See, for example, George W. Ball, "Cosmocorp: The Importance of Being Stateless," *Atlantic Community Quarterly*, vol. 6, no. 2 (Summer 1968), pp. 163–170; and his "Multinational Corporations and Nation States," *Atlantic Community Quarterly*, vol. 5, no. 2 (Summer 1967), pp. 247–253; Frank Tannenbaum, "The Survival of the Fittest," *Columbia Journal of World Business*, vol. 3, no. 2 (March–April 1968), pp. 13–20; Harry Johnson, "The Multi-National Corporation as an Agency of Economic Development: Some Exploratory Observations," in Barbara Ward et al., *The Widening Gap: Development in the 1970s* (New York: Columbia University Press, 1971), pp. 242–252; Howard Perlmutter, "The Tortuous Evolution of the Multi-national Corporation," *Columbia Journal of World Business*, vol. 4, no. 1 (January–February 1969), pp. 9–18. Most of this enthusiasm for the multi-national dates from the late 1960s. It was soon countered by a barrage of

criticism forecasting negative consequences from the expansion of multi-nationals, a literature that has grown in vigor during the 1970s, and which is both American and non-American in origin.

17 The most widely known statement of the globalist position is probably the report prepared for the Club of Rome by D. H. Meadows *et al., The Limits to Growth* (New York: Universe Books, 1972). This was based largely on a model developed by Jay W. Forrester, *World Dynamics* (Cambridge, Mass.: Wright-Allen Press, 1971). Other exponents of globalism include Harold and Margaret Sprout, *Toward a Politics of the Planet Earth* (New York: Van Nostrand Reinhold, 1971), and Lester R. Brown, *World Without Borders* (New York: Random House, 1972). The implications for international organization of the globalist position have been drawn in Philippe de Seynes, "Prospects for a Future Whole World," *International Organization,* vol. 26, no. 1 (Winter 1972), pp. 1–17, and Maurice F. Strong, "One Year After Stockholm: An Ecological Approach to Management," *Foreign Affairs,* vol. 51, no. 4 (July 1973), pp. 690–707.

18 The concept of hegemony in the form used here is derived from Antonio Gramsci, *Quaderni del carcere* (Turin: Einaudi, 1975).

19 For the concept of a "moderate" international system, see Stanley Hoffman, "International Organization and the International System," *International Organization,* vol. 24, no. 3 (Summer 1970), pp. 389–413.

20 This seems to have been the message contained in the circular telegram sent by the United States representative to the United Nations, Daniel P. Moynihan, to United States Secretary of State Henry Kissinger and to all American embassies which was "leaked" to the *New York Times* (January 28, 1976). The telegram referred to "a basic foreign policy goal of the United States, that of breaking up massive blocs of nations, mostly new nations, which for so long have been arrayed against us in international forums ... The nonaligned or the Group of 77, or whatever, are groups made up of extraordinarily disparate nations, with greatly disparate interests. Their recent bloc-like unity was artificial and was bound to break up ..." Roger D. Hansen, "The Political Economy of North–South Relations: How Much Change?," *International Organization,* vol. 29, no. 4 (Autumn 1975), discusses the likelihood of "the embourgeoisement of OPEC," i.e., of co-optation.

21 See, for instance, Arnold Beichman, *The "Other" State Department: The United States Mission to the United Nations – Its Role in the Making of Foreign Policy* (New York: Basic Books, 1967), and the extensive study sponsored by the Carnegie Endowment, *Les missions auprès des organisations internationales* (Brussels: Bruylent, 1971–76), 4 vols.

22 See especially Robert O. Keohane and Joseph S. Nye, "Transgovernmental Relations and International Organizations," *World Politics,* vol. 27, no. 1 (October 1974), pp. 39–62.

23 Of the literature on the role of executive heads, note Haas, *Beyond the Nation-State;* Robert W. Cox, "The Executive Head: An Essay on Leader-

ship in International Organization," chapter 16 in this volume; and a review article by Mark W. Zacher, "The Secretary-General: Some Comments on Recent Research," *International Organization*, vol. 23, no. 4 (Autumn 1969), pp. 932–930.

24 Mannheim, *Ideology and Utopia*, especially p. 154 and subsequently, in which he discusses the intelligentsia as "a relatively classless stratum," which implies that at least some members of this stratum would be capable of "dynamic mediation [*dynamische vermittlung*] of conflicting points of view" (p. 161).

25 There has been a dearth of attention to the relationship of public opinion to international organization, perhaps in large measure because it is but a latent phenomenon in most cases. William A. Scott's and Stephen B. Withey's early study, *The United States and the United Nations: The Public View, 1945–1955* (New York: Manhattan Publishing Company, 1958), remains one of the most detailed and conceptually elegant analyses. Not surprisingly, the European Communities have been most attentive to public opinion. A program of EEC-wide opinion polls has been conducted under the direction of Jacques-René Rabier, former director-general for press and information in the European Communities. See Commission des Communautés Européennes, *Les Européens et l'unification de l'Europe* (Brussels: General Directorate for Press and Information of the European Communities, 1972). The United Nations Institute for Training and Research (UNITAR) sponsored a study of press reaction to United Nations activities. See Alexander Szalai, *The United Nations and the News Media* (New York: United Nations Institute for Training and Research, 1971). In an imaginative piece of futurology, three Canadian professors of international law envisage a future world organization polarized between, on the one hand, an elite technocratic, computer-bound intrabureaucratic structure and, on the other hand, a world people's assembly of "interpopulism" directly representing a coalition of anti-bureaucratic, minority, and poor people's groups in rich countries with anti-capitalist, anti-imperialist groups in poor countries. See R. St. J. Macdonald, G. Morris, and D. Johnson, "International Law and Society in the Year 2000," *Canadian Bar Review*, vol. 51, no. 2 (May 1973), pp. 316–332.

18 Ideologies and the New International Economic Order: reflections on some recent literature (1979)

What is the NIEO literature about?

The demand for a New International Economic Order (NIEO), that can be formally dated from the Algiers conference of the nonaligned countries in 1973 and which has been pursued with the backing of these countries in the United Nations and other international institutions, has precipitated a reconsideration of the structure and processes of world political economy among all the principal interests.[a] This has resulted in a large and growing literature that to date, if it has not entirely clarified the problems and issues besetting the world political economy, has at least made it possible to identify certain salient currents of thought about them, each setting forth a mode of analysis and a strategy of action. This essay attempts to survey some of this literature. I take my stand not in some conception of objective science from which to allocate merits and demerits to particular authors, but rather as an observer of the confrontations of ideas, considering the role of ideas in relation to the positions of conflicting forces. The survey cannot claim to be comprehensive, though it does aim to be representative of different perspectives . . .

Ideological analysis is, of course, a critic's weapon and one most effectively used against the prevailing orthodoxies which, when stripped of their putative universality, become seen as special pleading for historically transient but presently entrenched interests. Social science is never neutral. It is, therefore, only fair to warn the reader that my purpose in undertaking this survey was to discover and encourage avenues of enquiry that might in the long run aid towards

[a] This is a substantially abbreviated version of this review. Cuts have been made to place emphasis on the organizing schema and analysis.

376

the transformation of power relations both within and among nations in the direction of greater social equity. Thus, I found the work of some of the radical neomercantilists and historical materialists discussed below more potentially valuable (though as yet very inadequately developed) than the more prestigious products of the western academic establishments.[1]

Some preliminary remarks are called for before getting to the books themselves. In the first place, what is the NIEO? Or, more specifically, what, in the broad, is this literature about? A number of answers are possible, all of which are in some measure correct. At a first level, the NIEO is a series of specific demands and considerations embodied in an impressive range and number of official documents adopted by international conferences. The extent of these can be measured by the size of a two-volume collection of official papers compiled by the librarians of the United Nations Institute for Training and Research which includes texts from the Group of 77 and its regional groups and the nonaligned countries as well as from the organizations of the United Nations family.[2]

At a second level, the NIEO is a negotiation process, broadly speaking, between countries of North and South but taking place through a variety of institutions and forums in which are represented wider or narrower ranges of functional and geographic interests. This negotiation process is concerned with the possibilities of agreement concerning both revised international policies and reformed or new institutions (including the power relationships governing these institutions). No one has yet attempted to plot the interinstitutional complex through which this negotiation process is taking place, though UNITAR and the Ford Foundation have sponsored a team project with Robert W. Gregg as principal investigator to "describe, explain, and analyze" this aspect.

At a third level, the NIEO has precipitated a debate about the real and desirable basic structure of world economic relations. Though the term "international" (consciously chosen in preference to "world" or "global" by the authors of the demand) connotes a limitation of the issue to relations among countries, the debate cannot be so artificially constrained and has ranged inevitably into domestic and transnational structural issues. Structures here encompass the relationships among regions within countries, among different industries and economic activities, among different modes of production, and among social classes, as well as those among countries of different groupings. This

377

debate brings into focus theories concerned with imperialism, with the causes of underdevelopment, and with the physical limits to growth.

Finally, at a fourth level, the debate becomes one about the form of knowledge appropriate to understanding these issues. In effect, the demand for a NIEO has mobilized a fresh challenge to the intellectual hegemony of liberal economics and its claims to an exclusive "rationality." For its critics, economics is an ideology derived from a particular historically determined set of power relations, not a science with absolute and universal scope, and the emergence of new power relations of which the NIEO is one manifestation calls for a reformulating of a more appropriate political economy.

The specific policy and institutional issues that are the subject of diplomatic negotiations and the theoretical and epistemological issues debated in academic seminars and symposia are indeed intimately related. Any general organization of power not only generates institutions and policy mechanisms but also sustains ideas which legitimate it. Such a dominant ideology justifies the existing order of power relations by indicating the benefits accruing (or accruable) to all the principal parties, including in particular the subordinate or less favored. So long as these latter acquiesce in the dominant mode of thought, their demands are likely to be reconcilable within the existing system of power. However, where there is a general challenge to the prevailing structure of power, then the articulation of counterideologies becomes a part of the action, and the possibility of reaching reasonably durable agreement on the practical issues of policies and institutions becomes bound up with the possibility of reaching a new consensus on theories and modes of analysis.

Moreover, in the case of the NIEO, there is a considerable overlap in the personnel concerned, on the one hand with the policy negotiations, and on the other hand with the debate about theory. This underlines the practical political importance of the theoretical issues and indeed gives the debate about a theory a certain logical priority in that its outcomes would provide the rationale for future policies. Many of the ideas to be discussed are the product of actual participants in the negotiations and are thus to be considered as political action, an aspect of a political process (rather than as independent, objective, or scientific analyses made by disinterested observers).

The intellectual participants who are politically active in the NIEO negotiations together with those academics who play a more indirect role can be seen as linked in a series of networks, each of which is mobilizing ideas around a certain partial consensus. There are, of course, disagreements among individuals within a particular network, but these disagreements are within a certain commonality of ideas or a basic common approach. There are also certain individuals who participate in more than one network and who are thus potential hinges or go-betweens. Such individuals might conceivably be important in exploring the possibility of broadening a partial consensus to encompass two or more networks, ultimately towards a new hegemonic ideology. The present state of the debate does not enable one to speculate about the shape of new hegemony, but it does make it possible to juxtapose the main networks and to place the various authors within this juxtaposition of perspectives or partial consensuses (while recognizing that individual authors may resist assimilation to a school). The political nature of the literature justifies this political mode of analysis.

These networks are not mere constructs of my imagination, classifications of authors whose ideas seem to have a certain community of spirit. Intellectual production is now organized like the production of goods or of other services. The material basis of networks is provided by formal (usually nongovernmental) organizations as mobilizing and coordinating agencies with research directors and funds (from sources sometimes more, sometimes less, visible) for commissioning studies, financing conferences, and symposia or informal luncheon discussions. The materially independent scholar is a rarity, though perhaps not quite extinct. The material basis of networks allows for a selection of participants which guarantees a certain homogeneity around a basic core of orthodoxy. However, since the object of the exercise is consensus building, narrow orthodoxy or exclusiveness would be a self-defeating criterion, and the activators of each network extend their search to those whose ideas reach the outer boundaries of what might ultimately be acceptable. Above and beyond material support, the organized network holds out to the intellectual the prospect of political influence, of being listened to by top decision makers and even of becoming part of the decision making team.

Five opinion clusters, some of which are more or less structured networks and some less formally structured orientations or approaches to the issues of North–South relations, can be identified from the literature concerning the NIEO:

(1) An "establishment" perspective that could be characterized as monopolistic liberalism is the dominant view in the industrialized countries. The Trilateral Commission is the most important formal organization coordinating the network. There is no need to embroider upon the variety of articles, journalistic and otherwise, that have underlined the potentially influential nature of this assemblage of political, business, and academic personalities from North America, western Europe, and Japan including a number of leading members of governments presently in power. The NIEO lies at the center of the Trilateral Commission's concerns and is the subject of several studies commissioned by it. One in particular, *Towards a Renovated International System* by Richard N. Cooper, Karl Kaiser, and Masataka Kosaka is extremely pertinent . . .[3] Basically these documents . . . take the existing structure of world economy as a starting point and ask what adjustments can be agreed upon by the dominant powers to gain wider acceptability. This is the view from the top.

(2) What can be described as a social democratic variant of the establishment view shares with it a basic commitment to the normative preference for a world economy with relatively free movement of capital, goods, and technology as well as an acceptance of the rationality of conventional economics, while putting more stress upon the needs of the poor. It represents, in other words, a broader and somewhat more generous view of the adjustments that can be made without fundamentally disturbing the existing hegemony. The network that is developing ideas consistent with this general perspective is less fully organized than the first one, though key groupings can be identified. The Club of Rome group presided over by Jan Tinbergen that produced the report *Reshaping the International Order* (or RIO report) represents a major statement of this viewpoint . . . .[4] By and large the social democratic perspective is that of First World understanding and sympathy with the Third World . . .

(3) There is a category of more or less official Third World representatives who have formalized a continuing network, the Third World Forum. I do not wish to suggest here that there is a single Third World viewpoint. The range of opinion among spokesmen for countries in the Third World is much wider

than that to be found among participants in this network, diversified as it is. Yet there is a body of thought-engaged-as-action that corresponds to the French adjective *tiers-mondiste* – a form of radical perspective shaped by abstract analytical categories, then by existential political struggle. Mahbub ul Haq, a senior official of the World Bank who was formerly responsible for economic planning in Pakistan at the time of General Ayub, places the origin of this grouping at the Stockholm conference on the environment in 1972. In his book *The Poverty Curtain: Choices for the Third World*, which is a kind of personal memoir of the evolution of thinking of a Yale-trained Third World economic-policy maker, he indicates how this organization grew out of informal discussions he had with Gamani Corea (of UNCTAD), Enrique Iglesias (of ECLA), and Samir Amin (of the UN Institute for Development Planning in Dakar), all of them high-level international officials and Third World intellectuals. The purpose, according to Mahbub ul Haq, was "intellectual self-reliance, both at the national and at the international level, which could give some form and substance to our [i.e., the Third World's] aimless search for appropriate development strategies at home and to our disorganized efforts to coordinate our negotiating positions abroad." [5] The Third World Forum took shape during 1972–73 at a time when the Third World countries' claims seemed to have been set aside by the First World in its concern with its own internal economic problems. The network was already in being when the succession of events of 1973, including the oil crisis, gave a new momentum to the Third World. President Echeverria of Mexico both gave his country a leading role in promoting the NIEO at the United Nations and put his personal support behind the Third World Forum, and the Third World Forum was not unassociated with his bid for the secretary-generalship of the UN. If since that time the Third World Forum seems to have been less active, its function may be revived through the proposal for a more formal Third World secretariat . . .

Ideologically, the Third World network of policy intellectuals shares the ambivalence of official Third World positions. Some, like Mahbub ul Haq himself, have impeccable liberal economics credentials, though experience with the practical problems of Third World development has led them to abandon faith in the market in favor of government intervention. Others, like Samir Amin, have a Marxist background. One senses a constant tension between intellectual analysis that leans towards a rejection of western models (and thus implicitly of the institutions that embody these models, such as the World Bank) and a hope for support from the western economies (which would be delivered through these same institutions), and tension also between a conviction that social and political revolution is a necessary condition for real development in the Third World and an unwillingness to allow First World economists and officials to use the ineffectiveness of existing governmental measures as an excuse for placing conditions of surveillance on resource transfers to the Third World. The ambivalence is acute in personal terms as these intellectuals, whose thinking tends to take a radical bent, are aware that their political influence depends upon the support of governments that cannot share their views. They face in an acute form the dilemma of the intellectual who seeks power and influence with power as an opportunity to put his ideas into practice, while knowing in his heart that the very power he solicits will be the contradiction of his goals.

(4) My fourth category can be designated neomercantilist. Unlike the first three it does not have a formal network, though at least one group of American policy thinkers, the group associated with the magazine *Commentary*, some of whose members have also enjoyed support from the Lehrman Institute in New York, may be seen as constituting something of a network within a much larger and more amorphous cluster. Whereas most of the authors in the first three categories considered here are in one way or another active in the negotiating process over NIEO policy issues, the neomercantilist works we have to consider here are those of individual observer-critics, not policy intellectuals.

The neomercantilist sees economic policy as an instrument of political goals – politics leads and economics follows. (In de Gaulle's phrase, *l'intendance suivra*.) Economic theory that makes an abstraction of economic behavior from politics is therefore to be rejected (as biased and misleading) in favor of a revival of political economy. The world is to be understood, not in terms of a market equilibrium model, but in terms of an organization of power; a world system in which economic processes are among the major manifestations of power.

Right-wing and left-wing neomercantilisms can be distinguished. The coming to power of the Trilateral Commission in the United States with the Carter election in effect displaced tendencies towards a right-wing mercantilism observable in the Kissinger–Nixon administration. The vision of a reunified Trilateral world as the anchor of a liberal world economy replaced the notion of a pentagonal organization of world power that seemed likely to become one of competing economic blocs. Kautsky's ultra-imperialism seemed to triumph over Lenin's rival imperialisms. Among the books considered here, the right of neomercantilism in the United States is represented by Robert W. Tucker's *The Inequality of Nations*.[6] He distrusts Trilateralism and argues for the defense of American power in a world in which the balance of power among nations has not ceased to operate. The left of neomercantilism recognize the same basic framework of power, but write from a standpoint of sympathy with those who are challenging dominant power in the world economy. Two recent works are worth noting.

Michael Hudson, an unconventional American radical, has written *Global Fracture: The New International Economic Order*. This is a sequel to his earlier *Superimperialism*, in which he argued that the United States had organized a dominant imperial system in which government financial management played the crucial role.[7] *Global Fracture* dates the decline of this empire from the crises of 1973 and the gradual emergence of a world of competing blocs (the US sphere receding to the American hemisphere, a western Europe–Arab–African complex, a Japanese sphere in Southeast Asia, the Soviet sphere, and China – each with its own center-periphery dialectic). Its title and its message are that powerful governments, not multinational corporations, are the dominant forces . . .

(5) The historical materialist current of thought likewise disdains the economics of liberalism as a mode of comprehending the issues posed by the NIEO, but, in distinction to neomercantilism which focuses upon the state, historical materialism directs attention in the first instance to the production process.

I prefer the term historical materialism to Marxism in this context, since Marxism carries so many conflicting connotations of doctrinal orthodoxies and political lines. In regard to the Third World and the problem of development, historical materialism is now a broad intellectual current within which a vigorous debate is taking place. Like neomercantilism, it is fragmented into a variety of groups and individuals, constituting an informal community of discourse rather than a formally organized network. Its members know and recognize each other and debate their differences in preference to engaging in polemics with those who do not share their own basic orientation. Like the neomercantilists considered here, the historical materialists are observer-critics generally far removed from influence upon current negotiations over international economic policies. (Samir Amin is a notable exception as a participant in the Third World network and link between it and the historical materialist current.)

The historical materialist position on development most familiar to those outside this school is that of Gunder Frank: the notion of a single all-embracing world capitalist system in which development at the center generates underdevelopment in the peripheries. Immanuel Wallerstein's refinement of this notion has also become fairly widely recognized. Less known by English-language readers is the work of Christian Palloix, whose thesis of the internationalization of capital seems consistent with the Frank–Wallerstein approach insofar as it envisages a globally unifying capitalist mode of production, but is inconsistent with Frank and Wallerstein in rejecting the center–periphery polarity with its implication that the revolutionary potential for transforming the system will come from the Third World . . .[8]

Quite different is the approach of those who see not one big capitalist mode of production, but rather a dominant capitalist mode articulated with other non-capitalist modes. The difference in viewpoint is not likely to be resolvable by refinements of deductive reasoning or further exegesis of the sacred texts (though many efforts are still being devoted to this form of Marxist scholasticism), but only by further study and observation of the actual development of production processes, especially in the Third World . . .

384

The central historical problem in the historical materialist perspective is how the world system may be transformed. One focus of interest is upon the crisis at the center – what the European left has for several years been calling *la crise* ... The other focus of interest is in the peripheries. Samir Amin ... argues that the present drive to promote industrialization in the Third World by the peripheral bourgeoisie is likely to lead only to a new phase of imperialism (based on export by the periphery of cheap manufactured goods) and that the only hope for a New International Economic Order would be if the Third World were to act collectively through mutual support of self-restraint projects and by reducing the flow of raw materials exports to the rich countries thereby forcing the center to adjust to a less unequal international division of labor ...[9]

Implicit though not developed in Amin's analysis is the question of the class structure of the peripheral countries and how this conditions the way they link into the world economy. The possibility of Samir Amin's preferred scenario depends upon the emergence of an autonomous "national" class in the Third World countries, whereas most Marxist analyses have pointed to the creation of local bourgeoisie dependent upon international capital ...

By considering this selection of recent literature under the five categories indicated above, it is possible to see, for each category or perspective, an intellectual framework or ideology that serves to define a particular problematic peculiar to that perspective. The internal debate within each of the five tendencies also gives an indication of the range of options in the negotiation process that may be seen as feasible from each of the main positions. Finally, since theory and practice are fused in regard to the NIEO, each intellectual position reveals a view of the structure of world power and a strategy of alliances or potential alliances.

The establishment perspective: monopolistic liberalism

... The fundamental commitment of the establishment perspective is to an open world market with relatively free movement of capital, goods, and technology. Government interventions should be of a kind that support this goal, and such interventions as would impede it are to be condemned. Powerful governments are to enforce this code of conduct upon weaker governments, using for this purpose especially the international organizations they control . . .

Since the NIEO is concerned with the direction of development, much of the thinking associated with it is prospective. The major schools of thought can be compared by the different shapes of the future they suggest. The liberal establishment studies portray a future with the same broad outlines, though with some differences in detail . . . It seems reasonably clear, however, that some change in relative incomes in favor of the poor countries is recognized in the establishment perspective as what the issue is all about.

The long current three-way division of the world into First (rich capitalist), Second (socialist), and Third (less-developed) countries has given way to a four-way division. The less-developed countries are now seen as falling into two groups, the Third World being limited to middle-income countries, including the OPEC countries and others like Brazil that are becoming industrialized, a group that Fred Bergsten refers to as "the new middle class,"[10] and the poorest countries, or Fourth World, whose indebtedness has increased as a result of the rise in energy and food imports uncompensated by any progress towards either industrialization or agricultural self-sufficiency. (The division into Third and Fourth Worlds is mainly a First World perspective. Promoters of Third World cohesion are bound to resist it. I have used "Third World" in the more comprehensive sense in this essay except for the discussion of the establishment perspective. This conceptual issue is basically political.) Leontief's classification, though more complex since it divides countries into fifteen regions, is compatible with the four-way division broadly accepted in the establishment analysis: developed market regions, developed centrally planned regions, medium-income developing regions, and low-income developing regions.[11]

Though the Soviet bloc is generally expected to play a bigger role in the world economy, no special problems or structural changes are considered likely in consequence. The real issues are those relating the First to the Third and Fourth Worlds. Capital investment will, in the establishment view, flow increasingly into the developing market economies – according to Leontief, the share of capital movements reaching these economies will rise from less than 20 percent to 57 percent by the year 2000.[12] A large portion of it should come from the OPEC countries. The Third World generally would receive capital on commercial terms. These countries would increase their manufactured exports to the rich countries and international trade in the products of light industry would in general show a substantial increase. The principal agencies of this development would be the multinational corporations, and therefore developing countries should avoid any actions likely to discourage these benefactors. All of the establishment texts considered here are quite firm on this point, though some recognition of the validity of criticisms of MNC conduct is recognized . . .

The Fourth World is accepted as a welfare burden. These countries are candidates for concessional aid and for measures of debt relief. It is recognized they cannot hold their own in the world economy. But the aid to which they may aspire would not be without conditions . . . Bhagwati writes that higher aid flows focused on the Fourth World would be "disbursed with diplomatic surveillance, performance criteria, and scrutiny that would make these more substantial flows acceptable to public opinion and parliamentary institutions of the donor countries."[13] The summer of 1978 has given a concrete illustration of the meaning of these general phrases as the consortium of countries administering the foreign debt of Zaire, following the rebel invasion of Shaba and counterattack by French and Belgian paratroops, agreed to refinance the debt on condition that International Monetary Fund and World Bank staff take over the internal management of the Zaire economy. One thinks back to the late nineteenth-century European consortium for the management of the Ottoman debt.[14]

What policies are developing countries, then, expected to follow? . . . Leontief is at pains to reject and set aside the implications of the first Club of Rome report on the limits to growth. He does not see population growth as an overwhelming obstacle to development but as a trend that will be corrected gradually during the next century. Minerals will not run out (except that lead and zinc will become scarce). Nor will the cost of combating pollution be exorbitant:

> The principal limits to sustained economic growth and accelerated developments are political, social, and institutional in character rather than physical. No insurmountable physical barriers exist within the twentieth century to the accelerated development of the developing regions . . . To ensure accelerated development two general conditions are necessary: first, far-reaching internal changes of

a social, political, and institutional character in the developing countries, and second, significant changes in the world economic order . . .[15]

The critical internal policies mentioned by Leontief are restraint on personal consumption and encouragement of a more equal distribution of income with a view to maximizing internal investment, and land reform and related institutional changes as indispensable to raising agricultural production. Self-sufficiency in food is, he argues, a necessary form of import substitution in view of the growing dependency of poor countries on imported foods. Leontief estimates that all underdeveloped regions have large reserves of arable land that could be brought under cultivation and that an increase in agricultural productivity of at least threefold would be possible . . .[16]

The food question leads to the idea of self-reliance. This term has become current in the discourse about development that takes place in international organizations. Originally, it seems to have been derived from the Chinese experience and became associated with a strategy of inward-looking development involving a break with the world economy, perceived as the source of dependency. What, however, is one to make of the endorsement of "self-reliance" by the World Bank and OECD? We must infer that it has a lot to do with Leontief's insistence on poor countries growing more of their own food and with aid directed as welfare assistance towards the poorest strata of population (in large part those living in rural areas). Self-reliance, in the establishment view, is a complement to the pattern of growth through a world economy which it advocates whereby manufacturing of consumption goods would shift towards the Third World, a complement that applies to that impoverished sector of world population that does not participate directly in this pattern of growth. Self-reliance, according to at least one segment of establishment opinion, is appropriate for the welfare sector, but, in the words of the Trilateral report, should not be allowed to "degenerate into a rejection of an integrated world economy."[17]

If the Bhagwati volume does not have much to say about specific development policies in poor countries, it is replete with moral judgement about governments in these countries. Bhagwati himself divides the moral critics into two camps: the "neoconservatives" (they sound like Daniel Patrick Moynihan, though he is not directly cited by Bhagwati) who argue that governments in less-developed countries that are undemocratic by American standards and are violators of human rights should not receive American aid; and the "liberals" (Richard Cooper is his exemplar) who argue that development is a matter of people, not governments, and that aid should only be given where policy performance criteria show that something is being done for the most disadvantaged groups (Richard Cooper adding that "it would be hard to rival a policy of liberal trade by developed and less developed countries alike as a mechanism for ensuring steady improvement in the real earnings of the poorest [healthy] residents of less developed countries."[18] The inference to be drawn in practice from both of these positions is justification of a reduction in resource transfers to elitist and oppressive regimes characteristic of Third and Fourth World countries. It was left to Ali Mazrui at the end of the Bhagwati volume to cut through the cant:

> Those who claim that the workers of Detroit should not be forced to subsidize the ruling elite of Kenya or Zaire are, unfortunately, the same ones who would be alarmed by the ruling elites of Kenya and Zaire going socialist. Salvador Allende paid with his life not because he was getting too elitist but because he was trying to transcend economic elitism in Chile.[19]

If the establishment view offers itself the moral luxury of criticizing elitism in poor countries, it is elitist indeed when it comes to power at the world level. "Should 150 countries participate in all or most of the matters of international discussion?," the Trilateral report asks rhetorically, and replies that this would "seriously impede the necessary cooperation." The Trilateralists then proceed to restate classic functionalism as the political route towards rebuilding an international economic order. The issues should be divided and dealt with separately by the governments most concerned with each, beginning with "those who have the largest stake in the issue." These are usually the Trilateral countries and particularly an inner core consisting of the United States, the Federal Republic of Germany, and Japan.

> Many issues can be handled through a series of circles of participation involving, in the outer rings, general consultation and discussion, and moving inward towards closer cooperation until, in the innermost rings, close collaboration and coordination of policies occurs among the inner group ... Such an approach is not anti-institutions, but rather seeks a more effective mode of reaching agreements in the proper institutional frameworks. Informal collaboration in the earlier stages of discussion would support eventual agreement in more formal institutional settings.

In case this is insufficiently clear, the report spells the point out again:

> ... [T]he main task of assuring consistency in the various fields will fall to the Trilateral nations which assume leadership in the system ... This need puts a premium on coherent policy making within each of these key countries and, especially, the United States, Japan, Germany, and one or two others. But it also calls for methods of coordinating their policy, at least informally. To formalize this function might well prove offensive to some of the Trilateral and other countries which do not take part. By exercising this role informally and by being responsive to others, the Trilateral countries can effectively help in coordinating the activities of various international agencies and in solving concrete problems relevant to many outsiders ... Some group of nations will have to take the responsibility for insuring [*sic*] that the international system functions effectively. No single nation appears to be likely to assume this role in the near term. The United States no longer seems willing to play it fully. Japan and the European Community are not yet ready to assume such leadership. Accordingly, it can be done collectively for some time by the members of the Trilateral region and notably some of its key states. They must act to provide the initiatives and proposals for wider acceptance. They must be on the watch to assure that the system does not break down as a result of the various tensions and pressures ...[20]

The reform proposals for the world economy likely to emerge from the Areopagus envisaged by the Trilateral Commission, if one may judge from the literature reviewed here, are likely to appear rather meager by comparison with Third World demands. There is some recognition of the legitimacy of stabilization of export earnings (on the lines of the Lomé convention), coupled with firm rejection of commodity "price rigging" (Harry Johnson) and indexation.[21] There is also the hint of a possible agreement to facilitate further processing of raw materials in less-developed countries through tariff deescalation and other measures to open rich-country markets wider to LDC manufactures, though this is linked by Fred Bergsten to securing LDC agreement on guaranteed access by developed countries to LDC raw materials and elimination of export controls.[22] The feasibility of the "link" whereby the creation of new SDRs through the IMF would be used as a means of resource transfer to LDCs, the industrialized countries then having to "earn" their reserves by exporting to the LDCs, is examined in a very frank analysis contributed to the Bhagwati symposium by John Williamson of the University of Warwick. He concludes that the scheme is likely to founder on the US veto, since the United States will be unwilling to forego in favor of the LDCs the seigniorage it derives from the present "nonsystem." The best results the LDCs are likely to get, in his view, would be by exploiting in their own interests the "nonsystem that presently exists and that seems likely to persist indefinitely," for example, by placing their reserves at higher rates in the Eurocurrency markets.[23] Beyond this small comfort is the trial balloon launched by Richard Cooper of a levy on deep-sea fishing and on ocean mineral rights to go to the LDCs (which would imply a renunciation on their part of claims to a 200-mile exclusive economic zone – there is no free lunch here).[24] And finally, a piece of fiscal gimmickry in the form of a proposed brain-drain tax that seems more calculated to alleviate the conscience problems of Third World emigrés than the resource deficiencies of Third World countries.

The social democratic perspective

During the later 1960s and early 1970s an alternative to the establishment perspective took shape in reaction to the apparent failure of development assistance programs to improve materially the conditions of the vast majority of people in the poor countries. Not only were the proclaimed targets of the UN Development Decade generally not achieved, but even in those few countries where economic growth did take place, it seemed to benefit only the rich of the poor countries. The strategy of giving priority to economic growth, which meant increasing the share of the rich in the national income and hoping for a trickle-down effect towards the poor to take place has been viewed with growing skepticism by many aid administrators and development planners, who began to think more and more in terms of projects directed specifically towards the poorest segments of the population. Faith in the market was abandoned and the need for governmental intervention recognized as a means of producing greater equity both within and among nations ... The new perspective, which arose mainly among international officials concerned with aid and specialists associated with them (whereas the establishment view is more characteristic of those close to the policy making of donor governments), stressed the satisfaction of simple basic needs of the poorest people, the expansion of employment opportunities among them, and the mobilization and participation of the poorest elements in the development effort. Where normatively the establishment view puts its emphasis on "economic efficiency," the new official perspective stresses an "equitable social order" and even hints that many of its promoters consider this to be achievable through "humanistic socialism." These phrases are drawn from the RIO report prepared by the committee sponsored by the Club of Rome under the chairmanship and influence of Jan Tinbergen which can be read as a consensual statement of this new quasi-official perspective on development. It is here referred to as the social democratic perspective not because of any self-proclaimed political affiliation but because of a general consistency with social democratic positions in the western political spectrum. Many of those who have contributed to formulating the new views on development come from the social democratic tradition and both Sweden and the Netherlands are prominent among the western models to which it refers.

The social democratic perspective in essence was a synthesis of some elements of a radical critique of existing development concepts with the central tenets of the liberal view of the world economy. The principal radical critique was the *dependencia* thesis, in particular André Gunder Frank's analysis of the "development of underdevelopment." The new targets of the basic-needs orientation represented a conscious effort to avert or at least alleviate the underdevelopment consequences of capitalist expansion, especially the marginalization of both rural and urban populations accompanying the spread of modern technology through foreign investment. The new synthesis rejected, however, the implication of the radical critique that autocentric or inward-looking development strategies that involved a break with the capitalist world economy were a necessary condition for overcoming underdevelopment. The essential conditions for an expanding world capitalism were to be preserved – relatively free movement of capital, goods, and technology, and an international division of labor based on the principle of comparative advantage – as the central strategy of world development, accompanied by policies designed to moderate the negative welfare effects this strategy had hitherto produced. Stated in these terms, there is only a nuance of difference between the establishment perspective and the social democratic perspective (since much of the basic-needs argument is now accepted by establishment opinion), though as a matter of practical emphasis in the current literature this nuance is important.

The analysis of the prospects of the world economy in the RIO

392

report is not dissimilar to that found in the establishment literature. The RIO report, like the Leontief report, begins from the limits to growth problematic and is at some pains to modify its pessimistic forecast. The RIO report attaches more seriousness to the prospects of population increase than does the Leontief report and it is not so sanguine concerning the availability of new land in Third World countries to be brought under cultivation. Like the Leontief report, it does not envisage that shortages of natural resources will be a major constraint upon development, though energy and water conservation will be important preoccupations.

Nor is the view of the future structure of the world economy significantly different in the two perspectives: there is the same vision of the less-developed countries becoming greater exporters to the rich countries of manufactured consumer goods, with the rich countries continuing to hold the edge in the export of producer goods. This internationally integrated world economy would be flanked by "self-reliance" sectors in the poor countries which would be directed towards self-sufficiency in production of food and other basic needs through "appropriate" technologies with labor-intensive processes. The RIO report is, indeed, quite explicit about the dualist nature of the national economies to be promoted in the Third World: a modern sector with increasing productivity enhancing the competitive position of Third World countries in world markets whose comparative advantage lies in an abundance of the labor factor; and a basic-needs sector attempting to cater for the welfare of those left outside of the world economy . . .

The comparative advantage notion is elaborated in the Herman study on the international division of labor prepared for the ILO's world employment program, which carries the imprimatur of Tinbergen. This deals only with one part of the dualism, that part integrated into the world economy. Indeed, it seems to ignore the basic-needs sector (though the world employment program had endorsed this approach) or even to reject it by the assertion that "inward-looking policies do not help to foster economic development mainly because of the large element of inefficiency that they allow" and that "no true development can be achieved if the harsh realities of the market mechanism are ignored."[25] The Herman study classifies countries according to their factor endowments – in particular capital-labor ratios – and groups industries according to typical factor requirements. The purpose of the exercise is summed up in the phrase that

393

"a country should specialise in the activities with factor requirements that match the country's factor endowment most closely" and that to do so would specifically achieve a maximization of employment.[26] This leads to some curious inferences, such as the grouping of Japan with Colombia, Greece, South Africa, and Venezuela in terms of factor endowments, and the finding that the United States has the comparative advantage for supplying the world with armaments, weapons, and aircraft.[27]

Tinbergen, in his foreword, regards this sort of thing as a "pioneering exercise" in world indicative planning. One can also read it in the context of the more sober judgement of Singer and Ansari (whose book shares much of the social democratic perspective) that it is misleading to put so much emphasis on factor endowment when more attention should be paid to factor *use*.[28] Trade in the modern world, they point out, does not reflect the assumptions of Ricardian theory,[29] assumptions which are taken over by Herman in his model.[30] Recent investments in less-developed countries, they point out, have not been guided in their factor use by the existing factor endowment; rather, imported technology has determined factor use, leading to dualism and unemployment.[31] All (Tinbergen, Singer and Ansari, and Herman), however, agree that rich countries should adopt adjustment policies to facilitate importation of an increasing proportion of their consumer manufactures from the less developed.

The multinational corporations are, of course, cast in the role of making use of the comparative advantage the less-developed countries have for producing standardized consumer manufacturers. The social democratic perspective does not, however, take an uncritical view of the MNCs. The RIO report envisages greater regulation and in a vague way the ultimate incorporation of the MNCs within some form of international corporatist-type structure:

> In the long terms, transnational enterprises will still form part of the world structure, in either their present form of private enterprises or in a renovated form comprising genuine international ventures ... The statutes of transnational enterprises should be under the supervision, and their profits taxed by, an inter- or supranational authority. Transnational enterprises should form part of an international framework of concrete economic activities and their labor conditions should be negotiated with representative national and international trade unions.[32]

Singer and Ansari foresee a mutual adjustment of LDCs and MNCs in which their divergent interests can be made compatible, since they are both "slowly grasping the fact that they cannot wish each other out of existence." They write: "Both the multinationals and the LDCs are relatively permanent units of economic activity in this second half of the twentieth century ... They must work towards compromises in which each party *sees* that its basic interests are being promoted."[33] ...

Samir Amin, writing from a standpoint of Marxian analysis, rejects this strategy of symbiosis between the MNCs and the LDCs as the doctrine of a new phase of imperialism. The RIO report specifically he interprets as an ideological maneuver:

> The fact is that the themes of the new order involve the aspiration to control natural resources and to strengthen national states, which imperialism does not accept. Imperialism would therefore like to substitute for the new order the "RIO Project" (Reshaping of the International Order!) which is an ideological formulation of the need to transfer some of the industries of the centers to the peripheries under the wing of the multinational.[34]

Singer and Ansari, more critically realistic than the authors of the RIO report though sharing many of their policy views, sense that something like this is indeed happening: the type of international economic integration advocated by western economists through trade liberalization, they write, "will tend to perpetuate the economic and technological dependence of the LDCs on the industrial centers and will increase the gap between the haves and have-nots on both a national and an international level."[35] They go on to argue that state power in the LDCs should be strengthened to counterbalance that of the MNCs, since "international integration based on cooperation between national states, conscious of development needs, will be preferred by the developing countries to the international integration that would result from an uninhibited expansion of profit-motivated foreign private investment."[36]

Visions of the future institutions of the world economy contrast markedly between the social democratic and establishment perspectives. In place of the "piecemeal functionalism" of the Trilateral Commission which would put the rich-dominated agencies like the IMF, the World Bank, and GATT at the center of the institutional picture, the RIO report envisages comprehensive planning on a world scale developed on the basis of the present United Nations ("the only machinery with the potential for constructing a fairer world"[37]), under the slogan of "decentralized planetary sovereignty." Functionalism becomes a principle of sovereignty that relates the appropriate level of decision making to the range of impact a decision will have rather than a recipe for fragmenting issues. It will lead to some issues being dealt with at the global level while others can be handled locally since they are only of local consequence. Participation in international institutions would not be limited to governments but should include non-governmental organizations of various kinds (MNCs and trade unions, for example – there is a corporatist bias in RIO prescriptions for planning). There would be a gradual transfer of power to certain functionally defined world authorities. International aid programs would evolve into a system of international taxation operating through a World Treasury. Monetary-reserves creation would take place through a World Central Bank. A World Food Authority would be created. And the United Nations would be restructured with broad economic powers as the center of a functional confederation of international organizations. Other contributors to the social democratic perspective more modestly advocate greater automaticity in resource transfers to poor countries . . .

These proposals are attenuated by the political naiveté that often characterizes social democratic literature and the RIO report in particular. This is not political economy in any sense; it is work written by professional economists who seem to think of politics as the domain of another set of specialists whose job it is to find a way putting the economists' own prescriptions into effect. The RIO report refers to a "power structure" as a kind of *deus ex machina* but never considers how economic policies are embedded in power positions that will have to be changed if material changes in policy are to be brought about. It is easy to say that LDCs should carry out land reforms, for example, without specifying how the balance of social and political forces can be shifted so as to achieve this goal, or how such a shift might affect the achievement of the other major goal, i.e., export-oriented industrialization through foreign investment. To consider the political dimension seriously would lead to the analysis of class struggles in poor countries and class alliances between poor and rich countries, and this the social democratic perspective avoids. "In the final analysis, our world is ruled by ideas – rational and ethical – and not by vested interests." So states the RIO report.[38] In such a view, politics is reduced to exhortation . . .

In the context of global politics of the NIEO, the Trilateral and RIO reports are the two faces of hegemony. They share the same fundamental assumptions about the progressive nature of world capitalism bringing about a new international division of labor, and both recognize the need in addition for an international welfare program to be carried out as far as possible by the poor themselves. Where the Trilateral report underlines the essential structure of power in the world political economy, the RIO report stresses those aspects of a new hegemonic consensus that deal with concessions and satisfaction for the subordinate. As an unofficial enterprise carried out by a number of people close to official decision making, the RIO project appears as a prospective exploration of the acceptable limits to adjusting the existing power structure in the world political economy to the demands of the poor countries . . . I for one would underscore the report's inadequacy: there is no analysis either of the causes of underdevelopment or of the nature of the crisis in the world political economy such as would be a precondition for realistic strategies for change. That this is so has something to do with the failure of the social democratic perspective to come to grips with political economy.

Third World perspective

Though sharing many of the specific proposals of the social democratic perspective, the ideas expressed by some Third World exponents of the NIEO have a quite different intellectual quality for being far more thoroughly conscious of politics. They are aware that the success of any program depends upon the political strength it can muster . . .

Mahbub ul Haq's personal rejection of the economic development credo he learned at Yale and which he had helped to apply in Pakistan with the support of the Harvard Development Advisory Group, through which, as he put it, "economic development had become warped in favor of a privileged minority,"[39] was a microcosm of a much broader revulsion of Third World opinion from western theses about development. In its purest form, this change was from one total view to another totally different. The Chinese experience offered a presumed point of reference for the new alternative, which was often presented in terms of a revolutionary change. Technology imported from the West created links of dependency. Financial aid from the West led Third World government leaders to take "soft options" requiring yet further foreign assistance and leading to deepening dependency. Growth policies promoted by the West led to absolute

impoverishment of the poorest groups and increasing income disparit-
ies within Third World countries. "The developing countries,"
Mahbub ul Haq told the International Development Conference in
Washington, D.C., in April 1972,

> have no choice but to turn inwards, in much the same way as China
> did twenty-three years ago, and to adopt a different style of life,
> seeking a consumption pattern more consistent with their own
> poverty – pots and pans and bicycles and simple consumption
> habits – without being seduced by the life styles of the rich. This
> requires a redefinition of economic and social objectives which is of
> truly staggering proportions, a liquidation of the privileged groups
> and vested interests which may well be impossible in many societies,
> and a redistribution of political and economic power which may only
> be achieved through revolution rather than through evolutionary
> change . . .[40]

How is one to interpret this talk of revolution coming from a high
official of the World Bank – and one who, despite the radical critiques
of the World Bank from many who would share his sympathy with
the revolutionary option, nevertheless is ready to give the Bank his
certificate of approval ("Over the last three decades, it [the Bank] has
shown considerable dynamism and brilliant improvisations in the
light of changing situations").[41]

Herein lies the ambivalence of the Third World perspective: on the
one hand, the prospect of revolution, rejection of western models and
western aid and pursuit of inward-looking development; on the other
hand, the menace of revolution as bargaining counter designed to
encourage further concessions from the West, perpetuating existing
structures with some incremental changes in poor countries . . .

Robert McNamara, president of the World Bank, seems to have
opted for the basic-needs orientation of development policy as a
means of preempting revolution, in a passage quoted approvingly by
Mahbub ul Haq:

> When the highly privileged are few and the desperately poor are
> many – and when the gap between them is worsening rather than
> improving – it is only a question of time before a decisive choice
> must be made between the political costs of reform and the political
> risks of rebellion. That is why policies specifically designed to reduce
> the deprivation among the poorest 40 percent in developing coun-
> tries are prescriptions not only of principle but of prudence. Social
> justice is not merely a moral imperative. It is a political imperative
> as well . . .[42]

These statements fairly clearly present basic needs as an element in strategies to sustain the status quo in transnational economic power relations, at least in the medium term. The argument skirts the issue that Marxists would describe as that of reproduction, i.e., that the pattern of power relations and organization of production characteristic of world capitalism tends to perpetuate itself and to continually recreate the inequalities of uneven development. A basic-needs approach that did not attack the issue of transforming world economic structures would accordingly be condemned to failure, though it might buy time. A basic-needs approach that did indeed become a strategy for structural change with an alternative pattern of development would challenge the establishment perspective's vision of a "moderate international order" . . . [43]

The neomercantilist perspective

Two characteristics justify the application of the term neomercantilism to the three very different authors treated here. One is that they recognize the state as the determining economic factor, like it or not, and view international economic relations as essentially relations among states. The other is that they leave aside formal economics in their search for an explanation of change in power relations – relations perceived, in other words, as history and to be analyzed through political economy. Within this "realist" approach, they have their own different normative preferences.

Robert W. Tucker's book is addressed to the defense of the national interest of the United States, but this national interest has to be understood with reference to a model of the international system. This, as Tucker sees it, is now a fragmented system with divisions among the democratic capitalist powers that enable Third World countries to press for advantages. The "poor power" of the South he dismisses as either romantic nonsense or the reflection of a failure of nerve in the North – but nothing objectively substantial in itself.[44] The fragmented condition has, however, resulted in a "growing disjunction between power and order," in which the capitalist countries still have the power but are no longer the principal guarantors of order, while the challengers do not have the power to create a new order.[45]

In many ways, this reads more like a book about morals than about economics – or rather, one might say it is about the moral fiber of the West and the United States in particular. It is written in terms of an extreme idealism that traces changes in the world system to ways of thinking rather than to changes in the relations of material forces. The chief culprit leading to the disjunction of power and order is what he calls the "new political sensibility" which is comprised of

> a rising disinclination to use or threaten force, whether from the belief that force is no longer expedient or from the conviction that force is no longer a legitimate instrument or, more likely, from a combination of the two; a view that the developed states are in many respects highly vulnerable; a persuasion that growing interdependence is threatened by inequalities that, if allowed to persist, will result in generalized chaos or war; a commitment generally to reducing international inequalities, though without a clear idea of – or, for that matter, interest in – the effects a redistribution of wealth would have on the redistribution of world power; and, finally, a sense of guilt over a past for which we are now thought to be paying the inevitable price.[46]

Tucker examines in turn and rejects to his satisfaction the foundations for each of these beliefs. Cumulatively, however, their impact on western and US policy in his view had been tantamount to an abdication of power, or (which amounts to the same) an unwillingness to do what is necessary to maintain the ordering function of power, and this is traceable to a change in moral values following World War I: "It was the belief in the intrinsic superiority of European civilization that from the start provided much of the self-assurance and elan of Western imperialism. In the interwar period, the self-assurance also began to erode in the solvent of an outlook that acknowledged the differences, though not the inequalities, of cultures" . . .

I come away from this book with the feeling that there may be a specifically American quality to this attempt to restate a "realist" view of world politics which distinguishes it from earlier non-American versions of realism, ranging from Albert Sorel's analysis of the eighteenth-century European balance of power to E. H. Carr's analysis of the interwar period (both cited favorably by Tucker) and including the well-known views of Charles de Gaulle (whom Tucker passes over in silence). All of the latter would have accorded more weight to the material sources of and constraints on power and less to ideology. I am left not so much with a sense of hard-headed realism as with the spectacle of an eighteenth-century natural-law liberal feeling increasingly alone in the world. Tucker is not a pessimist impressed with the constraints limiting human action; he is, to borrow Georges Sorel's categories, a disillusioned optimist who blames a failure of will. The "new conservatism," if that is what it is, is like nothing so much as the old liberalism.

Michael Hudson portrays the demand for a NIEO as born of the breakdown of United States hegemony, a hegemony that has operated through the mechanism of a "Treasury-bill standard." The United States was able to run a continuing balance-of-payments deficit through the 1960s and into the 1970s because its principal creditors – western Europe, Japan, and Canada – agreed to relend American debt to the US Treasury by holding their reserves in the form of Treasury bills. In this way, US involvement in Vietnam and the takeover of foreign businesses by US-based MNCs was financed by foreigners and US public debt came to be very largely foreign owned. The turning point came in 1973, in a series of four crises: the currency crisis in March that led to generalized adoption of floating rates; Europe's rejection of the Kissinger plan for a new Atlantic charter; the imposition of export embargoes by the United Nations on forty agricultural commodities and scrap metal during the summer; and the autumn Middle East war and attendant oil embargo. Hudson sees the NIEO as a reaction to these events by both Europe and the Third World (indeed, his view of the NIEO focuses rather more on Europe than on the Third World) in which both seek to become "independent of the US economic orbit and more closely integrated economically and politically with one another."[47]

The book is a coherent and challenging analysis, critical of US policy and sympathetic to European and Third World reactions to it. It is at times, however, difficult to distinguish between Hudson's perception of a tendency towards independence from the United States and an assertion that that independence has indeed become a reality. Hudson sees evidence of a new European independence in the creation of the "snake" – "the first major move" in breaking out of the US orbit – in the Pompidou–Jobert initiative towards a special relationship with the Arab world, and in the Tindemans report on the possibility of a European foreign policy. Another more skeptical author might have described all these initiatives as abortive or unsuccessful and the reality of Europe today as still very much bound into the American economic orbit . . . Hudson is cautious enough to qualify his indicators as marking only a threshold. The currency issue is for him the one which would ultimately define the reality of independence, which would require the creation of a European equivalent to the dollar and for this far more European integration than exists or is currently in prospect would be needed.[48]

Hudson also forecast the decline of the MNCs: "Ironically, economists chose to formulate a theory about multinational control over the direction of world economic development at the precise moment that the process began to deteriorate. (This is one more example of how the analysis of historical processes tends to be formulated at the end of these processes, generally when new ones are under way.)"[49] The MNCs are no longer the main channels of capital movement to the Third World. The private banks now play this role, and many Third World countries have become heavily indebted by borrowing in private financial markets. The rollover of this debt is now a matter of major concern in North–South intergovernmental relations and the US Treasury policy is to deal with it through the IMF and the World Bank, i.e., giving governmental policy supremacy over MNCs in controlling the allocation of world monetary resources.

Andre Tiano's *La dialectique de la dépendence* is, despite its title, a university textbook on international economic and financial relations...[50] English-speaking readers will turn to it less as a textbook than for the author's interpretation of the dependency question. Tiano rejects equally the liberal advocacy of free trade and comparative advantage, on the one hand, and the "break with the world economy" advocated by some Marxists (though only in rhetoric as he points out), on the other. For these, he substitutes the notion that dependency is a fact – though one which is difficult to define; indeed, by making underdevelopment its criterion he seems to have been caught in a circular definition – but a fact that can be changed through a dialectical process in which the dependent country exploits the weaknesses of the external forces upon which it is dependent. The leadership of the state in less developed countries is a necessary condition for pursuing this dialectic, and Tiano offers some examples of how it can be done: selective approval of foreign investment, the possibility of using export controls, for example, to encourage further processing, developing a national corps of engineering cadres both youthful and (especially) politicized so as to be committed supporters of the policy of working towards national economic independence. The critical issue for the LDC is to gain control over the productive apparatus of the country. This notion of a dialectic he regards as consistent with the Marxian tradition, though not with a certain Marxist sectarianism that advocates a dramatic break with dependency...

The realism of these neomercantilists is put to the service of change, not maintenance of the status quo. Tiano writes as a French socialist advocating a continuation of Gaullist policies for a Europe more independent of the United States, and confident that the European left would work hand in hand with the socialists of Third World countries dependent upon Europe towards facilitating the dialectical movement towards a more equal relationship. Hudson sees an exclusive Soviet–American detente, in which both parties seem to share an interest in preventing the unification and strengthening of the European left, as the greatest threat obstructing progress towards "economic independence from the United States and its Treasury-bill standard, its new wave of commercial protectionism, its self-centered foreign-aid philosophy and its tampering with the domestic political affairs of foreign countries."[51] He argues further that the costs of warfare are now prohibitive to all but a few Third World dictatorships, and that since the United States in particular cannot any more afford extensive overseas military involvement – Vietnam having led to the present crisis of the world economy – "repressive regimes will not be able to call upon the United States at will to support their power by overt or covert means as in the past. The path will thus be opened up for foreign economic, political, and social change that has been stifled for three decades."[52]

The perspectives of historical materialism

The characteristic feature of historical materialism is its focus on production as that of neomercantilism is its focus on the state. That is not to say that these are mutually exclusive or necessarily contradictory emphases or that other perspectives do not share either of them. It is largely a matter of points of departure. Questions of compatibility arise further down the road . . .

The use of the plural form of perspectives is particularly pertinent in the case of historical materialism. Bound for a long time in an orthodoxy confined to the Leninist view of imperialism and the contradictions of developed capitalism, the field of historical materialism has more recently been extended through a variety of attempts to respond to the challenge of the North–South problematic and particularly to found realistic strategies for the Third World countries . . .

The recent literature has raised a number of basic issues concerning concepts and approaches about which the historical materialists are divided amongst themselves. They are engaged in a debate that goes on quite apart from that in which most of the other orientations are involved. It revolves around three main cleavages.

The first concerns the relative emphasis to be given to productive forces as against the relations of production. The stress on productive forces can lead at one extreme to a technological determinism (modern industry, the historical work of capitalism, becomes a prior condition for the transition to socialism); that on relations of production at another extreme to a revolutionary voluntarism (revolution can reshape society independently of its technological base; indeed revolution will generate its own technology). In political terms, the former reflects the orthodoxy of Marxism particularly as exemplified by the Soviet model and the latter the Chinese road to socialism.

The second conceptual issue concerns the relative emphasis on modes of production versus social formations. Marx, of course, used both concepts but for different purposes. The mode of production was his deductive model that enabled him to explore the properties and dynamics mainly of capitalism and to a more limited extent of pre-capitalist forms, as in *Capital*. The social formation was his framework for analyzing the interaction of different forms of production and social classes in a particular historical conjuncture, for example, France following the revolution of 1848 in his *Eighteenth Brumaire of Louis Bonaparte*. The choice of concepts in the present historical conjuncture can lead in quite different directions. To pick the mode of production has led some to theorize about a world system defined as capitalism – the fate of the periphery being bound up with a crisis that is determined from the center. To pick the social formation, and specifically the peripheral or Third World country as a social formation, leads others to explore what they have called the "articulation of modes of production" or the complex interrelationship of capitalist and non-capitalist forms of production – or varieties of capitalist forms – in Third World countries and their linkages with the world economy. The view from the periphery via the social formation approach suggests a more complex world system and a greater range of choice in Third World strategies than does the center-based notion of a world-encompassing mode of production.

Finally, there are divergent epistemologies of positivism and historicism within the intellectual tradition of historical materialism. The positivist aspect has been most prominent recently among the French school from Althusser to Poulantzas who have tried to make Marxism into a universal general theory by rejecting in particular the Hegelian elements in Marx's thought – an attempt criticized by another historical materialist (with reference to Poulantzas in particular) as "structural-functionalism clothed in Marxist concepts."[53] The historicist aspect has been most prominent recently in Italian theory, especially that of Gramsci, but is also evident in the British historical works, for example, of Eric Hobsbawm and Perry Anderson.

These themes of debate can be seen running through the recent historical materialist literature. One is tempted to find an overlapping alignment between, on the one hand, those who stress the primacy of productive forces, reason in terms of a worldwide capitalist mode of production, and tend towards general theorizing, and, on the other hand, those who give their attention to the varieties of production relations to be found in peripheral social formations and who take a more concretely historical approach. But though there may be something in this, it oversimplifies a more complicated picture. It is more prudent to observe how these different themes arise in different authors.

The case for the primacy of productive forces is stated by Arghiri Emmanuel, whose work has been associated above all with the notion of unequal exchange based on difference in labor costs between center and periphery . . . [54] This is, in a sense, a Marxist defense of the historical role of the MNC and rejection of some current *dependencia* theses on underdevelopment. In effect, Emmanuel sets aside Gunder Frank's assertion that the "development of underdevelopment" is an effect of capitalism. Emmanuel observes that if you list countries in decreasing order of capital received and again in decreasing order of GNP per capita, the two lists coincide: "So either there is no causal link between foreign capital and underdevelopment, in which case the multinationals cannot be accused of having caused a deadlock at the periphery, or the deadlock occurred not because international capital flowed in but because it has stayed out."[55] He is contemptuous of "self-centered" development and "appropriate technology" ("An appropriate technology for poor countries can only be a poor technology . . . an anti-development technology.")[56] The progressive role of capitalism should not be forgotten by its critics:

> [C]apitalism is not a bad dream but a social system which has a historical part to play; a system which, as it developed, gave not only gadgets and pollution but also widespread literacy and an average life expectancy of seventy years instead of forty. And that, consequently, while awaiting the social revolution, it is by no means a

405

matter of indifference for people whether they live in India or the United States, no matter what similarity may be recognized between the production relations in these two countries.[57]

One is left with the feeling that "awaiting the social revolution" means awaiting the full development of a modern industrial base; but Emmanuel goes on to say that capitalism cannot bring this about in the Third World (apart possibly from some insignificant exceptional cases) so these countries must "skip the capitalist stage," an assertion that seems to contain a voluntaristic leap.

Christian Palloix grounds his analysis in the labor process. The labor process, as he understands the term in Marx's usage, has two components: one is the linkage between the different physical phases of production (capital goods, intermediate goods, consumer goods); and the other is the way in which human beings are organized into production and a labor supply is assured. He calls these respectively the objective and the subjective aspects, and deals mainly with the objective side. Palloix is at one with Emmanuel on the primacy of productive forces over relations of production. He rejects the (Chinese) thesis of the autonomy of production relations, i.e., the possibility of beginning a transition to socialism by a revolutionary change in the power position of social classes and in the way people are organized to do work, in the absence of any significant change in the quality or quantity of the physical apparatus of production. To ignore the constraint that productive forces impose upon the possibility of making the transition to socialism, he warns, is to lapse into idealism.[58] The inference is that LDCs should adopt strategies that emphasize acquiring the kinds of production activities which supply the means of production, in other words which would give them command over the labor process instead of remaining dependent upon the supply of these means of production from outside. Palloix here echoes views expressed by Samir Amin to the effect that LDCs should not follow the route of "comparative advantage" (in the sense used by liberal economists), since "if the international division of labor is unequal, the argument of comparative advantages loses its validity,"[59] and should instead put their efforts in areas of comparative disadvantage, in particular by developing basic industries. Amin's criticism of the RIO report (cited above) is on the grounds that it would perpetuate the structural inequality between center and periphery by maintaining control of the labor process in the center through its monopoly of the generation of the means of production. Amin sees the alternative road for the LDCs in terms of cooperation among themselves in raw materials exchange and in the development and sharing of technology.

A somewhat more pessimistic viewpoint is given by Norman Girvan in a collection of republished essays entitled *Corporate Imperialism: Conflict and Expropriation.*[60] Girvan's framework is one of overlapping and contradicting economies or policy areas: on the one hand MNCs, on the other LDCs, each struggling to maximize its control over the relationship and to become less dependent upon the other, with the LDCs losing out. At the present time, he notes an effort to co-opt the leadership of Third World countries into "a new model of dependent industrialization" which would involve an extended role for the state bureaucracies of the LDCs: "Co-optation of economic nationalism involves developing a new and enhanced role for the Third World state in the resource industries. Previously limited to the provision of infrastructure for the benefit of the corporations, which was paid for ultimately by the population, the state's functions can be expanded to embrace formal ownership, provision of capital, and administration of the labor force."[61] This new model requires a new set of political and class alliances and a new legitimizing ideology. This is meeting with some resistance within the center, notably resistance to the demands for a shift of decision-making power towards LDCs which is implied in the NIEO, yet, Girvan continues,

> it is difficult to interpret this demand as an assault on what we have called the system of corporate imperialism. There is no evidence that Third World states as a whole are seeking to reverse the process of concentration of private capital on a world scale, or that they wish to liquidate the role of the transnationals as the principal instruments of the international transfer of capital and technology.[62]

Girvan's call is for "subversion" of this new order in which Third World governments are accomplices of MNCs in a new phase of imperialism.

Other historical materialists study more optimistic and less apocalyptic scenarios. Tamás Szentes ... for example, envisages the possibility of Third World countries moving towards planned socialist development without any dramatic rupture in their international relations.[63] The decisive factor would be if the state were to follow policies to eliminate economic dualism by transforming agriculture, a task which could only be achieved by developing industry so as to provide the inputs for and interact with the rural sector. Like Emmanuel, Szentes recognizes the positive contribution of foreign capital and technology, but argues that the tendency of a private-investment-paced world economy to fragment national economies and integrate the pieces internationally should be resisted by the national state in the LDCs ... One can see here a potential convergence of historical materialist and neomercantilist approaches to the NIEO.

Strategies for overcoming underdevelopment in this more optimistic vein of historical materialism are being considered in the work of Hartmut Elsenhans.[64] Elsenhans appears to be exploring what Tiano called the dialectic of dependence, or how the LDCs can consciously use their links of dependency in order to gain more autonomy of development. Though his point of departure is in the productive forces, he, more than Emmanuel or Palloix, for example, arrives at a balance between production relations and productive forces rather than a subordination of the one to the other.

Elsenhans, by contrast with Emmanuel, for example, does endorse something like Gunder Frank's formulation: "Underdevelopment," he has written, "is not identical with non-development, but rather the result of the development of the capitalist mode of production."[65] This result takes the form of what he calls "structural heterogeneity" which, in the present historical conjuncture, takes place through the formation of "bridgeheads" of capitalism in peripheral countries. The economies of these countries become characterized by export of raw materials or standardized manufactures, import of capital goods (the means of work), import increasingly of the basic essentials, principally food, and a limited domestic demand because of the relatively small proportion of "bridgehead" income earners in relation to the whole population. Market force will not change this pattern so as to resolve structural heterogeneity into an all-embracing capitalism primarily because of the blockage of domestic demand arising from the structure of the labor force and incomes. The alternative way of resolving structural heterogeneity is by a state-led socialist development and it is towards devising a strategy for such a course that Elsenhans' work is directed.

Internally, the basic policy requisites are (1) an agricultural revolution that will increase production so as to satisfy the food needs of the population and eliminate dependency on imported foods, (2) an egalitarian incomes policy that will create a mass market for food and simple goods (cf. the "basic-needs" concept discussed in the first three sections of this essay), and (3) an industrial policy that produces inputs for the agricultural sector (fertilizers, tube wells, irrigation tubes, tractors, etc.) and simple manufactures for the aroused mass demand. All three are interdependent, but the first is particularly dependent upon the third. Industrial policy thus has a strategic leadership role, though the primary target is rural development. Like Emmanuel, Elsenhans rejects the argument (see especially the Third World perspective discussed above) in favor of labor-intensive technology, "intermediate" technology, or "appropriate" technology. The way in which the Chinese experience has been frequently depicted in these terms he sees as western romanticism. The technology question should rather be posed in terms of the proper combinations of capital- and labor-intensive processes and the ends to which they are put. A highly capital-intensive fertilizer plant that provides inputs for an agricultural revolution serves development, while a consumer goods factory producing for export that is labor-intensive by industrial country standards though relatively capital-intensive by LDC standards, consolidates structural heterogeneity.

Externally, Elsenhans eschews the myth of a break with the world economy and advocates for the LDC a combination of "associative" and "dissociative" behavior: a controlled cooperation with capitalist countries. It is this aspect that brings him closest to Tiano's dialectic. Elsenhans would not, for example, rule out LDCs cooperating with MNCs, but in any such cooperation the LDC government should bring the MNC activity into conformity with its own development goals – by requiring the MNC to increase its local procurement of inputs, for instance, and by taxation not only of profits but of employee earnings. Differences in time-dimension – the profit-making dimension of the MNC being somewhat shorter in time than the structural-change dimension of the LDC government – may allow for a certain transitory coexistence of MNC and LDC policies pursuing fundamentally different goals. Like a number of the other authors considered (Amin, Tiano, and Singer and Ansari included), Elsenhans also attaches importance to regional cooperation among LDCs.

Where Elsenhans seems to make an advance upon the other historical materialist authors so far considered is in pressing his enquiry beyond the realm of "productive forces" strictly speaking in order to consider the possible sociopolitical basis for the policy route towards overcoming development. Several points are worth making here.

First, there is the subjective dimension of political mobilization or political consciousness. A cultural revolution in thinking and attitudes on the part of the peasantry will be a necessary component of agricultural development. Relatively privileged workers in the "bridgehead" sector will have to be persuaded of the desirability of a more equitable incomes policy. Means will have to be found to mobilize the urban marginals. Elsenhans writes that the content of political consciousness is to be considered as a productive force, but he is here on the threshold of production relations.[66]

Second, there is an internal dialectic in addition to the external one Tiano pointed to. The necessary development of industry and importation of technology intended as the motor of change in agriculture will give strategic prominence to a relatively skilled labor force and will encourage income disparities that conflict with the goal of an egalitarian incomes policy. The way in which this contradiction (between material incentives for skill on the one hand and income solidarity on the other) is handled can be taken as a criterion of the developmental authenticity of a regime.

Third, there is the notion of the state class as the leader or potential leader of change and the question of the sociopolitical basis of this class, to which Elsenhans has devoted an (unpublished) manuscript . . . The emergence of a state class with authentic national development goals – both of capital accumulation and structural change – he considers to be a distinct possibility on condition that the underprivileged strata of society have been effectively mobilized, i.e., normally through a prolonged anti-colonial struggle. Developmental authenticity can only be maintained so long as this class remains under pressure of the disadvantaged strata, this pressure being constantly necessary since the leadership in the state class is in the nature of things held by relatively privileged groups (intellectuals and town-dwellers). Commitment to the agricultural revolution is itself one way of maintaining this pressure from below. Another source of pressure from the base of society upon the leadership arises in dialectical fashion out of rivalries within the state class itself. Subordinate groups within the state apparatus, impatient under the rule of established members of the class, seek external allies in the underprivileged groups which thus increases the pressure from below upon the leadership.

While Elsenhans looks to the state class in peripheral countries that have made an anti-colonial breakthrough as the initiators of a dialectic of development, others such as Girvan (as discussed above) picture new developments in the state machinery of LDCs as but the counterparts of a new phase of imperialism. Is there a contradiction here?

410

Not, I think, at least so far as Elsenhans is concerned. For him, there is nothing progressive per se in the state class. There is only a potential for developmental leadership if the historical conditions surround it with the necessary social pressures. Yet even in the case of a state class that colludes (RIO-like according to Amin) in the new MNC-directed international division of labor, Elsenhans would find scope for revolutionary praxis, by examining "how far the existence of islands of prosperity intensifies the revolutionary pressure of the underprivileged forcing, in turn, the state apparatus to introduce compensatory measures for the satisfaction of the needs of the underprivileged."[67] Here we join Samir Amin, who comments that "in theory" the new international division of labor does permit the co-opting of LDC ruling groups: "But only 'in theory,' because what counts in history are the unexpected accidents, and there can be some here and there in the peripheries and in the centers (and serious ones for capitalism) during the transition, laden with contradiction, ... to the new phase of imperialism."[68] We have come a good distance from the technological determinism implicit in Emmanuel towards a more voluntaristic view of revolutionary potential in the Third World, but one grounded nevertheless in the analysis of historical conditions.

The controversy about modes of production and social formations takes a rather different tangent from the historical materialist literature thus far discussed and presents some of the features of a level of analysis issue. On the one hand are those who write about the internationalization of capital as the homogenization of a world system in the form of the capitalist mode of production which has to be analyzed as a single whole. On the other, is the "new economic anthropology" examining the combinations of different modes of production in the peripheries, or what has been called by Pierre-Philippe Rey, one of the seminal thinkers of this school, "the articulation of modes of production."[69]

The world system approach, particularly in the form expressed by Immanuel Wallerstein (building on Gunder Frank and especially on Fernand Braudel's recently translated work) is now fairly well-known to American readers. Christian Palloix's work is probably less well known and, it must be added, intellectually less accessible (apart altogether from the language barrier, Palloix is often very obscure for French readers). Palloix's use of the labor process as an avenue of analysis is, however, relevant to the issues raised in the new economic anthropology even though he does not accept the notion of articulation of modes of production, since everything, for him, is explainable in term of capitalism. There are, for Palloix, two labor processes: (1) the labor process of capital or industrial mass-production (Taylorism for short) and (2) the domestic labor process or relatively simple production for use or immediate consumption as in the household. Up until the last decades of the nineteenth century capitalism grew on the basis of a labor supply that was sustained and replaced through the domestic labor process. The workers themselves came initially from rural villages; their food was produced in eastern Europe or Latin America by "pre-capitalist" methods; it was prepared and their workclothes mended by their wives at home; and they and their wives produced a new generation of workers. The "domestic labor process" is thus a convenient way of classifying the whole mixture of nonindustrial production processes as a subordinate category to the "labor process of capital." This (for capitalism) happy symbiosis between the two labor processes came to an end in the United States at the end of the century when waves of immigrants provided the labor for burgeoning American industry. As they were cut off from their native villages in eastern and southern Europe, the domestic labor process could no longer serve their needs so adequately. Capitalism moved in to fill the breach by progressively developing the labor process of capital to fulfil functions formerly exercised by the domestic labor process – by mechanizing agriculture (and thereby changing its labor process) and by penetrating the worker's household with mass-produced articles. In Palloix's somewhat ponderous formulation, capitalism interiorized the reproduction of labor power which had formerly been exterior to the labor process of capital. The massive inflow of immigrants also gave capital the opportunity to break the restrictiveness of old work patterns supported by traditional unions by moving altogether to Taylorism, thereby increasing capital's control over the labor process. A contradiction arises here, however, when labor acquired a degree of autonomy (e.g., more effective trade unions and political support) and was able to resist the tendencies of the labor process to deskill work and to increase its intensity (mass production and automation). The costs of interiorizing the domestic labor process became too high for capital which responded by segmenting the labor force into one part which is still "interiorized" with access to mass consumption goods and another part which is marginalized (the usual mechanism being racial segregation), and this led to profound social crisis within the capitalist city. Another response of capital, however, has been to shift production into the Third World in an attempt to restore the old nineteenth-century relationship between the labor process of capital and the domestic labor process which continues to exist in those areas. This, Palloix argues, is the basic reason behind the new international division of labor.

What does this historical interpretation tell us about the present structure of the world system? Like Wallerstein (not to mention Julius Caesar), Palloix divides it into three parts, although the ambiguity of Wallerstein's "semi-periphery" (which was the Italian city-states in the sixteenth century and is the Soviet Union in the twentieth) is absent. Most countries today, according to Palloix, are in an intermediate position in the global labor process, since they are at the same time dependent upon other countries for the importation of some of their producer goods (and likely the most critical ones) and are exporters of other producer goods to other countries. France, he says, is in such an intermediary status because it has lost control over the reproduction of its own productive system; while some Third World countries (he was speaking to Mexicans who might see themselves in this role) had moved into a position of supplying some capital goods to less-developed countries. The hierarchy, thus, could now be represented as (1) the hegemonic social formations (United States, Germany, Japan) which alone controlled the global labor process, (2) the intermediary formations, and (3) the underdeveloped formations (altogether dependent upon the outsider for producer goods). And the political issue, in consequence, could be defined as whether the NIEO would enlarge and consolidate the intermediary space (Palloix's version of what Amin argues is the RIO strategy) or whether the intermediary formation would ally with the underdeveloped in order to break with capitalism.[70] Thus for Palloix the dialectic is at the center of the system. Revolution must mean a change in the global system itself. There is no hint of the subtle dialectics à la Tiano or Elsenhans that could introduce change from the peripheries through exploiting the contradictions of the system.

If Palloix has in a sense sidestepped the challenge of the Third World by assimilating its variety of concrete conditions to the "domestic labor process," the new economic anthropology takes a more direct look at real conditions of production in the Third World, probing what Elsenhans refers to as structural heterogeneity. In a key work of this school, Pierre-Philippe Rey's *Les alliances de classes*, the author sees three stages in the impact of capitalism on a pre-capitalist peripheral formation. In a first stage a relationship is established through exchange, during which capitalism reinforces pre-capitalist modes of production. In a second stage, capitalism "takes root" within the peripheral formation and subordinates pre-capitalist forms without supplanting them, i.e., they continue to coexist symbiotically. In a third stage, not yet reached in the Third World, capitalism would absorb or eliminate everything else. The great advantage of this approach is that it directs attention to the study of actual production processes and to the complementarities and conflict between them. Initially, in terms of the subject matter, this arises for countries into which capitalism arrived from the outside; but by implication the same method might as well be applied to the study of the different forms of production process which have evolved in the industrialized countries. In short, it heralds a move from a debate over abstractions to a study of actual production. Aidan Foster-Carter underlines this possibility in his review of the debate in "The Modes of Production Controversy" and one can only applaud his sharpness in rooting out tendencies to reification: "It is already one level of abstraction to have 'classes' (rather than 'people') as the subject of history; but to endow so conceptual an entity as 'mode of production' with this role is idealism indeed. As modes of production are not the subject of history, so neither should they be the subject of sentences."[71]

This practical emphasis raises by implication the matter of clarifying just what a mode of production is. Foster-Carter points out that the question can be answered one way by defining it upwards, making it identical (à la Wallerstein or Palloix) with the world system – there is a single mode of production. It can be answered another way by defining it downwards to "on farm/in firm" relations at the point of production, thus, according again to Foster-Carter, "producing inevitable inflation and debasement of the coinage: each Andean valley has its own mode of production, and individuals may change them two or three times a week like underwear."[72] Nevertheless, it is in this latter direction that the most serious gap in the thought of historical materialism now seems to lie. Theorizing about the world system has achieved a certain academic status, but relatively little is being done towards a better understanding of the varieties of the real world of production – even where, as with the historical materialists, production is proclaimed to be the basis for both theory and action. Work in this direction should lend further subtlety and realism to the formulations of such as Tiano and Elsenhans. It would show historical materialism not as a refinement of dogma but as a method of work.

About a century and a quarter ago, Karl Marx wrote "Men make their own history, but they do not make it just as they please." He pointed both to the potentiality of human volition and the material limits of the possible. About another century and a quarter before that Giambattista Vico (whose thought Marx knew and seems to have appreciated) propounded the reverse of this proposition: that history makes men, or that what we call human nature is not something uniform and universal but is changing and shaped by history. These propositions are not mutually exclusive; they are reciprocally related: the mind that conceives and comprehends historical actions is itself molded by history; thought and action are bound together in a structural interrelationship that can only be understood historically. Both Vico and Marx would have agreed on that. The significant breaks or turning points in history are points at which mental constructs which have hitherto been recognized as generally valid science (because practically useful as guides to action under specific historical conditions) come to be seen as ideology.

It remains an open question whether the debate over the NIEO is such a turning point. Michael Hudson thinks it is, seeing in it a sequel to the first industrial revolution that produced the classical economics of Adam Smith and the second industrial revolution that engendered the economic and social theories now established in the western world counterposed to Marxism: "Today's cracking of international relations inevitably will be associated with a similar set of new ideological forms, rationalizations, and justifications."[73] Others see the NIEO not as a turning point but as an adjustment in an established ongoing hegemony, the co-opting or *embourgeoisement* of the Third World. As the quick survey of literature attempted here brings out, though the establishment still speaks with the authority of "science," the ideological foundations of the different positions are made more explicit by the radical critics, especially the neomercantilists and historical materialists.

Radical criticism is, in its nature, unfinished business. The themes advanced by the critics are potentially rich, and yet their work still has a very preliminary quality. Much remains to be done to give the lines of critical analysis opened up a fuller basis in empirical studies – a task that confronts the obstacle of the academic establishment's predominant control over resources for research. And out of this effort, if successfully pursued so as to overcome this and other obstacles, may come a new science that itself in due time will be perceived as ideology tied to historical foundations that have in turn become obsolete.

Notes

This text was first published in *International Organization*, vol. 33, no. 2 (Spring 1979), pp. 257–302.

1 Reviewers of this essay suggested that I make my political position clear at the outset, a request that is fair yet difficult for me to comply with since I do not sit comfortably under any political label. I have thought of myself as a conservative, but to accept this designation is to risk association with those who have appropriated it to cloak an egoistic defense of acquired privilege. My conservatism is in the first place historicism, or the sense that ideas and events are bound together in structural totalities that condition the possibilities of change – what I understand Machiavelli to have meant by *necessità*. My conservatism is also a commitment to a certain sense of right and equity for the underdog and a suspicion of the most recently established wealth and power – a pre-capitalist, Jacobite, anti-Whig conservatism. This makes me suspicious of all bureaucracies (though there are some good people who double as bureaucrats) whether governmental, corporate, international, or academic. I find some of the thought of the critical left (to be distinguished from the new scholasticism of the official left) more relevant to my concerns than anything on the right or center of today's political spectrum, though I am aware that many of those whose work I find helpful would regard my own historicism as a form of idealism. So much for the author's confessions.

The author is grateful for the critical comments offered by Robert Keohane, John Ruggie, and Peter Katzenstein.

2 United Nations Institute for Training and Research, *A New International Economic Order: Selected Documents 1945–1975*, vols. I and II, compiled by Alfred George Moss and Harry N. M. Winton (UNITAR Document Service No. 1).

3 Richard N. Cooper, Karl Kaiser, and Masataka Kosaka, *Toward a Renovated International System*, The Triangle Papers 14 (New York: The Trilateral Commission, 1977).

4 Club of Rome, *Reshaping the International Order: A Report to the Club of Rome*, Jan Tinbergen, coordinator, Antony J. Dolman, editor, Jan van Ettinger, director (New York: E. P. Dutton and Co., 1976).

5 Mahbub ul Haq, *The Poverty Curtain: Choice for the Third World* (New York: New York University Press, 1976), p. 84.

6 Robert W. Tucker, *The Inequality of Nations* (New York: Basic Books, 1977).

7 Michael Hudson, *Superimperialism: The Economic Strategy of the American*

Empire (New York: Holt, Rinehart, and Winston, 1972), and *Global Fracture: The New International Economic Order* (New York: Harper and Row, 1977).

8 Christian Palloix, *Travail et production* (Paris: Maspero, 1978).

9 Samir Amin, "Self-Reliance and the New International Economic Order," *Monthly Review*, vol. 29, no. 3 (July–August 1977), pp. 1–21.

10 C. Fred Bergsten, "Access to Supplies and the New International Economic Order," in Jagdish N. Bhagwati (ed.), *The New International Economic Order: The North–South Debate* (Cambridge, Mass.: Massachusetts Institute of Technology Press, 1977), pp. 199–218.

11 Wassily Leontief *et al.*, *The Future of the World Economy* (New York: United Nations/Oxford University Press, 1977).

12 Leontief, *Future of the World Economy*, p. 62.

13 Bhagwati, *New International Economic Order*, pp. 20–21.

14 See Herbert Feis, *Europe, the World's Banker, 1870–1914* (New Haven, Conn.: Yale University Press, 1930).

15 Leontief, *Future of the World Economy*, pp. 10–11.

16 Ibid., pp. 4–5, 7–8, 35, 41.

17 Cooper, Kaiser, and Kosaka, *Toward a Renovated International System*, p. 17.

18 Bhagwati, *New International Economic Order*, pp. 355–356.

19 Ibid., p. 374.

20 Cooper, Kaiser, and Kosaka, *Toward a Renovated International System*, pp. 34–38, 41–42.

21 Ibid., p. 25; Bhagwati, *New International Economic Order*, pp. 240–249.

22 Cooper, Kaiser, and Kosaka, *Toward a Renovated International System*, p. 26; Bhagwati, *New International Economic Order*, pp. 199–214.

23 Bhagwati, *New International Economic Order*, pp. 81–97.

24 Ibid., pp. 105–115.

25 Bohuslav Herman, *The Optimal International Division of Labour* (Geneva: International Labor Office, 1975), pp. 131, 132.

26 Ibid., p. 51.

27 Ibid., Appendix D.

28 Hans Singer and Jared Ansari, *Rich and Poor Countries* (London: George Allen and Unwin, 1977).

29 Ibid., pp. 65–66.

30 Herman, *Optimal International Division of Labour*, pp. 31–32.

31 Singer and Ansari, *Rich and Poor Countries*, p. 38.

32 Club of Rome, *Reshaping the International Order*, p. 160.

33 Singer and Ansari, *Rich and Poor Countries*, p. 196.

34 Amin, "Self-Reliance," p. 20.

35 Singer and Ansari, *Rich and Poor Countries*, p. 108.

36 Ibid., p. 212.

37 Club of Rome, *Reshaping the International Order*, p. 43.

38 Ibid., p. 107.

39 Mahbub ul Haq, *Poverty Curtain*, p. 6.

40 Ibid., pp. 40–41.

41 Ibid., p. 213.
42 McNamara to the Board of Governors of the World Bank, September 1972, cited in ibid., p. 10.
43 A "moderate international order" was the goal of a volume produced as a result of the 1980s project of the Council of Foreign Relations. Albert Fishlow, Carlos F. Diaz-Alejandro, Richard R. Fagen, and Roger D. Hansen, *Rich and Poor Nations in the World Economy* (New York: McGraw-Hill, 1978). The term should be read in the sense of Stanley Hoffmann's use of "moderate international system" as one that is not beset by revolutionary upheavals or extreme challenges and which allows considerable scope for accommodating issues through international organizations. See Hoffman, "International Organization and the International System," *International Organization*, vol. 24, no. 3 (Summer 1970), pp. 389–413.
44 Tucker, *Inequality of Nations*, p. 135.
45 Ibid., p. 93.
46 Ibid., p. 110.
47 Hudson, *Global Fracture*, p. 1.
48 Ibid., p. 33.
49 Ibid., p. 120.
50 André Tiano, *La dialectique de la dépendence: analyse des relations économiques et financières internationales* (Paris: Presses universitaires de France, 1977).
51 Hudson, *Global Fracture*, p. 166.
52 Ibid., pp. 225–226.
53 G. van Benthem van de Bergh, cited by Aidan Foster-Carter, "The Modes of Production Controversy," *New Left Review*, vol. 107 (January–February 1978), p. 56.
54 Arghiri Emmanuel, "The Multinational Corporation and Inequality of Development," *International Social Science Journal*, vol. 28, no. 4 (1976), pp. 743–772.
55 Emmanuel, "Multinational Corporation," p. 760.
56 Ibid., p. 764.
57 Ibid., p. 762.
58 Palloix, *Travail et production*, p. 72.
59 Amin, "Self-Reliance," p. 18.
60 Norman Girvan, *Corporate Imperialism: Conflict and Expropriation. Transnational Corporations and Economic Nationalism in the Third World* (White Plains, N.Y.: M. E. Sharpe, 1976).
61 Ibid., p. 6.
62 Ibid., p. 8.
63 Tamás Szentes, "Structural Roots of the Employment Problem," *International Social Science Journal*, vol. 28, no. 4 (1976), pp. 789–807.
64 Hartmut Elsenhans, "Overcoming Underdevelopment. A Research Paradigm," *Journal of Peace Research*, vol. 22, no. 4 (1975), pp. 293–313, and "The State Class in the Third World: For a New Conceptualization of Periphery Modes of Production" (unpublished).

65 Elsenhans, "Overcoming Underdevelopment," p. 294.
66 Ibid., p. 304.
67 Ibid., p. 309.
68 Amin, "Self-Reliance," p. 13.
69 Pierre-Philippe Rey, *Les alliances de classes* (Paris: Maspero, 1976).
70 Palloix, *Travail et production*, pp. 131–132.
71 Foster-Carter, "Modes of Production Controversy," p. 55.
72 Ibid., p. 74.
73 Hudson, *Superimperialism*, pp. 174–175.

19 Labor and hegemony (1977)

The issues examined here concern the relationship between the International Labor Organization (ILO) and the United States. None of the events considered has been of great intrinsic importance to the course of world affairs, though some have been of symbolic importance and the significance of symbols in political and social life must not be underrated. Participants in the ILO have said the issues are about "tripartism," evoking the principle of trade union and employer freedom from government control. Academic discussion of the ILO has hinged on "functionalism," a more esoteric reference to the potential for international integration deriving from autonomous social forces. Both concepts express the normative preference of the users, but are inadequate and inaccurate representations of basic social and political power relations. An effort to gain a more valid sense of these power relations must take account of changes in world production processes and in the social relations that arise in these processes, changes that will be seen as linked to the emergence of a corporative form of state with different manifestations in developed and underdeveloped countries. These basic relationships can, in turn, be seen as conditioning the problematic of economic and social development, the nature of American power in the world, and the contemporary process of international organization. The ILO's current predicament becomes something less interesting for its own sake than as a thread enabling us to trace these deeper tendencies. It becomes the occasion, not the real subject matter, of the enquiry.

This preliminary stage of mapping out a fresh view of basic structures of relations within which visible political action takes place, can best follow the historical method, regarding this method as did Collingwood when he wrote that "the events of history are never mere

420

phenomena, never mere spectacles for contemplation, but things which the historian looks, not at, but through, to discern the thought within them."[1]

Hegemony, corporatism, and the ILO

The United States government on November 5, 1975, gave notice of withdrawal from the International Labor Organization, a specialized agency of the United Nations of which the US has been a member since 1934. The period of notice is two years, after which the US will cease to be a member of the ILO unless the government meanwhile decides to withdraw its notice.[a]

The incident draws attention to a microcosm of world politics, the arena of international labor. Power, ideology, and personality shape events here as in the relations among states, but whereas power is an awesome constraint on ideological excess and personal idiosyncrasy in *grosspolitik*, ideology and personality sometimes seem to caricature power relations in labor affairs. The close observer is tempted to note that the real drama may nevertheless be unfolding here in the labor arena. The power struggles involving labor concern the control of production, the ultimate resource on which political power rests. Ideologies legitimate the control of production and the forms of social relations of the production process. The importance of the quarrel over the ILO lies in its ideological aspect: the ILO has symbolized a particular model of production relations.

Antonio Gramsci used the concept of hegemony to express a unity between objective material forces and ethico-political ideas in Marxian terms. A unity of structure and superstructure in which power based on dominance over production is rationalized through an ideology incorporating compromise or consensus between dominant and subordinate groups.[2] In the hegemonic consensus, the dominant groups make some concessions to satisfy the subordinate groups, but not such as to endanger their dominance. The language of consensus is a language of common interest expressed in universalist terms, though the structure of power underlying it is skewed in favor of the dominant groups.

[a] The United States withdrew from the ILO during the period November 1977–February 1980. For further discussion of the withdrawal see Mark F. Imber, *The USA, ILO, UNESCO, and IAEA: Politicisation and Withdrawal in the Specialised Agencies* (London: Macmillan, 1989).

In this Gramscian sense of the term, the ILO has been the expression of a global hegemony in production relations. At its origins in the making of the Versailles Treaty in 1919, the ILO was the response of the victorious powers to the menace of Bolshevism.[3] By creating the ILO, they offered organized labor participation in social and industrial reform within an accepted framework of capitalism. During the interwar period, the ILO was nourished by the spirit of reformist social democracy yet ever heedful of the practical limits imposed by dominant conservative forces.

The United States rejection of the Versailles Treaty precluded US membership in the ILO. In 1934, however, the Roosevelt administration passed over this obstacle and joined the ILO – an action taken rather quietly so as not to arouse an inattentive isolationism, and without any marked interest on the part of the American Federation of Labor.[4] The government's initiative sought to give an international dimension to the New Deal. From that moment, the United States took the lead in shaping the hegemonic consensus in the ILO. In 1944, by sponsoring a major ILO conference in Philadelphia, the Roosevelt administration appeared to encourage the organization to take on a prominent role in postwar international social policy. During the Cold War years, the ILO's emphasis on trade union freedom and collective bargaining expressed one ideological facet of America's dominant world position.

At present, the ILO lies under a cloud because the erstwhile hegemonic consensus seems to have come undone. There is no longer any firm cohesion among the more powerful forces (American, western European, and now Soviet as well), and no agreement on the concessions that can be made to those less powerful but of growing effectiveness (the Third and Fourth Worlds). The voice of American organized labor in particular has questioned whether a consensus acceptable to it can be put together again through the ILO, and by implication whether some alternative institutionalizing of hegemony in world production relations might be possible and preferable.[5] This is the meaning of the US notice of withdrawal, but to get to the meaning one has to strip away layers of polemic and place the incident in the global perspective of the forces affecting labor.

A principal reason given in the US letter of withdrawal was "fundamental concern" with the "erosion of the tripartite representation."[6] The ILO includes representatives of the trade union and employers of its member countries as well as of their governments. Although these labor and management representatives are appointed by the governments, they are supposed to be chosen after consultation with the most representative organizations, and they caucus and vote separately from governments at ILO conferences. This is the formal meaning of tripartite representation in the ILO. Those who drafted the letter signed by the secretary of state were saying that they did not think delegations from socialist countries and from many Third World countries represented trade unions and employers in the way they themselves understood the meaning of these terms.

The meaning of a concept has to be sought in the experience of those who use it. We may well ask, what is the *American* meaning of "tripartism" as a standard to judge the ILO? To answer, we must look away from the ILO's constitution and formal procedure and look towards the changing reality of labor in the evolution of the modern capitalist state.

Here mythology and reality diverge. The mythology of American business is the small entrepreneur of frontier free enterprise. The reality is the corporate bureaucrat with his executive attache case riding the metropolitan commuter train. The mythology of labor is heroic struggle for recognition and dignity against the bosses. The reality is legislative logrolling, bargaining tradeoffs with corporate management, and administrative processing of individual employee grievances.

New structures have emerged, slowly, hesitatingly, but continuously in America since the 1930s – the structures of an increasingly visible and effective corporative state in which organized labor forms an integrated whole with corporate management and government for the control of the American economy. The relationship within this structural unity is symbiotic – labor, management, and government shove and haul for the advancement of particular interests, but each needs the other and knows it. Conflict is held within the bounds of their common interest.[7]

The rise of the corporative state is the counterpart to the inability of electoral democracy to cope adequately with the increasingly complex issues of national economic policy. Where the corporative state was not explicitly imposed through formal institutions as in Fascist Italy, it appeared as a natural growth spawning less formal and more fluid procedures for associating economic interests with government. Although the same trend was visible in all industrialized capitalist states, the emergence of the corporative state in the United States has special importance because of the dominance of the United States economy in the world. The corporatist hegemony within the state is projected abroad as the form of America's global hegemony.

For organized labor in America, acceptance in practice of this new unifying structure of relationships has come about through the process that in the jargon of current American political science is called "modernization." "Modernization" conventionally implies a subordination of community or ethnic bonds to a more bureaucratized organization of material interests. Historically, unions in the United States have been among several agencies that have helped the lower strata of American society to merge into the mainstream of American life (others being big-city political machines and Mafia-type crime). During the Gompers era (1886–1924), Irish and German immigrants became prominent ethnic groups in the labor movement. The CIO's unionization of the mass-production industries in the 1930s reached out to include immigrant groups from southern and eastern Europe.[8] The 1960s might, as a continuation of this process, have been the phase of linking in blacks and hispanics, but the corporative state was approaching closure before this further extension of the labor movement was far advanced. During this latest period, American organized labor went through a critical phase of adjustment to the sophisticated, bureaucratized machinery of the corporative state.

With the emergence of these new structures, organized labor represented about one quarter of the American labor force, consisting of the better-off employees, middle-income people who in consumption terms and life styles see themselves as middle class.[9] For these people, it had achieved a fair degree of employment security, control over workplace conditions, and defense against arbitrary employer action. In addition to those protected by a stable union–management relationship is another group of employees in large public or private organizations who enjoy comparable conditions through a bureaucratized, impersonal paternalism in which the employee's security derives from corporate policies. This primarily white-collar group has recently become a major target of unionization. These two groups together may account for at most half the United States labor force, the half which has acquired a considerable stake in the economy.

The economy does much less well by the remaining half of the labor force. Largely non-union, heavily representative of women and minority people, whose employment is unstable and who have little or no career opportunities, this lower half is a human buffer softening the blow of an economic downturn for the more privileged upper half.[10] Acceptance of the corporative state by the leaders of organized labor means that unions have largely abandoned this lower half, or made only token efforts at unionization amongst it.[11]

Currently corporatism is advancing in two parallel movements. The first is towards more centralized negotiation over the organization of production, over the terms on which work is to be performed, and over the division of the product. All of this is a means of reducing uncertainties, controlling and making more predictable the economic environment – an aim shared by industry, union leaders, and government. From the point of view of union leaders, centralizing decisions seems to make the rank-and-file union worker more dependent upon those who participate in negotiations, while at the same time reducing the risk of having to call strikes. President of the AFL-CIO George Meany said a few years ago: "There is a growing feeling that strikes of people getting $7,500 a year or more just don't make sense . . . Now the workers have a little house, they may have a couple of kids going to college. You put them on strike, they're overboard within a week. So, we would like to eliminate strikes just on that basis alone."[12]

The second of these parallel movements is toward enterprise corporatism, a closer association of employee interests and loyalties with the big employer. IBM gives an example of enterprise corporatism without unions, but other big corporations have seen advantage in a somewhat more legitimate relationship, accepting unions and successfully tempting them into a symbiosis with management. The dualism of the labor market facilitated this form of corporatism among the upper half.

The personality presiding over this transformation of American trade unionism was George Meany, president of the AFL-CIO. Meany's career personifies organized labor's integration into the corporative state. Beginning as a labor legislative lobbyist, first in Albany, New York, then in Washington, he came at the height of his career to have access to presidents. Meany's experience with the War Labor Board of World War II and its Korean War counterpart gave him a positive view of tripartite machinery. No doctrinal reasons precluded Meany's collaboration in the Nixon attempts at an incomes policy. When he did come out against the Pay Board it was because he had become

convinced Nixon had "double-crossed" him by stacking its composition against labor. A pragmatist and no demagogue (Meany abhors
demonstrations and marches, the kind of happenings that give scope
to radicals), he favors tough bargaining in a closed room, and faithful
and disciplined adherence to bargains struck. He brought the personal
virtues of the old style of labor leader to the bureaucratized decision
making of the new corporatism. In the final judgement of his not
uncritical but on the whole sympathetic biographer, Joseph C.
Goulden, Meany is in essence an organization man[13] – a species that
finds its natural habitat in corporatism.

John Dunlop, Harvard professor of labor economics and secretary
of labor bridging the Nixon and Ford administrations during 1975–
76, though in public impact a lesser personality than Meany, has
been a prominent architect of the corporative state. Meany's proclaimed distrust of academics – an endearing quality of the old-style
labor leadership – makes exception for Dunlop whose academic
theorizing is held in check by the pragmatism of his experience in
the industrial relations of the building trades and also perhaps by
political ambitions. As secretary of labor, Dunlop was the perfect
complement to Meany.

Dunlop's work in government, consistent with his academic writings, has emphasized negotiation of issues among organized economic
interests. A. H. Raskin of the *New York Times* made this point on the
occasion of Dunlop's resignation as secretary of labor in January 1976,
writing that this departure "puts into mothballs the most ambitious
experiment ever undertaken in this country to establish a shadow
cabinet of top-level leaders in industry and labor as advisers to the
Federal Government in shaping national economic policy."

This "shadow cabinet" was the president's Labor Management
Committee, on which sat Meany and seven other leaders of major
trade unions, together with the heads of General Motors, General Elec-
tric, US Steel, Alcoa, Mobil Oil, the First National City Bank, the
Bechtel Group, and Sears Roebuck. With President Ford's initial
encouragement, Dunlop saw it as a means of reaching a consensus on
policy prior to executive or Congressional action. A related objective
of Dunlop's was to turn over the framing of regulations in such fields
as health and safety to labor–management negotiation. Thus the
industries and unions concerned would decide what should be done
about health risks to workers and to the public at large. Dunlop
argued that "regulation lessens incentives for private accommodation

426

of conflicting viewpoints."[15] Raskin did not miss the point that "exclusion from the new apparatus of voices representing such forces as consumers, environmentalists, small business and civil rights groups, could turn it into a device for collusion to advance monopoly interests at the expense of the general public."[16]

The project on which Dunlop was working at the time of his resignation – that inadvertently became the cause of his departure – envisaged a centralized tripartite bargaining structure for the building industry. This scheme would have taken power from the building-trades locals and the myriad small employers in the industry and placed it with the national unions and contractors' associations whose decisions would be reached under suasion from government to keep wages and costs in line with anti-inflation and growth goals of public policy. Such centralized decision making would have applied to unionized construction, not, of course, to the more than 50 percent of construction that is non-union.

These steps towards greater coherence in the structures of the corporative state were frustrated not by radical protest on the part of those excluded from corporatist hegemony but by the adherents to the mythology of free enterprise. The fire of the traditional right fell upon the "common situs" picketing provision that had been added to the new constitution for the building industry in order to consolidate labor support. The prospect of allowing one striking building-trades local to close down all work on a site was too much for the "right-to-work" lobby to swallow. Corporatism, a structure that shores up positions of acquired social power, depends upon the support of the pre-corporatist myths in which members of the dominant coalition were reared. In this case the hiatus between reality and myth became too evident. Dunlop was among the first sacrifices to Gerald Ford's fears of Ronald Reagan's rhetoric.

Tripartism can now be defined, in the perspective of the United States, as the reality of the corporative state veiled by the still vigorous myth of free enterprise. In the corporative state, organized labor – broadly representing the upper half of the work force – shares in the fruits and, through its union leaders, shares in the management of the economy. The other side of this reality is that the lower half of the work force has no secure status with the hegemonic coalition. In good times, the upper half supports social welfare to provide some solace for the most vulnerable among the lower half while at the same time keeping an eye on them. But in times of crisis, these social

427

programs are pared according to the exigencies of an economy conceived in terms of the interests of the dominant groups.

This structure of social power, skewed as it is in favor of the top half of society, joins with an ideology of pluralism. Pluralism says nothing directly about privilege. It extols the role of autonomous interest groups. But the more privileged are the better organized, the best able to profit by the interplay of interests, and among these business and established trade unions are most effective. Pluralism and tripartism are synonymous ideological terms expressing the corporative reality.

American labor's foreign policy

When George Meany, John Dunlop, and other American officials who have dealt with the ILO deplore the erosion of tripartism, they most probably express an honest concern for the autonomy of trade unions in countries where governments directly control or suppress unions. But the real meaning of an ideological statement is revealed more by actions than by words or intentions. This real meaning can be seen to be impatience at resistance to the expansion of American capitalism.

American organized labor has, indeed, since World War II, behaved abroad as an integral element in the global expansion of American capitalism. Whether consciously or unconsciously, its relationship to labor in other countries has been subordinated to this goal. American labor's foreign policy has stressed American interests first, international labor solidarity second – and indeed the second has been so far behind as hardly to count at all.

The AFL carried abroad its conviction of the fundamental soundness of American free enterprise, a distrust of foreign powers, and an implacable hostility towards the enemy it perceived in world communism. The AFL preceded the American government in fighting the Cold War. American labor's foreign policy actions have not infrequently appeared to conflict with the official positions of the State Department – but then so have the foreign actions of some agencies of US government, notably the CIA. American labor leaders themselves have at times seemed divided on foreign policy, witness the clash between George Meany and the late Walter Reuther.[b] In the

[b] On their clash over anti-communist policy, see Alfred O. Hero and Emil Starr, *The Reuther–Meany Foreign Policy Dispute: Union Leaders and Members View World Affairs* (Dobbs Ferry, N.Y.: Oceana Publications, 1970); John Barnard, *Walter Reuther and the*

larger perspective of America's world position, these seeming conflicts blend as complementary actions towards common goals. American labor's support for the expansion of American capitalism is demonstrated not by evidence of conspiratorial intent but by the consequences of its action abroad.

The historical roots can be traced to Samuel Gompers' support for President Woodrow Wilson during World War I. Government and organized labor learned then the mutual benefits of their alliance on both domestic and foreign fronts. The crucial support given by government to the expansion of the labor movement during the 1930s underlined once again the virtues of the alliance, this time profiting the CIO and for a time making of that organization a chosen partner of government.

During World War II, the CIO leaders broke the erstwhile AFL monopoly of representing American labor abroad by working with British and Soviet trade unions to create the World Federation of Trade Unions (WFTU), a grand alliance of world labor mirroring the grand alliance of nations against Germany and Japan. The AFL meanwhile cooperated with the US government in less visible action through the OSS – forerunner of the CIA – and built the weapons for its own Cold War through the Free Trade Union Committee, initially an offshoot of David Dubinsky's International Ladies Garment Workers Union. The FTUC under the direction of Jay Lovestone, a former secretary-general of the American Communist Party who had become determinedly anti-Stalinist, was from the 1940s the planning agency of AFL foreign policy.[17]

When the Marshall Plan began in 1947, the CIO policy of collaboration with the Soviet trade unions lost credibility and the AFL's anti-communist purity seemed justified. With the CIO discredited in the foreign policy arena, and occupied at home by a purge of communist sympathizers, the AFL regained the initiative. The resources the AFL could draw upon gave it great influence in selecting the leadership and thus shaping the development of trade unionism in postwar Germany, France, and Italy. In Germany, AFL agents put the American military government authorities on the defensive for being "soft on communism" and secured a position of advantage for their own proteges. In France, through the activity of Lovestone's lieutenant, Irving

Rise of the Auto Workers (Boston: Little, Brown, 1983); and Archie Robinson, *George Meany and His Times: A Biography* (New York: Simon and Schuster, 1981).

Brown, the AFL encouraged and financed the secession from the majority trade union, the communist-controlled CGT, of an anti-communist group that took the name of *Force Ouvrière*. Brown's activities extended from promoting dual unionism to hiring strong-arm squads of strike breakers to ensure passage of Marshall Plan supplies through French ports struck by CGT unions.

The links between the AFL and the CIA, which can be seen as an outgrowth of the wartime connection with the OSS, have been traced to this period. Though still formally denied by AFL-CIO president George Meany and by Irving Brown, the CIA connection is now acknowledged by some of the direct participants in AFL foreign-policy operations and accepted as fact by reasonably independent historians of the events.[18] Though much of the detail has yet to be divulged, there can no longer be any reasonable doubt that AFL and CIA worked in tandem in postwar western Europe and this mingling of labor and intelligence action extended later to Latin America, Asia, and Africa.[19]

The labor attaché program illustrated the ambiguity of the labor-government relationship in foreign policy, its pursuit of political goals under cover of trade union activities. Richard Deverall, one of the AFL-CIO foreign agents during this period (and one-time labor adviser to General MacArthur's military government in Japan) is reported by Meany's biographer Goulden as saying: "Classic examples of such activities can be found ... in Japan, where corrupt elements within the right-wing labor movement are given trips to America purely because they express pro-American sentiments to the labor attaches; or in the Philippines, where the US embassy has from the beginning supported a strange collection of gangsters, gamblers and parasites ..."[20]

From 1954, a yet closer and more open relationship between the merged AFL-CIO and US government developed. First, under the administration of President Eisenhower, George Meany gained a role in foreign aid, including influence over appointments to Foreign Operations Administration posts in Europe, the Near East, the Far East, and Latin America, and funds for training foreign labor activists. Such collaboration was intensified under President Kennedy. The AFL-CIO had thus acquired a regular and open flow of funds from AID, whereas for the earlier period interest focuses on the extent of covert financing through the CIA of some of the AFL's foreign operations.[21]

The role of the AFL-CIO as soldier of American capitalism abroad –

rather than merely as patriotic participant in American government foreign policy – became manifest during 1959–61, when the American Institute for Free Labor Development (AIFLD) was being set up. The AIFLD was conceived as an instrument of trade union penetration into Latin America, directly and fully controlled by Americans, disposing of abundant resources, and free from the restraints of even such subservient "international" trade union organizations as the Inter-American Regional Labor Organization (ORIT), a regional trade union body with Latin American affiliates, many of them not much more than their subsidized offices and officers, operating under the tutelage of the AFL-CIO. Placed on the board overseeing AIFLD activities, alongside President Meany and several trade union leaders, were representatives of American big business with interests in Latin America. The chairman of the board was J. Peter Grace of W. R. Grace Co. and a vice-chairman was Berent Friele, characterized by Goulden as the "Rockefeller family's house expert on Latin America."[22] Meany stated that the AFL-CIO executive council "decided unanimously that we should bring enlightened American business into this institution on the theory that they should have an interest in developing a friendly attitude toward the building of free societies in Latin America. They naturally want to do business there, and they certainly want to do business with countries that have viable economies."[23]

The record of AFL-CIO action to "build free societies" in Latin America is now quite extensive. Its recent history began with AFL-CIO participation in the CIA-led conspiracy which gave rise to the overthrow of the popularly elected Arbenz government of Guatemala in 1954, an action taken essentially in support of United Fruit Company interests and legitimated by the Eisenhower administration as reaction to the threat of a "communist bridgehead" in the western hemisphere. When Seraphino Romualdi, the AFL proconsul for Latin America, arrived in Guatemala City with the victorious forces of Castillo Armas, the first acts of the new regime were to suppress both the trade unions and the land reform instituted by Arbenz.[24] The effort to build "free societies" continued in 1963-64 with AIFLD participation in the overthrow of the Goulart government of Brazil – the last in that country to have any claims to constitutional legitimacy or labor support – and its replacement by a repressive military dictatorship.[25] The "communist bridgehead" fear worked again in 1963 to secure trade union cover for CIA operations to overthrow the elected government of Cheddi Jagan in British Guiana, this time using the American

Federation of State, County, and Municipal Employees along with the AIFLD as instruments of subversion.[26] In 1965, the AFL-CIO's client group in the Dominican Republic cooperated with US military intervention to overthrow the elected Bosch government. The full story about Chile is yet to be told.

Whatever intentions lay behind these foreign interventions by the AFL-CIO – and there is little point in disputing whether the union leaders have been naive dupes of their own ideology or cynical dissimulators of their true motives – the consequences have been to support the short-term interests of American investment.[27] These consequences have been uniformly disastrous for the Latin American working class.

The AIFLD was a model for similar action directed toward Asia and Africa. Irving Brown transferred his activities from western Europe to Africa in the pre-independence period and gave the AFL-CIO leverage with a number of African trade union leaders, like Tom Mboya of Kenya, who emerged into the political limelight in the early 1960s. And the Asian-American Free Labor Institute became a channel for AFL-CIO action in Vietnam. (Meany's wholehearted enthusiasm for LBJ's war hardly needs to recalled.)[28]

Apart from these foreign operations directly controlled by the AFL-CIO leadership in an integrated government–business–labor foreign policy, American organized labor has also participated in international trade union organizations. This relationship has never been an easy one. The CIO together with the British and other non-communist western trade unions withdrew from the WFTU when the lines of the Cold War were drawn. The AFL then joined with the secessionist group in setting up the International Confederation of Free Trade Unions (ICFTU) in 1949, the year of the North Atlantic Treaty, with Irving Brown serving as midwife. Meany's biographer, Goulden, wrote: "The AFL wanted to give legitimacy to the trade unions it was underwriting in Europe and elsewhere. The AFL wanted protective international coloration for some of the solely American activities it was conducting abroad. Finally, the AFL wanted a worldwide labor group with which to wage a propaganda battle with the now-avowedly Communist WFTU."[29] Such aims required compliant partners.

Not surprisingly, compliance was not always forthcoming. From the start, the British TUC was an alternative pole of influence within the ICFTU and one whose leaders did not altogether share Meany's world view. Through the 1950s, however, Meany had such prestige and resources that when he determined to mobilize them, he was able to have his way with the ICFTU. In 1953, he brushed aside British TUC influence, secured a place on the ICFTU executive for his ally, the Israeli Histadrut, imposed his own candidate as general secretary (a Belgian, Omer Becu, whose anti-communist credentials seemed impeccable as he had been an erstwhile associate of Dubinsky and Lovestone), and brought about a reorganization of the ICFTU that placed Irving Brown on its staff.[30]

But despite his power, Meany could never fully and continuously control the ICFTU the way he could control the AFL-CIO's own foreign activities. Europeans elected with his support had to make some show of independence in order to maintain credibility among other Europeans, and this not only cost them Meany's favor but incurred his active enmity. For Meany, a bureaucracy, whether an agency of the US government or an international organization like the ICFTU, was something to be controlled from outside by placing his own agents within. Yet any person placed in formal charge of a bureaucracy may be expected to try to assert his own control over the organization, to make it more effective and more autonomous, and to develop its own identity. Becu and his successor in the ICFTU both followed this course with varying success, but with predictable results as regards Meany's attitude. As the ICFTU tried to be more "international," so Meany became more impatient with it. At a press conference in 1965, Meany asserted the ICFTU was bureaucratic and ineffective, and implied that it was a haven for homosexuals.

Anti-communism was no longer a sufficient basis for common action among the non-communist European trade unions. Since this was Meany's criterion of "effectiveness," he was reluctant to trust them. The AFL-CIO worked more and more through its own directly controlled parallel international network rather than through the ICFTU, cooperating selectively with a very few foreign labor organizations, notably with the Histadrut. In 1969, the AFL-CIO withdrew from the ICFTU.

The US–ILO crisis of 1970: a dress rehearsal

The United States' relationship to the ILO has followed a similar course to that of the AFL-CIO to the ICFTU. In 1970, the US Congress suspended payment of contributions to the ILO in retaliation for the appointment of a Soviet citizen, Pavel Astapenko, as an assistant director-general.

Soviet representation in the various organs of the ILO had been an issue since the Soviet Union resumed membership in the organization in 1954. Those who opposed the Soviet presence argued that the Soviet system was incompatible with the ILO's tripartism, on the grounds that neither employers nor trade unions in the Soviet Union were independent of the government. Western employers rallied behind the banner of tripartism. So did the AFL-CIO. But other western trade unionists were more nuanced. The party that favored acceptance of Soviet membership, which included most of the western governments other than the United States, took its stand behind the slogan of universality arguing that all countries should be allowed to join. Both parties won and lost something. Universality was accepted as the rule for membership, while tripartism was ever more emphatically reasserted as the official ideology of the ILO.

To the adherents of tripartism, every step towards giving the Soviet Union the same degree of representation as other major powers seemed to undermine the ILO's ideological legitimacy. When the Soviet government demanded that it be treated like the other major powers in the allocation of top posts in the ILO and specifically that a Soviet citizen be appointed as an assistant director-general this issue immediately gained great symbolic importance.

In terms of practical consequences, this was a nonsense issue. Assistant directors-general are at most consultants and advisers to a director-general who wants to listen to them and at the least (the more usual case) are highly paid supernumeraries. The notion that some kind of communist infiltration and subversion was about to occur in the ILO was a fantasy lending some verisimilitude of reasonableness to American intransigence against the prospective appointment. If international agencies of broad membership were to be ranked according to the extent of western influence, the ILO would come close to the top, trailing only the International Monetary Fund and the World Bank (neither of which has the Soviet Union as a member) and leading by a wide margin the United Nations and bodies like UNCTAD. It was not lack of influence but the fact of diminishing influence that Meany and some other Americans resented, a situation viewed with greater equanimity by their European counterparts.

The Soviet Union had by 1970, in the minds of many government representatives, become the aggrieved party. Having served a fifteen-year apprenticeship in membership, it was still denied some of the accustomed prerogatives of a great power in the ILO, including an assistant director-general's post. The appointment of a Soviet citizen to such a post was by this time widely regarded as inevitable – an opinion shared by the leading US government personnel involved in ILO affairs – though everyone concerned recognized that Meany's steadfast opposition had to be taken into account. It was no longer a question of whether to do it, but of how and when – in particular, how to allow Meany some exit from his "this is the last straw" position.

A personality factor has to be introduced in explaining how this issue developed into an open crisis between the ILO and the United States. The US Congress' decision to cut off the ILO's funds in 1970 was the result of a conflict between Meany and the then-director-general of the ILO, an Englishman, Clarence Wilfred Jenks, two individuals who in fact never met but pursued their own separate collision courses. To say the Congress' action was a consequence of personalities is to imply it might have been avoidable. Possibly it might have been. Jenks' predecessor, David A. Morse, had spent ten years nursing the issue to avoid a confrontation. Morse, an American and an essentially political animal, understood the American viewpoints on the issues, including those with which he may not have agreed. Time had pretty well run out when Morse announced his resignation, and some interpreted his decision as an indication he had reached the limits of his ability to avoid a crisis. Nevertheless, the personality factor should not bear the full weight of the decision; it was more important in determining the manner and the occasion of the crisis than either its causes or outcome.

The political prelude to the Astapenko appointment was the campaign to elect a new director-general. Very little has been written about the electoral politics of international organizations, and when this does become a subject of scholarly study, the election process of the Holy Roman Empire will be found to be a better model than the mass-party politics of modern states. The real process of selecting a director-general is invisible almost entirely to nonparticipants, and most of it is obscure even to those directly involved in the process.

There were two leading candidates to succeed Morse: Jenks and Francis Blanchard. Both were senior serving ILO officials, Jenks of British, Blanchard of French nationality. Jenks was the insider's favorite. He wielded considerable influence in the small inner circle of the ILO's establishment. On Morse's behalf, Jenks had conducted the

435

regular business with members of the ILO's executive board – the Governing Body – which is the group that elects an ILO director-general. In this capacity, he had for a number of years past dispensed the rewards and penalties international secretariats dispose of in pursuit of their political objectives, notably in that form of patronage that consists of arranging the election of chairmen and the distribution of other "honors" prized by those whose careers are bound up with the work of international agencies. Jenks' frequently overbearing behavior in an apparently single-minded pursuit of what he construed to be the ILO's interest provoked a mixture of respect, resentment, and fear among those who had to deal with him. But Jenks and Morse were complementary personalities. Tempers ruffled by Jenks were in turn soothed by the understanding courtesy that characterized his chief. Another source of electoral support for Jenks came from a number of personalities in the international law field – amongst whom he was well known and was himself to be counted – a network of individuals having influential access to some of the governments with electoral votes.

Francis Blanchard was less well known to the ILO Governing Body members although he had served as a senior ILO official for many years. He had been in charge of ILO technical cooperation programs, and was a more familiar figure among the Third World government agencies that received ILO assistance than among the western government, employer, and trade union delegates who were the predominant influences in the Governing Body. Blanchard was the candidate of the French government and his campaign rested very largely on the considerable efforts made by French diplomacy on his behalf, efforts which in the final outcome failed where they should have been most effective, among France's partners in the European Economic Community. The British government by contrast seemed somewhat indifferent to Jenks' election prospects.

Just a few weeks before the election, Jenks had a critical conversation with the US government delegate, George Hildebrand, at which the US position opposing appointment of a Soviet assistant director-general was discussed. What transpired is not clear, but the outcome is.[31] The Americans thought they had a sympathetic understanding from Jenks. Jenks maintained afterwards he had not committed himself to anything, which was probably correct in a purely formal sense. American government, employer, and trade union support swung to Jenks. Meany's representative on the Governing Body, Rudy Faupl, the US worker representative, went to work on Jenks' behalf. Meany's man in the State Department, George P. Delaney, also came to Geneva during the election session.[32] Blanchard was supported by the Soviets, and so could be represented as likely to appoint a Soviet assistant director-general. Jenks, according to his active American supporters, was the candidate of the "free world." The Federal Republic of Germany's electors followed the American lead. So did the Japanese, until then undeclared. Jenks won by two votes over Blanchard. American support had been decisive.

Some four weeks later, Jenks convened George Hildebrand to review various items of business. As the interview drew to a close, Jenks casually (according to Hildebrand) said: "And by the way, I should tell you that as a result of administrative actions taken before I assumed this office, I am appointing a Russian to become assistant director-general."[33] Jenks made it clear to Hildebrand that he was being informed, not consulted. It was not Jenks' habit to expect much conversation from his visitors. Hildebrand absorbed the blow and left, and Jenks seems to have thought for a moment that his difficult moment was over.

When the news reached Washington, Meany was outraged. In his own frame of reference, he had been double-crossed – the ultimate offense in Meany's behavioral code. Even if Jenks had never made any explicit commitment, there certainly was, in the minds of Meany and the other Americans concerned, an implicit understanding. No one could accept the kind of arm-twisting electoral support they had provided without incurring an obligation to show some consideration for the terms they had stipulated. If this was not clear to Jenks, it was clear to anyone nurtured in the culture of American politics. It was not so much what Jenks had done that irked, but how he had done it, and the timing of his act. If he had waited a decent interval, if he had given some warning of his intentions, demonstrated the inevitability of the appointment, and allowed some of the steam to blow off, then there might have been some chance of getting past American objections. There might even have been a chance of arousing the sympathy of some Americans for his predicament. But the way the act was done, it appeared as a slap in the face, a declaration of independence from those to whom he owed most, a show of arrogance in the hubris of a power fantasy.

Meany did not hesitate. He called Congressman John J. Rooney, chairman of the subcommittee of the House Committee on

Appropriations that deals with the US contributions to international organizations. Rooney brought the subcommittee into session. Meany's statement was relatively restrained and statesmanlike. Rooney's performance had color. "Mr. Jenks needs to be rocked," he said. "I know of only one way to rock him, cut off his water."[34] And turning to Samuel DePalma, assistant secretary for International Organization Affairs in the State Department: "I am going . . . to ask Mr. DePalma to telephone to Ambassador Rimestad [head of the US permanent delegation to Geneva] and tell him to hotfoot it over to Mr. Jenks and tell him before nightfall that there will be no money for ILO as far as this subcommittee is concerned, and I think we can do it."[35] The subcommittee's action was supported by the House and the Senate. The United States ceased payment of its contributions to the ILO, and did not resume them until some two years later. The State Department made a formal gesture to tell the Congress that this action put the United States into an improper legal posture. For the Congress, the telling factor was that George Meany was displeased about a matter falling within his generally recognized sphere of influence, and the members were not going to change their stand until they had a signal from him.

Clarence Wilfred Jenks became an important figure in a most esoteric realm of politics, the interior world of international organizations. As these organizations increase in numbers and as their functions impinge upon public policies that affect the lives of people, there will be more demand for public scrutiny of their political processes and for accountability by their principal officers. Jenks' career ended on the threshold of such a development. He himself considered scrutiny and accountability with the gravest suspicion as likely to weaken and undermine the enterprise of building a future world order. Among those who gave Jenks their support, overawed by his personal energy and command of detail, very few probably had much insight into the workings of his mind.[36]

Central to his ideas was a vision of history as moving away from a world of nation-states, the lingering institutions of the past, towards a future world government. International organizations were the transition; the ILO in particular was to be thought of as a nucleus of future world government. But it would have to fulfil its destiny by stealth, since the true goals could not be openly proclaimed for fear of provoking obstructions. He disdained other international officials who did not seem entirely privy to this occult process. The ILO had been his whole adult life, since leaving Cambridge in the early 1930s, and he identified his person with this notion of its mission.

Jenks' concept of politics was that of the nineteenth-century *carbonari* – a conspiracy, exciting to the initiated, justified as being for the ultimate benefit of mankind, and requiring absolute loyalty and obedience to the cause. The members of this covert enterprise could be thought of as arranged in concentric circles, beginning at the outer edges with faithful executants who were allowed only the most general idea of the purposes they served, and moving through inner circles of initiates to whom a somewhat fuller version of its goals could be revealed. But only the chief really knew the whole purpose and ultimate goal.

In his legal writings, Jenks exalted the authority of the executive head and sought to limit severely any judicial control over the discretionary powers of the executive's administration. An international tribunal as a check or control upon executive authority, he wrote, "cannot substitute its conscience or sense of fairness for the conscience or sense of fairness of the administration."[37] Not only did he defend this authoritarianism in principle as a writer of legal treatises, but after he became director-general the tendency to secretiveness in his official behavior was exacerbated by his deteriorating relations with the United States, and he concentrated decision making in his own person.

In Max Weber's distinction between formal and substantive rationality, Jenks conformed to the formal type. He tried to bridge the hiatus between formal rationality and the conditions of the real world, by the manipulation of paradox, in two characteristic patterns. One pattern was to affirm a general rule, and then try to arrange the decisions of ILO committees so as to be consistent with this rule, despite the fact that formal observance of the rule might be contradicted by reality. Theoretical rules of law thus appeared to be given formal support though disregarded in substance. Much of his work in the field of legal protection of trade union rights followed this pattern; it built up a record of precedents through ILO decisions that may have impressed some international lawyers, but left many trade unionists and others skeptical as to practical results.[38] Repressive regimes could gain kudos from acquiescence in formal ILO procedures without making substantial changes in real conditions. The other pattern of manipulating paradox was to enunciate a general principle, and then to contradict it in an appended operational rule of conduct – giving the prudential exception priority over the principle affirmed.

As a political institution, the ILO was a limited monarchy.[39] Substantive initiative depended very largely on the director-general, and the political process consisted of an inflow of demands and influences upon the director-general, who had to determine what could be done with a keen sense of the possible, in an appraisal of his real limits. Jenks' actions in this office, however, conformed more to the different model of divine right monarchy. He sought counsel not to learn what he might be able to do but to gain support or acquiescence for doing what he was already clear in his own mind ought to be done. Though he was careful to secure proper approval for his actions, his energy and determination swayed the judgement of those who shared with him responsibility for decisions, and thus he may often have been misled as to the extent of real support he had. A psycho-historian might ponder the influences shaping such a personality in his formative years, but such speculations are beside the point here. What is important is that a person having such ideas, pursued with such personal vigor, should have assumed the executive leadership of the ILO at this critical juncture.

The contradictions of ideology

The rise of the corporative state, the spread of enterprise corporatism, and the international extension of American capitalism are the three salient and related structural tendencies already noted as affecting world labor relations. In the perspective of history, the issues between the ILO and the United States are of interest only insofar as they tell us something about these major movements, and the conflict of personalities only insofar as individuals may hasten or deter them. Ideology is the crux of the matter.

Through its history, the ILO's ideological commitment has retained a certain ambiguity. "Tripartism," the key concept, when considered in a broader and more general context than the specifically American one discussed above, can be interpreted to mean two very different things. One interpretation is the institutionalization of conflict, in other words a recognition that class struggle is a continuing feature of the production process, but that it can be regulated and moderated by collective bargaining and similar procedures.[40] The other possible interpretation of tripartism is non-conflictual, envisioning the integration of the worker with management in a harmony contrived or sustained by public policy; in other words, a corporatist interpretation. The latter, the corporatist version, has had the edge in recent times.

Managerial ideologies of production relations in both the United States and the Soviet Union are corporatist in essence, though neither American nor Soviet ideologies feel comfortable with the term.[41] American enterprise corporatism draws upon social psychology to make the worker feel more integrated within the enterprise. Soviet doctrine declares that the class struggle has been superseded under socialism. Dominant doctrines in continental western Europe, notably the "social partnership" concept consecrated in the official jargon of the European Communities, express the corporatist tendency. So does the "social contract" proclaimed by former prime minister Harold Wilson and chancellor of the exchequer Denis Healey in Britain in the 1960s and 1970s. In the industrialized enclaves of less-developed countries, two variants of corporatism prevail: one is an enterprise corporatism in the form of bureaucratic paternalism administered by the local branches of multinational corporations with or without compliant house unions; the other and growing form is a state corporatism in which unions are controlled by the political elites. The name "corporatism" still carries an aura of illegitimacy from its erstwhile association with Fascism, but the substance of the corporatist idea is triumphant.

The established trade unions in the leading western industrialized countries have not posed a serious challenge to the new corporatism. By and large, as established institutions, they have been susceptible to attraction into a more integrated relationship with business and government in the determination of economic policy. Opposition to the new corporatism is now apparent mainly in rank-and-file labor protest in western Europe. It may also be latent (though repressed) among workers in the industrializing areas of the Third World. In France and Italy, where unions have in the past been but weakly represented within plants, spontaneous protest has periodically erupted, pushing the union leadership along with it. The events of May 1968 were only the most widespread and explosive of a longer series of outbursts. British industrial relations have been characterized by wildcat strikes led by shop stewards in defiance of union leaders; indeed, the "social contract" can be interpreted as an attempt by a conservative established union leadership with support from industry and government to regain its slipping control over the labor movement.

All over Europe, there is evidence of radical rank-and-file challenge to established union leadership. Among the established union structures, only the Italian CGIL seems to date to have been able to respond effectively to this challenge. Despite the unstructured, unbureaucratized nature of the opposition movement, a communications network exists that carries the news of local worker actions, encourages a sense of common struggle, and mobilizes support. No opposition of comparable effectiveness confronts the American labor establishment.[42] None has gained entrance to the ILO.

From the late 1950s, a specifically American doctrine of industrial relations was given pride of place in the ILO as the rationale for its programs. Two books expressing this tendency of thought, both products of this period, were John Dunlop's *Industrial Relations Systems*[43] and the collaborative work, financed by the Ford Foundation, of Clark Kerr, John Dunlop, Frederick Harbison, and Charles Myers, entitled *Industrialism and Industrial Man*.[44] Both works owed something to the milieu of the ILO. Dunlop's was written in Geneva during a sabbatical leave; and the leaders of the Ford project held numerous conferences and consultations at the ILO in the course of preparing their book. But the main impact was in the other direction. The American scholars provided a reformulation of operational ideology for the ILO.

This ideology stressed cooperative problem solving between labor and management, and it deprecated conflict. Conflict may have been inevitable in the early stages of industrialization, but had ceased to be either necessary or significant. Industrializing elites – not labor movements – were the really significant factors in industrialization. They learned how to manage conflict. Technicians were increasingly important as accessories to the industrializing elites, helping the elites smooth out the rough spots and devise acceptable solutions. Where conflict occurred, it was often but a consequence of misperception: the necessities of development, the "logic of industrialism," had been misunderstood by someone, probably the workers. Better communication and more use of social psychology techniques could demonstrate to the workers the need to adapt and at the same time give them greater satisfaction in their work. This was the application to labor relations of the great conviction of American capitalism that advertising creates reality.

Any institution that endures runs the risk of becoming the prisoner of its own success. The ILO's tripartism had survived the ordeals to which the Great Depression and World War II subjected international organization, because the ILO represented the most powerful tendency of the time in sociopolitical structure, the emergence of the corporative form of state. The ILO's system of representation gave preeminence to the industrial establishments leading the movement towards corporatism; and during the 1960s, the ILO espoused an ideology (made in the US) consistent with this movement.

Acute social issues were, however, developing outside of the corporatist partnership, beyond the sphere of the industrial establishments, with which the ILO was ill-equipped to deal and even indisposed by its structure of representation and its dominant ideology to recognize. There was, first of all, the issue of land reform in the poor countries, which could affect a much more numerous though far less powerful body of producers than those with whose interests the industrial establishments were concerned. Second, there were the looming masses of social marginals, clustered in the burgeoning shantytowns, *bidonvilles, barrios, favelas* – different names assigned by particular cultures to this almost universal form of human misery. Third, and perhaps least recognized of all, was a tendency to design the production processes of modern industry so as to use increasing proportions of cheaper, more malleable, less effectively unionized semi-skilled labor.

Such issues were most unlikely to be raised through the formal structures of the ILO. The only real chance that they might intrude into the orthodoxy of conventional thinking would be through some elements within the ILO staff that had become sensitive to them; and any such staff members would have to be encouraged by a director-general ready and able to mobilize support for new initiatives from outside the range of interests conventionally represented in the ILO. For this reason, the substantive issues of policy were in practice often determined by decisions regarding bureaucratic management – decisions as to who was given scope to develop which kinds of programs – more than by votes on declarations of principle in ILO conferences.

One way in which an established institution can ward off the risk of arteriosclerosis and mental atrophy is to harbor in its midst a ginger group of critics whose acknowledged role is to challenge policy orthodoxy, to redefine issues, and to propose alternative methods of dealing with them. The International Institute for Labor Studies, founded within the framework of the ILO in 1960, might have performed a role of this kind.

443

The degree of autonomy the Institute should have within the framework of the ILO was a matter of dispute from the beginning. Autonomy was the necessary condition for a critical and independent attitude towards official doctrine. The United States representatives opposed autonomy and wanted the Institute to be an educational program controlled by the ILO administration. They also minimized the Institute's research role. Research would have constituted a capability for intellectual independence. The compromise decision did not close out the possibility of Institute autonomy, but fixed close administrative links to the ILO. Whether or not the Institute could perform the ginger-group role would depend more on how it was to develop than on its constitutional mandate.

During the early phase of its existence, the Institute did enjoy the tolerance of the ILO's formal structures, and the small staff of the Institute together with some outside scholars made modest progress towards perspectives alternative to those of the ILO's official ideology. This work was not inspired by any very coherent or preconceived viewpoint, but it was committed to a critical questioning of received opinion. From 1970, the main effort went into a study of future prospects in industrial relations. This study quickly found conventional notions of industrial relations to be too confining, and it began to broaden the notion so as to cover all of the structures of social relations that arise in production processes – pre-industrial and post-industrial as well as industrial. Estimates showed that the structures favored by the ILO, those characterized by collective bargaining, covered only some 9 percent of the world labor force, while other structures more or less screened out of the ILO's official consciousness governed the vast majority of the world's workers.[45] This study might have been one step towards redefining issues, but it was interrupted and discontinued in 1972.

The change in executive heads in 1970 demonstrated how the intellectual independence of the Institute had rested upon the fragile basis of an understanding between one director-general and the director of the Institute. Morse, though holding the office of director-general for more than twenty years, had always remained something of an outsider, critical of settled institutional routines and ready to encourage innovation. His was an American impatience to achieve something new, a desire to preside over a growing concern, rather than any fundamentally hostile regard towards the established hegemony. He saw the value of allowing expression of criticism, while at the same time

444

keeping a close control over its practical consequences. Jenks, by contrast, was the embodiment of the ILO's conventional doctrine, which he took pride in having personally articulated. He was the essence of the insider. In his speech to the ILO staff the day he became director-general, he made a point of declaring: "I am one of you." To his mind, the Institute could only be allowed to exist as a disciplined instrument to propagate the true and established faith. With characteristic hyperbole, he had declared: "The ILO has no ideology but it has ideals, and its ideals, which transcend ideologies, are fundamental, universal and eternal."[46]

Bureaucratic controls and cover-up: the mechanisms of hegemony

Since new program initiatives depended more on bureaucratic mandates than on the formal votes of conferences, they could be stifled by a conventional director-general even more easily than encouraged by an innovating one. The relative obscurity of these bureaucratic decisions has made of them means for the effective maintenance of hegemony. Several instances will illustrate this.

The new director-general set about to establish his personal control over the Institute, to eradicate its intellectual autonomy and propensity to take a critical view and to integrate it within the ILO bureaucracy. He used his control over administrative procedures to intervene in personnel matters and he exploited some latent resentments to gain support for intervention.

Some worker and employer members of the Governing Body thought of the Institute mainly as disposing of fellowships to finance attendance at courses given in Geneva, and there was a demand for study trips of this kind among officials of national employer associations and trade unions. "Tripartism" now became justification for control by the worker and employer group whips over the selection of Institute fellowship holders. Another source of latent opposition to the Institute took the form of a persistent suspicion of research. Research can be controversial, as Jenks was soon able to demonstrate. He capitulated with alacrity to the first criticism of an Institute publication that came before him.

This complaint came from a Brazilian government representative and concerned an article on efforts to organize the rural people of the

Nordeste written by a former Brazilian minister of labor in the Goulart government.[47] Jenks' statement to the Institute board in response to the complaint was a classic example of his use of paradox: "There can never be any question about the principle of freedom of expression in the ILO or in any body associated with the ILO . . . But, equally, there can never be any question that freedom of expression can be something altogether disruptive if it is not exercised in a responsible manner and that we have a quite special obligation as an international labor organization consisting of member states to practice a strict code of responsibility in the exercise of freedom of expression."[48] The practical consequence of this statement was the introduction of self-censorship in Institute publications comparable to that applied to ILO publications – a substantive denial of intellectual independence of the Institute accompanied by formal affirmation of its freedom of expression. The ultimate control was the director-general's insistence on pronouncing what Jenks called his *nihil obstat* upon all publications issued by the Institute and even on publications by Institute staff members in their personal capacities. Over this issue, the director of the Institute resigned, and he was replaced by one more compliant to the director-general's will.[49] The potential for independent criticism in the Institute was thereby stifled.

Soon thereafter the newly disciplined Institute became linked with an episode illustrating the spreading strength of enterprise corporatism. The events at the origin of this episode actually took place earlier, during 1970–71, when unions were endeavoring to organize the 40,000 white collar employees of the British-based chemical giant Imperial Chemical Industries (ICI), but the implications for the Institute of these events were revealed only between 1972 and 1974.

The major growth area for unions in the industrial countries has for some years past been among white-collar workers, and perhaps for this reason – because they have more ground to make up – white-collar unions have frequently been more radical than their blue-collar counterparts. Successful unionization of ICI's staff might have been a turning point in British industrial relations, tipping the balance not only towards effective organization of white-collar workers as a whole but also enhancing the strength of the more radical forces in the labor movement in general. Indeed, the issue was perceived by the ICI management as being significant for the future of industrial relations in Britain, and not merely as a problem specific to ICI. ICI's initial success in blocking the unions, conversely, represented a strengthening of enterprise corporatism.

This corporate success appears to have been achieved through a deliberate strategy. Management was aware of employee discontent with the staff representation scheme in ICI. Among the staff, some were in favor of reforming the existing scheme, some in favor of an in-house staff association, some for a union. ICI management arranged for an attitude survey or "consultative exercise" to be carried out among the staff on this issue. In order to achieve the result desired by management, three conditions had to be fulfilled. First, the staff had to be persuaded that management was ready to make some changes in the existing representation scheme, without moving to full collective bargaining. Thus the alternative in the minds of staff would not be either the union or the unsatisfactory existing scheme, but rather the union versus some future scheme of representation within the corporation which might be improved in undefined ways. Secondly, a third party should be introduced into the situation to conduct a survey of staff opinion on representation, a party that would have credentials as impartial and independent. A third and clinching aspect of the corporate strategy was to have this "independent" party sufficiently within management control so as both to manipulate and to legitimate the results of the survey.

The job of conducting the survey was contracted to the Tavistock Institute of Human Relations, but as part of the arrangement ICI inserted an outsider as "adviser" in the Tavistock survey team. Tavistock was required by the terms of the contract to consult this "adviser" on the formulation of the questionnaire, on the analysis and interpretation of the results of the survey, and in the writing of the reports emanating from the "consultation" of ICI staff. The person so inserted into the Tavistock team was ICI's guarantee the exercise would work out as envisaged.

The person who played this role was the same who later became the new director of the ILO Institute. At this time he was an ILO official and member of the Institute staff, though neither knew of his ICI contract. ICI management had represented him as an independent person – a "professor" from the ILO. To the officers of the union that was trying to organize the ICI staff, the Association of Scientific, Technical, and Managerial Staffs (ASTMS), headed by Clive Jenkins, he was introduced as a member of the Tavistock team. In fact, his

447

contract stipulated that his role was to work "opposite the other inter-ested parties, particularly the union," and management clearly regarded him as being on its side in devising "strategy opposite unions." The ASTMS had from the outset denounced the "consulta-tive exercise" as an anti-union trick and warned Tavistock against becoming involved in it. The survey produced the expected "find-ings" that a majority of ICI employees did not favor joining a union, a conclusion publicized by ICI in March 1971. (Subsequently, without benefit of a management-sponsored "consultation," the ICI staff voted overwhelmingly for unionization.)

The story of how the unions were undone at ICI on this occasion became public knowledge later, through an article published in the British weekly *New Statesman* in December 1972.[50] Clive Jenkins shortly thereafter demanded that the ILO repudiate the new Institute director for his role in the ICI affair. Jenks delayed replying to Jenkins and he officially ignored the *New Statesman* story as well as a second report with details of the incident that appeared in the *Sunday Times* in June 1973.[51] He reiterated expressions of confidence in the new Institute director to members of the Institute Board and to the officers of the ILO Governing Body. But Jenkins' tenacity matched Jenks' obstinacy. A meeting between the two was finally set for October 1973.

Before this meeting could take place, Jenks broke under the mount-ing pressures upon him. He was not only squeezed financially and criticized personally from the United States, but in addition was under attack from African representatives in the ILO Conference and Gov-erning Body over issues concerning the Portuguese African colonies. Rumors circulated, only to be denied, that he would leave to become a judge on the World Court or serve some other international legal function. The pressures upon him accentuated both his inherent pref-erence for centralized, secretive, personal management and also a compulsive speechmaking that led him to travel constantly to carry his message to any and every audience open to him. He collapsed and died suddenly in Rome during October 1973.

Jenks' notion of the conduct appropriate to the director-generalship was cut from the whole cloth of classic functionalism, in the spirit of David Mitrany; but the consequences of his actions demonstrated the *reductio ad absurdum* of functionalism.[c] Subjectively (in terms of

---

[c] Mitrany, a Romanian exile in London during the war, had been a critic of Marx from a rural perspective. While employed at Lever Brothers he wrote a seminal pamphlet on postwar world order, *A Working Peace System: An Argument for the Functional Devel-*

intentions), the goal Jenks pursued was to enhance the independent role of international organization through the monarchic authority of its executive head. Objectively (in consequences), Jenks' absolutist style undermined the authority of the office he held, his doctrine of tripartism made the ILO an international advocate of the corporative state, and his attitude in the ICI case encouraged enterprise corporatism. The ILO under his direction became more than ever before the expression of an ideology of production relations characteristic of dominant American capitalism – at the very time that United States political support for the organization was being withdrawn.

In the era of Watergate, American opinion became attuned to the idea that a cover-up of unethical or illegal political activity is a complex, consciously orchestrated, and unusual conspiracy. Watergate, in fact, was exceptional in making explicit and visible a process that goes on all the time in almost any durable power relationship, a process that is often barely conscious and is nearly always ignored or expunged from memory. Hegemony is supported by an opinion-molding activity that devises interpretations of events consistent with established power, that eliminates interpretations that contradict orthodoxy. Nearly everyone cooperates in this process. In practice it enables individuals to avoid the dilemma of deciding whether or not to take positions that might prove costly in personal terms. It makes life easier.

The ICI incident was a case in point. Apart from the two mentioned accounts in the British press, there was no public reference to it – although the *threat* of publicity influenced the handling of the matter. Given the stringency of British libel law, the amount of specific detail included in the *New Statesman* article indicated its author had some pretty hard evidence. But no public response ever came from the ILO. Jenks was widely considered to be a strict guardian of standards of conduct of the international civil service. One might have expected that he would have been most severe in his judgement. Criticism of the new Institute director's conduct could, in this case, however, be interpreted as being indirectly a criticism of Jenks, who had invested him with confidence, and thus, by confusion of persons and principles, as an attack on the standards Jenks claimed to represent. Jenks' own legal doctrine could be cited to strengthen his position; no legal

opment of International Organisation (London: Royal Institute of International Affairs/ Oxford University Press, 1943). Most recently he has been a professor in the Institute for Advanced Study at Princeton University.

enquiry into the case was in order because no other body is "entitled to substitute its own conscience and sense of fairness for the conscience and sense of fairness of the administration."[52] Had the Nixon administration been beneficiary to such a doctrine, recent American history might have been different.

The inner circle of the ILO Governing Body acquiesced in the avoidance of any official enquiry. This may seem surprising on the part of the trade unionists involved, who included Cyril Plant, the British labor delegate to the ILO, later to become chairman of the Trades Union Congress, and Joe Morris, the newly elected president of the Canadian Labor Congress and vice chairman of the Governing Body. How could such prominent trade unionists put themselves in a position that might appear as condoning anti-union activity? The most convincing explanation would be a "don't rock the boat" attitude. They were, after all, part of the ILO establishment, confronting jointly with Jenks the problem of American financial cutbacks. Their instinct was to support the director-general, for whom they showed great respect. These trade unionists were also representative of the larger establishment of the western world. Clive Jenkins was by comparison an upstart labor leader who was "rocking the boat" in Britain with his drive to organize white-collar workers, and furthermore, his radical style was irksome to more conventional members of the TUC General Council. Representatives of established labor could, in the cloistered conclave of the ILO, avoid having to take a public stand on such a potentially embarrassing issue, confident that the hegemonic process would screen out inconvenient facts and in effect make it a non-issue.[53]

ILO staff members also were confronted by a contradiction between, on the one hand, the standards of conduct which the vast majority of them were proud to observe scrupulously and, on the other, the published revelations about one of their colleagues recently promoted above the status to which a long service officer could reasonably aspire. Yet there was no general outcry in this quarter. Why? The cue from the director-general was to suppress comment in the interests of the organization. The interest of the organization has, indeed, become in the transnational world of multinational corporations and international bureaucracies what *raison d'état* was for the sixteenth century builders of the nation-state – the Machiavellism of a new elite. Loyalty required cover-up. Most officials resolved the conflict by preferring not to know about it. Some were denied this luxury. Administrators whose professional conscience urged the course of enquiry and defense of ethical principles of conduct were transformed by events into institutional instruments of obfuscation.

Not all members of the ILO and Institute staffs reacted in this way. For a very few the incident was an affront to the integrity of the international civil service. These were discouraged from expressing their opinion. One member of the Institute staff (a scholar whose independent work is published in Britain and the United States) did protest by addressing an internal factual memorandum to top ILO officials. Jenks' reaction was immediate. The protester was transferred to another department of the ILO at ten days' notice for "disturbing the serene atmosphere" of the Institute. No comment was made on the substance of his memorandum, but he was told by a senior ILO official that the memorandum was "improper" and that rather than seek to expose corruption he was duty-bound to "obey" his superior, the Institute director, as the director-general could be relied upon to deal with improper conduct. He very shortly thereafter left the ILO; and though he continued to seek redress, it was more in outrage at the travesty on the integrity both of social science and of international civil service ethics that he had witnessed than because of any real hope the shabby treatment he had received would be remedied.

This and other acts of protest cannot, however, be regarded as entirely without effect. Many people witness to these events, some of quite modest circumstances, took personal risks in collecting and piecing together and then in bringing forward the evidence. They showed that weak though the challenge may be, hegemony no longer goes unchallenged, and that the cover-up process in large organizations has become more difficult.

Jenks' former rival, Francis Blanchard, was elected to succeed him as director-general. Clive Jenkins, waiting a decent interval, renewed his complaint and threatened public disclosure if the ILO did not rectify the situation. Blanchard ultimately forced the offending official's resignation. Jenkins obtained satisfaction. ILO people expunged the incident from memory. The *dramatis personae* – dead or departed – might never have existed. Harmony prevailed.

The experience of the Institute tested the possibilities of critical perspectives developing within an established organization framework; but the Institute's resources were small and its work did not impinge directly on ILO programs and policy. The World Employment Program (WEP), by contrast, was an ILO program to which a considerable portion of ILO resources were allocated, and it did have direct policy implications. The WEP illustrates another way in which hegemony has worked through tripartism to constrain and control innovation in the ILO.

The WEP was presented as the centerpiece of the ILO's fiftieth anniversary celebration in 1969, as a demonstration that the organization was alive and well and ready to deal with vital issues of world social policy. In its origins, the WEP was linked to the first United Nations Development Decade, that of the 1960s, and ILO officials hoped it would become a central aim of the second development decade – by making employment expansion a major goal of economic development. The program differed from conventional technical assistance (which was concerned piecemeal with a list of specialized services), by its comprehensive approach towards defining a coherent set of measures to make the attainment of employment objectives an integral part of the overall national economic policy. The program was directed as much towards a more equitable income distribution as towards employment; indeed, the rationale for employment expansion was that jobs are the most effective way of providing incomes to the poorest segment of the population.

It did not take long for the WEP to encounter obstructions from the ILO's tripartite structure. One of the program's first ventures, a policy study for the government of Colombia made under the direction of Dudley Seers of the University of Sussex Development Institute, recommended restraint on wage increases for workers in the industrial enclaves as a means of expanding investment to generate employment outside these enclaves.[54] The report was attacked by one of the Colombian trade unions – organizers of enclave workers – and this criticism was echoed among members of the ILO Governing Body. The issue served notice that any further employment-policy missions would be expected to work through the organized employer and labor interests, which, of course, meant those already satisfied with regard to employment. There was an implicit contradiction here between the goal of a program that implied change in social structures to attain greater social equality, and the operational or political requirement that the program work through the existing structures. The then-director-general, Wilfred Jenks, gave the necessary assurances that tripartism would be observed in the further development of the program.

The latent contradiction could not but recur. The program's underlying rationale recognized that its objective could only be attained if new social forces became actively aroused in working for it. Organizing the unorganized, and particularly the poor in rural and urban centers of the Third World, became a theme of the WEP. So did land reform, the one measure likely to put sufficient resources into the hands of the poor to enable them to produce for themselves. Furthermore, considerations critical of multinational corporations crept into the literature of the WEP: the record suggested that expansion of multinationals into the Third World had, indeed, not been very effective in expanding employment, whatever other benefits might be adduced.[55] All these points met with strong opposition in the American "tripartite" circles dealing with the ILO, as being inconsistent with the expansion of private investment in a liberal world economy that US policy maintained is the only admissible world-development strategy. American delegates were also suspicious that the staff of the WEP was working closely with the Group of 77, UNCTAD fashion, and sought to snuff out this tendency before it had a chance to develop. (The fact that ILO documents now linked the WEP with United Nations' resolutions for a New International Economic Order seemed to confirm these suspicions.) The issue became acute, following the US notice of withdrawal, in connection with a World Employment Conference convened in Geneva in June 1976.[56]

The World Employment Conference itself was hardly determining for the future of the program. It became a negotiation between the Group of 77, on the one hand, which presented a set of proposals, and governments, employers, and worker delegates representative of the industrial establishments of the rich countries, on the other. A long text recounting principles and program objectives was ultimately adopted by consensus, being a much watered-down version reluctantly acceptable to the rich countries of what was wanted by the poor-country delegates.[57] In this, the conference differed in no way from other international conferences dealing with world economy questions. The text itself is probably of little consequence, except as an indicator of the minimum of consensus attainable. Of more practical importance was the leadership and orientation of future ILO work on the WEP. And in this respect, important changes were made by Director-General Blanchard following the conference. The director of the program, Louis Emmerij, left the ILO for an academic post in the Netherlands, and his departure was followed by that of one of his principal collaborators, Keith Griffin, an American scholar from

Oxford.[58] Together they had given entrepreneurial and intellectual leadership to the WEP and made the program's staff into a dynamic and distinctive nucleus within the staid bureaucracy of the ILO. The new management has a mandate to reduce the scale of the WEP and to bring it into line with ILO orthodoxy. In the WEP as in the case of the Institute, hegemony avoids open confrontation on clear issues, and works more subtly and effectively through bureaucratic channels and personnel changes.

One further instance illustrates the connection between ideological orientation and bureaucratic changes. This concerns the International Industrial Relations Association (IIRA) which is a professional and academic group, analogous to international associations of economists, sociologists, and political scientists, but combining those disciplines that bear upon the industrial relations field. The Institute played a critical role in bringing the IIRA into existence in 1966 and the director of the Institute was elected secretary of the association. At first, the Institute promoted a continuing enlargement of the IIRA from an initial base that had been rooted in a predominantly Anglo-Saxon view of industrial relations towards a broader representation of the range of differing perspectives such as was expressed in the Institute's own work. After the crisis recounted above that reduced the Institute to conformity, the incentive to broaden and diversify was removed, and the IIRA remained a reflection of the dominant ideology of "industrial relations." John Dunlop was president of the IIRA during the year in which, as United States secretary of labor, he was a party to the US notice of withdrawal from the ILO.

In 1974, Albert Tévoédjre, the senior African official of the ILO and unsuccessful rival to Francis Blanchard for the director-generalship, was appointed director of the Institute by Blanchard. Tévoédjre convened in January 1976 an international symposium on the social implications of a New International Economic Order. This initiative was the subject of grumbling within the ILO establishment because it seemed to give a somewhat larger voice to the Third World opinions and to the more radical labor movements of western Europe than had been usual in ILO "expert" meetings. Blanchard dissociated himself from this initiative. The office-holders of the IIRA were clearly unhappy now in continuing the link with the Institute and Blanchard agreed to have a unit of the regular ILO bureaucracy take over the work of the IIRA secretariat.[59] Tévoédjre, now cut off from the IIRA, launched through the Institute a world association for the study of social perspectives that leans towards a Third World constituency.

Inferences

Some inferences are to be drawn from the foregoing.

First, how important was executive leadership? The executive heads were witting or unwitting instruments of hegemony, not shapers of hegemony. Jenks made gestures of independent leadership and took more verbal initiatives than anyone now cares to remember. Blanchard affected the lower profile of consensus seeker, never straying far from a cautious orthodoxy. Apart from these differences in style and in the ways individuals reacted to these two men, the practical consequences of their respective tenures of office have been virtually identical. Jenks may have crystallized American discontent by his manner; but Blanchard was powerless to alter the course of American policy on withdrawal, despite his more conciliatory nature. Both ensured that the ILO bureaucracy and the ideology that guided its work conformed to dominant American perspectives. With the United States on the verge of withdrawal, the ILO remained more than ever an expression of American world power. Personal satisfactions apart, it did not seem to matter very much who the director-general was.

Second, will the fact that hegemony prevails lead the United States to remain as a member of the ILO by scrapping its notice of withdrawal before it becomes effective in the autumn of 1977? Beyond underlining the imprudence of predicting something that will be decided a few months at most from the (initial) date of publication of this essay, it can be pointed out that the two questions are not necessarily linked. Hegemony could well prevail *and* the United States leave. The US government's letter of withdrawal from the ILO purports to be a bargaining ploy. It holds out the prospect that if sufficient satisfaction were to be given to the United States, the withdrawal procedure might be stopped. What exactly might constitute such satisfaction is by no means clear from the letter – no specifics are itemized. The responsible US officials are free to declare themselves satisfied or dissatisfied. The decision in practice rests with George Meany, whose political credit derives from AFL-CIO support for Governor Carter in his campaign for the presidency of the United States. Since Meany has not been able to gain satisfaction on more substantial issues, presumably the Carter administration would be reluctant to challenge his writ in ILO matters. Meany's past record suggests a preference for unilateral control of international labor relationships through structures like the AIFLD.

Third, how would a US withdrawal from the ILO fit into the broader picture of US participation in international organization? There is much current evidence that US policy is tending to limit commitment to existing universal international organizations, and to move selectively towards the use of agencies (old, new, or ad hoc) more effectively under US control. The World Bank is a case of an old agency still substantially controlled by the United States. The International Atomic Energy Agency is an example of a new one. These agencies are important because they deal in real material resources. But the same tendency can be noted in respect of what may be thought of as ideological resources. The AFL-CIO retreat, first from the ICFTU and now from the ILO, towards increasing reliance upon a network directly controlled by an American union–business–government complex shows a movement along a parallel course. The State Department viewpoint has been one of caution and prudence with regard to the United States abandoning its position in any major international forum, including the ILO. The revisionist policy expressed by former US representative to the United Nations (now US Senator from New York), Daniel P. Moynihan, finds selective unilateralism, of which withdrawal from the ILO would be an instance, a convenient way of signaling a tougher stance on international relations generally.

Fourth, supposing the United States did leave the ILO – and the credibility of the revisionist policy might suffer if the United States did not leave after all – what would be the consequences for the ILO, particularly as regards its future orientation? There would, of course, be a considerable budget reduction to adjust to, since other states are not likely to want to make up the 25 percent US contribution. The budget cut seems likely to be dramatic because the ILO administrators have not made use of the two-year period of notice to scale down expenses significantly, apparently taking the position, in public at any rate, that US withdrawal was unthinkable. But assuming the budget crisis could be managed successfully over a transition, a deeper question concerns the future structure of influence in an ILO lacking US participation.

The tripartite structure of representation has given the ILO a western bias, despite its universal membership. The ILO was never able to gain support in Third World countries comparable to that which made

UNCTAD and UNIDO *their* organizations. The experience with the WEP suggests that an option of Third World political support was effectively closed out. Nor can executive leadership and the ILO bureaucracy be counted upon as a possible source of innovation and renewal. The monarchic structure centered in the director-generalship was greatly weakened by the Jenks incumbency, and the consequence of guarding against a repetition of chaotic verbal initiatives has been to enclose the director-generalship in an unprecedented mediocrity of talent. The myth of Soviet influence, alive in the imaginations of American delegates, must also be discounted.

This leaves the countries of western Europe as the mainstay of the ILO. From them came the original impetus and sustaining support for the organization. There is every indication that western Europe, and particularly the Federal Republic of Germany and the *Deutsche Gewerkschaftsbund* (German Confederation of Trade Unions, or DGB), are ready to assume the mantle of leadership. Setting aside the consequences for individual careers (about which much of the activity of bureaucratic politics is concerned), the broader political structures would remain largely unaffected by such an outcome. Hegemony, reconstructed a little on the surface, would remain substantially undisturbed. Even American influence, so potent during the period of withdrawal notice, would seem likely to remain effective, since the ILO would continue to court American reaffiliation. Such influence far outweighs the formal voting rights of a member in good standing.[d]

Fifth, if hegemony will determine the future role of the ILO with or without US membership, what are the prospects of a change in hegemony? The question leads beyond the scope of the present article. Suffice it to state the opinion that the trend towards the consolidation of different forms of corporatism remains dominant in both rich and poor countries. This presages possibly some adjustments in the nature of hegemony, but most likely no fundamental reversal of its current form. In the United States, the movement towards an ever more fully formed corporative state, interrupted in the latter days of the Ford administration, seems likely to resume under President Carter. Societal corporatism is likewise ascendant in Britain, France, and the Federal Republic of Germany.

[d] This essay was written on the eve of a change in hegemony not contemplated here. The emerging prominence of hyperliberalism turned public policy against corporatism. See "The Global Political Economy and Social Choice," chapter 10 in this volume, and "Global *Perestroika*," included as chapter 15.

The principal force urging an adjustment of hegemony now lies in demands from Third World countries for a New International Economic Order. Most of these countries have a state corporatist form of production relations. If Third World countries are successful in increasing their bargaining power on the issues of international economic relations which have priority, then there is a probability that this bargaining strength would be reflected in altered orientations for the ILO. A critical indicator would be the question of multinational corporations, on which no consensus could be reached at the ILO's World Employment Conference. Hitherto, this question was posed within the framework of enterprise corporatism: for example, regarding the personnel policies and industrial relations practices of MNCs, including the prospects of multinational unionism. If Third World countries gain significantly greater leverage in the world economy, the question is in the future more likely to be pressed in a state corporatist framework: more benefits exacted from MNCs by governments of host countries and administered as regards employment impact and working conditions through locally controlled workers' organizations.

Sixth (and finally), what prospect, even remote, is there of a more radical challenge to hegemony? The western Europe likely to have a predominant influence in the ILO according to the preceding scenario is the corporatist Europe of the industrial establishment. This particular Europe is challenged on its own ground by rank-and-file labor protest in industry and also by the emergence of a stronger political left in southern Europe and in France, forces that have been excluded from the ILO at least until comparatively recently.

In the Third World, authentic voices of labor are hardly to be heard. Worker organizations are either manipulated from outside by the labor organizations of the world's industrial core, or are controlled by the political leaders of the periphery. Nevertheless, should there be during the coming decades any significant shift in the international division of labor, with manufacturing production moving to peripheral countries to make use of abundant supplies of relatively cheap labor – and current developments in production technologies place this in the cards – then conditions would be created that could make newly mobilized industrial workers of the periphery receptive to a more radical leadership.

Some conjunction of radical forces in core and periphery would be the condition for an effective challenge to or reversal of existing world social power relations. Just to spell out this possibility is to realize how remote it is. Yet the prospect may survive to fire the imagination of those crying out against the continuing hegemony of triumphant corporatism.

Notes

This text was first published in *International Organization*, vol. 31, no. 3 (Summer 1977), pp. 385–424.

1 R. G. Collingwood, *The Idea of History* (Oxford: Clarendon Press, 1946), p. 214. Each person who undertakes to penetrate events so as to make them reveal their deeper structures is likely to have some body of direct experience that facilitates access to the broader picture. My point of entry is through the ILO, with which I was associated for twenty-five years, between 1948 and 1972, during the latter period as director of the International Institute for Labor Studies with the rank of assistant director-general. Though it is thus informed by personal experience, the present account rests upon evidence of a kind accessible to historians. It should also be emphasized that the analytical perspective subsequently acquired as an outside observer since 1972 has enabled me to place within a broader context events in which I had earlier participated directly. It hardly need be added that my analysis in no way reflects an official ILO perspective.

2 A complete critical edition of Gramsci's prison notebooks has been published under the auspices of the Instituto Gramsci: Antonio Gramsci, *Quaderni del carcere* (Turin: Einaudi, 1975).

3 This is evident from the testimony of those involved in the peace negotiations. See, for example, Harold Butler, *Confident Morning* (London: Faber and Faber, 1950), p. 175.

4 The fullest account of this episode is in Daniel P. Moynihan, "The United States and the International Labor Organization," Ph.D dissertation, Fletcher School of Diplomacy, 1960.

5 For example, as stated in the AFL-CIO Platform Proposals presented to the Democratic and Republican National Conventions in 1976.

6 The letter and accompanying supporting news releases from the Chamber of Commerce of the United States and the AFL-CIO, both dated November 6, 1976, were circulated by the Department of Labor. For an analysis of factors behind the decision to give notice of withdrawal, see John P. Windmuller, "US Participation in the ILO: The Political Dimension," in *Proceedings of the 27th Annual Meeting of the Industrial Relations Research Association* (1974), pp. 100–108.

7 Philippe C. Schmitter has performed a public service in attempting to define corporatism in such a way as to give it precise meaning in social science discourse. He sees corporatism as a structure of interest representation (thereby separating it analytically from a form of political domination, for example, authoritarianism). For Schmitter corporatism is one of four ideal types of interest representation, the others being pluralism, monism, and syndicalism. His formal definition is: "a system of interest

representation in which the constituent units are organized into a limited number of singular, compulsory, noncompetitive, hierarchically ordered and functionally differentiated categories, recognized or licensed (if not created) by the state and granted a deliberate representational monopoly within their respective categories in exchange for observing certain controls on their selection of leaders and articulation of demands and supports": Phillipe C. Schmitter, "Still the Century of Corporatism?," in Frederick B. Pike and Thomas Stritch (eds.), *The New Corporatism: Social-Political Structures in the Iberian World* (Notre Dame, Ind.: University of Notre Dame Press, 1974), pp. 93–94. Schmitter's usage is thus confined to the state level. My own differs slightly from his (but, I think, includes his): corporatism, as I use the term, is in essence a form of production relations, one based on an ideology of non-antagonistic class relations and on bureaucratized structures of representation and control. As such, it may exist at the enterprise level as well as at the state level (enterprise corporatism is a distinctive mode of social relations of production). At the state level, I refer to the general category of the corporative state, which takes two main forms historically corresponding to what Schmitter has called societal and state corporatism. Tripartism is historically linked to the societal form, emerging in countries of advanced capitalism (out of what Schmitter describes as "the slow, almost imperceptible decay of advanced pluralism": p. 106); state corporatism characteristically has been associated with dependent capitalism. Note that the corporatist concept at the enterprise level applies to Soviet production relations, although the structure of central planning at the state level must be differentiated from tripartism. I have attempted to develop the meaning of the concepts as used here in R. W. Cox, "Pour une étude prospective des relations de production," *Sociologie du Travail* (March 1977), pp. 113–137.

There is a growing literature on corporatism and the modern state. Several salient works merit mention as influencing the notion presented here. Andrew Shonfield, *Modern Capitalism* (London: Oxford University Press, 1965), discerned common structural characteristics in the countries of advanced capitalism during the post-World War II period. The antecedents of the contemporary corporative state, as they emerged in France, Germany, and Italy following World War I, are traced in a comparative history by Charles S. Maier, *Recasting Bourgeois Europe: Stabilization in France, Germany, and Italy in the Decade After World War I* (Princeton, N.J.: Princeton University Press, 1975). In the United States, the growth of the corporative state can be traced in a succession of waves: World War I, the first phase of the New Deal, World War II, and the Johnson and Nixon administrations. The New Deal phase is observable through Arthur M. Schlesinger, Jr.'s history, *The Age of Roosevelt*, especially Vol. II, *The Coming of the New Deal* (Boston: Houghton Mifflin, 1959), pp. 87–176.

8 See Schlesinger, *Coming of the New Deal* pp. 371–406.

9 The picture of union labor as a middle-class group – of middle income, not

notably disposed towards economic and social change, more supportive of the Vietnam War and tough action against crime than of social welfare and the war on poverty – is drawn in an establishment view of American labor: Derek C. Bok and John T. Dunlop, *Labor and the American Community* (New York: Simon and Schuster, 1970), especially pp. 43, 47, 121, 134.

10 A growing number of studies deal with the duality of labor markets in the United States, most arising from concern with the characteristics of poverty. Early instances of this fairly recent discovery of the existence of two largely separate kinds of labor market are P. Doeringer and M. Piore, *Internal Labor Markets and Manpower Analysis* (Lexington, Mass.: D. C. Heath, 1971); and David M. Gordon, "Class, Productivity and the Ghetto," Ph.D dissertation, Harvard University, 1971. An empirical study applying statistical techniques to effect a binary split according to primary and secondary labor-market characteristics within a sample of 1023 individuals (data collected by the Institute for Social Research of the University of Michigan) was carried out by Howard M. Wachtel and Charles Betsey, "Low Wage Workers and the Dual Labor Market: An Empirical Investigation," *Review of Black Political Economy*, vol. 5, no. 3 (Spring 1975), pp. 288–301. A summary of the state of dual labor-market theory among radical economists in the US is by Michael Reich, David M. Gordon, and Richard C. Edwards, "A Theory of Labor Market Segmentation," *Papers and Proceedings of the 85th Annual Meeting of the American Economic Association*, Toronto, December 1972, vol. 63, no. 2 (May 1973), pp. 359–365. Peter Doeringer has investigated the extent to which duality in labor markets exists in Great Britain, Japan, and Sweden as well as in the United States, and finds a similar pattern of stratification, except for the case of Sweden, where the vast majority of workers are included in the primary labor market (Doeringer, "Low Pay, Labor Market Dualism, and Industrial Relations Systems," (unpublished) Discussion Paper No. 271, Harvard Institute of Economic Research, Harvard University, January 1973). Insofar as the sample used by Wachtel and Betsey may be representative of the labor force as a whole (it was collected for a survey of consumer finances and consists of individual heads of households or dwelling units), the primary labor market would encompass substantially less than half, in effect about 35 percent of the labor force.

11 While unions have become ever more centralized and union leaders more ready to be integrated into the tripartite management of the economy, there have, since the 1960s, been increasing signs of restiveness among the secondary labor-market workers in the United States. Young, black, and women workers in particular have acted against the policies of union leaders, mainly with the aim of gaining more direct control over the work process (while union leaders have cooperated with management in supporting productivity drives and concentrated on the wage claims more popular with older and more skilled primary labor-market workers). The protest movements have frequently taken place outside of union structures

in wildcat strikes, sabotage, and absenteeism, but seem not as yet to have acquired a focused and coherent ideology. In a thoughtful analysis, Stanley Aronowitz, "Arthritic Unionism: Corporate Labor in America," *Social Policy* (May–June 1972), pp. 40–52, concludes that out of the likely continuing confrontation between established unions and the workers' revolt "one can expect that the trade unions will fortify their role as the representatives of the most privileged, the most socially integrated, and the oldest sections of the working class" (p. 52).

12 From *US News and World Report*, February 21, 1972, p. 28. Meany's figure of $7,500 is strikingly close to the mean annual earnings of primary labor-market workers found by Wachtel and Betsey ("Low-Wage Workers," fn. 9), which was $7,634. The mean annual earnings of secondary labor-market workers was $5,478 (p. 296).

13 Joseph C. Goulden, *Meany* (New York: Atheneum, 1972).

14 A. H. Raskin, "After Dunlop," *New York Times*, February 3, 1976, p. 31.

15 David Burnham, *New York Times*, November 9, 1975.

16 Raskin, "After Dunlop."

17 See especially John P. Windmuller, *American Labor and the International Labor Movement, 1940 to 1953*, Cornell International Industrial and Labor Relations Reports, No. 2 (Ithaca, N.Y.: Institute of International Industrial and Labor Relations, Cornell University, 1954). Lovestone's break with communism is covered in Theodore Draper, *American Communism and Soviet Russia* (New York: Viking Press, 1960). Ronald Radosh, *American Labor and United States Foreign Policy* (New York: Random House, 1969), is a "revisionist" interpretation.

18 Meany's biographer Goulden, for example, gives an account of the CIA connection, pp. 127–131. Various accounts of AFL and AFL-CIO foreign operations have been published that deal with the CIA connection; see, for example, Sidney Lens, "American Labor Abroad: Lovestone Diplomacy," *Nation*, July 5, 1965, pp. 10–28; and Roy Godson, "Nongovernmental Organizations in World Politics: The American Federation of Labor in France, 1945–1952," *World Affairs*, vol. 136, no. 3 (Winter 1973–74), pp. 208–231.

The involvement of the CIA in American labor's actions abroad, especially through Lovestone and Brown, was a matter of accepted common knowledge among European trade unionists active in international labor affairs, long before any public proofs were available. The matter was put into public print by Thomas W. Braden, a former CIA official, in an article in the *Saturday Evening Post* (May 20, 1967). Braden explained how he had passed CIA money to Brown, some of which was used to pay "strong-arm squads in Mediterranean ports, so that American supplies could be unloaded against the opposition of Communist dock workers." Braden reported he had also given CIA money to Walter Reuther (a revelation seemingly provoked by the fact that Victor Reuther had been criticizing Lovestone and Brown for taking CIA funds). Braden estimated that Lovestone had been paying the breakaway unions in France and Italy nearly two million dollars annually. Goulden cites evidence from Richard L. G. Deverall, AFL proconsul in the Far East, who told him: "I don't think Meany knew where Lovestone was getting the money. Of course, it's all pretty much common knowledge now, and I don't see anything wrong with it" (Goulden, *Meany*, p. 130). Further confirmation came in a document that in 1971 fell into the hands of radical students occupying the building in Cambridge, Mass., that houses the Harvard University Center for International Affairs. This was a confidential record of a meeting held at the Council on Foreign Relations in New York, on January 8, 1968; the document was subsequently published in Victor Marchetti and John D. Marks, *The CIA and the Cult of Intelligence* (New York: Alfred Knopf, 1974). One of the participants in the meeting, Meyer Bernstein, director of international affairs of the United Steelworkers of America, was reported as commenting:

> [B]efore May 1967 it was common knowledge that there had been some CIA support for labor programs, but first Ramparts and then Tom Braden spelled out this support in public. Those in international labor affairs were dismayed, and certain newspapers confounded their difficulties by confusing AID with the CIA, and claiming that the AFL-CIO's Free Labor Development program was tainted. Since these disclosures, the turn of events has been unexpected. First, there hasn't been any real trouble with international labor programs. Indeed, there has been an increase in demand for US labor programs and the strain on our capacity has been embarrassing. Formerly, these foreign labor unions knew we were short of funds, but now they all assume we have secret CIA money, and they ask for more help.

And Bernstein concluded: "We've come to accept CIA, like sin." (Quoted in Marchetti and Marks, *CIA and the Cult of Intelligence*, pp. 51–52, 395.)

19 Philip Agee, *Inside the Company: CIA Diary* (Harmondsworth, Middlesex: Penguin, 1975), includes many accounts of CIA use of trade union cover for work in Latin America, particularly in attempting to organize non-communist unions. Agee reports from his briefings in the CIA that Meany as well as Lovestone and Brown were "effective and witting collaborators" of the agency (p. 75).

20 Goulden, *Meany*, pp. 136–137. The question of control by the AFL-CIO over the appointment of labor attachés was raised by Senator J. W. Fulbright in hearings before the Senate Committee on Foreign Relations in 1969, to which Meany responded: "Control, no. We make suggestions. I would not say we control it at all. But we have recommended a number of people and they have been accepted and are serving abroad, yes" (American Institute for Free Labor Development, *Hearing Before the Committee on Foreign Relations, United States Senate, 91st Congress, 1st session, with George Meany, President, AFL-CIO, 1 August 1969* (Washington, D.C.:

US Government Printing Office, 1969, hereinafter referred to as *AIFLD Hearing*), p. 58).

21 Much of the questioning of Meany by Senator Fulbright in the aforementioned hearing concerned the substitution of AID funds for previous CIA financing. Meany continued to deny that the AFL-CIO had received funds from the CIA (*AIFLD Hearing*, pp. 23–24). Fulbright cited press reports in the *St. Louis Post-Dispatch* by its chief Washington correspondent, Richard Dudman, published in the editions of April 13 and 14, 1969, which reported how AID had "picked up the tab" for some "CIA orphans." "The new conduits, taking the place of the mysterious foundations that transmitted the CIA money, are a group of regional labor institutes financed mainly by AID and operated by the AFL-CIO" (*AIFLD Hearing*, p. 24). A similar report was published in the *Washington Post*, April 28, 1969, by Bernard Nossiter (*AIFLD Hearing*, pp. 74–76). Senator Fulbright commented: "I know of no precedent in which a private organization similar to yours is likewise given money to go out and to influence governments and to lobby in foreign parliaments and to try to influence foreign policy" (*AIFLD Hearing*, p. 46). Meany steadfastly maintained "We don't do any of those things and you cannot prove that we do" (p. 47).

22 Goulden, *Meany*, p. 330.

23 *AIFLD Hearing*, p. 6. Among the contributors to the AIFLD were International Telephone and Telegraph, Kennecott Copper Corp., The Anaconda Co., The United Fruit Co., the First National City Bank, and the Chase Manhattan Bank.

24 Goulden, *Meany*, pp. 223–225. Romualdi, in a memoir that is consistently Manichaean in its anti-communist vision of the world, affected surprise at the repression of labor following Castillo Armas' victory, and blames it on "reactionary forces" that "eventually gained the upper hand" despite the good intentions of Castillo Armas himself: Seraphino Romualdi, *Presidents and Peons* (New York: Funk and Wagnall, 1967), pp. 244–247.

25 William Doherty, then director of the Social Projects Department of the AIFLD and subsequently executive director of the AIFLD, in a comment broadcast over the Mutual Broadcasting System on July 12, 1964, referred to AIFLD trainees from Brazil who, on their return had become involved in the overthrow of the Goulart government:

> Some of them were so active that they became intimately involved in some of the clandestine operations of the revolution before it took place on April 1. What happened in Brazil on April 1 did not just happen – it was planned – and planned months in advance. Many of the trade union leaders – some of whom were actually trained in our institute – were involved in the revolution, and in the overthrow of the Goulart regime.
>
> (*AIFLD Hearing*, p. 29)

26 Goulden, *Meany*, pp. 333–334. The confidential document published in Marchetti and Marks included the statement that "British Guiana's labor

unions were supported through CIA conduits." The *New York Times* published a letter from Dr. Cheddi Jagan in July 1963 charging that the AIFLD was involved in the attempt to overthrow his government, a charge borne out by information that later became available. Serephino Romualdi (then executive director of the AIFLD), who was specifically mentioned by Jagan as the leading instigator, gives his account of the events (including his putting six graduates of AIFLD at the service of the anti-Jagan movement) as an episode in his worldwide struggle with communism (Romualdi, *Presidents and Peons*, pp. 345–352).

27 A detailed study of US trade union action in support of US business interests in Jamaica is to be found in Jeffrey Harrod, *Trade Union Foreign Policy: A Study of British and American Unions in Jamaica* (London: Macmillan, 1972).

28 In response to a question from Senator Fulbright referring explicitly, but not exclusively, to the Vietnam War, Meany said: "Our activities in this respect, Mr. Chairman, are part of the activities of our Government . . . When we help the Vietnamese trade union, which is certainly on our side, we feel we are furthering the policy of our own Government . . . We think we are doing what good citizens would do to help their country in these affairs" (*AIFLD Hearing*, p. 37).

29 Goulden, *Meany*, p. 133.

30 John P. Windmuller has written extensively about AFL and AFL-CIO relations with the ICFTU. See especially "Leadership and Administration in the ICFTU: A New Phase of Development," *British Journal of Industrial Relations*, vol. 1, no. 2 (June 1963), pp. 147–169; "The Foreign Policy Conflict in American Labor," *Political Science Quarterly*, vol. 82, no. 2 (June 1967), pp. 205–234; and "Internationalism in Eclipse: The ICFTU after Two Decades," *Industrial and Labor Relations Review*, vol. 23, no. 4 (July 1970), pp. 510–527.

31 The conversation took place at Caracas, Venezuela, during an ILO regional conference that was a turning point for Jenks' campaign. The timing of the conference (which had been delayed from its original timetable) and the fact that Blanchard was absent as he had no official reason to be there, gave Jenks an advantage with Latin American delegates who might on balance have been thought likely to be more favorable to Blanchard's candidacy. Furthermore, Jenks' personal relations with top Venezuelan leaders helped him in this setting. His success in acquiring US support at this time consolidated his candidacy.

32 The career of George P. Delaney illustrates an aspect of "tripartism." At the time of these events he was special assistant to the secretary in the Department of State. Delaney's role in the State Department was the subject of enquiries by Senator Fulbright (*AIFLD Hearing*, pp. 58–59), particularly with regard to appointment of labor attachés. Senator Fulbright asked Meany whether Delaney had not been formerly an official of the AFL-CIO. Meany denied this, adding: "He was a Representative, a workers' rep-

resentative, on the ILO representing the US Government. He worked in the Labor Department. He has been in Government service to my knowledge for over 20 years." This may have been a Freudian slip. Meany could hardly have forgotten that Delaney had been AFL International Representative, and a workers' member of the ILO Governing Body representing US labor throughout the Cold War years. He later joined the Labor Department as assistant to Secretary of Labor James P. Mitchell, in the Eisenhower administration, before joining the Department of State.

33 Reported by George H. Hildebrand in *Departments of State, Justice and Commerce, the Judiciary, and Related Agencies Appropriations for 1971. Hearings before a Subcommittee of the Committee on Appropriations, House of Representatives, 91st Congress, 2nd session. Part 5. Additional Testimony on the International Labor Organization* (Washington, D.C.: US Government Printing Office, 1970, hereinafter referred to as *ILO Hearings*), p. 71. The reference to "administrative actions taken before I assumed this office" was a rather lame attempt to place the responsibility for the decision on Morse. In the hearings, Meany stated that the decision "could not have been made by David Morse because he would not have gone out of his office without announcing a decision he had made. It had to be made by Mr. Jenks" (ibid., p. 77).

34 Ibid., p. 69.

35 Ibid., p. 76.

36 People with whom Jenks had working relationships can be divided into three groups: ILO officials, persons connected in a representative way with the ILO, and international law specialists. A few, but very few, bridged these three groups, and these few should have been in the best position to understand his thought processes. No attempt is made here to analyze Jenks' extensive legal writings, a task that is best left to some diligent researcher in international law. It is not irrelevant to the matter at hand, however, to point to a style characteristic of his written work. The reader is impressed in the first instance by the massive accumulation of quotations and references and the breadth of topics covered. Admiration for the industry and power of memory that has gone into the construction of the work yields place, on reflection, to perplexity over the eclecticism with which now one, now another basis of argument is marshaled in support of the author's contentions – now the opinions of revered authorities, now evidence of precedent or practice in a variety of legal systems, now appeals to moral sentiment, depending upon which material seems most convenient to the purpose. It further becomes increasingly evident that the reader's labor of assimilating all these elements is not disclosing some objective reality of law revealed through history, but is disclosing rather an intensity of volition revealed in the author – his lists of "we must" do this and that, his appeals for "bold and vigorous action" assorted with vague exhortations to meet "a challenge to evolve procedures of consensus and techniques of responsibility within a context of dynamic action" (*A*

466

New World of Law?, London: Longmans, 1969, p. 231). Jenks' invoking of "the intellectual rigour and vigour" of the law, accompanied by condescending if not downright disparaging references to other disciplines, cannot obliterate the critical reader's sense of the essentially subjective nature of his work: it proceeds from an inner vision of a future world, couched in phrases drawn from the past like the "parliament of man" and the "common law of mankind." The subjectivity of the work is the more troubling in that the author seems to be utterly devoid of any awareness of the extent to which his own imagination is the product of his personal history. This is a rather flagrant case of what Vico called "the conceit of scholars" that takes the form of asserting one's own historically conditioned thoughts as being of universal validity. No detailed exegesis of Jenks' writings would be useful in the context of the present discussion. What I am concerned with here is the expression of Jenks' ideas in his actions as an international official.

37 C. Wilfred Jenks, *The Proper Law of International Organisations* (London: Stevens, 1962), p. 113.

38 See for example, C. Wilfred Jenks, *Trade Union Freedom* (London: Stevens, 1957).

39 I have attempted to analyze the ILO as a political system in ch. 4 of Robert W. Cox and Harold K. Jacobson, *The Anatomy of Influence: Decision Making in International Organization* (New Haven, Conn.: Yale University Press, 1972), pp. 102–138.

40 For example, as developed in Ralf Dahrendorf, *Class and Class Conflict in Industrial Society* (Stanford, Calif.: Stanford University Press, 1959). Original German edition published 1957. Dahrendorf did not use the term "tripartism."

41 Reinhard Bendix, *Work and Authority in Industry* (New York: John Wiley, 1956), compares managerial ideologies in Britain and Russia during the nineteenth century and in the United States and the German Democratic Republic in recent times. He does not use the term corporatism, but his analysis points to the characteristics I have linked to this concept, in particular, managerial authority, bureaucratized relations between management and labor, and a doctrine of harmony of interests. I have distinguished between corporatism in production relations, and corporatism in the form of the state.

42 Evidence of worker protest in the United States was referred to above. The challenge during 1976 to the leadership of the United Steelworkers of America, which had shown a particular propensity for integration within the structures of the corporative state, may be seen as evidence of opposition to the corporative state among American workers.

43 John Dunlop, *Industrial Relations Systems* (New York: Holt-Dryden, 1958).

44 Clark Kerr, John T. Dunlop, Frederick H. Harbison, and Charles A. Myers, *Industrialism and Industrial Man* (Cambridge, Mass.: Harvard University Press, 1960).

Approaches to world order

45 Issued by the International Institute for Labor Studies as *Future Industrial Relations: An Interim Report* (Geneva: IILS, 1972).

46 From a lecture at the Graduate Institute of International Studies, Geneva, October 27, 1969, published in *Annals of International Studies*, 1970 (Geneva: Alumni Association of the Graduate Institute of International Studies, 1970), p. 60. Jenks was obviously pleased with this passage because he quoted it in his address of welcome to the Congress of the International Industrial Relations Association (ILO press release, September 1, 1970). The speech by Jenks to the ILO staff was distributed in ILO Circular No. 61, June 3, 1970.

47 Almino Affonso, "El sindicato campesino agente de cambio," *Boletin 8* (Geneva: IILS, 1971). Affonso, at the time of writing this article, was living in exile in Chile, employed by the United Nations as a technical assistance expert. Philip Agee, a former CIA agent, wrote much later (in 1975) that the CIA had joined with the Brazilian ambassador in Montevideo, where Affonso spent the first period of his exile after the overthrow of the Goulart government, to have Affonso expelled from Uruguay. See Agee, *Inside the Company*, pp. 402, 405, 408.

48 Draft verbatim record of the meeting of the Board of the Institute held on March 4, 1972.

49 In my letter of resignation, dated June 12, 1972, I went into the issue of intellectual independence in some detail and indicated a series of incidents which in my judgement cumulatively negated that independence and made it impossible for me to continue as director. I also made the point that criticism of accepted doctrine could be helpful towards enabling an international organization like the ILO to adjust to the demands of a changing world. (This point was taken up by Georges-Henri Martin, editor, in *La Tribune de Genève*, June 16, 1972.) The term *nihil obstat* had been habitually used by Jenks to refer to what he considered to be a director-general's prerogative to pass judgement on any writing for an audience by an ILO official. He had used it specifically in seeking to prevent me from publishing the chapter about the ILO I had written for *Anatomy of Influence*. The term was taken up by the new director of the Institute who used it in a letter to a staff member requiring him to submit all his writings for official approval. ILO publications policy operated under such constraints as the prohibition on publishing anything about a country that was not written by a national of that country – a rule that was interpreted (as the fuss over the Affonso article showed) to mean a national who was *persona grata* with the government.

50 Peter Patterson, "ICI's Last Stand," *New Statesman*, December 1, 1972, pp. 806–807.

51 Vincent Hanna, "Storm Grows as ICI Fights Off Unions," *Sunday Times*, June 3, 1973.

52 Jenks, *Proper Law*, p. 113.

53 The fact that an organization like the ILO disposes of what in local politics

would be called patronage can also act as an incentive to conformity. There
have been numbers of cases of members of the Governing Body being
appointed to ILO staff jobs. Anyone who had such a future in mind would
want to keep his slate clean with the organization's executive head. To
take a public position on some policy issue is one thing, but to antagonize
a director-general in a personnel matter he considered to lie within his
discretionary domain would be quite another. To take just one case of this
kind of relationship, the directorships of the ILO's branch offices have very
frequently been filled by former members of the ILO Governing Body,
when they retire from their national civil service jobs. The London office
in particular has been filled by a succession of retired government members of the Governing Body. These are all, like Brutus, honorable men,
and no one imputes wrong-doing on their part. But the practice certainly
creates expectations hardly conducive to pursuing issues that would turn
out to be unpopular with an executive head. Appointments to the Paris
office of the ILO have been an exception, in that the French government
very early acquired control over them. The importance of the question
may be gauged from the fact that this assertion of control by the French
government in the 1930s provoked the resignation of the ILO's then-
executive head (see "The Executive Head: An Essay on Leadership in
International Organization," chapter 16 in this volume). The practice
whereby an executive head can appoint members of his executive board
to jobs – and especially post-retirement jobs – in the organization constitutes one of the ways in which high office-holders in international institutions can influence those to whom they are formally accountable. These
same office-holders are not, of course, powerful in their own right, but
their relative freedom from accountability enhances the facility with which
they can act as agents of hegemony.

54 ILO, *Towards Full Employment: A Programme for Colombia, Prepared by an
Inter-Agency Team Organised by the International Labour Office* (Geneva: ILO,
1970).
55 Tripartite World Conference on Employment, Income Distribution, and
Social Progress, and the International Division of Labor, *Employment,
Growth, and Basic Needs: A One World Problem*, Report of the Director-
General of the International Labor Office (Geneva: ILO, 1976).
56 Indications of official US displeasure with the ILO staff in regard to the
WEP are to be found in articles by A. H. Raskin in the *New York Times*,
June 17, 18, and 19, 1976. In the article of June 17, Raskin wrote: "The
government, employer and worker representatives in the United States
delegation to the job conference made no secret from the start that [*sic*]
their belief that the position papers prepared by the ILO staff have a strong
Marxist bias and that the probable affect [*sic*] of a program based on them
would be a sharing of poverty rather than a general lifting of economic
standards." An editorial in the *New York Times* of June 16, 1976, referred
to "ridiculous position papers by the ILO staff." The US government del-

egate told the conference his government "was not in accord with the basic needs strategy as formulated in the Conference document" and that the report prepared for the conference (*Employment, Growth, and Basic Needs*) "did not pay sufficient attention to the need for individual initiative, free enterprise, and a market economy such as had contributed to the growth of this country" (ILO World Employment Conference, Geneva, June 1976, *Summary Record* 5, p. V/9). Such opposition to the ILO staff proposals put the United States delegation in a minority position, although US delegates aligned themselves with a larger body of conciliatory western industrial-country opinion in the negotiating process. The United States worker representative was Irving Brown, who was also the US labor member of the Governing Body.

57 ILO, World Employment Conference, Geneva, June 1976, *Summary Record* 20, Report of the Committee of the Whole.

58 Keith Griffin's book, *The Political Economy of Agrarian Change: An Essay on the Green Revolution* (Cambridge, Mass.: Harvard University Press, 1974), shows the depth of his analysis of the rural problem in the Third World. His resignation from the ILO was commented on in the *Guardian* (October 6, 1976) by Rod Chapman, who wrote: "Tripartism is one of the sacred cows of the ILO but a number of officials argue that a fetish with tripartism means that concepts such as a world employment programme to help the rural poor in developing countries are given a back seat." The article noted a disposition of the ILO to please the US and added that, "The ILO may even be anticipating objections that the US will not make for fear of being isolated." When the ILO Governing Body met soon after this article had appeared. Griffin was a target of criticism by Joe Morris, the Canadian labor delegate, and by Irving Brown, the US labor delegate.

59 Gossip circulated in Geneva ILO circles during the summer of 1976 that John Dunlop might again become US secretary of labor, this time in a future Carter administration. Whatever probability they accorded such gossip, top ILO administrators were inclined to be helpful regarding Dunlop's interest in the IIRA. This may be seen as an instance of hegemonic influence at work through bureaucratic decisions. That the rumors were not without foundation became clear late in 1976, when Dunlop emerged as the leading candidate for secretary of labor in the Carter cabinet, strongly backed by Meany and the AFL-CIO. His appointment was blocked when it encountered strong opposition from groups representing women and blacks who criticized Dunlop's record on equal employment opportunity (see Eileen Shanahan in the *New York Times*, December 11, 1976).

20 Labor and hegemony: a reply (1980)

When I wrote "Labor and Hegemony," I anticipated two kinds of critical reaction: one on the ground that the method and approach was at variance with mainstream political science; the other in defense of two institutional establishments whose ideological foundations were challenged in the article, the ILO and the AFL-CIO. Both these organizational establishments place great stock in the idea of tripartism, representing it as a form of pluralism or a bargaining relationship of independent actors – unions, employers, and government. In "Labor and Hegemony," I argued that this appearance of independence has to be understood as the ideological expression of a particular structure of social power, a particular form of hegemony that is found in advanced capitalist societies with the emergence of a corporative form of state. This *blocco storico* is the proper object of study,[1] and since it has international as well as national dimensions its study can be a fruitful approach to international affairs and international organization.

A response from ILO quarters came in the form of a letter signed by a retired ILO official.[2] It did not really require substantive comment from me since it did not deal with the basic questions I had raised. The letter purported to find inaccuracies in my account, though it merely presented some additional facts that were either irrelevant to or would have supported my argument had they been put into a fuller context. The letter can best be understood as an exercise in self-justification by a few ILO officials whose functions had involved them in a cover-up described in the article. The comment printed in this issue by William A. Douglas and Roy S. Godson is a defense of the AFL-CIO foreign-policy makers.[a] It raises some more basic questions

---

[a] William A. Douglas and Roy S. Godson, "Labor and Hegemony: A Critique," *International Organization*, vol. 34, no. 1 (Winter, 1980), pp. 149–158.

that merit a fuller response. These questions arise at different levels: ideological, epistemological, structural, and factual. I shall try to deal with each in turn, though the need for brevity may serve to broaden rather than to conclude the debate.

Perspectives

It is important to underline at the outset the difference in perspectives which separates us. Douglas and Godson categorize me as a "revisionist" and advocate of a "corporate unionist" thesis. These are their words, not mine. "Corporate unionism" I do not understand. I used the term "corporatism," which is not equivalent. Revisionism implies an orthodoxy that has been challenged by a new orthodoxy – as used variously by Bolsheviks, Maoists, and American Cold War protagonists. "Labor and Hegemony" was not written without commitment, but it was not a commitment to any new or old orthodoxy. I would, of course, prefer that readers refer to the essay rather than accept any rather facile labels with such connotations as may attach to them.

The perspective of the Douglas and Godson comment is to a degree apparent from their taking up the challenge of what they perceive as revisionism (which I take to refer to the Cold War debate) and from their *parti pris* for AFL-CIO foreign policy. A more explicit statement of perspective is to be found in Godson's book about AFL intervention in Europe in the post-World War II period, in which he argued that "the AFL helped maintain the postwar balance of power by helping to prevent the Soviet Union from dominating the European continent," and that the AFL leadership acted from the motive of "preventing the Russians from gaining control of Western Europe and either precipitating war with the United States or, ultimately, destroying democracy and genuine trade unionism in the United States."[3] The book is devoted mainly to the activities in postwar France of Irving Brown, the AFL representative widely recognized among European unionists as the principal conduit for CIA funds used to finance the split in the French labor movement. Brown has, indeed, been the most prominent agent of the Meany–Lovestone foreign policy; he has a long and successful record of splitting minorities away from labor movements deemed to be under communist influence in order to set up organizations under AFL or AFL-CIO influence (activities that extended from France to Italy, to various African countries, and recently to Portugal).

Godson's main point in the book is that the AFL intervention in postwar France is a good illustration of how to fight communism in Europe today. He asserts that the Soviet threat (and he equates communism with Soviet influence) has grown during the 1970s. He sees the formation of the European Confederation of Trade Unions – an effort to achieve some practical cooperation among the major national trade union organizations in the EEC irrespective of their doctrinal or political affiliations – as a notable Soviet "success"; but he is most concerned with the strength of communism in southern Europe. The book concludes by envisaging a renewed AFL-CIO intervention in southern Europe on the lines of postwar France – and announcing Irving Brown's availability for the job.[4]

My own perspective differs from the foregoing in several respects, which I can summarize thus: (1) apart altogether from the merits of "revisionist" interpretations of the Cold War, it is oversimplification to reduce or subordinate the variety of issues and conflicts that have beset labor movements in Europe and the Third World since World War II to a single struggle between communism and what AFL-CIO foreign-policy makers call "democracy"; (2) to regard both the attempt during the 1970s to achieve some degree of common action among the diverse labor movements of western Europe and the development of the left during the same period in southern Europe as manifestations of Soviet influence rather arrogantly underestimates the strength of indigenous social and political movements; and (3) to accept at face value the explanations for their actions offered by AFL-CIO leaders, agents, and ideologues, while seeing nothing but Soviet manipulation behind those they worked against, makes for insufficiently critical political analysis.

Of course, one's perception of the meaning of particular events is conditioned by one's view of the whole of which these events are a part. I can understand Godson's view of the whole from his book. I do not have the same basis for understanding Douglas' perspective, but I have to assume a certain compatibility with Godson's. "Labor and Hegemony" was an effort on my part to present a different view of the whole, to delineate a basic structure of social and political forces and the mechanisms that maintain this structure, and to suggest by way of illustration how this enables one to understand particular events. Since we have different perspectives, it is not surprising that we perceive events differently. Where Douglas and Godson perceive beneficent help to foreigners in combating an evil world force, I see intrusions supporting a status quo and obstructing autochthonous forces for change. These appraisals derive from our views of what is significant in the whole, and it would trivialize the issue to focus only on the parts – i.e., particular events. It is possible to interpret the same events differently when they are viewed from different perspectives. It is also possible to impose interpretations that have no relationship with reality. The factual points raised by Douglas and Godson have to be considered in the light of these two possibilities.

Method in social science

We seem to differ also in our ways of understanding the processes of reasoning in social science. Douglas and Godson consider (or write as though they consider) as data for the study of politics: actors, the motives that can be attributed to actors, and events or "cases" produced by the interactions of the actors. Each of these kinds of data they treat as fragmented and separated out from the social matrix in which they arise, and as separately classifiable under categories relevant to their research. Thus, there are cases in which the AFL-CIO has opposed popularly elected left-leaning foreign governments, there are cases in which the AFL-CIO has opposed multinationals, and there are cases in which the Soviet Union has favored relations with US multinationals. Douglas and Godson think that a comparison of these cases will support their contention that the consistent motive of the actor concerned, the AFL-CLO, is defense of "democratic freedoms," rather than the motive they read me (incorrectly, I was not discussing motives) as attributing to that actor, namely, defense of capitalism (which they, again incorrectly in my view, equate with the interests of US multinationals). (As Douglas and Godson say, "To determine which explanation of labor's anti-communism is correct . . . we need a test case in which communists actually *favored* some US corporate activities abroad" "Labour and Hegemony: a Critique," p.154.) In this form of reasoning they are consistent with a certain mainstream political science.

Once again, I must contrast my own approach very summarily as follows: (1) action is not fragmented into a sequence of discrete events but always presupposes a context which gives it meaning (events without such meaning are mere programmed responses to specific stimuli); (2) the first task of analysis is to discern the context or historical structure of social reality within which action takes place, a struc-

474

ture that consists objectively of power relations and subjectively of a web of shared meanings; (3) ideological analysis, or the attempt to reconstruct the mental frameworks through which individuals and groups perceive their fields of action, is the best means of access towards knowledge about the historical structure, knowledge that must be approximated by critically confronting and not just passively accepting the perspective of one group or another; and (4) the further task of political analysis is to know whether actions tend to reinforce or alternatively to transform a historical structure, and this can only be understood in terms of the consequences of actions rather than the motivations behind them.

The Douglas–Godson line of criticism does not really come to grips with my argument. For instance, they compare interventions in Latin America through the American Institute for Free Labor Development (AIFLD) in the early 1960s with AFL-CIO criticism in the 1970s of "runaway shops" set up abroad by US-based multinationals. These events cannot, however, be considered in abstraction from their contexts as separable cases to "test" some general proposition about AFL-CIO motives on a stimulus-response basis. The context of the first set of events was different from that of the second. In the first, there was convergence of perceived interests between AFL-CIO foreign-policy makers, the multinationals active in Latin America that were represented on the board of the AIFLD, and the government agencies that provided most of the funding. In the second, the difference between the AFL-CIO leaders and some US-based multinationals have to be understood in terms of contradictions arising through the further internationalizing of production which deepened the division of US capital into internationally and domestically oriented segments and aligned organized labor with the latter segment of capital in favoring neomercantilist policies. Established labor's opposition to multinationals, as it has developed in the 1970s, is directed to displacement of manufacturing. It does not apply in the same way to raw materials extraction, since labor, like domestic manufacturers, has an interest in uninterrupted supply of raw materials. The US interests mainly involved in the Latin America cases cited were primarily in raw materials. In both sets of cases, US organized labor was acting consistently with the interests of segments of US capital.

Douglas and Godson also cite a number of cases in which the AFL-CIO favored governments that imposed some restrictions on US investments as refuting my contention that AFL-CIO foreign policy has served the interests of American capitalism. Once again, the flaw in the argument lies in the stimulus-response model which ignores the context or structure in which the events occurred. The "Chileaniz-ation" of copper under the Frei government, which they cite, was not an attack on American capital; indeed it was welcomed by some US interests anxious to divest without losing effective control.[5] US government, business, and labor made a considerable political invest-ment in the election of Frei and support of his government. (Nor did the acquisition of lands and of majority holding in bauxite enterprises and increasing of rents on mined bauxite by the Jamaican government constitute a hostile act towards US interests. Multinational managerial control remained intact, the companies acquired additional financing from host-country acquisition of assets – which in some cases exceeded the host country's equity earnings – and there was no threat of reduction in supplies of bauxite to importing countries.)[6] These and similar events are best understood in the context of a new structure of relationships between the governments of some mineral export countries and the center economies to which they are linked, which emerged in the late 1960s and early 1970s: a new phase of capitalist relationships in which the host governments assumed a greater role and acquired a greater return from their links with the center without disrupting the basic relationship between peripheral and center econ-omies and without undermining multinational managerial control or market power.[7] The Allende government's measures did, however, break with this new pattern and thus did constitute a challenge to American capitalism which the other instances cited by Douglas and Godson did not.

Social-political structures

The fragmentation approach to the study of social and political pro-cesses faces a problem of how to organize data. Its solution is to find a framework on which to hang the pieces; but this is only an apparent solution because the framework often turns out to be a mere ideology, that is to say, a perceptual screen which distorts social reality by seeing only what is in accordance with dominant interests. Douglas and Godson do not propose any particular framework in the forego-ing comment, but Godson, in the book cited above, has opted for a form of a transnational relations framework, in which trade unions

476

are defined as nongovernmental organizations that are supposed to operate independently of governments.

This raises implicitly the more general problem of the models of social reality that are the necessary ground for any social or political analysis. The current debate about this problem derives from the distinction between state and civil society inherited from late eighteenth- and early nineteenth-century Europe. Civil society – a notion rich in its implications of citizenship, individual pursuit of interests, and contractual relationships – marked a contrast to the status society of the old regime; and the state could be distinguished from this civil society in turn when its activity was conceived both as fixing a framework of law for the interplay of particular interests and of standing over these particular interests as the embodiment of a general interest. Of course, the clarity of the distinction between state and civil society was eroded in practice throughout the later nineteenth century and during the twentieth. The dichotomous model was perpetuated rather anachronistically in foreign-policy studies into our own times by those who saw only the activity of states, while analysts of domestic politics had become converted to a view of the state as the instrument of competing societal pressures. The state-centric bias in foreign-policy studies led to a reaction focusing on non-state forces at work in international affairs, through such notions as functionalism and transnational relations. It would not do justice to this corrective swing in scholarship to take it – as Godson appeared to – for a simple assertion of the autonomy of nongovernmental agencies. Rather was it a signal of the need for a more realistic assessment of the structure of social reality. "Labor and Hegemony" is addressed primarily to this problem. Douglas and Godson do not refer to it explicitly, but since they find my approach "simplistic" it behooves me to discuss the issue briefly as a prelude to considering the factual points they raise.

I can best do so by referring to a recent contribution to the search for an adequate structural model, namely Stephen Krasner's effort to rehabilitate the idea of the state as autonomous actor, distinct from and acting upon society.[8] Krasner discusses four competing models: (1) liberalism, in which the state is manipulated by competing societal pressures and has itself been disintegrated into a set of competing interests by the bureaucratic politics paradigm; (2) instrumental Marxism (which others may call "vulgar" Marxism) in which the state is manipulated by members of a coherent capitalist class; (3) structural Marxism, in which the state appears as autonomous and performs the function of supporting the capitalist system, which may lead it to act against the interests of particular capitalists or groups of capital – for example, by enacting social policies and giving status to trade unions which, though seemingly in conflict with the immediate interests of capitalists, legitimate the system for its subordinate elements; and (4) statism, in which the state is autonomous in relation to society and its polices are determined by central decision makers with a view to the utility of the community (i.e., guided by their own values, these decision makers express a judgement about the well-being of the community as a whole as distinct from a summation of the preferences of its individual members).

Liberalism (to which the transnational concept can be linked) and vulgar Marxism have certain similarities in their instrumental view of the state, and differ mainly in that Marxism posits explicit power relationships in society whereas liberalism obscures the matter of power. Krasner easily rules out both these models but has difficulty in distinguishing between structural Marxism and the statism he considers to be a more accurate model of reality. Ultimately, the difference turns upon the degree of rationality in state behavior. Marxists, so Krasner argues, overestimate the rationality of state actions and underestimate the extent of what Pareto (whom Krasner prefers to Marx) called nonlogical conduct. His proof of the validity of the statist model rests on the finding, from his analysis of US foreign policy in the raw materials sector, that American leaders "persistently exaggerated the importance of communist elements in foreign countries," pursued ideological goals without means–ends calculations as though their resources were infinite, and by so doing seriously damaged the internal fabric of American society (through the Vietnam War). Since such conduct could not be rational in defense of the capitalist system (indeed it weakened that system), he concludes that the statist model must be a more accurate one.

The argument is intriguing, and yet I find it unsatisfying or incomplete. The inference to be drawn from Krasner's work, though he does not explicitly draw it himself – perhaps because it would remove him from the field of analysis to that of policy – is a plea for a more realistic assessment of the US national interest. The question naturally comes to mind: supposing nonlogical behavior attributable to the hubris of power were eliminated, would state behavior then appear more consistent with the structural Marxist model? There still remains, of course, the difference between Krasner's conviction that men make

478

history by acting out their values (and in consequence often make a botch of it), and the Marxist identification of more impersonal social forces as the source of movement, in other words, looking more at cumulative consequences than at individual motivations. For a Marxist, Krasner's work could be seen as a dialectical moment correcting the errors and excesses of one now-transcended phase of American capitalism.

In "Labor and Hegemony," Gramsci's concept of hegemony was offered as the key structural idea. It offers a way of getting beyond the state/civil society dichotomy by stressing the historicity of models. The search, after all, is not for the one correct model on which to found a universal science of international relations, but rather for a model or models which best represent and help us to understand contemporary historical structures of world politics. Douglas and Godson have, I think, misunderstood the idea of hegemony by equating it with hierarchical dominance or a superior–subordinate relationship between state and trade union. Hegemony arises in civil society and expresses a structure of social power in which one class is dominant, but in which that class consents to concessions in favor of subordinate classes such as to make the structure tolerable to them, thereby creating a broadly based consensus in its favor. The ideology through which this social power relationship represents itself excludes options which would be in contradiction to the basic power relations, while at the same time obscuring the existence of the power factor – to take two specific and complementary manifestations, Friedmanian economics[b] and the political theory of pluralism.

The problem of defining precisely the position of the state within the hegemonic situation is more difficult.[9] The state is autonomous in the sense that it can act against particular interests and on behalf of Krasner's general interest, or Pareto's utility of the community, or Rousseau's *volonté générale*. But it is also constrained within the configuration of hegemony and therefore of something which contains both state and social classes, an entity which can be called the social formation. It is extremely difficult to distinguish clear boundaries between state and civil society in a hegemonic formation; there appears to be a fusion or interpenetration between the two. In the nonhegemonic formation, on the other hand, the distinction is clear and the dominance of the state over civil society is evident. The state

[b] i.e., monetarism.

479

establishes by force the order which an absence of hegemony makes it impossible to establish by consensus. The fully autonomous state imposes its order upon civil society; and yet since this order works in favor of one class, even though that class has not been sufficiently powerful to establish its own hegemony and cannot be said to control the state, the state may appear to be the instrument of that class. The notions of autonomy or instrumentality of the state are thus extremely elusive; yet hegemony, in its treatment of the relationship of state to civil society, gives a clear criterion for distinguishing, for example, pluralist from fascist forms of capitalism, to give them their ideological names. In institutional and policy terms, the distinction is that which Philippe Schmitter made between societal corporatism (the hegemonic form) and state corporatism (the nonhegemonic).[10]

AFL-CIO foreign policy and the hegemonic corporatist model

My contention in "Labor and Hegemony" is that the hegemonic corporatist model most adequately accounts for the foreign-policy behavior of the AFL-CIO. In such a structure there is a high degree of interpenetration of trade union, government, and business, accompanied by a division of labor in the pursuit of common goals. There may well be tensions or conflicts among these various agencies and interests, but such conflicts will be subordinated to the maintenance of cohesion vis-à-vis the rest of domestic society outside the corporatist coalition and vis-à-vis foreigners whose actions are perceived as challenging the international extensions of this hegemony. One might expect a high degree of conscious planning in such a concentration, but too much overt planning would contradict the ideological basis of hegemony, namely pluralism. Thus concertation is more likely to remain implicit, often embarrassed, and sometimes deliberately obscured. Ultimately, the proof of the pudding is in the eating – i.e., in the digestive consequences rather than in the proclaimed intentions of the cooks.

Three features of the model are easily demonstrable in this case: (1) the policy coherence and operational interpenetration of the foreign activities of the AFL-CIO and US government agencies; (2) the remoteness and manipulative relationship of US labor vis-à-vis foreign labor; and (3) the practical nonaccountability of AFL-CIO foreign-policy makers to forces in the domestic society inside or outside the labor movement.

Douglas and Godson speak of "fundamental" differences of foreign policy between the AFL-CIO and US government, but the instances they give are of complementarity or division of labor, not of conflicting goals or strategies. There were no fundamental differences. The fact that the AFL entered the Cold War actively ahead of the US government (incidentally, I did not "admit" this as though it were something I would have preferred to deny) could be attributed to a variety of factors. One could argue, for instance, that David Dubinsky developed a hostility to communists from his experience of faction fights in the New York garment district, which he then projected onto the world scale in hostility to the Soviet Union; and that he then hired as his principal agent Jay Lovestone, an ex-communist leader who was pursuing a personal struggle against Stalin for reasons obscurely connected with the purge of Bukharin. Something of a case could be made out in this sense towards an explanation of events in terms of the motives of the actors.[11] Yet this is not a serious way of understanding history. There are always a wide range of motivations and individual actions at work, but only some become attached to historically significant events, and to attribute causality to those that do is to take accident for reason. Tolstoy covered the point in his parody on the battle of Borodino.[12] The crucial factor in this instance was the convergence of AFL foreign policy with US government concern to mobilize domestic support in western Europe behind the Marshall Plan. The CIO, whose different foreign policy had been more salient internationally than the AFL's during the phase of the Grand Alliance, now had to withdraw from the international scene.[13] The Lovestone–Brown operations were able to penetrate western European labor movements in ways the US foreign service could not. There was a similar complementarity in AFL-CIO activities in colonial territories approaching independence. The recruitment of potentially influential supporters among trade union leaders in pre-independence societies was certainly convergent with longer-range US goals, though it was obviously in conflict with conventional diplomatic usage in relation to allies. Division of labor involving nongovernmental agencies playing roles which would be out of character for diplomatic agents is a common feature of contemporary international relations.

As to the operational integration of AFL-CIO with government foreign policy, I cited (in notes) some instances from an enquiry conducted by former US Senator William Fulbright through the Senate Committee on Foreign Relations.[14] This enquiry, during 1968–69, was directed particularly to allegations that funding of international labor activities, formerly done secretly by the CIA, had subsequently been taken over by AID. Articles in such newspapers as the *Washington Post* and *St. Louis Post-Dispatch* reported that AID funds were being passed through the AIFLD and its counterparts for Asia and Africa and subcontracted to unions such as the International Federation of Petroleum and Chemical Workers, Retail Clerks International Association, Communications Workers, and Brotherhood of Railway Clerks, to the accompaniment of efforts to obscure this rather complex "laundering" of government money. Meany's oral testimony was inadvertently revealing. Concerning AFL-CIO direct financing of the Vietnamese Confederation of Labor (CTV), Meany said: "Our activities in this respect, Mr. Chairman, are part of the activities of our government...When we helped the Vietnamese trade union, which is certainly on our side, we feel we are furthering the policy of our own Government." And, placing the initiative with the government, he added: "If you object to Government people making these requests you had better take it up with State Department, not with us. We think we are doing what good citizens should do to help their country in these affairs."[15] Meany was also asked about the role of one George P. Delaney, special adviser to the secretary of state, with purview over all international labor activities whether channeled through State, Labor, or AID. Delaney, as was surmised by those concerned with such matters, was Meany's man inside the State Department. In the exchange, Meany denied that Delaney was formerly an official of the AFL-CIO, and when pressed said: "He was a representative, a worker's representative, on the ILO representing the US Government. He worked in the Labor Department. He has been in Government service to my knowledge for over 20 years."[16] Despite Meany's confusion, Delaney's career is a clear indication of the degree of practical interpenetration of AFL-CIO and government foreign policy in labor matters. Delaney had, in fact, represented *both* US labor and the US government in the ILO, first as international representative of the AFL (and then the AFL-CIO) as a worker member of the ILO Governing Body from 1949 to 1958, and later as a voting member of the US government delegations during the 1960s. In the Labor Department and then subsequently in the State Department, he was a key figure in the effective integration of trade union and government foreign policies.

A more recent enquiry by the US Senate into intelligence activities, mentioned by Douglas and Godson, is also revealing.[17] The final report of this enquiry asserts that CIA support of "counterfront" labor organizations began in western Europe in the 1940s and became more prevalent and more internationally widespread in the 1950s and 1960s, during which time labor, student, and media projects constituted the "greatest single concentration of covert political and propaganda activities," reaching a peak in the years 1964–67, since when, as a result of disclosures and risks of disclosures, these activities have decreased. The report also noted the inefficiencies inherent in covert support for foreign labor unions (along with support for political leaders, parties, and media). "In some cases, it has encouraged a debilitating dependence on United States covert support, and made those receiving such support vulnerable to repudiation in their own society when their covert ties are exposed."[18]

The greatest concern underlying this enquiry was with the adverse impact on the image of American society from revelations that government agencies had used voluntary organizations as fronts or channels for covert foreign activities – a concern arising, in the words of the report, "because of the importance Americans attach to the independence of private institutions."[19] Nevertheless, despite the fact that the general passages of this document refer consistently to labor unions along with universities, student, religious, and cultural organizations, and that the conclusions mention CIA collaboration with an anonymous "American trade union federation,"[20] the more specific discussion of CIA impact on domestic nongovernmental institutions is limited to universities, the media, and religious institutions, passing over the acknowledged trade union involvement without further comment or elaboration. In this respect, the document raises more questions than it answers. Is there less public concern for the independence of trade unions than for that of universities, the press, or religious groups? Would fuller reference to covert labor-intelligence activity have been prejudicial to ongoing projects? Were the interested parties more easily able to maintain cover for lack of mobilized opinion demanding disclosure? The indication is that it is easier and more readily acceptable to bend the principle of pluralism so as to admit a certain union–government concertation of action than it would be in the case of other cherished private institutions.

The second feature of the model concerns the relationship of US labor to foreign labor movements. No reasonably independent student can fail to be impressed by (1) the relative isolation of US labor from the major strongly based worker organizations in other countries (the Israeli Histadrut being probably the only case of continuous close relations with the AFL-CIO), and (2) the clear preference of the AFL-CIO foreign-policy makers for dominant–subordinate, controlled, or manipulated relationships over more equal or multilateral relationships. The conflictual nature of AFL-CIO relations with the ICFTU leading up to withdrawal in 1969, and the markedly bilateral character of relations with Third World labor through agencies like the AIFLD and its counterparts for Asia and Africa give clear evidence. Together, these persistent tendencies show the use of terms like "transnational" and "tripartite" to be purely ideological in the sense that they distort the meaning of the social reality to which they refer. These terms imply a free and equal relationship among trade unions from different countries, all independent of their governments, when the reality is a hegemonic corporatist structure of power with a national base and international extensions. By what name should we call this structure? I used the term "American capitalism," despite misgivings as to the adequacy of the word "capitalism," which is variously and often loosely used. The question of name is just a shorthand for the problem of achieving a fuller and better understanding of the historical structure to which it refers.

The third facet is the remoteness of the AFL-CIO foreign-policy makers from the social groups for whom they claim to speak. A minority of US workers are members of trade unions, a minority consisting mainly of established or primary labor-market workers.[21] The most disadvantaged social groups are largely outside unions. There has been a predominant tendency towards bureaucratization of the government of individual unions, which are the economic power centers in the US labor movement – i.e., management by self-perpetuating bureaucracies, punctuated on occasion by rank-and-file revolts which have so far failed to change the basic tendency but relapse relatively quickly into new self-perpetuating oligarchies. (Anyone familiar with recent trade union history can fill in the examples.) Labor foreign policy, remote even from these oligarchies, has been the royal prerogative of the president of the AFL-CIO and in practice (as Godson himself allows)[22] has been conducted by a handful of people responsible only to Meany. This sequential series of removals of policy making from the rank and file of labor has facilitated the meshing of AFL-CIO international activities with those of government. AFL-CIO foreign policy has not "represented" American working people in the sense that they would be consciously aware of and actively supportive of this policy. (This is not to say they would necessarily have been opposed to it had they known about it.) The point is that AFL-CIO foreign policy has been made in conditions similar to governmental foreign policy, by a limited number of people, having monopoly access to the same kinds of often secret information, sharing the same world view and many of the same biases. Each knows what the other is doing, can bargain with the other about what is to be done, and complement the other's activity. Government and labor foreign-policy makers have much more in common with each other than with the American public and rank-and-file working people.

Matters of fact: the Chilean case

Space precludes attention to all of the several factual points raised by Douglas and Godson. Each would have to be discussed at some length to show why I think their interpretations must be rejected. The obstacles to critical research in these matters have to be underlined. Information is secret for the most part, though the substance of what is going on tends to be fairly quickly known or surmised among those engaged in the highly political quasi-covert realm of international labor activities on whatever side of the struggle they may be. Researchers who are given privileged access to some of this information are likely to be those who share the perspectives of the people who accord access, and thus risk themselves becoming agents of hegemony. Otherwise, the independent researcher is dependent upon fortuitous events (like the discovery of documents during the student occupation of the Harvard Center for International Affairs) or indiscretions (like ex-CIA agent Philip Agee's memoirs).[23] Furthermore, we are not dealing here with data – i.e., "givens" of unquestionable authenticity and solidity. The documents that can be cited as authority are themselves part of the action. They must be questioned by the researchers critically so as to make them reveal things they do not explicitly state, namely their meanings. Inference is the process of acquiring knowledge in such situations; and inference, let it be stressed contrary to what Douglas and Godson imply, leads to a higher not a lower level of certainty, through the application of critical method to biased sources.

I shall deal here, for purpose of illustration, only with events in Chile preceding and following the Pinochet coup and assassination of

President Salvatore Allende in September 1973. In "Labor and Hegemony," I wrote that the full story had not been told, to which Douglas and Godson retorted that indeed it had and referred me to *Covert Action in Chile*, the staff report to the Senate committee whose final report I mentioned above, which, they write, "diligently investigated rumors of AIFLD involvement, but found none to report." It is not as simple as that. There are a number of elements with which the outline of the picture of the AFL-CIO involvement can be pieced together.

In the first place, there certainly was an AFL-CIO effort, principally through the AIFLD, to penetrate the labor movement in Chile as in other Latin American countries, an effort operating with high-level political protection in the United States, though it was accepted with less enthusiasm by some US diplomatic quarters in the field. As early as 1963, for instance, the US embassy was aware of opposition to these activities from Chilean Christian Democratic quarters on the grounds that US labor activities were backed by multinational business and by the US government and were opposed to the Latin American organization of Christian trade unions (CLASC), which Meany regarded as being crypto-communist. Nevertheless, labor projects were undertaken during the later 1960s in an attempt to undermine the principal Chilean trade union federation (CUTCh). Subsequent CIA evaluations, mentioned in the staff report cited, indicated that these projects were unsuccessful, since "neither of the labor projects was able to find a nucleus of legitimate Chilean labor leaders to compete effectively with the communist-dominated CUTCh."[24] An American sociologist who has studied Chilean labor at close hand, Professor Henry Landsberger, testified: "At one time I was quite familiar with early efforts by the AIFLD to build up a rival trade union movement in Chile. Despite the existence of large anti-Marxist sectors in labor at that time and the spending of very considerable sums of money by the AIFLD obtained from AID, these efforts were then an almost total failure. Cooperating with us and with the kinds of groups we sponsored was distasteful to Chilean trade union leaders."[25]

AFL-CIO efforts to penetrate Chilean labor have to be placed in the context of the development of the Chilean labor movement. Chile is not a typical underdeveloped country with a small industrial labor force and weak and easily penetrable union structures. Its industrial, agricultural, and white-collar labor had experienced a rapid growth in authentic union organization during the mid-1960s, in organizations of both Marxist and Christian ideology, encompassing close to 20 percent of the labor force, a proportion approximating that in the United States. In addition to political and ideological divisions, the labor movement was in practice divided on the issue of pursuing the interests of particular groups of workers versus solidarity with the goals of national development and more equitable wage spread. Alongside mass-based organizations of manual workers was a middle class movement of *gremios* or trade and professional associations. It was among the latter that the AIFLD efforts struck what limited success they had, particularly among some elements in the Chilean Maritime Federation (COMACh) and the Confederation of Chilean Professionals (CUPROCh), and also among some workers in the copper mines (whose wage demands Allende challenged as those of a "labor aristocracy") and airline employees.

AIFLD practice has been to bring selected potential labor influentials to the United States for training and indoctrination and then to retain them on AIFLD pay for nine months after their return to their country. In intelligence terminology, these would be "agents of influence," and an investment in possible future intelligence or political action.[26] There would have been a number of such agents of influence available, and there is no question but that labor disruptions in the copper mines, the strike of self-employed truck drivers and shopkeepers, and a last-minute pre-coup action by airline pilots were factors in the downfall of Allende. The effective struggle leading to the overthrow of the constitutional government was between the *gremios* attacking the regime and the mass-based worker organizations by and large defending it – and AIFLD contacts were with the former. The *New York Times* later revealed that most of the $8 million authorized for clandestine CIA activity in Chile was used in 1972 and 1973 to provide strike benefits and other means of support for anti-Allende strikers – a sum that converted at black-market rates would have had an impact of $40 million[27] – and the staff report to the Senate committee mentioned confirmed that, though there was no official decision in Washington to provide covert support to truck-owners or other strikers, "the US passed money to private sector groups which supported the strikers."[28] One cannot, however, infer from all this that AIFLD penetration was a major factor in the outcome – i.e., the fall and assassination of Allende. The AIFLD had utterly failed to develop any worker-based organizational support in Chile, and ultimately its impact could have been only that of a conspiratorial fringe, marginally effective in a condition of crisis.

The significant thing was not the determining importance of what the AIFLD may or may not have done through its contacts, but rather the kinds of people and interests it was supporting. These associations continued after the coup. AIFLD graduates were among those allowed by the Pinochet junta to constitute a labor front for the regime following its dissolution of the CUTCh.[29] Almost immediately following the coup, world trade union confederations of all tendencies – the ICFTU and World Labor Confederation, as well as the World Federation of Trade Unions with which the CUTCh had been affiliated – condemned the coup and the dismantling of authentic Chilean trade union organizations, which the junta undertook, and gave hospitality and financial support to the CUTCh in exile. AFL-CIO leaders were alone among world trade union leaders in condoning the coup.[30] While demurring at the "excesses" of the Pinochet regime, AFL-CIO pronouncements continued to devote their emphasis to condemnation of the Allende regime and approval of the coup.[30] In the United States, it was the United Auto Workers, not the AFL-CIO and its affiliates, which first began to focus criticism on the Chilean junta. An apparent change in the AFL-CIO attitude took place more than three years after the coup (at a time, it may be noted, when especially following the Letelier affair,[c] the newly-elected US government was taking its distance from the junta), in a statement by Meany in February 1977 condemning the repression of human rights in Chile.[31] This came in a curious manner as a response to an overture to Meany from the Chilean minister of labor proposing cooperation with the AFL-CIO on human rights. Douglas and Godson state, as evidence of its opposition to right-wing dictators, that the AFL-CIO in 1978 sent a mission to Chile that

---

[c] Orlando Letelier was the Chilean Ambassador to the United States during the government of Salvador Allende. He was imprisoned by the military junta which took power in Chile in the 1973 coup. Subsequently, he worked as director of the Transnational Institute, the international program of the Institute for Policy Studies in Washington, DC. A week before his assassination in September 1976 by agents of DINA, the Chilean secret police, he had published an article in the *Nation* which argued that the Chilean junta's human rights violations were linked to the US-sponsored "Chicago-school" economic model implemented in Chile by the junta. See John Dingles and Saul Landau, *Assassination on Embassy Row* (New York: Pantheon, 1980), and Donald Freed with Dr. Fred Simon Landis, *Death in Washington: The Murder of Orlando Letelier* (Westport, Conn.: Lawrence Hill and Company, 1980). The authors of the assassination have been tried and convicted under the post-Pinochet regime.

protested suppression of trade union rights. They do not say why it took the AFL-CIO leadership so long to see what other union leaders had seen more than three or four years earlier, nor why the Chilean minister of labor might have had reason as late as 1977 to think of Meany as a potential ally. Having totally failed in the pre-coup conditions of constitutionality and open society to attract a significant labor following, the AFL-CIO foreign-policy makers rejoiced in the elimination by the Pinochet regime of the existing Chilean trade union leadership, and were apparently able to secure some minimal conditions under the dictatorship for the activity of some of their AIFLD associates. Subsequently, the AFL-CIO foreign-policy group has aimed to enhance the status within the Chilean system of the people they support and to counter the criticism their position has evoked among the labor and social democratic forces in Europe.[32] Pious hopes for a return to constitutional freedom in Chile are, however, overshadowed in their policy thinking by apprehension lest overthrow of the dictatorship result in the return of the former trade union leadership or others of similar persuasion.[33] They cannot approve the junta, but neither can they safely do without it. In this respect, the AFL-CIO is caught in the same contradiction as US foreign policy and American capitalism, a contradiction between the ideology of hegemonic corporatism in the center and the structural need of its international dimension for nonhegemonic forms of control in the periphery. The issue of human rights is the manifestation of this contradiction.

Douglas and Godson represent the AFL-CIO as a champion of the "democratic left." This may be the way AFL-CIO leaders would like to represent themselves. It is probably the way many American trade union members feel about their own political preferences. But in the discourse of political analysis one is entitled to require that words have some commonly accepted meanings and that there be some correspondence between meanings and reality. If European social democratic trade unionists are to be considered as of the democratic left, not many of them would recognize the present AFL-CIO leaders as their political companions. Among Third World union activists of various tendencies – socialist, communist, religious, or populist – this characterization of the AFL-CIO's international activity could hardly be taken seriously. The common meaning evaporates. What of the correspondence with reality? The US Senate's staff report on *Covert Action in Chile* speaks of CIA-sponsored projects to support "democratic labor groups,"[34] which is routine AFL-CIO jargon. "Democratic" cannot mean majority unions, since the projects were designed to undermine the majority unions. Nor can it refer to rank-and-file support, since in a time of growing worker mobilization the AIFLD was unable to find a following. "Democratic" in this context can only be a code word designating anyone who can be bought or persuaded to work with the penetrating power's foreign policy. If, as pointed out above, "tripartite" and "transnational" are terms which can carry a surreptitious load of ideological distortion, "democratic" when applied to the client groups promoted by AFL-CIO foreign policy is a flagrant form of Newspeak.

I agree with Douglas and Godson that more research about the international dimension of trade unionism is desirable. Unfortunately, much previous work has been ideologically tied to one or other of the institutional interests active in the field. Some good and honestly independent research has been done, though it is not abundant and sometimes remains unacknowledged, so pervasively effective is the working of hegemony in this sphere.[35] Lack of sophistication of paradigms is not the main problem. More rare is the personal courage to undertake critical study in the certain knowledge that it will be read as a challenge to established positions of power and will leave the researcher virtually devoid of public and institutional support. Academic careers are not easily made that way. The chief intellectual requirement I would list is a talent for ideological analysis, ability to cut through to the meanings of documents – in other words, to know the difference between research and public relations.

Notes

This text was first published in *International Organization*, vol. 34, no. 1 (Winter 1980), pp. 159–176.

1 On the derivation and meaning of the concept, see A. Gramsci, *Quaderni del carcere* (Turin: Einaudi, 1975), vol. II, pp. 1051–1052, 1237–1238, 1300, 1321, and vol. IV, p. 2632.

2 H. A. Dunning, "Communications," *International Organization*, vol. 32, no. 2 (Spring 1978), pp. 576–578; R. W. Cox, "Communications," *International Organization*, vol. 32, no. 2 (Spring 1978), p. 579.

3 Roy Godson, *American Labor and European Politics: The AFL as a Transnational Force* (New York: Crane, Russak, 1976). This is a published version of a dissertation accepted by Columbia University in 1972 for a Ph.D in political science.

4 Ibid., pp. 149, 157–159, 161.

5 Stephen Krasner, *Defending the National Interest: Raw Materials Investment and US Foreign Policy* (Princeton, N.J.: Princeton University Press, 1978),

writes of the Frei measures: "The companies, particularly Kennecott, were generously compensated through tax reductions, new financing from the state, and liberal provisions for the expatriation of foreign exchange earnings" (p. 230). Norman Girvan, *Corporate Imperialism: Conflict and Expropriation. Transnational Corporations and Economic Nationalism in the Third World* (White Plains, N.Y.: M. E. Sharpe, 1976), writes: "Kennecott willingly agreed to Chileanization – indeed, the company claimed to have taken the initiative in suggesting it to the government – and it secured a favorable price considerably in excess of the book value for the equity sold to the government" (p. 69). The less perceptive management of Anaconda resisted Chileanization at the outset but later did a complete volte-face and asked to be fully nationalized. Both companies retained effective managerial control under formal Chilean state ownership.

6 Girvan, *Corporate Imperialism*, pp. 136–156.

7 This thesis is developed by Girvan, *Corporate Imperialism*, pp. 152–156. A more comprehensive analysis of this phase of the world economy broadly consistent with Girvan's thesis, though emphasizing manufacturing more than minerals extraction, is Charles-Albert Michalet, *Le capitalisme mondiale* (Paris: Presses universitaires de France, 1976).

8 Krasner, *Defending the National Interest*.

9 This is discussed in Perry Anderson, "The Antinomies of Antonio Gramsci," *New Left Review*, vol. 100 (November 1976–January 1977).

10 Philippe C. Schmitter, "Still the Century of Corporatism?," in Frederick B. Pike and Thomas Stritch (eds.), *The New Corporatism: Social-Political Structures in the Iberian World* (Notre Dame, Ind.: University of Notre Dame Press, 1974).

11 Godson seemed to take this approach but satisfied himself with the platitudes politicians are wont to offer as explanations of their conduct. He wrote that since the 1880s, American trade union leaders "have been seeking an amalgam of what they have regarded as worldwide democracy and free trade unionism, peace and stability, and economic and social justice" (*American Labor and European Politics*, p. 55).

12 L. Tolstoy, *War and Peace*, Book III, pt. II, ch. 28. The setback to the French forces at Borodino was attributed to the fact that Napoleon had caught cold, which adversely affected the genius of his military dispositions. The cause of his cold might thus have been traced to the valet who had not properly dried his boots, and the valet would thereby bear responsibility for the turning point in the war and ultimate defeat of the Empire.

13 This period is well analyzed in John P. Windmuller, *American Labor and the International Labor Movement, 1940 to 1953*, Cornell International Industrial and Labor Relations Reports, No. 2 (Ithaca, N.Y.: Institute of International Industrial and Labor Relations, Cornell University, 1954).

14 See "Labor and Hegemony," included in this volume (chapter 19).

15 American Institute for Free Labor Development, *Hearing Before the Committee on Foreign Relations, United States Senate, 91st Congress, 1st session,*

with George Meany, President, AFL-CIO, 1 August 1969 (Washington, D.C.: US Government Printing Office, 1969), pp. 46–47.

16 Ibid., pp. 58–59.

17 *Foreign and Military Intelligence*, Book 1, *Final Report of the Select Committee to Study Governmental Operations with Respect to Intelligence Activities. United States Senate, 26 April 1976* (Washington, D.C.: US Government Printing Office, 1976). See especially pp. 145–149, 445–446.

18 Ibid., p. 179.

19 Ibid., p. 451.

20 Ibid.

21 I refer the reader back to "Labor and Hegemony" (chapter 19), for a discussion of this dualism in the labor force.

22 Godson, *American Labor and European Politics*, pp. 52–53.

23 It should be noted that Douglas and Godson do not challenge my assertion that the AFL and AFL-CIO worked with and were subsidized by the CIA. Nor do they challenge my reference to Agee as a source, though they do appear to cast doubt upon the value of other references, namely Goulden's biography of Meany and Romualdi's memoir, both, incidentally, cited in reference by Godson in his book.

24 *Covert Action in Chile, 1963–1973. Staff Report of the Select Committee to Study Governmental Operations with Respect to Intelligence Activities. United States Senate* (Washington, D.C.: US Government Printing Office, 1975), p. 19.

25 *Hearings before the Sub-Committee on Inter-American Affairs, House of Representatives*, August 5, September 17, 18, 1974 (Washington, D.C.: US Government Printing Office, 1975), p. 229.

26 *Foreign and Military Intelligence*, p. 146.

27 Seymour M. Hersh, *New York Times*, September 20, 1974.

28 *Covert Action*, p. 2.

29 Information about the roles of AIFLD contacts in Pinochet's Chile has been collected by concerned groups and investigative reporters – for example, North American Congress on Latin America, Berkeley, Calif.; Northern California Chile Coalition, Berkeley, Calif.; Research Associates International, Marina del Rey, Calif. The substance of what these sources have reported is confirmed in an article by Andrew McLellan, Interamerican Representative of the AFL-CIO, published in *AFL-CIO Free Trade Union News*, December 1975; namely, that AIFLD associates are "the surviving nucleus" of Chilean trade unionism, and that the AIFLD "serves as a rallying point and source of encouragement" for them. The same issue of *Free Trade Union News* carries with editorial approval a statement by Eduardo Rios Arias, an AIFLD associate who was placed by the military in charge of the Maritime Confederation of Chile after they had removed the elected CUT-oriented officers. Rios was appointed by the junta to represent Chilean labor at the ILO Conference.

30 In a resolution adopted by the AFL-CIO Executive Board at its meeting of August 5–6, 1974, and adopted again in substantially the same terms by

the AFL-CIO Convention in October 1975, it is stated that "a majority of the Chilean people . . . accepted the coup as a necessary act," and that "the desire of the people . . . was, and is, a return to the freely elected and constitutional government" (*AFL-CIO Free Trade Union News*, September 1974 and December 1975). In documents of this sort, one cannot imagine even a touch of irony, having regard to the fact that the overthrown government and assassinated president were both constitutional and freely elected.

31 *AFL-CIO Free Trade Union News*, February 1977.

32 Andrew McLellan, in the article cited above, criticized the ICFTU for its support of "Communist and Maoist exiles" of the CUT and for all but disowning its regional affiliate, the ORIT. Though technically an organ of the ICFTU, the ORIT has in fact been a creature of the AFL-CIO.

33 A theme developed in another article written by Stuart Elliot in the December 1975 issue of *Free Trade Union News* – the same which contained the McLellan and Rios statements. Godson, *American Labor and European Politics*, p. 42, pointed out that Irving Brown is the author of the doctrine that the overthrow of right-wing dictatorships creates a most dangerous situation favoring communist takeover.

34 *Covert Action*, p. 9.

35 There is the considerable work of John Windmuller, who has maintained a consistent scholarly detachment. Jeffrey Harrod's *Trade Union Foreign Policy: A Study of British and American Unions in Jamaica* (London: Macmillan, 1972), a study of British and US trade union penetration in Jamaica, was a path-breaking study that has suffered an almost systematic lack of recognition.

21 Multilateralism and world order (1992)

"World order" has become a current catchphrase of political discourse and journalism. "Multilateralism" has become something of a growth sector in academic studies. What current events have brought into prominence, scholarship has an obligation to subject to critical analysis. This essay raises some of the questions that should be probed in this analysis.

The two concepts are interrelated. Multilateralism appears in one aspect as the subordinate concept. Multilateralism can only be understood within the context in which it exists, and that context is the historical structure of world order. But multilateralism is not just a passive, dependent activity. It can appear in another aspect as an active force shaping world order. The agent/structure dilemma is a chicken-and-egg proposition.

To understand the potential for change that multilateralism holds, it is first necessary to place the study of multilateralism within the analysis of global power relations. I deliberately avoid using a term like "international relations" since it embodies certain assumptions about global power relations that need to be questioned. "International relations" implies the Westphalian state system as its basic framework, and this may no longer be an entirely adequate basis since there are forms of power other than state power that enter into global relations. "World order" is neutral as regards the nature of the entities that constitute power; it designates an historically specific configuration of power of whatever kind.

The dominant tendencies in existing world order can be examined within a global system having three principal components: a global political economy, an inter-state system, and the biosphere or global ecosystem. These three components are both autonomous in having their own inherent dynamics, and at the same time, interdependent with each other. Contradictions are generated within each of the three spheres, and contradictions arise in the interrelationships among the three spheres.

In conventional diplomatic usage, the term multilateral refers to states. It covers relationships among more than two states with respect to some specific issue or set of issues.[1] Another usage of "multilateral" has long been current in international economic relations, i.e., the notion of multilateral trade and payments. Multilateralism in this sense was synonymous with the most-favored-nation principle in international trade and the movement towards convertibility of currencies and freedom of capital flows.[2]

The first of these meanings of "multilateral" derives from the inter-state system. It is limited to relations among states through diplomatic channels or inter-state organizations. The second refers to relations among the economic actors of civil society within a framework regulated by states and international organizations. It pertains to an historically specific form of capitalist market economy, that in which civil society is separate and distinct from the state, and the agents of civil society are presumed to act within a system of rationally deducible behavioral laws. It would have little or no meaning for the relationships among what Karl Polanyi called redistributive societies, whether ancient empires or modern centrally planned economies.[3]

The specific context out of which the economic concept of multilateralism emerged was negotiation essentially between the United States and Britain for the constitution of the post-World War II economic order. The United States used its economic leverage to pressure Britain to abandon the preferential trade and payments system encompassing the Commonwealth and Empire under the Ottawa Agreements of 1933, which was one of several attempts to cope with the worldwide depression of the 1930s by protectionism within an economic bloc. When these Anglo-American negotiations took place, Europe and the Soviet Union were devastated by war and what later became known as the Third World was inarticulate in international economic affairs. These countries were not effective participants in the definition of the concept or in giving substance to it.

In that context, economic multilateralism meant the structure of world economy most conducive to capital expansion on a world scale; and political multilateralism meant the institutionalized arrangements made at that time and in those conditions for inter-state cooperation on common problems. There was, for some people, an implicit compatibility, even identity, between economic and political aspects of multilateralism: political multilateralism had as a primary goal the security and maintenance of economic multilateralism, the underpinning of growth in the world capitalist economy. This was the vision of Cordell Hull, President Franklin D. Roosevelt's secretary of state. Others saw contradiction between economic and political aspects: political multilateralism for them existed to correct the inequities that resulted from the world economy, leading, for instance, in the 1960s, to a demand for the institutionalization of a New International Economic Order. This view came to be expressed by leaders of Third World nations.

The relative simplicity of the idea of a world order consisting of a state system and a capitalist world economy may, however, be inadequate to encompass the totality of forces capable of influencing structural change at the close of the twentieth century. An enlarged conception of global society would include economic and social forces, more or less institutionalized, that cut across state boundaries – forces of international production and global finance that operate with great autonomy outside of state regulation, and other forces concerned with ecology, peace, gender, ethnicities, human rights, the defense of the dispossessed, and the advancement of the disadvantaged that also act independently of states. Multilateralism has to be considered from the standpoint of its ability to represent the forces at work in the world at the local level as well as at the global level. What about aspirations for autonomy and a voice in world affairs by micro-regions or fragments of existing states? How can the less powerful be represented effectively? Who will negotiate for the biosphere which humanity shares interdependently with other forms of life?

To define a meaning of multilateralism for today and tomorrow, we must begin with an assessment of the present and emerging future condition of the world system, with the power relationships that will give contextual meaning to the term. In the most general statement of the problem of multilateralism, these questions are posed:

— What kinds of entities are involved in multilateral relations?
— What kind of system connects these entities?
— What specific condition of the system gives the contextual meaning to the terms multilateral and multilateralism?
— What kind of knowledge is appropriate to understanding the phenomenon of multilateralism?

Multilateralism can be examined from two main standpoints: one, as the institutionalization and regulation of established order; the other, as the locus of interactions for the transformation of existing order. Multilateralism, in practice, is both, but these two aspects find their bases in different parts of the overall structure of multilateralism and pursue different tactics. A comprehensive enquiry into multilateralism at the present time cannot afford to focus on the one to the detriment of the other. Indeed, the question of transformation is the more compelling of the two.

The "crisis of multilateralism"

Before tackling these questions, we must consider further the circumstances leading to this revived concern with multilateralism on the threshold of the 1990s. Why is multilateralism a matter of such concern today? In a preface to a collection of articles by Dutch officials and scholars published in 1988 entitled *The UN Under Attack*,[4] Sir Shridath Ramphal, secretary-general of the Commonwealth, wrote:

> [T]he paradox – and the tragedy – of recent times is that even as the need for better management of relations between nations and for a multilateral approach to global problems has become more manifest, support for internationalism has weakened – eroded by some of the strongest nations whose position behooves them to be at its vanguard and who have in the past acknowledged that obligation of leadership. This is most true, of course, of the United States, whose recent behaviour has served actually to weaken the structures of multilateralism, including the United Nations itself.

Ramphal then referred to some of the advances in international cooperation, particularly with reference to Third World problems, since Bretton Woods and San Francisco, and continued:

> They were possible because of the emergence of a global consensus which responded in some fashion to the consciousness that we were all part of one world community – neighbours needing an ethic of partnership for living together. That enlightened consensus has become a casualty in the drift towards dominance and the ascendancy of unilateralism in world affairs ... Recently there have been moves towards coordination of economic policy among leading industrial countries. This is, in principle, better than wholly uncoordinated national action. But cooperation within a directorate of powerful countries is hardly the answer to the world's needs, the needs of all its nations. In fact, it could well have the result of reinforcing the dominance of the few over the many.[5]

497

In this perspective, the crisis of multilateralism emerged in the 1980s in a tendency on the part of the United States and some other powerful countries to reject the United Nations as a vehicle for international action and a movement on the part of these countries towards either unilateralism or collective dominance in world economic and political matters. The context in which this shift occurred was the economic crisis of the mid-1970s which led among other things to a reduced willingness on the part of the rich countries to finance aid to the Third World, and an increased tendency on their part to insist upon free-market, deregulating, and privatizing economic policies both at home and abroad. This was accompanied by their suspicion that the United Nations system was an unfriendly political forum and a potential obstacle to economic liberalization.

There thus occurred a cleavage between the old economic multilateralism, perceived as a support to a liberal economic order and institutionally located in the principal agencies of the western-dominated world economy, i.e., the International Monetary Fund (IMF) and the World Bank; and a more political multilateralism, symbolically located in the UN General Assembly, and perceived by these powerful states as harboring an unfriendly Third World majority.

During the late 1980s and early 1990s, the configuration of power giving context to multilateralism changed again. The Soviet Union, beset by economic crisis at home and undergoing a major transformation of its political being, proclaimed "new thinking" about world relationships and the United Nations system. In substance, the key factor for the Soviet Union became the maintenance of friendly relations with the United States and the corollaries of a shift of resources from military to civilian purposes, a turning inward to face political and economic crises within the union, and a withdrawal of support for Third World opposition to US international objectives.

The vacancy of Soviet power as a countervailing balance to US power together with the economic and political weakening of the Third World generated a new potential for the UN Security Council, an opportunity seized by the United States. Cooperative relationships between the five permanent members of the Security Council emerged significantly with regard to the Iran–Iraq war. For Britain and France the new relationship among the permanent five was an opportunity to regain a privileged position at the center of world power. They needed the United States but the United States also evidently needed them. For China, the new situation was a means of attenuating the relative ostracism it had suffered in the wake of the Tiananmen Square incidents of 1989. The Gulf crisis of the summer of 1990 and the military action that followed delineated a new configuration of forces that US President George Bush has repeatedly referred to as the "new world order."

From a position of reluctant member of the United Nations, expecting little support for its policies in that organization, the United States, with Soviet acquiescence, took the initiative against Iraq and gained legitimacy for it from the Security Council. The reversals of attitude towards the United Nations by both the United States and the Soviet Union had been followed by measures to begin payment of the considerable arrears owed by both states to the UN, although repayments were stretched out over time sufficiently to constitute a continuing leverage for compliant behavior by the organization.

The US success in the Security Council posed the problem of multilateralism in a different way, contrasting with the way it was presented by Ramphal in the passage cited above. The problem was no longer how the UN could survive without the political and financial support of the United States. It became whether the UN could function as a world organization if it came to be perceived as the instrument of its most powerful member. The Security Council's action could be seen as legitimating a US initiative already decided, not as the independent source of a genuinely international policy.

This question concerns particularly the Third World countries that had wielded considerable influence over United Nations decisions in the General Assembly. This apprehension is strengthened by the effect of global economic structures in weakening the capacity for resistance by poor countries to the disciplinary market effects generated by forces of global finance and production in an economic system organised and sustained by the rich countries. If Third World countries can no longer seek even symbolic support through collective action in the United Nations, what recourse will they have to express an alternative vision of world order?

The present world political-economic context raises both potentially and more and more explicitly a number of new issues for multilateralism. One concerns the process through which the Security Council majority and the military coalition for the Gulf War was put together. These were ad hoc diplomatic constructs built with country-specific pressures and incentives. The cost to the United States in material and diplomatic concessions to secure both Security Council votes and participation in the military coalition was offset by the ability of the United States to extract funding from Japan and Germany, Saudi Arabia and Kuwait. Such measures could work in the Security Council with its limited membership but could hardly be expected to work in the larger General Assembly. The process hardly compares with the "enlightened consensus" of a continuing character evoked by Ramphal with respect to the earlier period. Would it likely lead to a polarization within UN multilateralism between the dominant few and the relatively powerless many, eventually between the Security Council and the General Assembly?

There is also the question how far a state can act militarily for the United Nations in the absence of any United Nations command and regular accountability to the Security Council or of any defined role for the secretary-general. The Gulf case seemed to open an institutional void, creating an uncertain and potentially dangerous precedent.

A further issue is the relationship between governments and domestic forces. In a number of countries in the Islamic world, sentiment in the streets favored Iraq and fueled resentment against US and other western intervention forces in the heartland of Islam, despite the official positions of Arab government members of the coalition. Popular Islamism may also be read as a metaphor for a more widespread Third World resentment against the economic and political dominance of the capitalist West, more forcibly felt since the 1980s as a consequence of the Third World debt crisis among other causes. Furthermore, domestic opposition to the war was manifested in the more powerful countries as well, including initially in the United States. How far can the existence of widespread domestic opposition undermine the legitimating function of the United Nations? Is there any way in which multilateralism can take account of the level of popular forces as well as the level of governments?

The Gulf crisis also brought into focus the issue of the environmental consequences of war. The warnings of environmental disaster from a conference of scientists in London just prior to the beginning of hostilities were quickly realized by oil spills and fires. This particular disaster underscored the problem of achieving some means of managing the relationship between the natural environment and human actions determined by politics in the interests of the biosphere which humanity shares as a part of nature. The implications of multilateralism extend beyond humanity, whether expressed at state or popular or individual behavior levels, to include non-human forces which will affect prospects for human survival.

Thus, the "crisis of multilateralism" in its two recent phases, presents an additional set of questions:

— How can national interest as perceived by the most powerful state be reconciled with multilateralism? Must there be a choice between weakening multilateralism through its rejection by the unilateralism of a powerful state, and weakening of multilateralism through its instrumental use by a powerful state?

— What are the conditions for global consensus as a basis for multilateralism? One form of consent may be acquiescence in the leadership of a powerful state insofar as that state is widely perceived to embody universally acceptable principles of order. Another may be through recognition of the coexistence of different value systems where the principles of each value system are brought to bear in the achievement of a solution to common problems.

— What is the relationship between economic multilateralism, i.e., the processes of global liberal economic structures sustained by the most powerful capitalist states; and political multilateralism or the aspiration for consensual control over global economic processes empowering less-privileged countries, for example, as was envisaged in the abortive demands for a New International Economic Order?

— What role could popular movements either mobilized by events or around longer-term issues (for example, peace, social justice, environmentalism, or feminism), play in multilateralism?

— What role does multilateralism play in the relationship between the biosphere and human political and economic organization?

Intellectual approaches to multilateralism

The current crisis of multilateralism represents the problematic of our study. This problematic can be viewed through a number of different lenses, each a different intellectual perspective. These perspectives are differentiated by epistemologies and ontologies. They express different conceptions of how knowledge in human affairs can be acquired and for what purposes; and they posit different conceptions of what constitutes the field of enquiry, what the basic entities and basic relationships are. Some of the principal perspectives can be reviewed to illustrate this point.

To represent these different perspectives is, in practice, to construct them as ideal types. Here, the perspective becomes separated from the perceiver. The work of certain authors helps to define the logically coherent forms of ideal types; but many authors share more than one perspective. My intention is not to put people into boxes. It is rather to show how a satisfactory perspective may draw upon several of the main theoretical traditions.

Realism

The starting point for contemporary theorizing about global power relations is the realist tradition. Realism puts a primary emphasis upon states and the analysis of the historical behavior of states but, I shall argue, does not limit its vision to states. Realism, in its more sophisticated manifestations, is also concerned with the economic and social underpinnings of states and how the nature of states changes. In classical realism, the state is no absolute; the state is historicized.

However, let us begin by assuming a world in which states are the only significantly powerful entities engaged in global power relations, and in which each state is constrained in its ambitions only by the threat of retaliation by other states. In such a world, multilateralism is conceivable at most as a series of transitory arrangements designed to achieve collective purposes among a group of states that find a temporary common interest. The moving forces in such a system are changes in the relative powers of the states and redefinitions of state interests. These could change the composition of groupings of states that are able to discover common or compatible purposes.

International institutions and general principles of international law or behavior are not absent from the realist conception of world order, but they have what a Marxist might call a superstructural character. That is, they are not to be taken at face value but to be seen as means of achieving ends that derive from the real conflicts of interest at the heart of the system. E. H. Carr, whose work remains a classic exposition of realist thinking, wrote: "Just as the ruling class in a community prays for domestic peace, which guarantees its own security and predominance, and denounces class war, which might threaten them, so international peace becomes a special vested interest of pre-dominant Powers."[6] And: "[I]nternational government is, in effect, government by that state which supplies the power necessary for the purpose of governing."[7]

In the realist perspective, there is room for a considerable prolifer-ation of international institutions, but little room for any cumulative acquisition of authority by these institutions. International organiza-tions will have no real autonomy as agencies capable of articulating collective purposes and mobilizing resources to pursue these pur-poses. They will remain mechanisms for putting into effect, or merely for publicly endorsing, purposes that have been arrived at and are given effect by those states that dispose of the resources necessary for attaining them. International institutions are a public ritual designed to legitimate privately determined measures. The general principles used to legitimate these measures in the enactment of ritual are sus-pect as rationalizations of ulterior motives. The critical realist analyst is enjoined to strip away the cloak of public respectability so as to reveal the basic purposes at work. Argument on the grounds of the principles invoked would be an irrelevant distraction from the real issue which is to reveal the basic interests at work. Only by laying bare these interests can effective counteracting forces be put together, forces which, in turn, might make use of international institutions and principles of law and morality to further their different purposes.

Classical realism is capable of recognizing its own limitations; and these limitations arise with the phenomenon of moral sentiment. The fact that the powerful appeal to moral principles in order to secure acquiescence from the less powerful suggests that moral sentiments do have a certain force in human and even inter-state affairs. Even though the state is a purely fictitious person, the fact that people ascribe moral claims to state behavior as though the state were a person has some effect in constraining the state. Moreover, moral sen-timents may enter into the formulation of state purposes. The realist will, however, beware of placing too heavy a burden of practice upon moral sentiment and will be alive to the hypocrisy with which moral sentiment cloaks egoistic intents.

Classical realism remains remarkable in the extent to which it is capable of accounting for the condition of multilateralism and in par-ticular for the crisis of multilateralism discussed above. It provides an explanation for United States aloofness from the UN system during the 1970s phase of the crisis, in the perception that a Soviet blocking ability in the Security Council and a Third World majority in the General Assembly negated the endorsement of US goals in these bodies. Meanwhile, economic forces in which US interests remained predominant, were weakening both the Soviet bloc and the Third World. The United States could virtually ignore the United Nations as a center of multilateral activity and allow economic forces to continue to shift power relations in its favor.

Classical realism also provides an explanation for the second phase of the crisis of multilateralism. The withdrawal of Soviet power as a counterweight to US power and the alignment of Soviet with US positions in the Security Council, coupled with continuing financial pressures on Third World countries guaranteed a docile response to US initiative in the Security Council. Most Third World countries were constrained by financial pressures of external debt to open their economies further to the penetration of the dominant forces in the world economy protected by the United States. A Third World country that sought to control its economic resources in its own interest in contradiction to external market forces posed a challenge to the global economic system that, even if not substantively threatening, might become contagious. Chile and Nicaragua were not alone to suffer the consequences. A Security Council under US dominance could authorize military action that would stand as a warning to any Third World country disposed to build a military challenge to the system. The real reasons for the US initiation of war against Iraq, in a realist interpretation, remained obscured by the public ritual in the Security Council.

The epistemological foundations of classical realism are historicist and hermeneutic. Classical realism is a critical theory in that it does not accept appearances at face value but seeks to penetrate to the meaning within. It takes account of historical structures as well as of events. The term historical structures designates those persisting patterns of thought and actions that define the frameworks within which people and states act. These structures are shaped and reshaped slowly over time – the *longue durée* of Fernand Braudel.[8] They are the intersubjective realities of world politics. The critical analysis of classical realism is the process of discerning the meaning of events within these historically determined frameworks for action.

A critical theory is more at the service of the weak than of the strong. Machiavelli may be accorded the status of first critical theorist of European thought. (I would argue that Ibn Khaldun, the fourteenth-century Islamic diplomat and scholar was the first critical theorist of his civilization;[a] and I expect other instances of critical theory can be discovered in other traditions of civilization.) In form, Machiavelli's *Prince* appears to be addressed to the powerful, to the *palazzo*. In effect, his work instructs the outsiders in the mechanisms of power – it enlightens the *piazza*. Classical realism is to be seen as a means of empowerment of the less powerful, a means of demystification of the manipulative instruments of power.

There is a distortion of classical realism called neorealism that severs realism from its critical roots and converts it into a problem-solving device for the foreign-policy makers of the most powerful states.[9] This neorealism, which is very largely an American product of the Cold War, attempts to construct a technology of state power.[10] It computes the components of power of individual states, and assesses the relative chances of moves in the game of power politics. Its epistemology is positivist and it lacks any dimension of historical structural change. The world of inter-state relations is a given world, identical in its basic structure over time. There are no changes of the system, only changes within the system.[11]

Liberal institutionalism

From the moment of drafting of the UN Charter until the present time a different current of theories has centered attention upon multilateralism, endeavoring to discern in it the emergence of institutions that would transform world order by progressively bringing the state system within some form of authoritative regulation. This current has thrown up a whole sequence of theoretical formulations, each of which appears to have been superseded by its successor.

The earliest formulation was the functionalism of David Mitrany.[12] Functionalism, despairing of progress through the world federalist approach to constructing world government, envisaged an alternative route through the "low politics" of functional or technical agencies. Its principal argument was that by associating professionals and technicians who were primarily concerned with solving practical problems of everyday life – from delivering the mail on time to promoting health, education, and welfare – in international agencies charged with these matters, the conflictual sphere of "high politics"

[a] See "Towards a Posthegemonic Conceptualization of World Order: Reflections on the Relevancy of Ibn Khaldun," chapter 8 in this volume.

monopolized by diplomats and political leaders would be outflanked and diminished by the cooperative sphere of functionalism. World government would arrive by stealth rather than by design.

Functionalism became embodied in the specialized agencies revived or established as component parts of the UN system. The thought behind it appeared to gain relevancy when the UN system, from the 1960s, expanded its technical assistance work in less-developed countries. The world system was, in a sense, helping to build the state structures upon which it formally was to rest.

Functionalism, however, though it distinguished "low" from "high" politics in order to focus upon the former with the implication that in the long run low politics was the more fundamental, offered no theory of how a more centralized world authority would come about. Neofunctionalist theory filled this gap. According to its proponents, the scope and authority of international institutions would be increased through a conscious strategy of leadership. Any major field of functional competence entrusted to an international institution was likely to impinge upon linked fields in which no international authority had been assigned. Innovative leadership could manipulate an impasse in which action was blocked at the margin of an institution's existing authority into a consensus for the expansion of authority into the bordering field that would enable action to advance. This was called "spillover." Neofunctionalism also expanded the range of relevant actors to include elements of civil society: trade unions, industrial associations, consumer groups and other advocacy groups, and also political parties. The orientation of these various interests towards international institutions would enhance the authority of these institutions.[13]

The broadening of scope and authority of international institutions was considered by neofunctionalists as a process of integration. Karl W. Deutsch, in a somewhat different approach, defined integration as the formation of a "security community" within which groups of people enjoyed institutions and practices of a kind that allowed for a reasonable expectation that change would proceed by peaceful rather than violent means.[14] Deutsch's approach gave more emphasis to modes of common understanding and communication without placing the condition of integration necessarily upon the creation of an authoritative central power.[15]

Neofunctionalism had its greatest success in studies of the process of European economic integration.[16] The apparent fit with the western

European experience prompted its adaptation to non-European situations. With regard to Latin America, the importance of autonomous interest groups and political parties was replaced by an emphasis on the technocratic elites.[17] Neofunctionalism was also applied, though with somewhat lesser plausibility, to the world as a whole.[18]

Both functionalism and neofunctionalism were challenged by events. The East–West conflicts of the Cold War and the North–South political issues that remained after the decolonization of the 1960s (notably southern African and the Arab–Israeli conflicts) could not be set aside by technical cooperation. These issues kept resurfacing within specialized agencies as well as in the UN General Assembly. Functionalism then appeared as an ideology of the western capitalist powers which sought to resist what they perceived as "politicization" of technical work by Soviet and Third World diplomats.

Neofunctionalism encountered its negation in the defeat of the proposed European Defense Community in 1954 when the French National Assembly refused to ratify the treaty establishing it. It was negated again during the 1960s in the personality of General Charles de Gaulle, who stood as an obstacle to the accumulation of further authority by the Community bureaucracy in Brussels. Neofunctionalist analysts who had previously envisaged "spillover" of authority from one functionalist sphere to another, now began to write of "spillback."[19] What had hitherto been represented an an irreversible process now appeared to be stalled and quite possibly reversed.

As functionalism and neofunctionalism lost theoretical luster, liberal institutionalism shifted ground. It focused less on the prospect of superseding the state though some larger regional or world process of integration, in order to concentrate more upon processes through which cooperative arrangements at the international level are constructed.

From the early 1970s, interest shifted to transnational relations.[20] This approach magnified the emphasis neofunctionalism had placed upon civil society as a network of linkages both extending and circumscribing in some ways the autonomy of state action. The world economy was the center of attention, in terms both of the business organizations that operated on a global scale and of the emergence of a transnational form of society among those people most directly involved. Alongside interest groups, emphasis in the liberal institutionalist tradition has been placed more recently on "epistemic communities" or transnational networks of specialists who evolve amongst themselves a way of conceiving and defining global problems in particular spheres of concern.[21]

Corresponding to this prominence of transnational civil society came a stress on the fragmentation of the state. States, following the lead given by the "bureaucratic politics" analysis of national policy making, were perceived as systems of competing agencies, where an agency in one state might build a coalition with like agencies in other states in order to enhance its domestic influence within its own state.[22] International institutions now looked more complex: they were both constrained by the transnational linkages of global civil society such as the networks of influence generated by international production and global finance; and they had become vehicles for transgovernmental coalitions constructed by bureaucratic segments within the various states.

This vision of "complex interdependence"[23] led to a fresh round of research into international "regimes."[24] Without reproducing any exhaustive definition of a regime, it is sufficient to describe it as a set of norms or rules accepted by a group of states as a means of dealing with a certain sphere of common concerns. The notion goes to the heart of the question of how cooperation is achieved and sustained, without necessarily tying this to the existence of formal international organizations. Moreover, it is concerned with cooperation, not with superseding the state system as the repository of authority. Regime theory focuses upon "rational actors" acting in conditions of "bounded rationality," i.e., in the absence of the impossible conditions of full information and continuous calculation of self-interest, relying rather on procedures that have worked reasonably well in the past. One probable consequence of the predominance of regime theory in recent liberal institutionalism has been a shift of emphasis back more exclusively to states as the principal actors.

A central issue in regime theory is the thesis of "hegemonic stability" according to which regimes have been constituted under the protection of dominant powers. The question is: can regimes founded in such conditions survive the decline of such powers? Robert Keohane has constructed an argument based on rational-choice assumptions to suggest that existing forms of cooperation may indeed survive because they continue to provide states with cost-saving, uncertainty-reducing, and flexible means of achieving the results of cooperation.[25]

Another theoretical basis of regime theory seems to be derived from Durkheim's thesis that the growth of the division of labor bringing about increased interdependencies among the actors in society will lead to disruptive consequences – he mentioned specifically economic crises and class struggle – unless the growth of interdependence is matched by adequate regulation.[26] Applied to the international level, regimes are the means of introducing such regulation – the counterpart to what Durkheim envisaged as the role for corporatism in national society. In the current world economy, some spheres of activity have been covered by regimes that are being maintained or amended more or less effectively, for example, in trade with GATT, while other spheres of activity, for example, finance and production, are very largely unregulated.

This current approach of liberal institutionalism pursues answers to these questions: do international institutions make a difference? Why are some spheres of activity internationally regulated while others are not? Does the density of transborder interactions in a particular area predict the formation of a regime in that area? What determines membership and non-membership in a regime?[27]

Liberal institutionalism through its various developmental phases has certain basic characteristics. Its epistemology has remained both positivist and rational-deductive insofar as its objects of enquiry are actors and interactions and as it attempts to account for their behavior according to models of rational choice. It has lacked the historical structural dimension of classical realism which is concerned with the frameworks or structures within which actors and interactions take place and the meanings inherent in the relationship of actions to the preexisting whole. Liberal institutionalism takes the existing order as given, as something to be made to work more smoothly, not as something to be criticized and changed.

In effect, liberal institutionalism has its starting point in the coexistence of state system and world capitalist economy. The problems with which it deals are those of rendering compatible these two global structures and of ensuring stability and predictability to the world economy. Thus regime theory has much to say about economic cooperation among the G7 and other groupings of advanced capitalist countries with regard to problems common to them. It has correspondingly less to say about attempts to change the structure of world economy, for example, in the Third World demand for a New International Economic Order. Indeed, regimes are designed to stabilize the world economy and have the effect, as Keohane has underlined in his work, of inhibiting and deterring states from initiating radical departures from economic orthodoxy, for example, through socialism.[28]

The current implications of liberal institutionalism are that new regimes or international institutions may be more difficult to initiate or even to change in the absence of a dominant power able and willing to commit resources to them, but that existing regimes may survive and evolve to the extent that they provide information and facilities for dealing with matters among their members. These regimes and institutions facilitate the interaction of states and components of civil society within their spheres. This approach to multilateralism is consistent with a conservatively adaptive attitude towards the existing structures of world order.

World-system structuralism

World-system theories, unlike liberal institutionalist theories, have not been directed explicitly towards the study of international organization, though they do provide an explanatory framework for multilateralism. These theories begin with a conception of the totality of the world system. This conception takes states for the constitutive units, as does realism, but sees these units as having a structural relationship predetermined by the world economy – a relationship expressed in terms of core and periphery, with an intermediate category of semi-periphery.

The concept "state" designates the political aspect of an entity conceived primarily in economic terms. Core economies are dominant over peripheral economies; they determine the conditions in which peripheral economies produce and they extract surplus from peripheral production for the enhancement of the core.[29] Thus, the core produces underdevelopment in the periphery through the economic relations linking the two.[30] Semi-periphery economies are strong enough to protect themselves from this kind of exploitation, and they struggle to attain core status.

States and inter-state relations are the political structures that maintain in place the exploitative core–periphery relationship of economies. Periphery states are weak in relation to core states and penetrated by them. A principal weapon in the struggle of semi-peripheral countries is, accordingly, to strengthen the semi-peripheral state so that it can gain autonomy in relation to the core states. Economic protectionism, economic nationalism, and national planning, whether socialist or state capitalist, are characteristic of the semi-peripheral struggle for greater local control over development.[31]

The core–periphery structure of dominance is maintained not just by external pressures but also by support from dominant classes or elites in the periphery country who benefit from the relationship. State, military, and economic elites in the periphery country are critical factors in maintaining the relationship. They count on material and ideological support from the core. They maintain their position internally by exclusion or manipulation of the domestic social forces from political and economic power, for example, by suppressing opposition or allowing only "domesticated" opposition parties, suppressing or controlling trade unions, etc. Where this peripheral structure of power is overthrown, its components can count on the resources of the core (financial, intelligence, and ultimately military) to destabilize and subvert the forces that have taken power from them.

This political structure of domination is coupled to a socioeconomic structure that orients the peripheral economies towards the world economy shaped by the core. The core requires that the periphery economy be open to foreign investment, to imports of core goods and services, and to export of profits. Peripheral structures of labor control differ from those in the core; they ensure a supply of docile and cheap labor, since the economic function of the periphery is to supply inputs to the higher value added production of the core as well as to absorb part of the core's output. This relative subordination of periphery labor contributes to maintaining terms of trade favorable to the core while at the same time separating the interests of core labor (which benefits from the core–periphery relationship) from periphery labor. Within the periphery economy, too, a minority of labor employed in foreign-owned undertakings is integrated into the world-economy networks, while the mass of local labor remains relatively deprived. The structure perpetuates itself by dividing the potential opposition forces.

Even though multilateralism does not have the central position in world-system theory that it has in liberal institutionalism, this theory has obvious implications for multilateralism. Multilateralism is seen, first, as an instrument for institutionalizing the core–periphery structure of domination. The role of the world-economy agencies, the IMF and the World Bank, is to enforce the practice of openness to world-economy forces upon peripheral economies, to maintain the outward economic orientation of periphery-country economic policy as against any locally inspired tendencies toward autocentric development.[32]

These international economic agencies operate under majority control by the core countries. They have become the means of collective imposition of core-oriented policies upon peripheral countries, while financial relations among core countries are dealt with through other mechanisms.[33] In effect, a two-tier system of economic regulation in the world economy was put in place during the 1960s: a top level comprising only the advanced capitalist countries, and a bottom level through which the advanced capitalist countries collectively imposed financial conditions upon Third World countries.

Moreover, technical assistance through international agencies under the influence of core countries became a means of adjusting the internal structures of the periphery countries to the exigencies of the world economy. International and bilateral aid, in the theory of the world-system structuralism, is seen as part of the total mechanism of subordination of the Third World, in which internal structures of dominance and dependency reinforce external pressures.[34]

Secondarily, however, in the world-system perspective, multilateralism is seen as a terrain of struggle between core and periphery, a terrain in which the grievances of the periphery can be aggregated into collective demands upon the core for structural change in the world economy. The demand raised in the 1970s for a New International Economic Order had this aspect.[35]

The two phases in the crisis of multilateralism are explainable to a considerable extent within the framework of world-economy structuralism. The quasi-withdrawal of the United States from commitment to the UN system during the late 1970s and the 1980s can be seen as a response to a perception that peripheral countries were using their majority in the major assemblies and conferences in disregard of world-economy-oriented policy and behavior. The United States and other core countries allowed the pressures of international finance to wreak their toll upon a debt-ridden Third World, while offering palliatives to avoid any Third World disruption of the system. The United States also contributed to destabilizing revolutionary movements in Central America. By the threshold of the 1990s, economic discipline had very widely been restored in the Third World, where regimes favorable to policies of adjustment to the world economy were in place. The immediate threat of concerted opposition to core-country goals within the major international organizations seemed abated. The longer-term problem remained one of sustaining favorable governments in Third World countries and of mounting a deterrent warning against particular instances of radical deviation. The Gulf crisis signaled that the ultimate sanction against defiance of the world-economy hierarchy is military. In these matters, world-system structuralism is close to the critical analysis of classical realism.

In world-system structuralism, formal multilateralism, that is, what goes on through international organizations, is only the institutionally visible part of a more complex total system of relationships linking the First and Third Worlds. The advanced capitalist countries dispose of many means of intervention (financial, intelligence, communications, and military) within Third World countries and have the support of class allies in these countries. A threat to any aspect of this complex structure of dependency would provoke retaliatory response, including response through multilateral institutions. Classical realism also probes the less visible processes of this power relationship in particular cases; but world-system structuralism offers a more systematic and generalized heuristic hypothesis. Both differ from liberal institutionalism which more readily takes state actions and multilateral processes at face value.

Epistemologically, world-system analysis has a structural-functional character. It posits the existence of a structure of relationships that are coherent and self-reproducing. Within that framework, it accounts for economic practices and social forces as well as states. Thus it embraces a larger sphere of human activity than does a realism which focuses more exclusively upon states. Realism does take account of economic capabilities as the resource underpinning state power, but tends to perceive economics as segmented into national compartments whereas world-system theory stresses the transnational linkages of economies in dominant–dependent relationships.

The weakness of world-system theory is the limitation of functionalism. Functionalism can account for synchronic relationships in a given system that has coherence. It cannot explain how that system came into existence; nor is it adequate to explain how it may be transformed.[36] What world-system theory lacks is an ability to explain change, to explain structural transformation. For this reason, it is appropriate to describe world-system theory as a structural*ism*. This structuralism can be contrasted with or complemented by a dialectical transformation of historical structures.

Historical dialectic[37]

Historical structures, as noted above in the discussion of realism, are persistent patterns of human activity and thought that endure for relatively long periods of time. They are the result of collective responses to certain common problems – whether these relate to the satisfaction of material wants (economics), the organization of cooperation and security (politics), or the explanation of the human condition and purpose (religion and ideology) – which become congealed in practices, institutions, and intersubjective meanings for a significant group of people. These practices and meanings in turn constitute the objective world for these people.

These structures are historical because they come into existence in particular historical circumstances and can be explained as responses to these circumstances. Similarly, they are transformed when material circumstances have changed or prevailing meanings and purposes have been challenged by new practices. This historical malleability of structures differentiates them from a structural*ism* that posits fixed and immutable structures, for example, like those of neorealism.

The dialectical approach to the understanding of change was concisely expressed by Ralf Dahrendorf: "The idea of a society which produces in its structure the antagonisms that lead to its modification appears as an appropriate model for the analysis of change in general."[38] The method set forth here is thus both dialectical in its explanation of change, and hermeneutic insofar as it enquires into purposes and meanings, and links subjectivity and objectivity to explain a socially constructed world order and multilateralism.

This approach can be seen in one aspect as a deepening of classical realism. Where realism focuses upon the state and the state system, historical dialectic enquires into the social processes that create and transform forms of state and the state system itself, and into the alterations in perceptions and meanings that constitute and reconstitute the objective world order.

The approach, therefore, begins with an assessment of the dominant tendencies in existing world order, and proceeds to an identification of the antagonisms generated within that order which could develop into turning points for structural transformation. Multilateralism, in this context, will be perceived as in part the institutionalization and regulation of existing order, and in part the site of struggle between conservative and transformative forces. Multilateralism's meanings and purposes, and thus the new or changed structures which multilateralism may help to create, are to be derived from its relationship to the stresses and conflicts in world order.

Karl Polanyi gave a dialectical interpretation of European economic and social history in the nineteenth century in what he called a double movement.[39] The first phase of movement was the introduction of the self-regulating market: what Polanyi saw as an utopian vision backed by the force of the state. The second phase of movement was society's unplanned and unpredicted response of self-preservation against the disintegrating and alienating consequences of market-oriented behavior. Society set about to tame and civilize the market.

The approach of historical dialectic discerns a recurrence of the double movement in the late twentieth century. A powerful globalizing economic trend thrusts toward the achievement of the market utopia on a world scale, opening national economies and deregulating transactions. At the present moment, the protective responses of societies at the national level are being weakened by the trend, while a protective response at the level of global society has yet to take form. Yet the elements of opposition to the socially disruptive consequences of globalization are visible. The question remains open as to what form these may take, as to whether and how they may become more coherent and more powerful, so that historical thesis and antithesis may lead to a new synthesis. In this context, multilateralism will become an arena of conflict between the endeavor to buttress the freedom of movement of powerful homogenizing economic forces, and efforts to build a new structure of regulation protecting diversity and the less powerful.

The global economy has become something distinct from international economic relations, i.e., from transborder economic flows assumed to be subject to state control and regulation.[40] Global production and global finance now constitute distinct spheres of power relations which constrain the state system at least as much as they are influenced by it.[41] They are bringing about a new social structure of production relations superseding the nation-centered labor–capital relations of the past. Decentralizing of production organizations and mass migratory movements from South to North are generating global patterns of social cleavage and bringing new sources of conflict within national borders.

It is less and less pertinent to think of societies as confined within territorial limits, more and more necessary to think of a stratified global society in which global elites have the impetus in shaping the social order, including the ideology in which it is grounded, and other social groups are in a position of relative powerlessness, either acquiescent or frustrated. The concepts of core and periphery, introduced by world-system analysis with a geographical meaning, are coming more and more to have a meaning of social differentiation within and across territorial boundaries.[42] The elites of globalization merge into a common structural force, even when they compete amongst themselves for primacy in the common movement.[43] The relatively powerless are fragmented by nationality, ethnicity, religion, and gender – all obstacles to greater cohesion – but their subordination is a manifestation of the formation of global society. The problem of how their concerns will be articulated is critical for the future of multilateralism.

Global finance limits drastically the capacity of states to conduct autonomous economic and social policies for the protection of their populations. The state system of the late twentieth century is coming to act more as a support to the opening of the world to global finance and global production, less as a means of defense of the welfare of local populations. Indeed, where states try to act in the protective mode they face retaliation, initially financial, ultimately perhaps military, from the changed state system. The state system skews the distribution of benefits and costs of an increasingly globalized society in favor of the economically powerful within the dominant states. (In this sense, world-system analysis retains validity within the framework of historical dialectic.) The centers of financial power and military power are located in these states. These forms of power sustain the globalizing world economy, even while the processes of global society are introducing the social cleavages and latent conflicts of First and Third Worlds *within* these centers of world power, in a process that has been called the "peripheralization of the core."

The biosphere suffers the impact of both the global economy and the state system. The global economy, activated by profit maximization, has not been constrained to moderate its destructive ecological effects. There is no authoritative regulator, so far only several interventions through the inter-state system to achieve agreement on avoidance of specific noxious practices. The state system itself is capable of massive ecological destruction through war.

The ecosystem is no longer to be thought of as an inert, passive limit to human activity. It has to be thought of as a non-human active force capable of dramatic interventions affecting human conditions and survival. Humanity is only one contingent element in the biosphere. A valid paradigm for the investigation of global change would need to include the historical interaction of human organization with the other elements in nature. The biosphere has its own automatic enforcers, for instance in the consequences of global warming; but who will negotiate on behalf of the biosphere? That must be one of the questions overshadowing future multilateralism.

The dominant economically based globalizing tendencies are accompanied and accelerated by a process of cultural homogenization emanating from the centers that give impetus to globalization. They are spread by the world media, and sustained by a convergence in modes of thought and practices among business and political elites. Yet this homogenizing tendency is countered by the affirmation of distinct identities and distinct cultural traditions. The changes taking place in state roles in the globalizing economy give new opportunity for self-expression by nationalities that have no state of their own, in movements for separation or autonomy; and the same tendencies encourage ethnicities and religiously defined groups that straddle state boundaries to express their identities in global politics. Social movements like environmentalism, feminism, and the peace movement also transcend territorial boundaries. Transnational cooperation among indigenous peoples enhances their force within particular states. These various developments augur modification of the pure Westphalian concept of inter-state system into something that might be more like what Hedley Bull envisaged as a "new medievalism," a multi-level system of political authorities with micro- and macro-regionalisms and transborder identities interacting in a more complex political process.[44]

The cultural challenge goes to the heart of the question of hegemony. "Hegemony" is used here in the Gramscian meaning of a structure of values and understandings about the nature of order that permeates a whole society, in this case a world society composed of states and non-state corporate entities.[45] In a hegemonic order these values and understandings are relatively stable and unquestioned. They appear to most actors as the natural order of things. They are the intersubjective meanings that constitute the order itself. Such a structure of meanings is underpinned by a structure of power, in which most probably one state is dominant but that state's dominance is not sufficient by itself to create hegemony. Hegemony derives from the ways of doing and thinking of the dominant social strata of the

517

dominant state or states insofar as these ways of doing and thinking have inspired emulation or acquired the acquiescence of the dominant social strata of other states. These social practices and the ideologies that explain and legitimize them constitute the foundation of the hegemonic order. Hegemony frames thought and thereby circumscribes action.

Today there is an apparent disjunction between military power, in which the United States is dominant, and economic power, in which the US advantage is lessening. Neither military nor economic power alone, or even in combination, necessarily implies hegemony. In the structure of hegemony, cultural and ideological factors are decisive. Whether or not the hegemonic order of *pax americana* is in decline, is a matter of current debate.[46] The very fact that it is called in question indicates a weakening of the ideological dimensions of hegemony, even if it proves nothing about the material power relations underpinning hegemony.

Supposing hegemony to be in decline, several logical possibilities for the future are: (a) a revival of the declining hegemony;[47] (b) a revival of the universals of the declining hegemony underpinned not by one state but by an oligarchy of powerful states that would have to concert their powers;[48] (c) the founding of a new hegemony by another state successfully universalizing its own principles of order;[49] (d) a nonhegemonic order lacking effective universal principles of order and functioning as an interplay of rival powerful states, each with their client states, most probably based on an organization of rival world regions;[50] and (e) a counterhegemonic order anchored in a broader diffusion of power, in which a large number of collective forces, including states, achieve some agreement upon universal principles of an alternative order without dominance. Quite obviously, the likelihood of these logical possibilities seems weighted in favor of some more than others. Equally obviously, the role and possibilities of multilateralism would be very different in each. The most unlikely prospects are (a) and (c) – the era of dominant single powers founding hegemony seems now past; there are no plausible successors to *pax britannica* and *pax americana*. The globalizing trend of the present would, at least in the medium term, give most probability to (b), with a distinct possibility, in case of breakdown, for example, through major financial crisis, of (d). In the much longer run, (e) will remain as a possibility, and for many of the world's less powerful, an aspiration.

Previous hegemonic orders have derived their universals from the dominant society, itself the product of a dominant civilization. A posthegemonic order would have to derive its normative content in a search for common ground among constituent traditions of civilization. What might be this common ground?

A first condition would be mutual recognition of distinct traditions of civilization, perhaps the most difficult step especially for those who have shared a common hegemonic perspective, and who are unprepared to forsake the security of belief in a natural order that is historically based on universalizing from one position of power in one form of civilization. The difficulty is underlined by the way political change outside the West is perceived and reported in the West; the tendency to view everything through western concepts which can lead, as an example, to a conclusion that the "end of history" is upon us as the apotheosis of a late western capitalist civilization. Mutual recognition implies a readiness to try to understand others in their own terms.

A second condition for a posthegemonic order would be to move beyond the point of mutual recognition towards a kind of supra-intersubjectivity that would provide a bridge among the distinct and separate intersubjectivities of the different coexisting traditions of civilization. One can speculate that the grounds for this might be (1) recognition of the requisites for survival and sustained equilibrium in global ecology, though the specific inferences to be drawn from this may remain subjects of discord; (2) mutual acceptance of restraint in the use of violence to decide conflicts, not that this would eliminate organized political violence, though it might raise the costs of resorting to violence; and (3) common agreement to explore the sources of conflict and to develop procedures for coping with conflict that would take account of distinct coexisting normative perspectives.

Historical dialectic crosses the threshold of the present from past to future. Its mode of reasoning moves from an appraisal of the forces that have historically developed to interact in the present, towards an anticipation of the points of crisis and the real options for the future. It draws upon the three preceding perspectives – realism, liberal institutionalism, and world-system analysis – while appropriating their insights within its own hermeneutic method. It approaches the problem of multilateralism as a problem in the making of a new world order.

Notes

This text was first published in *Review of International Studies*, vol. 18, no. 2 (April 1992), pp. 161–180. A first version was prepared as a "concept" paper for a symposium on perspectives on multilateralism as part of the United

Nations University program on Multilateralism and the United Nations System (MUNS). It was also presented and discussed at the International Political Science Association Congress, Buenos Aires, July 1991. I am especially grateful to Edward Appathurai, Stephen Gill, Michael Schechter, and Pat Sewell for reading and commenting on the early draft, and to three anonymous readers for the *Review of International Studies* for their helpful comments.

1 Johan Kaufmann, *Conference Diplomacy: An Introductory Analysis* (Leiden, Netherlands: A. W. Sitjoff, 1968).

2 Richard N. Gardner, *Sterling–Dollar Diplomacy: The Origins and Prospects of Our International Economic Order* (New York: McGraw-Hill, 1969).

3 Karl Polanyi, Conrad M. Arensberg, and Harry W. Pearson (eds.), *Trade and Market in the Early Empires* (Chicago: Henry Regnery, 1957).

4 Jeffrey Harrod and Nico Schrijver (eds.), *The UN Under Attack* (Aldershot, Hampshire: Gower, 1988).

5 Sir Shridath Ramphal, preface to Harrod and Schrijver, *UN Under Attack*.

6 E. H. Carr, *The Twenty Years' Crisis, 1919–1939* (London: Macmillan, 1946), p. 82. Other notable authors who could be included in the realist tradition include Hans Morgenthau, Reinhold Neibuhr, Raymond Aron, and William T. R. Fox. They do, of course, differ in their relative emphasis, particularly on the role of morality in politics; but they participate in a common discourse.

7 Ibid., p. 107.

8 Fernand Braudel, *Civilisation matérielle, économie, et capitalisme, XVe–XVIIIe siècle*, vol. 1: *Les structures du quotidien: le possible et l'impossible* (Paris: Armand Colin, 1979), and "History and the Social Sciences: The *Longue Durée*," in Braudel, *On History*, trans. by Sarah Matthews (Chicago: University of Chicago Press, 1980), pp. 25–54.

9 I have discussed the distinction between problem-solving theories and critical theories in another essay. See Robert W. Cox, "Social Forces, States, and World Orders: Beyond International Relations Theory" included in this volume (chapter 6).

10 See, for example, Kenneth Waltz, *Theory of International Politics* (Reading, Mass.: Addison-Wesley, 1979); Robert O. Keohane (ed.), *Neorealism and Its Critics* (New York: Columbia University Press, 1986).

11 I am using "neorealism" to represent a perspective perhaps best expressed in the work of Kenneth Waltz (see, for example, Keohane, *Neorealism and Its Critics*). The term has also been used more broadly to include the theorizing of cooperation among interest-pursuing states in such forms as "regimes." See, for example, Fox, who had in mind the work of John Ruggie and Stephen Krasner. I think this is better treated as one of the modifications of liberal institutionalism, although it does show the influence of neorealism upon the liberal institutionalist tradition in American scholarship of the Cold War era (W. T. R. Fox, "E. H. Carr and Political Realism: Vision and Revision," Department of International Politics, University College of Wales, Aberystwyth, E. H. Carr Memorial Lecture No. 1, n.d.).

12 David Mitrany, *A Working Peace System: An Argument for the Functional Development of International Organization* (London: Royal Institute of International Affairs/Oxford University Press, 1943).

13 Ernst B. Haas, *Beyond the Nation-State: Functionalism and International Organization* (Stanford, Calif.: Stanford University Press, 1964), especially Part I. Also see the discussion in Cox, "The Executive Head: An Essay on Leadership in International Organization", chapter 16 in this volume.

14 Karl W. Deutsch, *et al.*, *Political Economy in the North Atlantic Area: International Organization in the Light of Historical Experience* (Princeton, N.J.: Princeton University Press, 1957).

15 Karl W. Deutsch, *Nationalism and Social Communication: An Enquiry into the Foundations of Nationality* (New York: Wiley, 1953).

16 Ernst B. Haas, *The Uniting of Europe* (Stanford, Calif.: Stanford University Press, 1958).

17 Ernst B. Haas and Philippe Schmitter, "Economics and Differential Patterns of Political Integration: Projections about Unity in Latin America," *International Organization*, vol. 18 (Fall 1964), pp. 705–737.

18 Haas, *Beyond the Nation-State.*

19 Leon N. Lindberg and Stuart A. Scheingold, *Europe's Would-be Polity: Patterns of Change in the European Community* (Englewood Cliffs, N.J.: Prentice-Hall, 1970).

20 Robert O. Keohane and Joseph S. Nye (eds.), *Transnational Relations and World Politics* (Cambridge, Mass.: Harvard University Press, 1972).

21 Peter M. Haas, "Obtaining International Environmental Protection Through Epistemic Consensus," *Millennium: Journal of International Studies*, vol. 19, no. 3 (Winter 1990).

22 Robert O. Keohane and Joseph S. Nye, "Transgovernmental Relations and International Organizations," *World Politics*, vol. 27, no. 1 (October 1974), pp. 39–62.

23 Robert O. Keohane and Joseph S. Nye, *Power and Interdependence* (Boston: Little, Brown, 1977).

24 Stephen Krasner (ed.), "International Regimes," special issue of *International Organization*, vol. 36, no. 2 (1982).

25 Robert O. Keohane, *After Hegemony: Cooperation and Discord in the World Political Economy* (Princeton, N.J.: Princeton University Press, 1984).

26 Emile Durkheim, *The Division of Labor in Society*, trans. by W. D. Halls (New York: Free Press, 1984).

27 Robert O. Keohane, "Multilateralism: An Agenda for Research," *International Journal*, vol. 45, no. 4 (Autumn 1990), pp. 731–764; Oran R. Young, *International Cooperation: Building Regimes for Natural Resources* (Ithaca, N.Y.: Cornell University Press, 1989).

28 Keohane, *After Hegemony*, pp. 119–120, 254.

29 Immanuel Wallerstein, *The Modern World-System: Capitalist Agriculture and the Origins of the European World-Economy in the Sixteenth Century* (New York: Academic Press, 1974).

30 André Gunder Frank, *Capitalism and Underdevelopment in Latin America. Historical Studies of Chile and Brazil* (New York: Monthly Review, 1969).

31 Immanuel Wallerstein, "The Rise and Future Demise of the World Capitalist System: Concepts for Comparative Analysis," *Comparative Studies in Society and History*, vol. 16, no. 4 (September 1974), pp. 387–415.

32 Theresa Hayter, *Aid as Imperialism* (Harmondsworth, Middlesex: Penguin, 1971); Cheryl Payer, *The Debt Trap: The International Monetary Fund and the Third World* (New York: Monthly Review, 1974); James H. Mittelman, "International Monetary Institutions and Policies of Socialism and Self-Reliance: Are They Compatible? The Tanzanian Experience," *Social Research*, vol. 47, no. 1 (1980), pp. 141–165.

33 Robert W. Cox and Harold K. Jacobson, *The Anatomy of Influence: Decision Making in International Organization* (New Haven, Conn.: Yale University Press, 1972).

34 Brigitte Erler, *L'aide qui tue* (Lausanne, Switzerland: Editions d'en bas, 1987); James H. Mittelman, *Out from Underdevelopment: Aspects for the Third World* (London: Macmillan, 1988).

35 Robert W. Cox, "Ideologies and the New International Economic Order: Reflections on Some Recent Literature," chapter 18 in this volume; Stephen Krasner, *Structural Conflict: The Third World Against Global Liberalism* (Berkeley, Calif.: University of California Press, 1985).

36 W. G. Runciman, *Social Science and Political Theory* (Cambridge: Cambridge University Press, 1965), pp. 109–134; Robert Brenner, "The Origins of Capitalist Development: A Critique of Neo-Smithian Marxism," *New Left Review*, vol. 104 (July–August 1977), pp. 25–92.

37 I have discussed this concept more fully in earlier articles. See Robert W. Cox, "On Thinking About Future World Order" and "Social Forces, States, and World Orders: Beyond International Relations Theory," chapters 5 and 6 in this volume.

38 Ralf Dahrendorf, *Class and Class Conflict in Industrial Society* (Stanford, Calif.: Stanford University Press, 1959), pp. 125–126.

39 Karl Polanyi, *The Great Transformation: The Political and Economic Origins of Our Time* (Boston: Beacon, 1957).

40 Bernadette Madeuf and Charles Albert Michalet, "A New Approach to International Economics," *International Social Science Journal*, vol. 30, no. 2 (1978), pp. 253–283.

41 Susan Strange, *States and Markets: An Introduction to International Political Economy* (London: Pinter, 1988).

42 Robert W. Cox, *Production, Power, and World Order: Social Forces in the Making of History* (New York: Columbia University Press, 1987), ch. 9.

43 Stephen Gill, *American Hegemony and the Trilateral Commission* (Cambridge: Cambridge University Press, 1990); Kees van der Pijl, *The Making of an Atlantic Ruling Class* (London: Verso, 1984).

44 Hedley Bull, *The Anarchical Society: A Study of Order in World Politics* (New York: Columbia University Press, 1977), pp. 254–255.

45 Robert W. Cox, "Gramsci, Hegemony, and International Relations: An Essay in Method," included in this volume (chapter 7).

46 On this issue, see for example, Paul Kennedy, *The Rise and Fall of the Great Powers* (New York: Random House, 1987); Joseph S. Nye, Jr., *Bound to Lead: The Changing Nature of American Power* (New York: Basic Books, 1990); Susan Strange, "The Persistent Myth of Lost Hegemony," *International Organization*, vol. 41, no. 4 (Autumn 1987), pp. 551–574; and Stephen Gill, *American Hegemony*.

47 This would seem to be Nye's thesis in *Bound to Lead*.

48 Envisaged notably in Keohane, *After Hegemony*.

49 For example, speculations about a *pax nipponica*: see Ezra Vogel, "Pax Nipponica?," *Foreign Affairs*, vol. 64, no. 4 (Spring 1986), pp. 752–767, and a skeptical comment by Robert W. Cox, "Middlepowermanship, Japan, and Future World Order," included in this volume (chapter 13).

50 For example, Robert Gilpin, *The Political Economy of International Relations* (Princeton, N.J.: Princeton University Press, 1987).

22 Globalization, multilateralism, and democracy (1992)

I am particularly grateful for quite personal reasons to be able to give the John Holmes Memorial Lecture. It was John Holmes who opened the way for me to return to Canada after some thirty years away. During that time, Canada had become for me more of an idea than a place on the map, an idea embodied in a few people amongst whom John Holmes was an archetype.

He was a diplomat, an historian, and a master craftsman of the English language. He had that sense of duration that gives precedence to the long run over the immediate and transitory. He valued cooperation more than competition. He had a firm sense of right and wrong, but he expressed this through what Max Weber called an ethic of responsibility – always concerned in the first place about the effects of a word or an action, forsaking the satisfactions of self-proclaimed moral rectitude. He was intimately involved in the Cold War from its very beginnings in the Gouzenko affair but he never succumbed to the Manichaeism that corrupted politics and distorted mentalities for two generations.[a]

Holmes spoke somewhat ironically about "middlepowermanship" as the vocation of Canadian foreign policy. He did not mean to suggest that there is a special virtue in being neither too big nor too small. Middlepowermanship really had nothing to do with size. It defined a conception of a country's role in the world. What he had in mind

---

[a] Igor Gouzenko was a low-ranking official in the Soviet Embassy in Ottawa at the end of World War II. His defection in late 1945 exposed a wide network of Soviet agents in the civil service, military, and scientific establishments of Canada, the United States, and Great Britain. According to Granatstein and Stafford, this defection was "substantial in creating the atmosphere of crisis, betrayal, and fear that heralded the coming of the Cold War": J. L. Granatstein and David Stafford, *Spy Wars; Espionage and Canada from Gouzenko to Glasnost* (Toronto: Key Porter, 1990), p. 63.

was the initiative and the restraint of the power *in the middle*. This perspective would identify national interest with the creation and maintenance of a predictable world order with rules that are intended to be binding upon the big as well as the small. This is the *realpolitik* of the middle power. It is why John Holmes saw the United Nations as the focus of international relations.

I would like to take your time today to reflect upon issues presented by a world that has changed since the founding of the United Nations, but first I should say something about how I conceive the relationship between academic research and the practical work of international organization. The difference is not just one between theoretician and practitioner. It is a difference that involves two kinds of time and two kinds of theory.

There is the time of immediacy, the problems that press for an immediate response; and there is the time of medium-term and longer-term change. The relationship between the two times is the relationship of agency to structure.

Two kinds of theory correspond to the two kinds of time. There is problem-solving theory which takes the present as given and reasons about how to deal with particular problems within the existing order of things. Then there is what, for want of a better term, I shall call critical theory. Critical theory stands back from the existing order of things to ask how that order came into being, how it may be changing, and how that change may be influenced or channeled. Where problem-solving theory focuses synchronically upon the immediate and reasons in terms of fixed relationships, critical theory works in a more historical and diachronic dimension. Its aim is the understanding of structural change.

There are also, correspondingly, two main functions of international organization: one, to respond effectively to the pressing problems of the present; the other, to be concerned with longer-term questions of global structural change and with how international organization – or we can use the broader term "multilateralism" – can help shape that change in a consensually desirable direction.

In an ideal perspective, both functions should be united in the top direction of international institutions. In practice, the top levels of responsibility are overwhelmed by the pressure of immediate problems and events. However much the executive head may aspire to the role of long-term planner, there is little time for it. The present is always more urgent. And furthermore, the existing political pressures bear in most forcefully upon the top authority. Tolstoy wrote: "A king is history's slave."

The UN system today is a vast organizational complex. It has more of a segmented than a hierarchically coordinated structure. There are those who would like more centralized control; but the great advantage of the segmented structure is openness, flexibility, room for initiative. Centers of reflection, of longer-term structural thinking, can arise within it. I can think of the ECE during the early Cold War years under the directorship of Gunnar Myrdal, or the ECLA under Raul Prebisch, and one could add to the list.

I do not discern any logic or pattern in how and when and where such creative and innovative segments appeared. Yet their appearance has been important in the development and transformation of the UN system and to the system's influence. Once active, they do not continue to perform indefinitely the reflective-creative function. It might be a useful exercise to make a study of the conditions of their existence and duration.

Looking at the other side of the relationship, the role of the academic, I would suggest that the essence of the scholarly responsibility lies in the sphere of critical theory – the ability to place the process of international organization in the framework of global change, to take the structural, diachronic approach. This critical perspective is particularly necessary in a moment of world history when there is a whole series of interacting fundamental changes.

How should one approach the understanding of global structural change having the future of international organization in mind? The point of departure, which governs the kind of questions we should be asking, is either optimistic or pessimistic. The optimist sees the end of the Cold War as the beginning of a new beneficent era. The pessimist sees rather the strains and stresses of a declining order. The optimistic viewpoint, promoted in the current discourse of western political leadership and media, speaks of a "new world order," the "end of history," the apotheosis of western capitalism, and the return of the United Nations to its "initially intended functions."

As a matter of prudence as well as reasoning from the evidence, I take the pessimistic perspective as my starting point. The world about us is full of conflicts and inequities, some long obscured by the Cold War, and some generated or accelerated by more recent developments. Furthermore, we should be alive to the gravity of the dangers to the United Nations system inherent in the new political relationships and in their ineffective grasp upon mounting social and ecological risks. My point is not to spread gloom. As one master thinker of the twentieth century prescribed: "Pessimism of the intellect; optimism of the will."

The longer-range issues are best approached in the realm of political economy. The evidence today indicates a worldwide expansion of a certain type of capitalism. Although the ideology in which the new capitalism is grounded proclaims a universality exclusive of other types, this particular type is historically specific and of fairly recent origin in the United States and Britain. It has made some impact in Europe and in Japan, although different forms of capitalism, with their own distinctive historical conditioning, retain strong roots there. The new capitalism seems now to be carrying all before it in Latin America, Africa, and the geographic zone that has just recently abandoned so-called "real socialism."

Capitalism, as the French historian Fernand Braudel emphasized, is not just a way of organizing an economy. Capitalism, in each of its different historical forms, has also been a distinct system of values, pattern of consumption, social structure, and form of state. Each form has also projected a conception of world order. The new capitalism with its global vocation encompasses all of these things. So do alternative capitalisms, anchored in European and Japanese traditions, and possibly other forms of economic organization that could be based in less developed areas.

It is said that those who ignore history are condemned to repeat it. Karl Polanyi, whose work is ignored in current neoliberal economics but who bears rereading for his historical analysis, illustrates the point. Polanyi examined what he called substantive economics, that is to say economic processes embedded in specific historical societies – how these societies organized themselves to satisfy their material wants. There are, of course, a variety of substantive economies. He distinguished this study from formal economics, which is based upon an analytical separation of economic behavior from other human activities and is grounded upon certain postulated human characteristics assumed to be universal – the classical concept of economic man. Substantive economics orients thinking in an historical diachronic dimension. Formal economics, in its quest for universally valid rules, follows a synchronic logic.

In *The Great Transformation*, Polanyi's analysis of the development

527

of capitalism from the industrial revolution through the first half of the twentieth century, he discerned a double movement.[1] In the first phase, the state was evacuated from substantive economic activity, but took on the role of enforcer of the rules of the market. The market was assumed to be self-regulating; and its automaticity, through the instrumentality of the invisible hand, was assumed by theory to promote the general good.

The second phase of the double movement was society's response to the socially destructive consequences, unanticipated in theory, of the self-regulating market – the response to the Dickensian picture of a society torn apart by competition and greed. This response relegitimated the state as regulator of the economy and as guarantor of a modicum of social equity. Conservative politicians like Bismarck and Disraeli, who understood that the state required a strong social base (unlike the so-called neoconservatives today), initiated this second phase; and it continued through the action of labor and socialist movements, culminating in the welfare state and the idea of social democracy.

Polanyi did not live to see the crisis of this second phase of the double movement. We can trace it to the late 1960s and early 1970s when the pattern of regulation built up through the second phase of his double movement seemed to reach its limits in stagflation and fiscal crisis.

In retrospect, this crisis appears as the consequence of a transition from an international economy to a global economy. In the international economy, states retained a good deal of control over their national economies and could regulate their relationship to the external world economy. The Bretton Woods institutions were conceived as a means of achieving cooperation among states in carrying out this regulatory function. In the emerging global economy, this autonomous capacity of states has been reduced for all states, although in a greater degree for some than for others. States are, by and large, reduced to the role of adjusting national economies to the dynamics of an unregulated global economy. We are back again to the beginning of Polanyi's first phase of movement, but now at the global rather than the national level.

The new capitalism is conceived in this historical context. Its basic instinct is to free itself from any form of state control or intervention. Its thrust is deregulation, privatization, and the dismantling of state protection for the vulnerable elements of society. It preaches that the unregulated global market is good for everybody, although some may reap its benefits earlier than others. The state retains a function as enforcer of contracts and as instrument of political leverage to secure access to resources and markets worldwide. It is also at times expected to salvage reckless enterprises, if they are big enough, and to compensate an innocent public for plunder by unscrupulous financial operators. But, by and large, the state is conceived as subordinate to the economy. Competitiveness in the global economy is the ultimate criterion of public policy.

During the 1980s, this new form of capitalism seemed ubiquitously triumphant. Critics in its homelands could be plausibly represented as clinging to an irrelevant past. The aura of superstar surrounded its heroes, some of whom subsequently went to jail. The doctrines and practices of the new capitalism brought about a revolution in economic policy in the countries of Latin America and Africa whose governments had hitherto put their faith in more autocentric, state-directed development. Third World initiatives from the 1960s and 1970s towards collective management of world economic relations – the New International Economic Order and UNCTAD – became marginalized. And the collapse of "real socialism" unleashed a feverish rush to emulate the most extreme versions of new capitalist theory.

The euphoria has been challenged rather abruptly more recently. We have been made vividly aware of the socially destructive consequences of the new capitalism, both in its homelands and in its global reach. These consequences can be enumerated:

In the first place there has been an accentuation of social polarization between rich and poor. UNDP's *Human Development Report* for 1992[2] dwells upon this. The report attempts to measure the increasing gap between rich and poor, not only in country aggregates but also in terms of incomes of social categories on a global basis. It estimates that between 1960 and 1989 there was an eight-fold increase in the absolute difference in incomes between the richest fifth and the poorest fifth of the world population. This polarization is manifest in the poorer areas of Africa and Latin America, and it has appeared in ex-socialist countries converted to the new capitalism, but it is present in rich countries as well. Other sources indicate that during the past decade, the income of the bottom 40 million Americans declined by 10 percent.[3] During the same period, the US prison population doubled; and the numbers of private security guards now exceeds the numbers of publicly employed police.[4] All over the world, the rich are getting fewer and richer and the poor poorer and more numerous.

The explanation of this increasing gap between rich and poor is traceable to globalization. Those segments of the populations in both rich and poor countries that are linked most directly to the global economy have fared well, but they are relatively very small. Those with a more local economic orientation, whether they are among the upper classes or the lower classes, have fared badly. The salaried middle classes have lost ground, as have most of the peasantry, except for a few relatively prosperous commercial farmers. Increasing numbers of people have entered the informal economy.[5]

Another factor is that the relationship between finance and production has become problematic. Peter Drucker spoke of a "decoupling" of the "symbolic economy" of money from the real economy of production and distribution.[6] There is a marked disproportion in the level of activity between symbolic and real economies. Foreign exchange trading in the world's financial centers is about forty times the amount of world trade every day.[7] The relative autonomy of finance and the tendency for finance to feed upon itself has some negative effects on production. New financial mechanisms that facilitate changes in ownership (LBOs and junk bonds) also lead to asset stripping and bankruptcies that are destructive of production. Poor countries have been incurring new debt in order to service old debt, without being able to invest significantly in new productive resources.[8] Transnationalized corporate and state debt is a heavy obstacle to the revival of production. Moreover, the synchronic mode of thought characteristic of the symbolic economy (cash flow and quick returns) squeezes out the diachronic planning essential to productive investment.

Nevertheless, production is being restructured as an integral aspect of economic globalization, very largely through the agency of multinational corporations that have been able to escape these financial constraints. This restructuring has very significant social consequences. The mass-production assembly-line industries that maximized economies of scale (and which incidentally were the basis for trade union strength in the advanced economies) are being phased out in favor of a more flexible combination of smaller production units capable of producing a greater variety of products for much more diversified demand. These new methods use smaller core workforces, skilled and securely employed, but also a larger more precariously employed secondary workforce. Some of this secondary workforce are support staff in main plants and others work in a multitude of production units spread across the globe. The obstacles to collective action are formidable among these workers who are separated by geography, nationality, ethnicity, religion, and gender. The global restructuring of production has undermined the power of labor in relation to capital.

Not only is capital moving to set up production organizations that are global in extent, but people are moving from South to North and from East to West, and so providing a steady flow of recruits to the secondary workforce in the richer countries. The ability of states to control this movement of peoples is limited, while it often arouses xenophobic reactions, particularly among unemployed and downgraded workers in the countries the migrants come to. Migration is a growing but also increasingly conflictual aspect of globalization.

The terms "core" and "periphery" were introduced into political economy as geographical terms, distinguishing dominant and rich national economies from dependent and poor ones – broadly, North from South. While this geographical and state-centered distinction remains valid, the terms "core" and "periphery" have acquired a new meaning indicative of the polarized structure of a global society. The North is generating its own internal South; and the South has formed a thin layer of society that is fully integrated into the economic North. The social core and the social periphery cut across national boundaries.

The pattern of growth and of consumption of the new capitalism has some drastic ecological implications. To posit the continuing extension of its consumption model in terms of energy use and greenhouse effects makes no sense; and yet the political obstacles to changing these habits entrenched in the richer countries are intractable. In poorer areas of the world, integration into the global economy may provide more foreign exchange to service accumulated debt, but it often has grave implications for local populations. The most fertile lands are given over to export crops, while desertification and famine attack subsistence farmers, who incidentally happen in most cases to be women. The power relations of the global economy are very clear and peasant women are near the bottom of the scale. The contradictions between economic globalization and ecological balance ultimately threaten everybody.

All of these tendencies, which confirm my pessimistic point of departure, have implications for political life. One hopeful sign is that democratization seems to have been on an upward swing. "Democracy" is a term with several meanings.

The classic meaning of liberal democracy separates the political and economic spheres. Democracy applies to the political sphere in which individual citizens are recognized as equal in their civil and political rights. In the economic sphere, property, not the individual citizen, enjoys rights. Individuals experience the hierarchical subordination of the labor market. This democracy risks becoming formal, while the reality of daily life is determined by the power relations of the market. The distinction between the economic and political spheres became somewhat blurred during the second phase of Polanyi's double movement when people used their political rights to limit and to channel the rights of property – to correct the inequities of the market. Now, the new capitalism is reviving the distinction between economic and political spheres in a more rigorous form. Efforts are being made to protect the economic sphere from political intervention through legislative and constitutional limitations. The new capitalism is haunted by the specter of revived political controls.

There is another meaning of democracy that corresponds to this fear. It is what we may call "populist democracy," that is to say a form of politics that does not recognize any barriers to entry into the economic sphere. This is no doubt what the ideologues of the Trilateral Commission had in mind when they warned about the "ungovernability of democracies."[9] They feared that popular demands were overloading the capacity of governments to respond, leading to inflation and deepening fiscal crisis. The implication of their warning was that more unemployment and more fiscal restraint would correct the problem.

Today, a different kind of crisis affects democracies: a disillusionment of people with political leadership, a turning away from politics with a certain disgust, an association of politics with corruption, a sense that politics doesn't really matter except to the politicians, a widespread depoliticization. This phenomenon is more evident in some countries than others, and it is most evident among that part of the population that is poorest and most adversely affected by the social consequences of the new capitalism.

It is difficult not to see a correlation between the success of the new capitalism and this effect of depoliticization. By removing the economic sphere from political control – whether this is achieved by law or by ideology – what determines the condition of people in their everyday lives is removed from their control. Politics becomes irrelevant. The sense of civic efficacy is removed, and many people, the most disadvantaged, are left in the futility of alienation. Their rage is unchanneled, ineffective, self-consuming. It marks an impasse. It does not herald the construction of a future.

If this condition foreshadows the end of a cycle of world history, what may be the possibilities of a new beginning? Let me say here that I am no believer in historical inevitability. People, collectively, may be confronted with opportunity, but whether or not they take it is up to them. Human agency, conditioned by past experience, is the ultimate maker of history. The way out of the impasse created by economic deregulation and depoliticization is reregulation and repoliticization attuned to the changed global structures. This can hardly come about in one country at a time, since each country is caught in the net of economic globalization. Secession or isolationism on a country basis will be self-defeating. It seems as though the cure can only come, perhaps as a first stage, through world regions, and ultimately at the global level; and it can only come there if it is firmly based in global society. A dual approach is involved: the building of a sufficient foundation in social organization at the base; and a creative response and initiative through multilateralism.

Reregulation on this basis would imply revision of currently dominant economic ideology and reform of economic practices:

— competitiveness as the criterion of economic action would be subordinated to forms of regulation intended to manage economic growth in a manner consistent with ecological balance and social equity;
— consumption models would be evolved which are more respectful of ecological balance;
— finance would be regulated so as to serve the real economy and to curb speculation, destructive asset stripping, and corruption.

Such changes are not likely to come about as a result of moral exhortation or utopian schemes of institutional reform. They are more likely to come about through two currently observable historical processes. One is the struggle between rival forms of substantive economy – rival capitalisms.[10] The other is the recomposition of civil society that is taking place in response to the disruptive consequences of the new capitalism. Both tendencies merit much more attention than they have received.

The first underlines the importance of challenging the "end of history" thesis. There is not one universal form of capitalism, henceforth perpetual and triumphant. There are several forms, of which one – the new capitalism – appears now to have the dominant influence but whose warts and weaknesses are more and more apparent. There are also persistent traditions of social market or social democratic forms of capitalism most resilient in parts of Europe, a Japanese capitalism that has yet other social and international consequences, and a rising concern for devising a more ecologically conscious mode of production and consumption. Current debates in the European Community about entrenching guarantees for a "social Europe" and about overcoming the perceived "democratic deficit" in the Community's institutions may become a first test of strength of rival conceptions of economic and social organization.

The social forces challenging the new capitalism are perhaps stronger and better organized in Europe than elsewhere; but challenges could come from many places. Trade unions have been weakened in relation to management; but the labor movement retains an organizational capability that can be valuable to a broader social coalition. Neighborhood and self-help organizations have been formed to deal with basic needs of marginalized groups in both rich and poor countries. Women are especially prominent in the new basic organizations of self-help and self-defense.[11] People are dropping out of the world market, and the formal structures of national economies, to seek their survival in the informal sector. It results in a lowering of incomes and a worsening of safety and health conditions. But it can also become a stimulus to new forms of cooperation and self-governance. Loss of confidence in the state can, in a measure, be compensated by growth in civil society. One African scholar has described these developments as a "silent revolution."[12]

There is a meaning of democracy that could be built upon such a development of civil society – a "participative democracy," the organization of civic life upon the basis of a variety of self-governing groups that deal with the whole range of people's substantive concerns.

Multilateralism, if it is to seize the opportunity opened by these developments, will be schizophrenic – one part of its being involved in the present predicaments of the state system, another part probing the social and political foundations of a future order. This second part can only exist within the shadow of the first. It can only develop when shielded from the day-to-day constraints of inter-state politics.

The responsibility of this second sector of international institutions is to become the point of contact, the interlocutor, for the new social forces. The debate about alternative forms of economic organization, about alternative development strategies, will also be a debate within the UN system. Different segments of the system develop policy approaches that respond to the interests and needs of different social groups. I have in mind particularly the needs of the relatively disadvantaged and the imperative of ecological sustainability. The segments of multilateralism that take on the task of envisaging a world order in this perspective will also foster linkage among supportive social forces in different countries and thereby help to build a political base for a globally coherent alternative set of policies.

Institutional change, I would suggest, is more likely to follow than to precede a new direction in global economic and social policy. The new order will have to be built from the bottom up, when the present order falters in its attempt to hold things in place from the top down. Freedom of initiative and freedom to build are the critical conditions for the emergence of the new order. This is also the practical meaning of democracy in international organization.

Notes

This text was originally delivered as the John Holmes Memorial Lecture to the 1992 conference of the Academic Council on the United States System, Washington, D.C., June 19, 1992 in the headquarters of the International Monetary Fund. It was published for distribution to ACUNS members. See the complete bibliography of works included in this volume.

1 Karl Polanyi, *The Great Transformation: The Political and Economic Origins of Our Time* (Boston: Beacon Press, 1957).
2 United Nations Development Program, *Human Development Report* (New York: Oxford University Press for the UNDP, 1992), p. 35.
3 US Bureau of the Census and Congressional Budget Office figures cited in Michel Albert, *Capitalisme contre capitalisme* (Paris: Seuil, 1991), pp. 53–55.
4 Kenneth Galbraith, *The Culture of Contentment* (Boston: Houghton Mifflin, 1992), p. 45.
5 Dharam Ghai (ed.), *The IMF and the South* (London: Zed Books for UNRISD, 1991), p. 45.
6 Peter Drucker, "The Changed World Economy," *Foreign Affairs*, vol. 64, no. 4 (Spring 1986).

7 Jeff Frieden, "Invested Interests: The Politics of National Economic Policies in a World of Global Finance," *International Organization*, vol. 45, no. 4 (Autumn 1991), p. 426.

8 UNDP, *Human Development Report*, pp. 4, 45–47.

9 Michel J. Crozier, Samuel P. Huntington, and Joji Watanuki, *The Crisis of Democracy: Report on the Governability of Democracies to the Trilateral Commission* (New York: New York University Press, 1975).

10 Robert W. Cox, *Production, Power, and World Order: Social Forces in the Making of History* (New York: Columbia University Press, 1987), ch. 8; also Albert, *Capitalisme contre capitalisme.*

11 Ghai, *IMF and the South*, pp. 33–39; also Rosalinda Pineda-Ofreneo, *The Philippines: Debt and Poverty* (Oxford: Oxfam, 1991).

12 Fantu Cheru, *The Silent Revolution in Africa* (London: Zed Books, 1989).

Complete bibliography of works by Robert W. Cox to 1995

1948
"The Quebec Provincial Election of 1886," MA thesis, McGill University (unpublished)

1952
"Some Human Problems of Industrial Development," *International Labour Review*, vol. 66, no. 3 (September), pp. 246–267

1953
"The Idea of International Labour Regulation," *International Labour Review*, vol. 67, no. 2 (February), pp. 191–196

1954
"English Workers and Middle Classes," *International Labour Review*, vol. 69, no. 1 (January), pp. 77–82

1958
"Some International Aspects of Labour Relations," in *Labour Relations Trends: Retrospect and Prospect* (McGill University, Industrial Relations Centre, Tenth Annual Conference, September 11 and 12), pp. 83–89

1964
"Idéologies de l'organisation internationale," published inaugural lecture at the Graduate Institute of International Studies (Geneva)

1965
"The Study of European Institutions: Some Problems of Economic and Political Organization," *Journal of Common Market Studies* (Oxford), vol. 3, no. 2 (February), pp. 102–117

"Social and Labour Policy in the European Economic Community," *British Journal of Industrial Relations*, vol. 1, no. 1, pp. 5–22

"Towards a General Theory of International Organization," review of Ernst

Bibliography

B. Haas, *Beyond the Nation State, Industrial and Labor Relations Review*, vol. 19, no. 1 (October), pp. 99–106

1966
"Trade Unions, Employers, and the Formation of National Economic Policy," in Arthur M. Ross (ed.), *Industrial Relations and Economic Development* (London: Macmillan, for the International Institute for Labor Studies), pp. 229–251

1968
"Education for Development," *International Organization*, vol. 22, no. 1, pp. 310–331; also in Richard N. Gardner and Max Millikan (eds.), *The Global Partnership* (New York: Praeger, 1968), pp. 310–331

1969
"The Executive Head: An Essay on Leadership in International Organization," *International Organization*, vol. 23, no. 2 (Spring), pp. 205–230; republished in Leland H. Goodrich and David Kay (eds.), *International Organization: Politics and Process* (Madison, Wis.: University of Wisconsin Press, 1973), pp. 155–180

(edited) *International Organization: World Politics. Studies in Economic and Social Agencies* (London: Macmillan); US edition was published with the title *The Politics of International Organization* (New York: Praeger, 1970)

1970
(with Harold K. Jacobson) "Decision Making in International Organizations: A Report on a Joint Project," prepared for delivery at the VIII World Congress of the International Political Science Association, Munich, August–September

1971
"Approaches to a Futurology of Industrial Relations," *Bulletin*, no. 8 (Geneva: International Institute for Labor Studies)

(under the initials N. M.) "International Labor in Crisis," *Foreign Affairs*, vol. 49, no. 3, pp. 519–532

1972
"The Pearson and Jackson Reports in the Context of Development Ideologies," *Yearbook of World Affairs, 1972*, vol. 26 (London: Stevens) pp. 187–202; Spanish version of this article, "Los informes Pearson y Jackson: un análisis ideológico de las doctrinas de asistencia al desarrollo," was published in *Foro Internacional* (Mexico City), vol. 13, no. 3 (1973)

(with Harold K. Jacobson, Gerard and Victoria Curzon, Joseph S. Nye, Lawrence Scheinman, James P. Sewell, and Susan Strange) *The Anatomy of Influence: Decision Making in International Organization* (New Haven, Conn.: Yale University Press); paperback edition, 1975; chapter 1, pp. 73–103, by Cox and Jacobson, is being reproduced in Oran R. Young (ed.), The International Political Economy and International Institutions (Cheltenham: Edward Elgar, 1995) (with Jeffrey Harrod *et al.*) *Future Industrial Relations: An Interim Report* (Geneva: International Institute for Labor Studies)

"Industrial Relations and Rapid Industrialization: Some Far Eastern Cases" *Bulletin*, no. 10 (Geneva: International Institute for Labor Studies), pp. 5–47

"Labor and Transnational Relations," in Robert O. Keohane and Joseph S. Nye, Jr. (eds.), *Transnational Relations and World Politics* (Cambridge, Mass.: Harvard University Press), pp. 204–234

1973
"Labour Relations and Public Policy: Perspectives on the Future," *Dalhousie Law Journal*, vol. 1, no. 1, pp. 82–104

(with Harold K. Jacobson) "States, People, and Wealth in the Global Political System" (unpublished)

1974
(with Stuart Jamieson) "Canadian Labor in the Continental Perspective," *International Organization*, vol. 28, no. 4, pp. 804–826

(with Harold K. Jacobson) "Structural Aspects of the Global Political System, 1950–1970" (xeroxed, unpublished)

1975
"Labor and French Canadian Nationalism" (unpublished)

1976
"Labor and the Multinationals," *Foreign Affairs*, vol. 54, no. 2, pp. 344–365; republished in George Modelski (ed.), *Transnational Corporations and World Order* (San Francisco: Freeman, 1979), pp. 414–429; Japanese translation has also been published

"On Thinking about Future World Order," *World Politics*, vol. 28, no. 2 (January), pp. 175–196

1977
(with Harold K. Jacobson) "Decision Making" in *International Social Science Journal*, special issue on "Approaches to the Study of International Organizations," vol. 29, no. 1, pp. 115–135; republished as "The Decision-making Approach to the Study of International Organization," in Georges Abi-Saab (ed.), *The Concept of International Organization* (Paris: UNESCO, 1981), pp. 79–104, and in French translation as "Une première approche: l'analyse de la prise de décision," in Georges Abi-Saab (ed.), *Le concept d'organisation internationale* (Paris: UNESCO, 1980), pp. 81–110

"Labor and Hegemony," *International Organization*, vol. 31, no. 3 (Summer), pp. 385–424

"La participation: considérations sur la signification des expériences européennes," in *Participation et négotiation collective* (Québec: Université Laval, Département de relations industrielles), pp. 37–51

Bibliography

"Pour une étude prospective des relations de production," *Sociologie du Travail*, vol. 2, pp. 113–137

1978
"Labour and Employment in the Late Twentieth Century," in R. St. J. Macdonald *et al.* (eds.), *The International Law and Policy of Human Welfare* (Leiden, The Netherlands; Sijtoff and Noordhoff), pp. 525–548

"Labour and the Multinationals: Elements for Strategic Planning," mimeo, Instituto de estudios transnacionales, Mexico City

"Le Procès de l'état moderne se fera sur le terrain des relations de travail," public lecture to the 9th conference of the School of Industrial Relations, l'Université de Montréal, published in *Le Devoir*, November 23, cahier spécial XII

1979
"Employment, Labour and Future Political Structures" in R. B. Byers and Robert W. Reford (eds.), *Canada Challenged* (Toronto: Canadian Institute of International Affairs), pp. 262–292

"Ideologies and the New International Economic Order: Reflections on Some Recent Literature," *International Organization*, vol. 33, no. 2 (Spring), pp. 257–302; republished as a chapter in Michael Smith, Richard Little, and Michael Shackelton (eds.), *Perspectives on World Politics: A Reader* (London: Croom Helm for the Open University, 1981), pp. 413–424

1980
"The Crisis of World Order and the Problems of International Organization in the 1980s," *International Journal*, vol. 35, no. 2 (Spring), pp. 370–395

"Labor and Hegemony: A Reply," *International Organization*, vol. 34, no. 1 (Winter), pp. 159–176

"Production Relations and the Third World", in Louis Lefeber and Liisa North (eds.), *Democracy and Development in Latin America* (Toronto: York University, Latin American Research Unit), pp. 77–92

1981
"In Search of International Political Economy," *New Political Science*, no. 5–6 (Winter–Spring), pp. 59–77

"Social Forces, States, and World Orders: Beyond International Relations Theory," *Millennium: Journal of International Studies*, vol. 10, no. 2 (Summer), pp. 126–155; republished in R. B. J. Walker (ed.), *Culture, Ideology, and World Order* (Boulder, Colo.: Westview Press, 1984), pp. 258–299; in Robert O. Keohane (ed.), *Neorealism and Its Critics* (New York: Columbia University Press, 1986), pp. 204–254; abridged in John A. Vasquez (ed.), *Classics of International Relations*, Second Edition (Englewood Cliffs, N.J.: Prentice Hall, 1990), pp. 116–124; in Howard Williams, Moorhead Wright, and Tony Evans, (eds.), *A Reader in International Relations and Political Theory* (Buckingham: Open University

Press, 1993), pp. 274–308; and in Friedrich Kratochwil and Edward Mansfield (eds.), *International Organization: A Reader* (New York: Harper Collins, 1993), pp. 343–364

1982

"Production and Hegemony: Towards a Political Economy of World Order," in Harold K. Jacobson and Dusan Sidjanski (eds.), *The Emerging International Economic Order: Dynamic Processes, Constraints, and Opportunities* (Beverly Hills, Calif.: Sage, for the International Political Science Association), pp. 37–58

(with Harold K. Jacobson) "The United States and World Order: On Structure of World Power and Structural Transformation," prepared for delivery to the Research Committee on the Emerging International Economic Order at the Twelfth World Congress of the International Political Science Association, Rio de Janeiro, Brazil, August

1983

"Gramsci, Hegemony, and International Relations: An Essay in Method," *Millennium: Journal of International Studies*, vol. 12, no. 2 (Summer), pp. 162–175; republished in Stephen Gill (ed.), *Gramsci, Historical Materialism, and International Relations* (Cambridge: Cambridge University Press, 1993), pp. 49–66

"Problems of Global Management," in Toby Trister Gati (ed.), *The US, the UN, and the Management of Global Change* (New York: New York University Press, for the United Nations Association of the USA), pp. 64–81

1984

"The Alleviation of Poverty: A Comment," in John Trent and Paul Lamy (eds.), *Global Crises and the Social Sciences: North American Perspectives* (Ottawa: University of Ottawa Press/UNESCO), pp. 113–118

1985

"China: A Redistributive System in the World Political Economy," paper prepared for the World Congress of the International Political Science Association, Paris, July

1986

"Social Forces, States, and World Orders: Beyond International Relations Theory," with a Postscript, in Robert O. Keohane (ed.), *Neorealism and Its Critics* (New York: Columbia University Press), pp. 204–254

1987

Production, Power, and World Order: Social Forces in the Making of History (New York: Columbia University Press); extract included in Edward Weisband (ed.), *Poverty Amidst Plenty: World Political Economy and Distributive Justice* (Boulder, Colo.: Westview Press, 1989), pp. 186–196

1988

"Economic Reform and the Social Structure of Accumulation in Socialist

Bibliography

Countries," paper prepared for the XIVth World Congress of the International Political Science Association, Washington, D.C., August–September

1989
"The Global Political Economy and National Options," paper prepared for the Conference on Export-led Growth, Uneven Development, and State Policy: the Cases of Canada and Italy, April, University of Pisa, Pisa, Italy

"Middlepowermanship, Japan, and Future World Order" *International Journal* (Canadian Institute of International Affairs), vol. 44, no. 4 (Autumn), pp. 823–862

"Production, the State, and Change in World Order," in Ernst-Otto Czempiel and James Rosenau (eds.), *Global Changes and Theoretical Challenges. Approaches to World Politics for the 1990s* (Lexington, Mass.: Lexington Books), pp. 37–50

"Programme Outline: Multilateralism and the United Nations System," prepared at the request of the United Nations University, September

"The United Nations System: Multilateralism Reappraised. Some Suggestions for an Approach to Defining a Programme," paper prepared for the United Nations University Meeting on Peace and Governance, April, Barcelona, Spain

1990
"Dialectique de l'économie-monde en fin de siècle" *Etudes Internationales*, vol. 21, no. 4 (December), pp. 693–703

"Globalization, Multilateralism and Social Choice," *Work in Progress*, vol. 13, no. 1, July (Tokyo: United Nations University Press), p. 2

"Towards a Counterhegemonic Conceptualization of World Order," prepared for the Governance-without-Government Workshop, convened by James Rosenau and E.-O. Czempiel, Ojai, California, February

1991
"The Global Political Economy and Social Choice," in Daniel Drache and Meric S. Gertler (eds.), *The New Era of Global Competition: State Policy and Market Power* (Montreal and Kingston: McGill-Queen's University Press), pp. 335–350

"Perspectives on Multilateralism" (Tokyo: United Nations University, April); substantially reproduced in "Multilateralism and World Order" (see 1992)

Programme on Multilateralism and the United Nations System, 1990–1995 (Tokyo: United Nations University Press)

" 'Real socialism' in historical perspective," in Ralph Miliband and Leo Panitch (eds.), *Socialist Register 1991* (London: Merlin Press), pp. 169–193

"Structural Issues of Global Governance: Implications for Europe," paper prepared for the international conference on "A New Europe in the Changing Global System," organized by the United Nations University in collaboration with the Hungarian Academy of Sciences, Velence, Hungary, September; a revised version is in Stephen Gill (ed.), *Gramsci, Historical Materialism, and International Relations* (see 1993)

1992
"Global *Perestroika*," in Ralph Miliband and Leo Panitch (eds.), *Socialist Register 1992* (London: Merlin Press), pp. 26–43; shortened and slightly amended version included in Richard Stubbs and Geoffrey R. D. Underhill (eds.), *Political Economy and the Changing Global Order* as "Global Restructuring: Making Sense of the Changing International Political Economy" (Toronto: McClelland and Stewart, 1994), pp. 45–59

"Globalization, Multilateralism, and Democracy," John Holmes Memorial Lecture delivered to the annual conference of the Academic Council on the United Nations System, Washington, D.C., June, in the headquarters of the International Monetary Fund (Brown University, Providence, R.I.: Academic Council on the United Nations System, Reports and Papers)

"Multilateralism and World Order," *Review of International Studies*, vol. 18, no. 2 (April), pp. 161–180

Program on Multilateralism and the United Nations System, 1990–1995: Interim Report (Tokyo: United Nations University Press)

" 'Take Six Eggs': Theory, Finance, and the Real Economy in the Work of Susan Strange," paper presented to the International Studies Association Conference, Atlanta, March–April

"Towards a Post-hegemonic Conceptualization of World Order; Reflections on the Relevancy of Ibn Khaldun," in James N. Rosenau and Ernst-Otto Czempiel (eds.), *Governance Without Government; Order and Change in World Politics* (Cambridge: Cambridge University Press), pp. 132–159

1993
"Critical Political Economy," lecture given to the United Nations University Conference on Emerging Trends in *Political Economy and International Relations Theory*, Oslo, Norway, August, p. 4; published as chapter in Björn Hettne (ed.), *International Political Economy: Understanding Global Disorder* (London: Zed Books, 1995)

"Production and Security," in David Dewitt, David Hagland, and John Kirton (eds.), *Building a New Global Order: Emerging Trends in International Security* (Toronto: Oxford University Press), pp. 141–158

"Realism, Political Economy, and the Future World," in Roger Morgan, Jochen Lorentzen, Anna Leander, and Stefano Guzzini (eds.), *New Diplomacy in the Post-Cold War World: Essays for Susan Strange* (London: Macmillan Press), pp. 27–44

Bibliography

"Structural Issues of Global Governance: Implications for Europe," in Stephen Gill (ed.), *Gramsci, Historical Materialism, and International Relations* (Cambridge: Cambridge University Press), pp. 259–289; for original text, see 1991

"Multilateralism and the Democratization of World Order," paper for the Symposium on Sources of Innovation in Multilateralism (Lausanne, Switzerland, May 1994) organized within the framework of the United Nations University program on multilateralism and the United Nations system

Program on Multilateralism and the United Nations System, 1990–1995: Second Interim Report (Tokyo: United Nations University Press)

1994

"The Crisis in World Order and the Challenge to International Organisation," *Cooperation and Conflict. Nordic Journal of International Studies*, vol. 29, no. 2 (June 1994), pp. 99–113; substantially taken from the John Holmes lecture to ACUNS (see 1992)

1995

"Civilizations: Encounters and Transformations," *Studies in Political Economy*, no. 47 (Summer 1995), pp. 7–31

Index of names

Index of names

Index of subjects

CAMBRIDGE STUDIES IN INTERNATIONAL RELATIONS

CAMBRIDGE STUDIES IN INTERNATIONAL RELATIONS

CAMBRIDGE STUDIES IN INTERNATIONAL RELATIONS